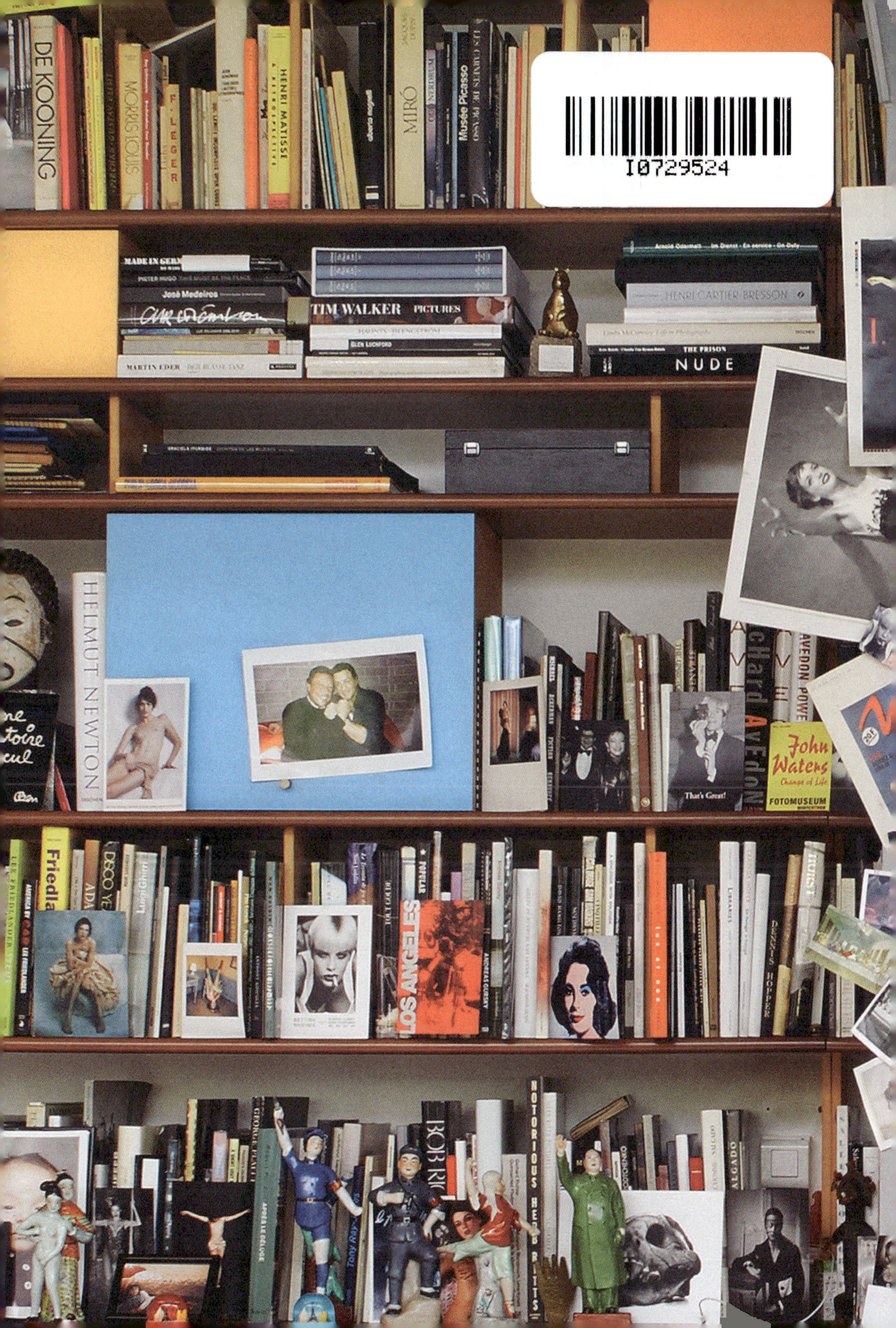

BETTINA
RHEIMS

BETTINA RHEIMS

TASCHEN

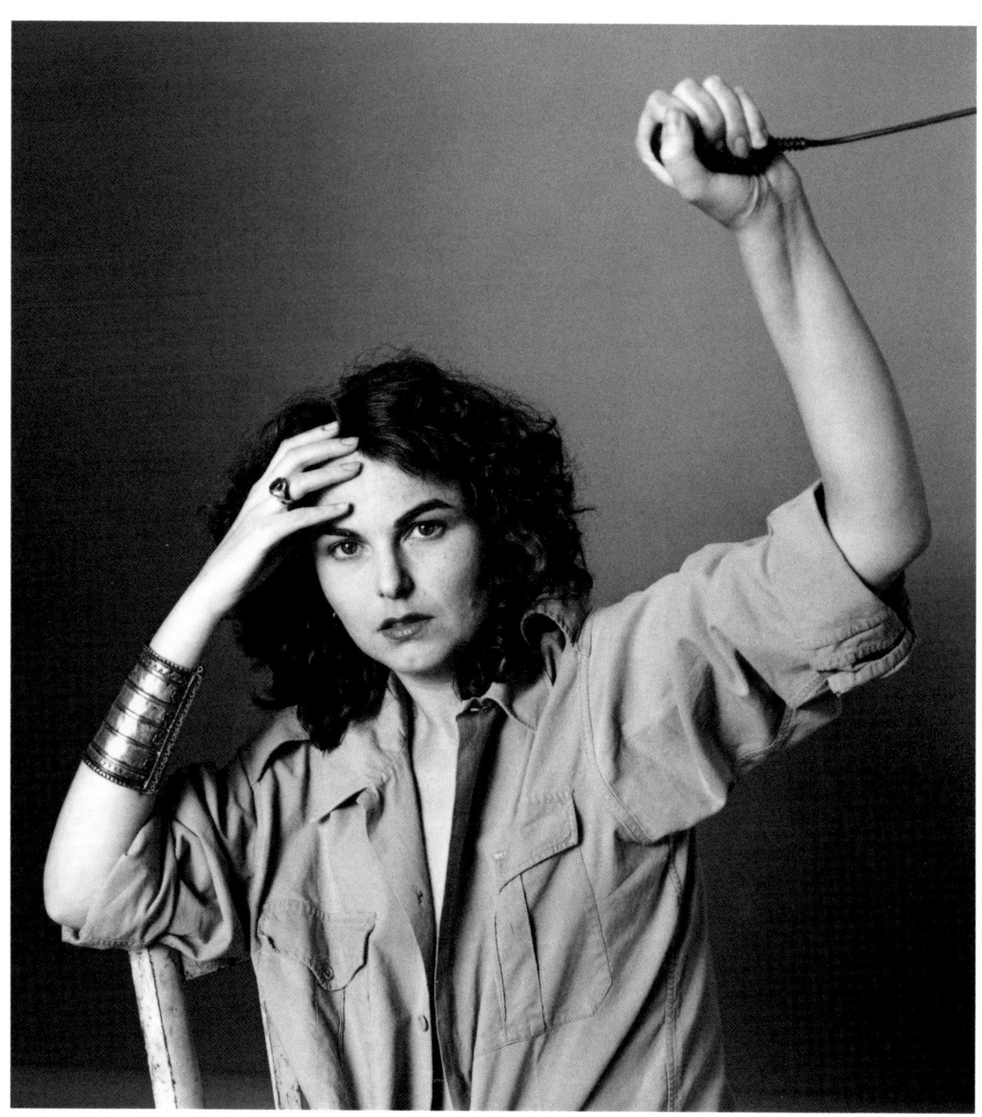

Autoportrait, 1982, Paris

Pour Jean-Michel

Close-up of Karolína Kurková, the most beautiful girl in town, December 2001, Paris

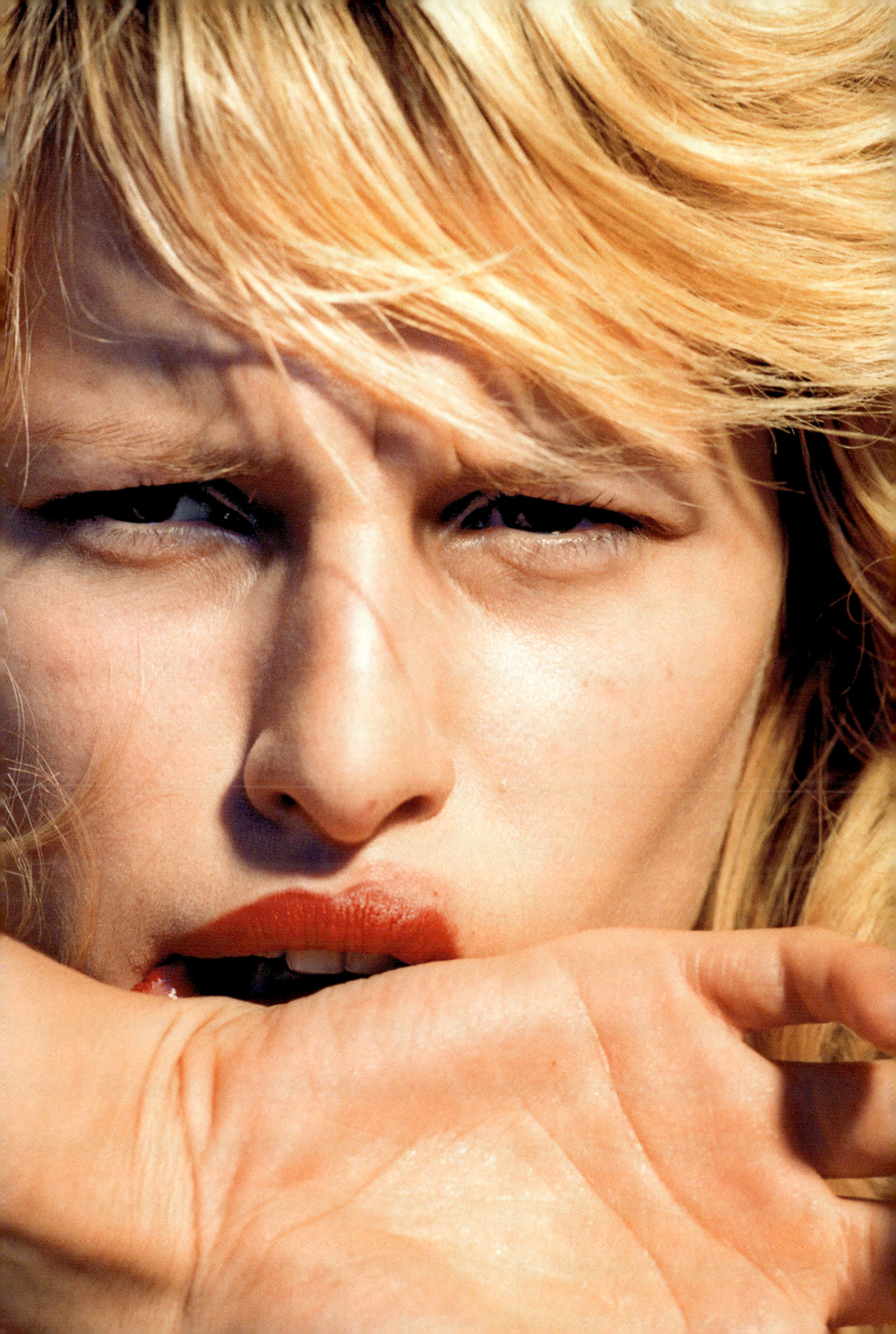

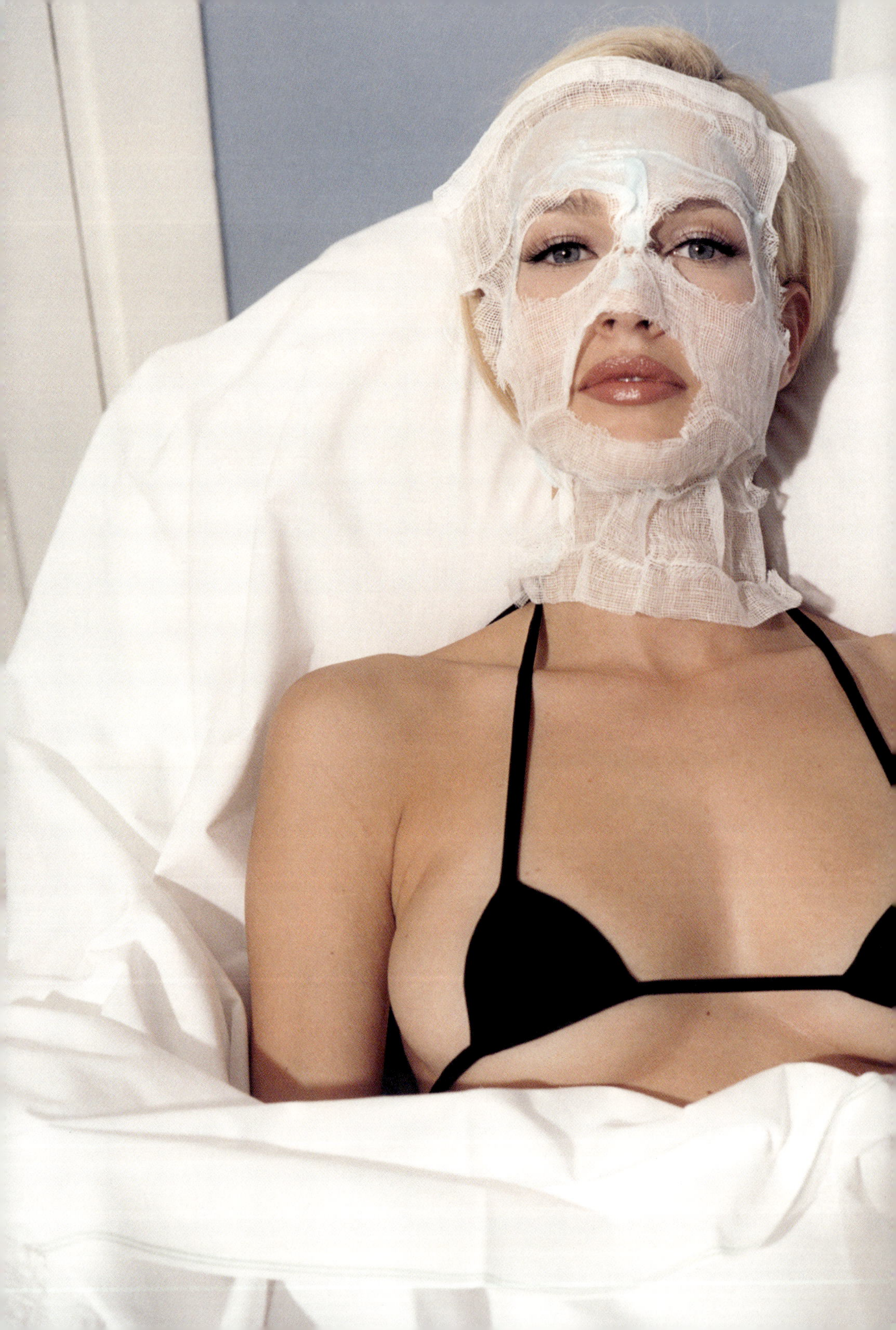

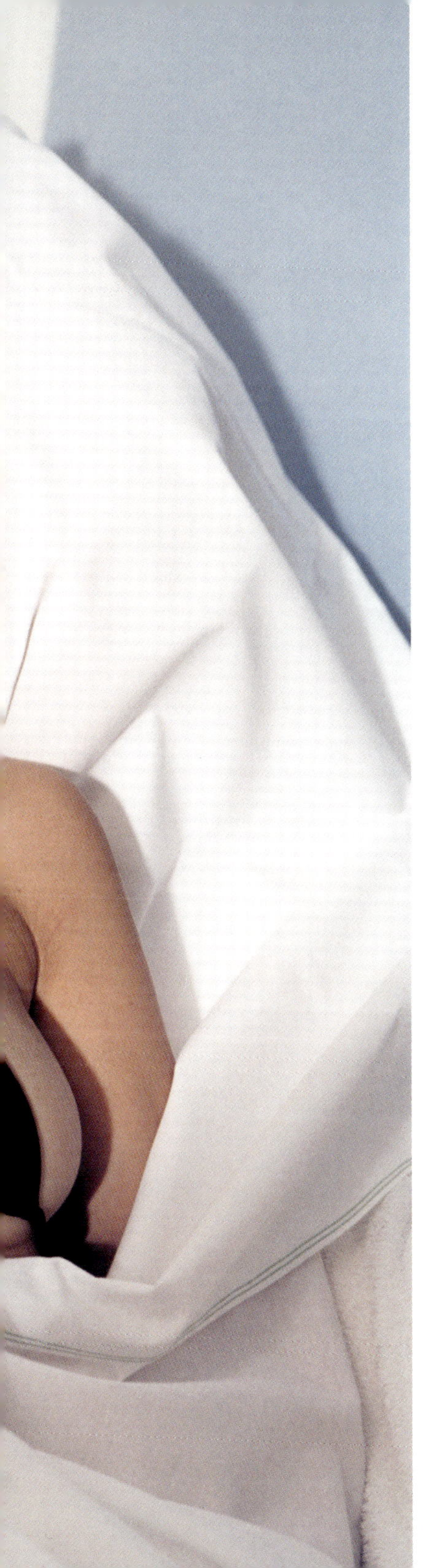

Karen Mulder with a very small Chanel bra, January 1996, Paris

Bettina Rheims never steals, never takes anything by force or surprise. She prepares the space like a dance floor, on to which she invites – how can I put it? – a partner, whom stylist, hairdresser and make-up artist have brought to perfection. When the music starts, the lens catches her gaze and never lets it go. A few steps to warm up, getting used to each other; then camera and model start to dance under the strobes of flash, eye to eye: a tango.

Bettina Rheims ne vole pas, ne prend rien de force ni par surprise. Elle prépare un espace, comme une piste de danse, où elle convie – comment dire? – un partenaire, que la styliste, le coiffeur, le maquilleur ont mis *en tenue*. Tandis qu'on envoie la musique, l'objectif capte son regard, pour ne plus le lâcher. Quelques pas d'échauffement, on s'habitue l'un à l'autre ; puis appareil et modèle tournoient sous les parapluies des flashs, les yeux dans les yeux, comme dans un tango.

Bettina Rheims stiehlt nicht, erzwingt nichts und überrumpelt niemanden. Sie bereitet einen Raum wie eine Tanzfläche vor, in den sie – wie soll ich sagen? – einen Partner einlädt, den die Stylistin, der Friseur, der Maskenbildner zurechtgemacht haben. Sobald die Musik einsetzt, fängt das Objektiv den Blick des Gegenübers ein und lässt ihn nicht mehr los. Ein paar Schritte zum Aufwärmen, um sich aneinander zu gewöhnen; dann kreisen Kamera und Modell unter den Blitzschirmen umeinander und sehen sich tief in die Augen, wie beim Tango.

Serge Bramly, in *Bettina Rheims*, 1987

Autoportrait de Valeria Golino par moi-même, April 1991, Los Angeles

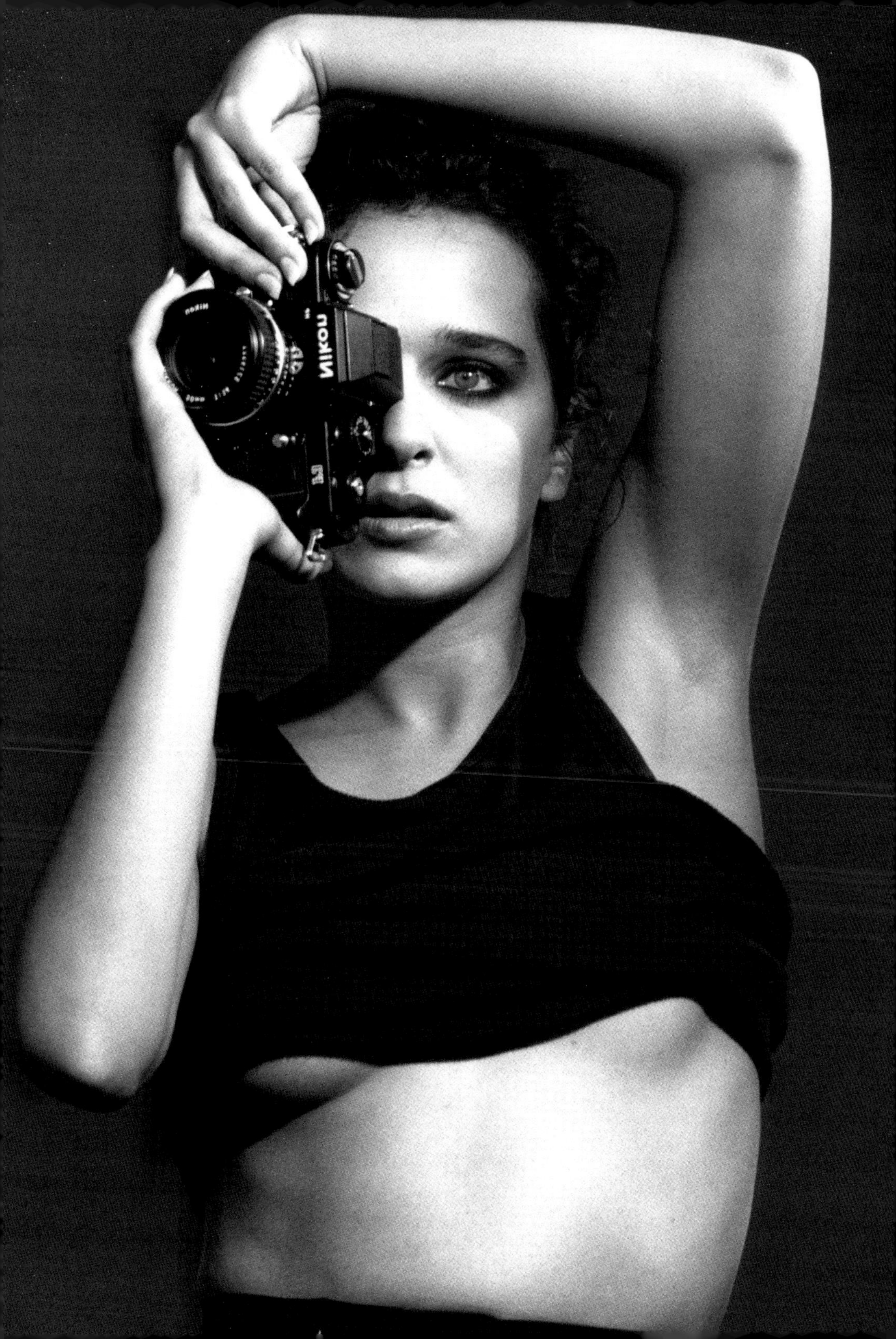

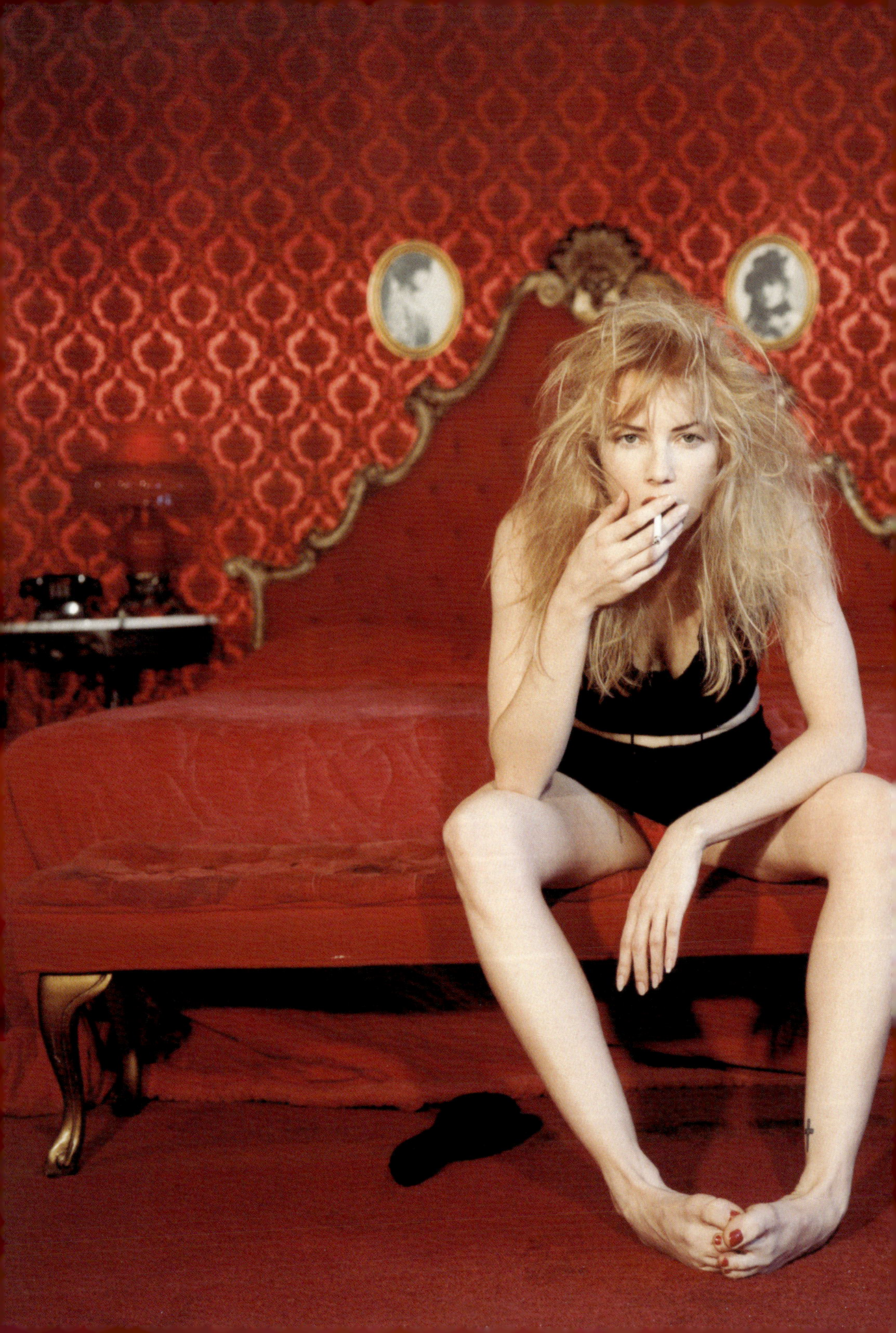

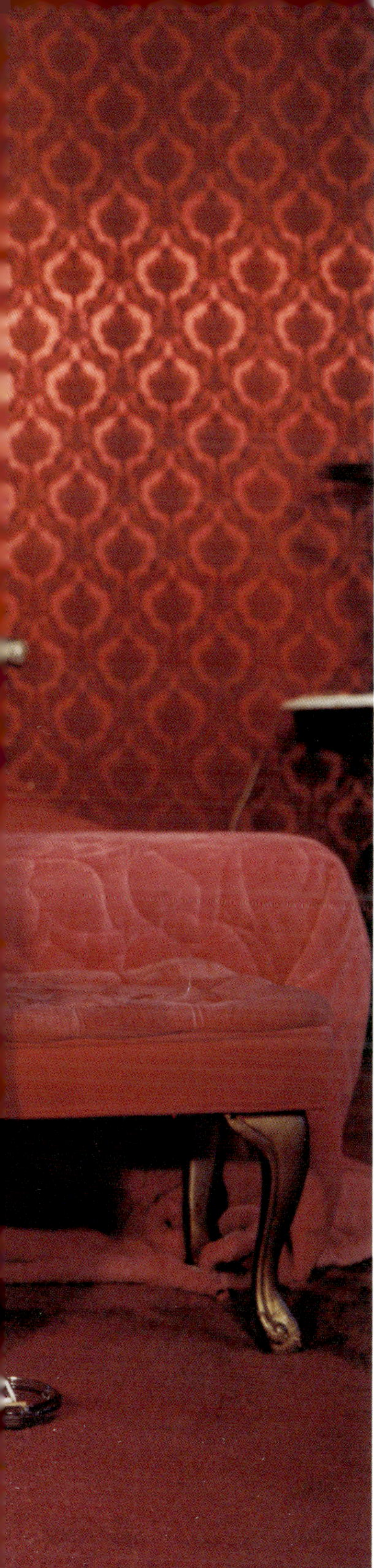

Traci Lords smoking a cigarette in the Valentino Room of the Alexandria Hotel, April 1994, Los Angeles
Following double page — *Madonna blue, smiling in shiny blue underpants*, September 1994, New York

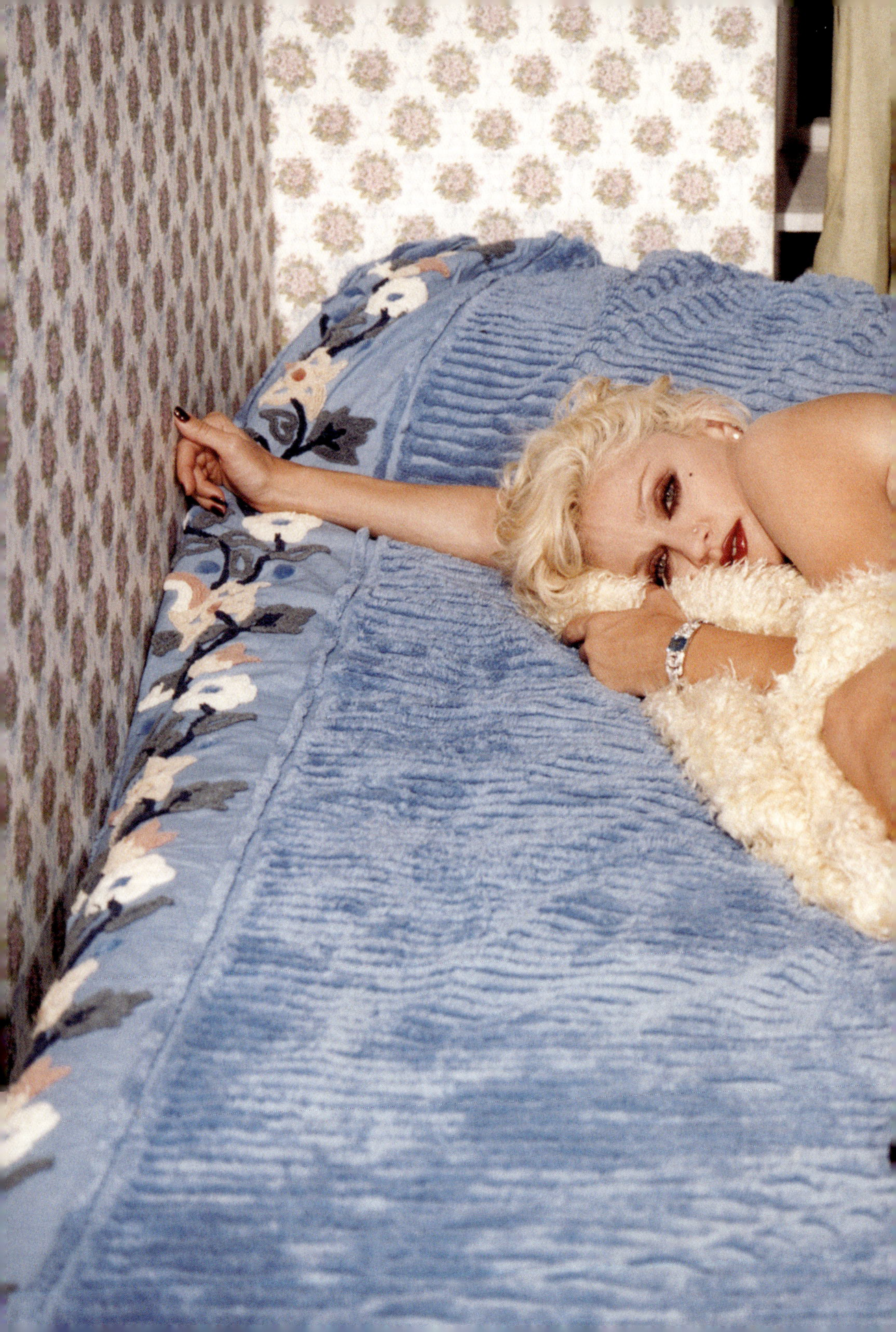

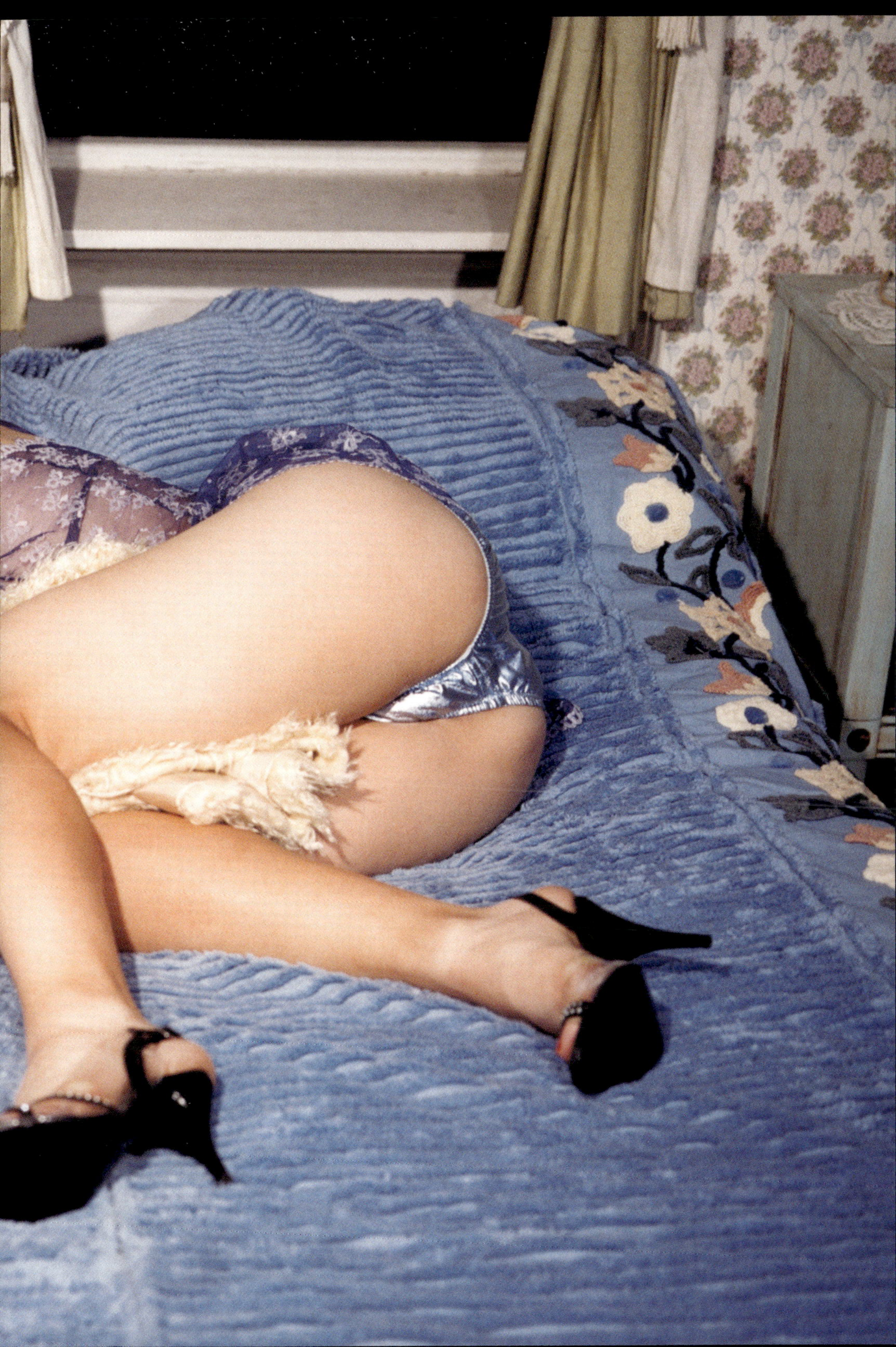

Breakfast with Monica Bellucci, November 1995, Paris
Page 18 — *Claudia covered with babypowder II*, May 2000, London
Page 19 — *Zhou Xun, dans une limousine*, November 2002,
Shanghai

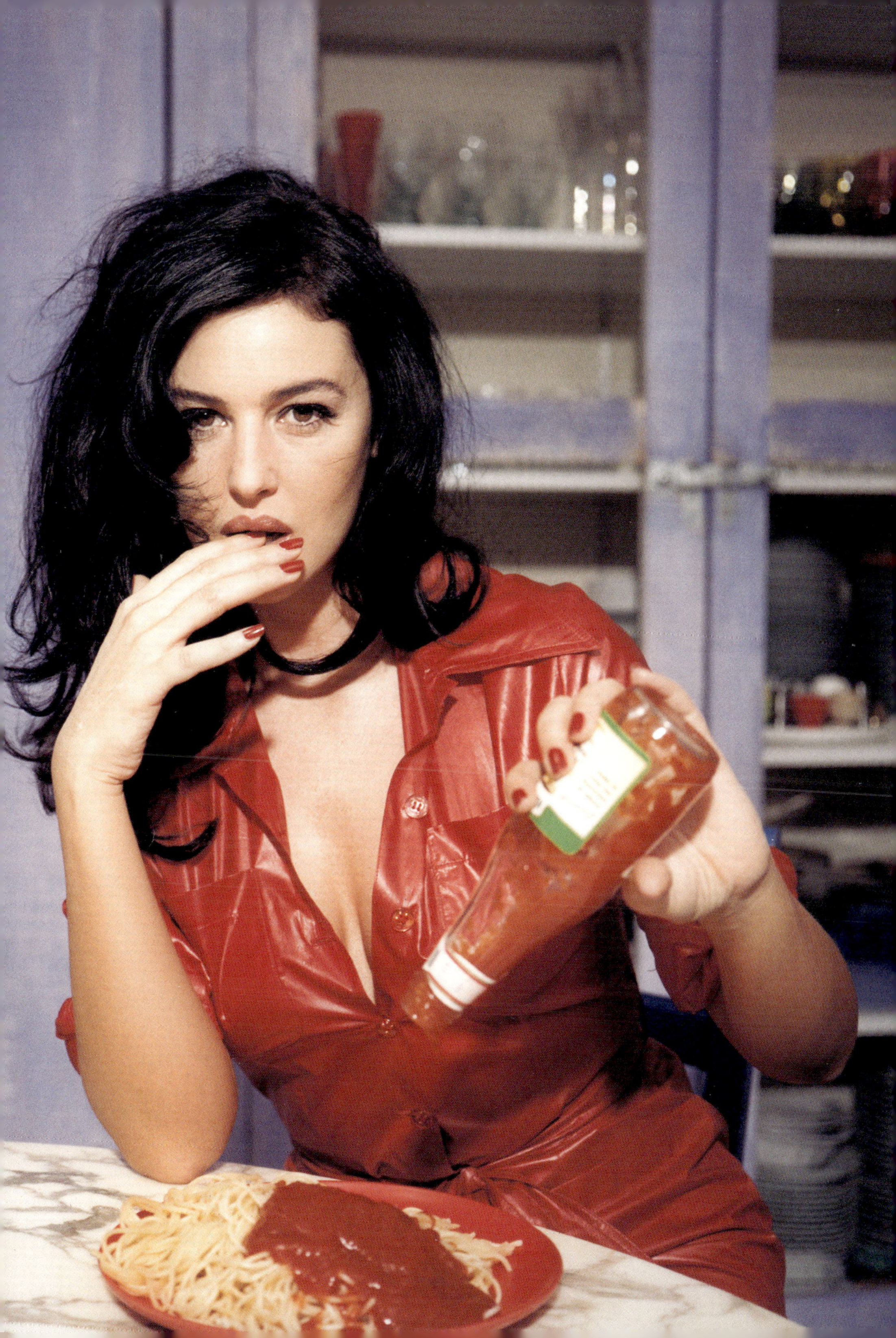

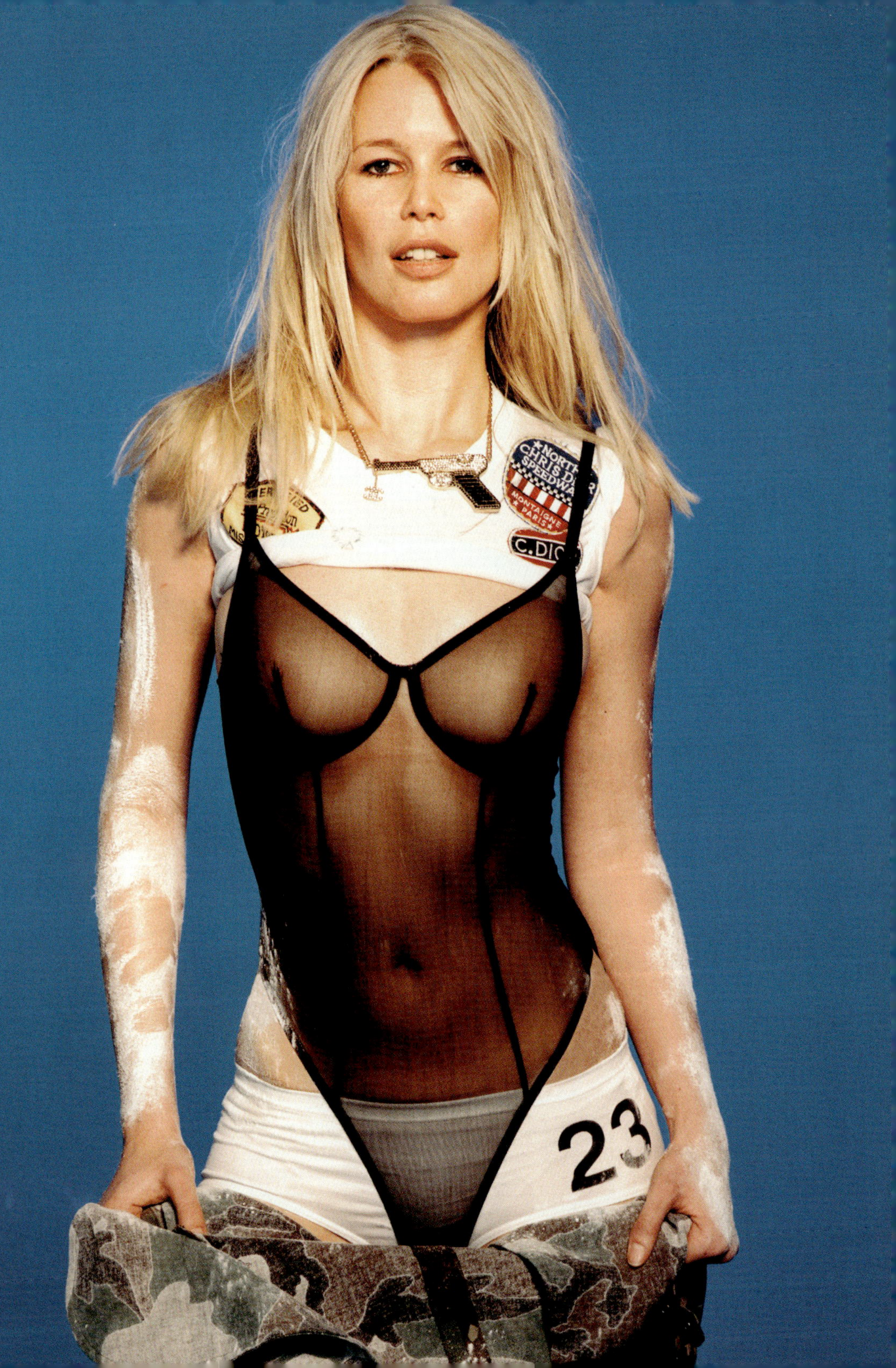

NORTH
CHRIS DIOR
SPEEDWAY
MONTAIGNE
PARIS
C. DIOR
23

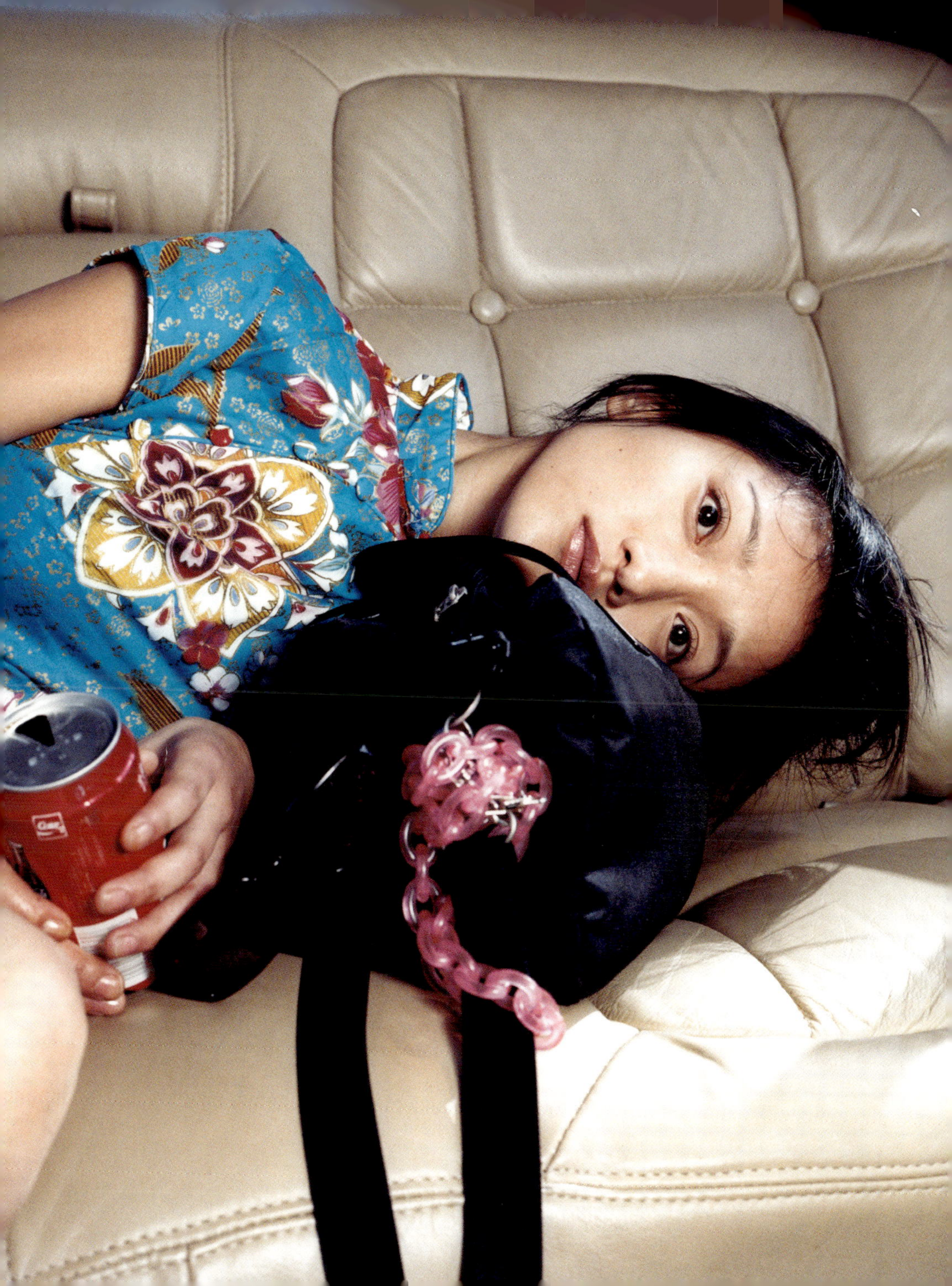

Bettina Rheims is a Renaissance painter who undresses her models with a bread knife. In her work, rock, punk and rap explode on to the ceiling of the Sistine Chapel.

Bettina Rheims est un peintre de la Renaissance qui aurait déshabillé, à l'aide d'un couteau à pain, ses modèles. C'est l'irruption de la culture rock, punk et rap sur le plafond de la chapelle Sixtine.

Bettina Rheims ist eine Renaissance-Malerin, die ihre Modelle mit einem Brotmesser entkleidet hat. In ihrem Werk explodieren Rock, Punk und Rap an der Decke der Sixtinischen Kapelle.

Patrick Besson, in *Paris Match*, 1996

Rose McGowan sinking in a bath of roses, September 1996, New York

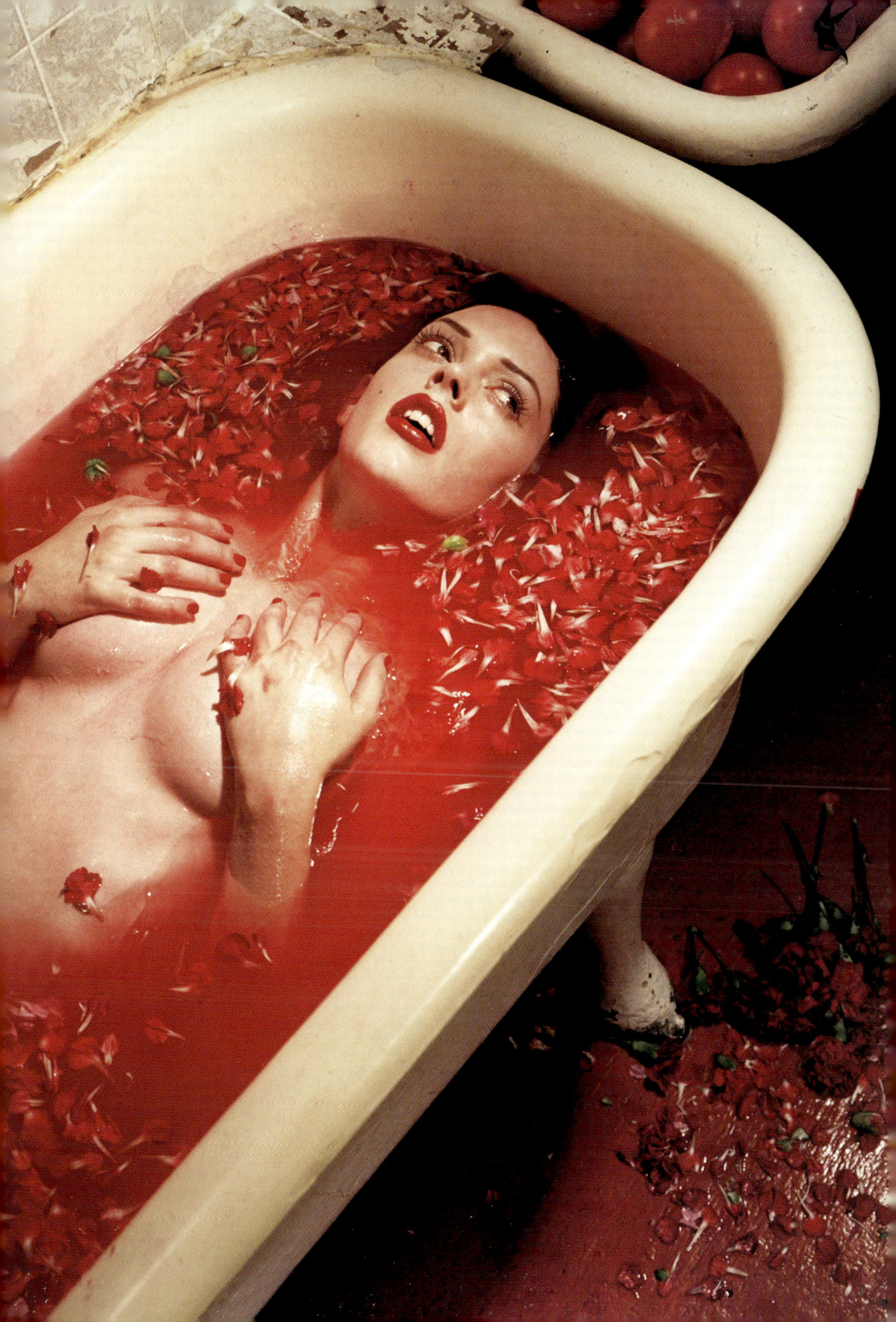

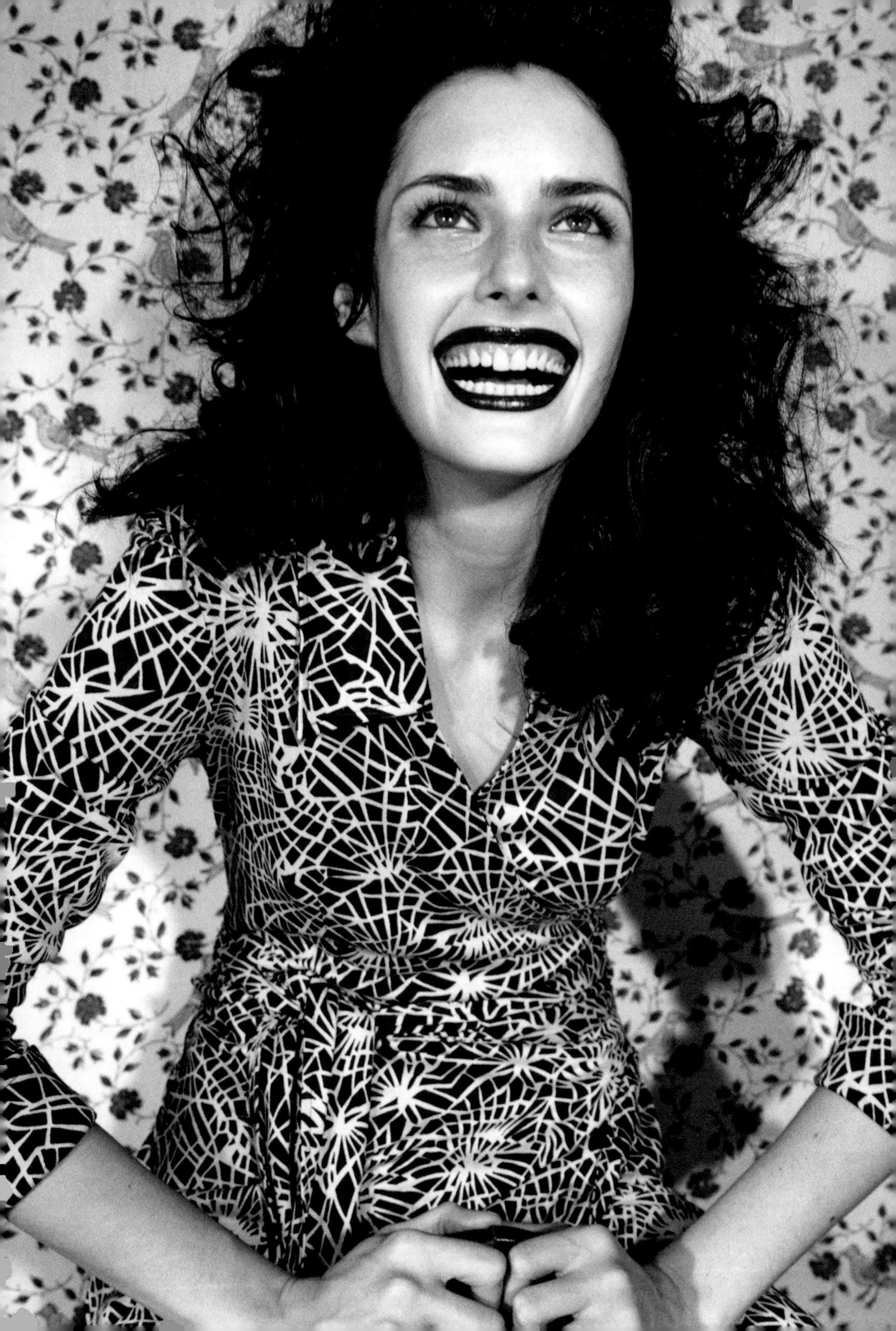

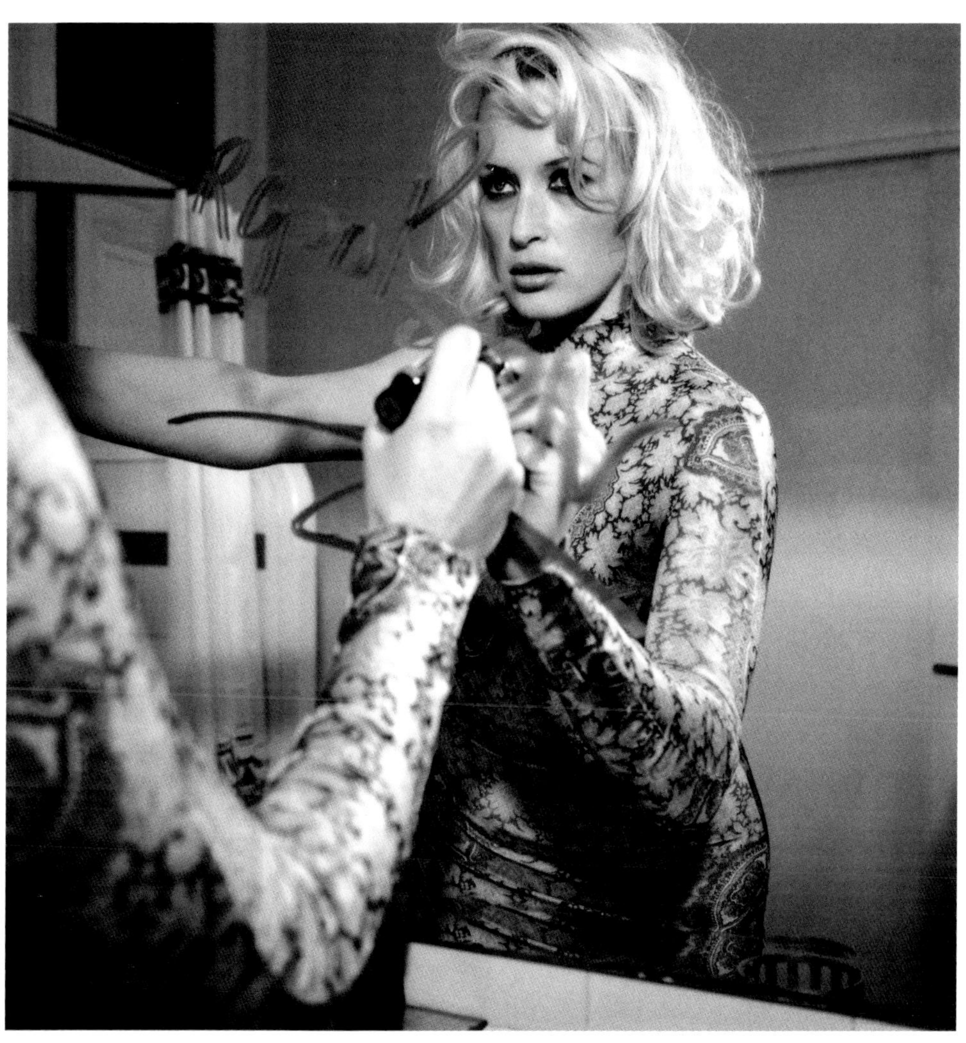

Above — *«Répulsion» avec Estelle Hallyday II*, January 1996, Paris
Opposite page — *Laughing ad for Diane von Fürstenberg*, May 1997, Paris

Karen Elson, nue couronnée de fleurs, October 2000, Paris

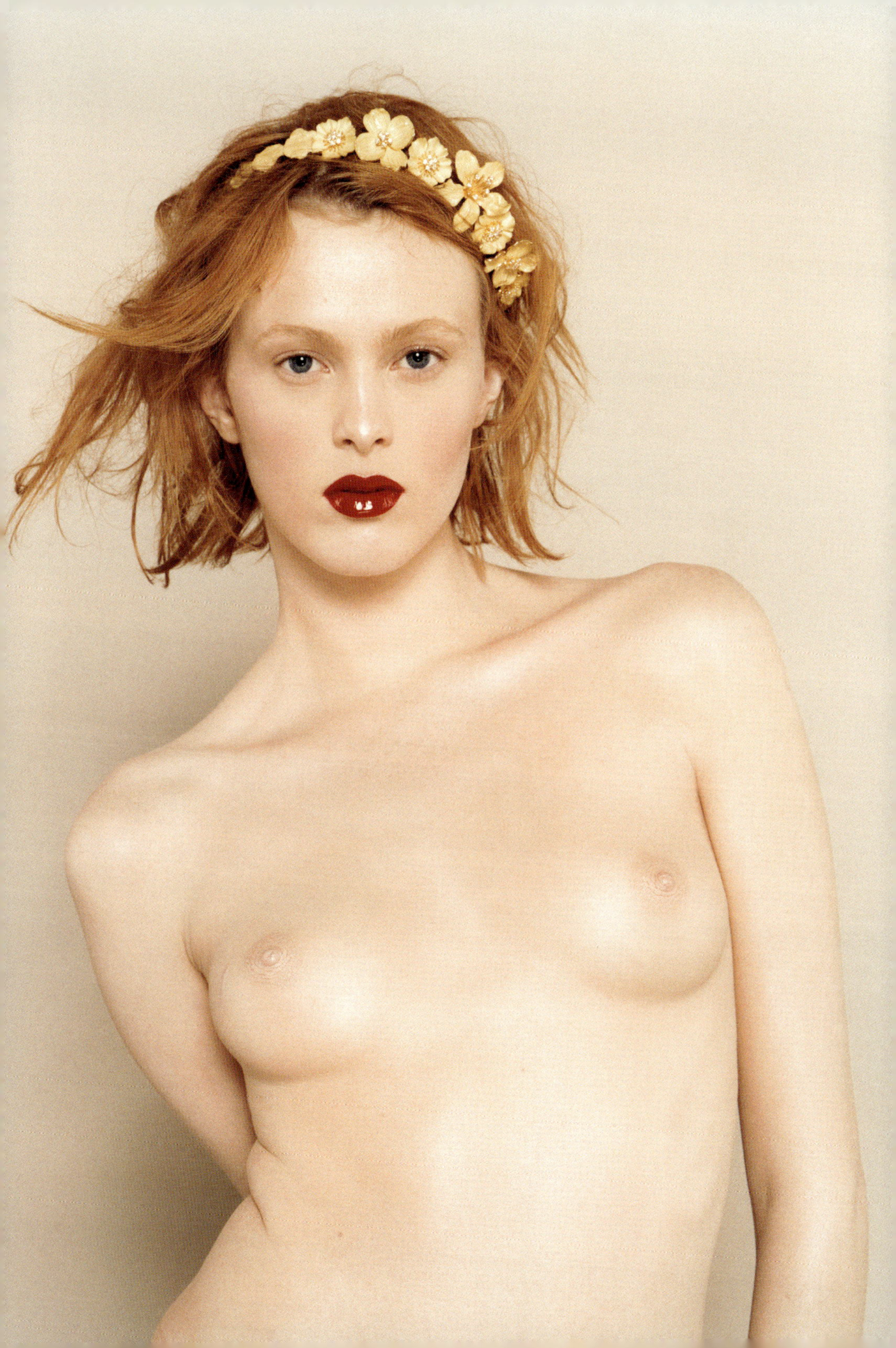

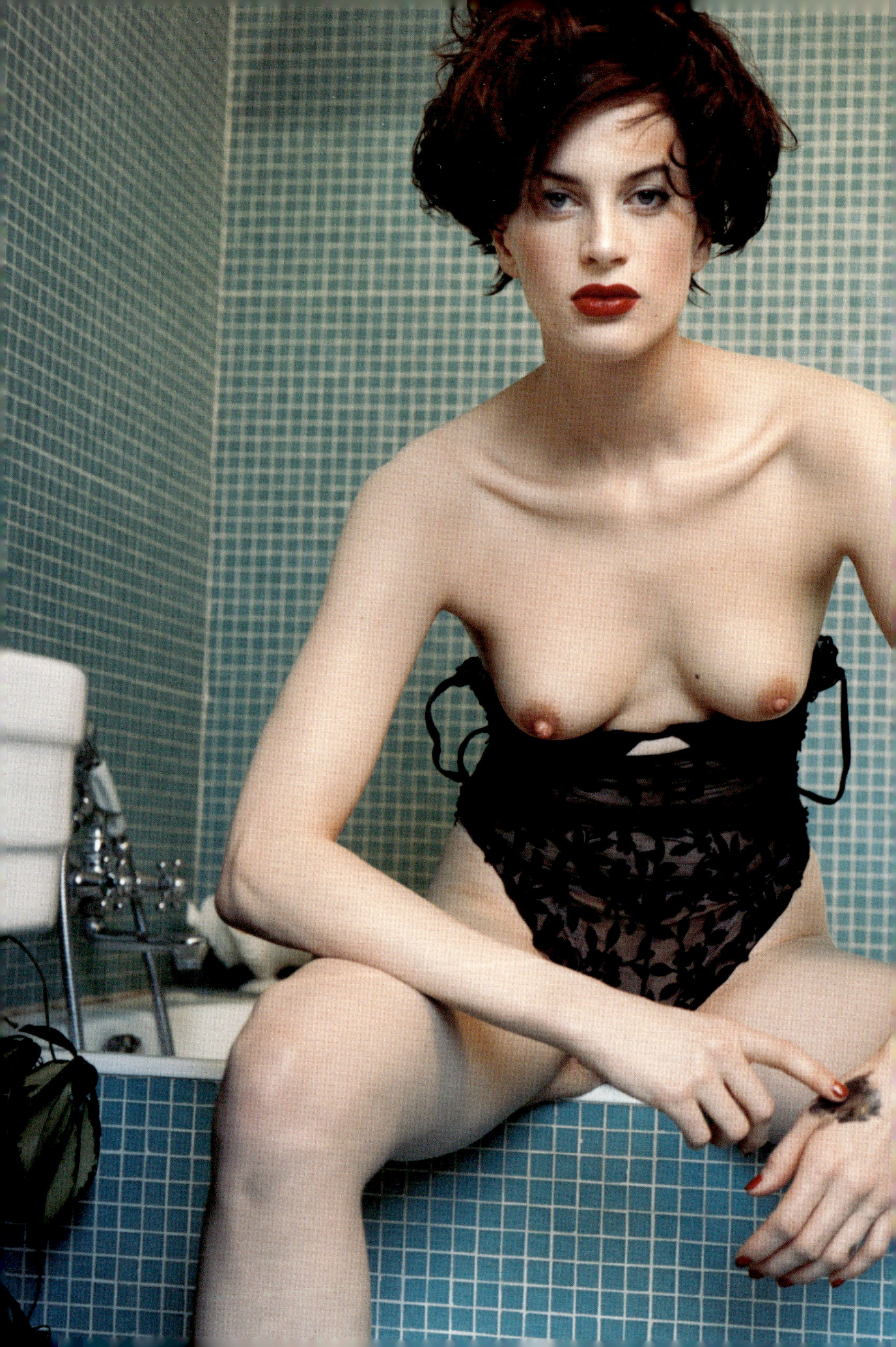

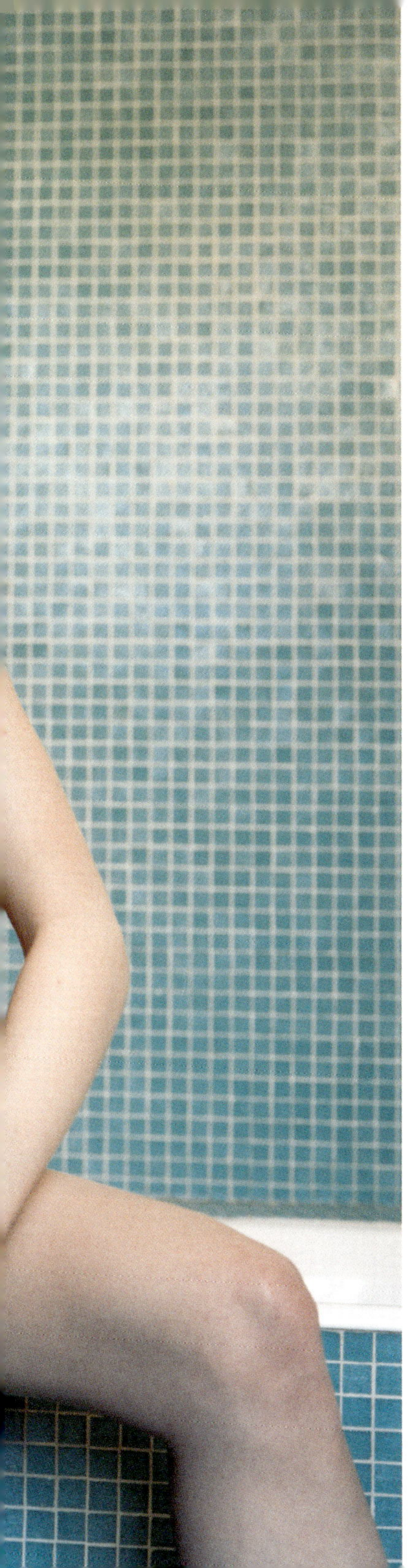

Kristen McMenamy with black make-up on her hand,
June 1994, Paris

27

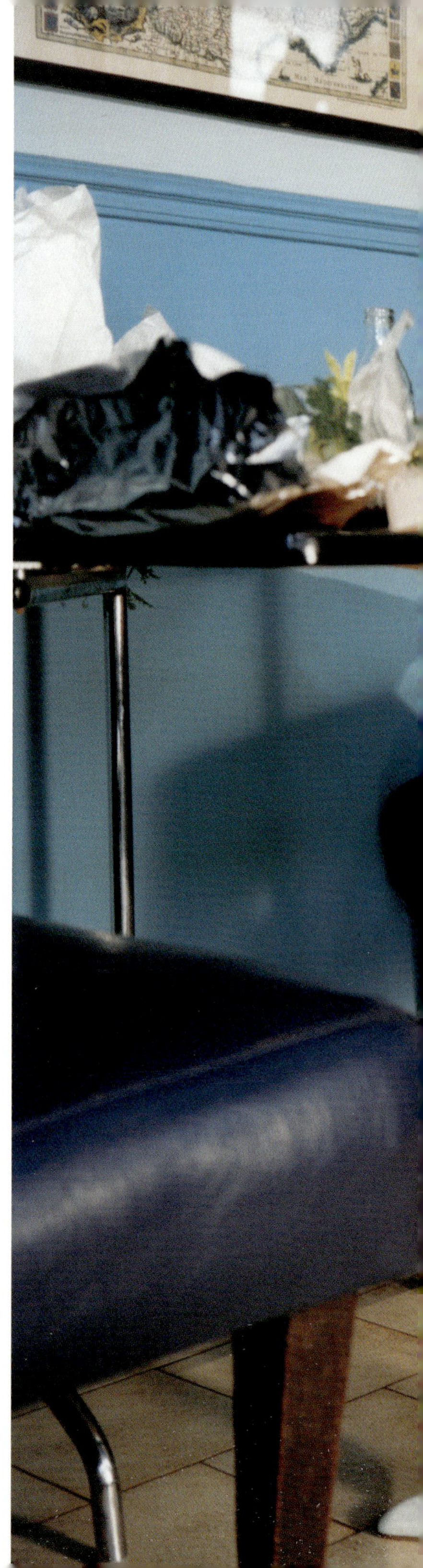

Martina for German Playboy, April 1993, Paris

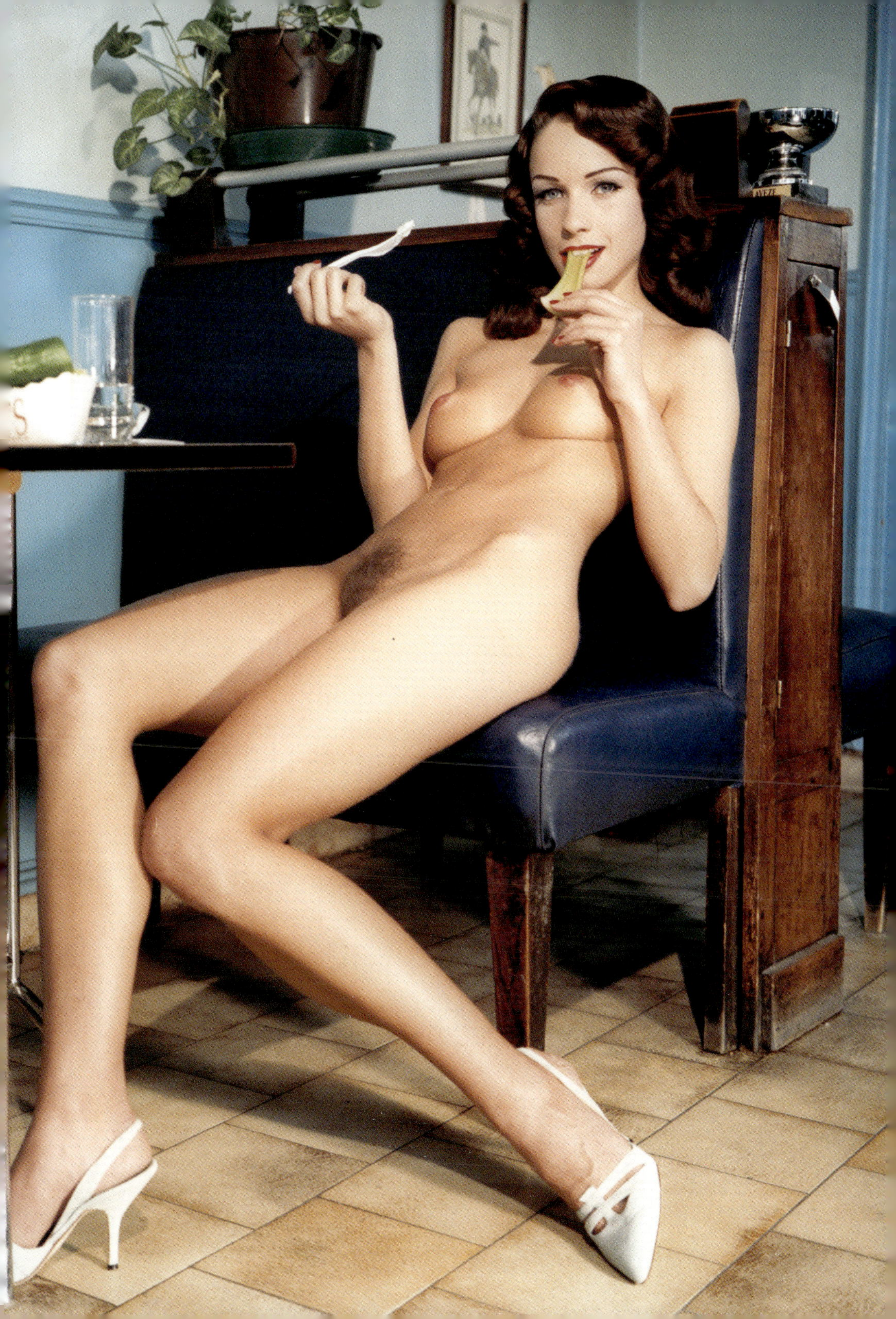

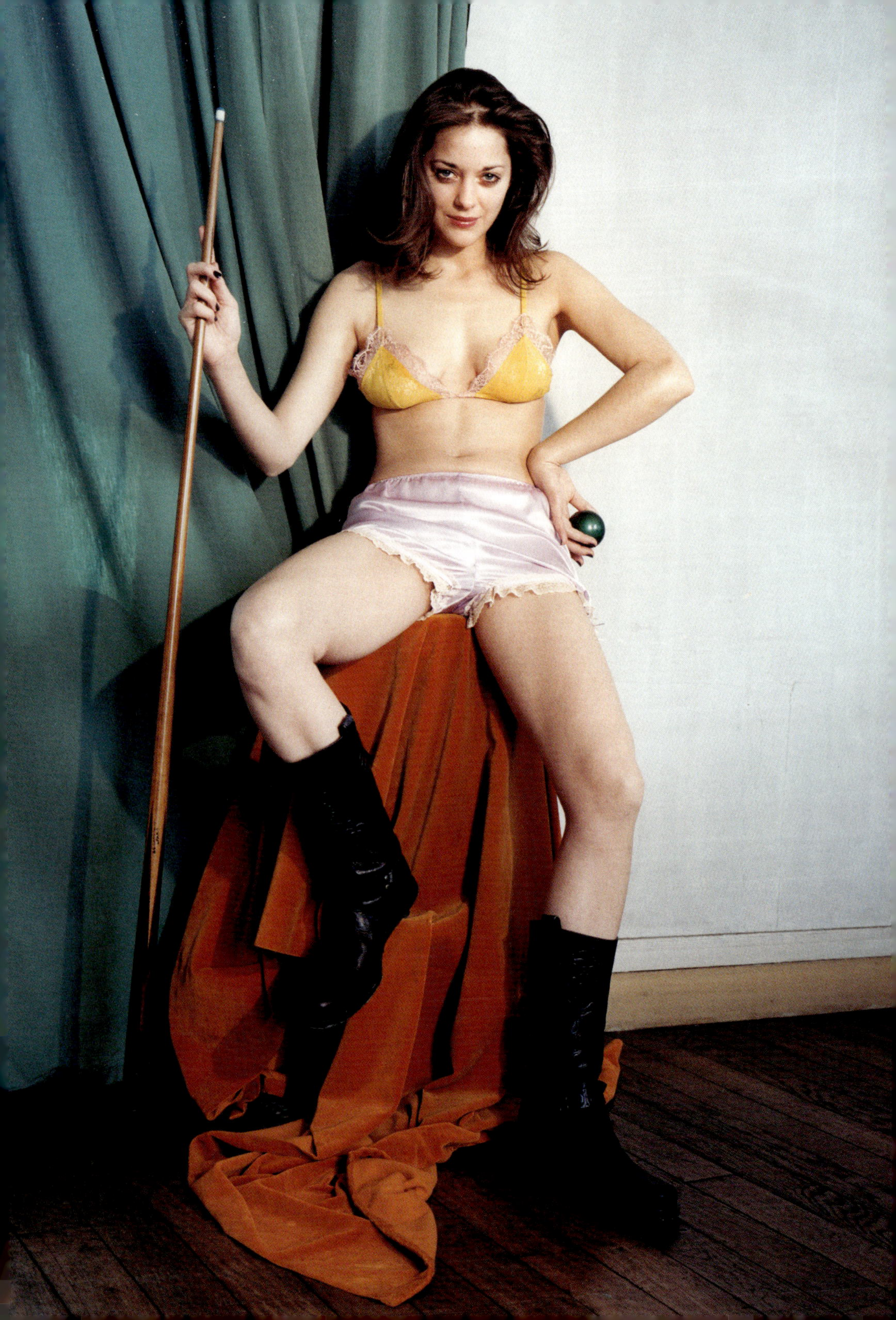

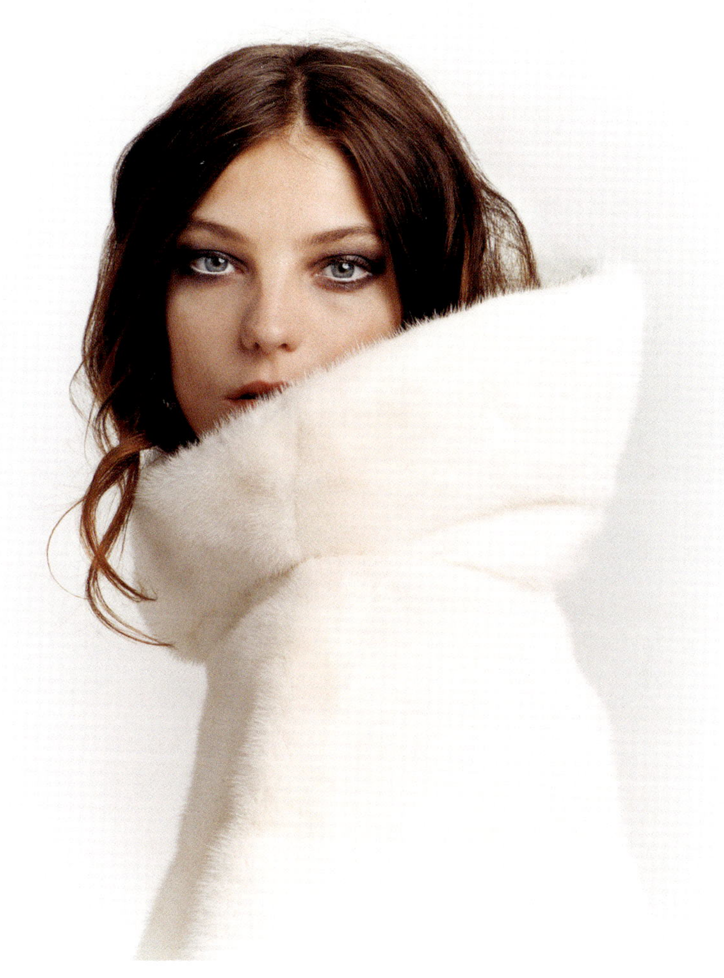

Above — *Portrait de Daria au vison blanc II*, September 2006, Paris
Opposite page — *La sublime joueuse de billard, Marion Cotillard*, June 2002, Maisons-Laffitte

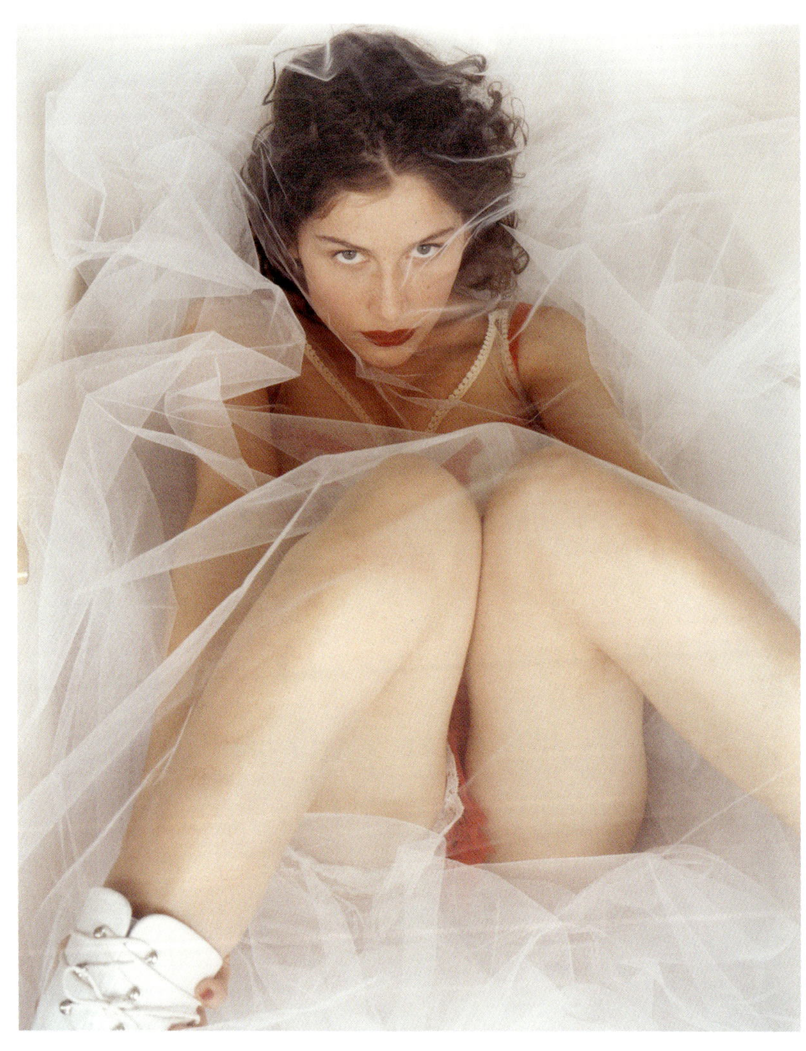

Above — *Laetitia Casta prend un bain de tulle à l'hôtel George V*, June 2002, Paris
 Opposite page — *Rose McGowan nailed on a rundown wall*, October 1995, Los Angeles

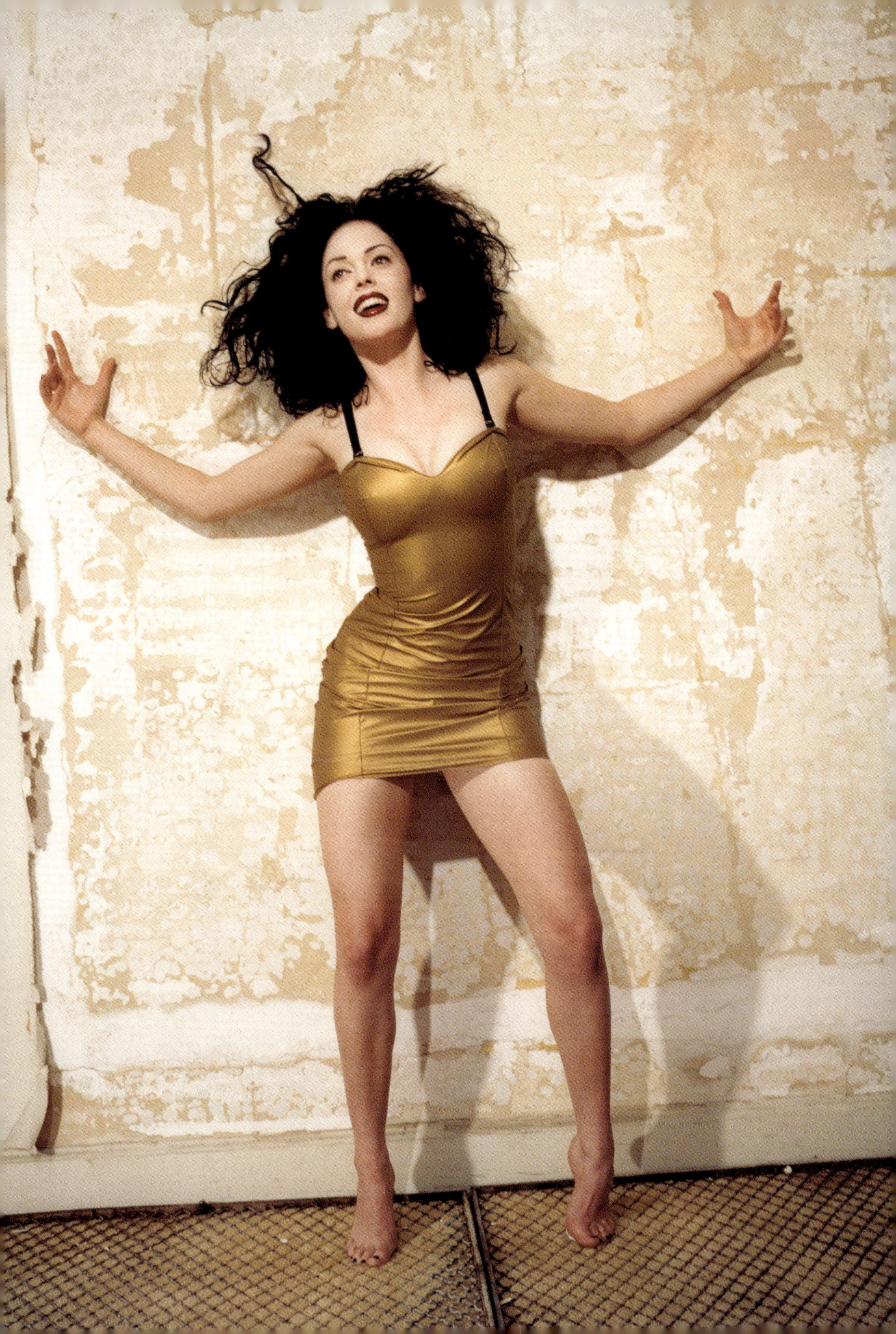

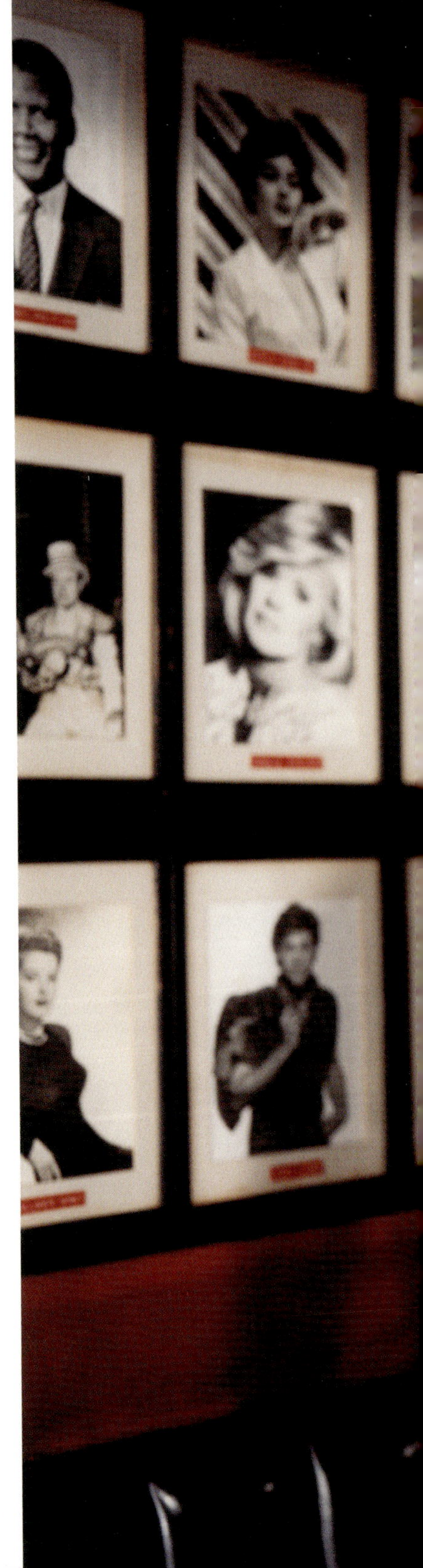

Claire Stansfield crying in the Formosa Café, February 1994, Los Angeles

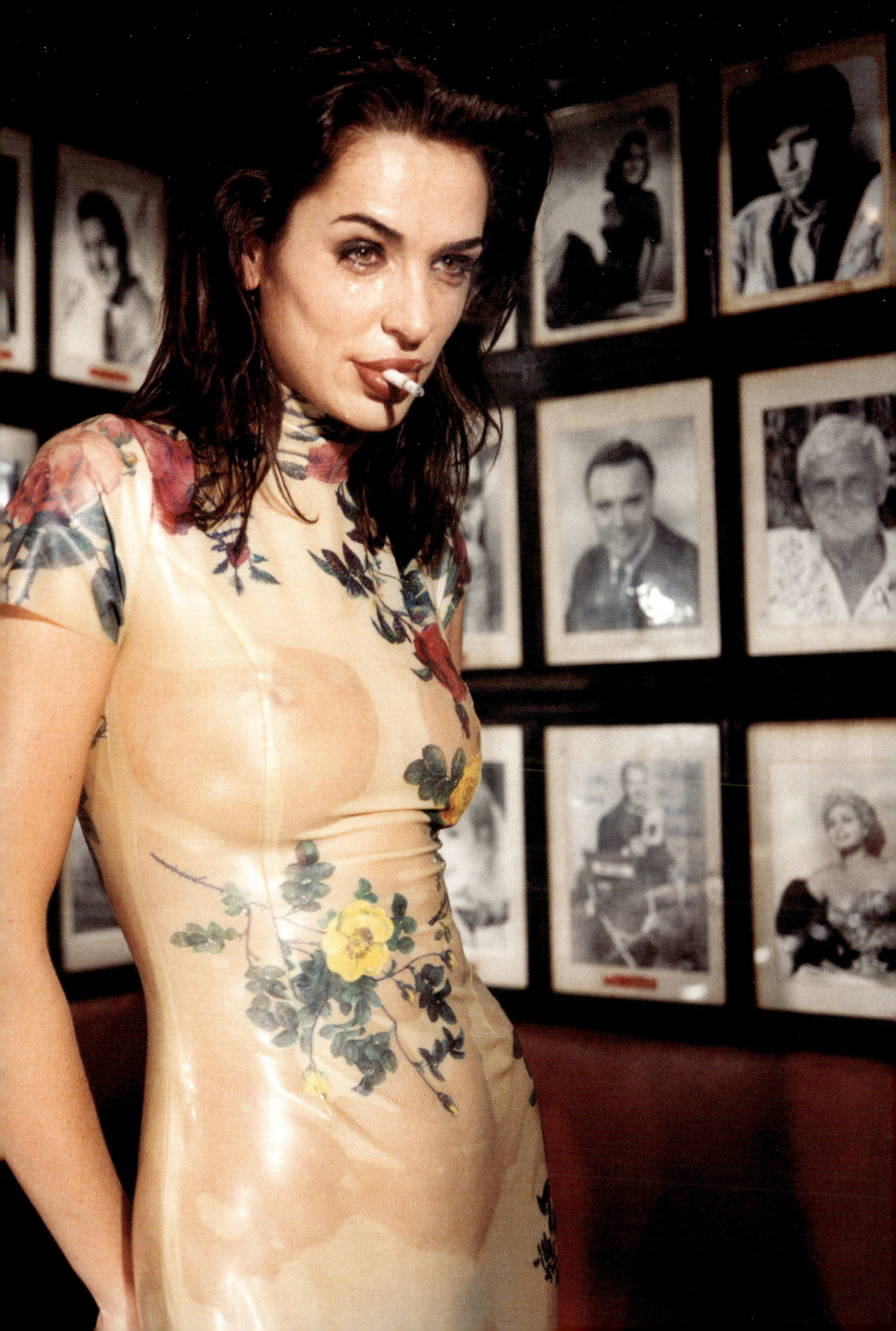

This ambiguity belongs to the artist, who has photographed
respectable young women the way a prostitute would undress,
beauty icons with their bodies covered with sweat and bruises,
symbols of life that turn out to be stuffed animals, or again, the
mutant bodies of those who have chosen to change sex. She has
understood that this is what she does: show equivocal moments,
but show them raw.

Cette ambivalence appartient à l'artiste, à celle qui a photographié
des jeunes filles convenables dans les conditions de déshabillage
d'une prostituée, des icônes de la beauté quand leur corps est
couvert de sueur et de bleus, des symboles de vie qui se révèlent
être des animaux empaillés, ou encore le corps mutant de ceux
qui choisissent de changer de sexe. Elle a compris que son métier,
c'était cela: montrer les moments de flottement, mais les montrer
crûment.

Diese Ambivalenz ist charakteristisch für die Künstlerin, die brave
junge Mädchen fotografiert hat, die sich wie Prostituierte entkleiden,
Ikonen der Schönheit, wenn ihre Körper von Schweiß und blauen
Flecken bedeckt sind, Symbole des Lebens, die sich als ausgestopfte
Tiere entpuppen. Oder auch die mutierenden Körper jener, die
beschlossen haben, ihr Geschlecht zu wechseln. Sie hat erkannt, dass
genau das ihre Berufung ist: zweideutige Situationen zu zeigen – aller-
dings schonungslos.

Catherine Millet, 2008, Paris

     Catherine Deneuve au George V, May 1988, Paris

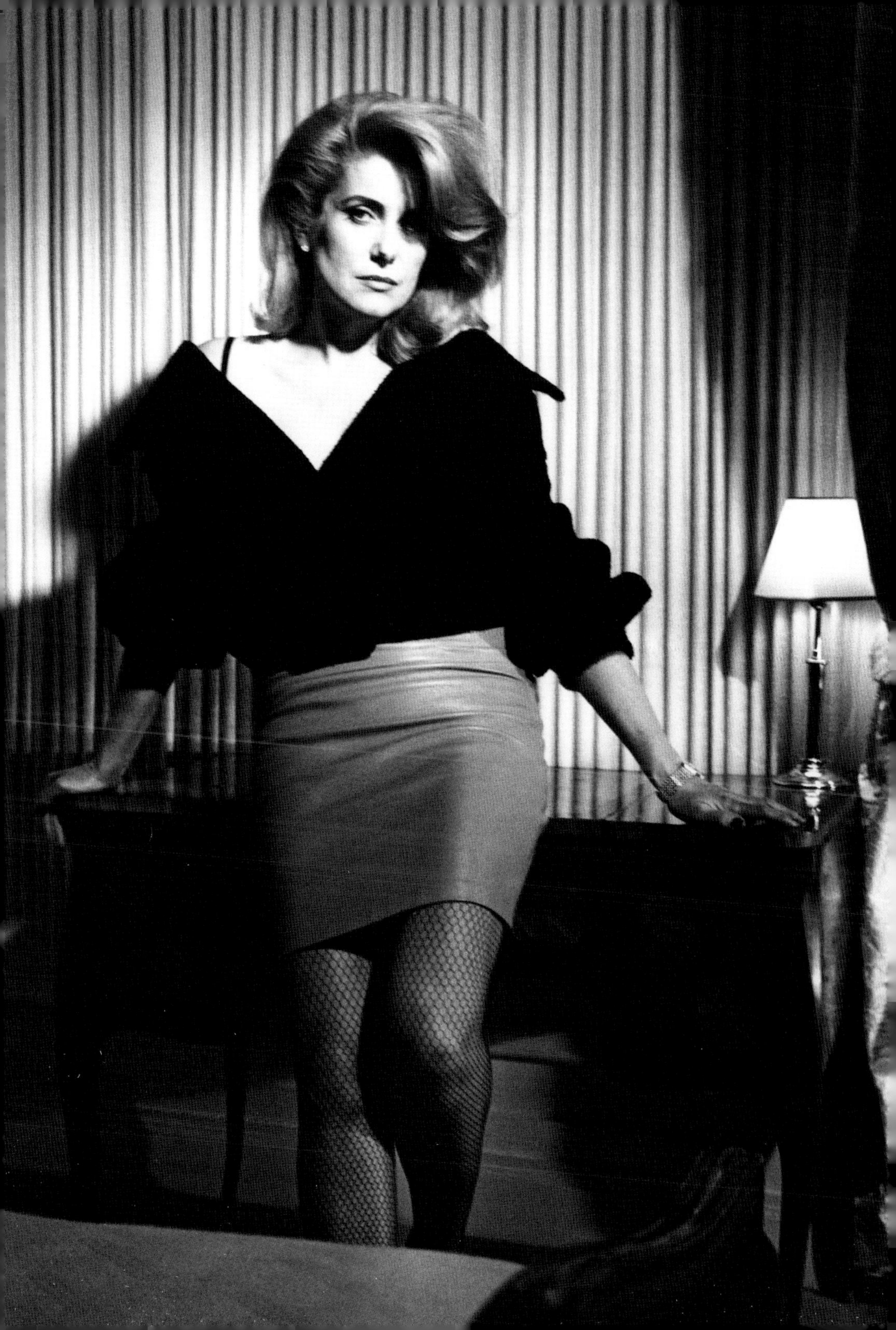

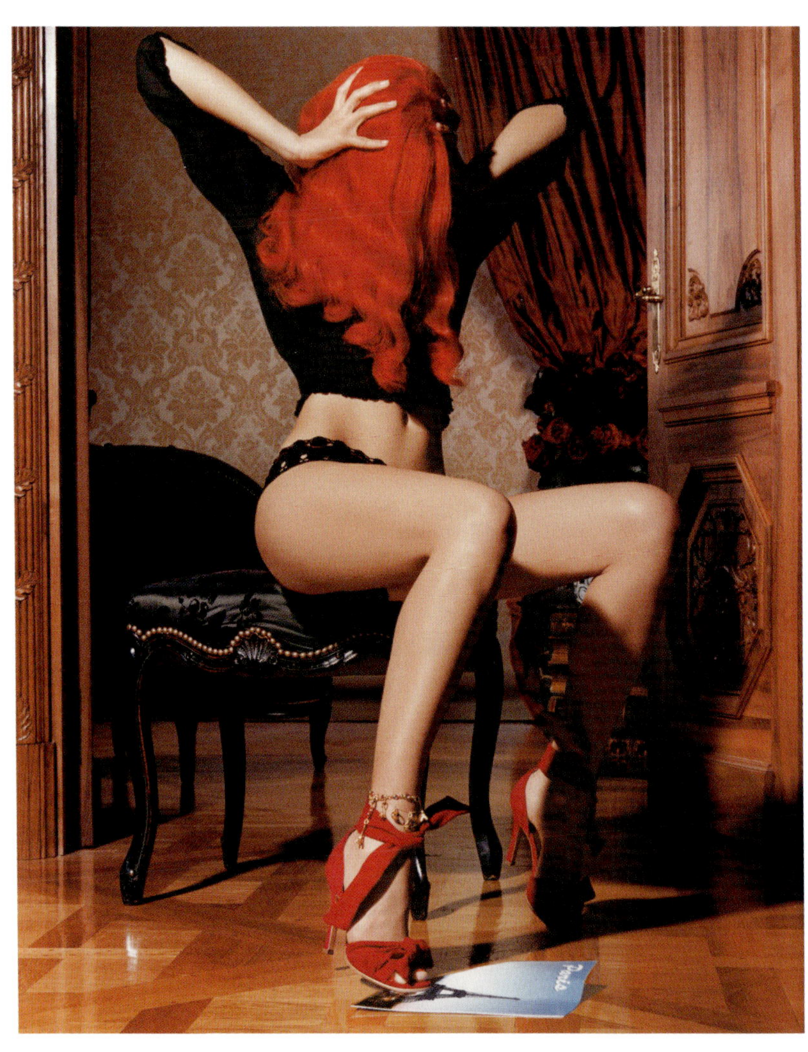

Above — *La fille aux cheveux rouges porte des chaussures rouges Charles Jourdan*, June 2006, Paris
Opposite page — *Elizabeth Berkley in a coucou's nest*, February 1996, Los Angeles
Page 40 — *Cérémonie VI, eyes wide open*, February 1999, Paris
Page 41 — *Kim Peers as a boy trying to be a girl*, January 2001, Paris

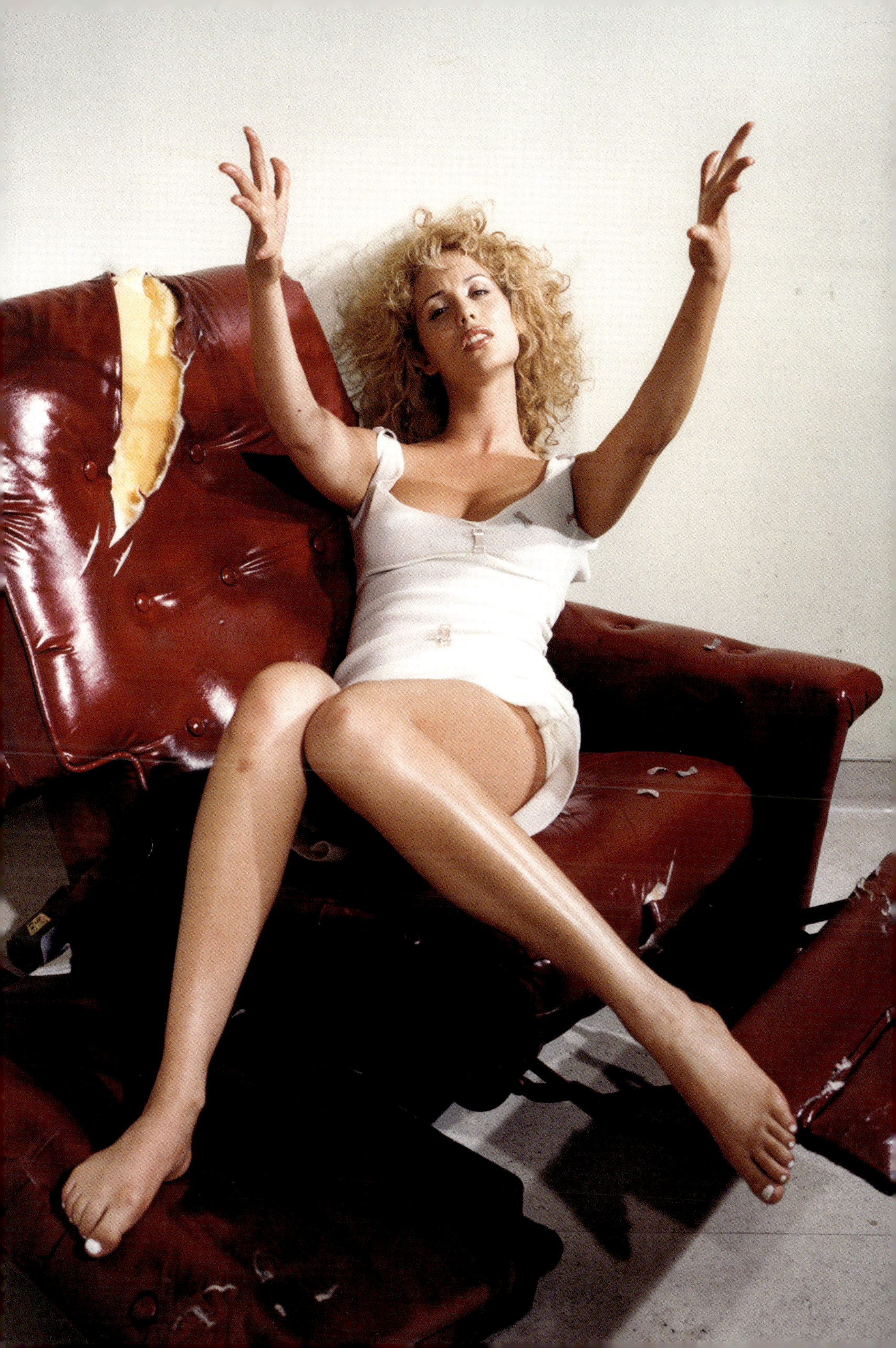

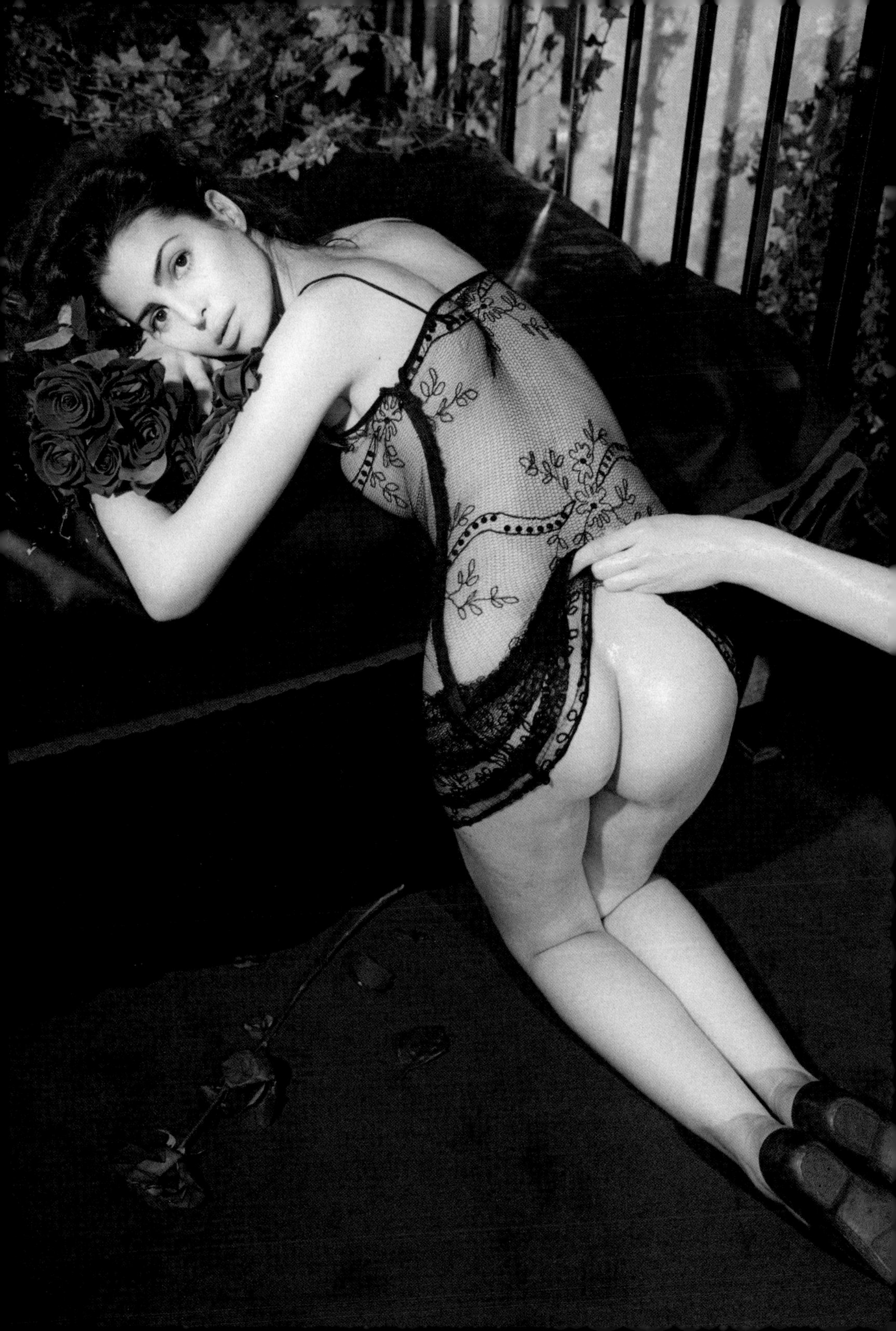

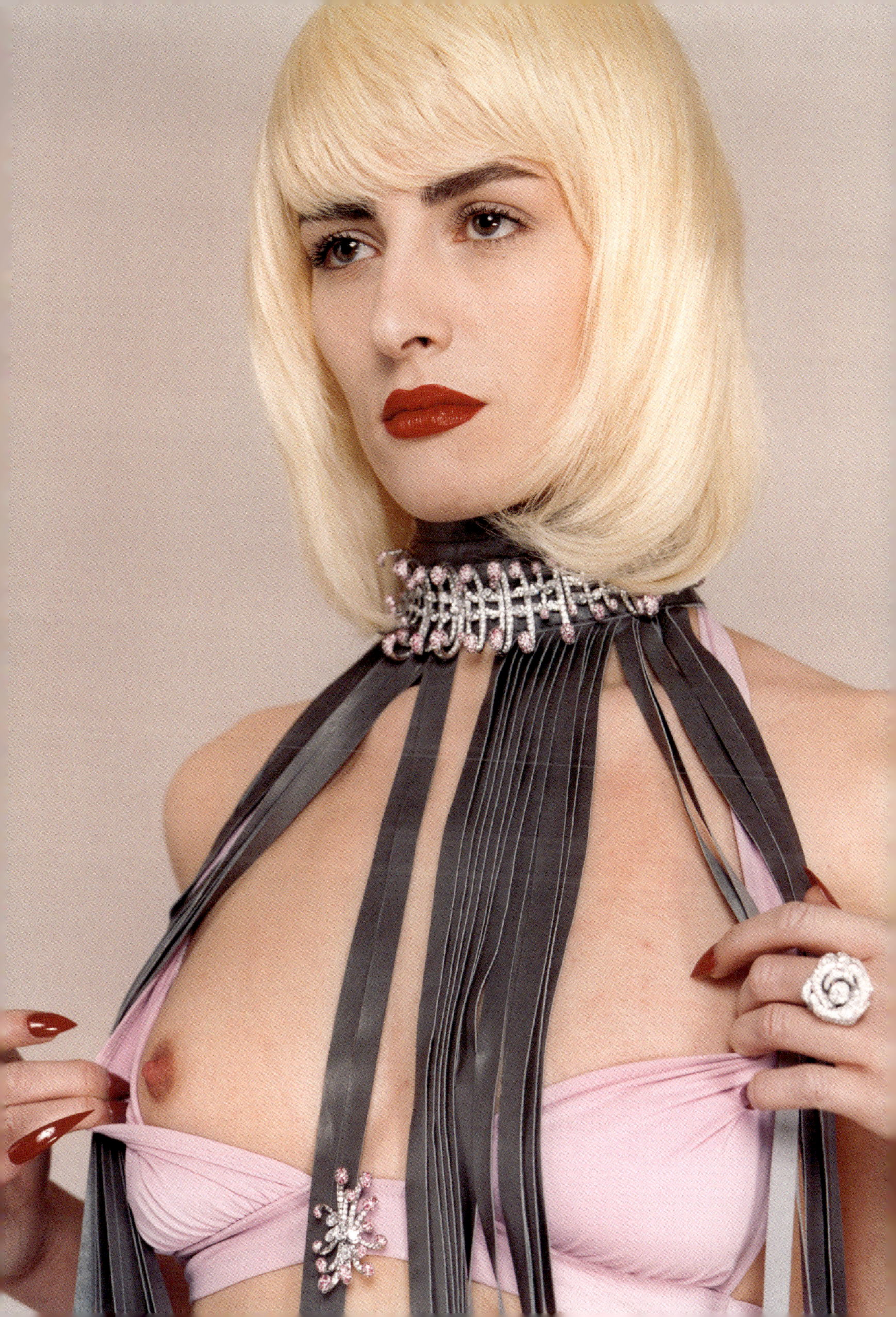

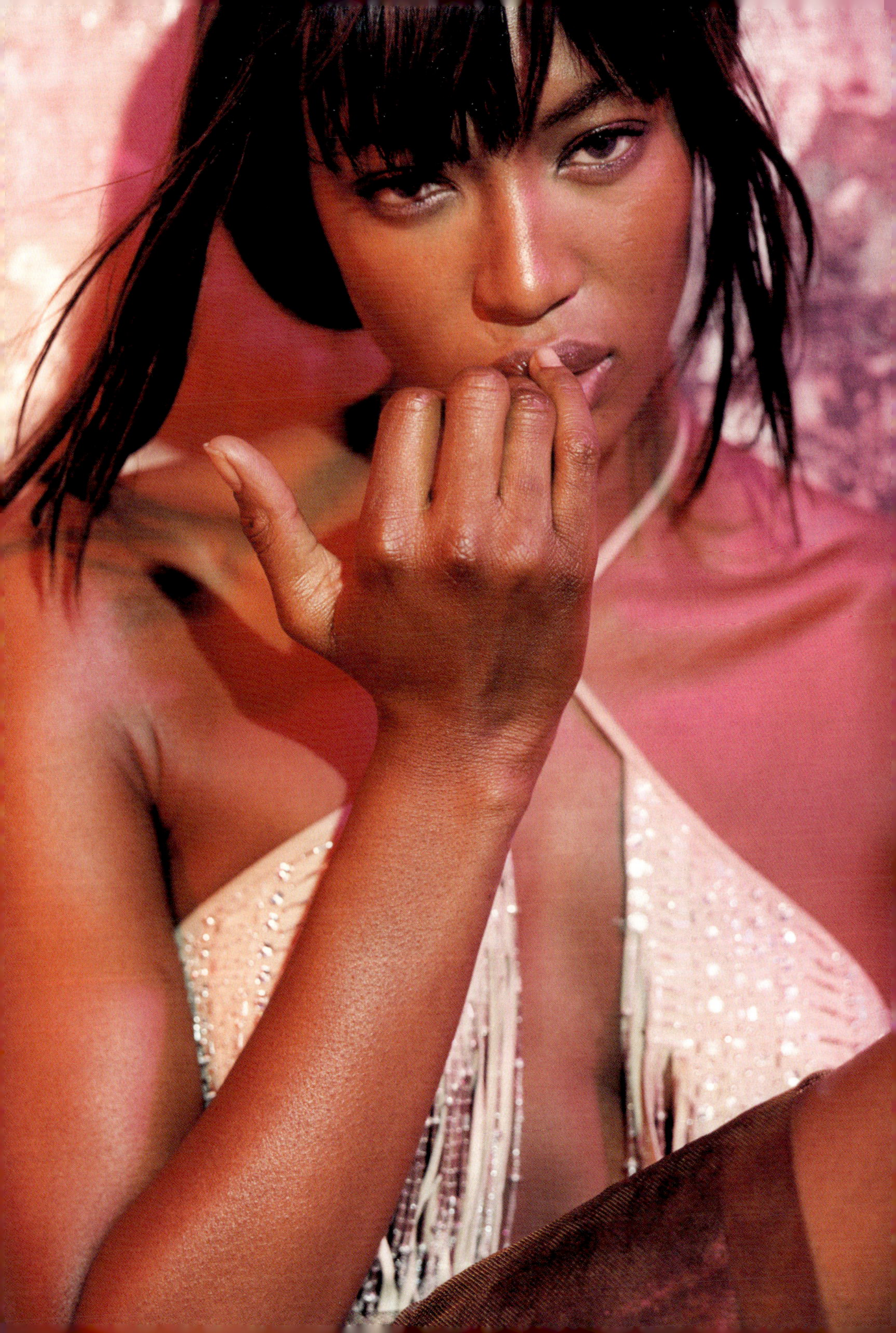

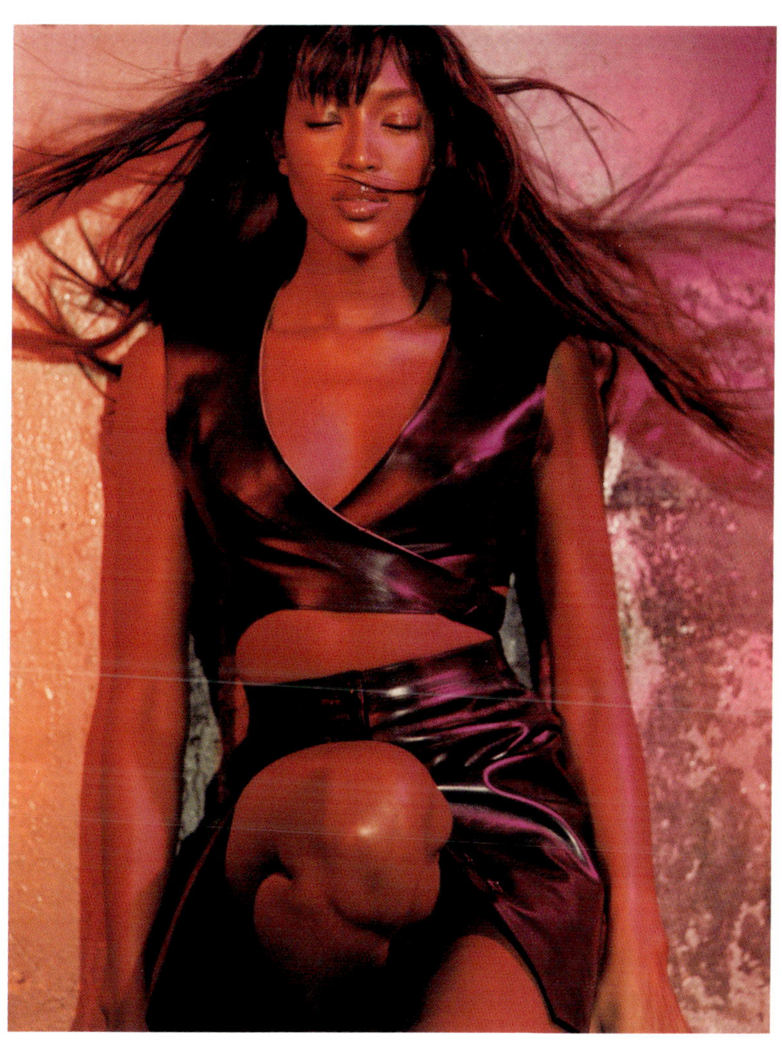

Above — *Naomi Campbell*, March 1999, Paris
Opposite page — *Naomi Campbell, portrait of a lady*, March 1999, Paris

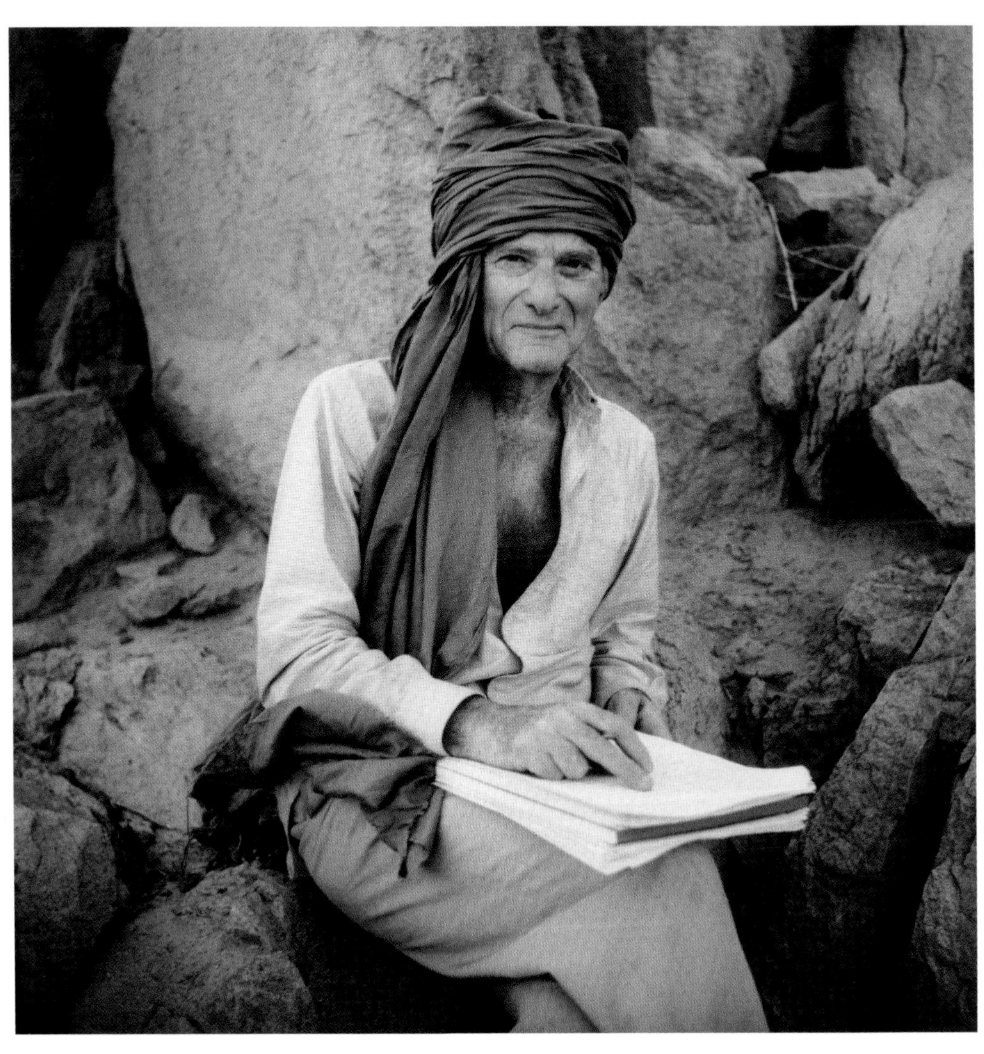

Above — *Maurice Rheims dans le désert*, February 1982, Agadez, Nigeria
Opposite page — *L'immortel*, March 2009, Place du Calvaire, Paris

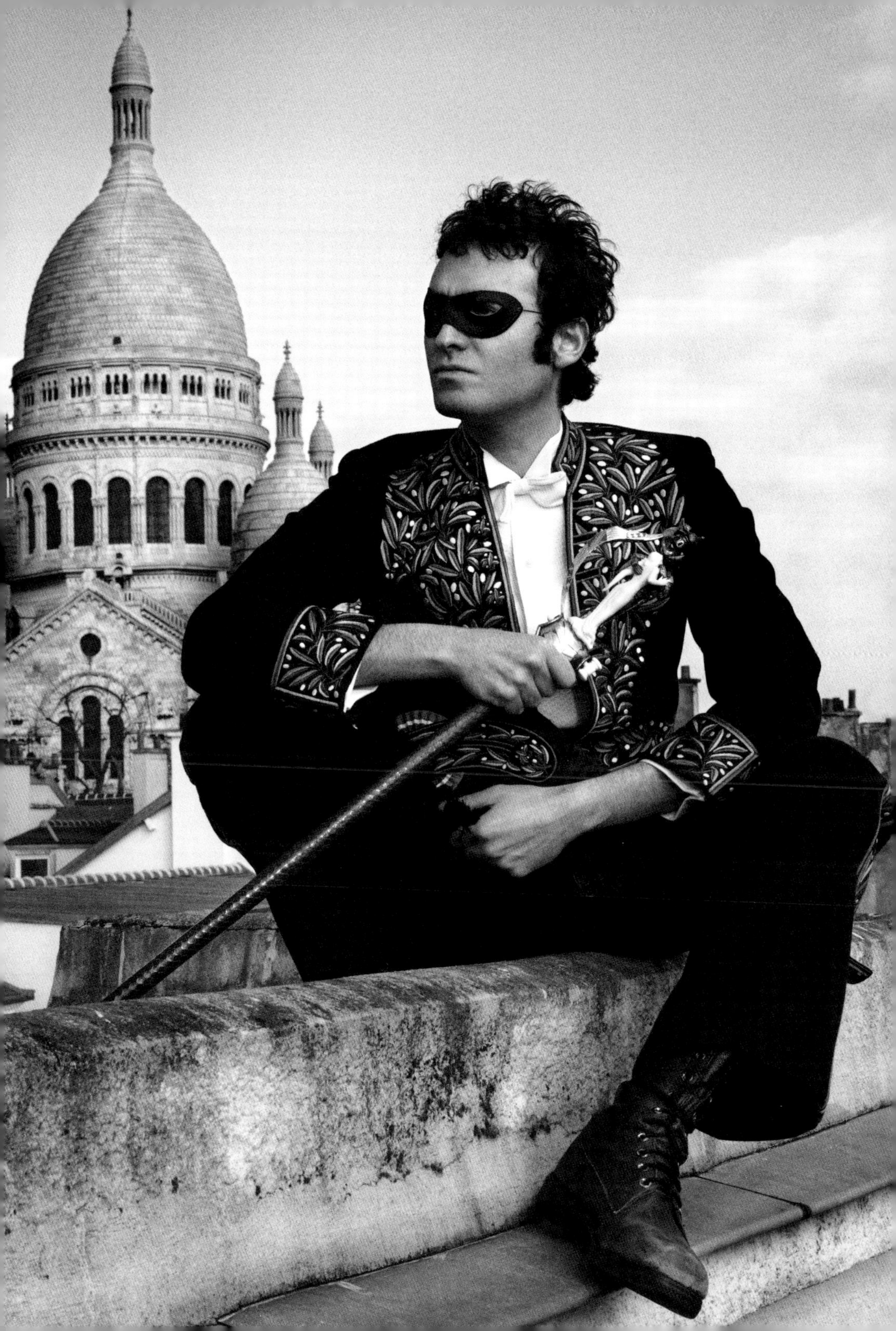

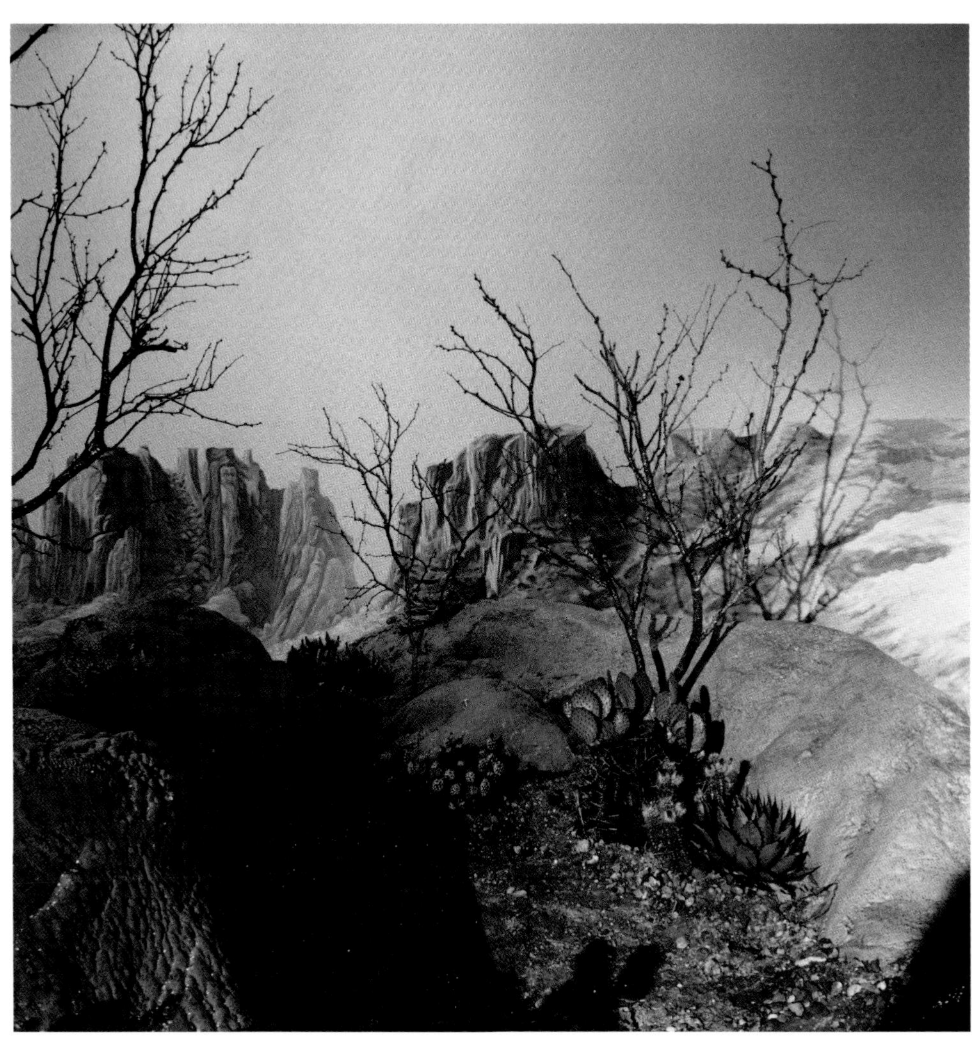

 Arizona landscape, May 1991, Arizona

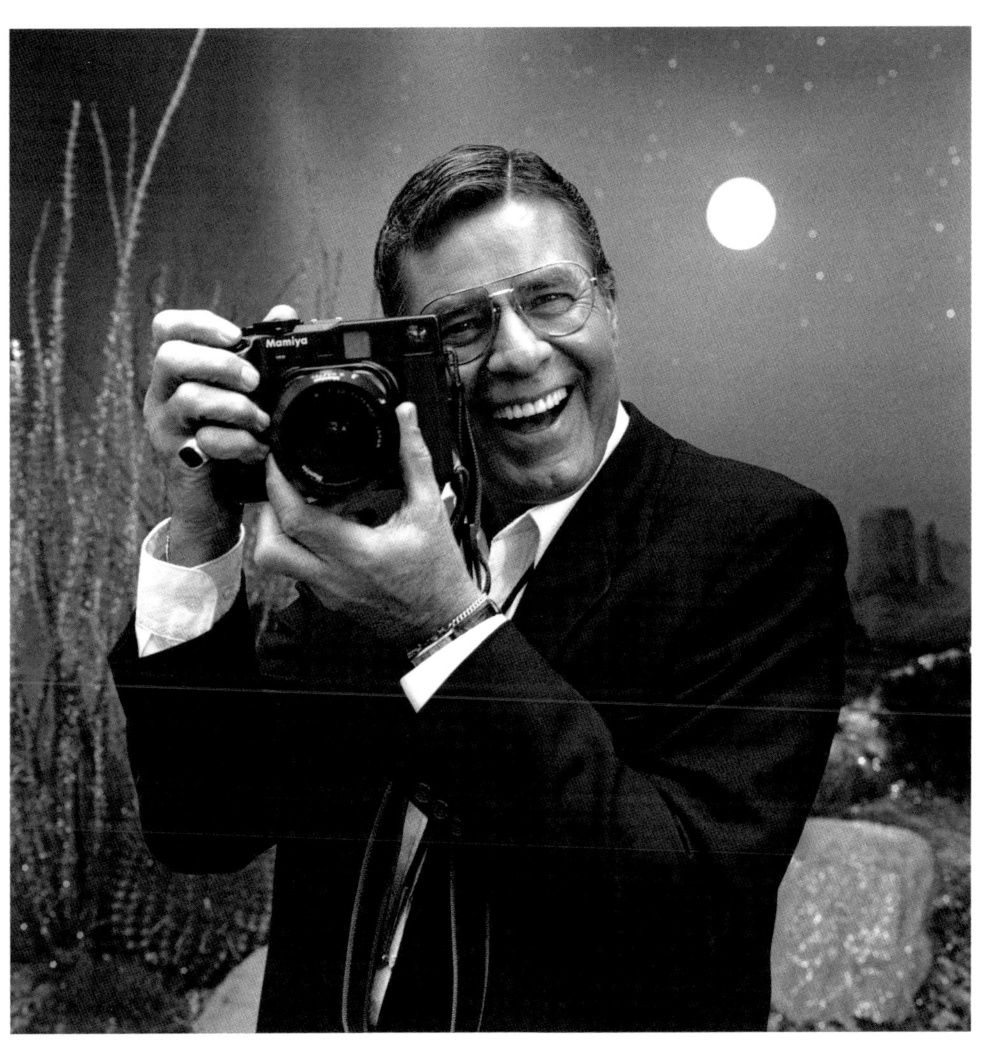

Jerry Lewis fait mon potrtrait, May 1991, Arizona

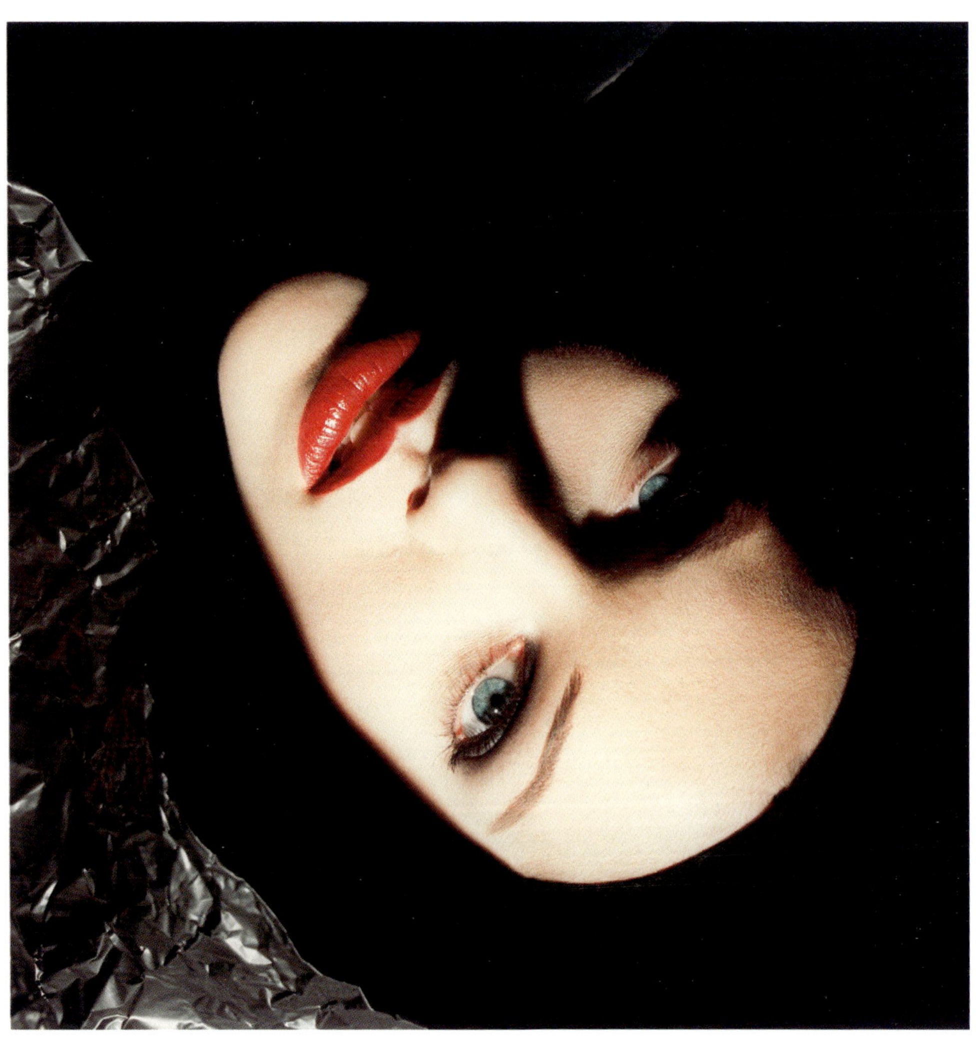

Above — *Put the blame on Mame, par Chanel*, November 1992, Venice
Opposite page — *Anna T. caresse une étrange fleur — Anthurium*, June 2007, Paris

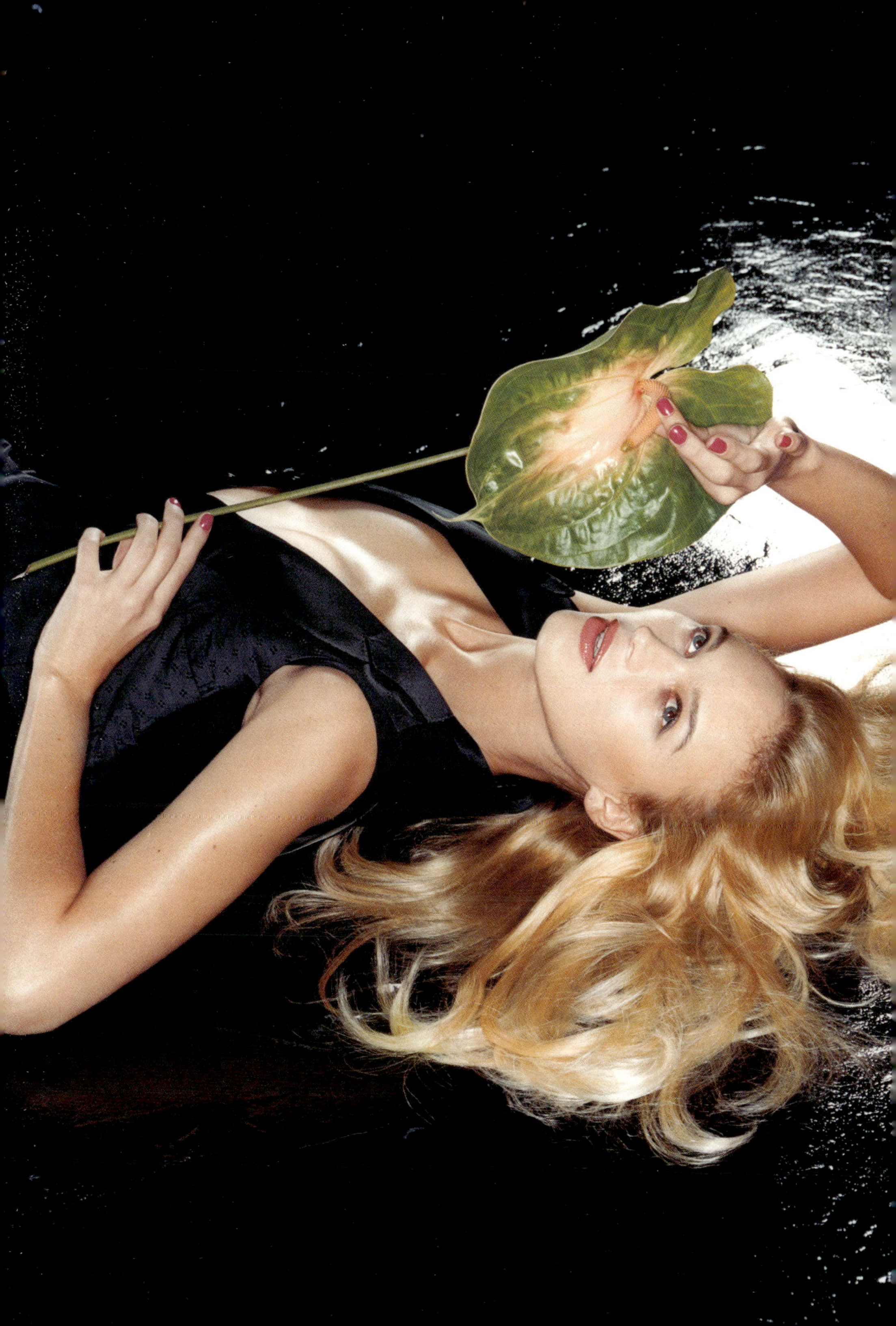

Michael Douglas and Jeanne Tripplehorn in «Basic Instinct», July 1991, Los Angeles

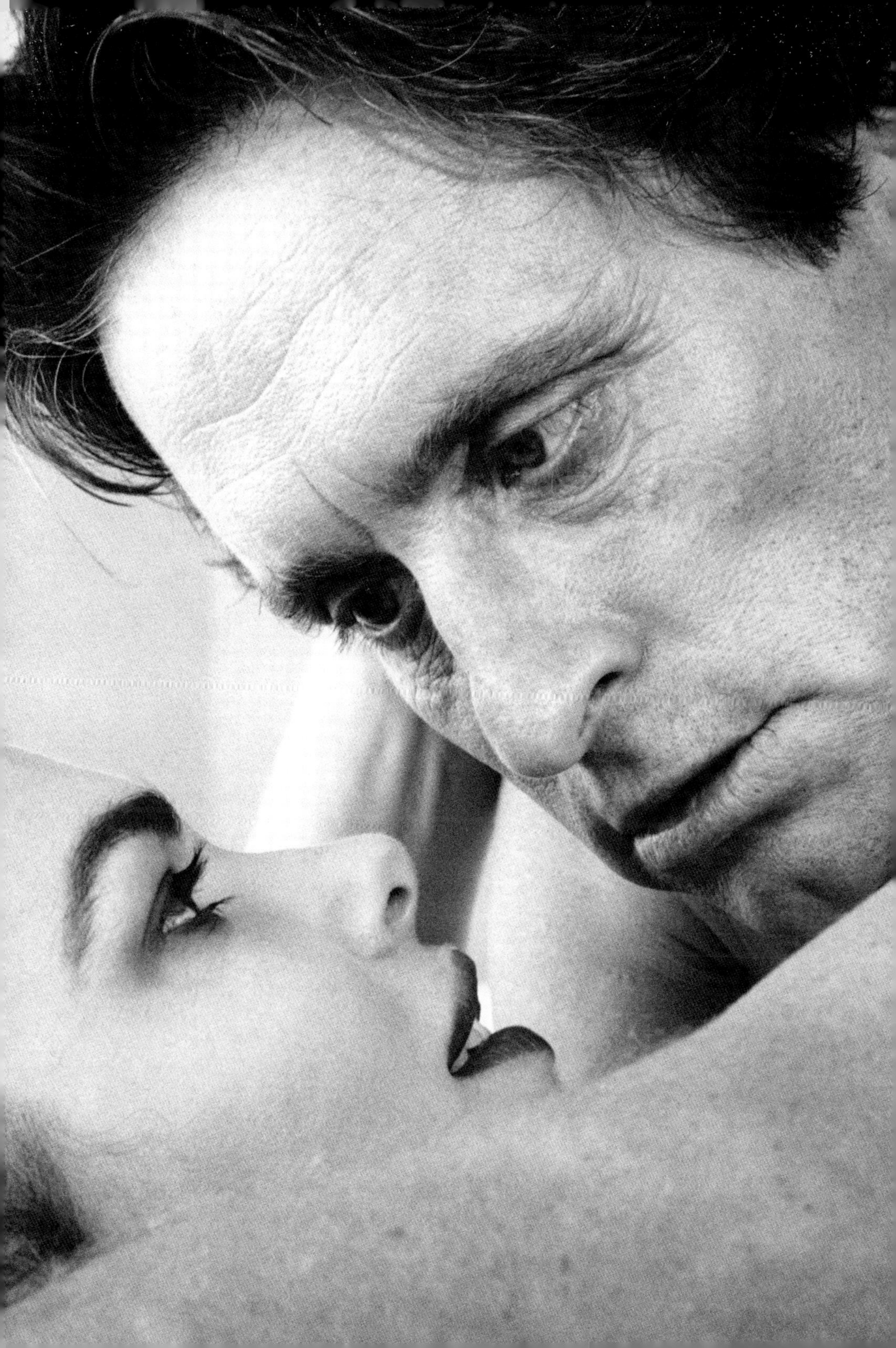

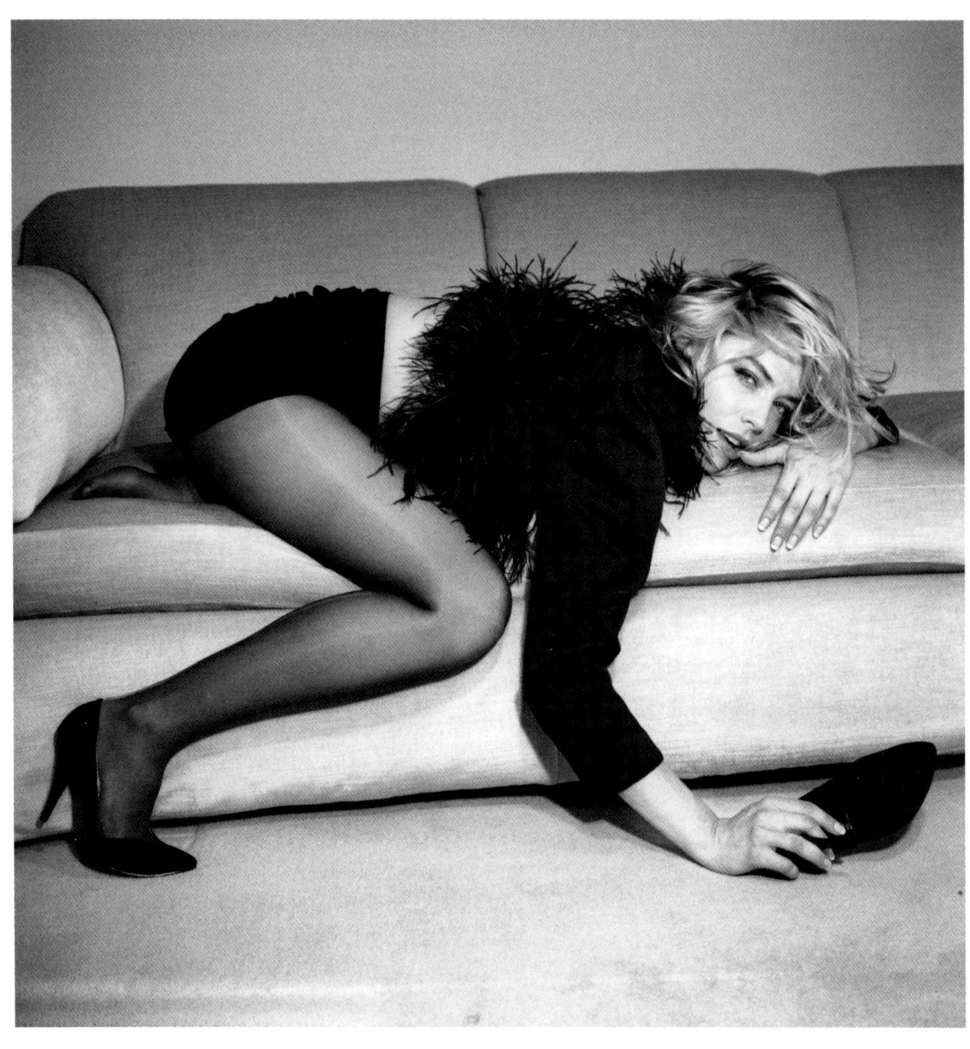

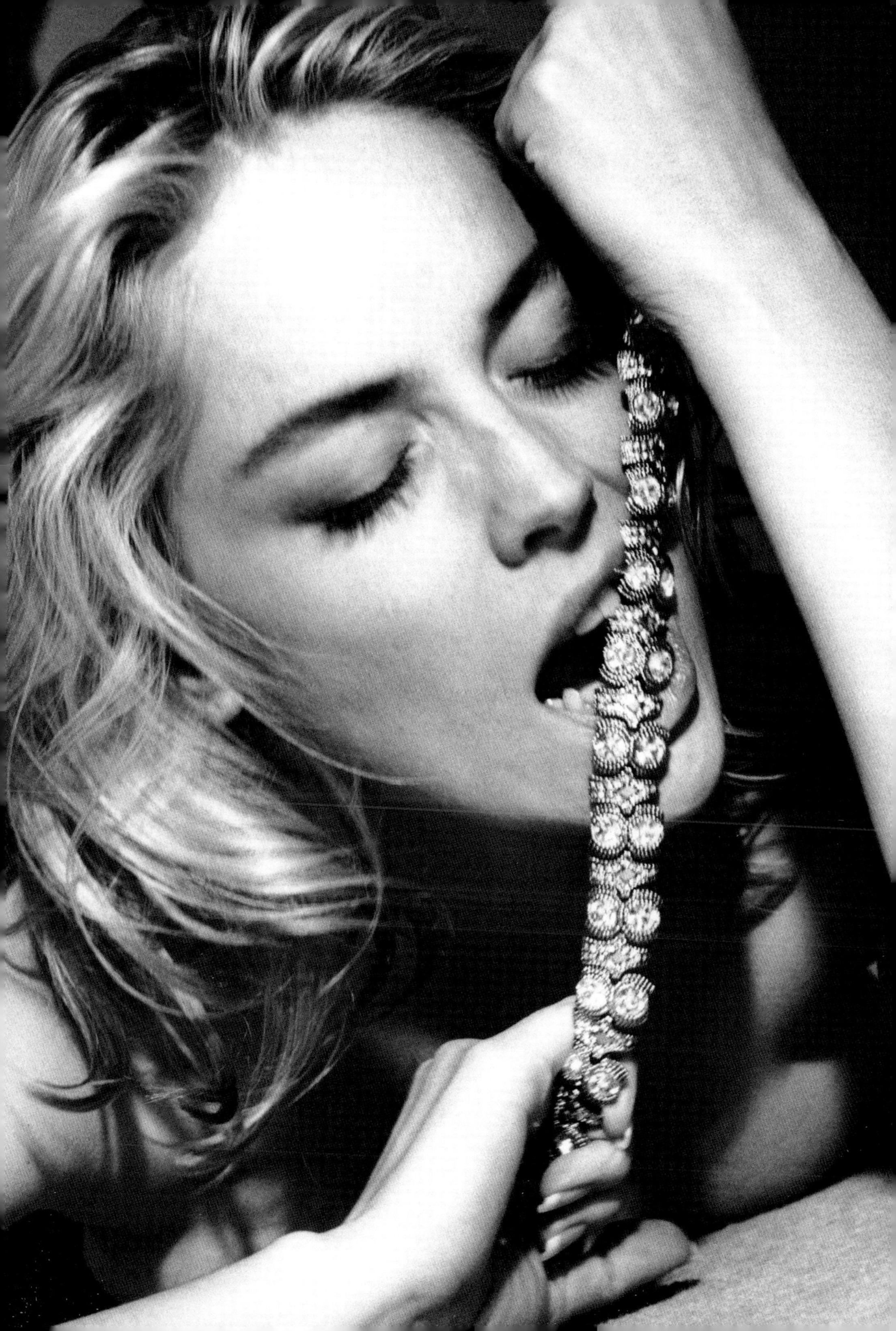

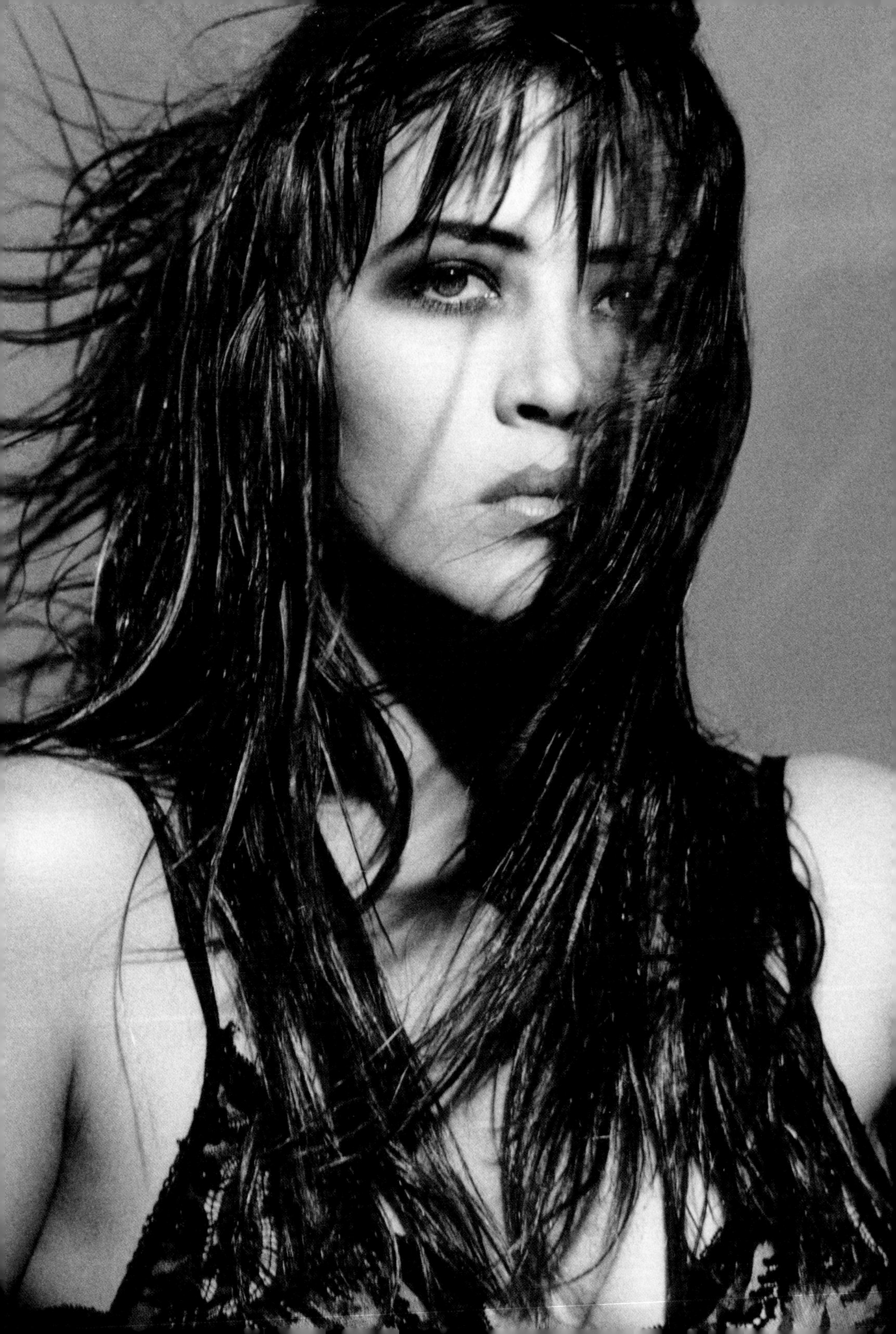

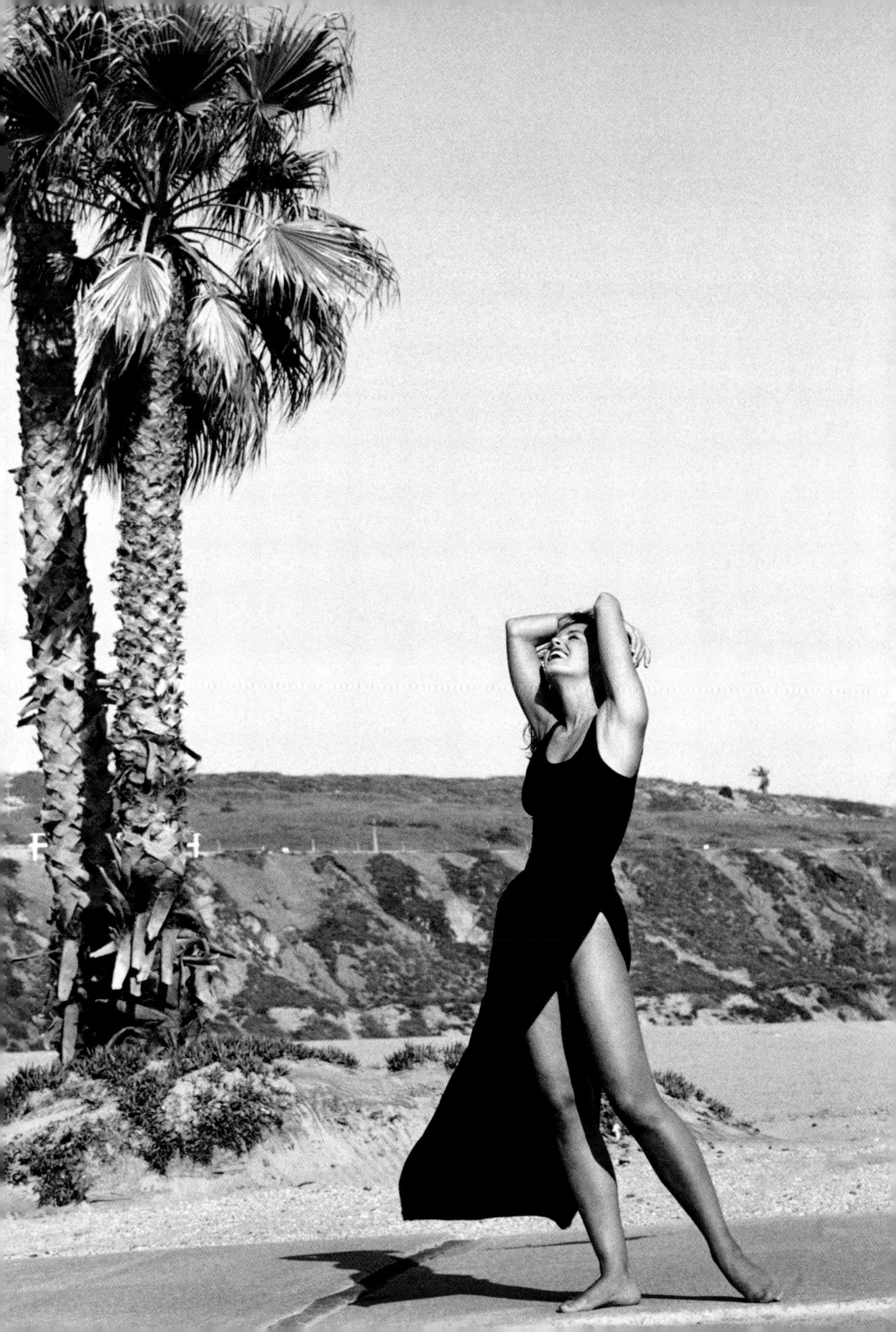

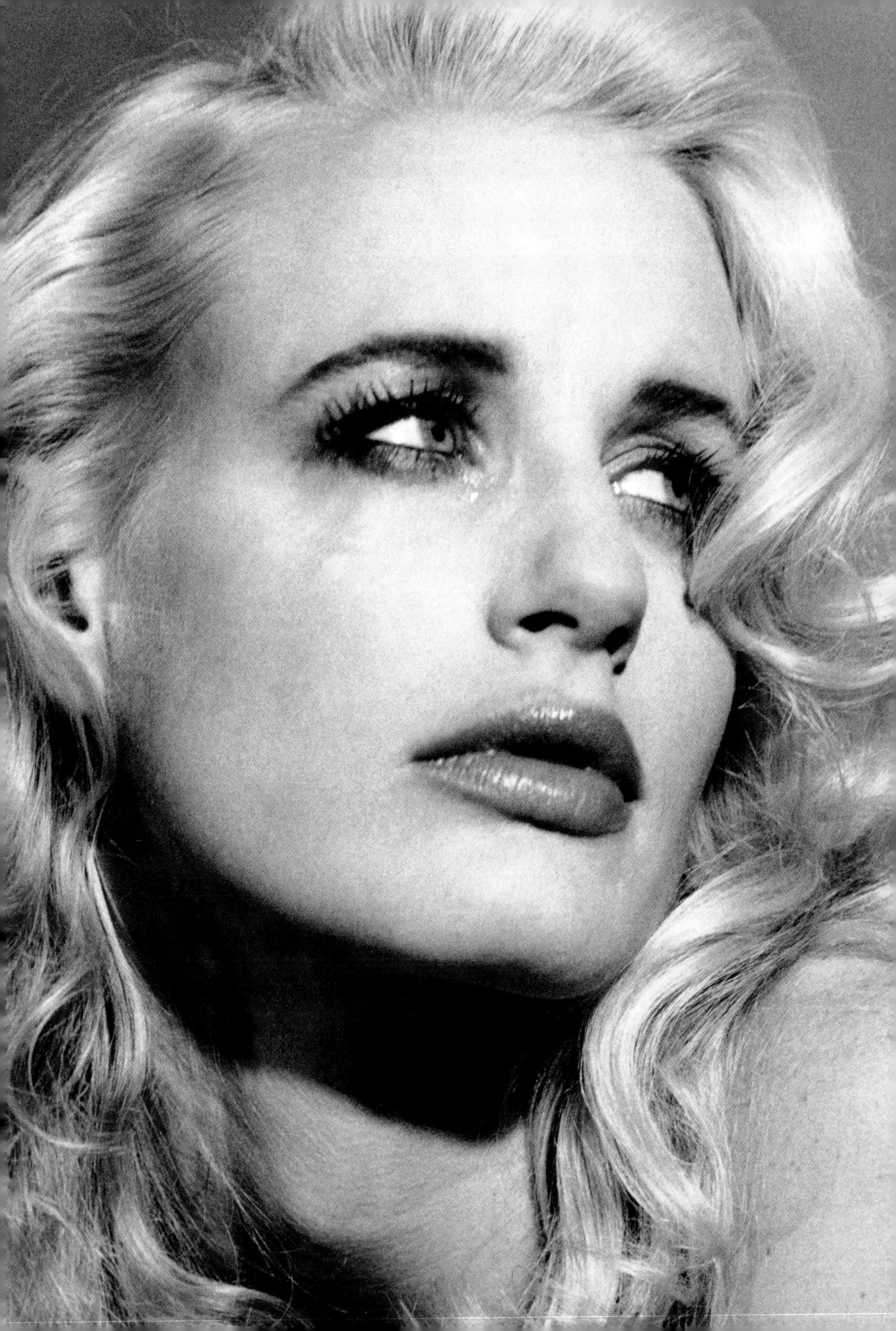

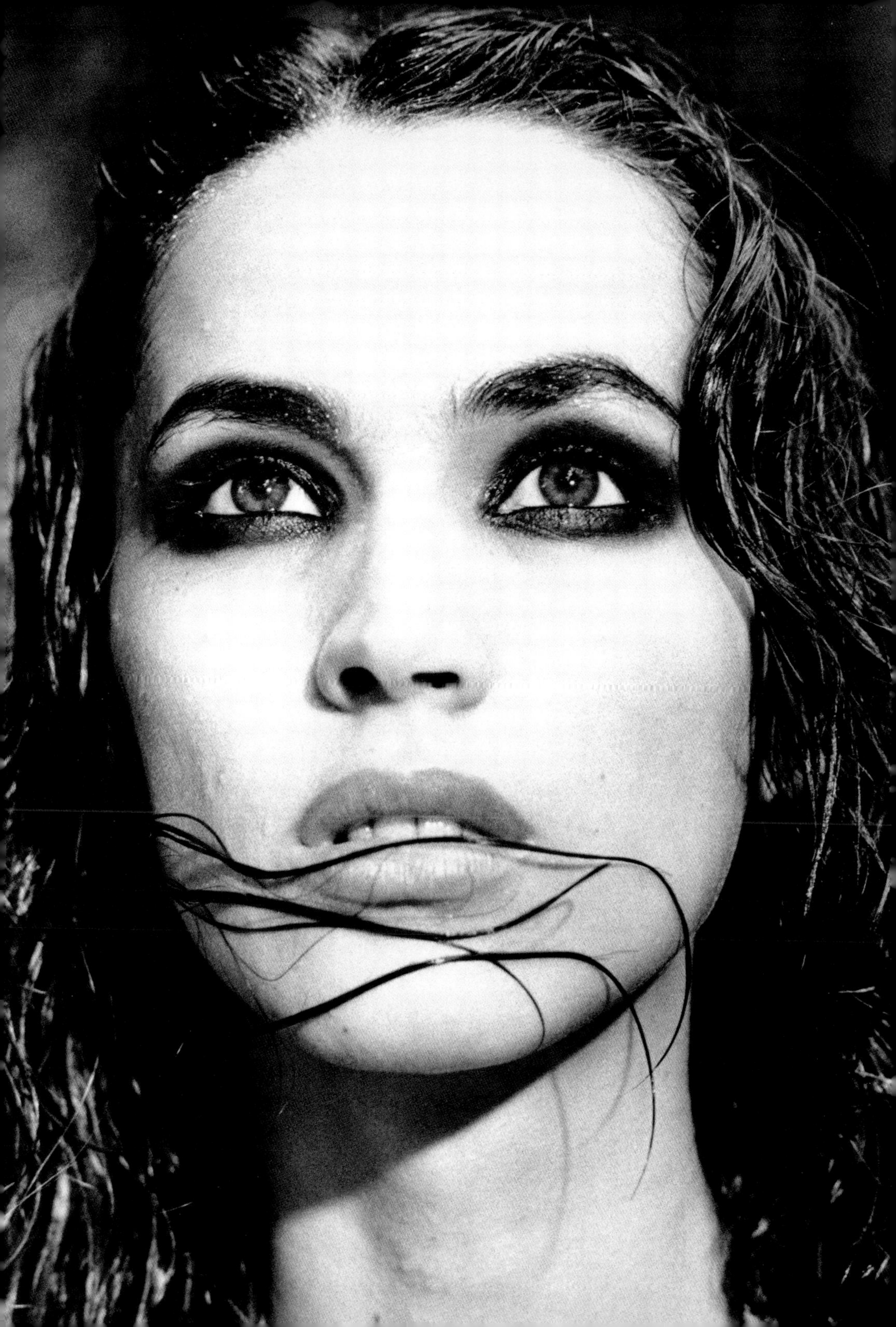

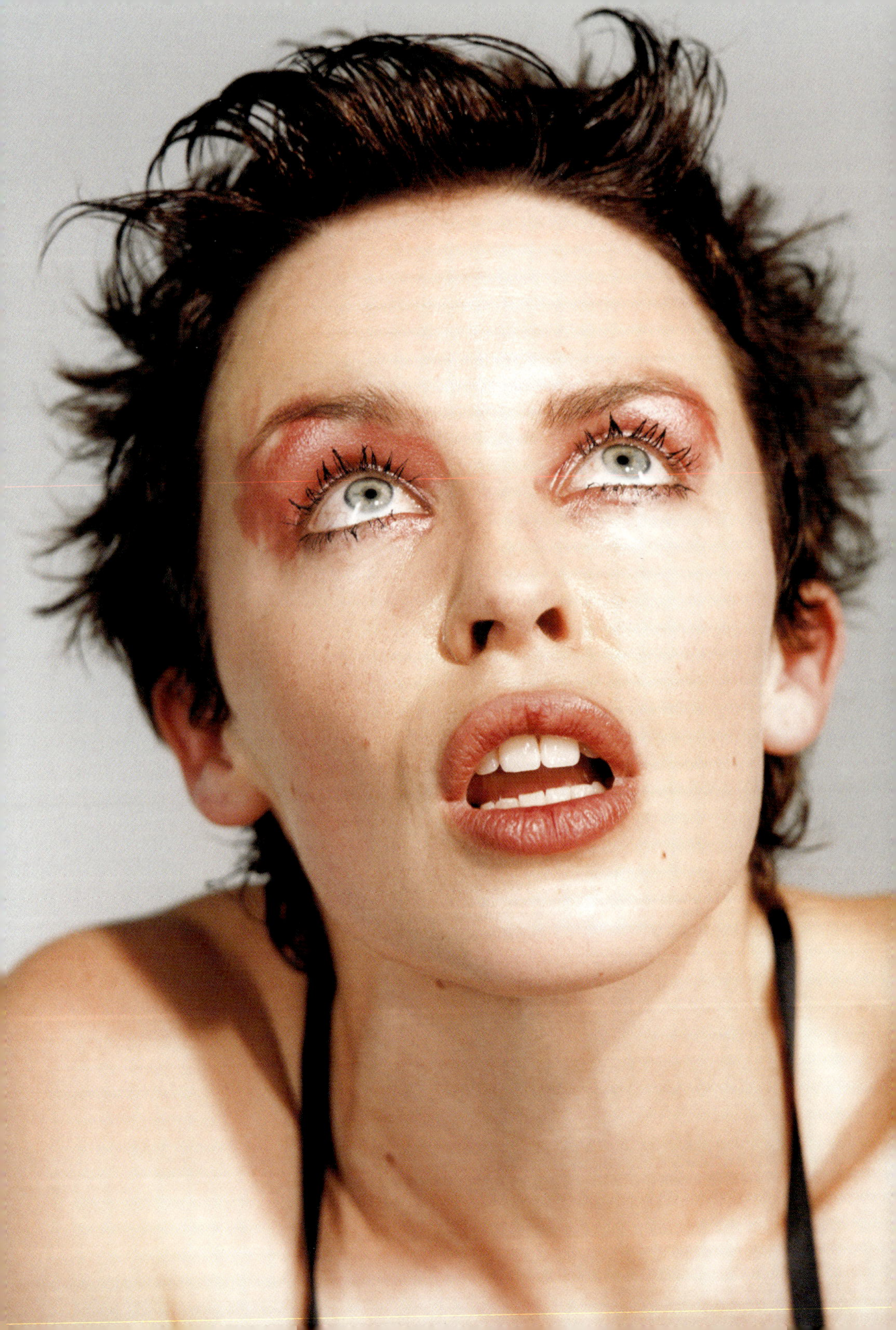

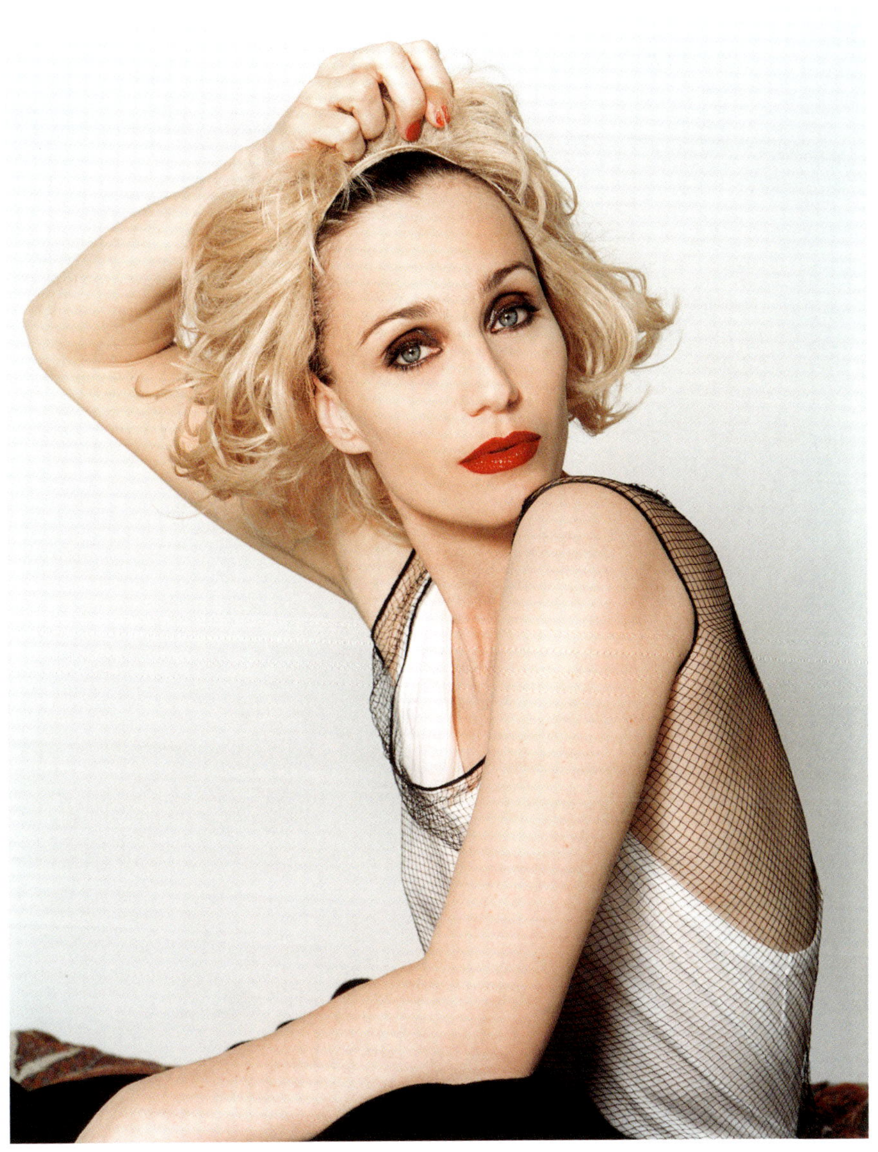

Above — *Kristin Scott Thomas playing with a blond wig I*, May 2002, Paris
Opposite page — *Kylie Minogue looking to the sky*, April 1996, New York
Page 60 — *Michael Douglas dans « Basic Instinct » avec un bas sur la tête*, July 1991, Los Angeles
Page 61 — *Photo de mode aux gants noirs*, March 1991, Paris

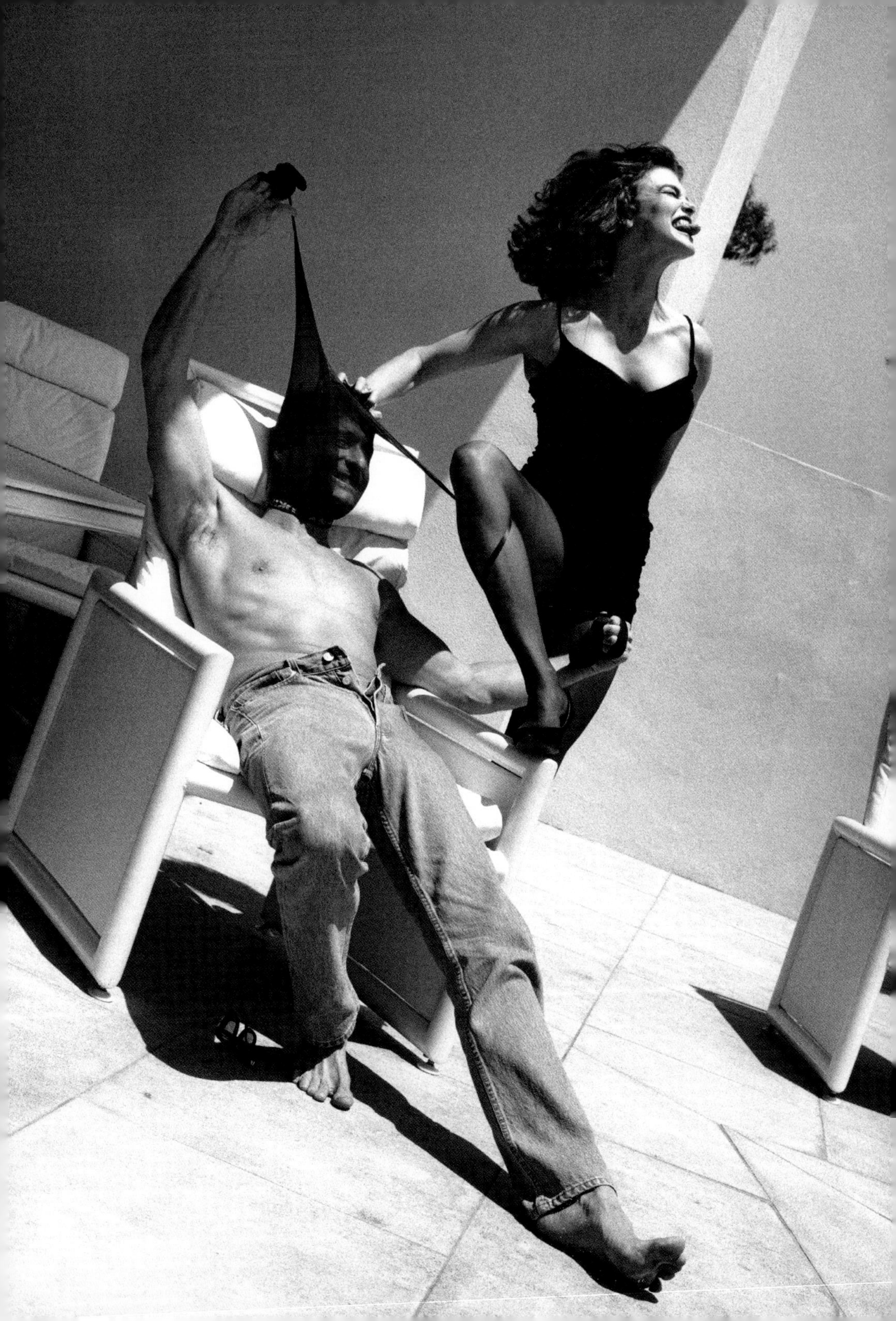

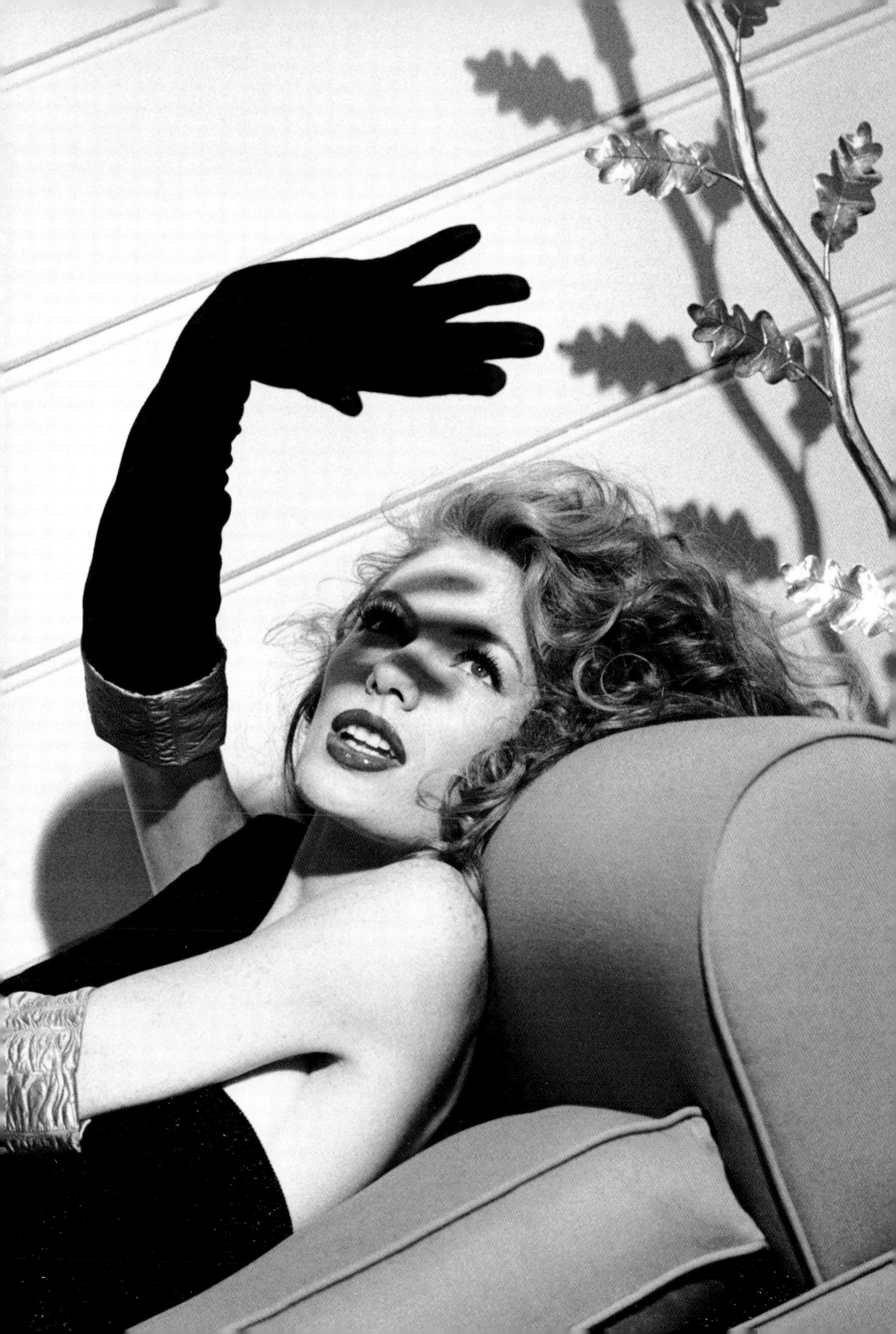

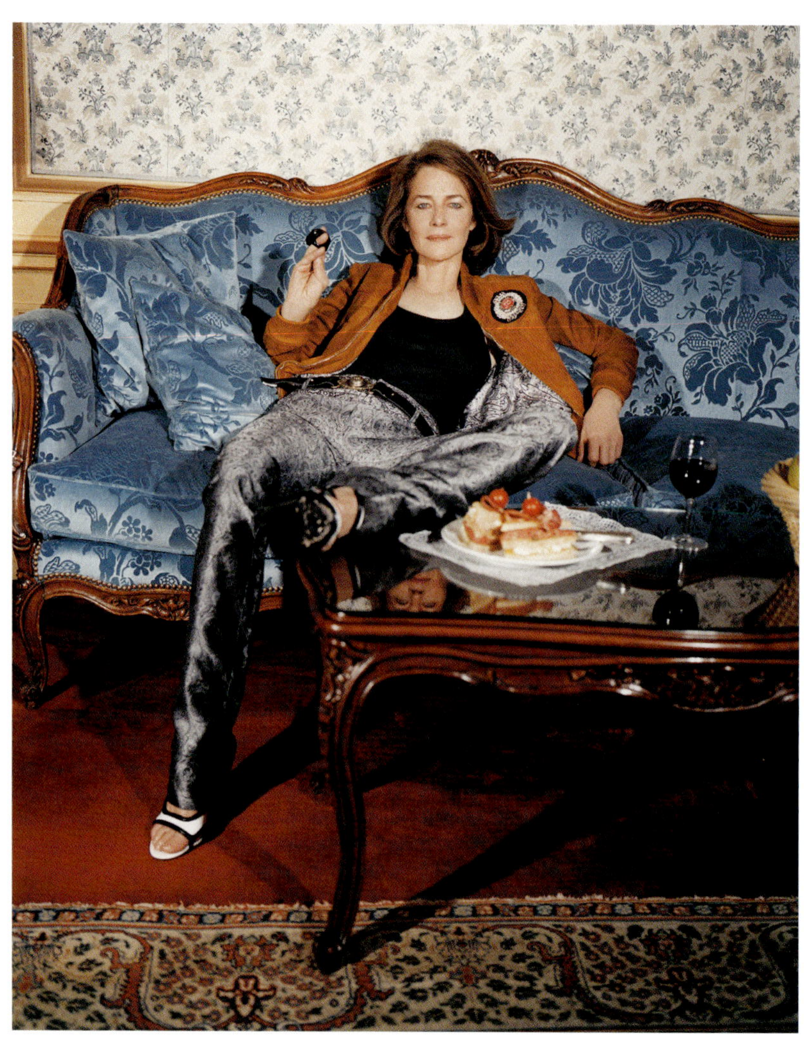

Above — *Charlotte Rampling at the Hotel Raphael*, February 2006, Paris
Opposite page — *Charlotte Rampling at the Hotel Raphael*, February 2006, Paris
Page 64 — *Inés Sastre had too many strawberries*, October 2010, Paris
Page 65 — *Tenue de gala*, February 2009, Hotel Le Meurice, Paris

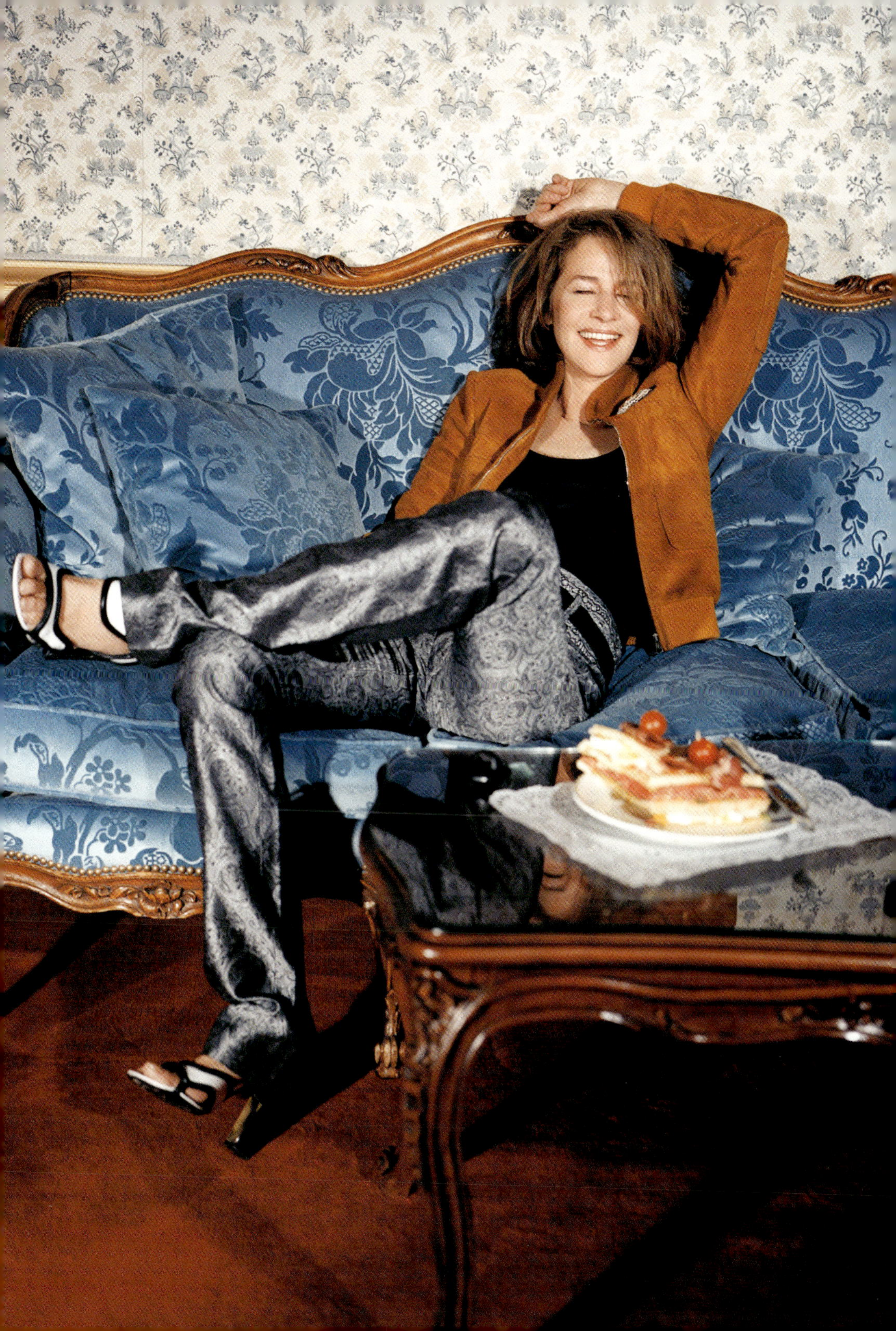

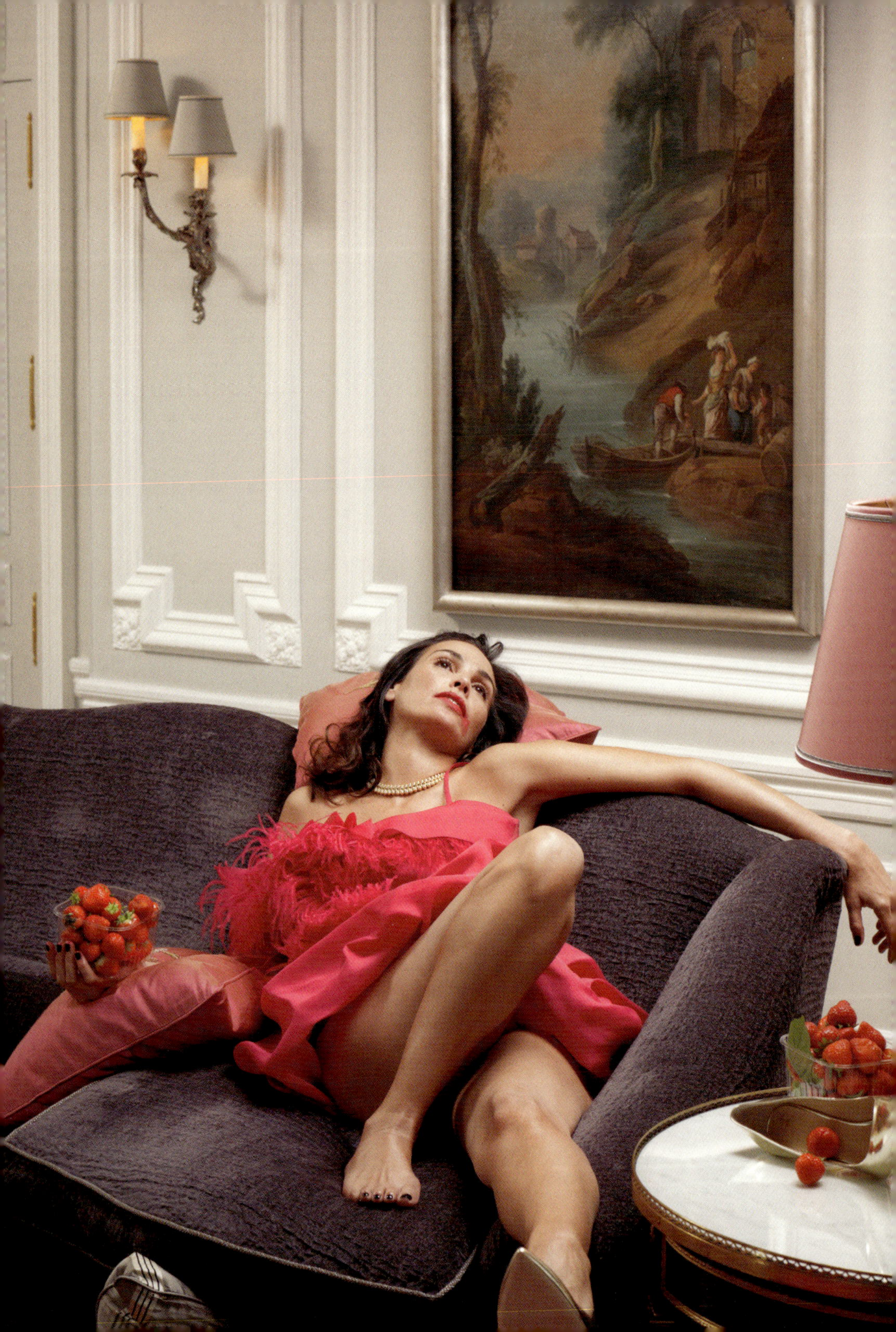

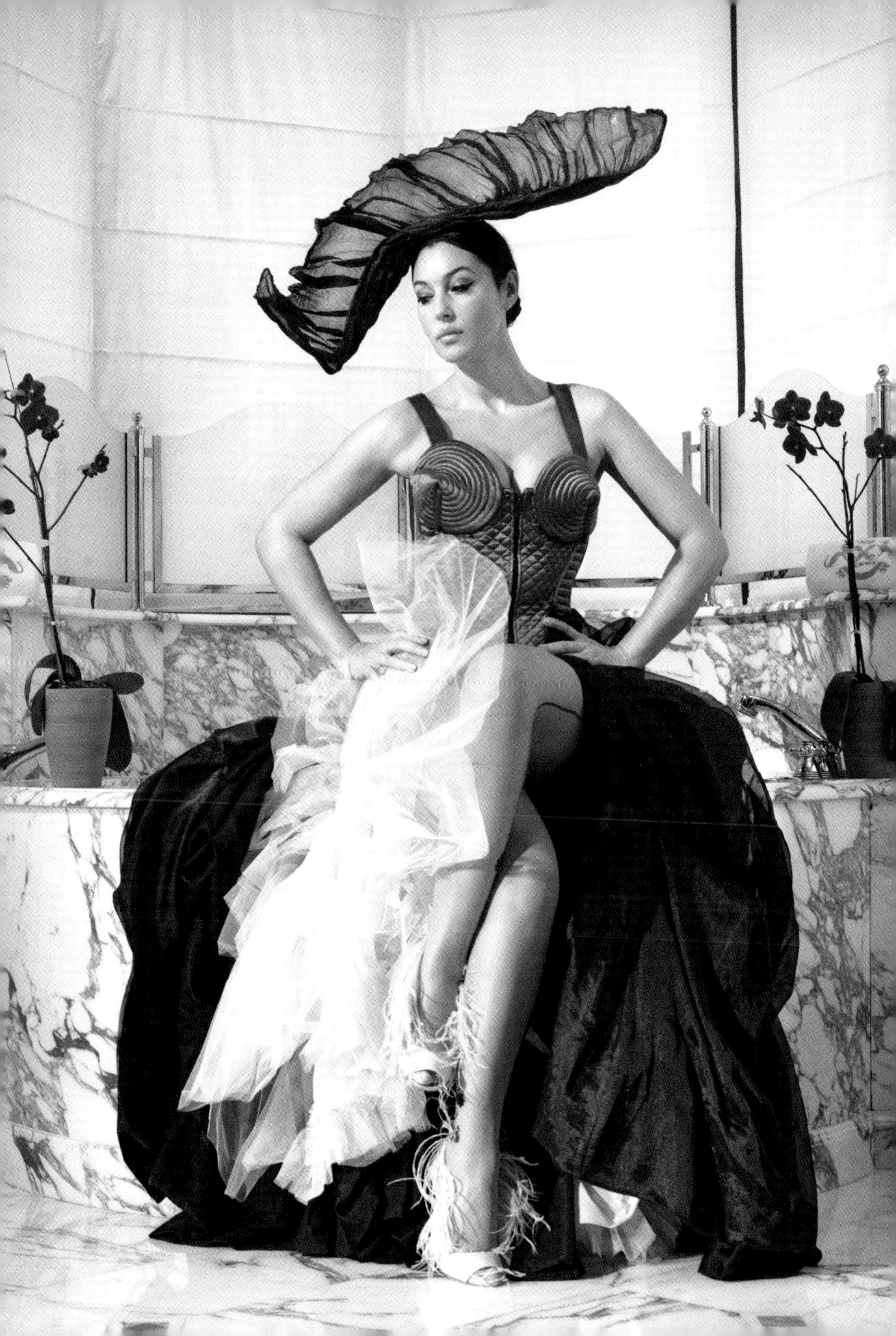

Anna T., salie de fleurs et de peinture, plus belle encore, June 2007, Paris
Following double page — *Gina and Elizabeth kissing,* March 1995, Los Angeles

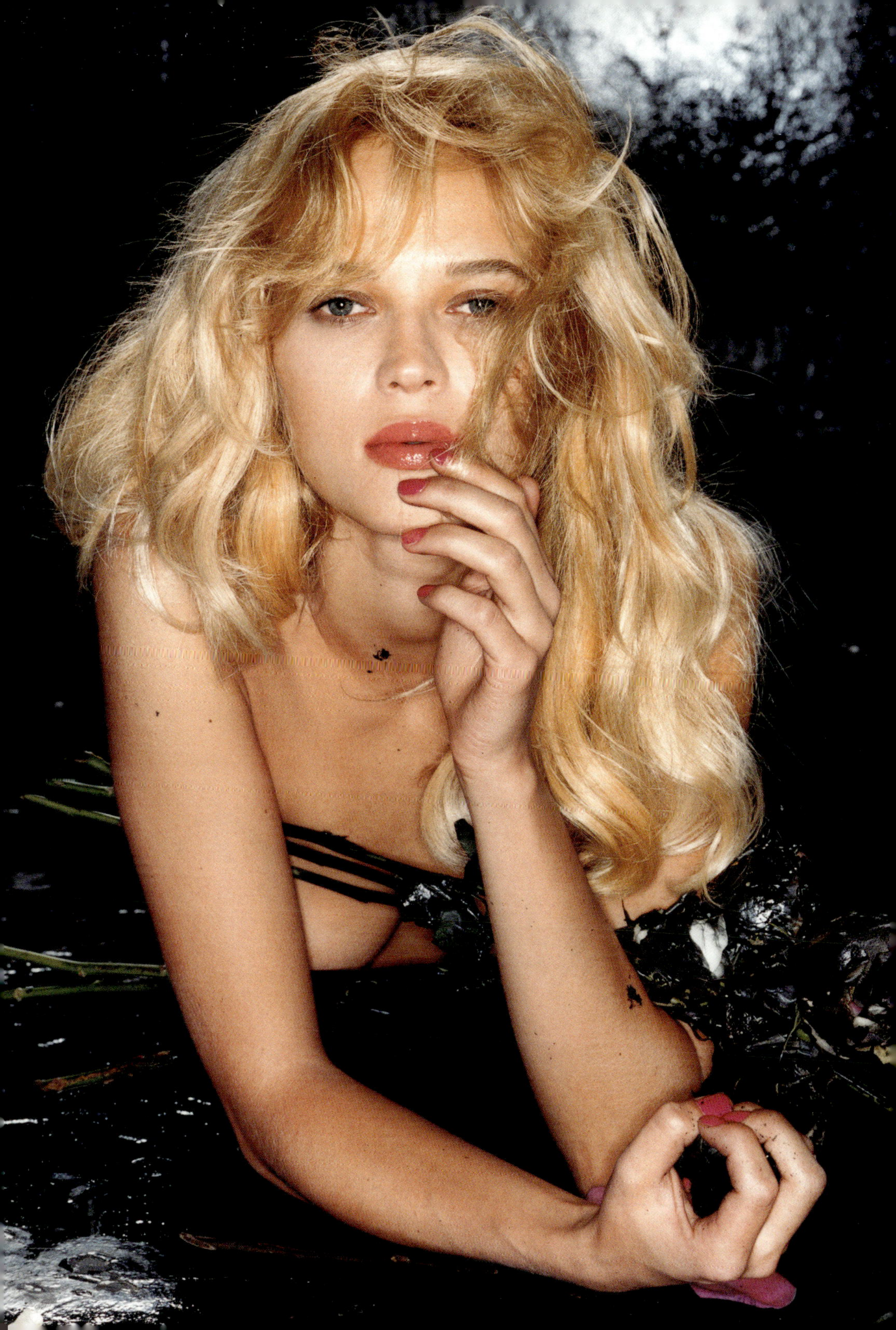

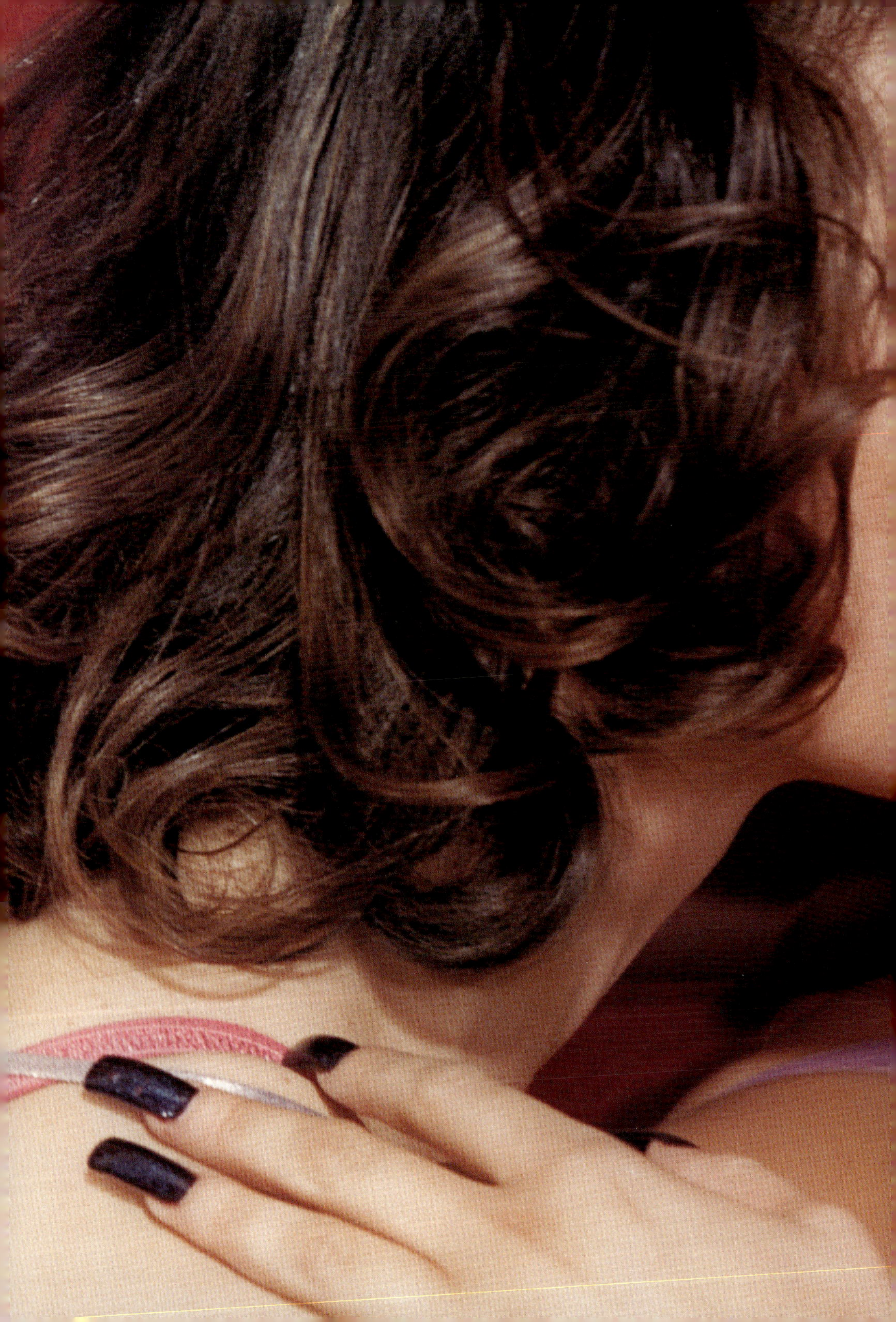

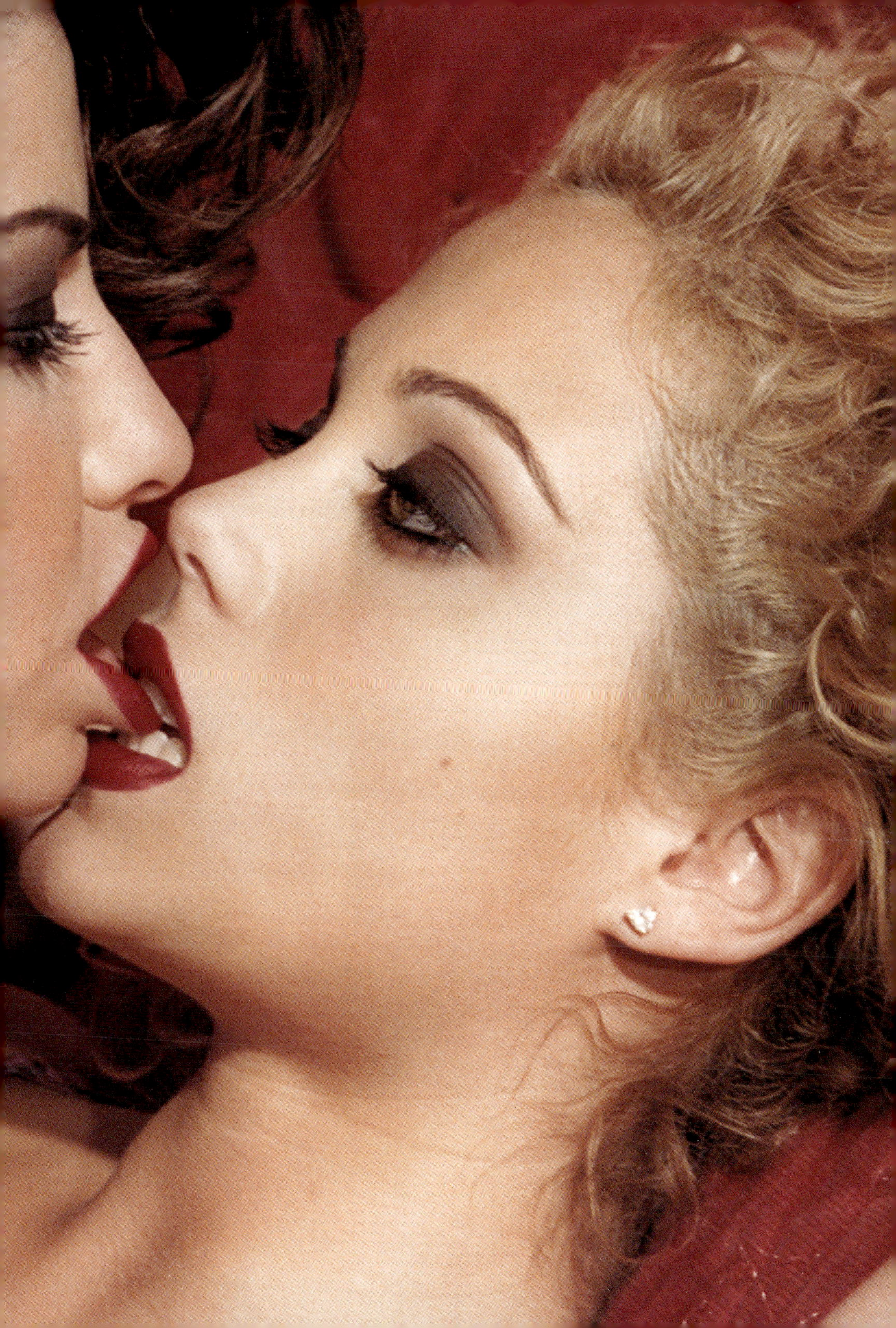

For Bettina Rheims photography was primarily constructed
in black and white, founded on an intimate approach to the
other, choosing itinerant strippers and acrobats, (...) using performance to touch on what is normally concealed. And already
one perceived a quality that became her trademark: recreating,
reinventing – whether in the studio or elsewhere – a true space
of encounter.

Pour Bettina Rheims la photographie s'est construite d'abord en
noir et blanc, sur une approche intime de l'autre, en choisissant
des artistes foraines, des acrobates, (...), afin de toucher par le
biais de la performance ce qui normalement ne se montre pas. Et
déjà apparaissait cette particularité qui allait devenir sa marque:
recréer, réinventer – en studio, ailleurs – l'espace de la rencontre.

Für Bettina Rheims entstand Fotografie zunächst in Schwarz-Weiß,
als intime Annäherung an das Andere, wobei sie oft Stripperinnen
und Akrobatinnen wählte (...), um bei deren Performance das einzufan-
gen, was normalerweise nicht gezeigt wird. Und schon damals zeigte
sich diese Besonderheit, die ihr Markenzeichen werden sollte: ihre
Fähigkeit, den Raum der Begegnung – im Studio oder anderswo – neu
zu erschaffen, neu zu erfinden.

Serge Bramly, in *Rétrospective*, 2004

Paysage photographique, August 1981, Paris
Page 72 – *Anthéna avec une perruque*, January 1980, Paris
Page 73 – *Maral debout*, October 1980, Paris

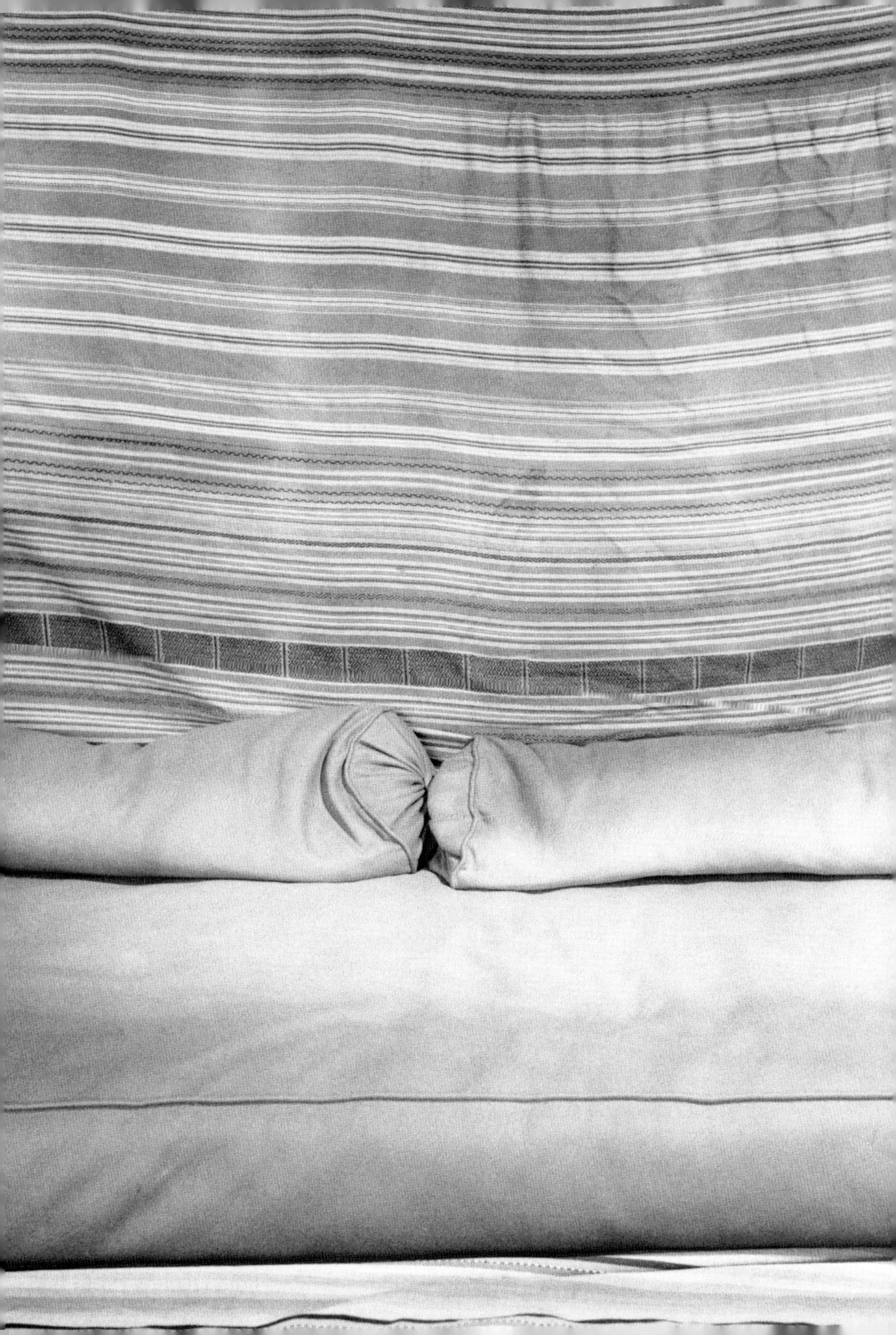

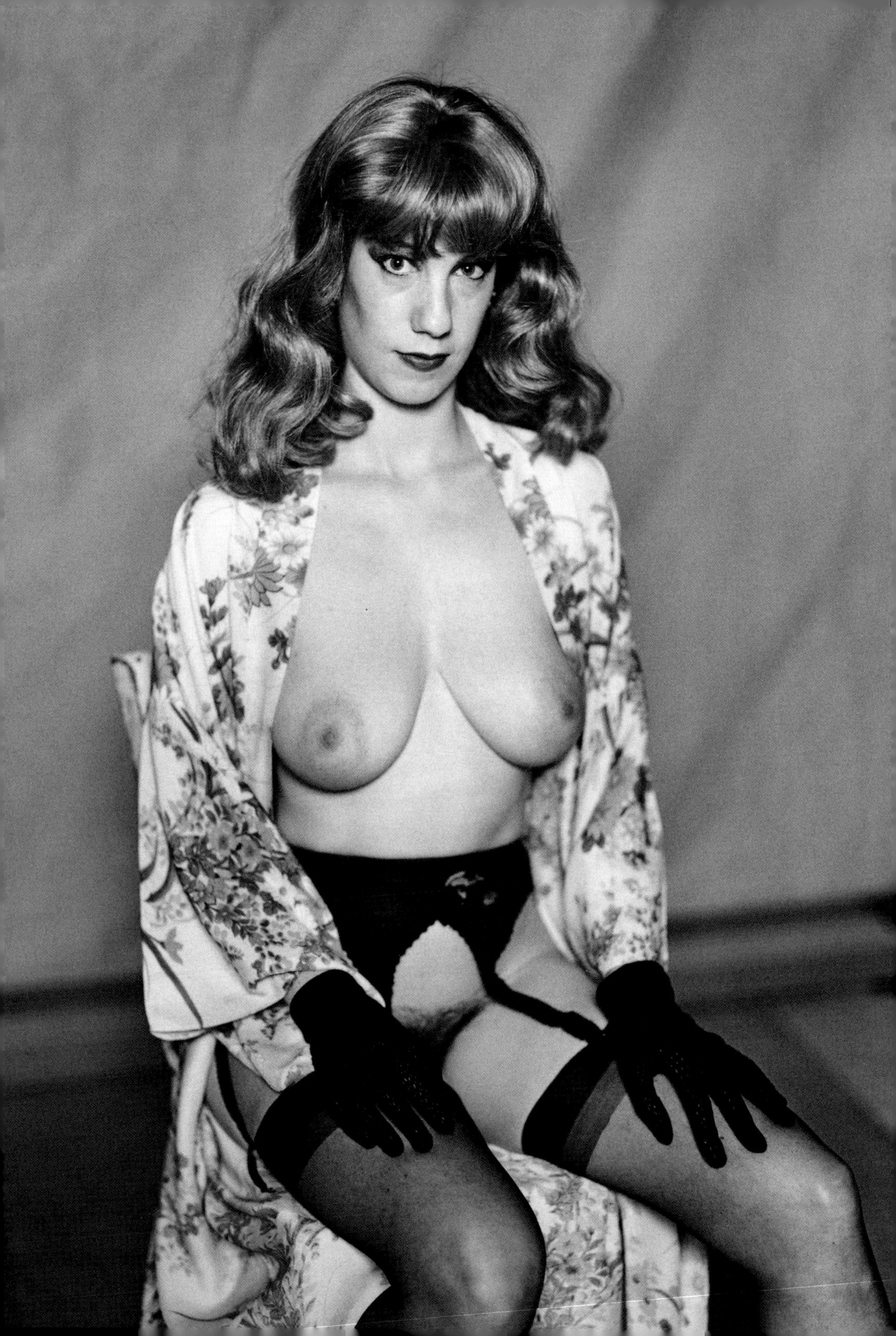

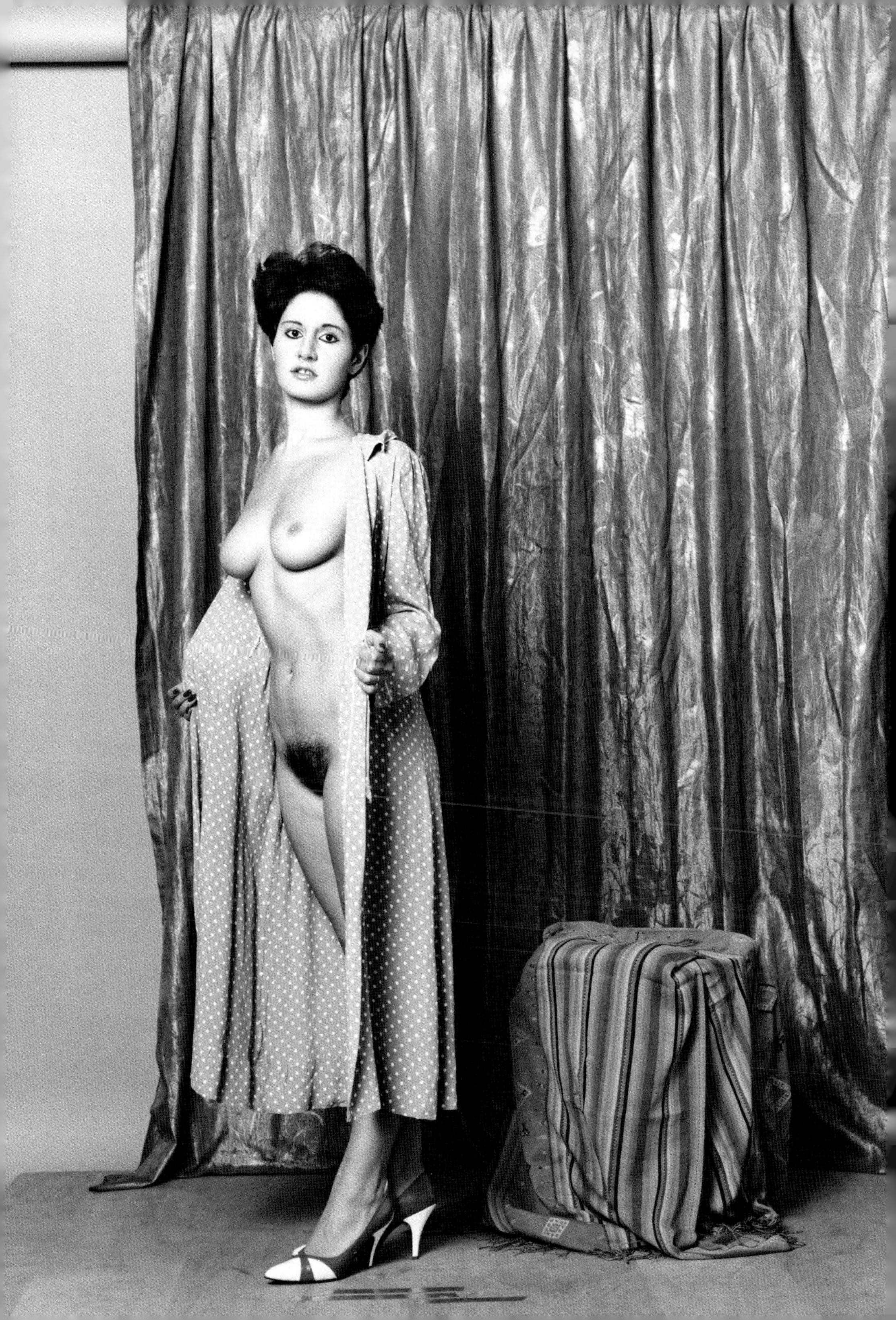

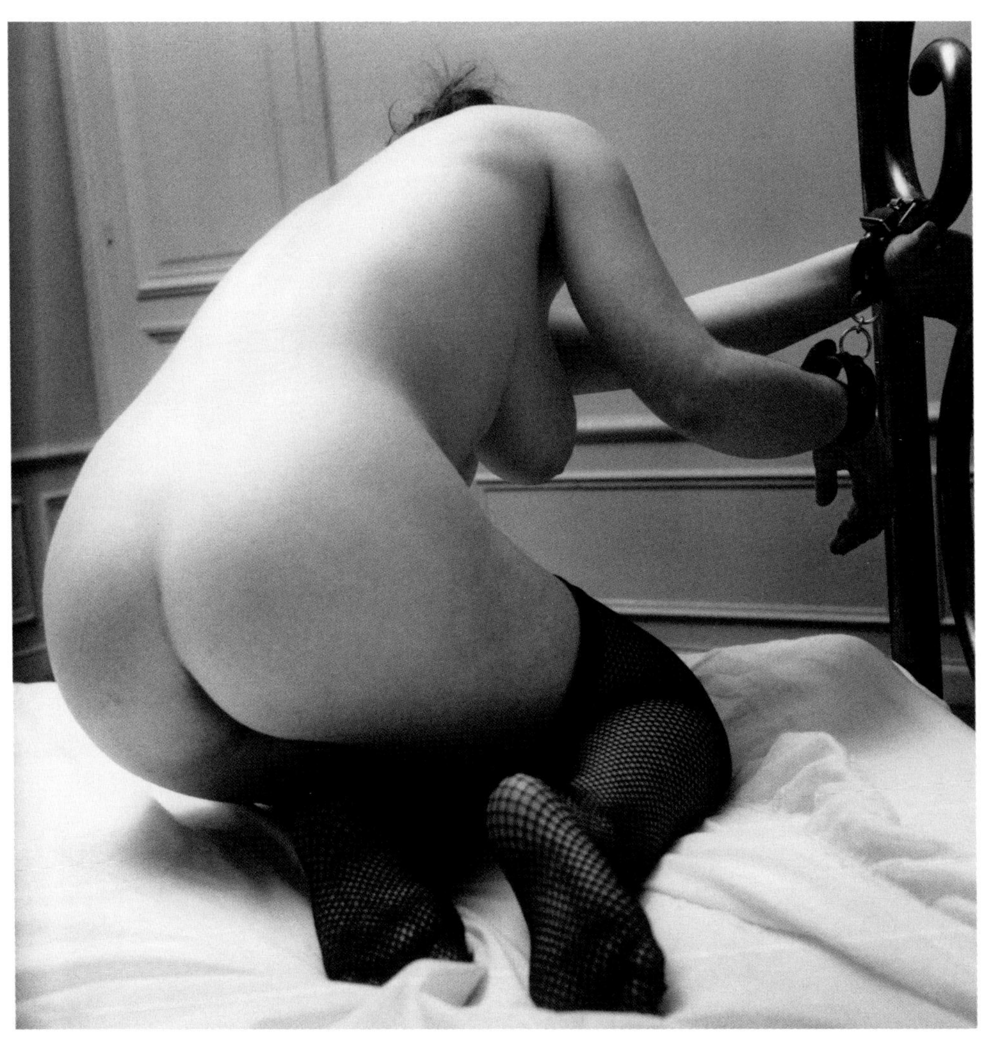

Above — *Nu de dos attaché à mon lit*, February 1981, Paris
Opposite page — *C. au radiateur*, February 1981, Paris

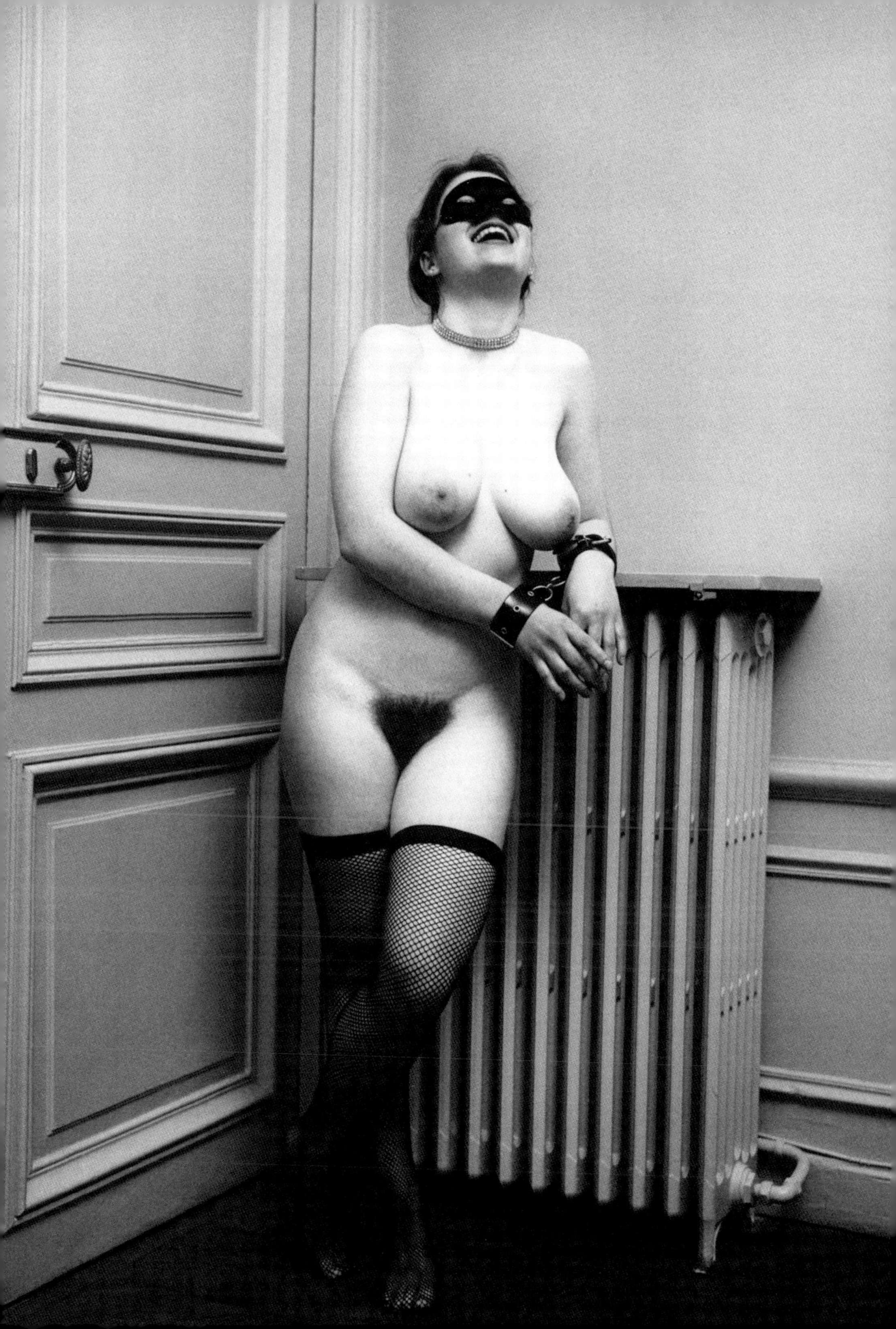

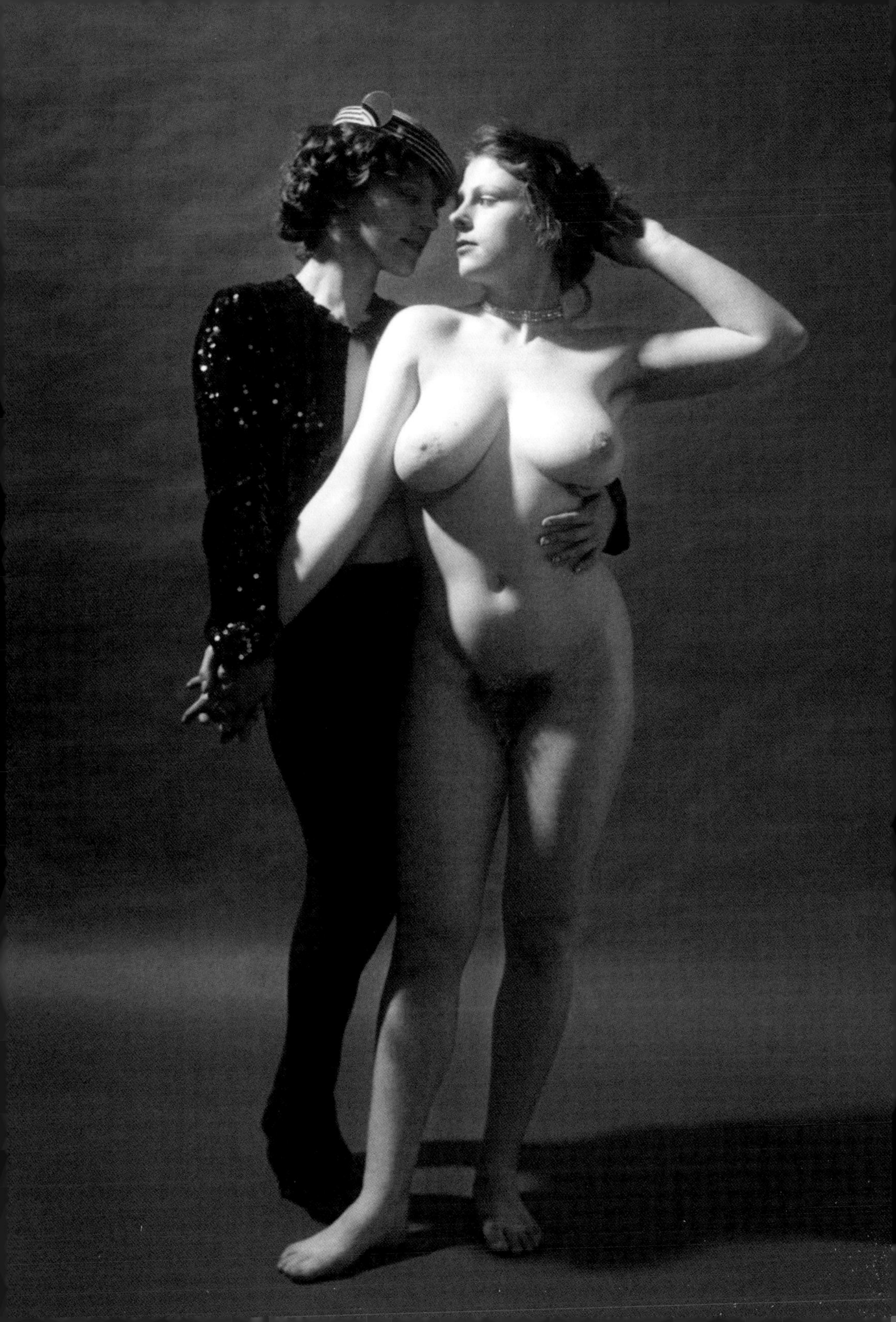

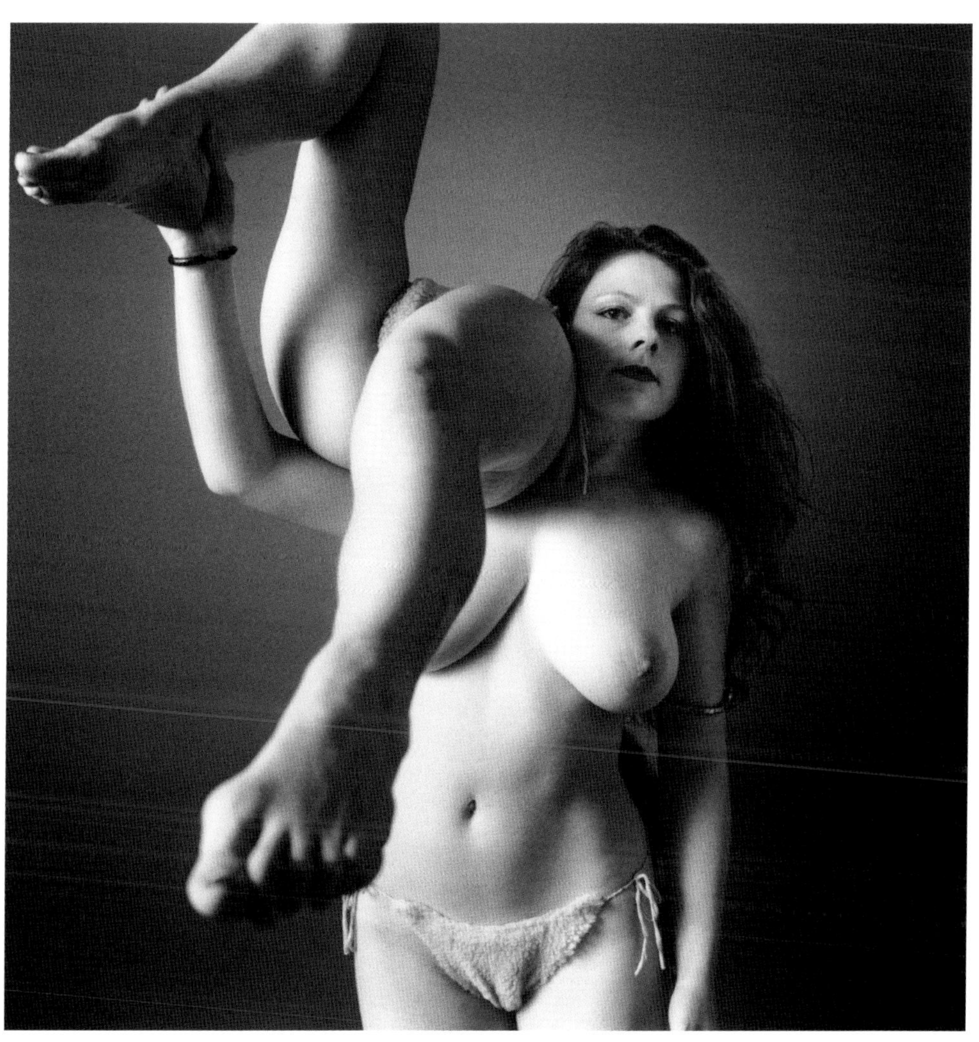

Above — *Acrobates III*, March 1981, Paris
Opposite page — *Cliché romantique*, February 1981, Paris
Page 78 — *Gwen Stefani from No Doubt*, April 1996, New York
Page 79 — *Mary J. Blige nous a oublié*, April 1996, New York

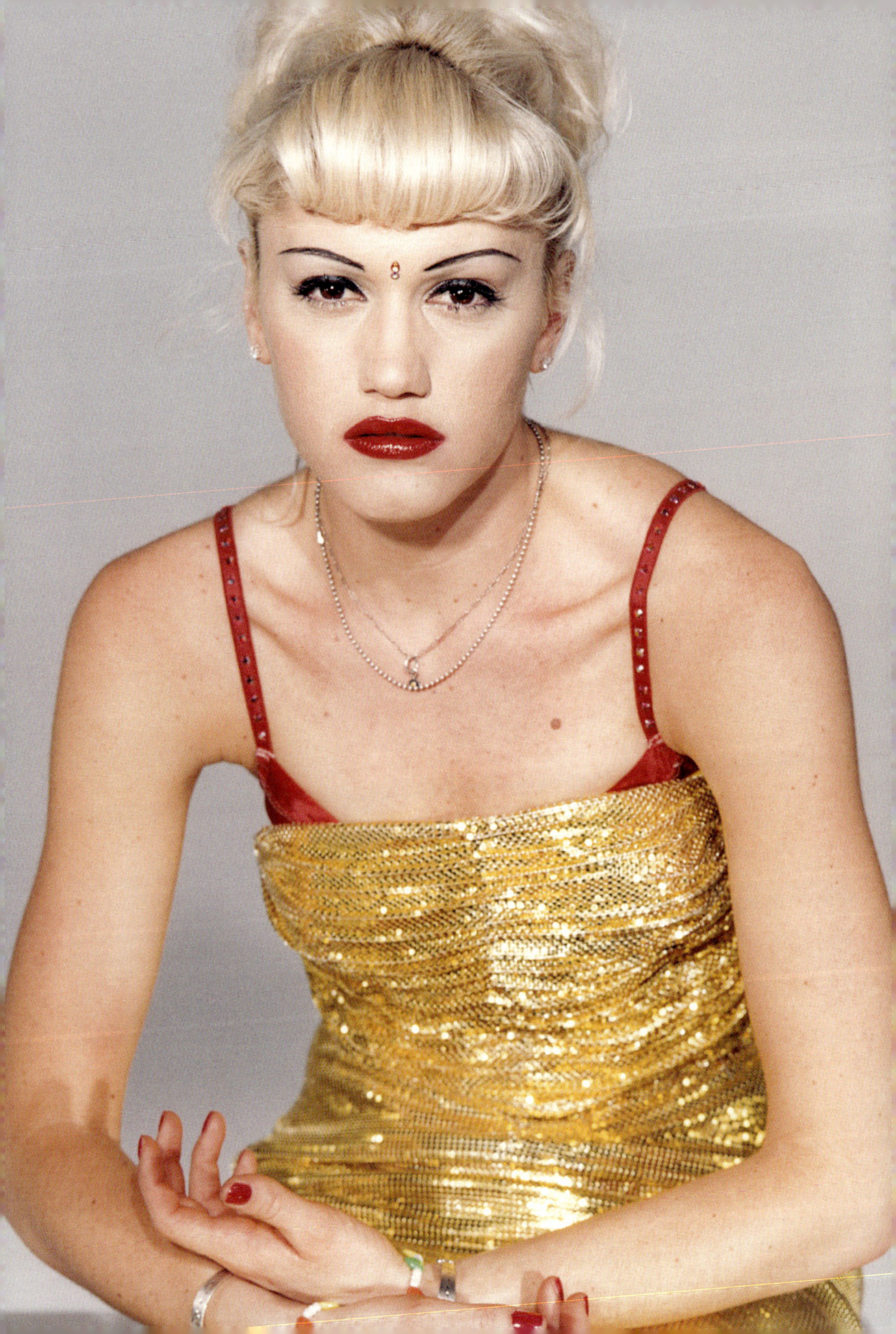

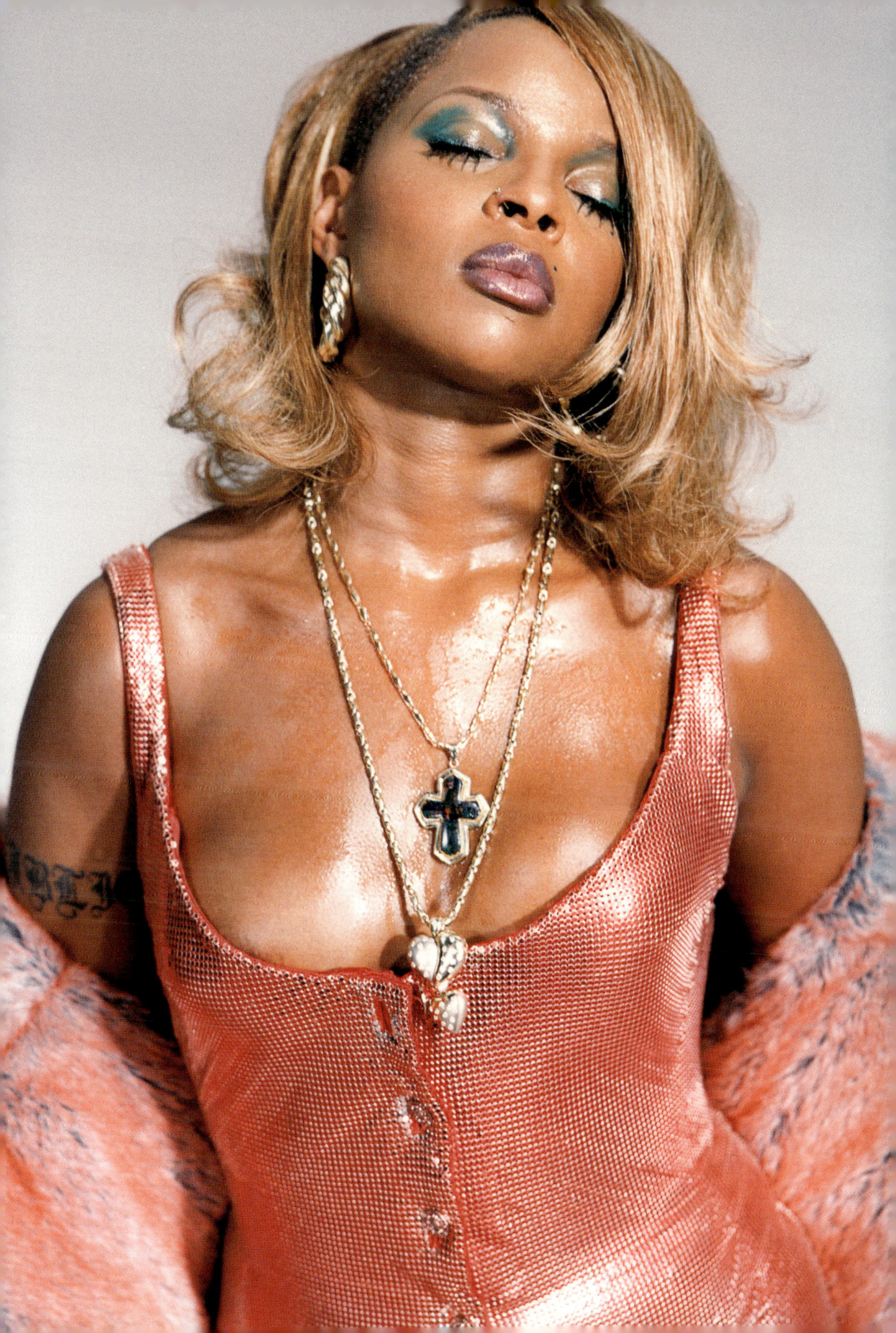

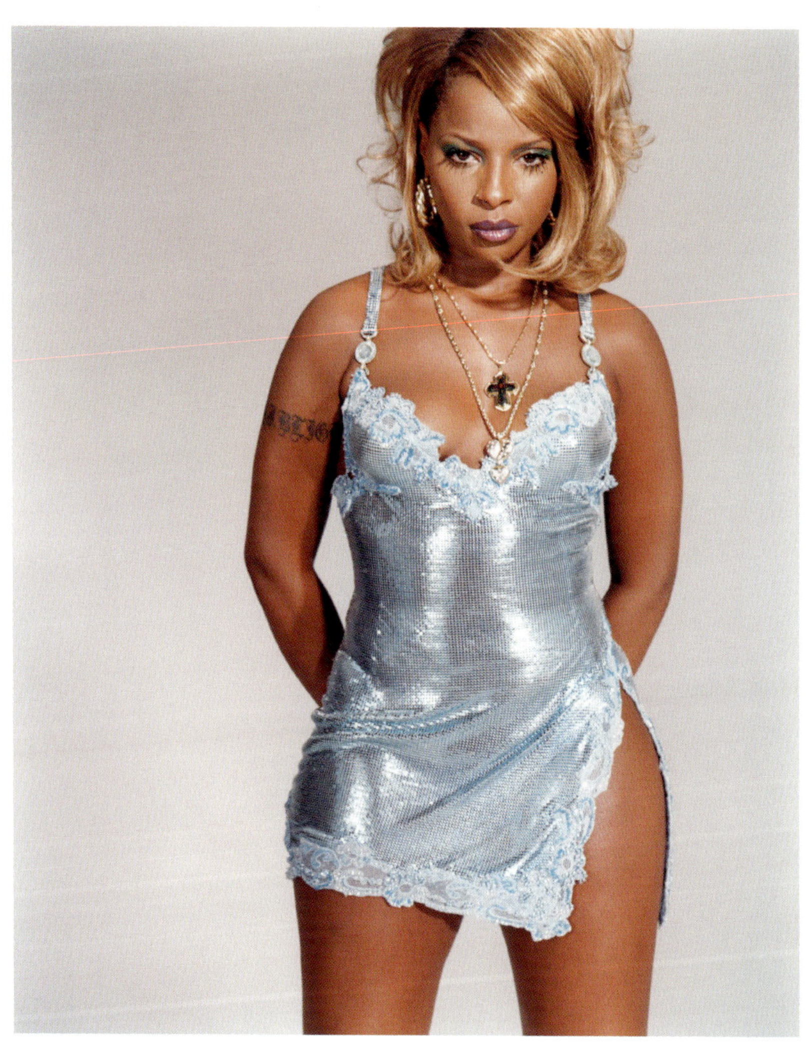

Above — *Mary J. Blige so nasty in a Versace dress,* April 1996, New York
Opposite page — *Lil' Kim from Junior M.A.F.I.A.,* April 1996, New York

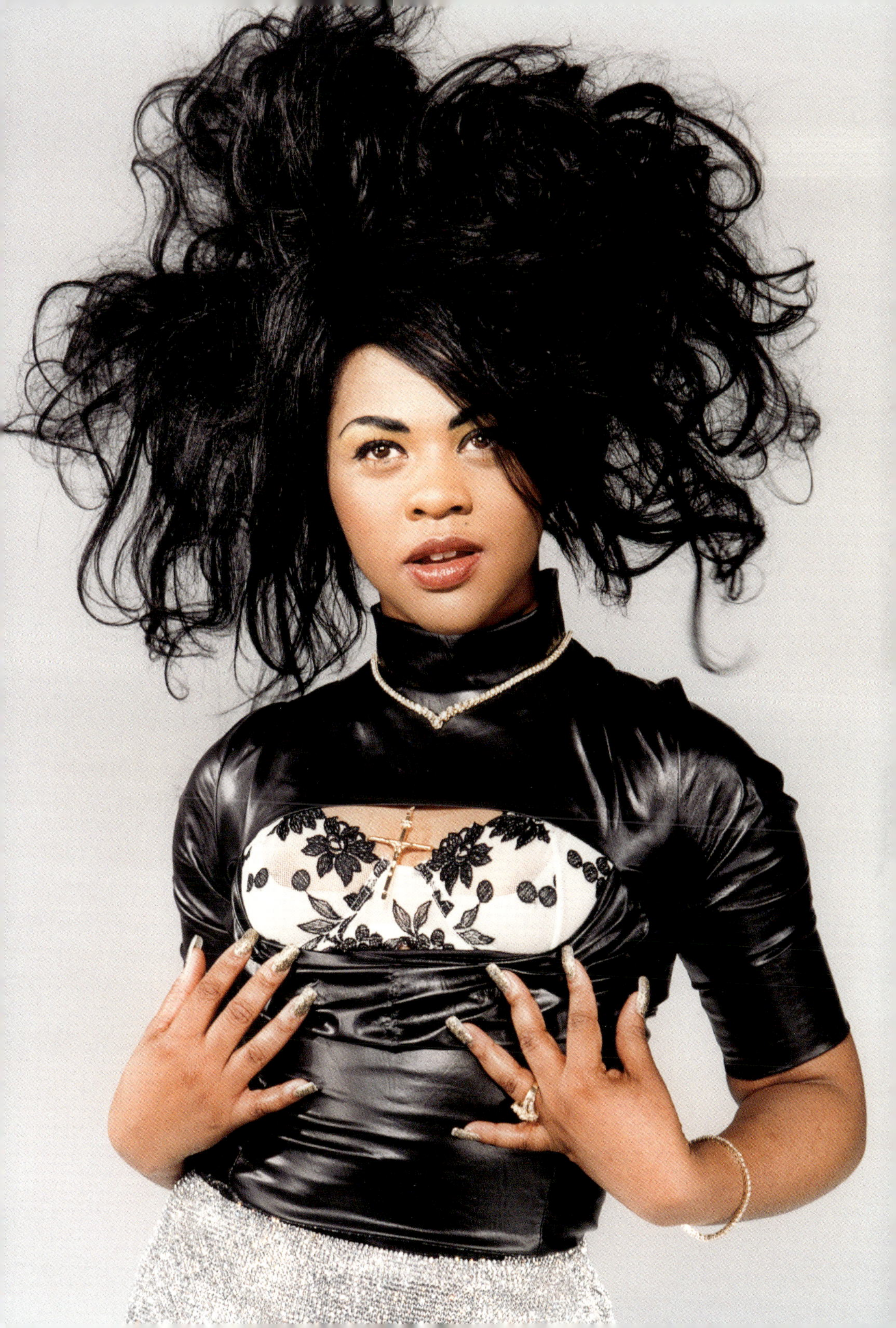

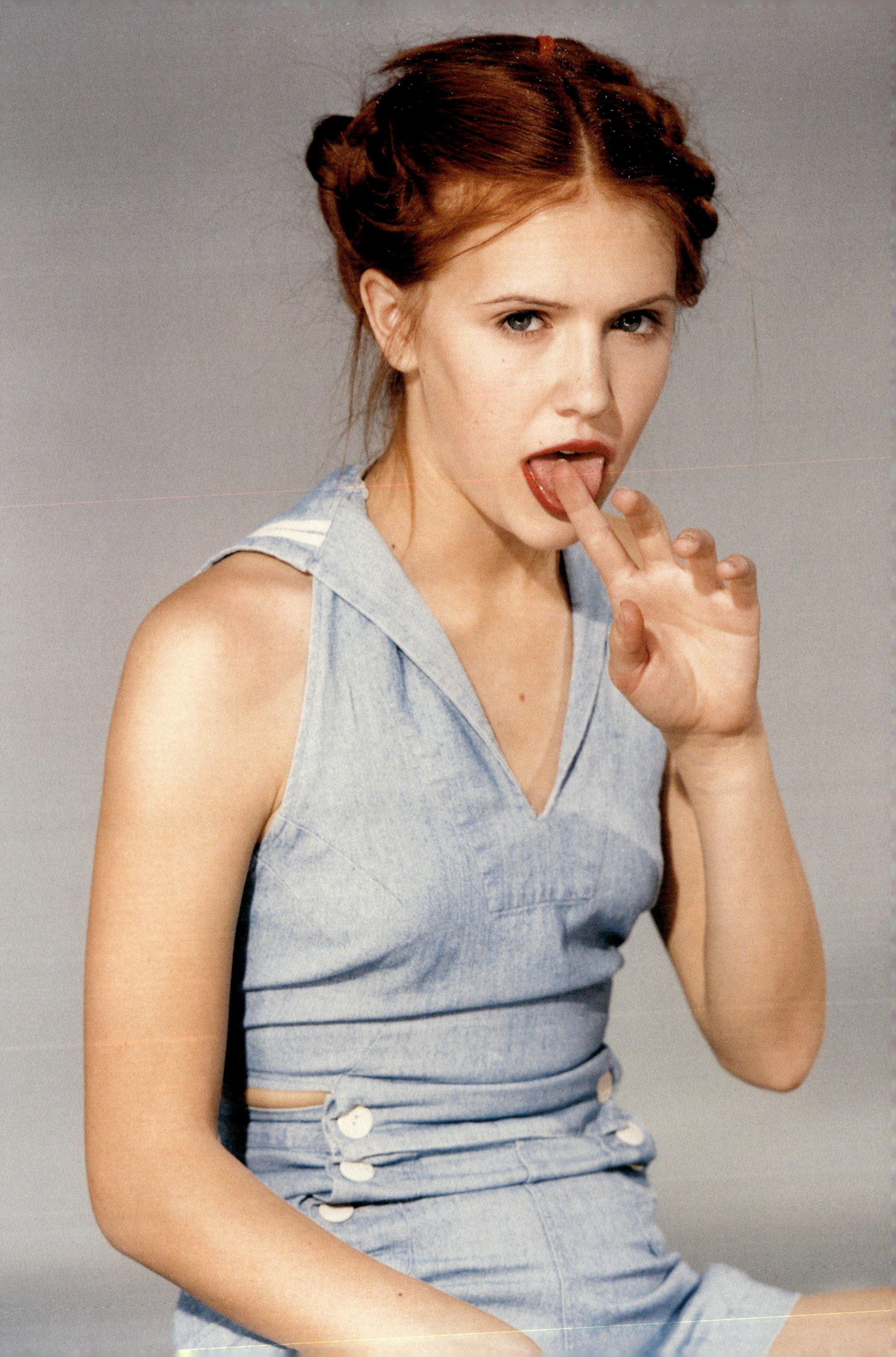

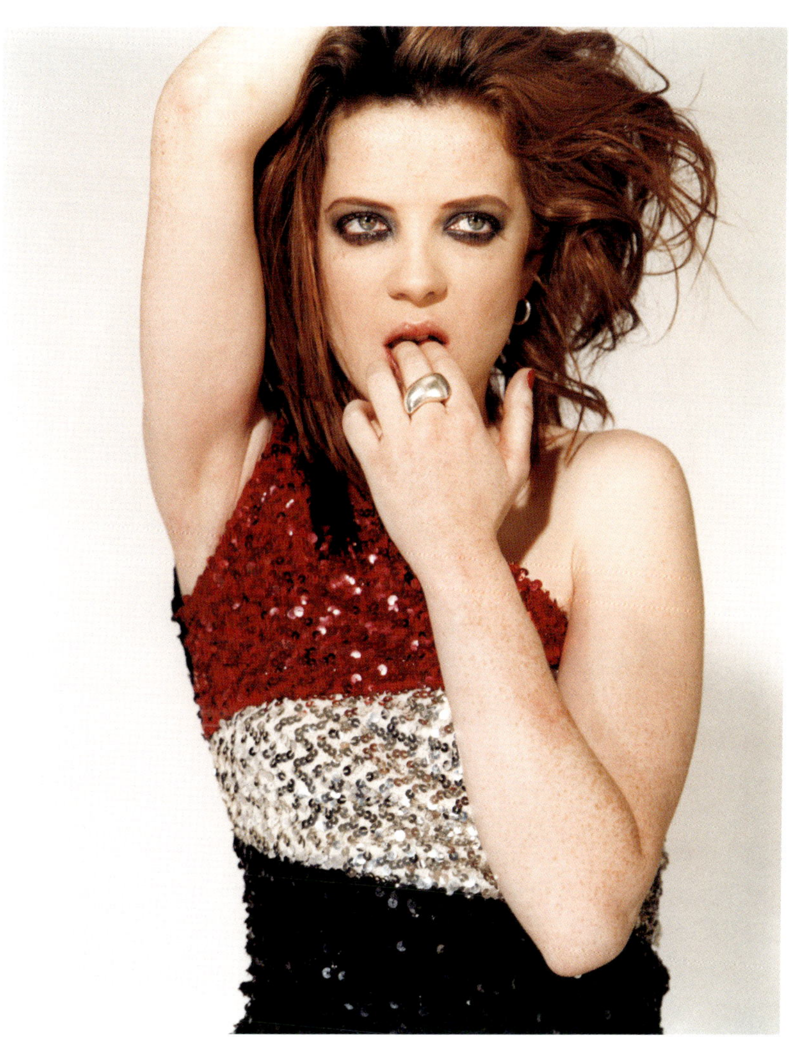

Above — *Shirley Manson from «Garbage» wearing a Helmut Lang flag*, March 1996, Paris
Opposite page — *Dominique Swain as «Lolita» IV*, March 1996, London

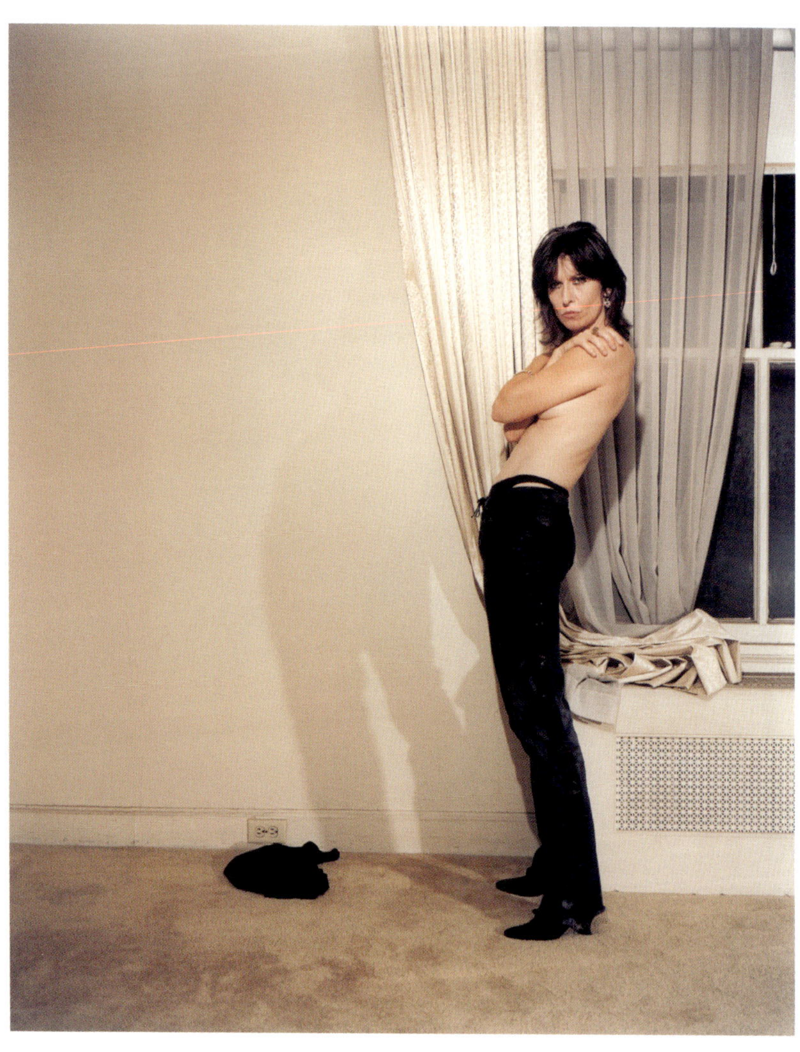

Above — *Chrissie Hynde being very difficult*, October 1995, Los Angeles
Opposite page — *The kiss of the Cramps*, April 1994, Los Angeles

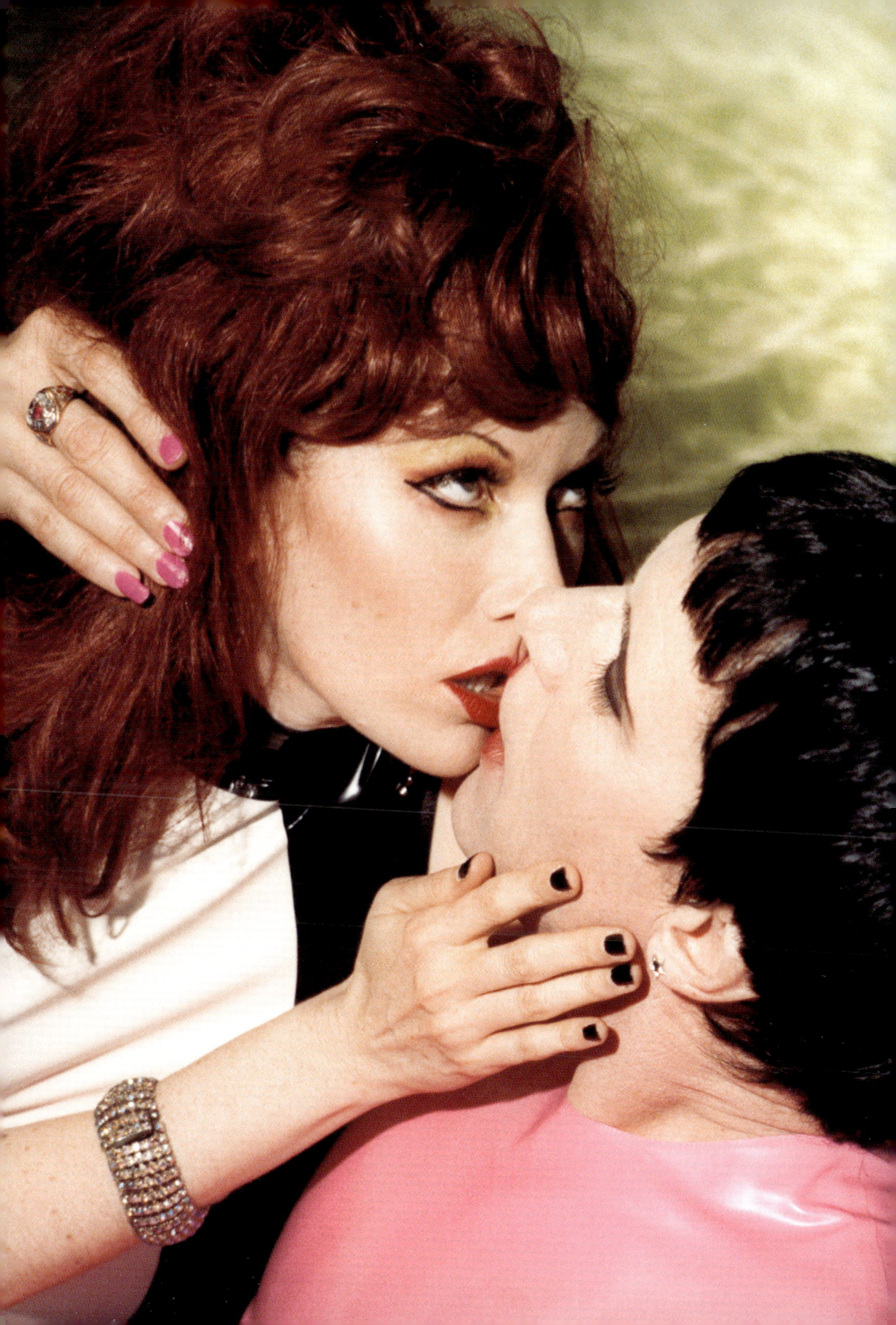

Marilyn Manson as a «little red riding hood», September 1996, Cleveland, Ohio

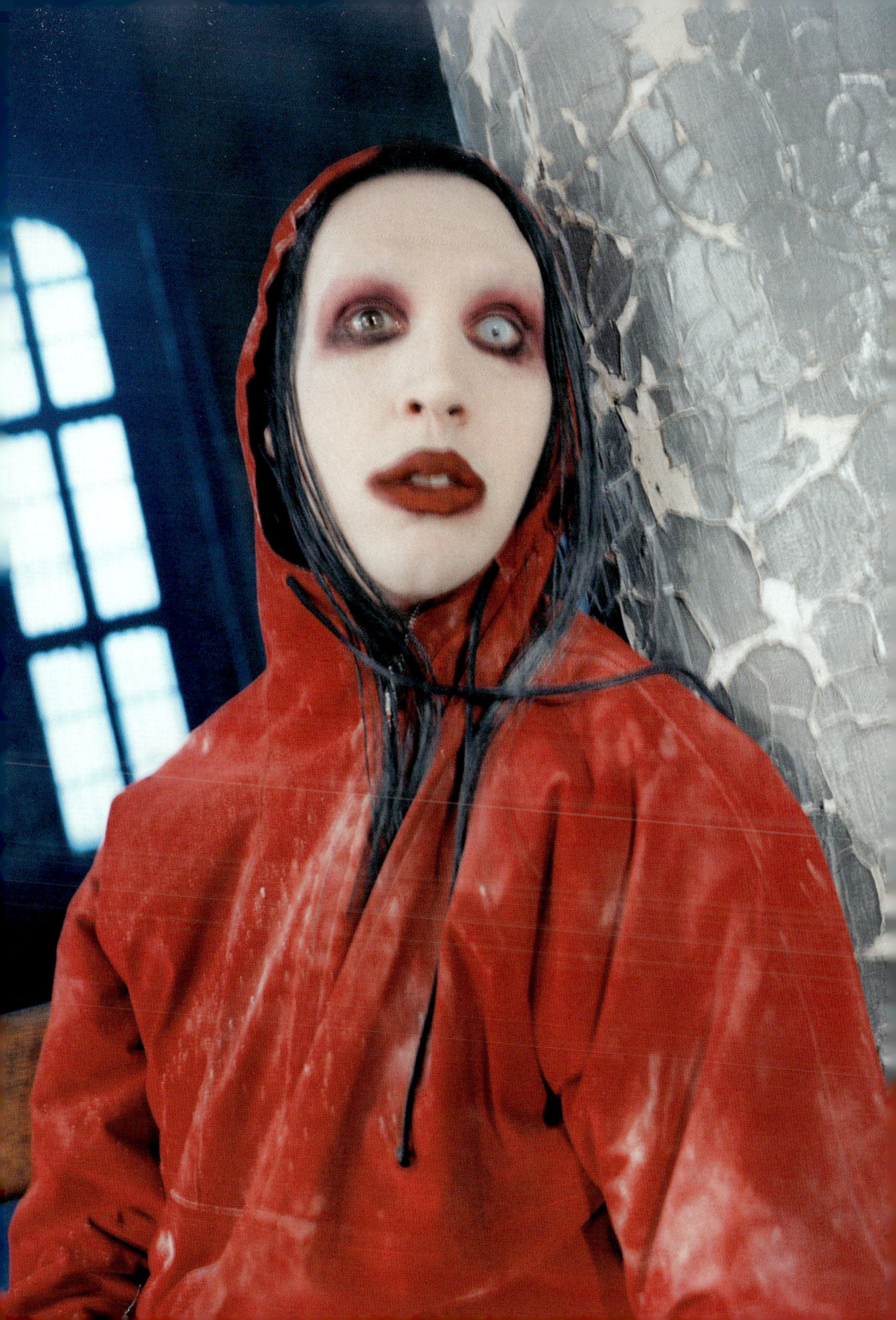

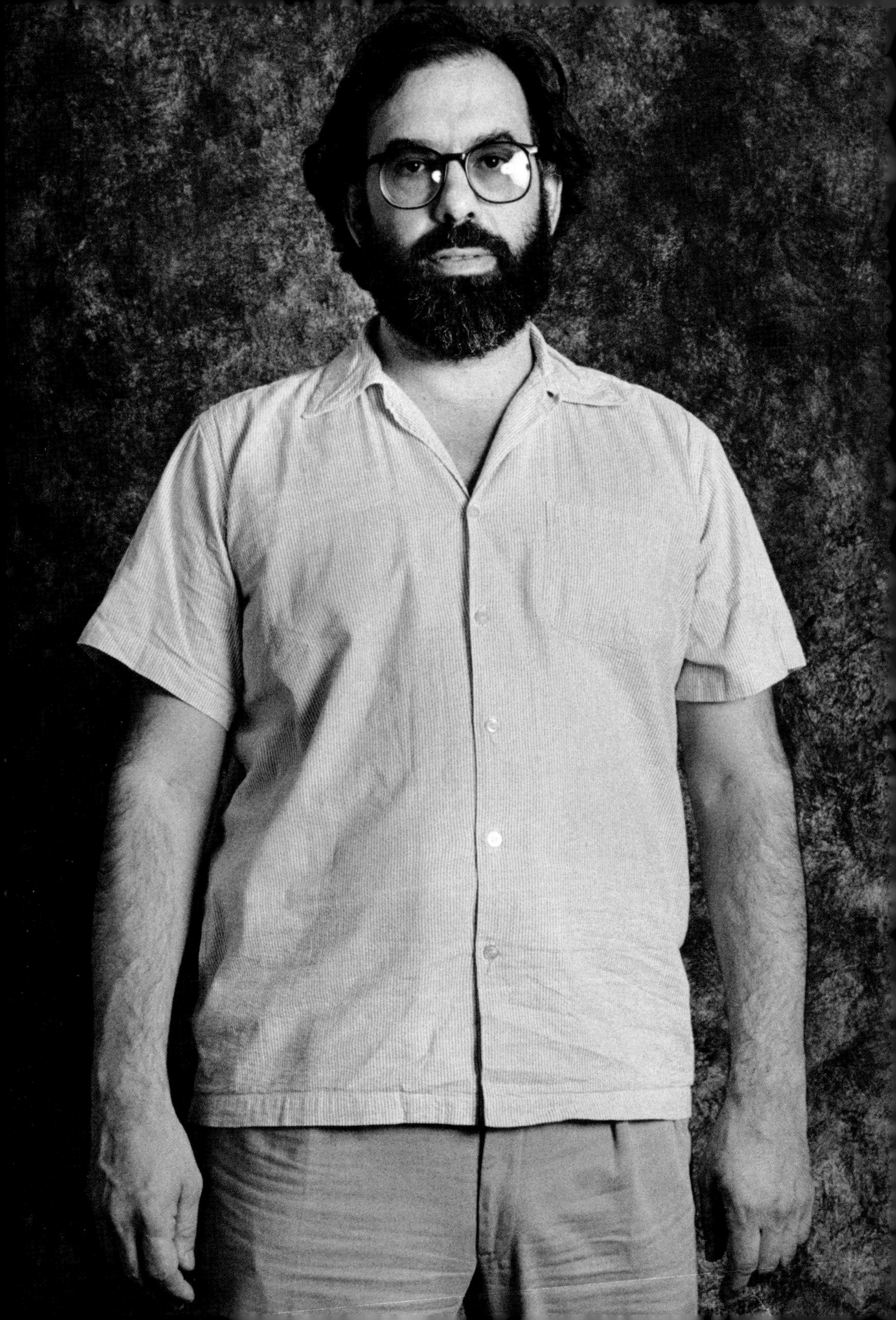

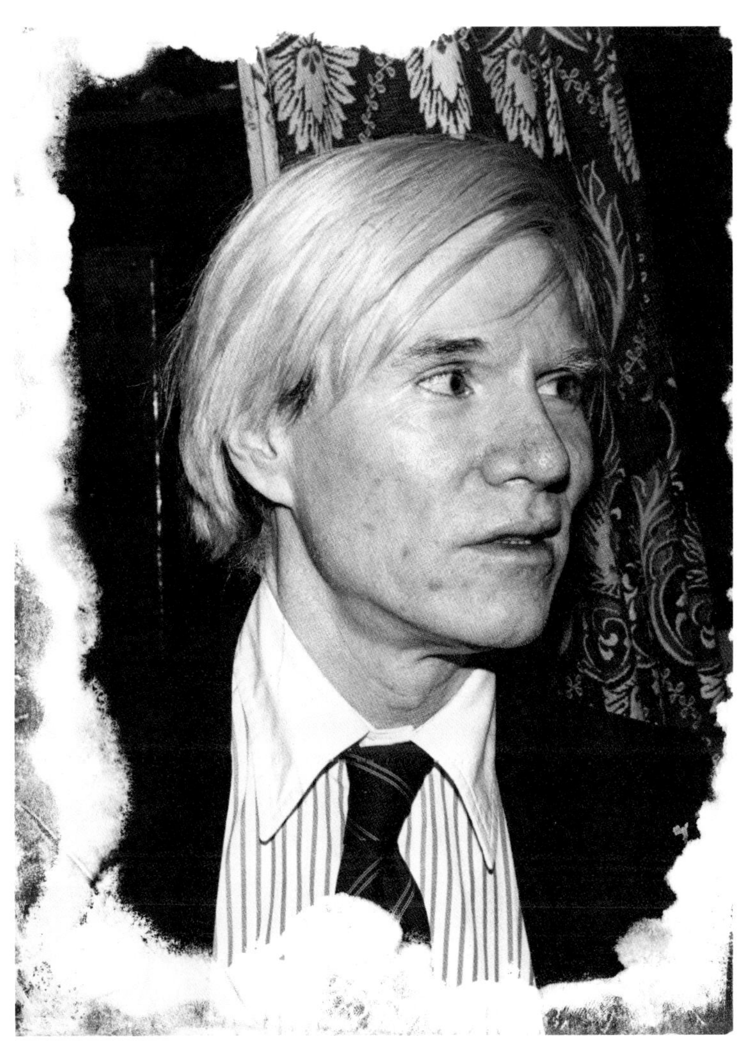

Above — *Andy Warhol*, 1978, Paris
Opposite page — *Francis Ford Coppola*, June 1979, Paris

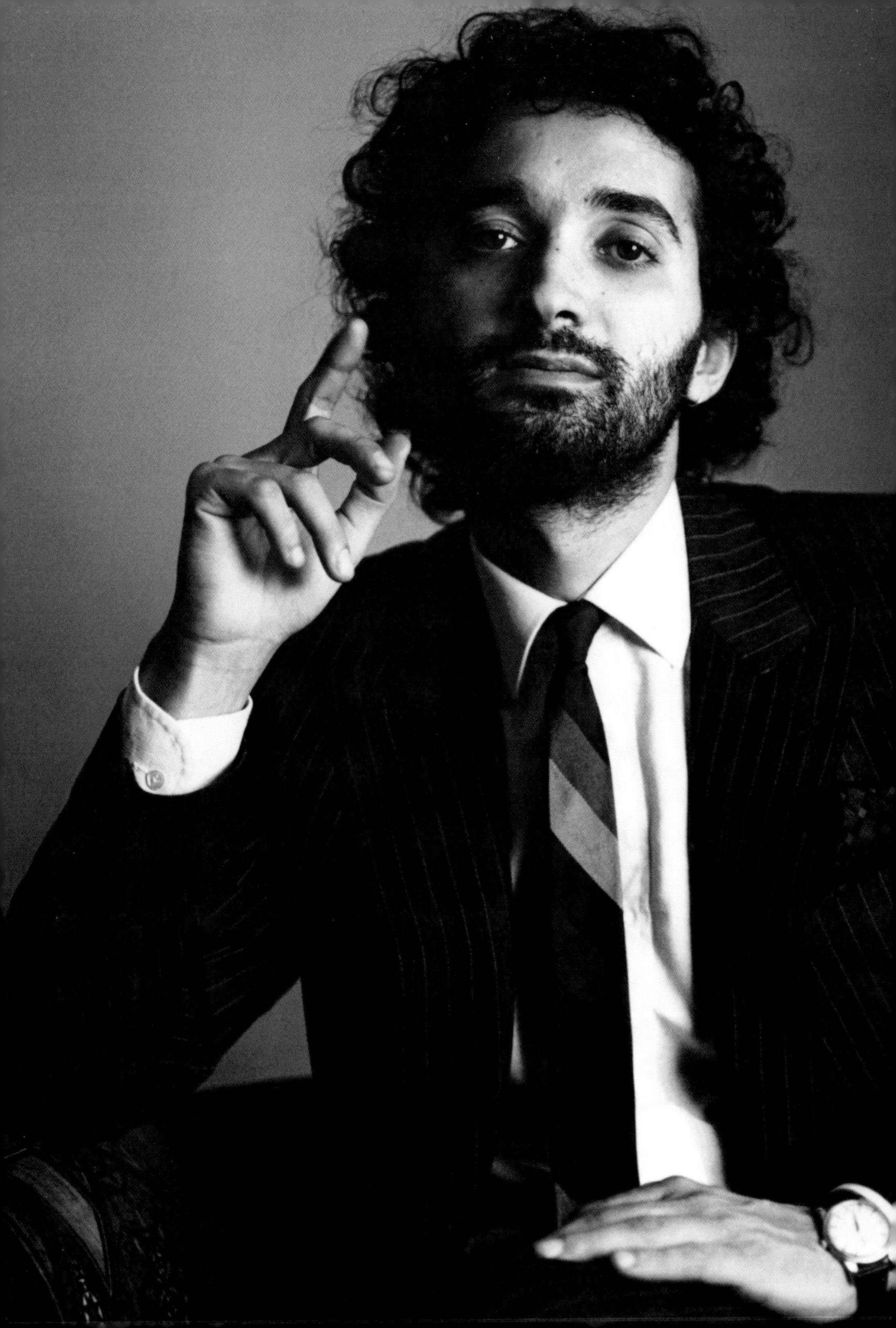

LA CROISIÈRE BLEUE
1987, Paris

Charity ball given by Hélène Rochas

Baronne Inès Reille au bal de la «Croisière bleue», December 1987, Paris
Pages 94/95 — *Leslie Caron et des amis au bal de la «Croisière bleue»*, December 1987, Paris
Page 96 — *Alexis de Redé, Hélène Rochas et Madison Cox au bal de la «Croisière bleue»*, December 1987, Paris
Page 97 — *Anouk Aimée au bal de la «Croisière bleue»*, December 1987, Paris

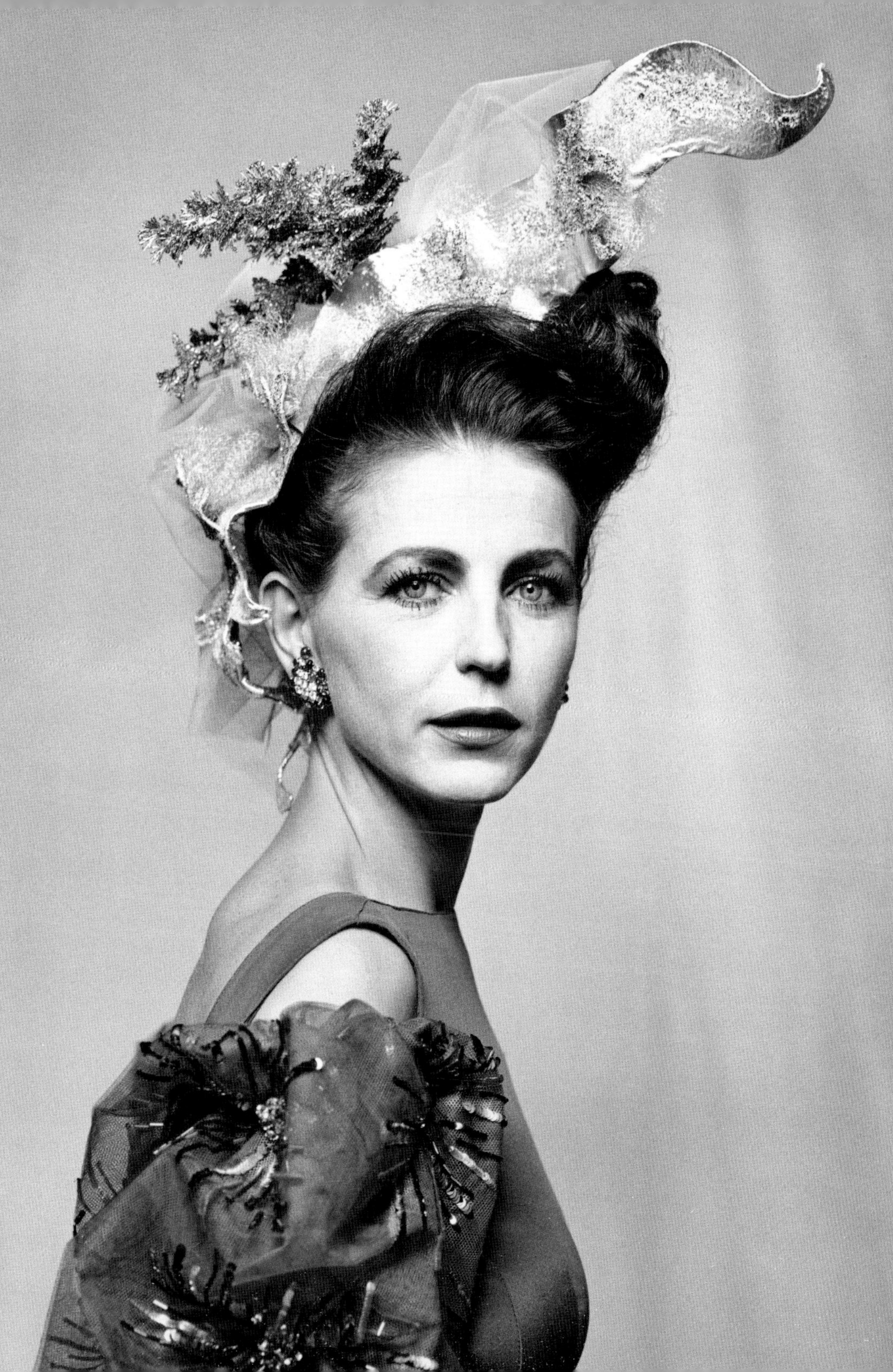

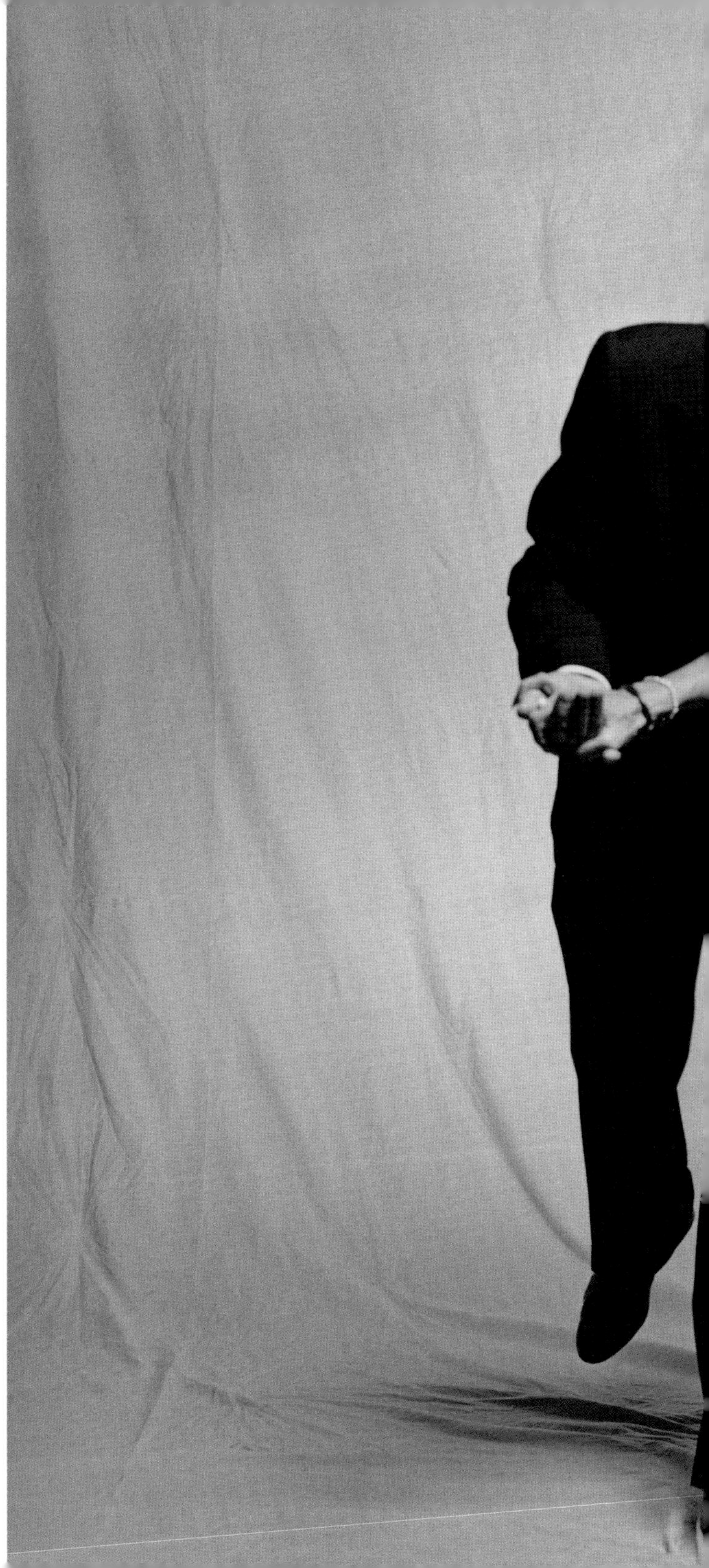

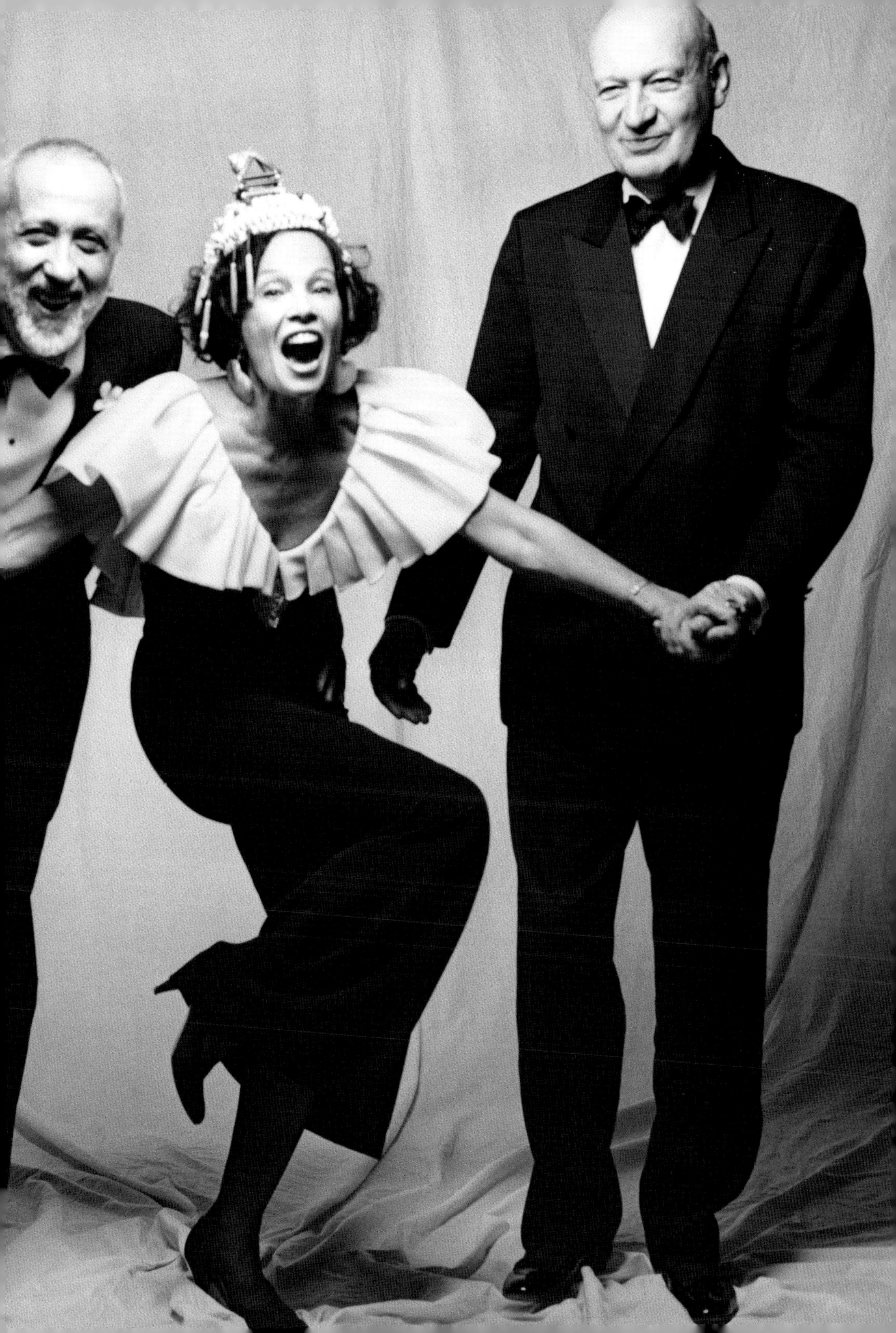

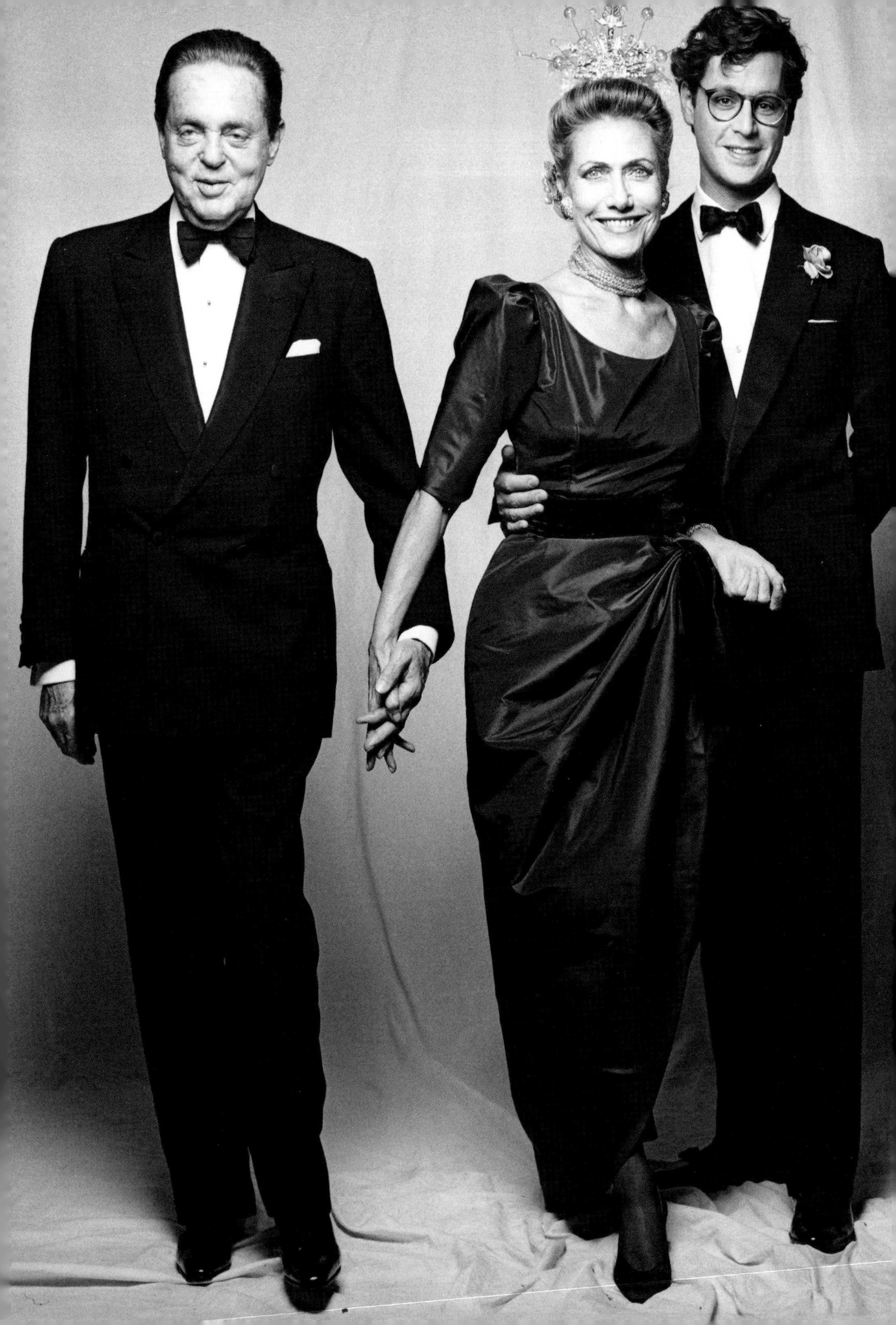

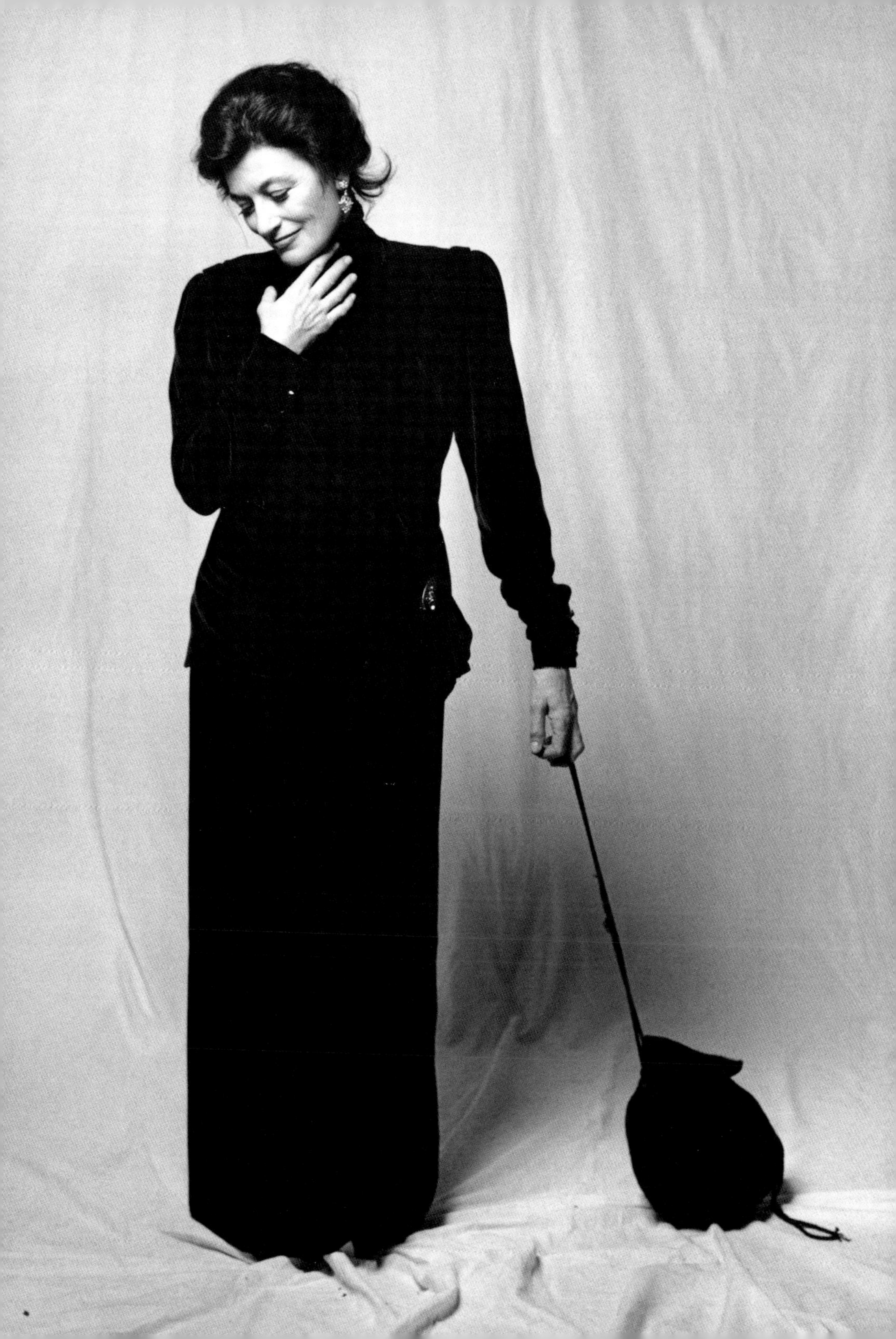

Au bal de la « Croisière bleue », December 1987, Paris

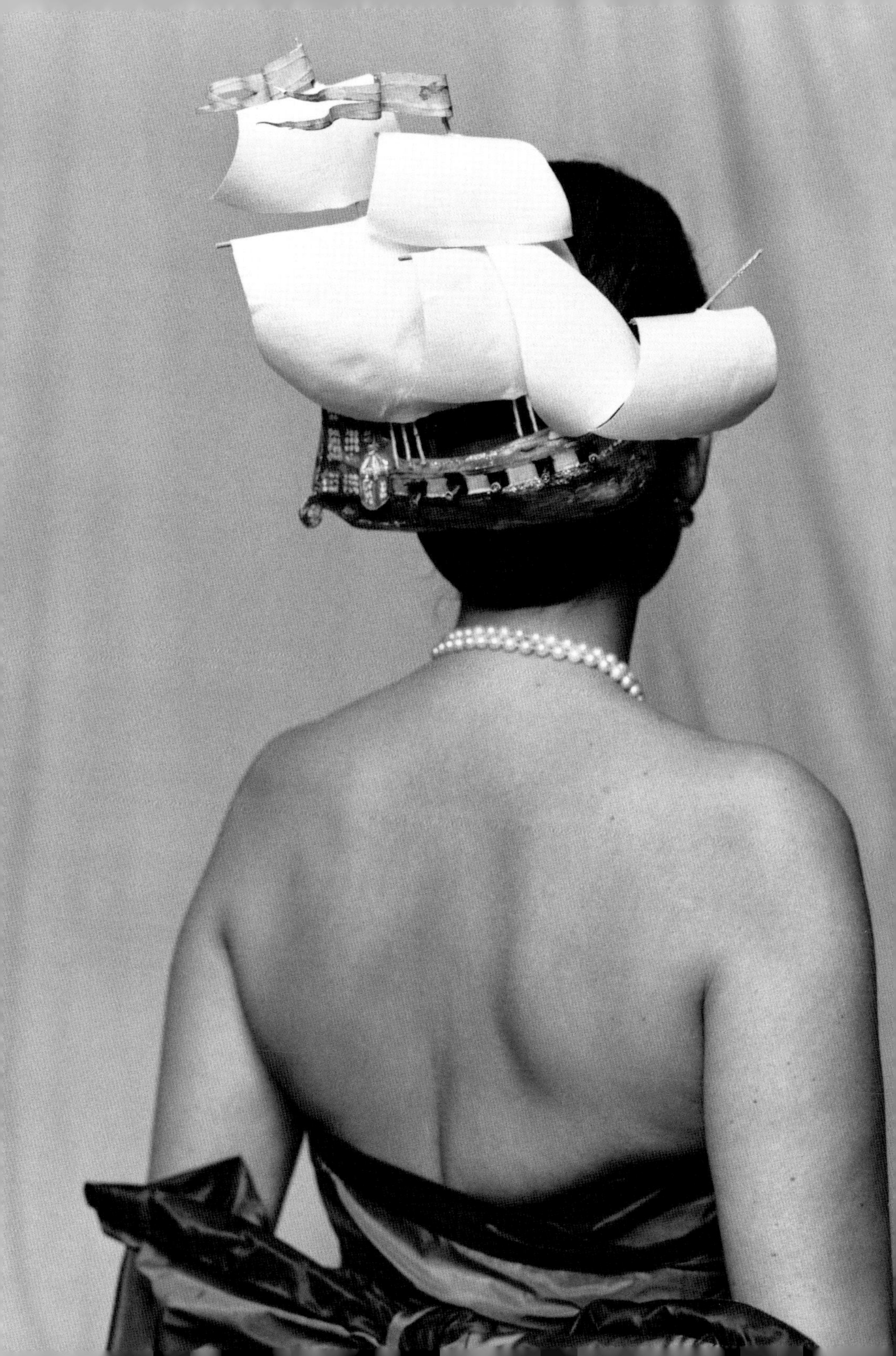

Sibyl rouge avec un chandail vert, January 1996, Paris

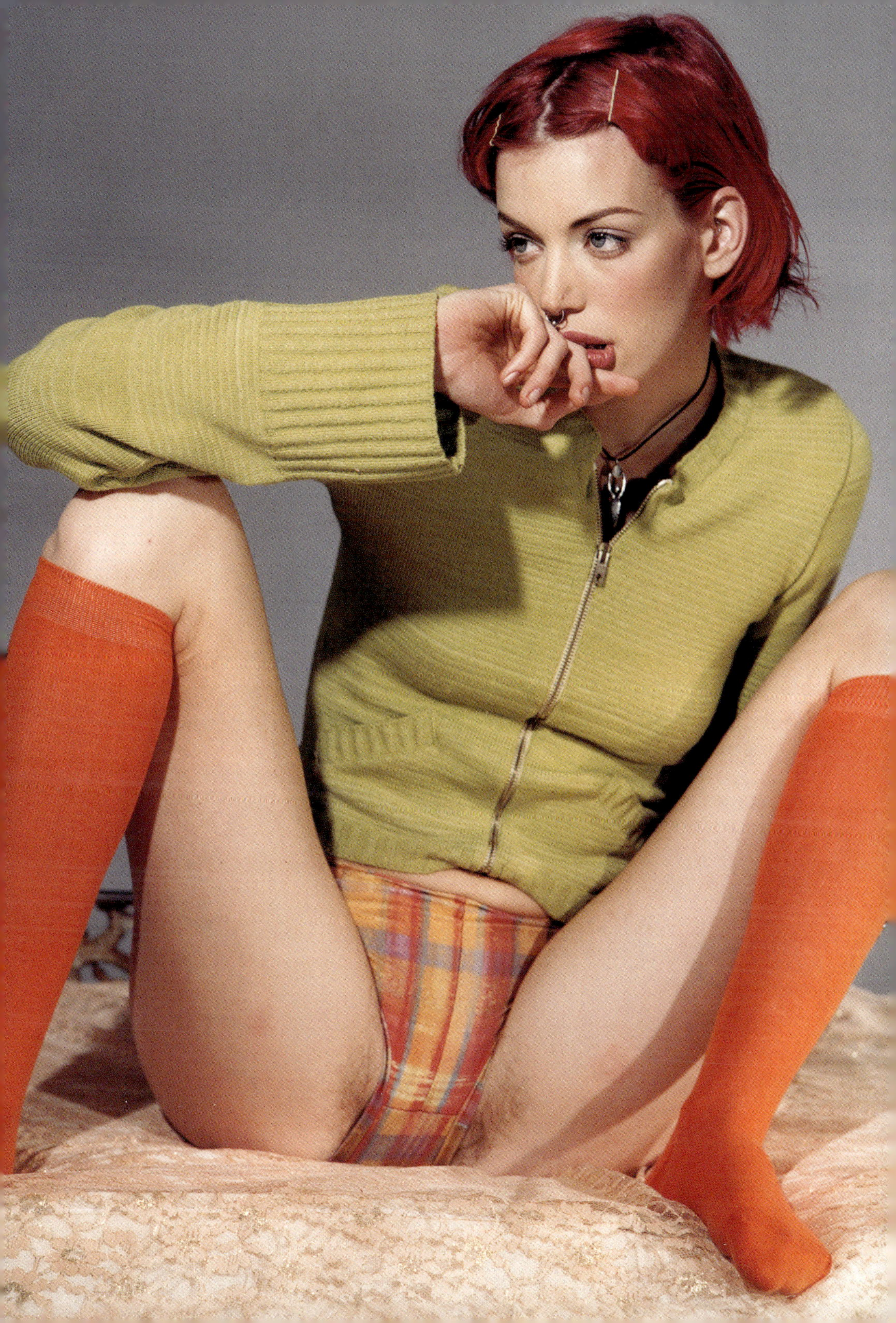

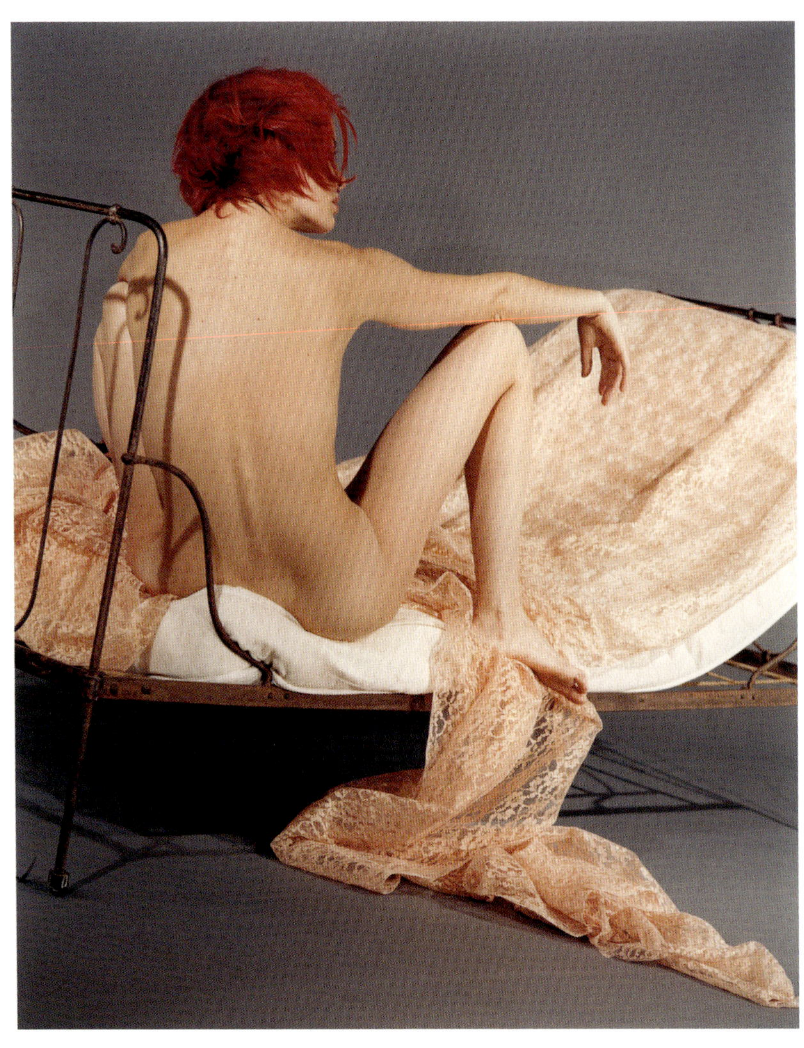

Above — *Sibyl Buck in my studio sitting on an iron bed*, January 1996, Paris
Opposite page — *Sibyl Buck la joue écrasée sur un lit*, January 1996, Paris

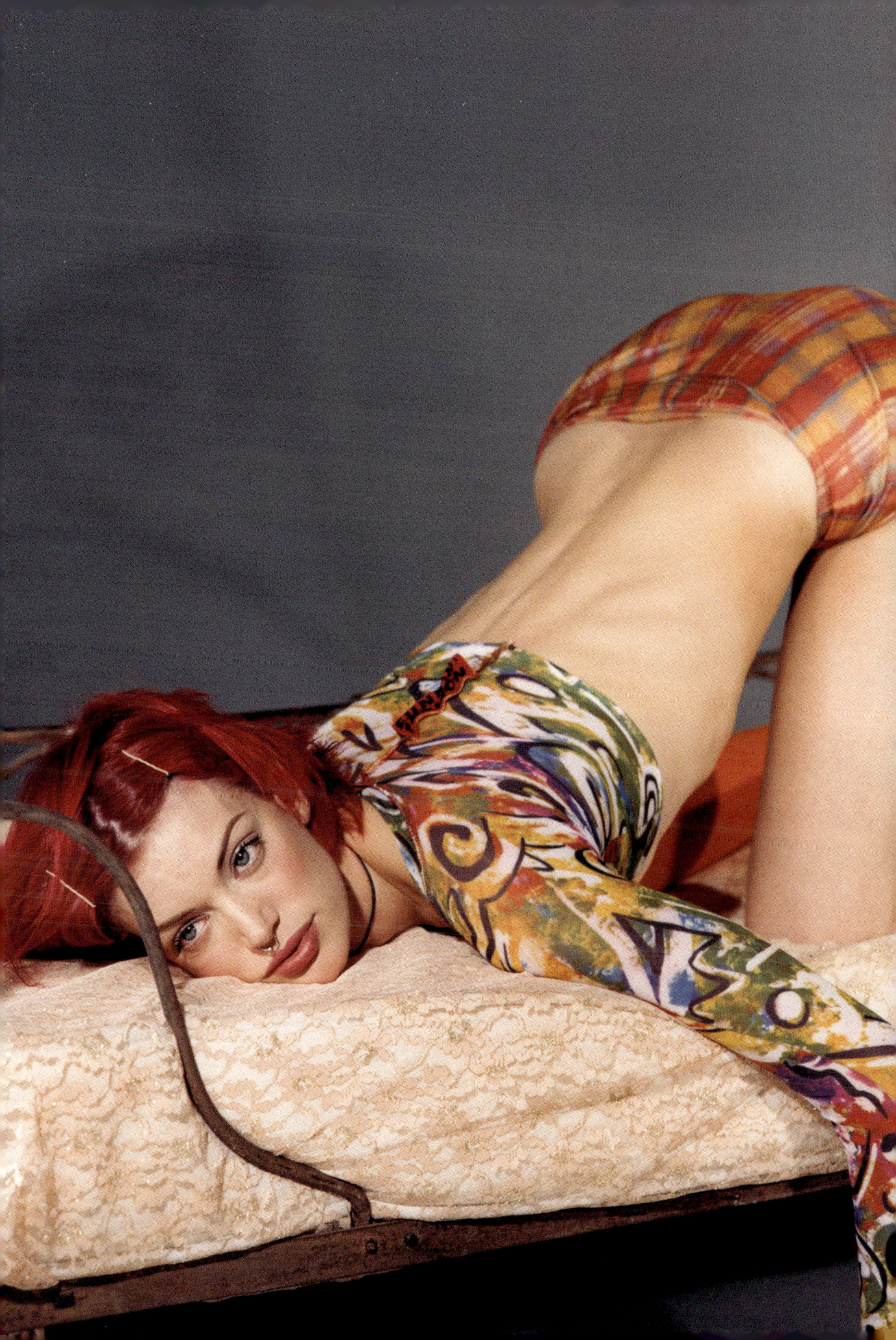

ANIMAL
1982–1985, Paris

Death fascinates the photographer because it is the unspoken driving force behind her art. An instant – the fraction of the second during which the shutter opens – perfectly illustrates the brevity of our existence in an ocean of eternity. (...) Joyful as it may seem, every photograph is a *memento mori*.

La mort fascine le photographe parce qu'elle est le moteur secret de son art. Un instantané; cette fraction de seconde pendant laquelle s'ouvre le diaphragme symbolise à merveille la longueur de notre existence au sein de l'éternité. (...) Tout cliché, aussi joyeux soit-il, constitue un *memento mori*.

Der Tod fasziniert die Fotografin, denn er ist die geheime Triebkraft ihrer Kunst. Ein Schnappschuss – dieser Sekundenbruchteil, für den sich die Blende öffnet – ist ein wunderbares Sinnbild für die Dauer unseres Daseins im Angesicht der Ewigkeit. (...) Jedes Bild, und mag es noch so fröhlich sein, ist ein *Memento mori*.

Serge Bramly, in *Animal*, 1994

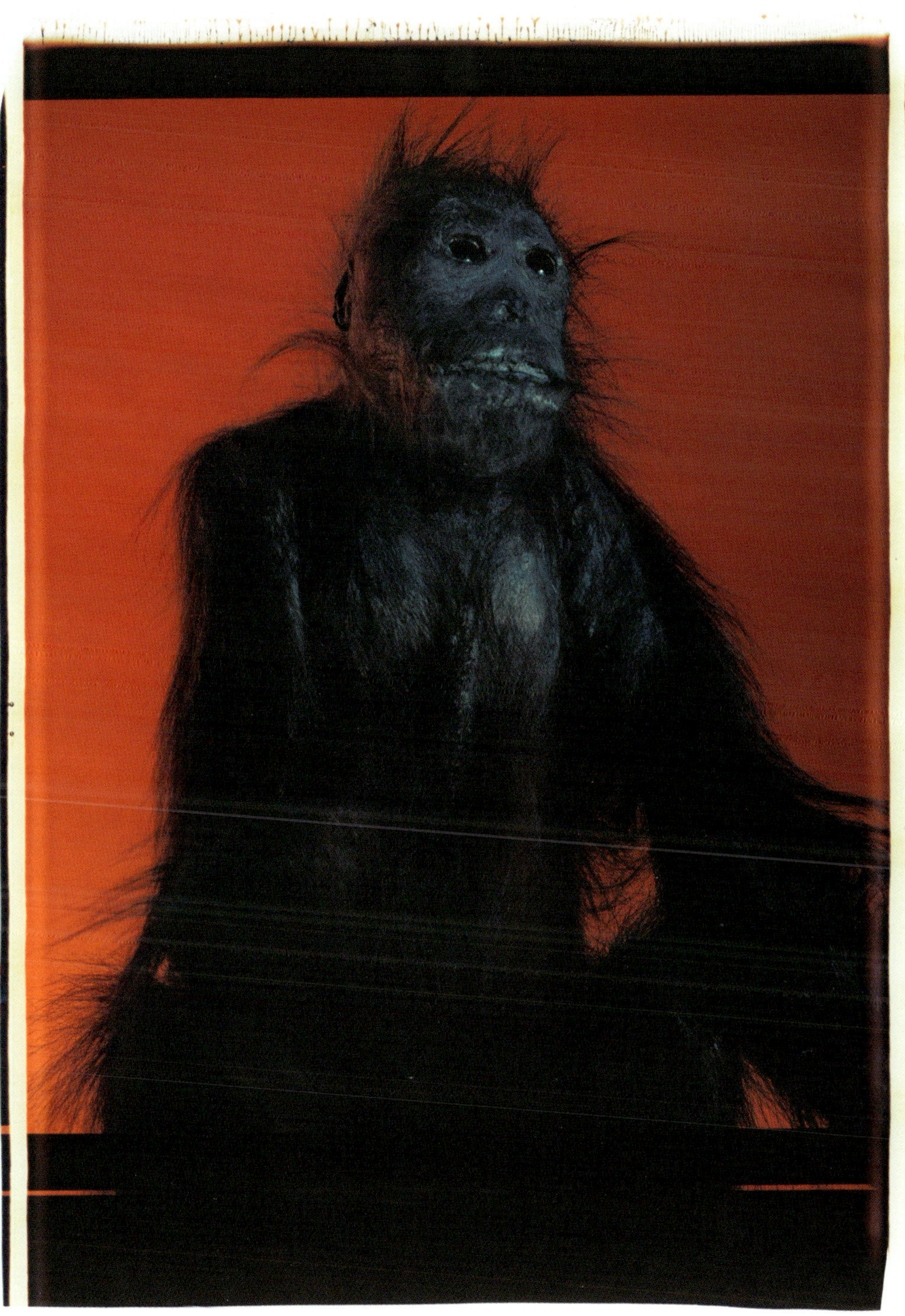

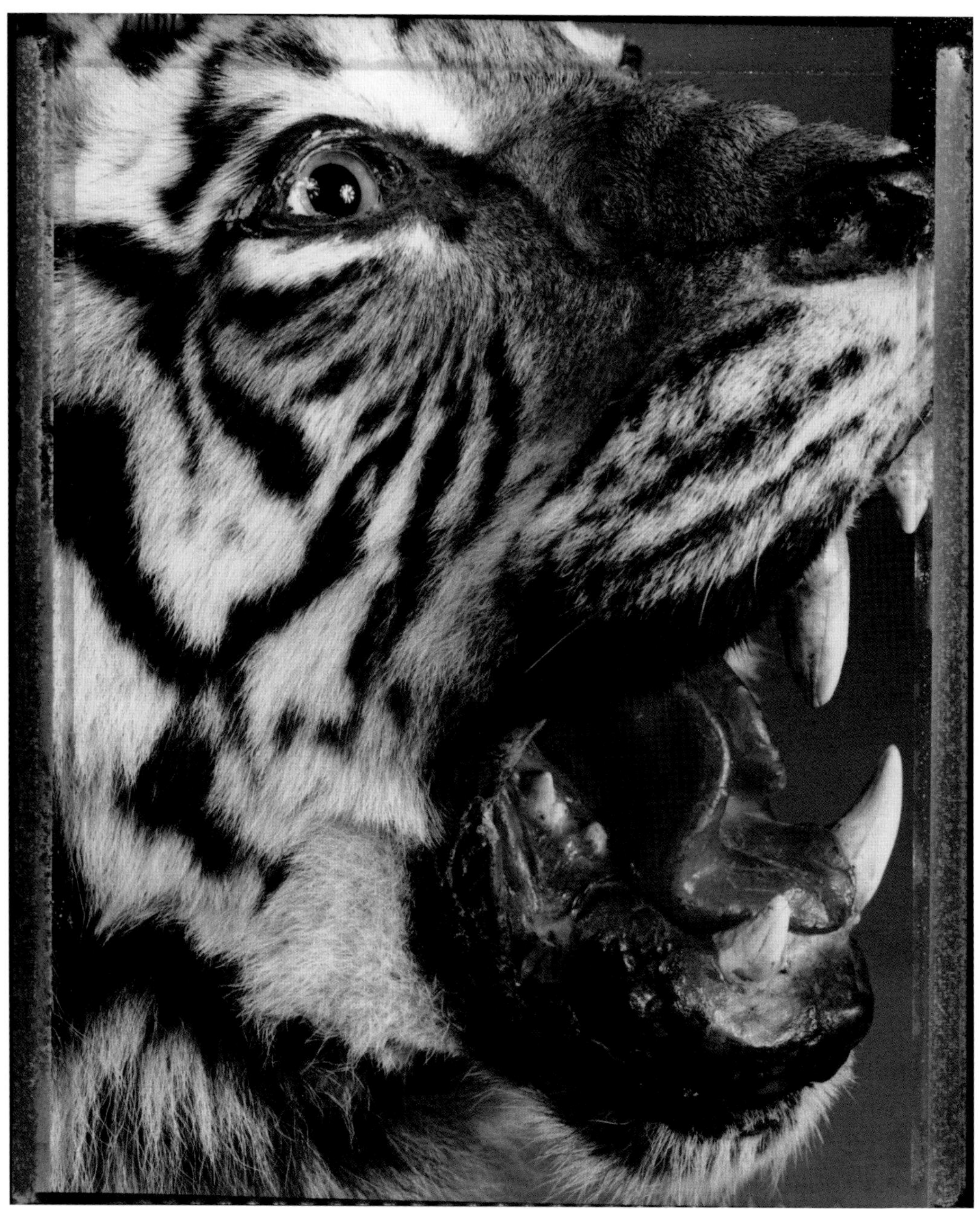

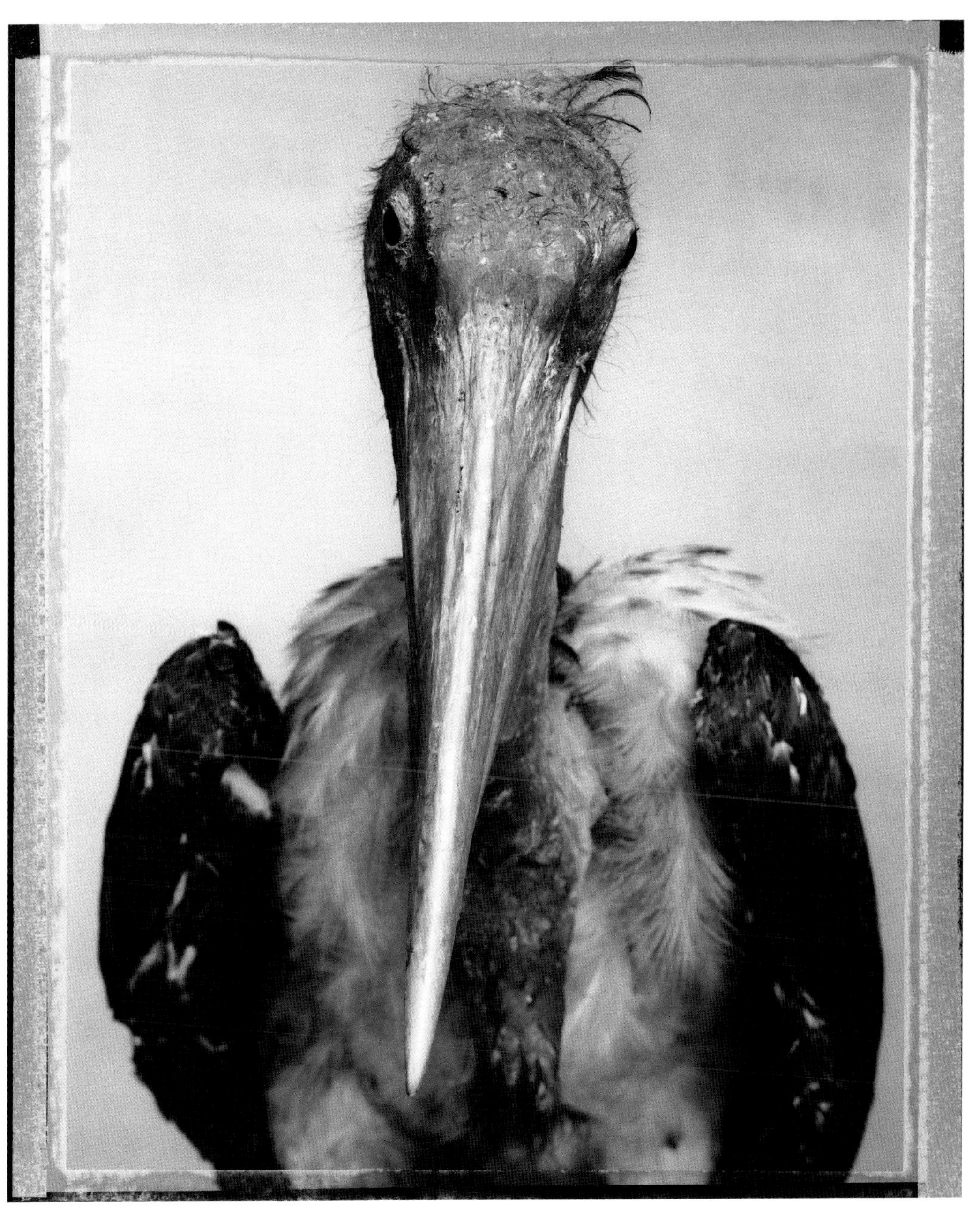

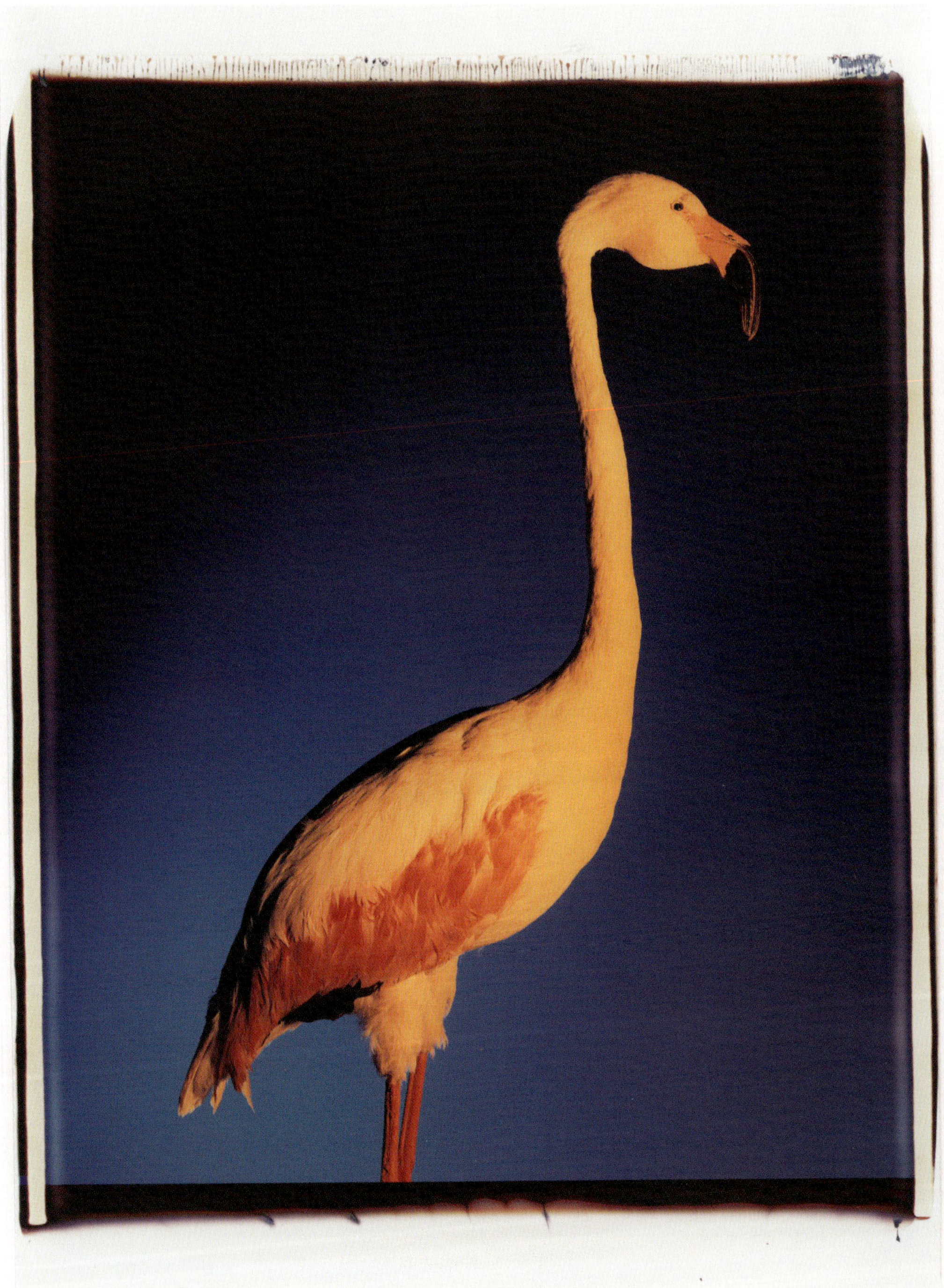

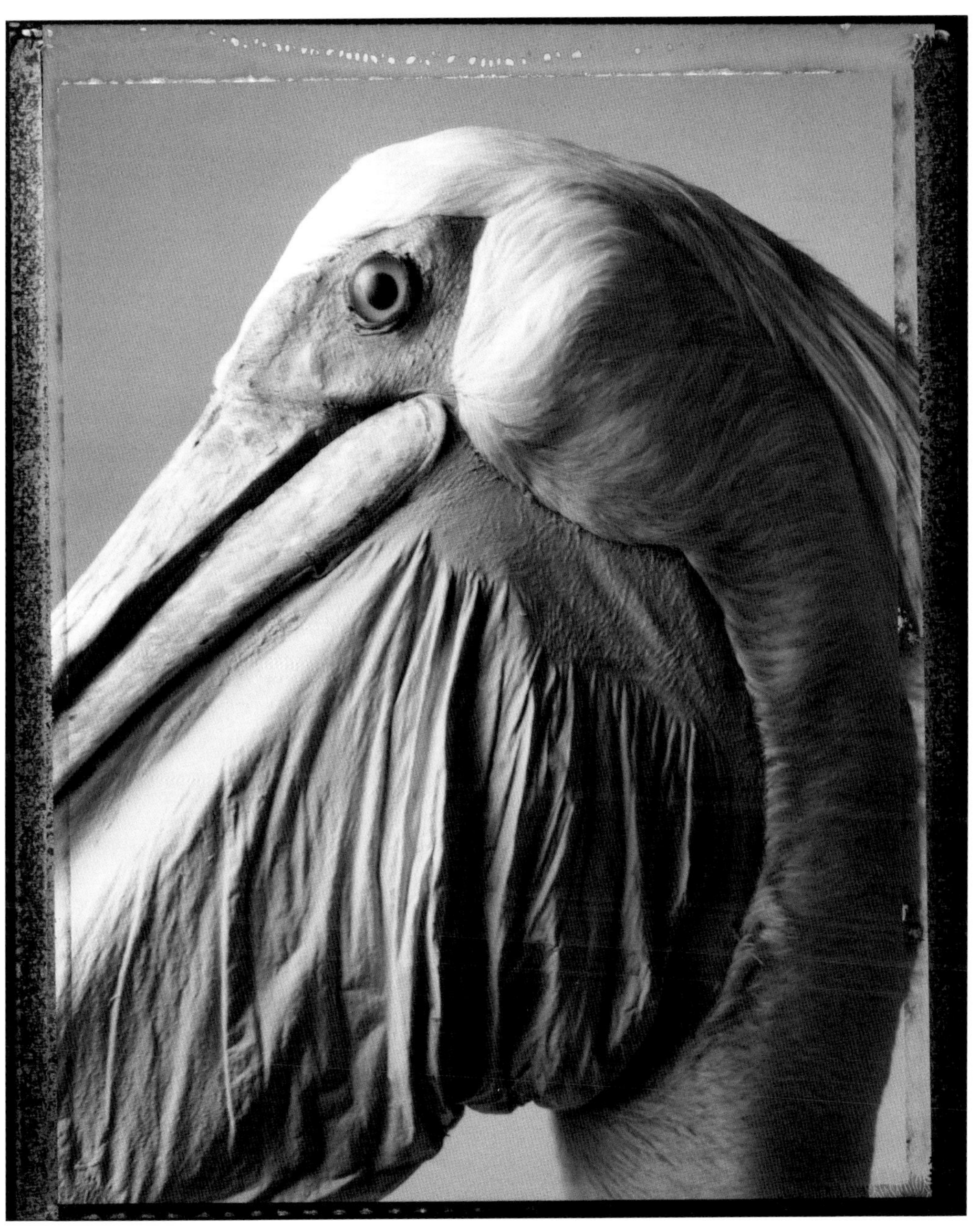

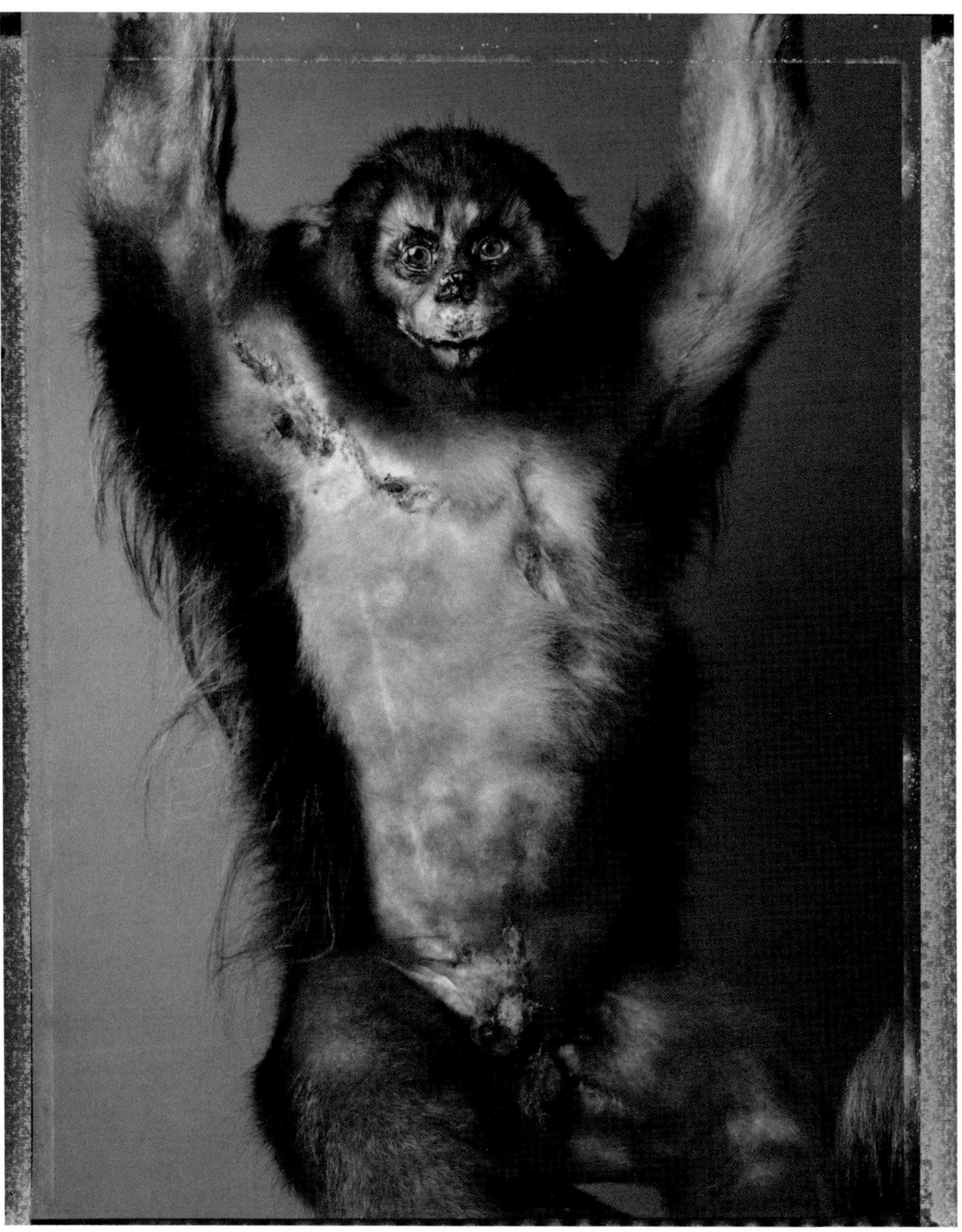

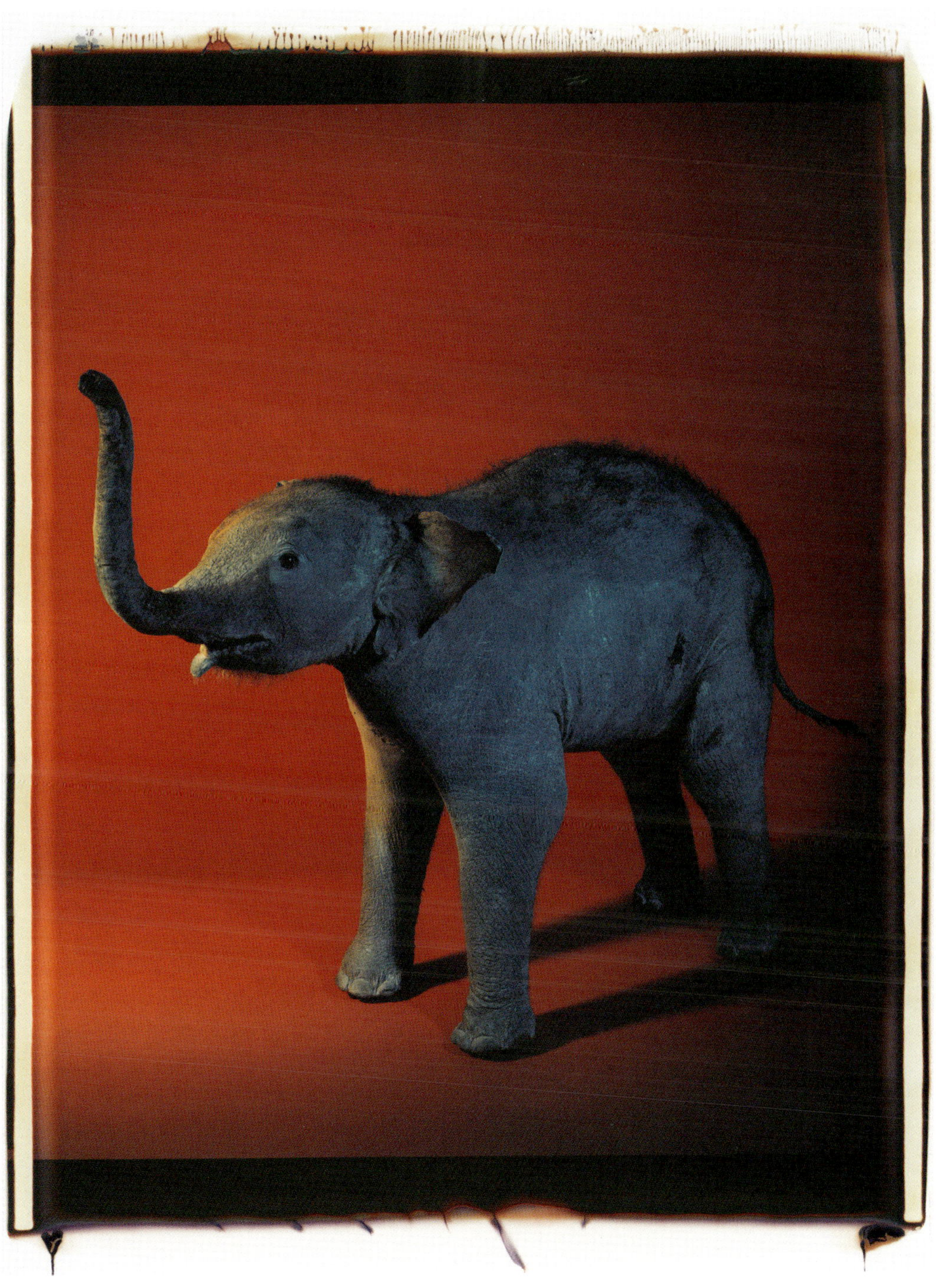

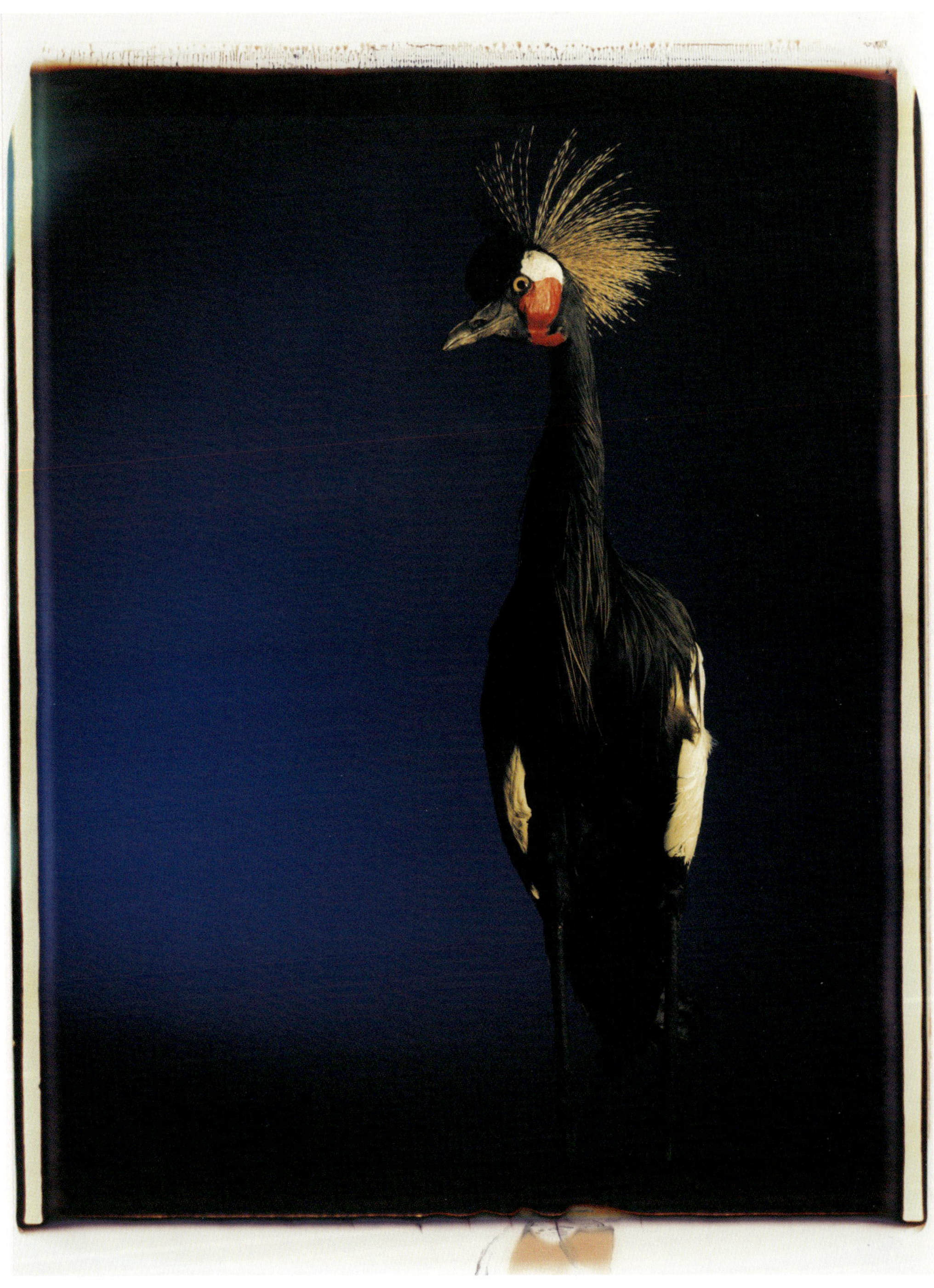

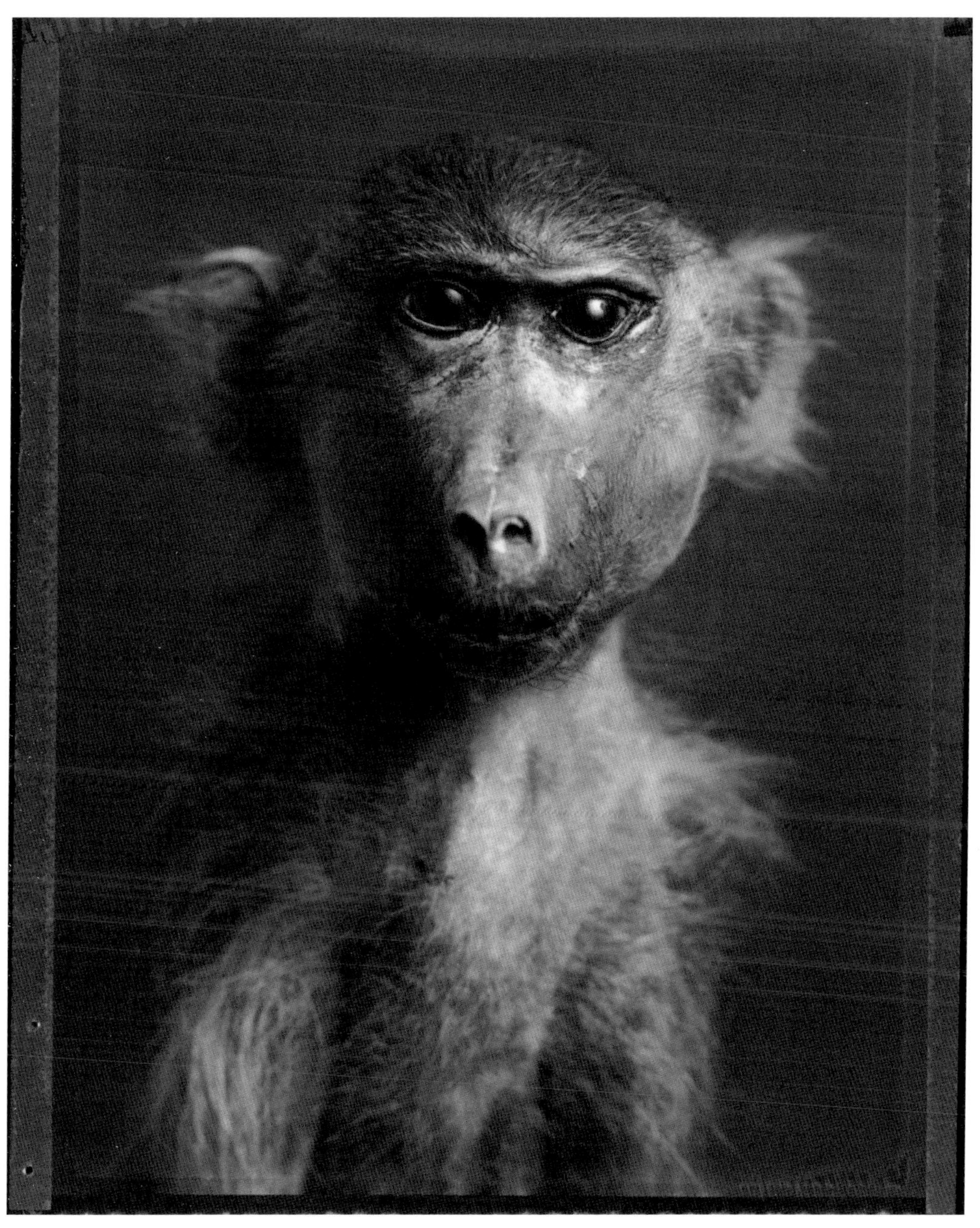

CHAMBRE CLOSE
IN COLLABORATION WITH SERGE BRAMLY
1991–1993, Paris

Chambre close invented the life and work of some distinguished amateur bent over the viewfinder of his camera as if over a keyhole: here are his pleasures, his trophies; this is a Don Juan whose conquests are made on film. I gave him a voice, Bettina gave him a vision.

Chambre close inventait la vie et l'œuvre d'un amateur distingué penché sur le viseur de son appareil comme sur un trou de serrure: voilà ses plaisirs, voilà ses trophées, ce Don Juan jouit des femmes en les exposant sur de la pellicule: tandis que je lui donnais une voix, Bettina lui imaginait un regard.

Mit *Chambre close* erfanden wir Leben und Werk eines distinguierten Liebhabers, der sich über den Sucher seiner Kamera beugt wie über ein Schlüsselloch: Da sind sie, seine Freuden, seine Trophäen; dieser Don Juan genießt die Frauen, indem er sie auf Film bannt. Ich verlieh ihm die Stimme, und Bettina stellte sich seinen Blick vor.

Serge Bramly, in *Rétrospective*, 2004

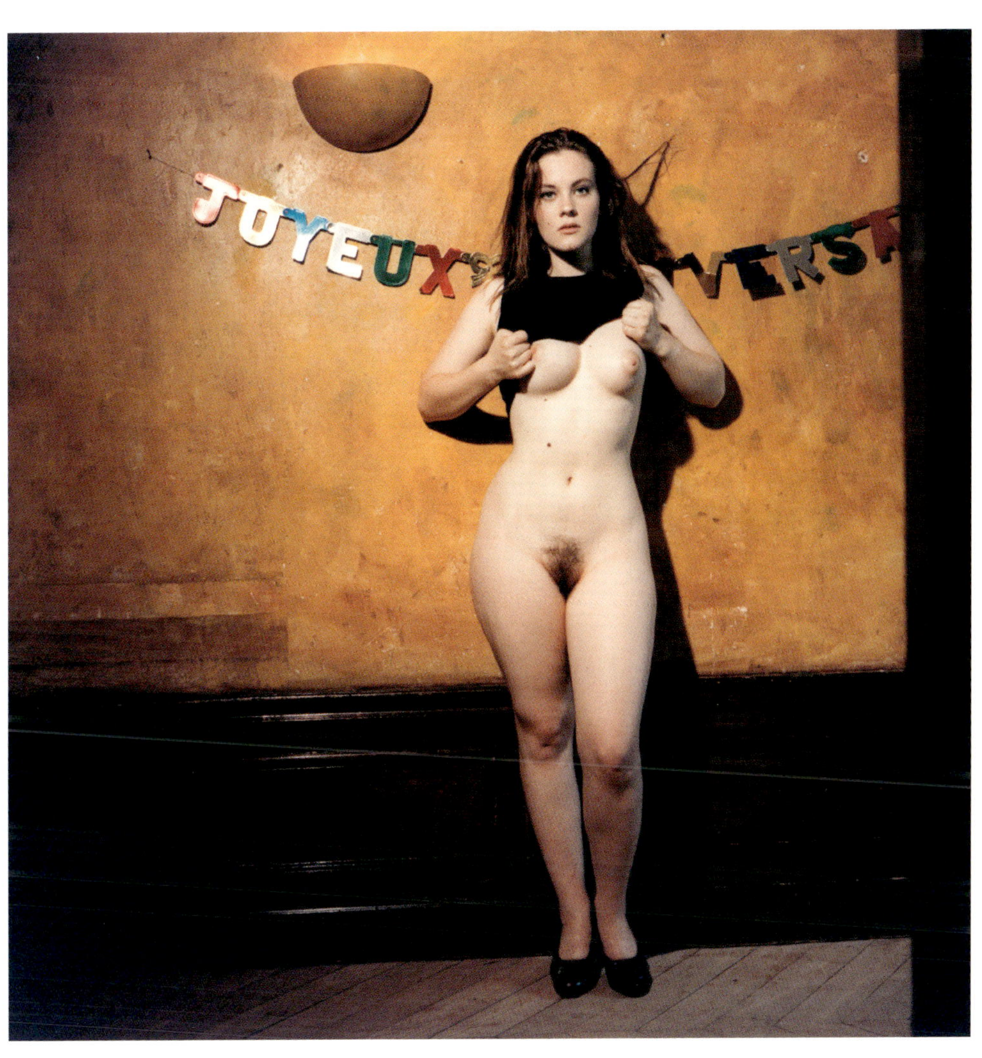

18 décembre, September 1991, Paris

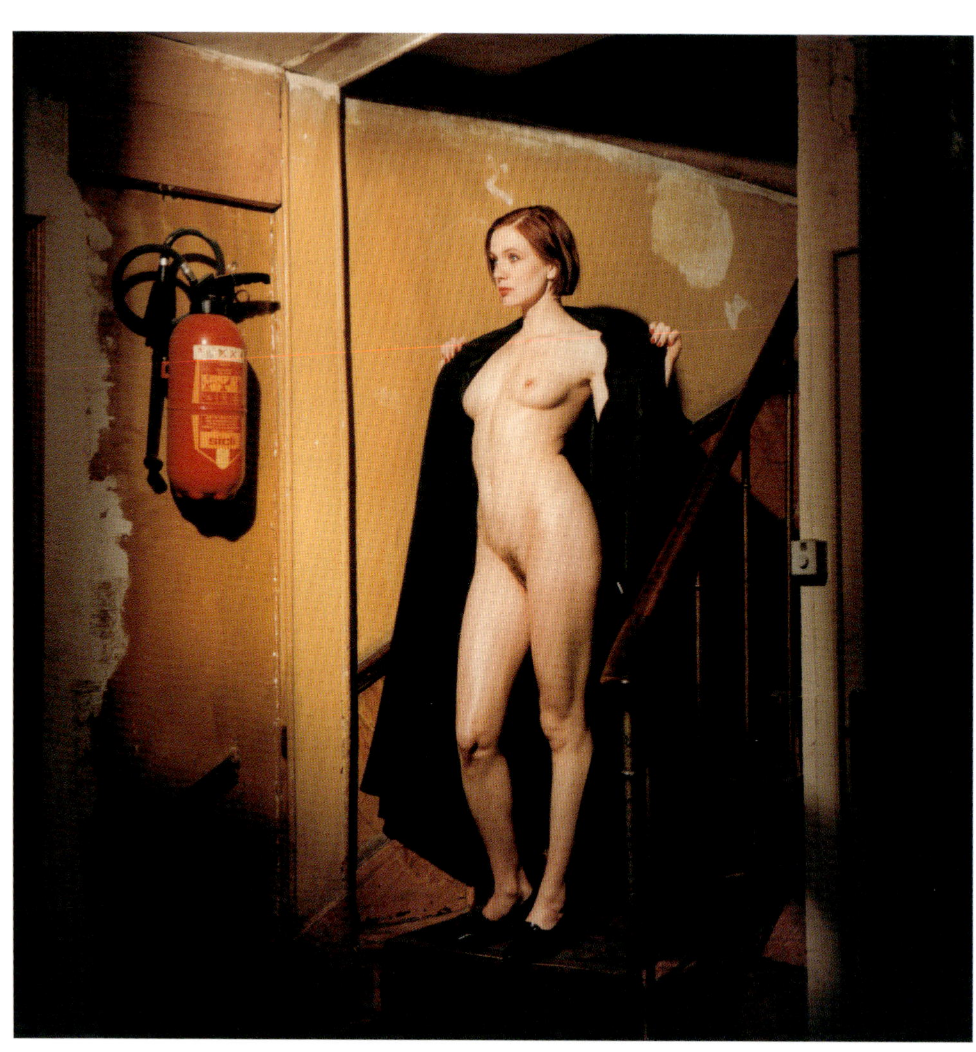

 15 août, June 1991, Paris

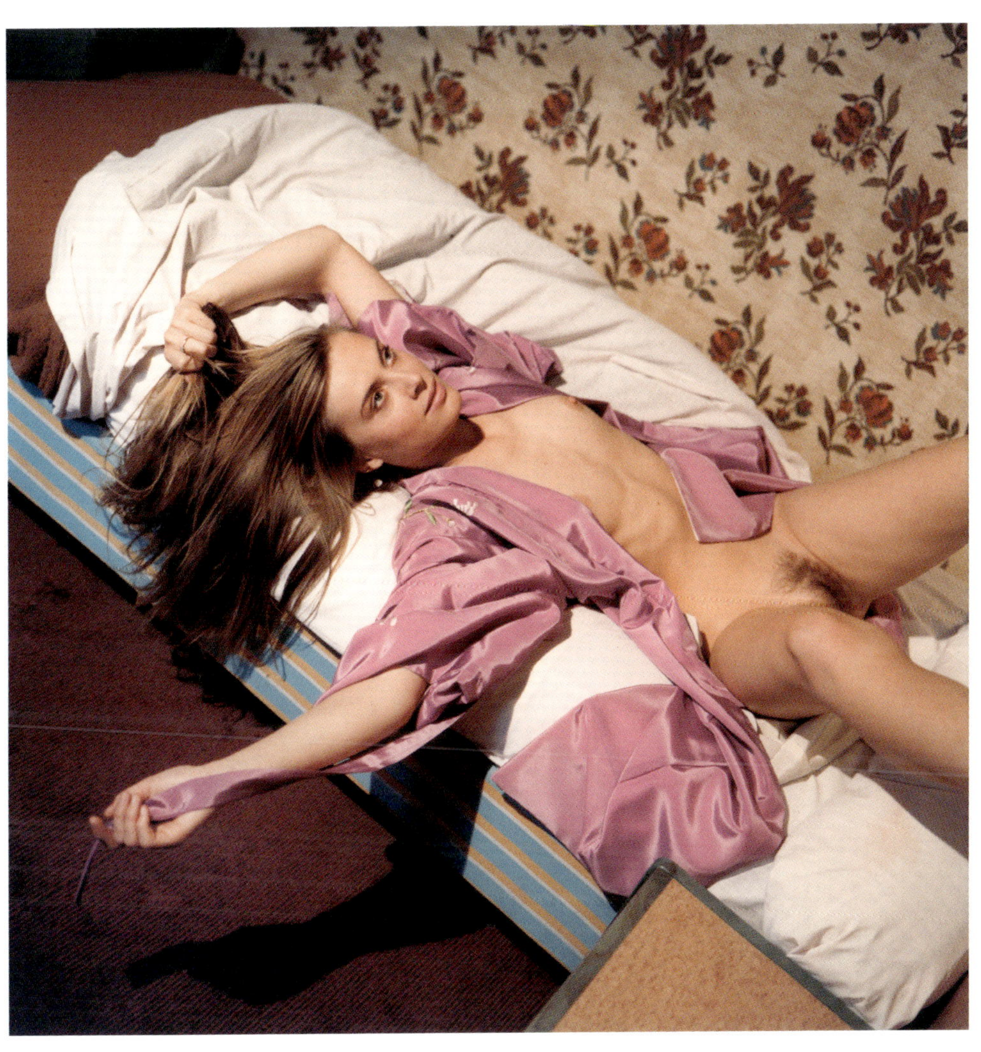

26 juin II, June 1991, Paris

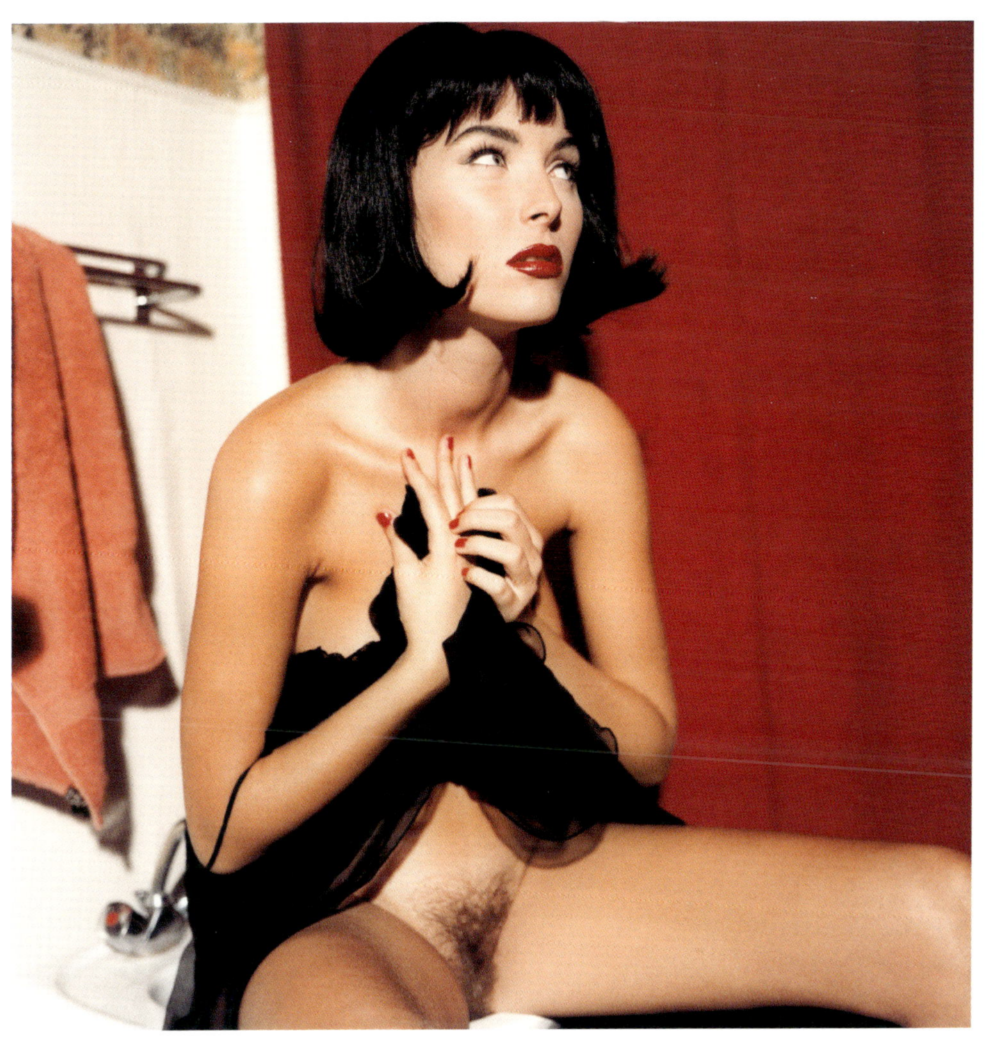

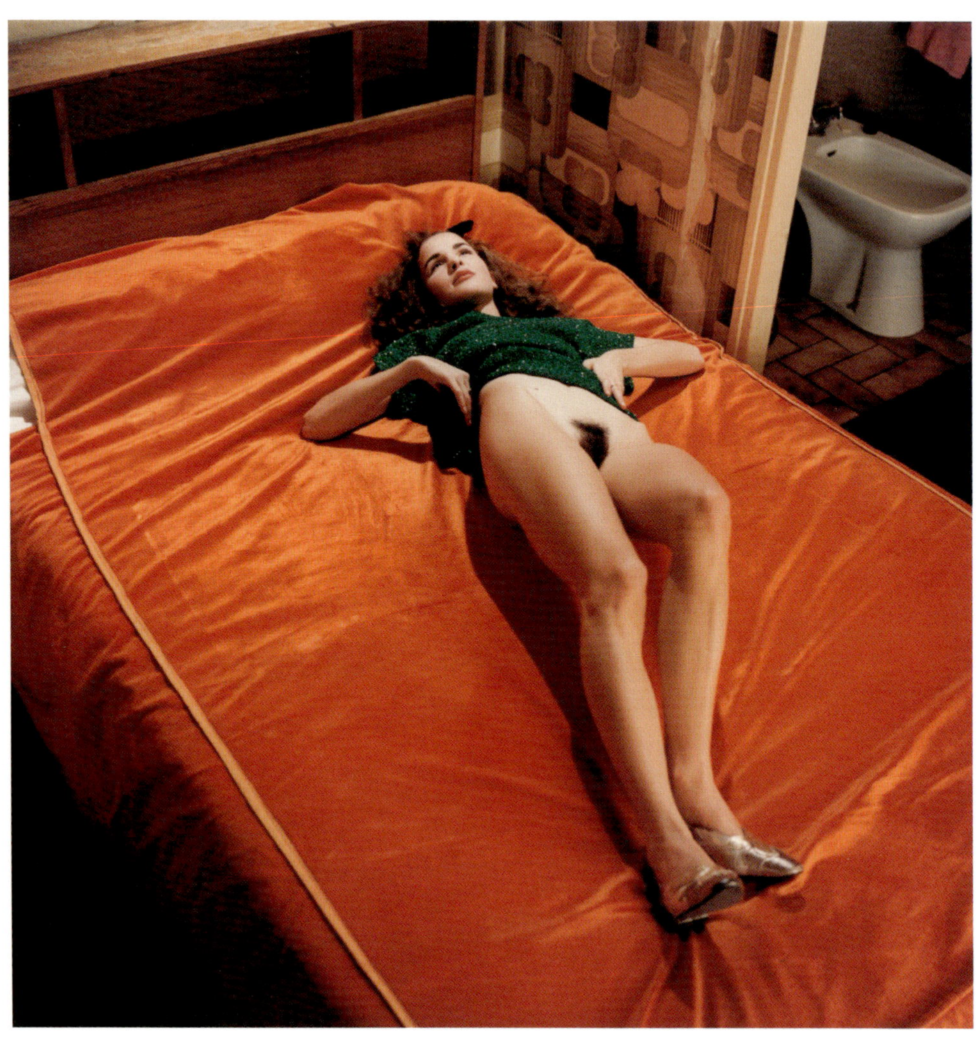

     21 avril, November 1991, Paris

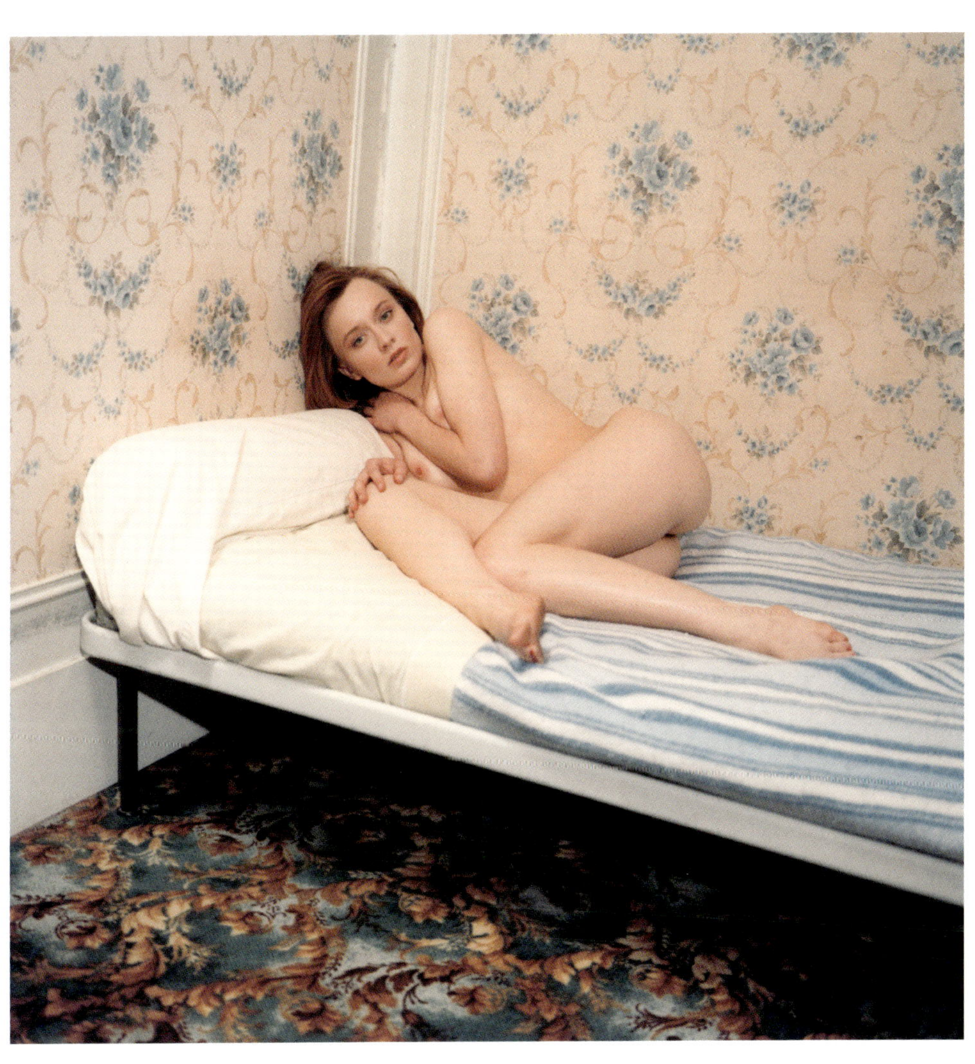

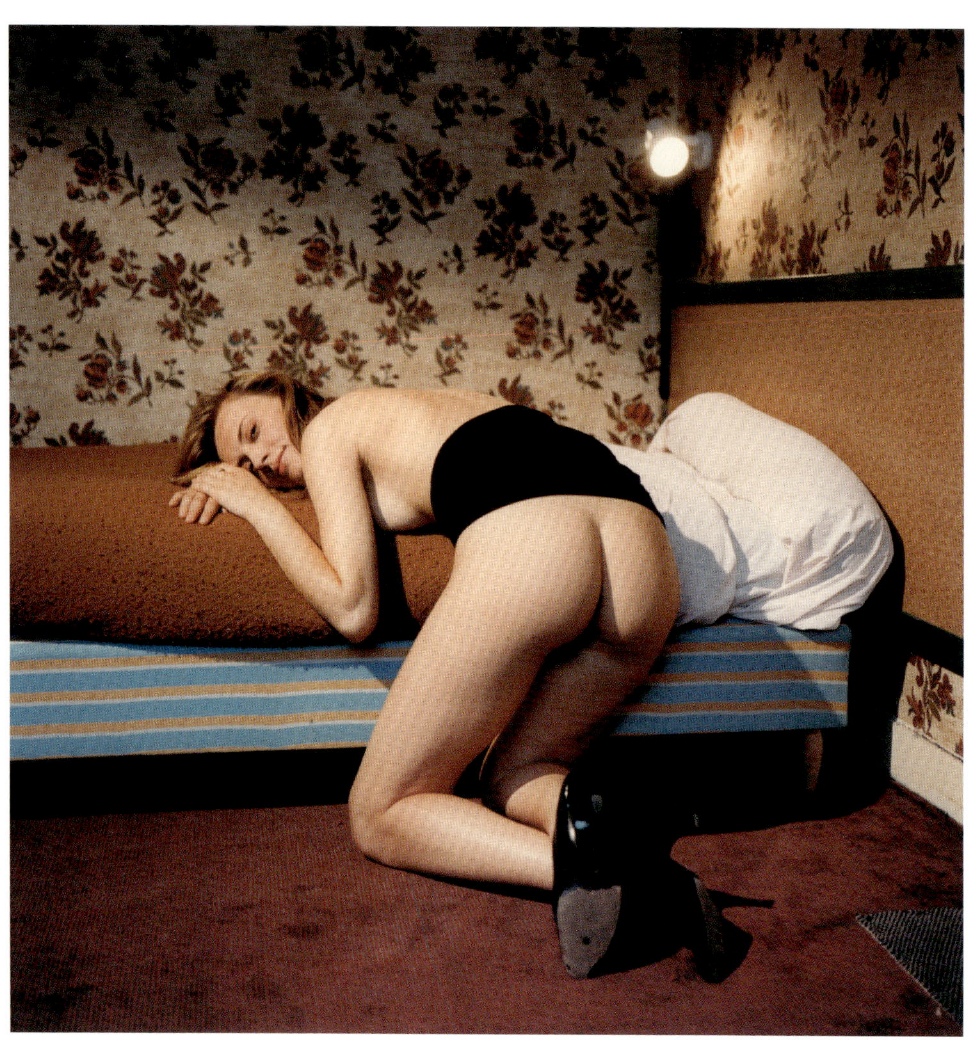

26 juin I, June 1991, Paris

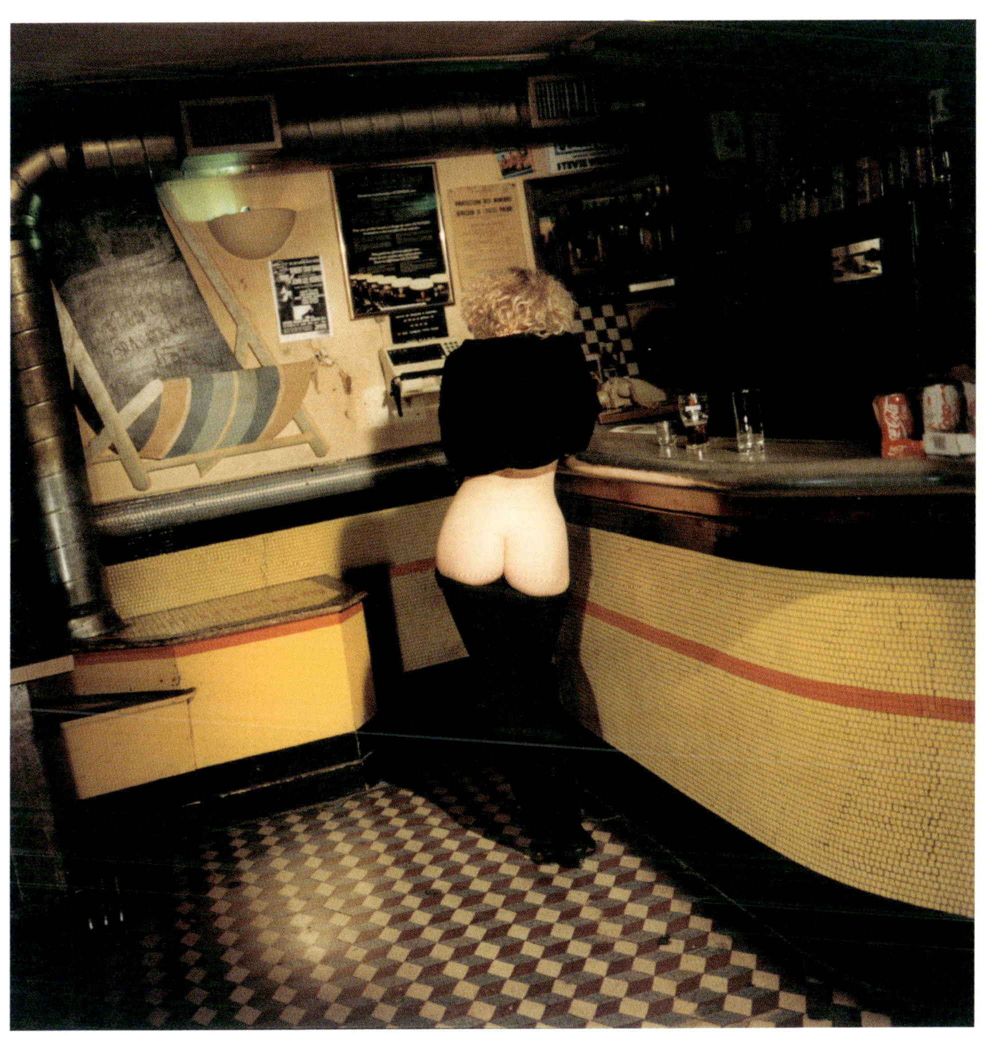

14 juillet, June 1991, Paris

(...) the body is broad and rather heavy and seems, by contrast, the
more stable and static: a sort of sculpture in the flesh, its volumes
broad and round – the curve of the shoulders, the curve of the
forearms, the curve of the buttocks whose inflection is outlined
by the rounding out of the skirt, which has slipped down over
the hips, already so low that the parting of the buttocks is uncov-
ered – this detail alone suggests every erotic situation one might
care to imagine.

(...) le corps, assez large, plutôt lourd apparaît par contraste
d'autant plus stable et statique: une sorte de sculpture de chair,
aux volumes larges et ronds: courbes des épaules, courbes des
avant-bras, courbes des fesses dont le galbe est dessiné par l'arrondi
d'une jupe descendue sur les hanches, si bas déjà que la raie des
fesses se dévoile – ce détail suggère toutes les situations érotiques
que l'on peut avoir plaisir à imaginer.

(...) der ziemlich breite und eher schwere Körper wirkt durch den
Gegensatz noch stabiler und statuenhafter: eine Art Skulptur
aus Fleisch und Blut, mit üppigen, runden Formen. Die Kurven
der Schultern, die Kurven der Unterarme, die Kurven des Hinterns,
dessen Wölbung sich in der Rundung eines auf die Hüften gerutschten
Rockes abzeichnet, der schon so tief sitzt, dass der Spalt zwischen den
Pobacken sichtbar wird – dieses Detail verheißt alle möglichen eroti-
schen Situationen, die man sich gern vorstellen mag.

Philippe Dagen, in *Can you find happiness*, 2008

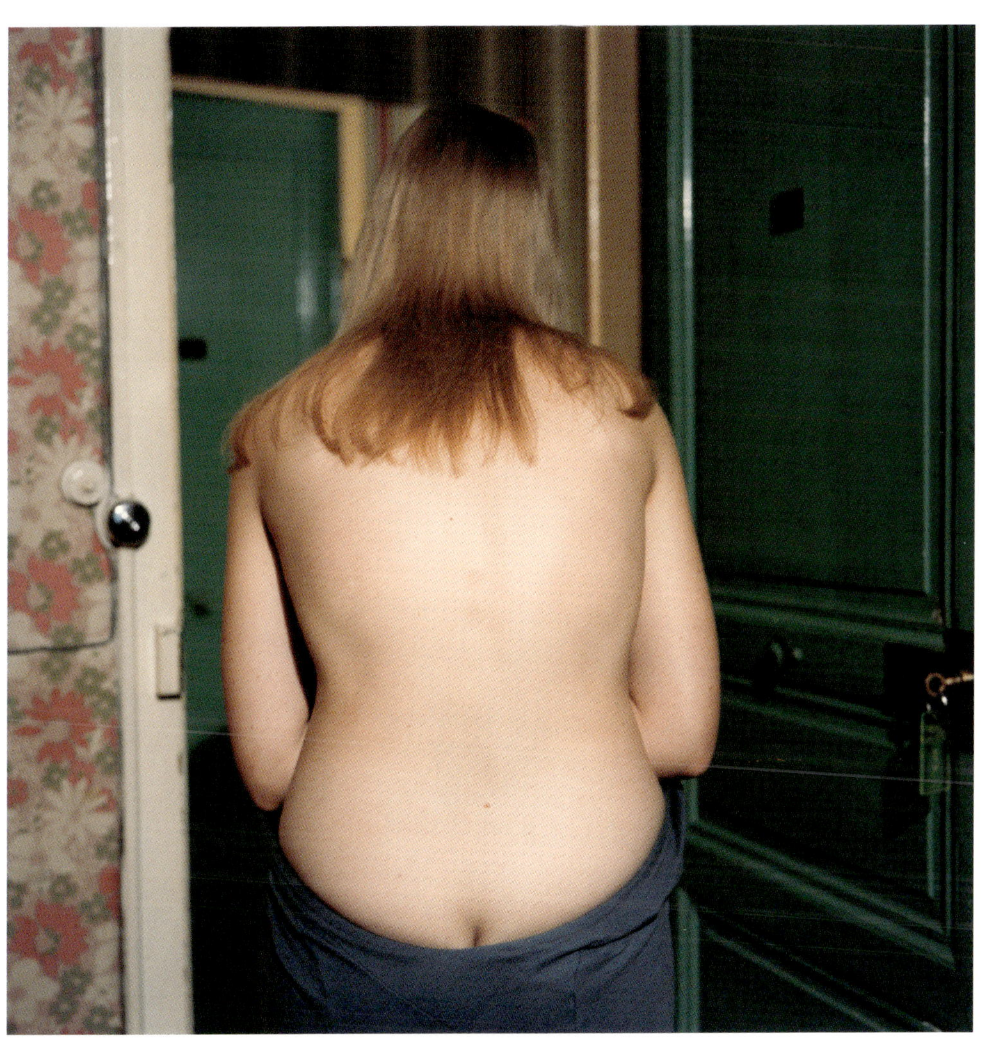

17 juillet, October 1991, Paris

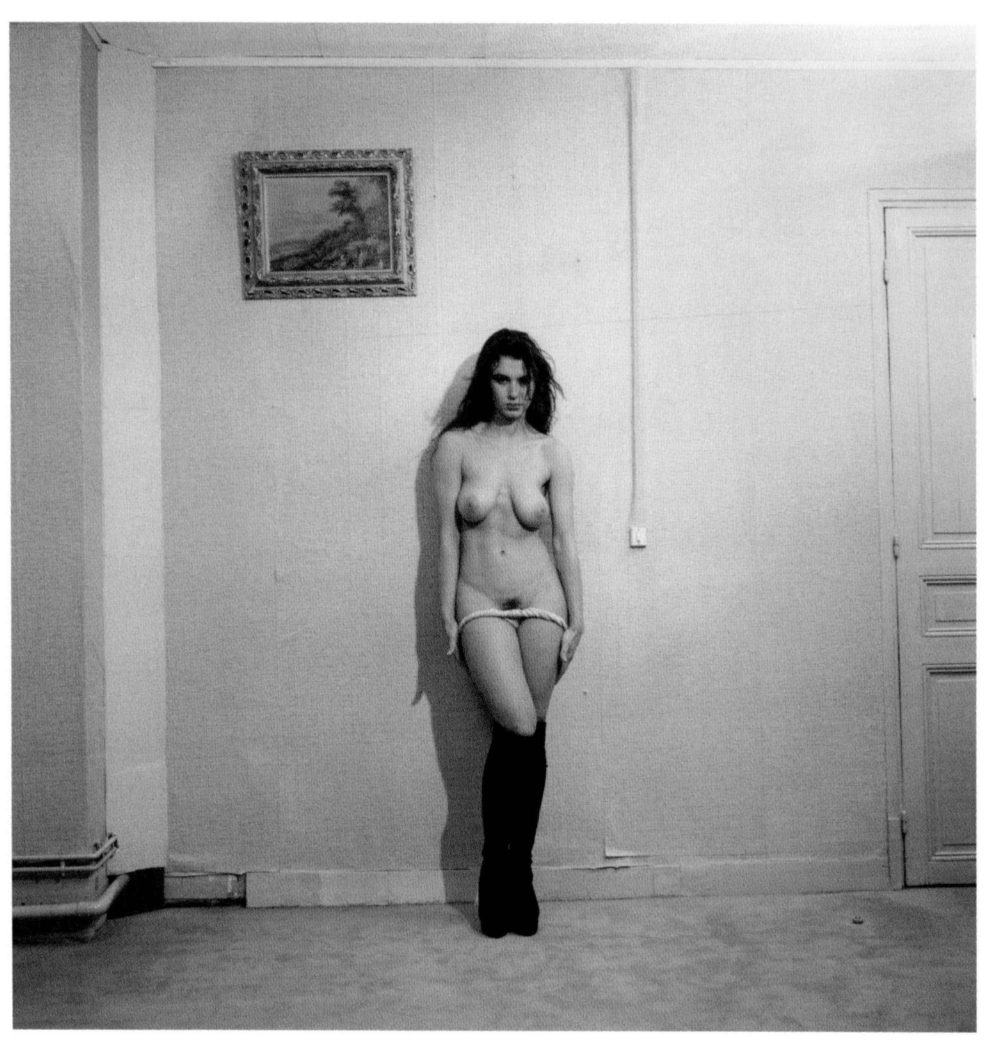

 20 février I, February 1991, Paris

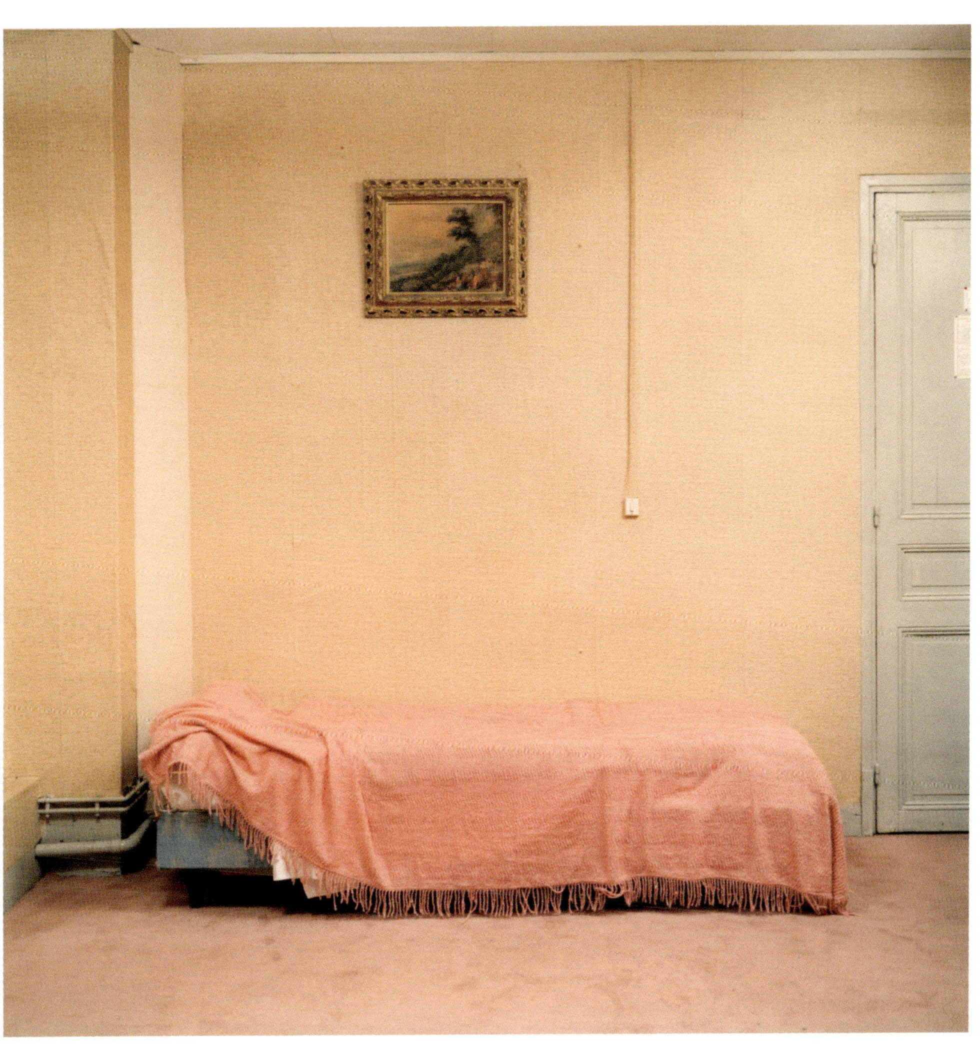

20 février II, February 1991, Paris 127

«Vivement dimanche» III, June 1993, Paris
Page 130 — *Mickey Rourke I*, July 1991, Los Angeles
Page 131 — *S.A.S. la princesse Caroline de Monaco sur une plage*, April 1988, Monaco

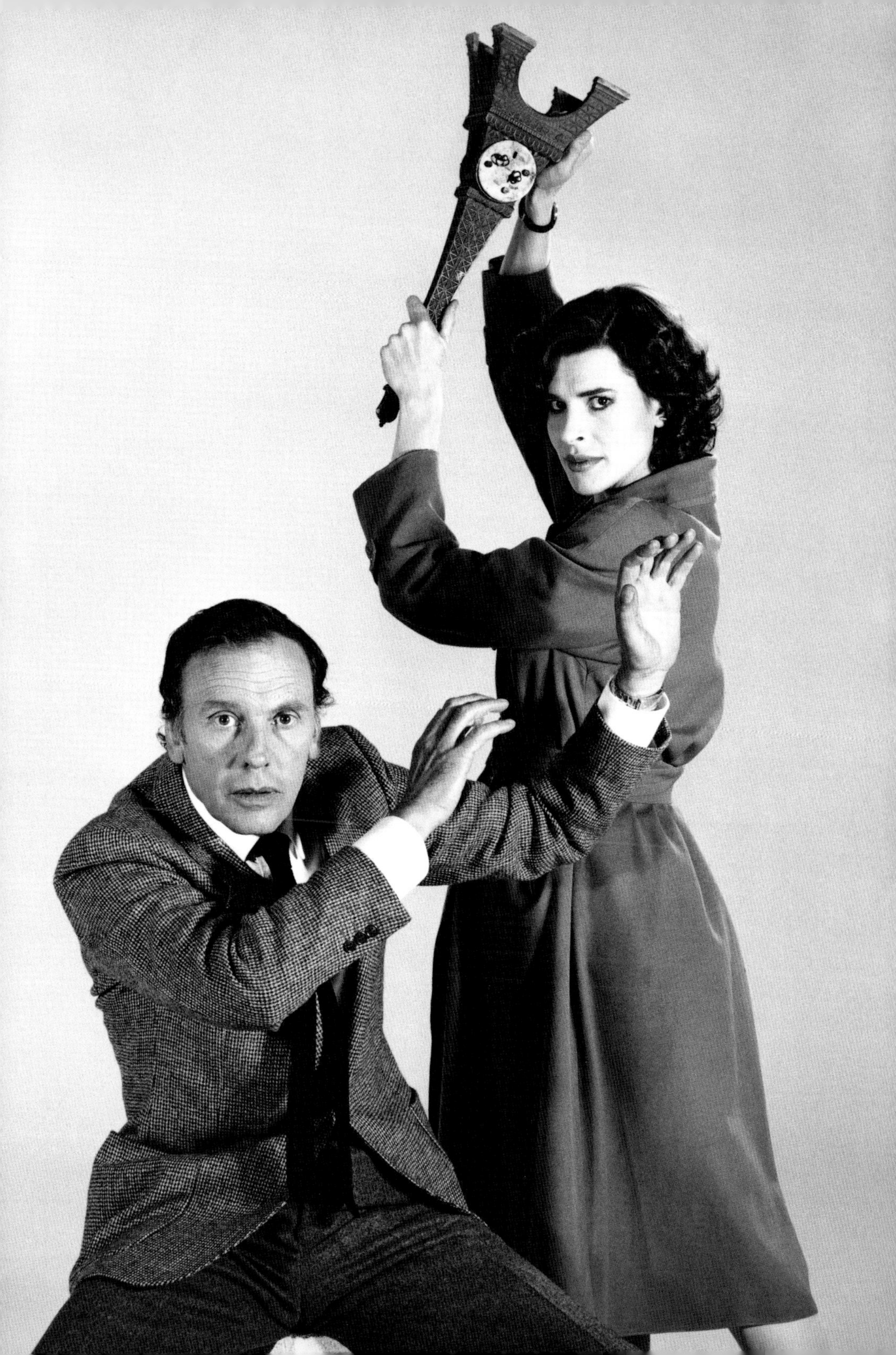

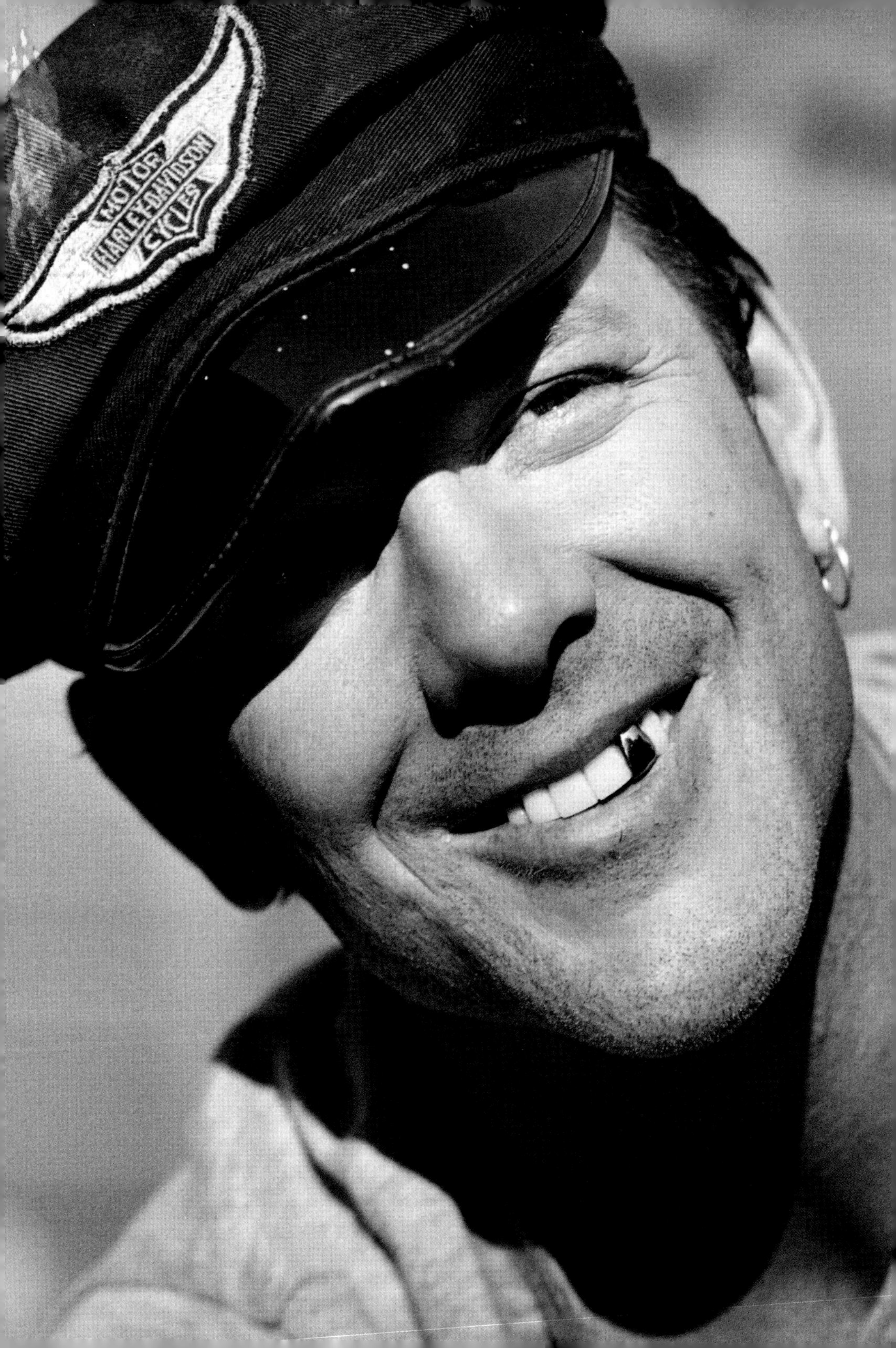

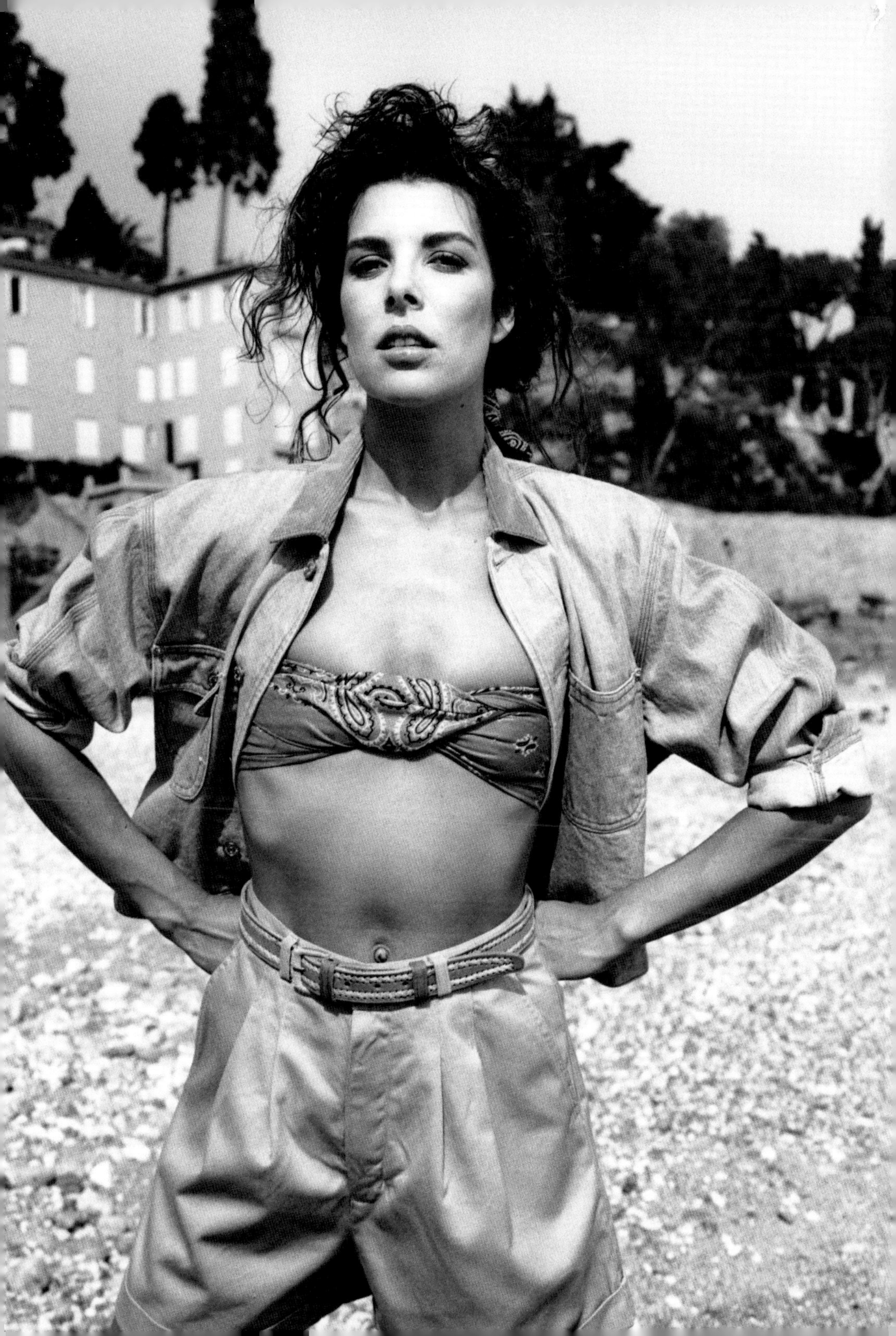

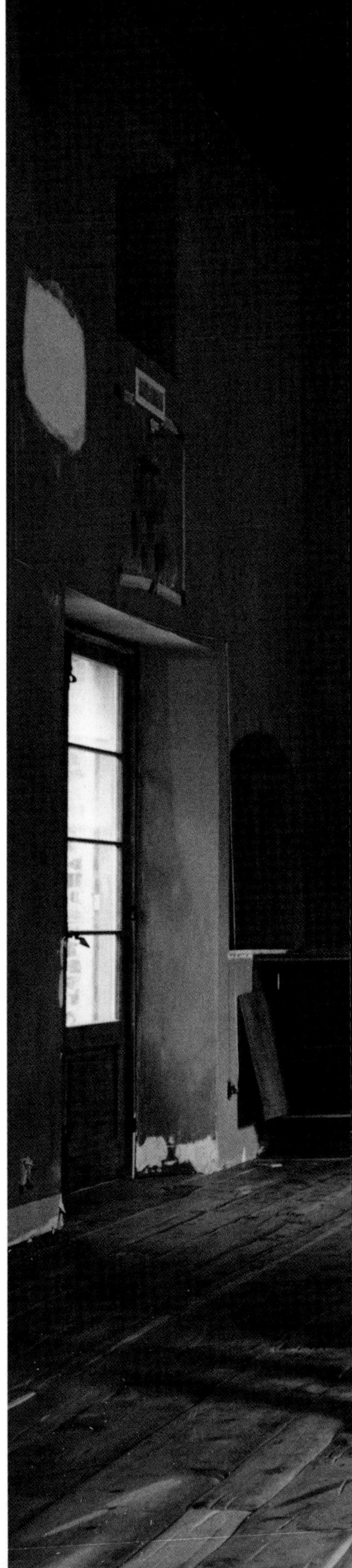

Mickey Rourke et ses copains dans le chantier de sa maison en construction, July 1991, Los Angeles
Page 134 — *Catherine Millet par Jacques Henric photographiée par Bettina Rheims*, July 2008, Paris
Page 135 — *Claude Lévi-Strauss*, June 1985, Paris
Pages 136/137 — *Barbara à son piano*, May 1987, Précy-sur-Marne
Pages 138/139 — *Eugène Ionesco*, March 1986, Paris

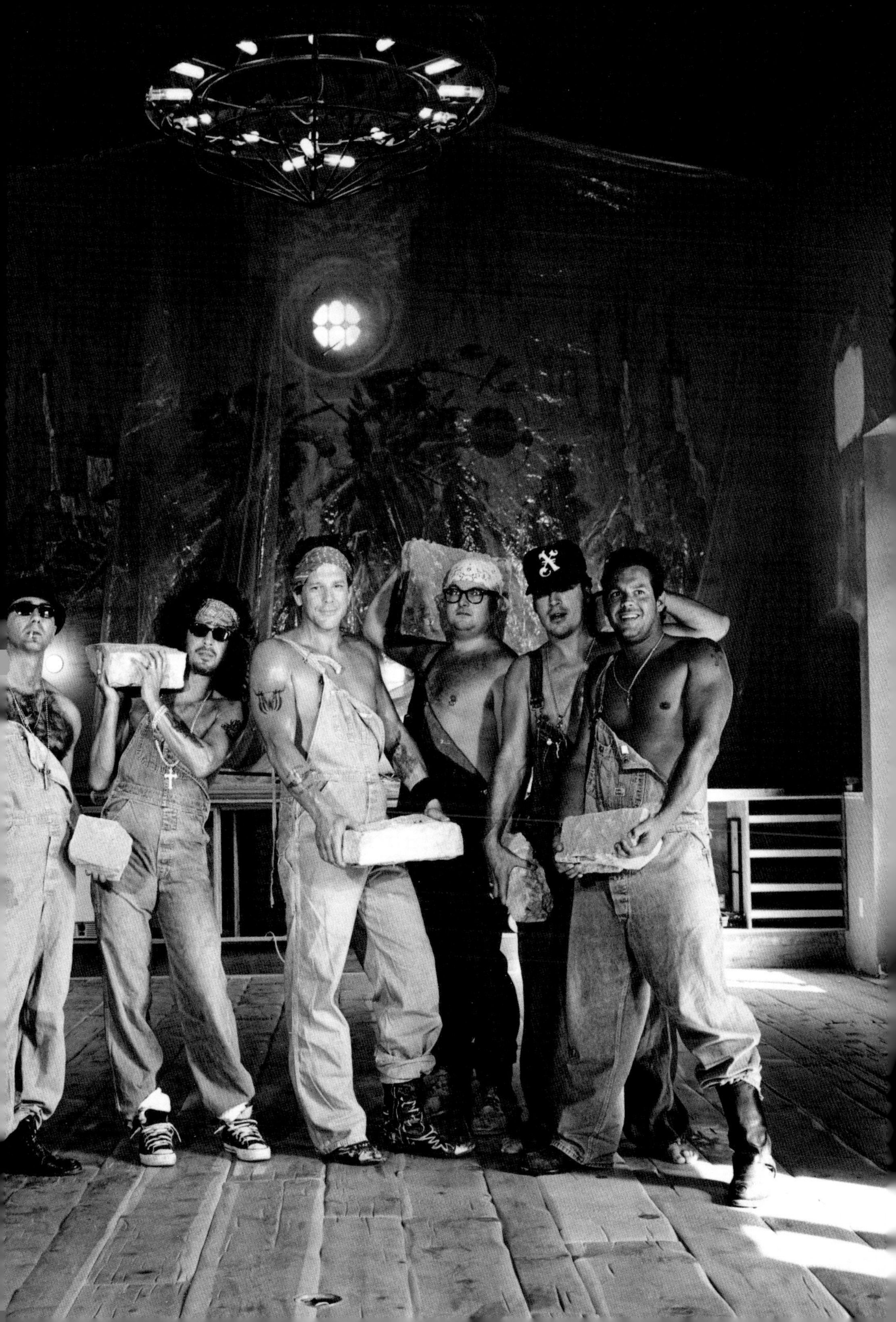

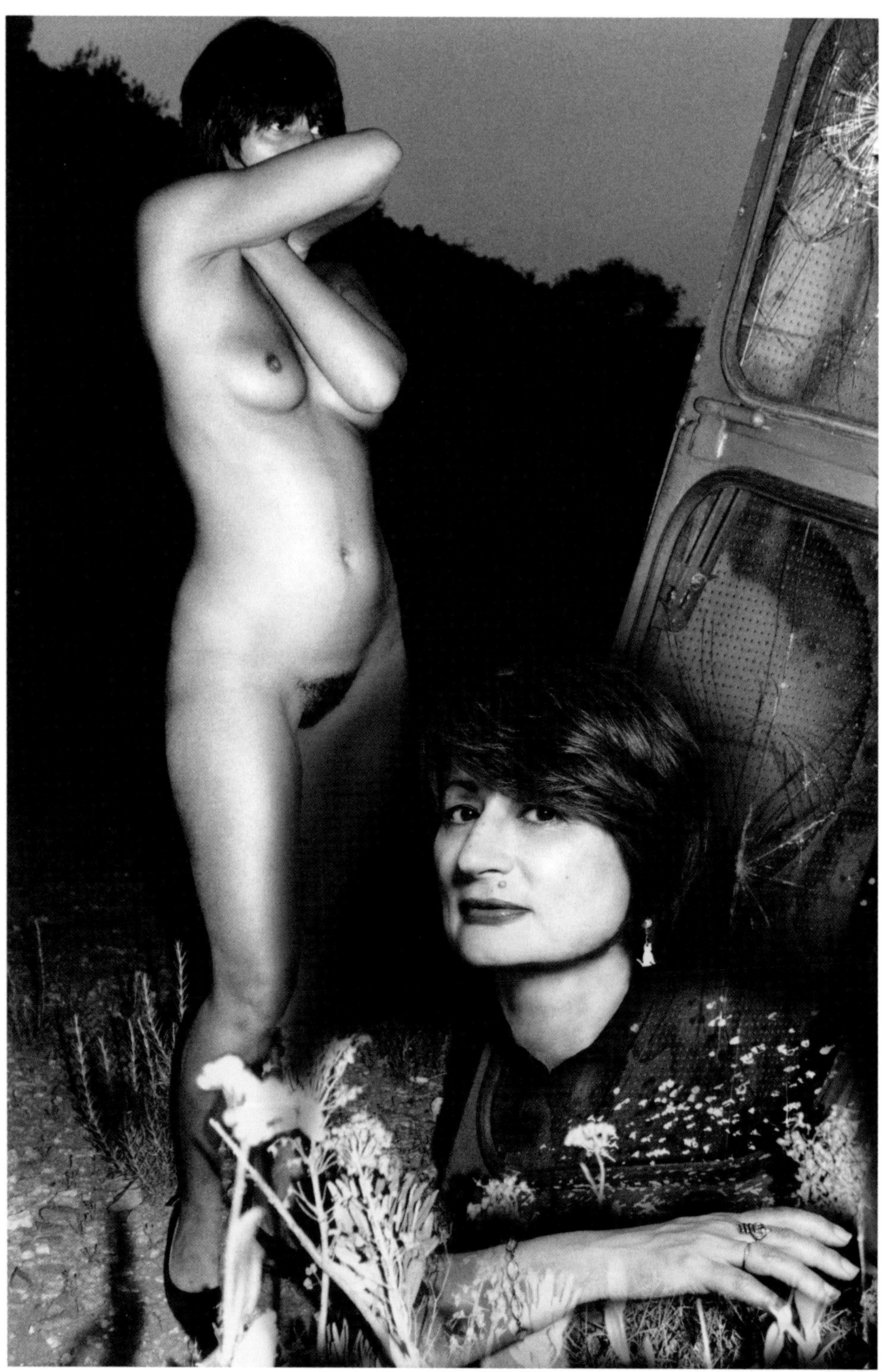

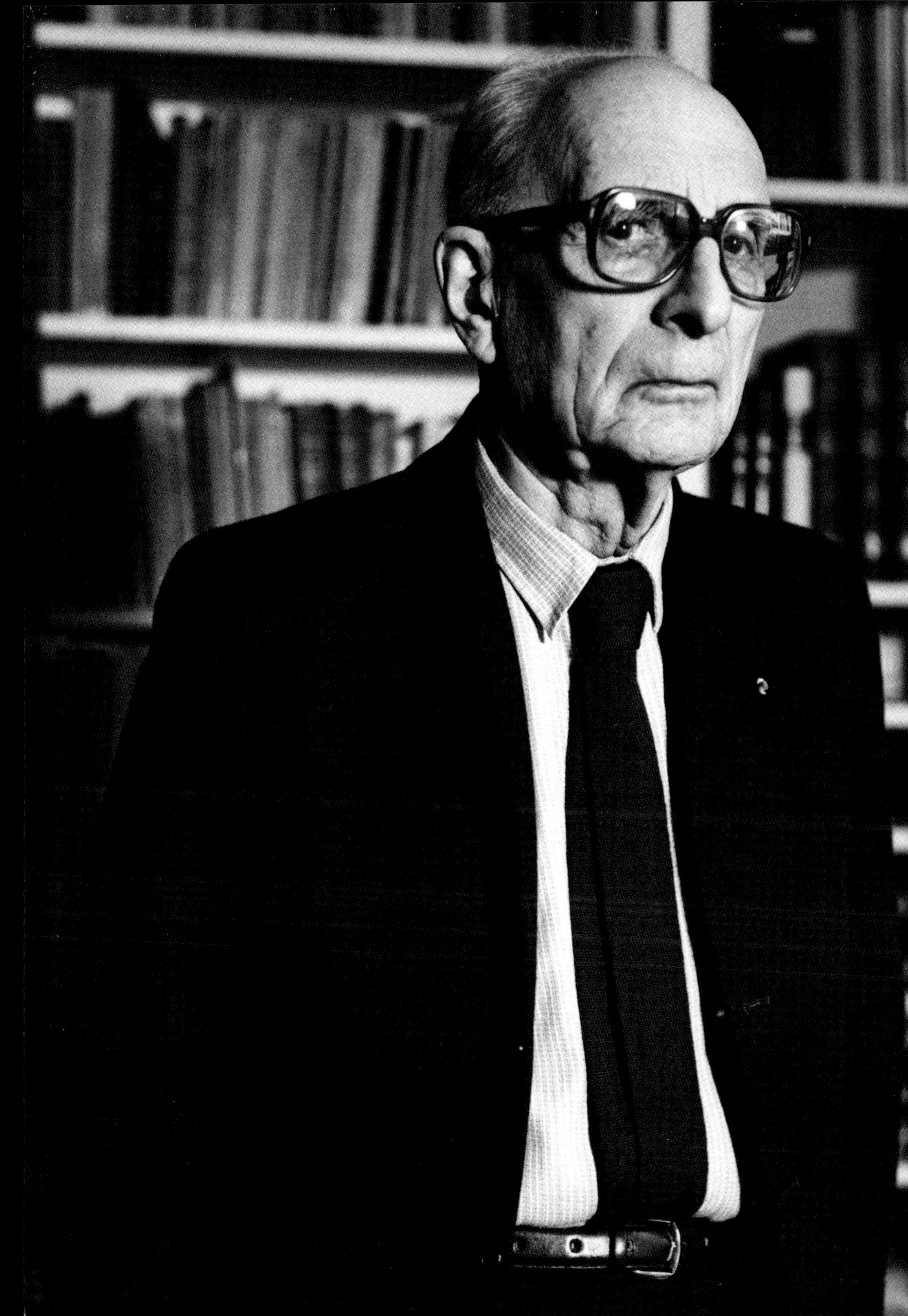

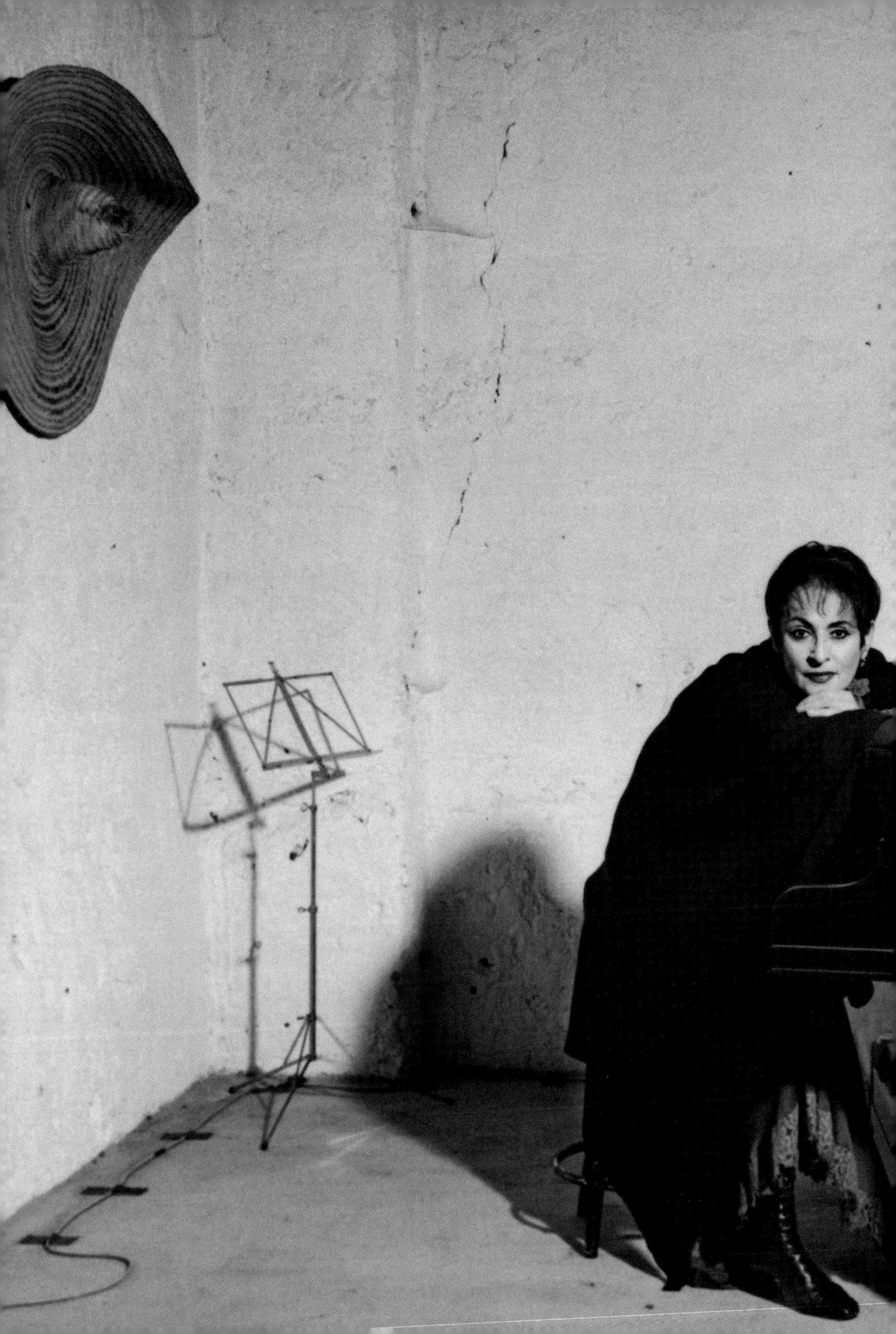

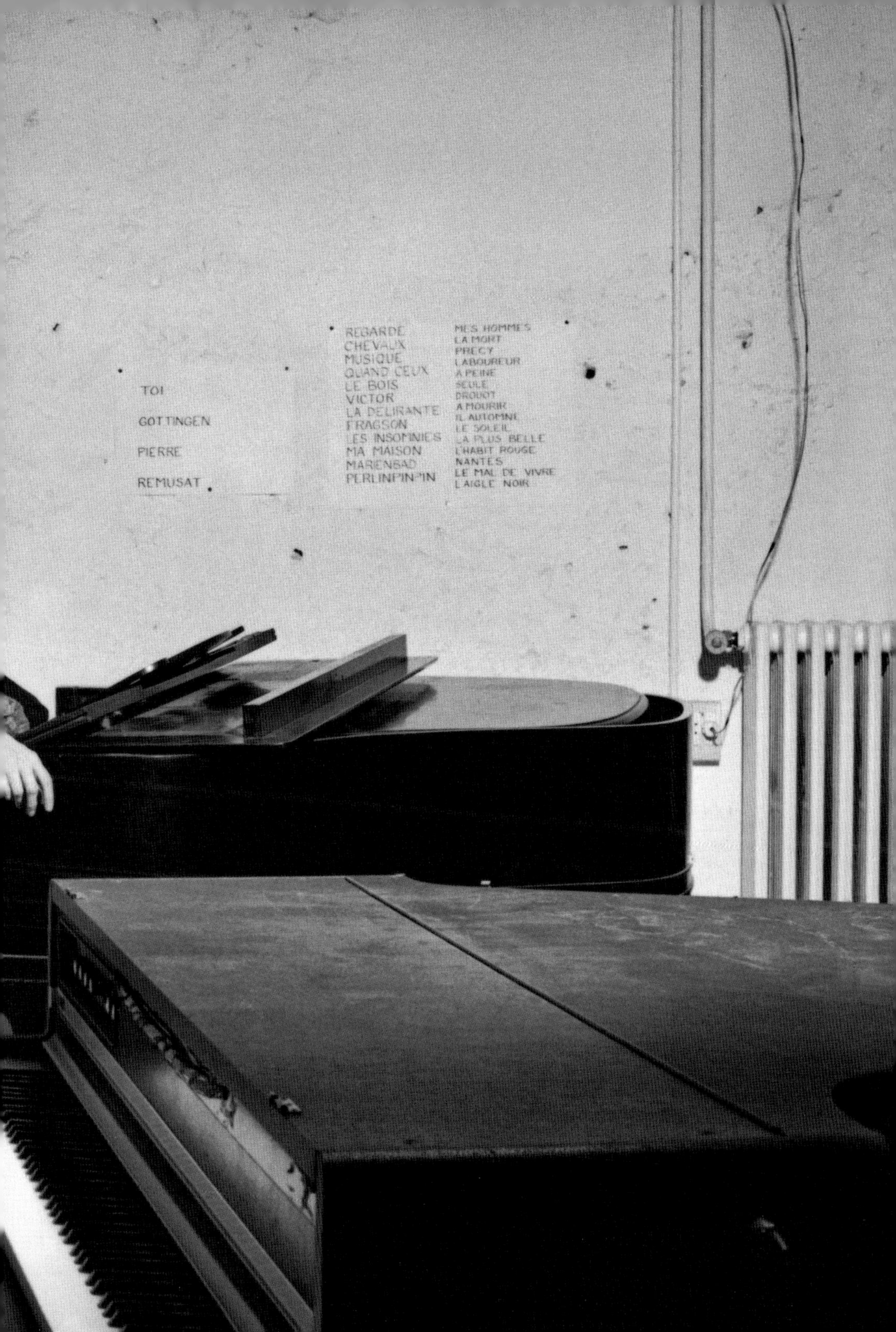

TOI
GOTTINGEN
PIERRE
REMUSAT

REGARDE
CHEVAUX
MUSIQUE
QUAND CEUX
LE BOIS
VICTOR
LA DELIRANTE
FRAGSON
LES INSOMNIES
MA MAISON
MARENBAD
PERLINPIN-PIN

MES HOMMES
LA MORT
PRECY
LABOUREUR
A PEINE
SEULE
DROUOT
A MOURIR
IL AUTOMNE
LE SOLEIL
LA PLUS BELLE
L'HABIT ROUGE
NANTES
LE MAL DE VIVRE
L'AIGLE NOIR

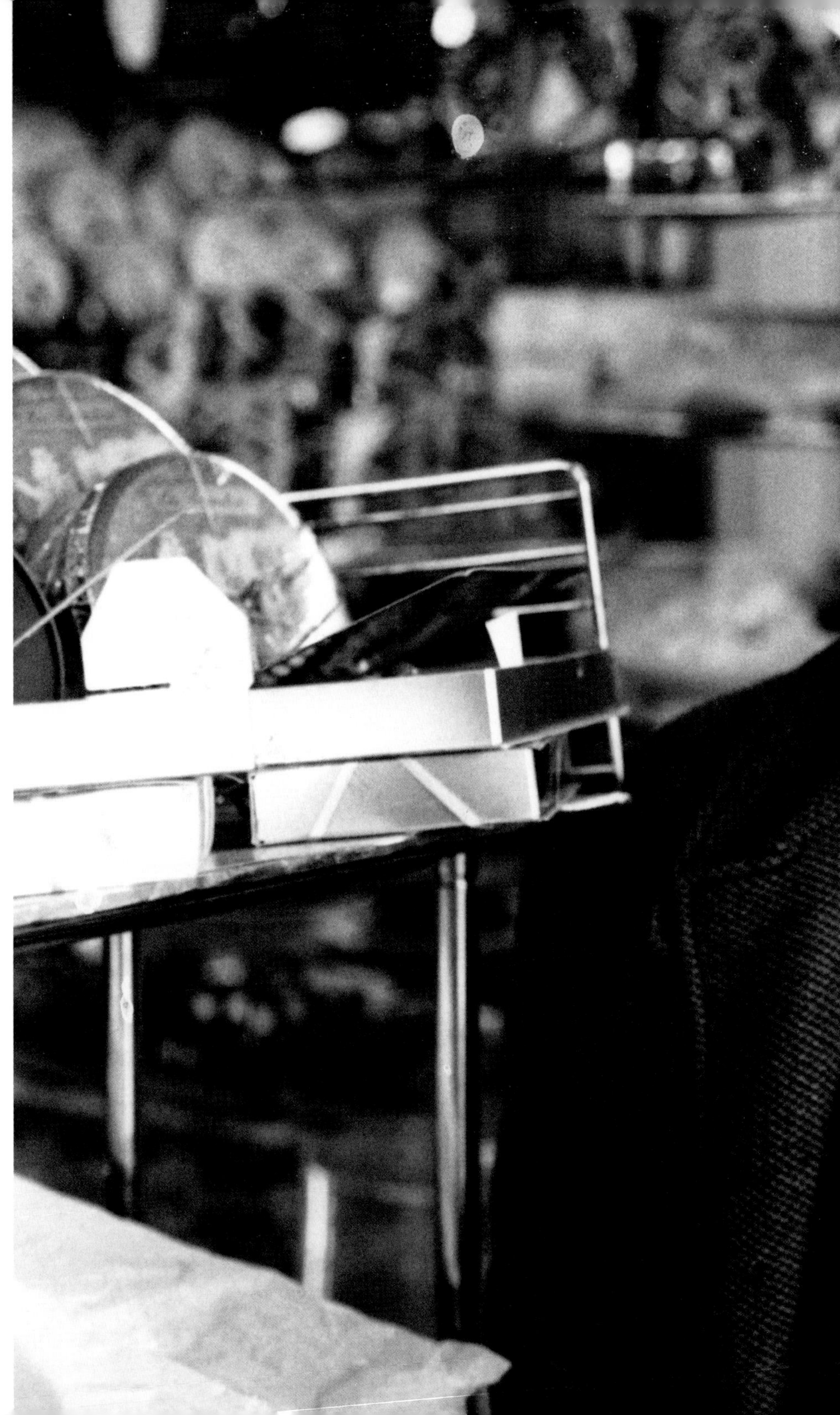

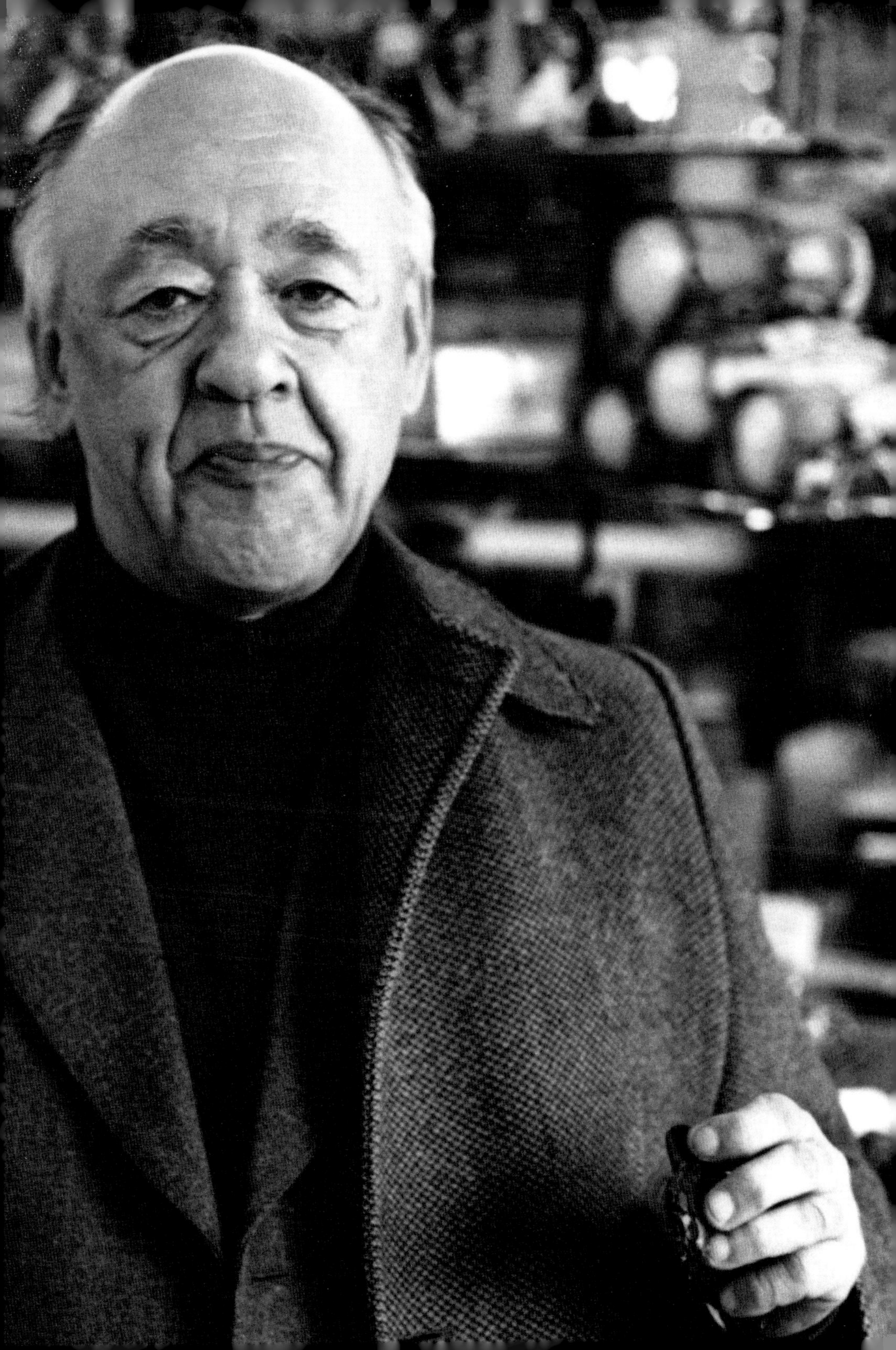

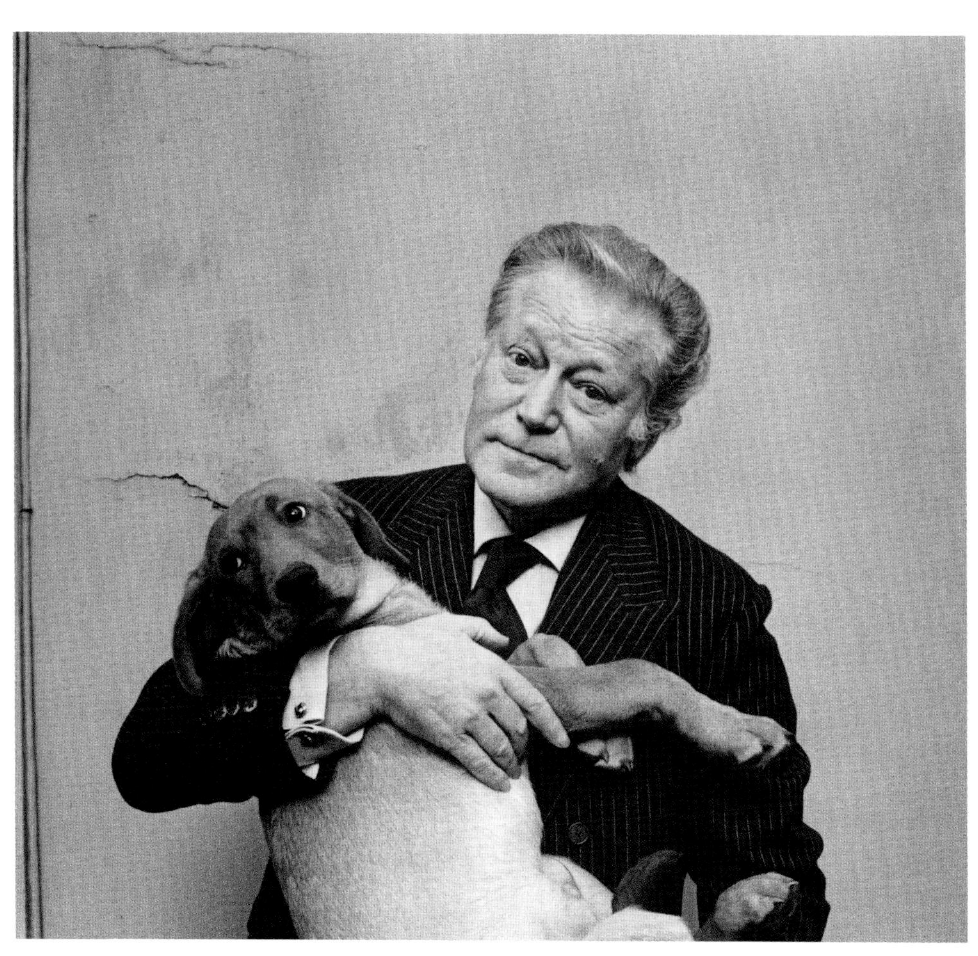

Above — *Maurice Druon*, November 1977, Paris
Opposite page — *Jackie Chan standing on a bed holding a rose*, November 1998, Paris
Page 142 — *Gina Gershon publicity shoot for «Showgirls»*, March 1995, Los Angeles
Page 143 — *Elizabeth Berkley publicity shoot for «Showgirls»*, March 1995, Los Angeles
Pages 144/145 — *Léah au canapé rose pour Anne Valérie Hash II*, October 2006, Paris
Pages 146/147 — *Léah, au téléphone*, October 2006, Paris

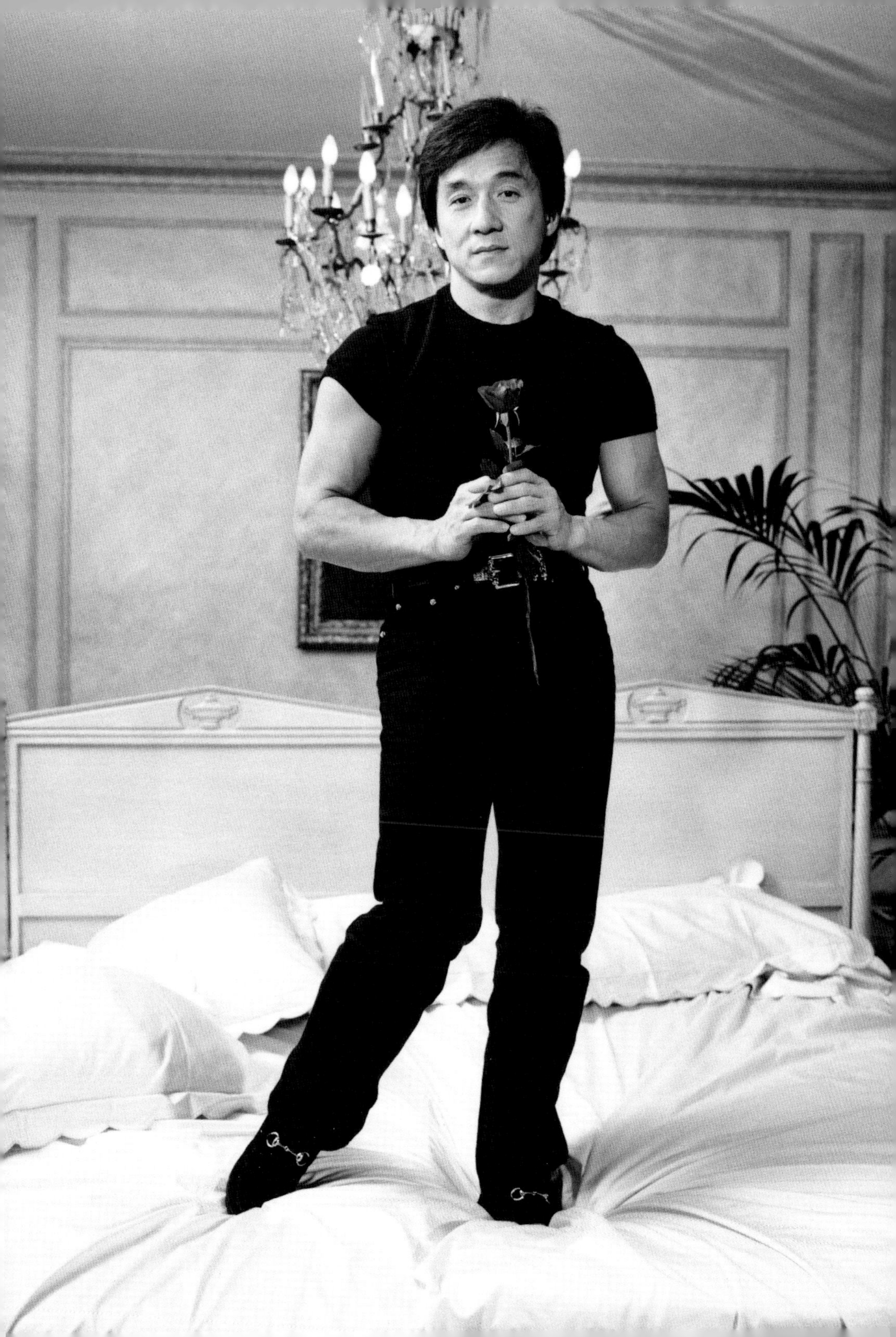

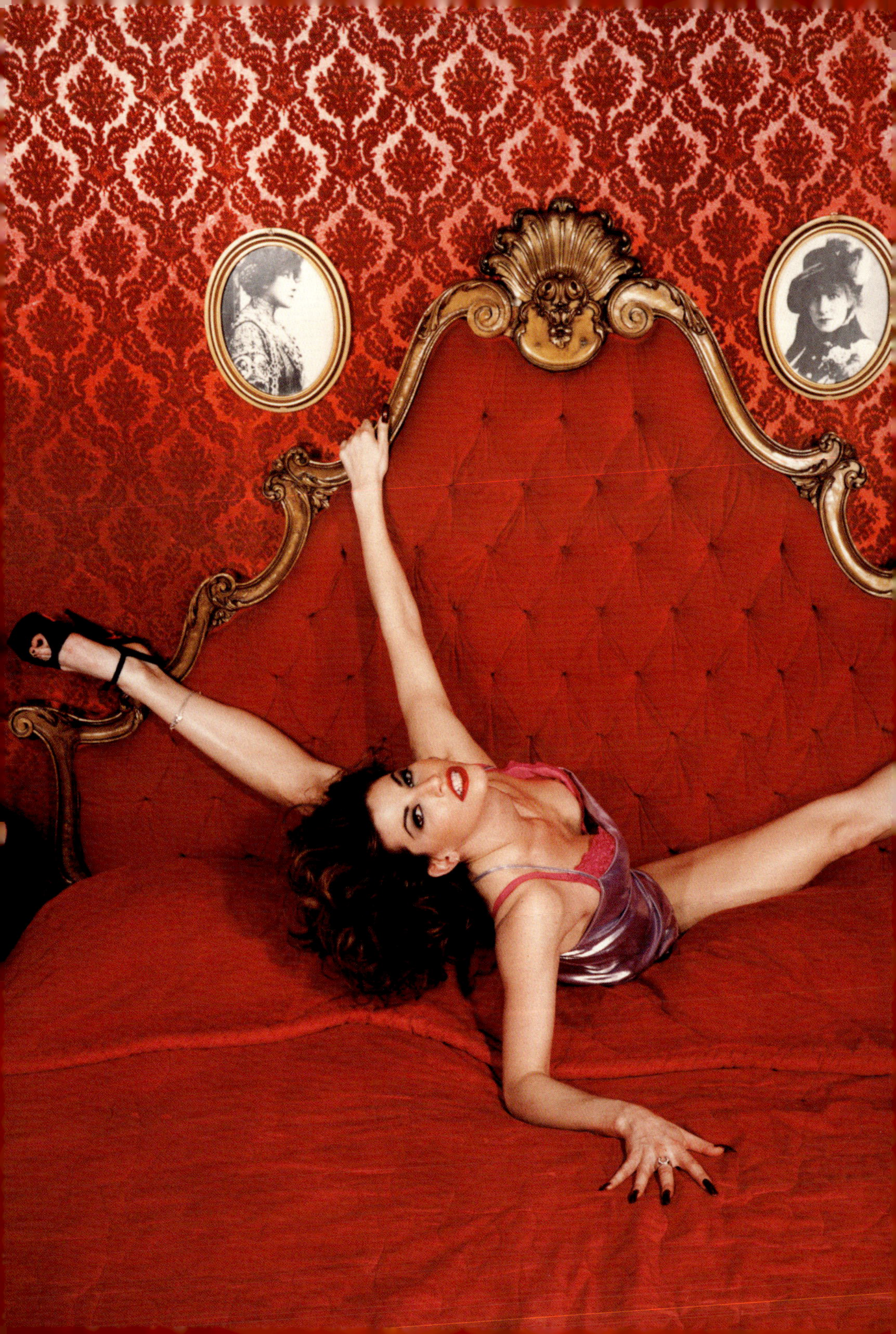

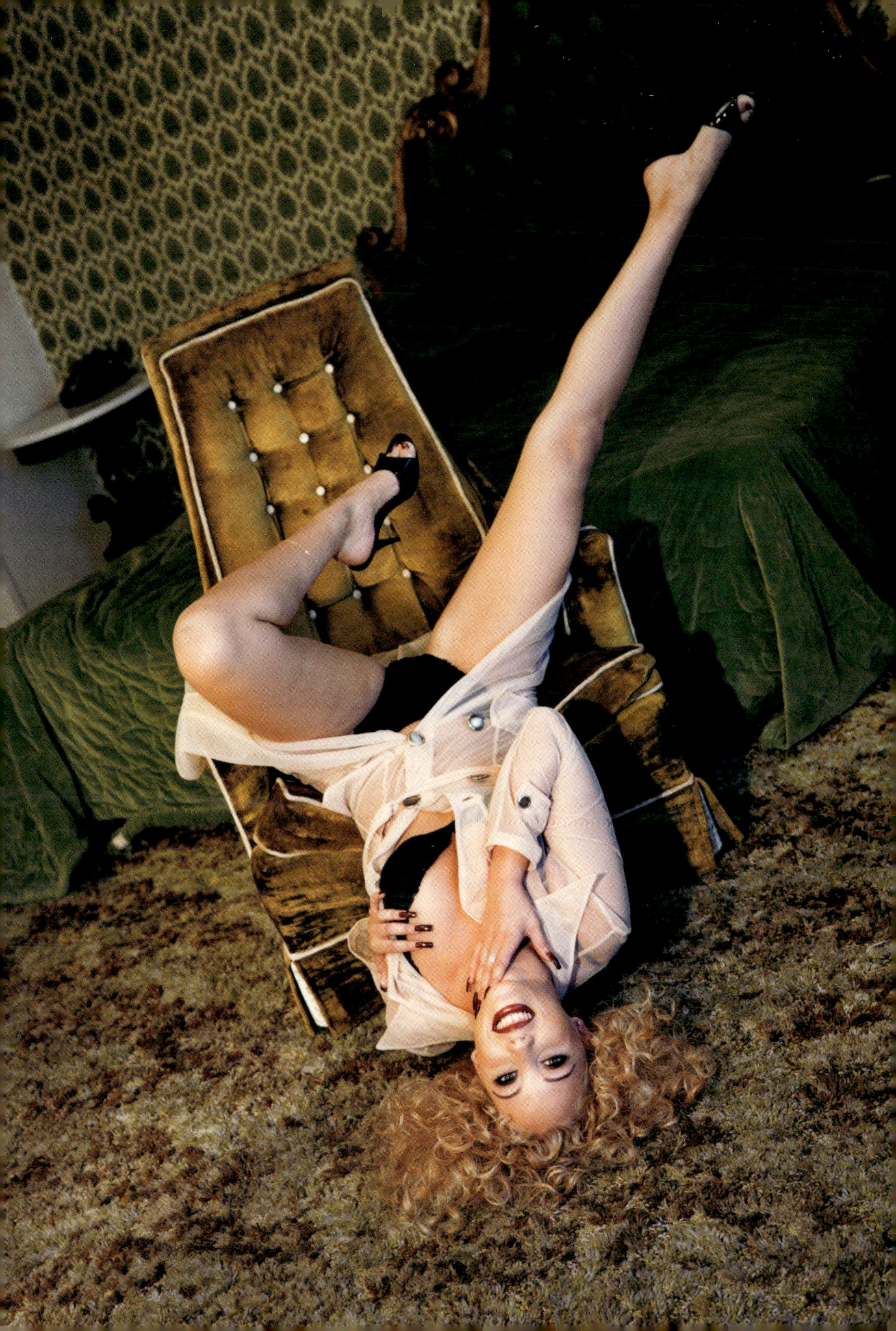

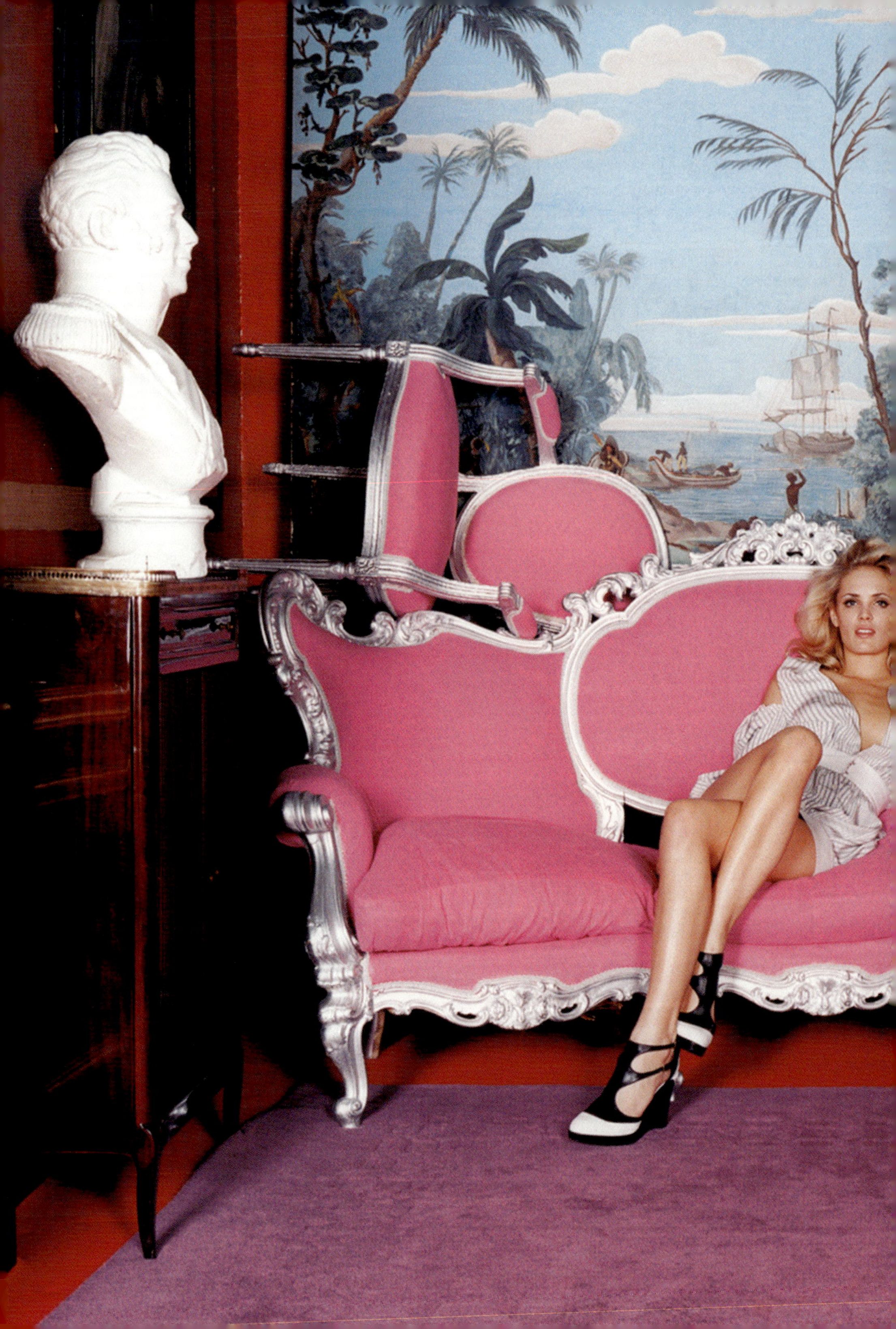

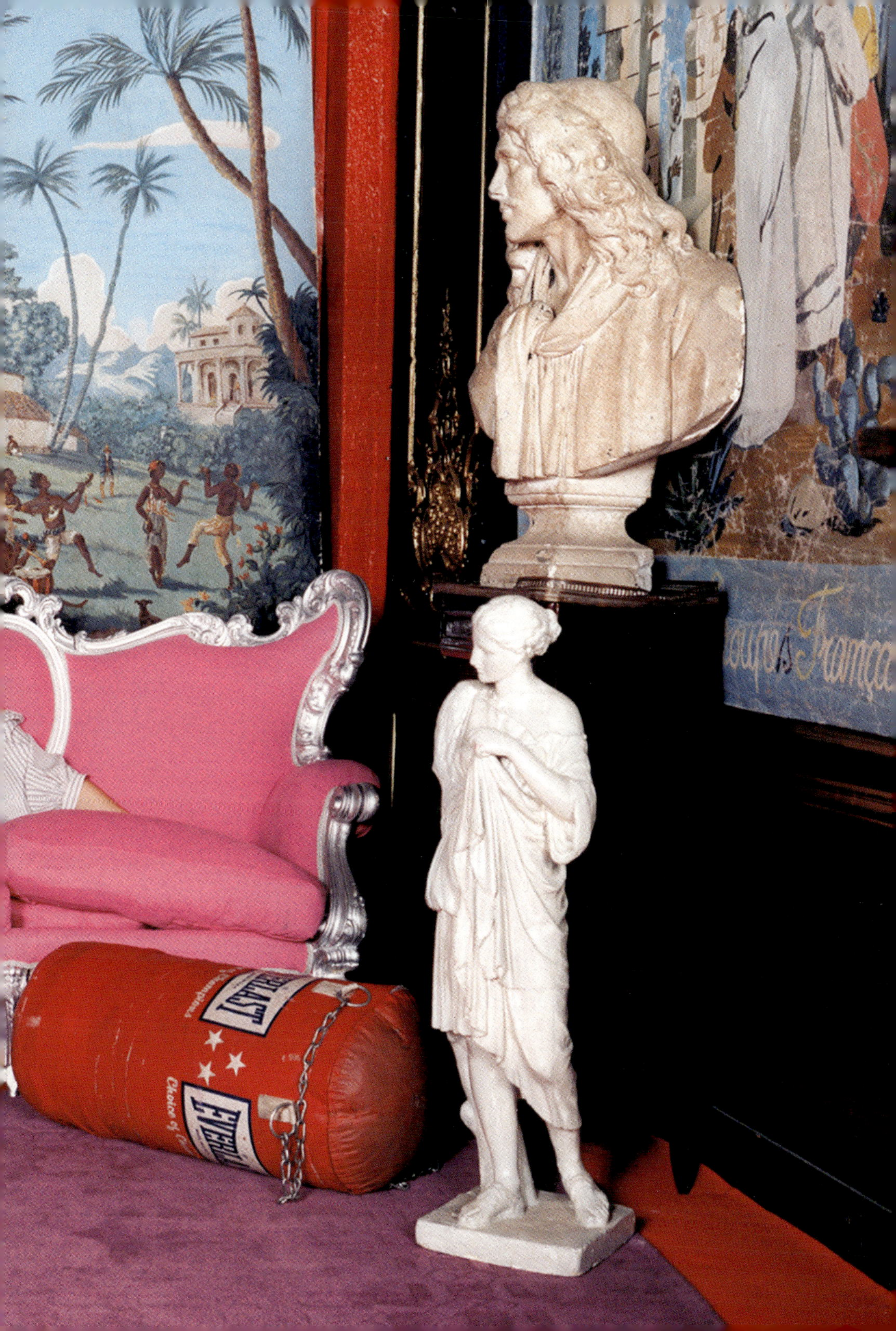
EVERLAST
EVERLAST
Choice of

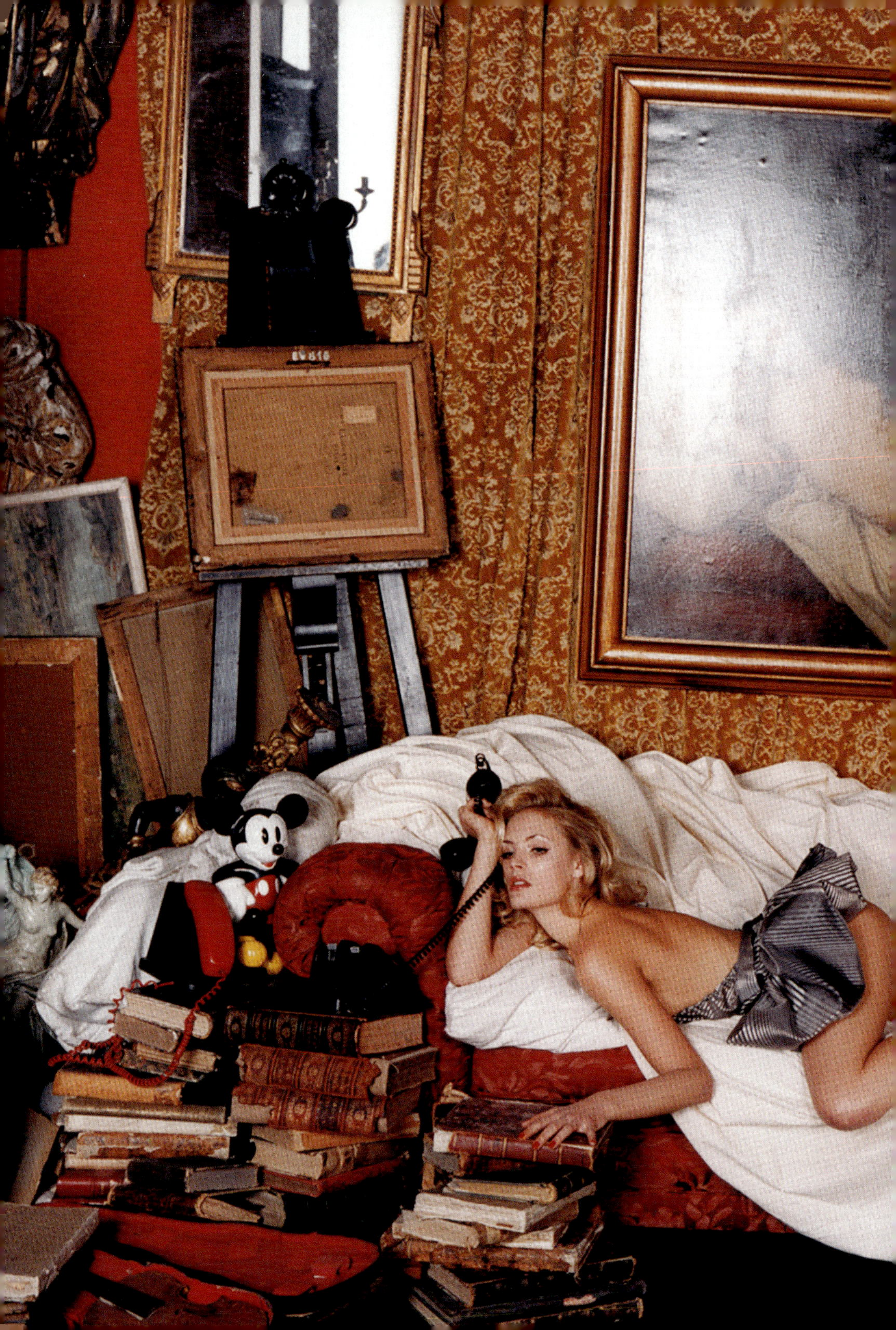

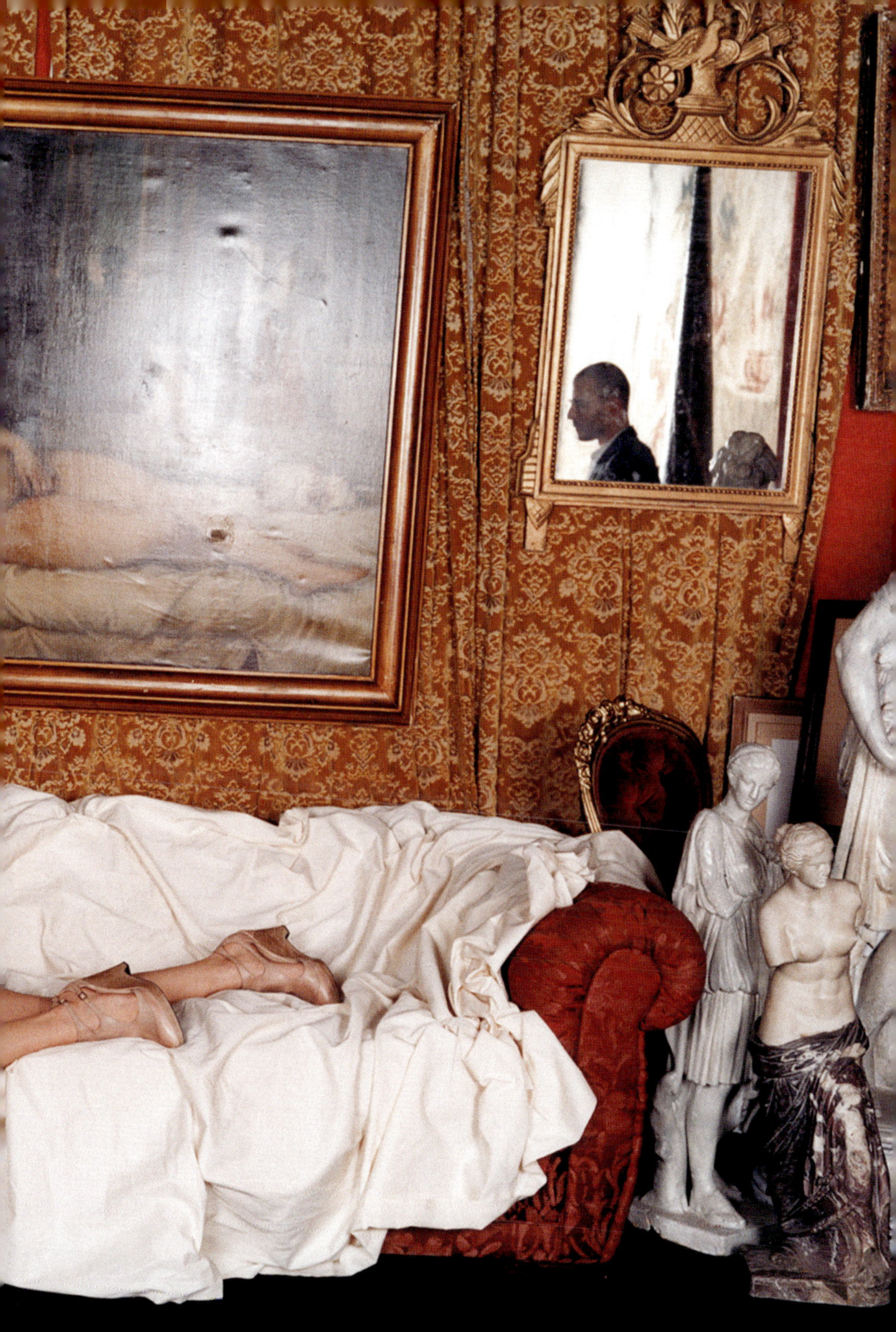

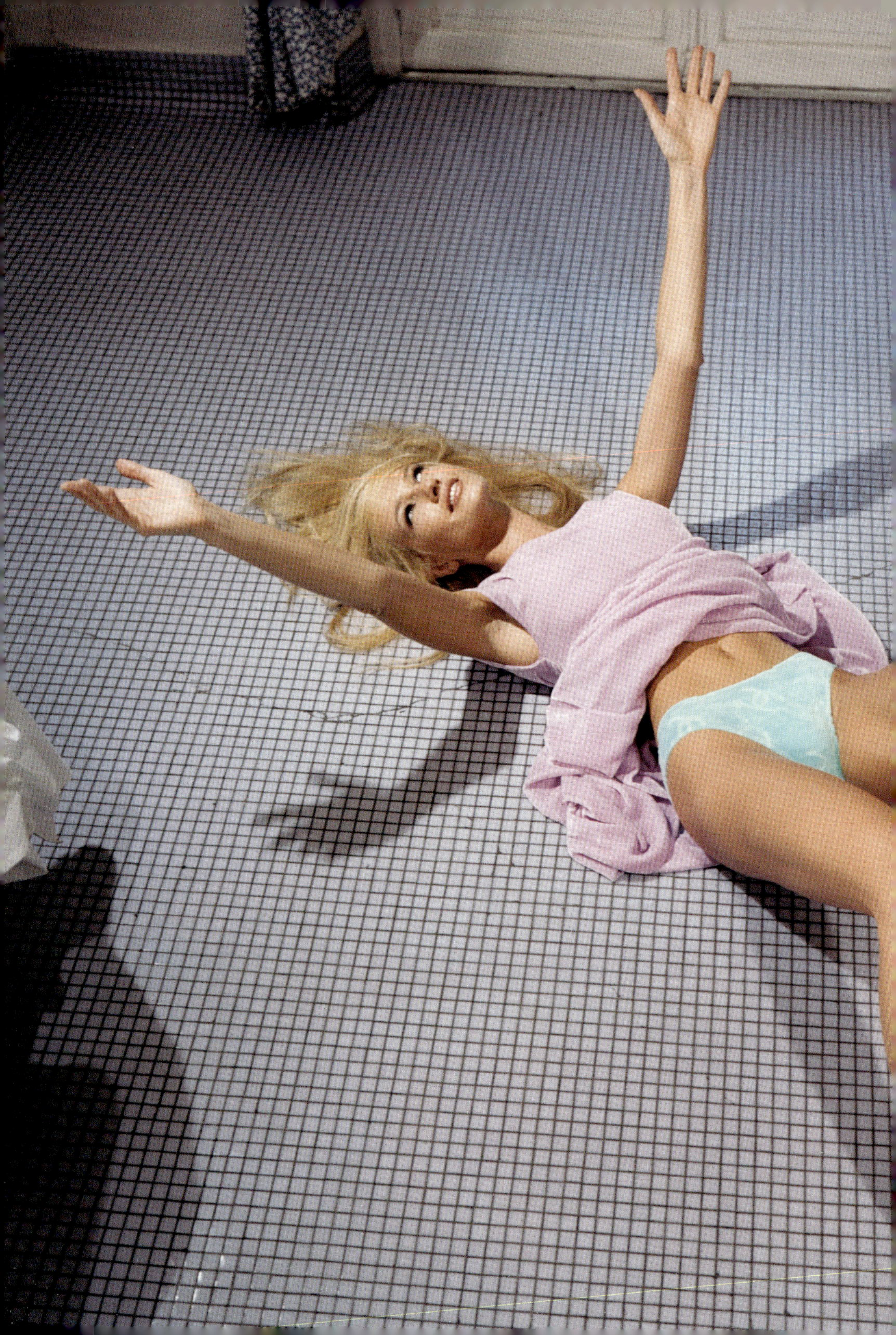

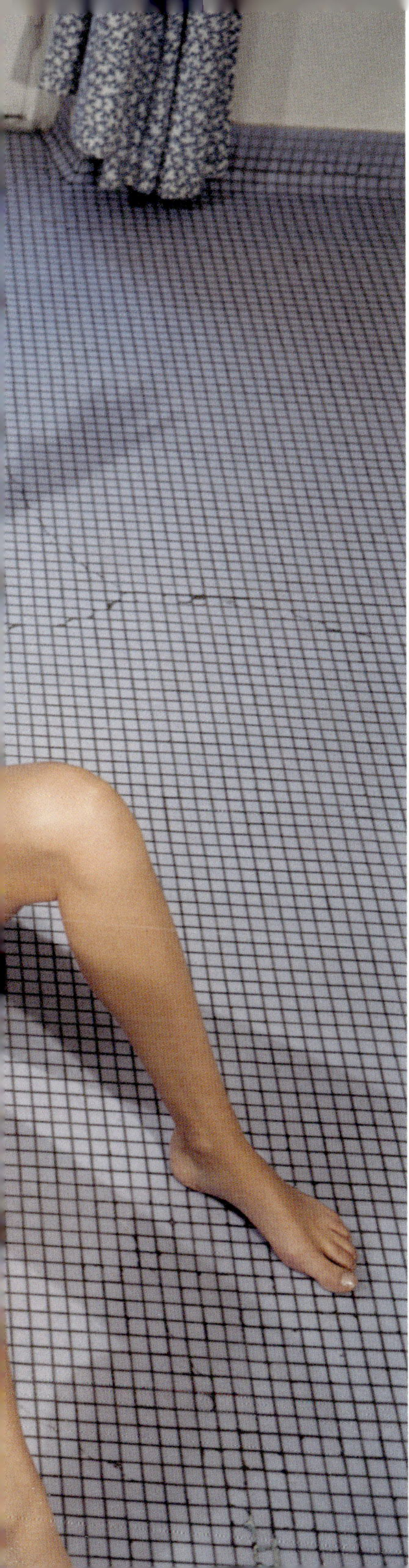

Karen Mulder as a doll lying on the floor of a beauty parlour,
January 1996, Paris

LES AVEUGLES
1992

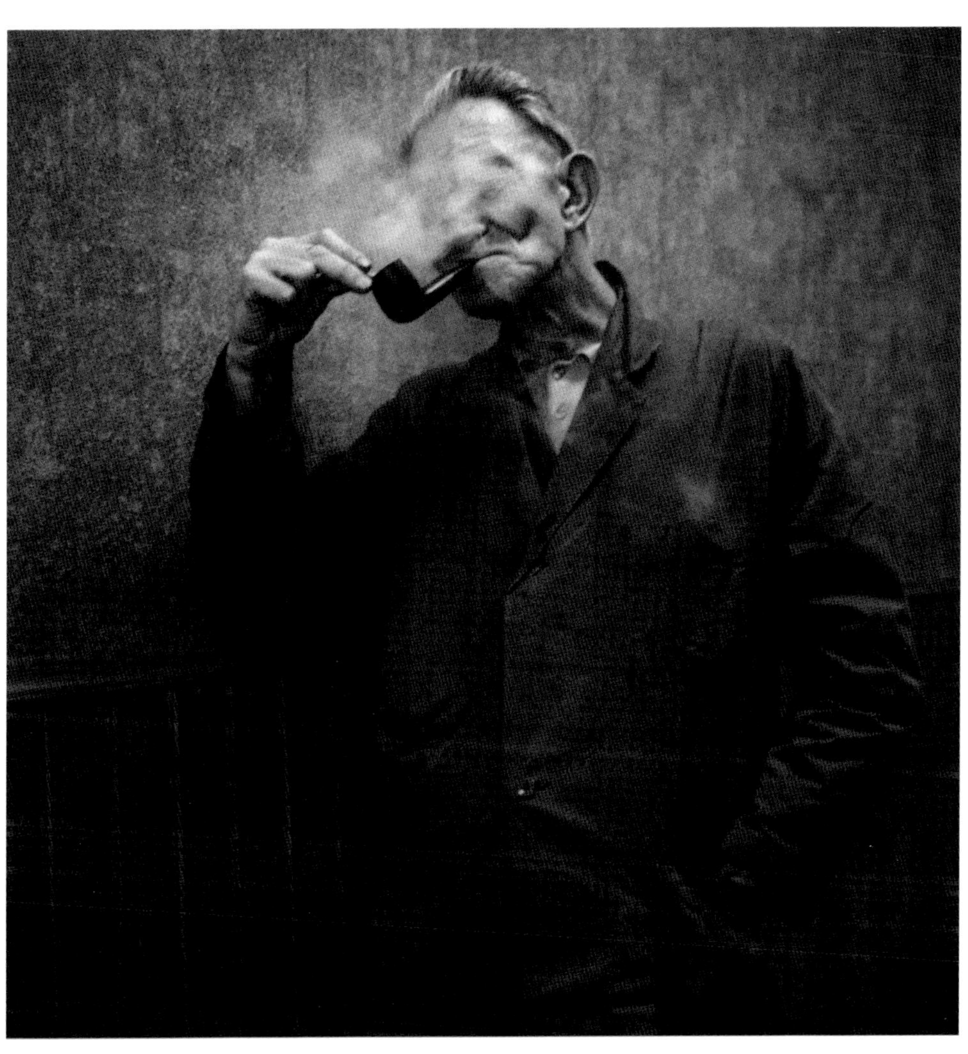

Portrait d'un fumeur de pipe aveugle I, February 1992, Versailles

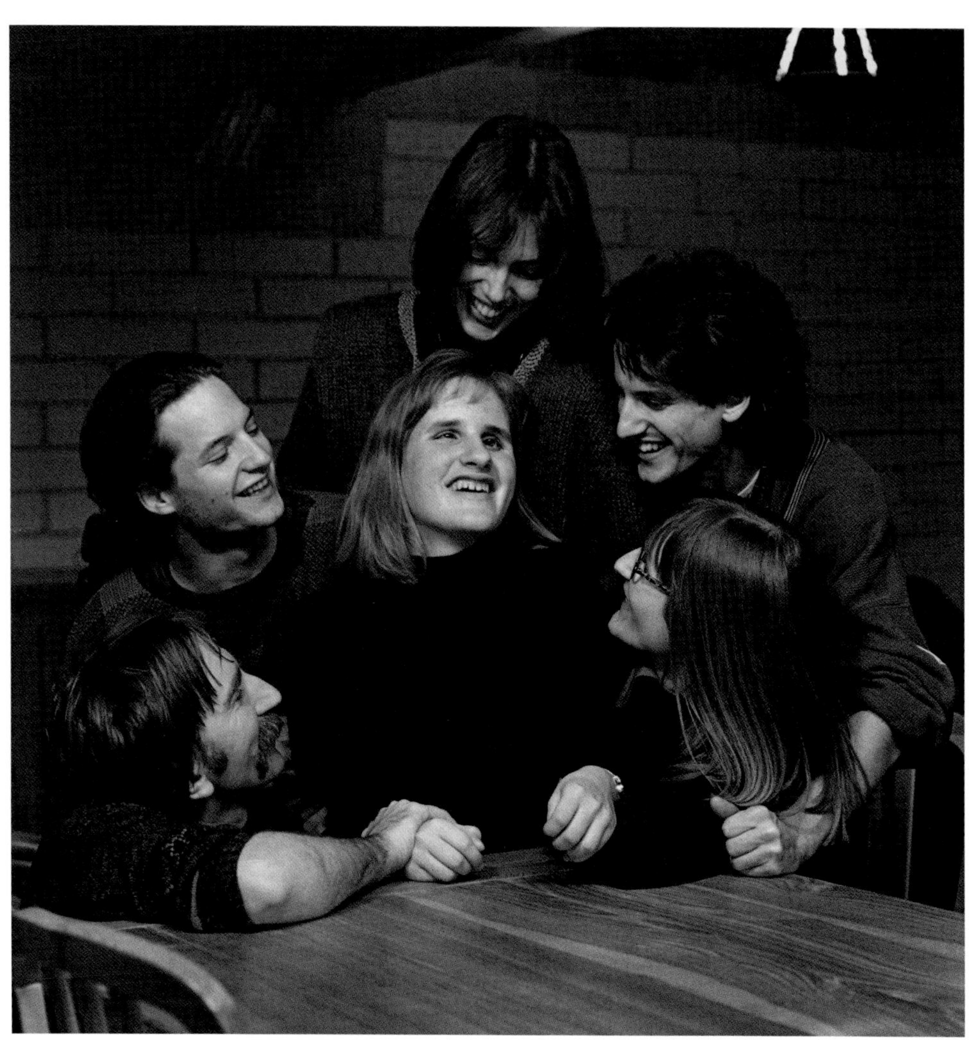

 Jeanne Leroux entourée de sa famille, February 1992, Ramonville

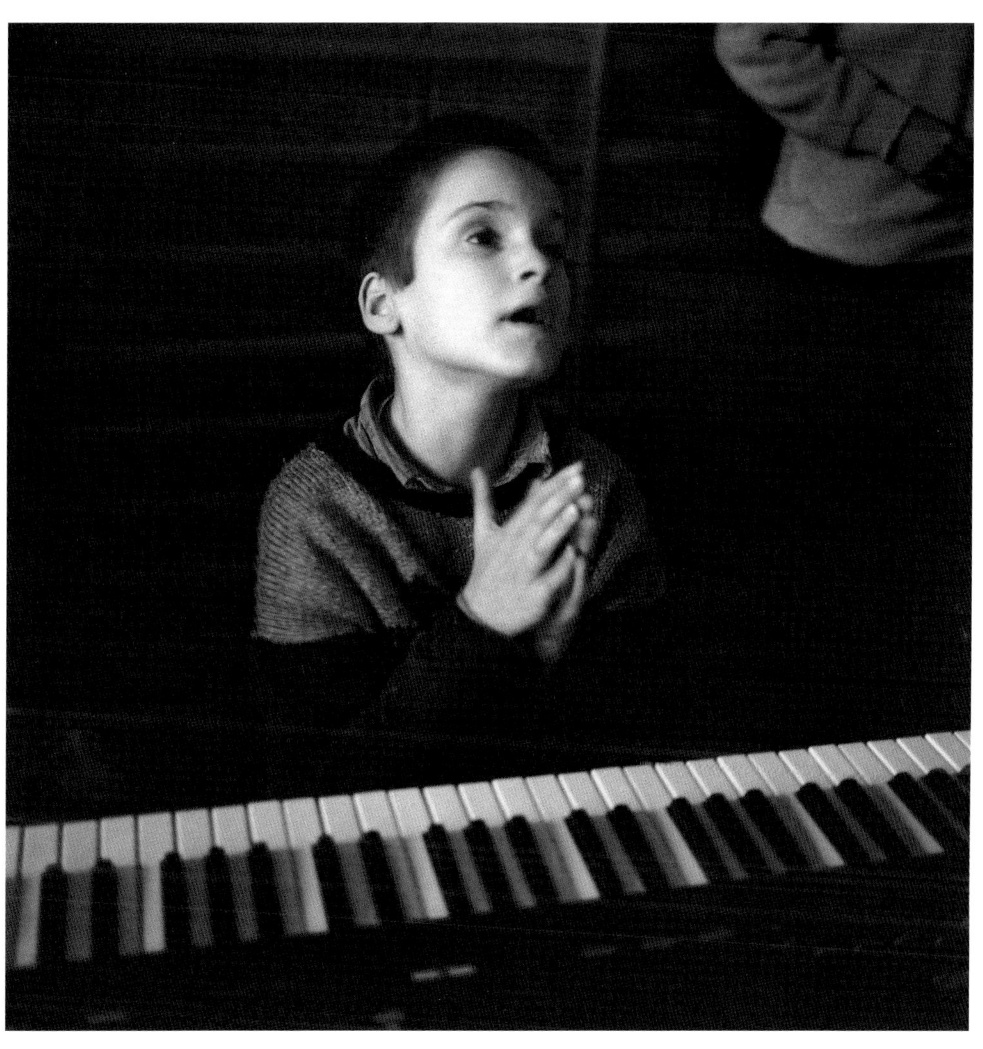

Sylvain, autiste et musicien, February 1992, Paris

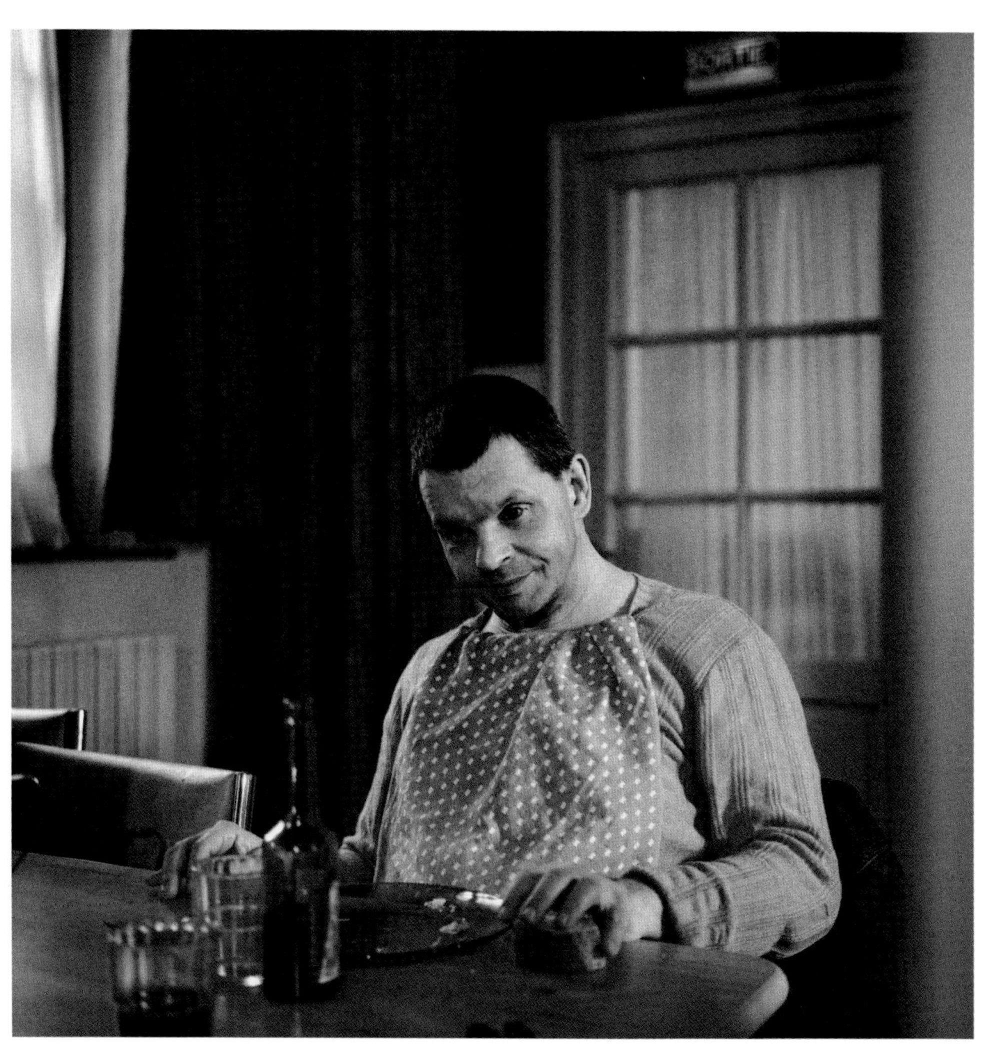

 Déjeuner à la cantine de la maison de retraite Darnel pour aveugles, February 1992, Versailles

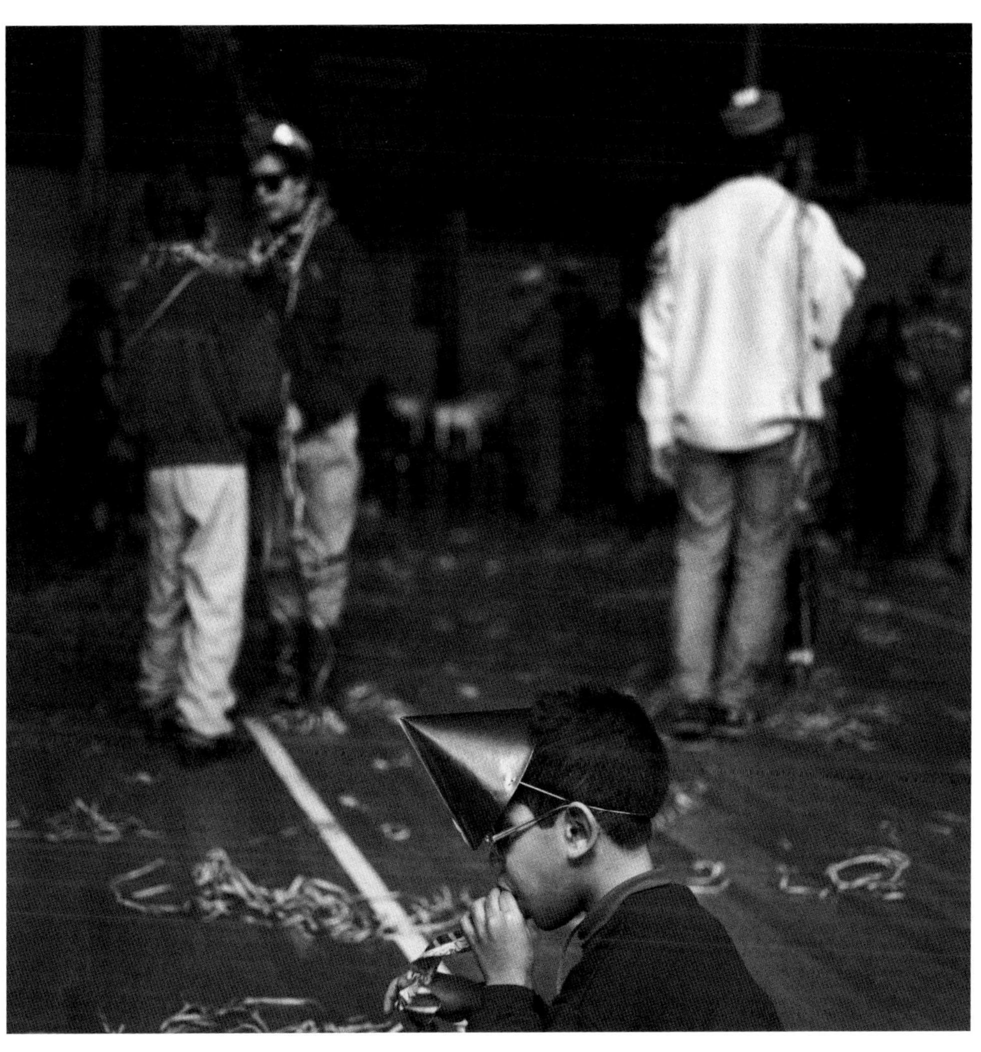

Fête du Centre de l'Estrade, February 1992, Toulouse

MODERN LOVERS
1989–1990

There was a moment, a single moment, when they became at once man and woman. I'd no sooner pressed the button than this fleeting impression was gone. (...) Things happened in the beat of an eyelid. And when I transfixed the models in that flat light, it was as if I were pinning butterflies on to cork.

Il y avait un moment, un seul, où ils devenaient homme et femme à la fois. J'avais juste le temps d'appuyer sur le bouton avant que cette impression ne disparaisse. (...) Les choses se passaient en une fraction de seconde. Et quand je fixais les modèles dans cette lumière plate, j'avais le sentiment d'épingler des papillons sur du liège.

Es gab einen einzigen Moment, in dem sie zugleich Mann und Frau waren. Ich hatte gerade noch Zeit, auf den Auslöser zu drücken, bevor sich dieser Eindruck auch schon wieder verflüchtigte. (...) Alles geschah im Bruchteil einer Sekunde. Und wenn ich die Modelle in diesem flachen Licht fixierte, hatte ich das Gefühl, Schmetterlinge auf Kork zu spießen.

Bettina Rheims, in *Modern Lovers*, 1990

Josie I, September 1989, Paris

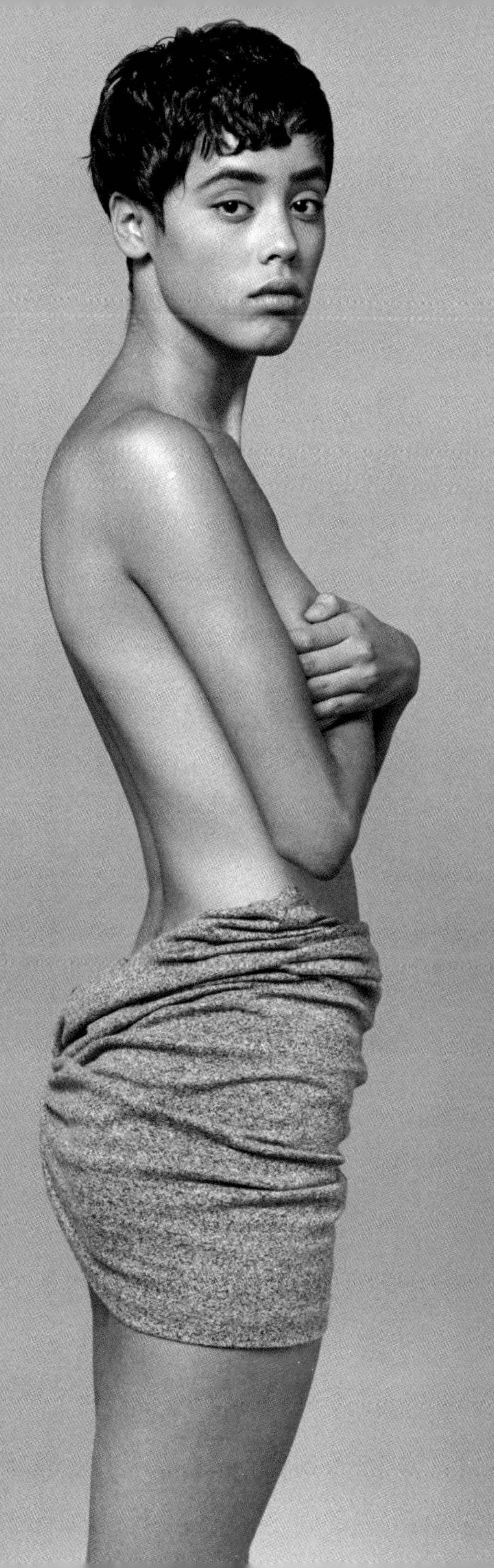

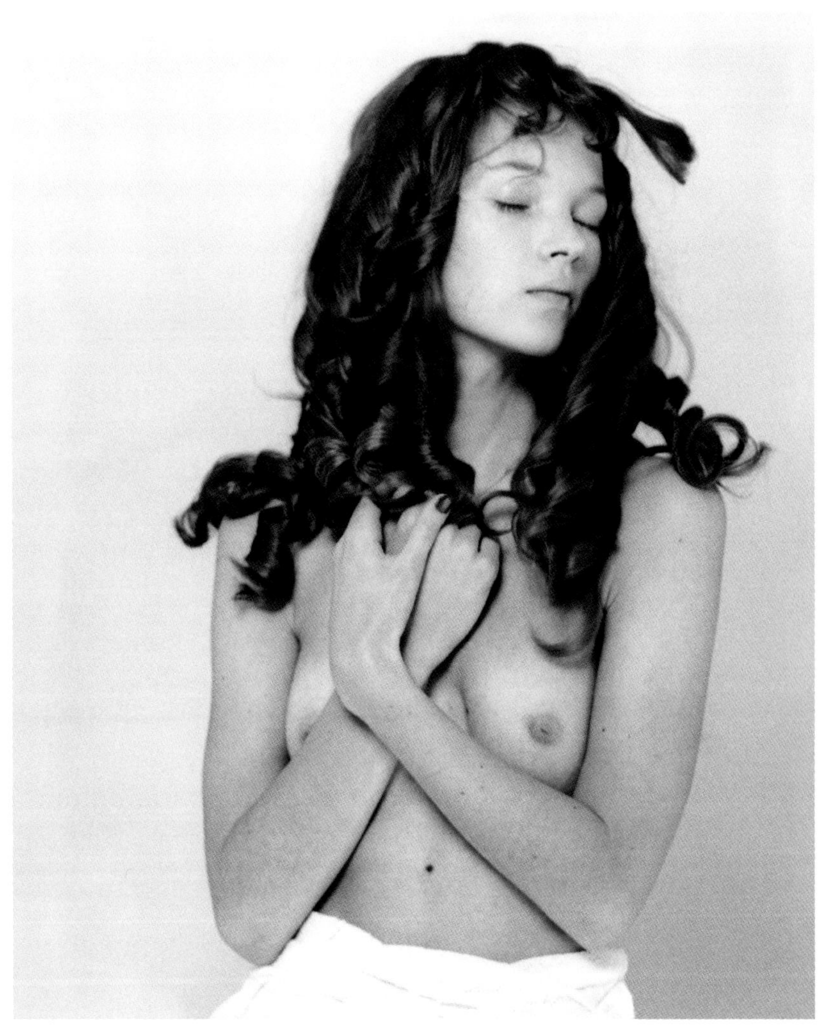

Above — *Kate before she became Kate Moss*, December 1989, London
Opposite page — *Kate before she became Kate Moss II*, December 1989, London
Page 160 — *Kira C. III, in "Gender Studies"*, June 2011, Paris
Page 161 — *Eloy I. II, in "Gender Studies"*, June 2011, Paris

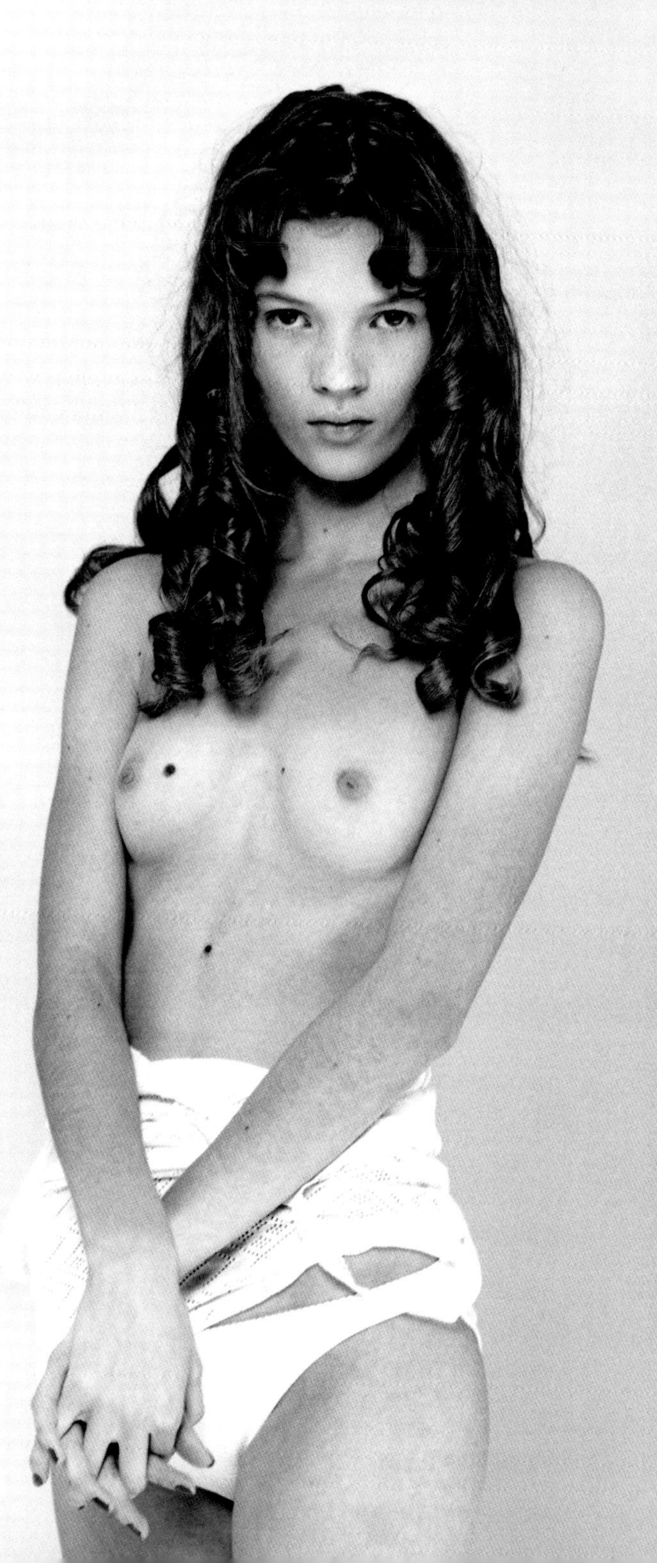

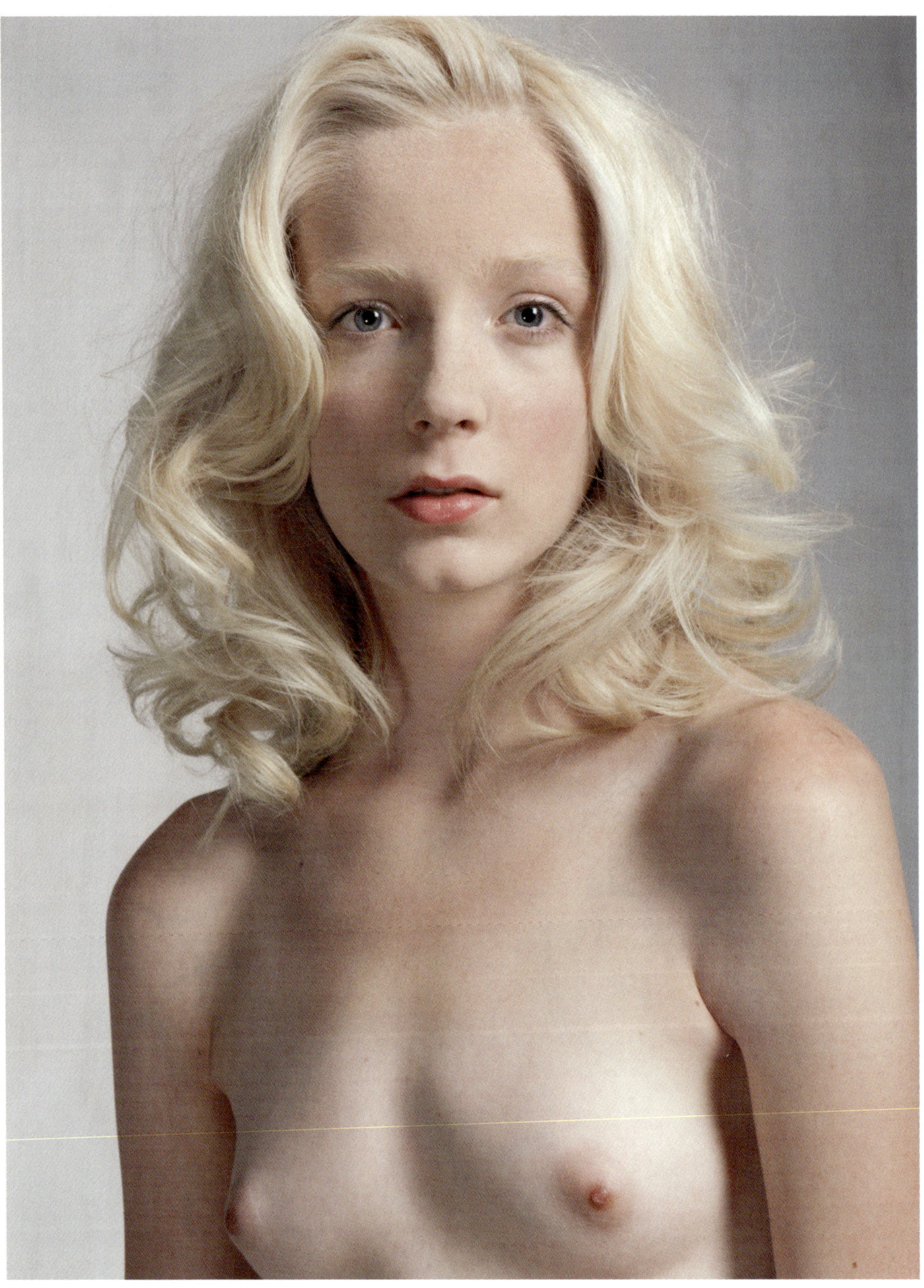

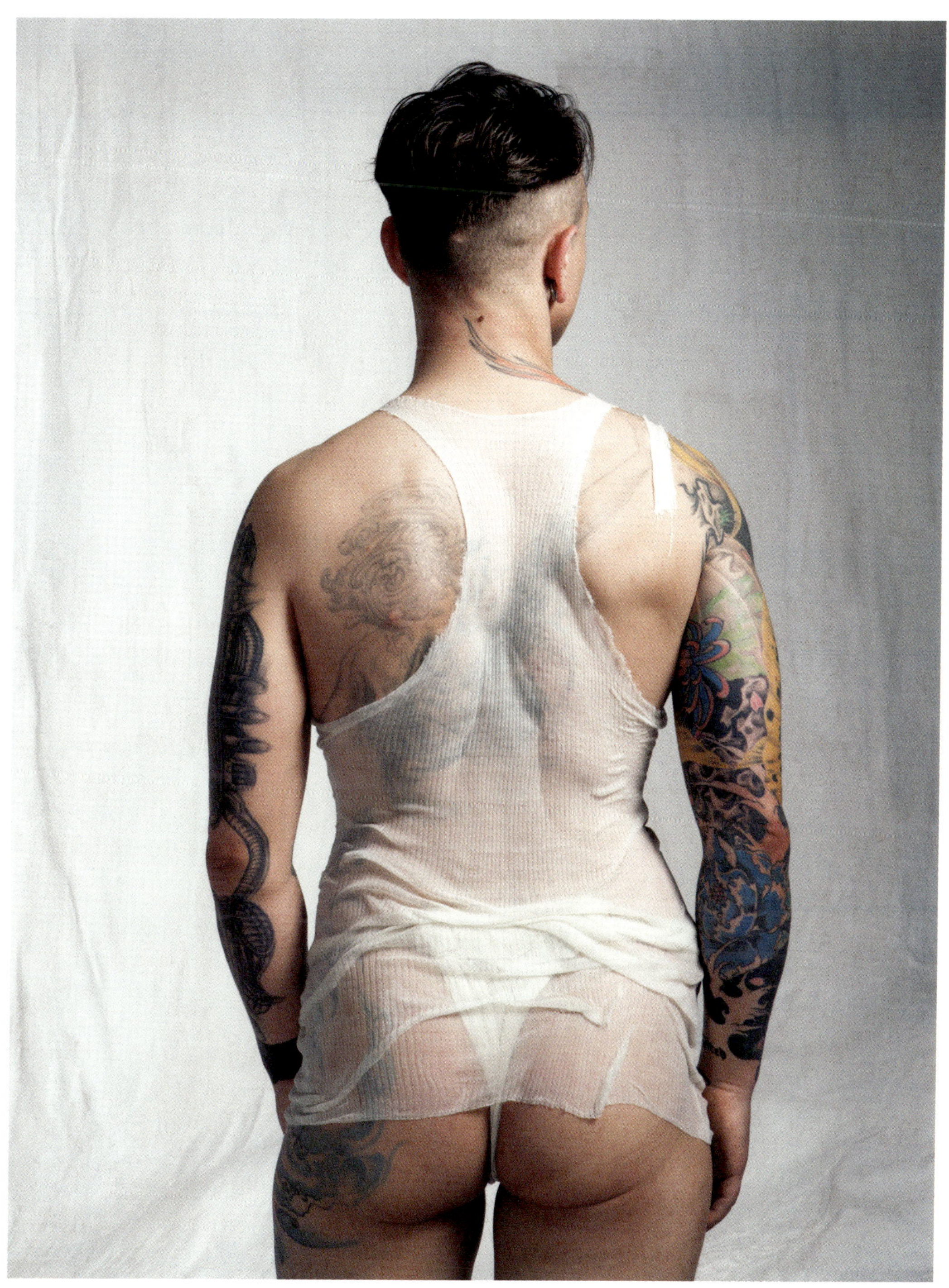

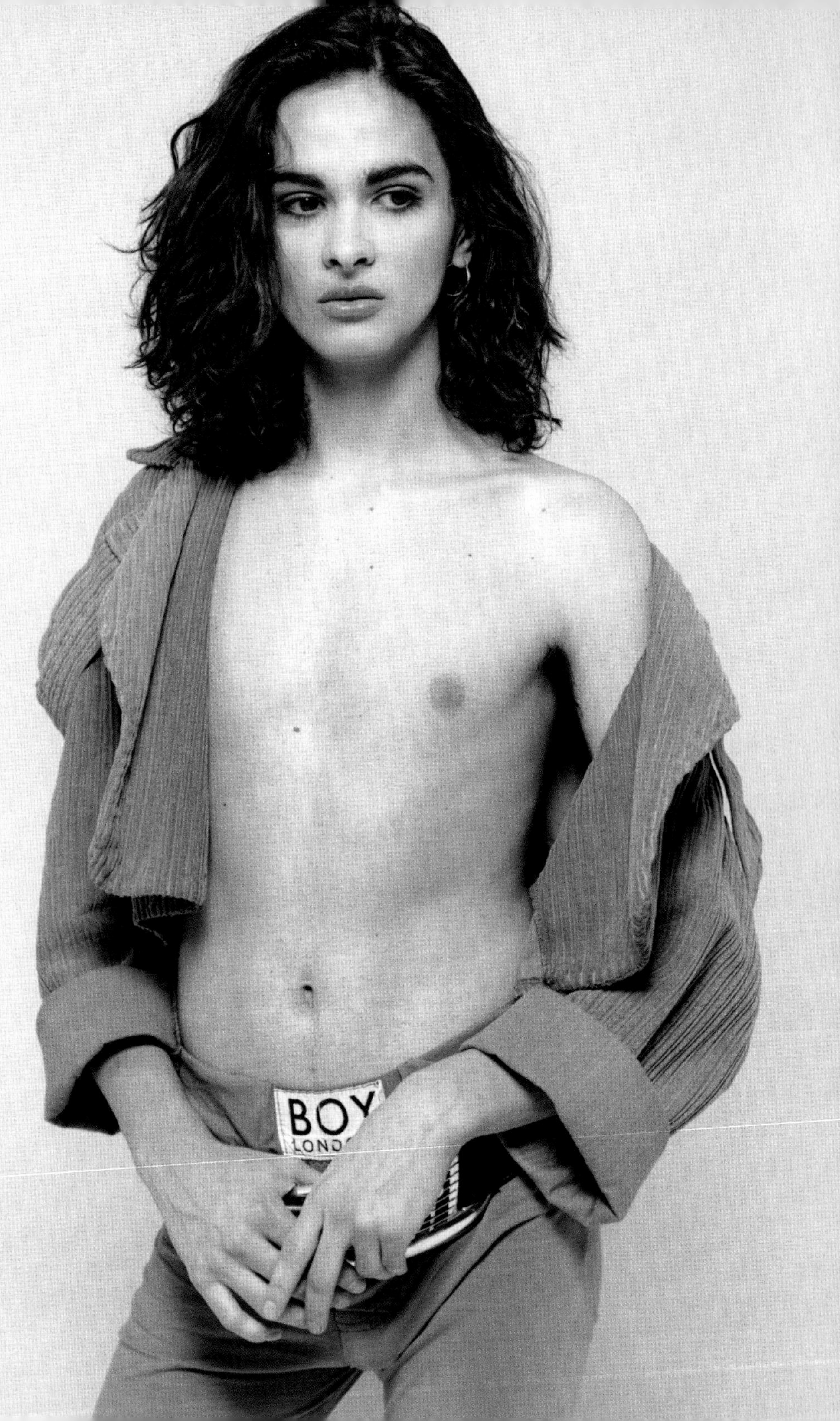
BOY
LONDON

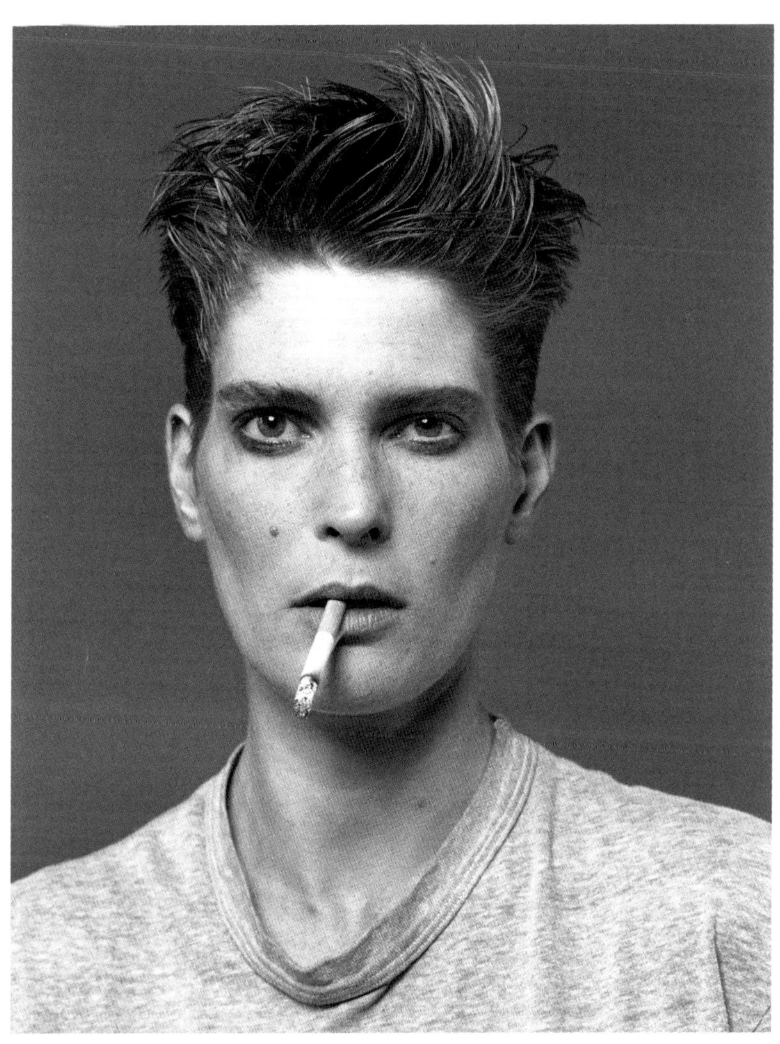

Above — *Leslie*, October 1990, Paris
Opposite page — *William*, July 1990, Paris
Page 164 — *Sasha*, December 1989, London
Page 165 — *Andy B., in "Gender Studies"*, June 2011, Paris

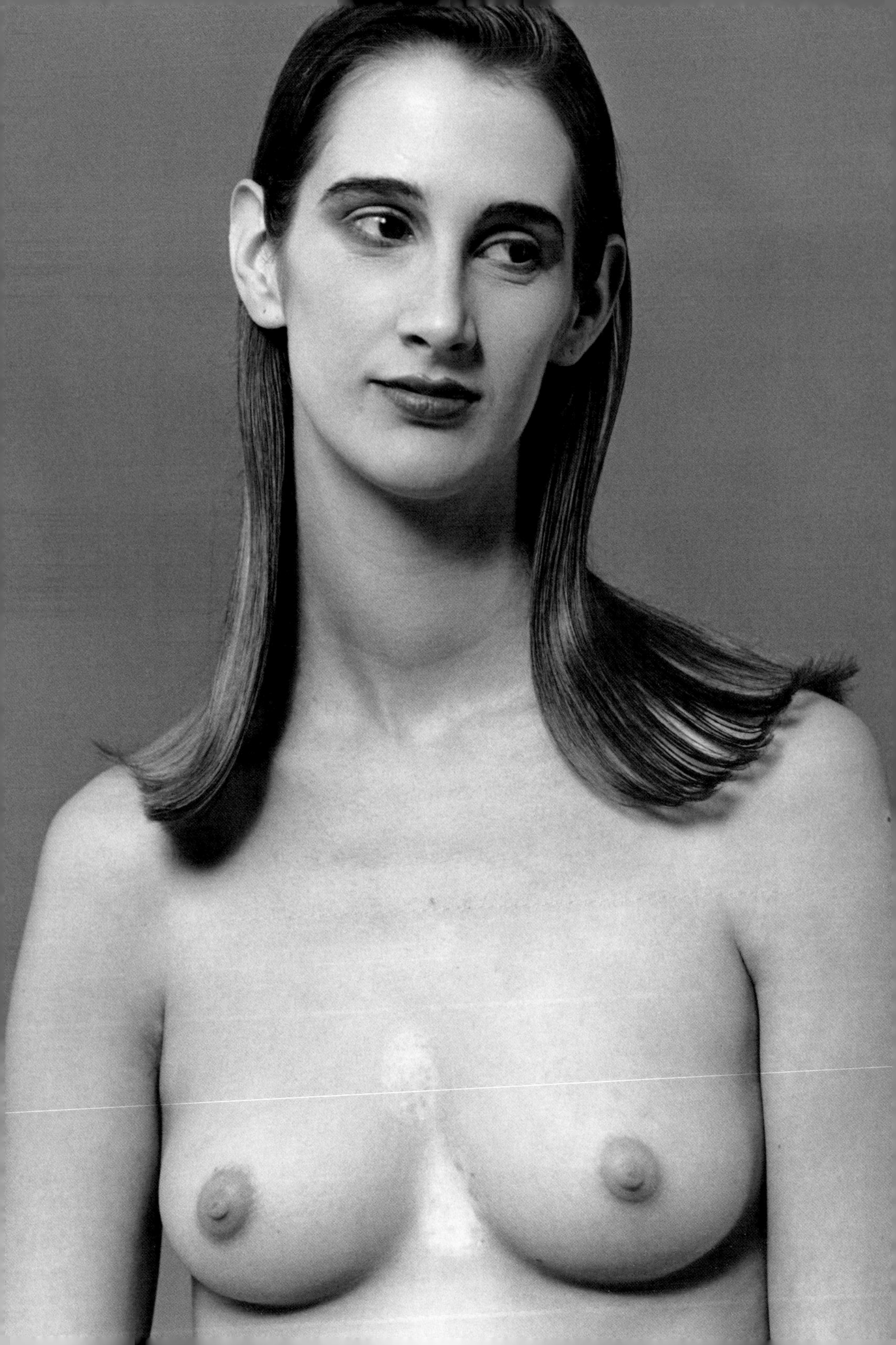

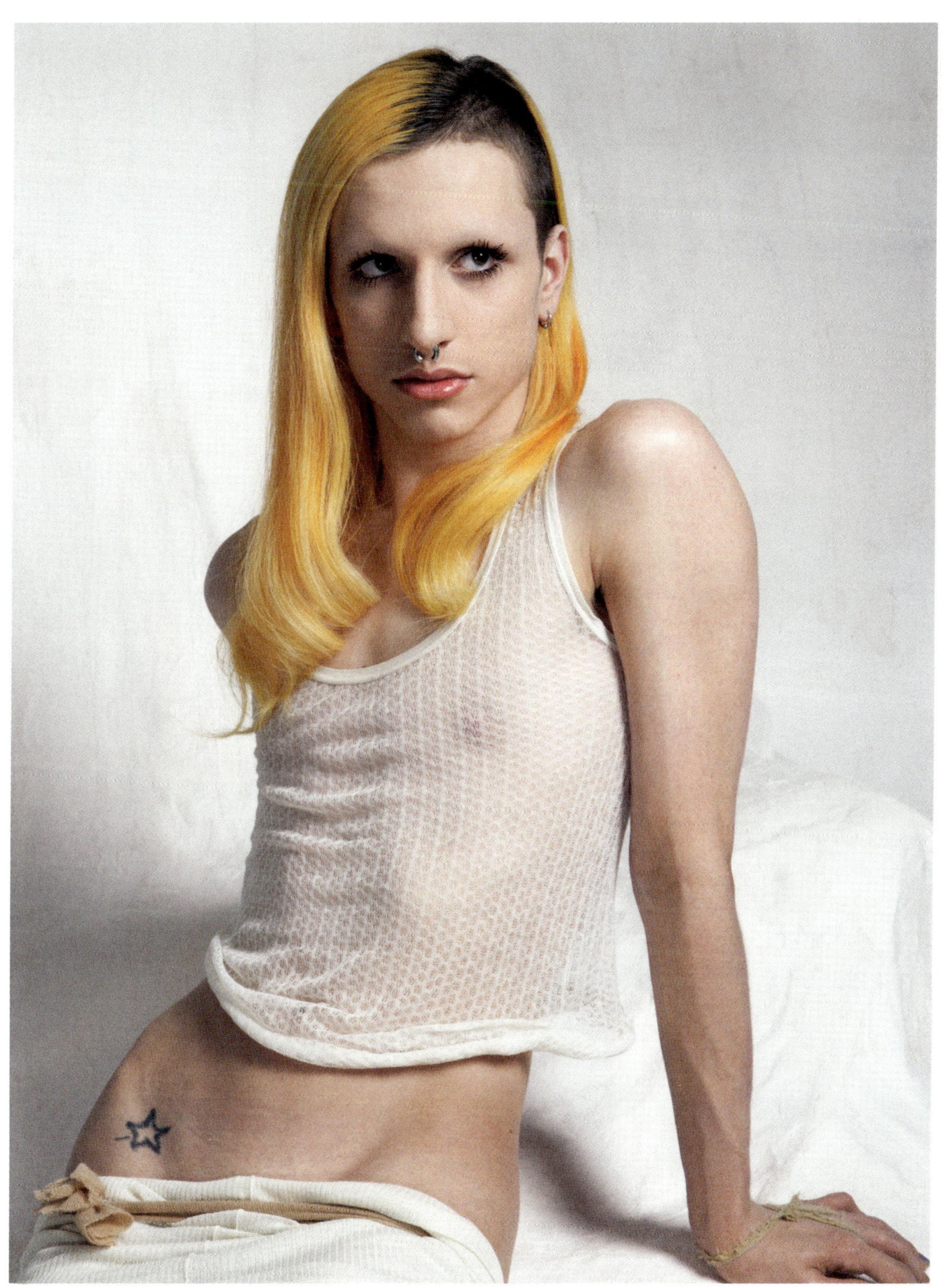

KIM

1991, Paris

I nevertheless felt (...) ready to give her all of myself; for this subject I had to forget my excessive femininity and awaken the boy who is, in spite of every effort, still present within me; I tried to use my eyes and my muscles; I so much wanted to give Bettina what she was looking for that over those two days I did nothing but exacerbate everything that I had struggled against for years.

Malgré tout je me sentais (...) prête à me donner totalement, pour ce sujet il me fallait oublier ma trop grande féminité et réveiller ce garçon qui est malgré tout un petit peu en moi, j'essayais d'utiliser mes yeux et mes muscles, je voulais tellement donner à Bettina ce qu'elle recherchait et pendant deux jours je n'ai fait qu'exacerber ce contre quoi j'avais lutté pendant des années.

Trotz allem fühlte ich mich (...) bereit, mein Bestes zu geben. Für dieses Thema musste ich meine starke Weiblichkeit unterdrücken und den jungen Mann in mir hervorkehren, der trotz allem noch irgendwo tief in mir steckt. Ich bemühte mich, vor allem meine Augen und meine Muskeln zur Geltung zu bringen; so sehr wollte ich Bettina das geben, wonach sie suchte. Zwei Tage lang tat ich nichts anderes, als genau das an die Oberfläche kommen zu lassen, gegen das ich jahrelang angekämpft hatte.

Kim Harlow, in *Kim*, 1994

Kim dans le miroir de la salle de bains IV, January 1991, Paris
Page 168 — *Kim Harlow de dos II*, January 1991, Paris
Page 169 — *Kim Harlow, portrait d'un jeune homme*, January 1991, Paris
Page 170 — *Kaplan II*, February 1990, Paris
Page 171 — *Kaël T. B. I, in "Gender Studies"*, June 2011, Paris

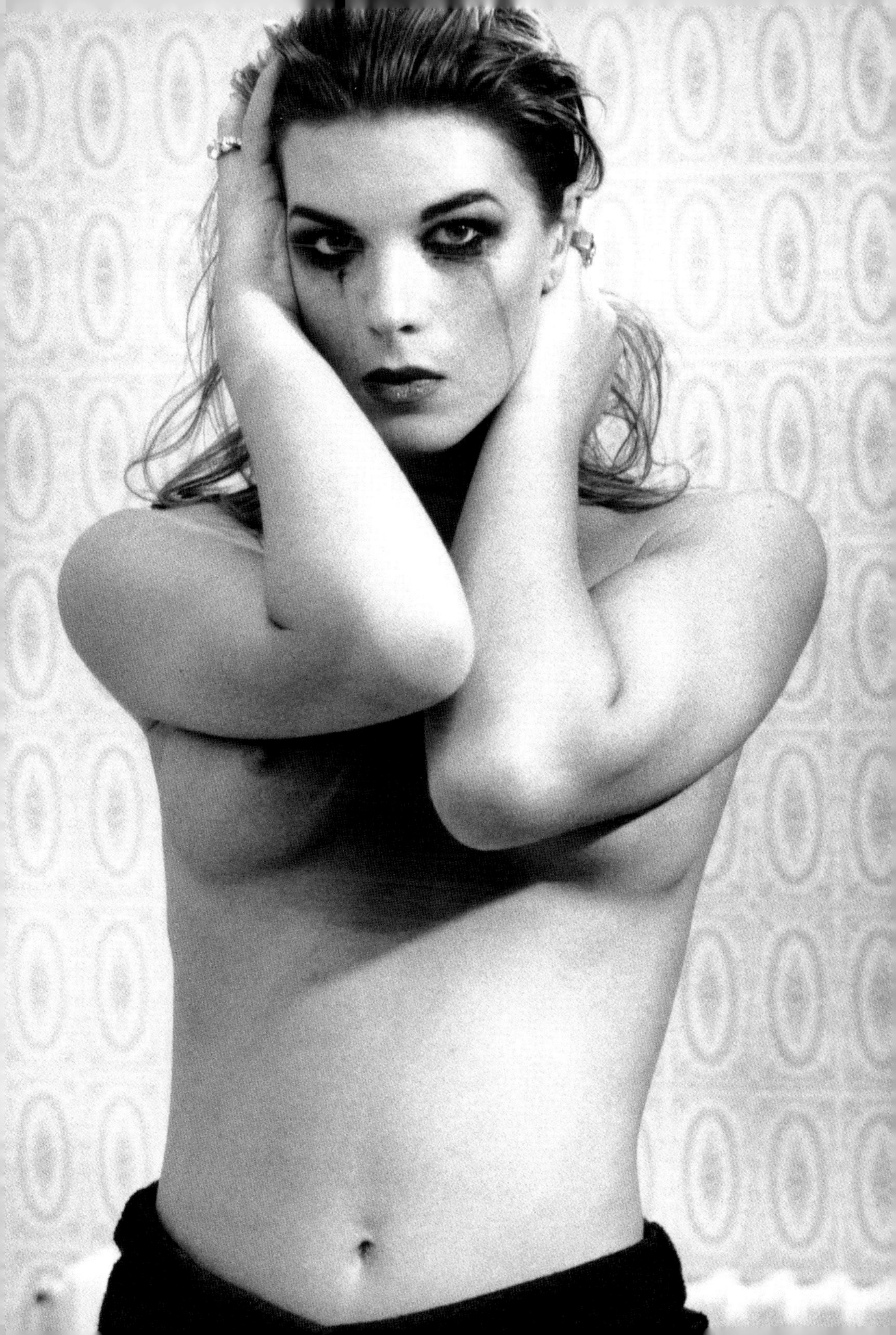

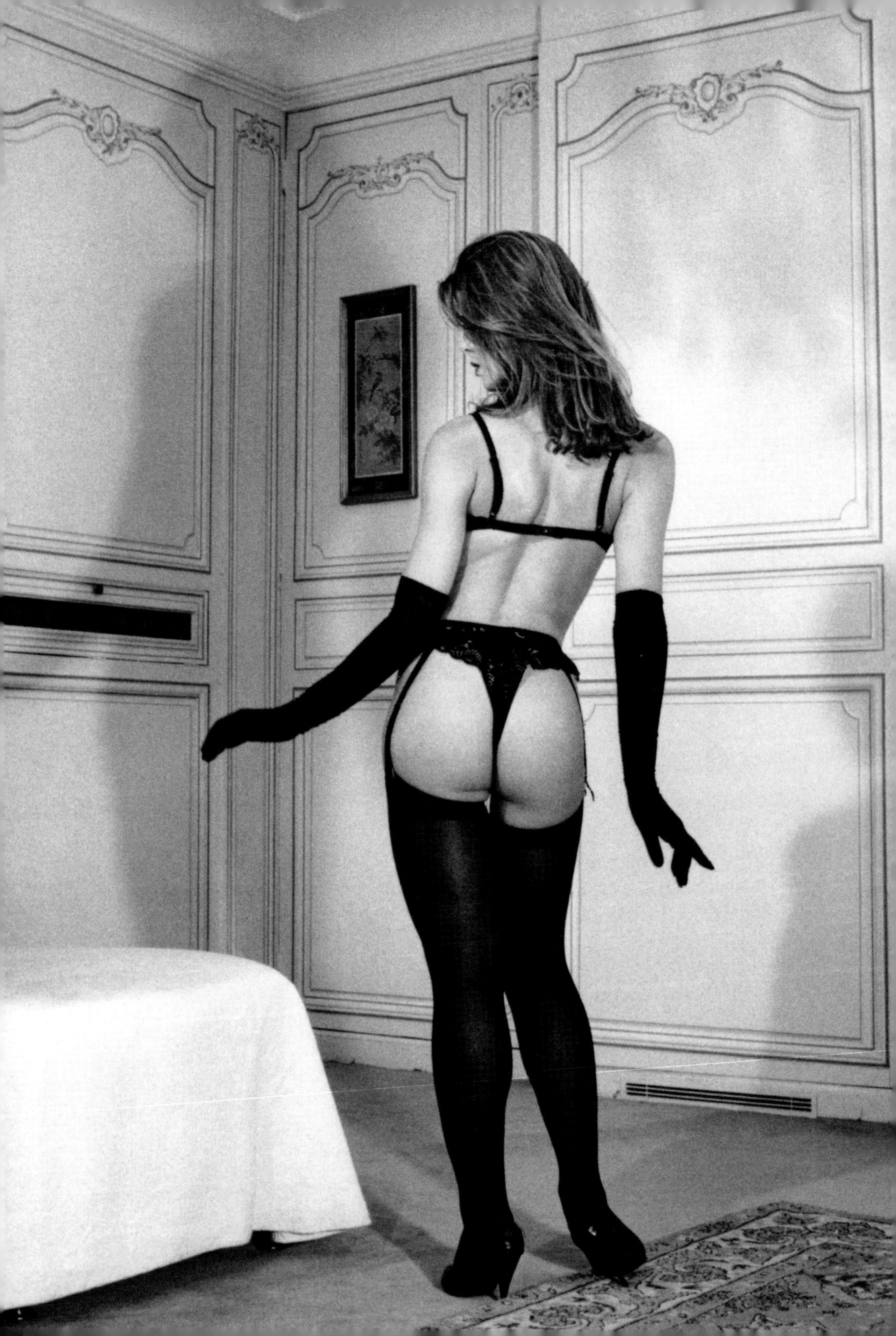

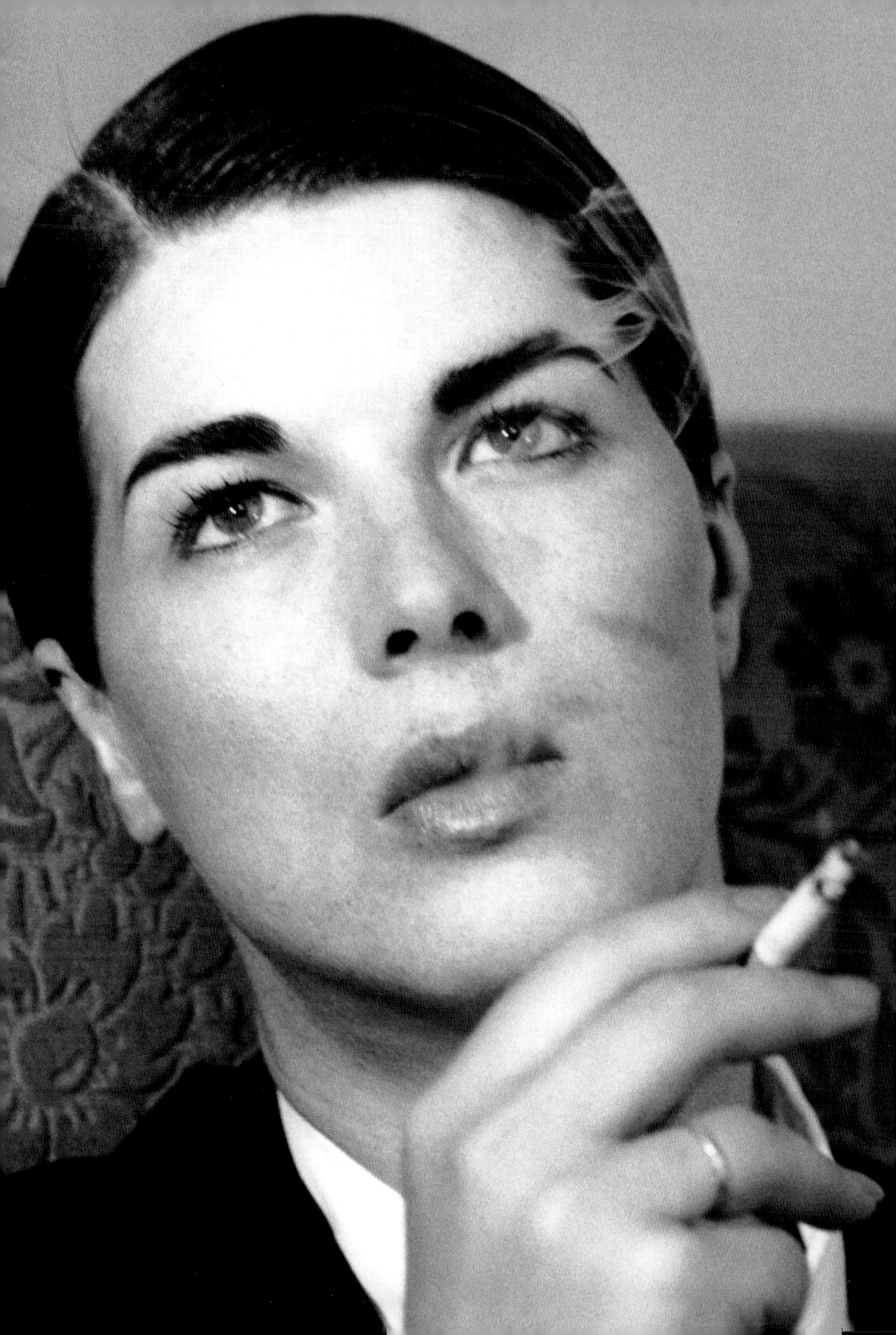

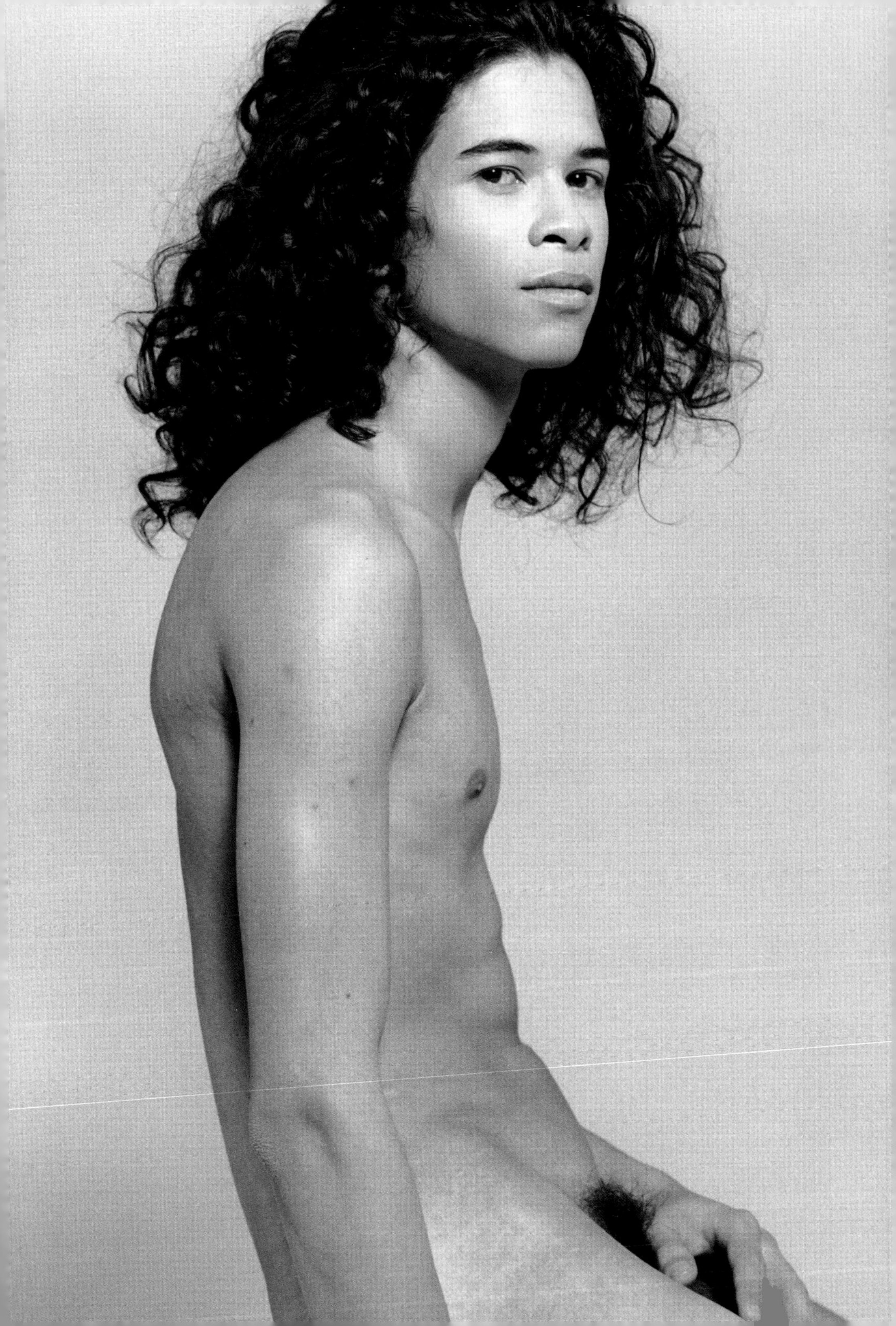

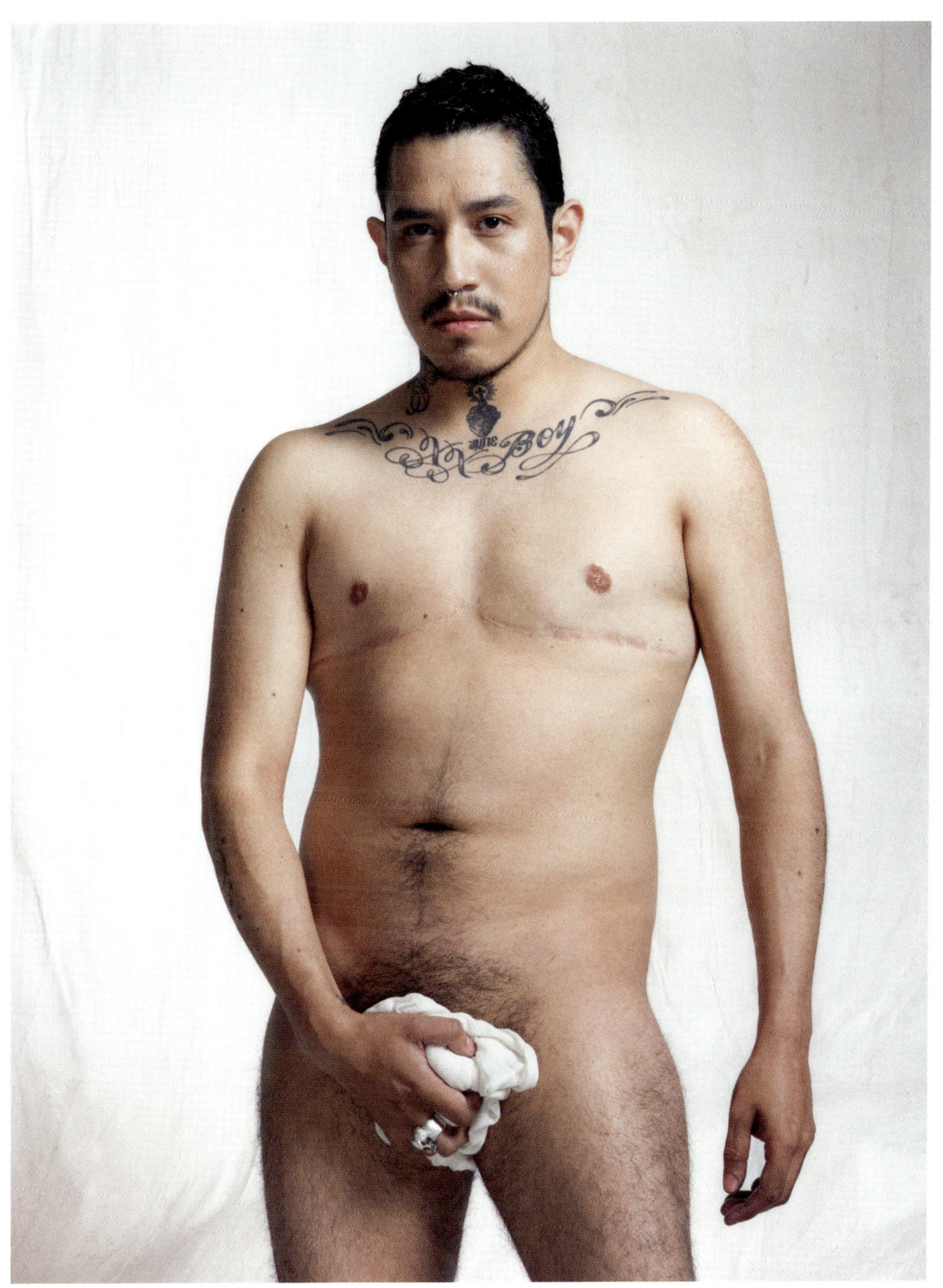

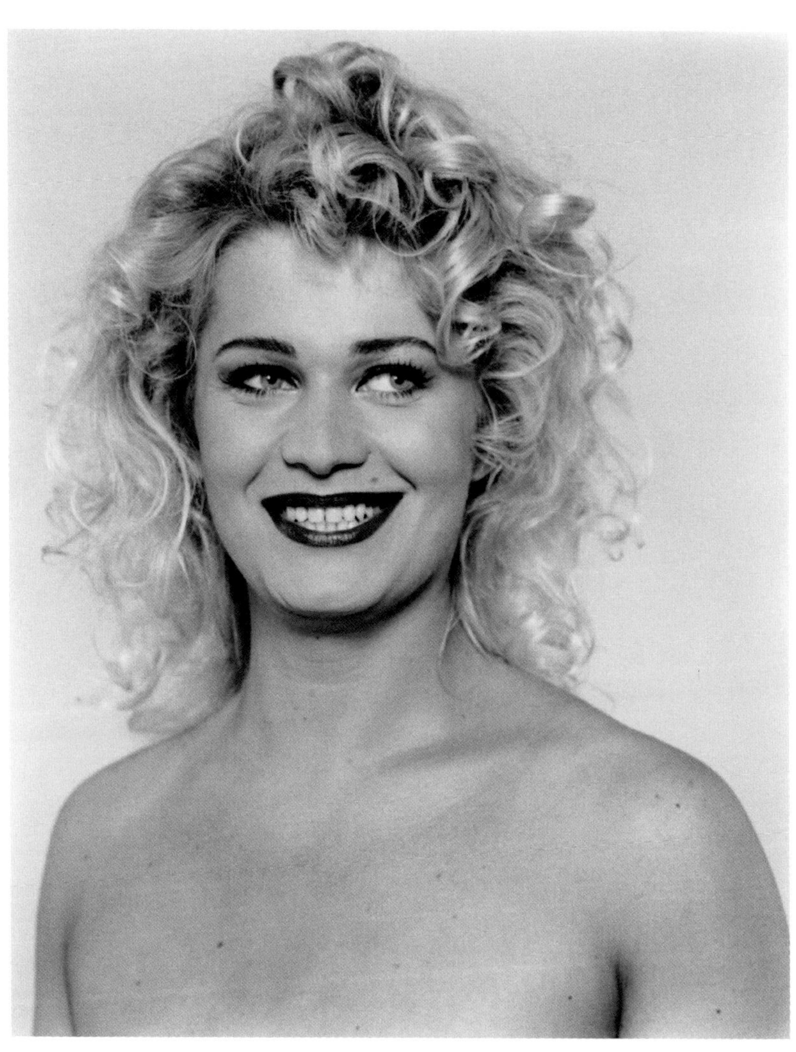

Above — *Mika I, in "Les Espionnes"*, June 1991, Paris
Opposite page — *Valérie I, in "Les Espionnes"*, June 1991, Paris

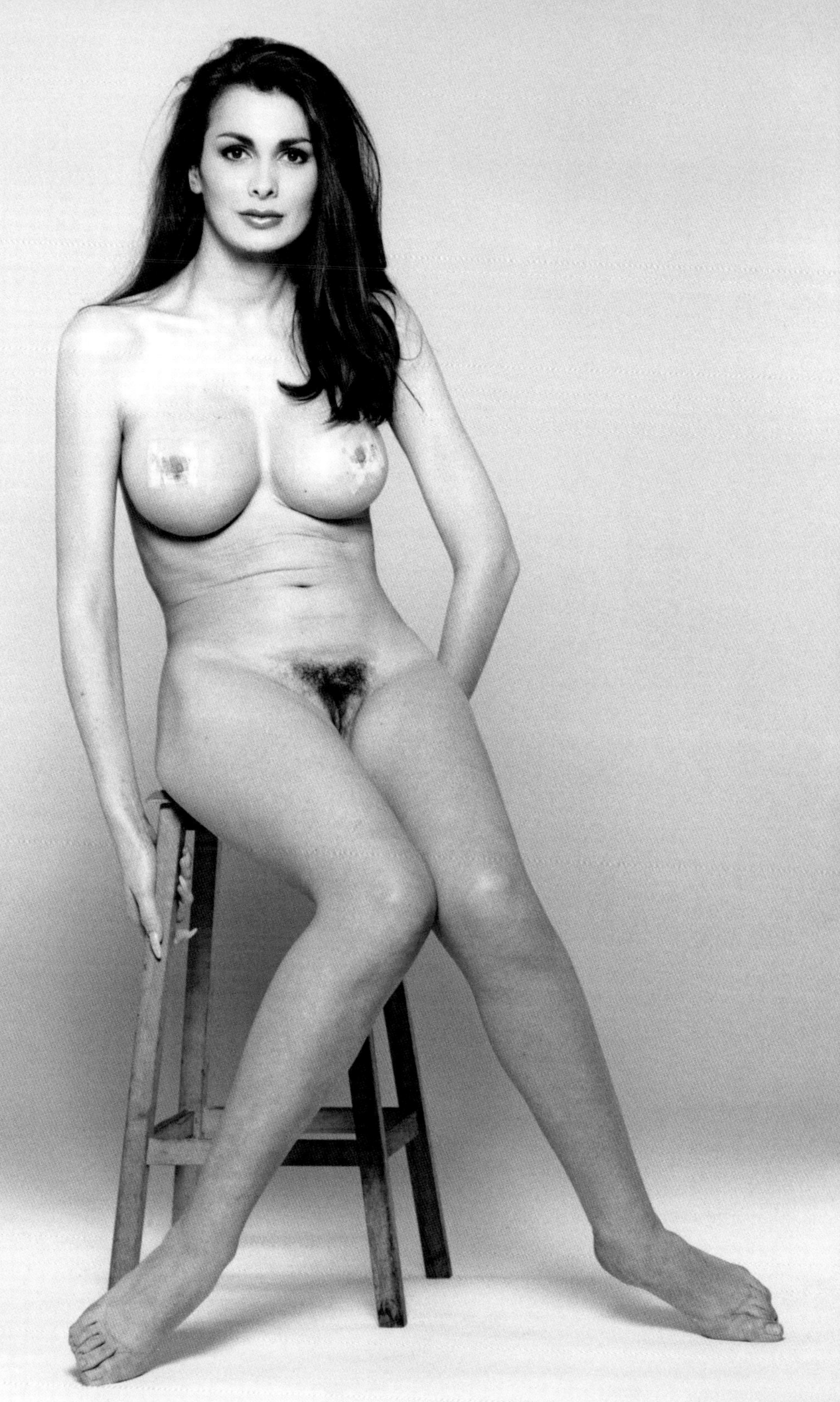

Dione smoking, July 1990, Paris

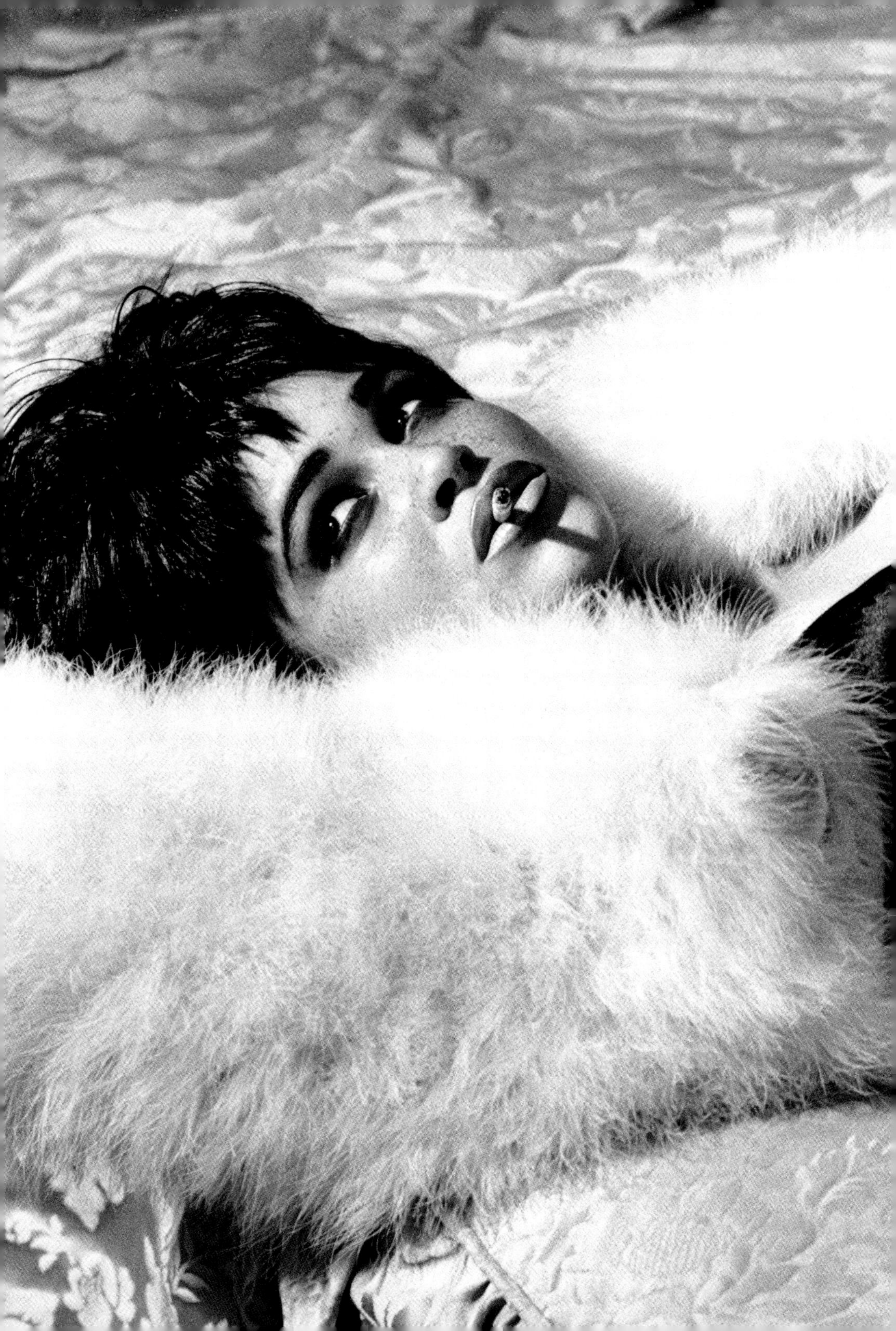

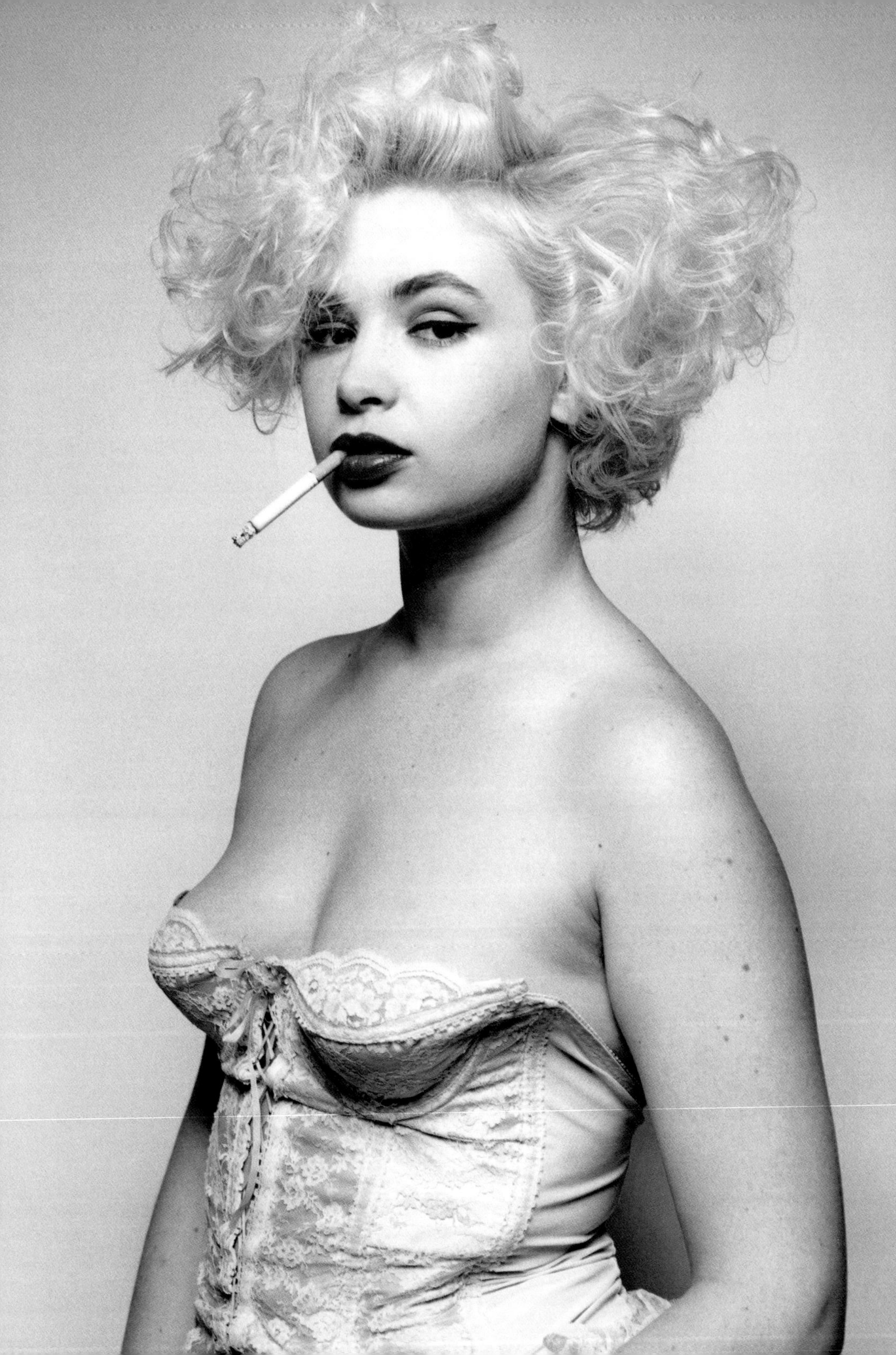

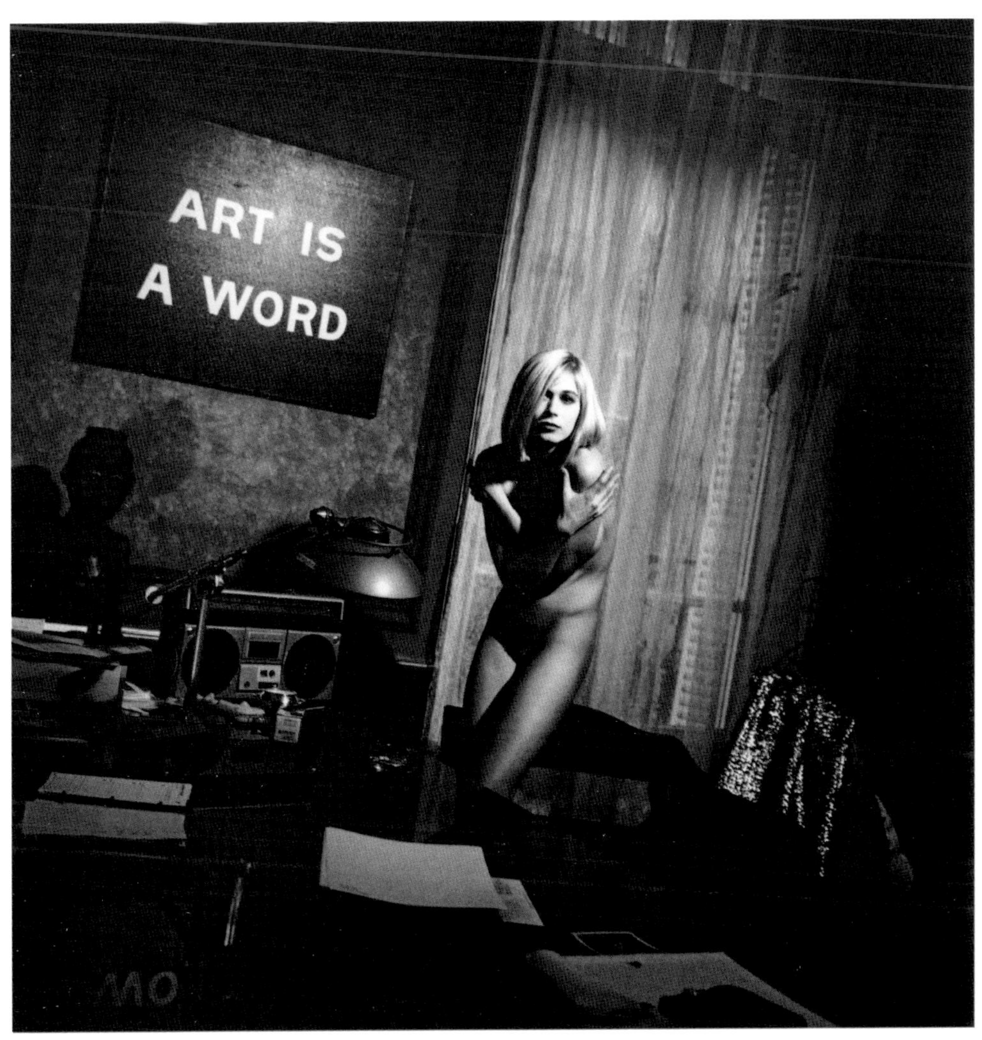

Above — *Art is a word*, November 1988, Paris
Opposite page — *Marthe en guêpière*, February 1987, Paris
Page 178 — *Anna Karina II*, October 1988, Paris
Page 179 — *Sofia à la cigarette*, May 1989, Paris
Pages 180/181 — *Cordula et la peau de zèbre*, May 2000, New York
Page 182 — *Portrait of Vivien Solari hoping to be a cover*, November 2000, Paris
Page 183 — *Catherine Robbe-Grillet avec les cendres de son mari, Alain*, May 2013, Château du Mesnil, Normandy   177

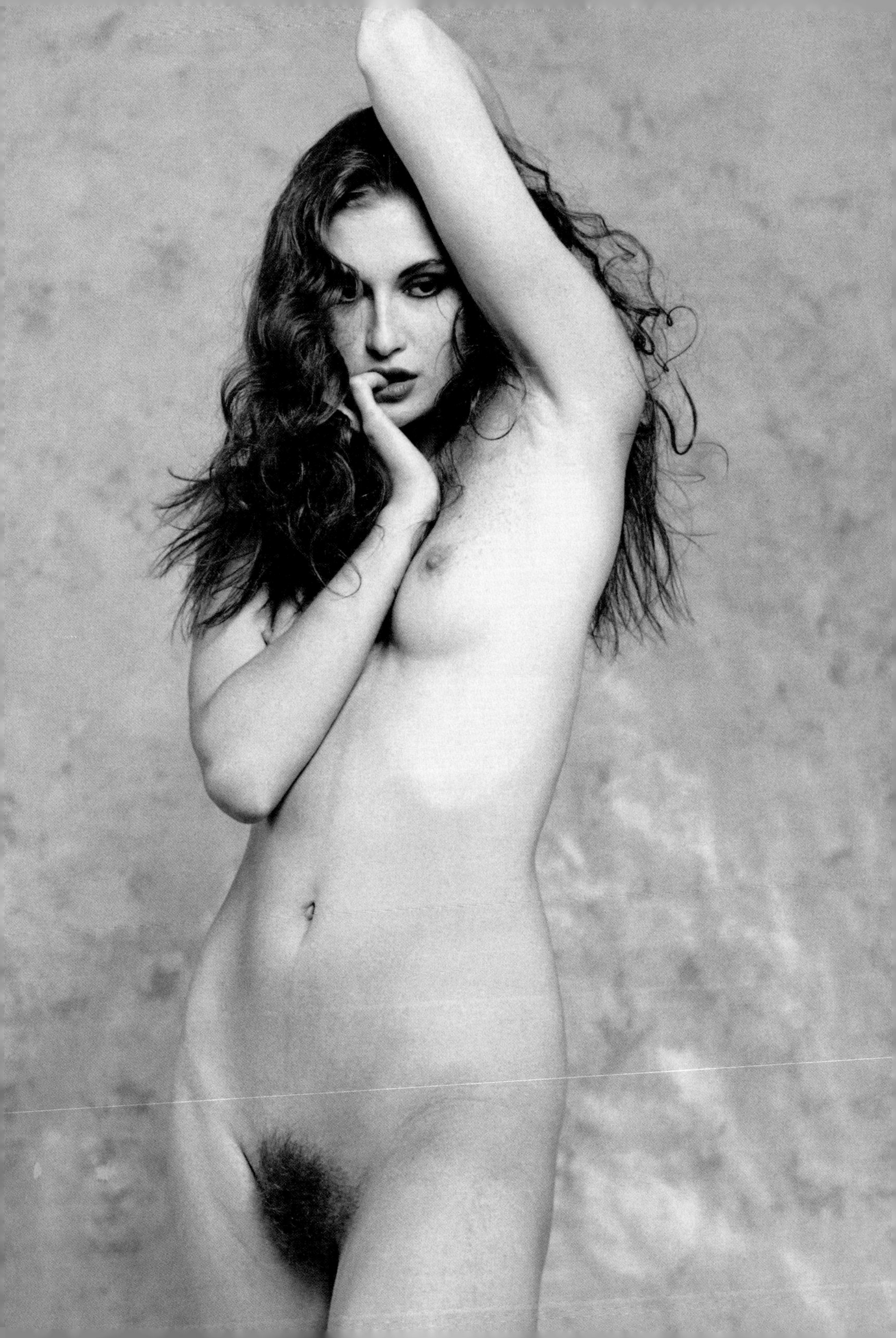

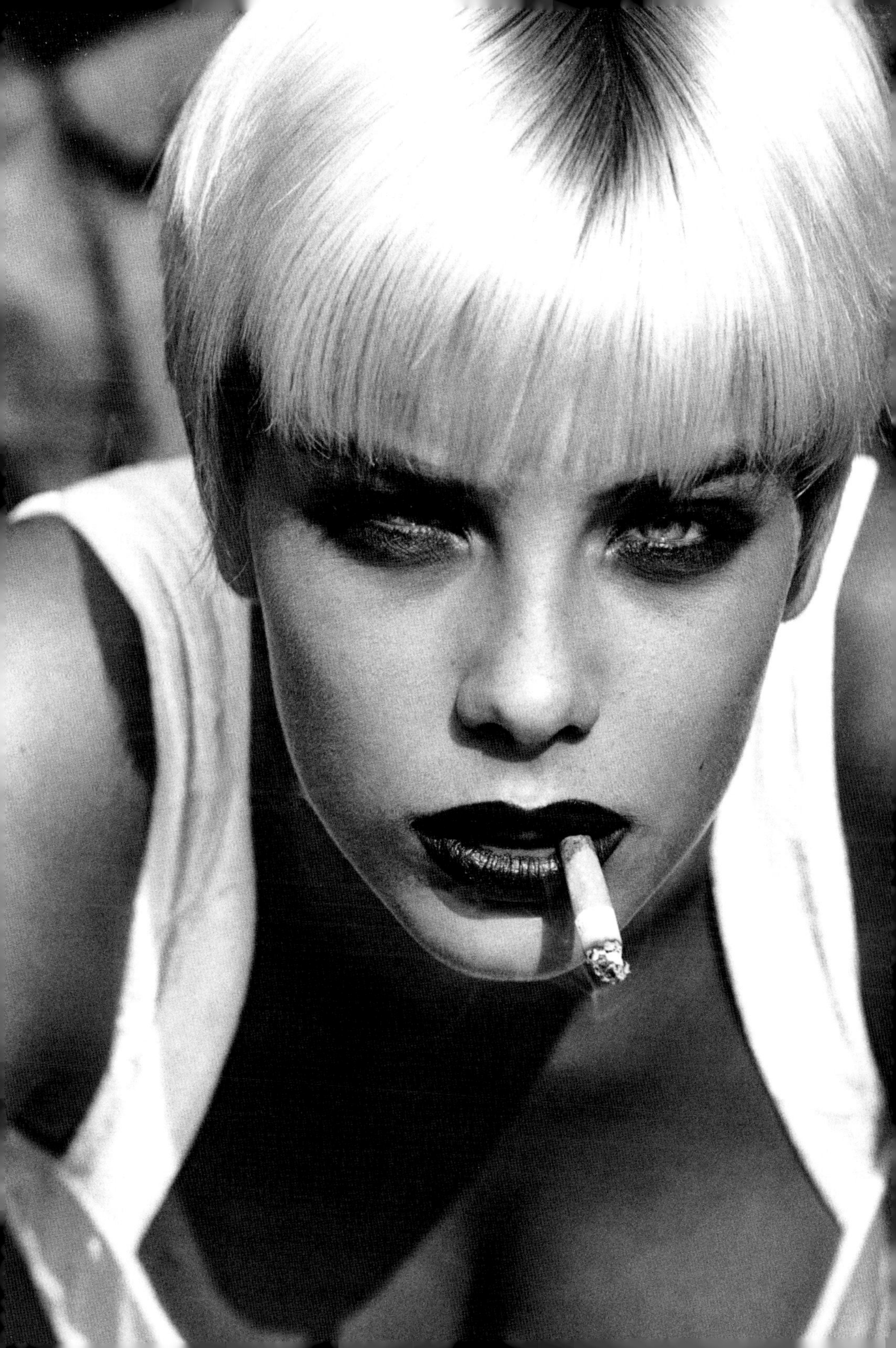

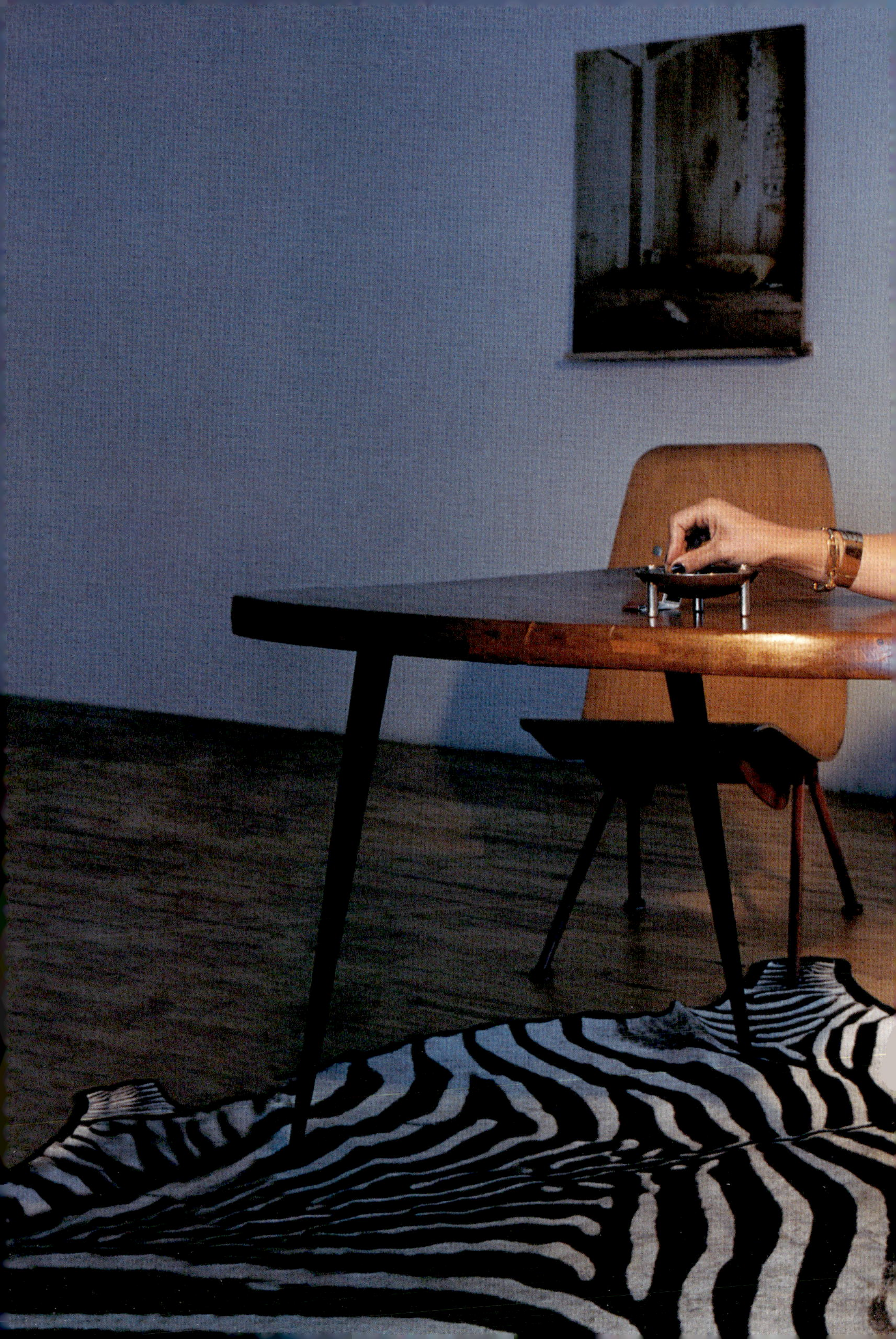

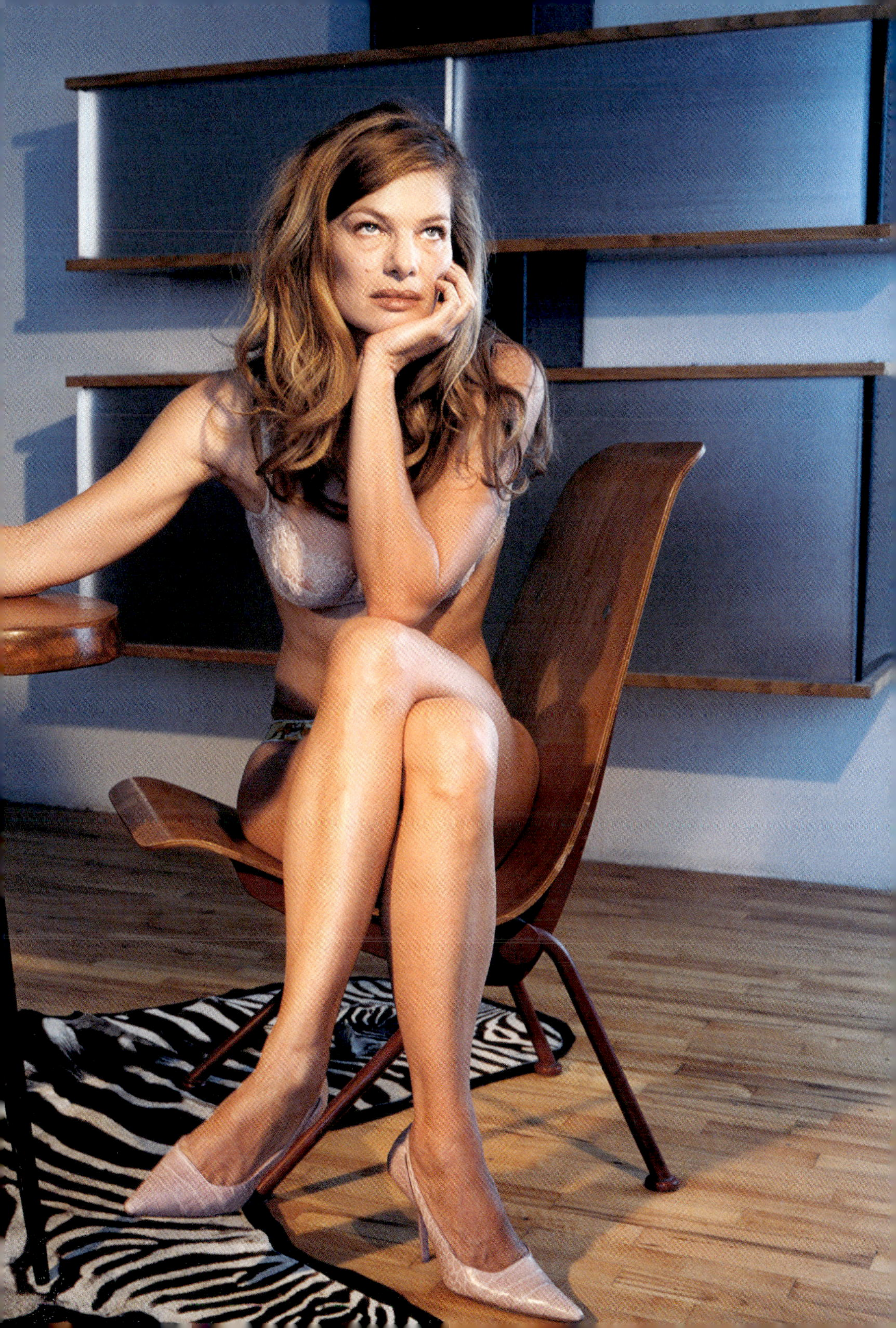

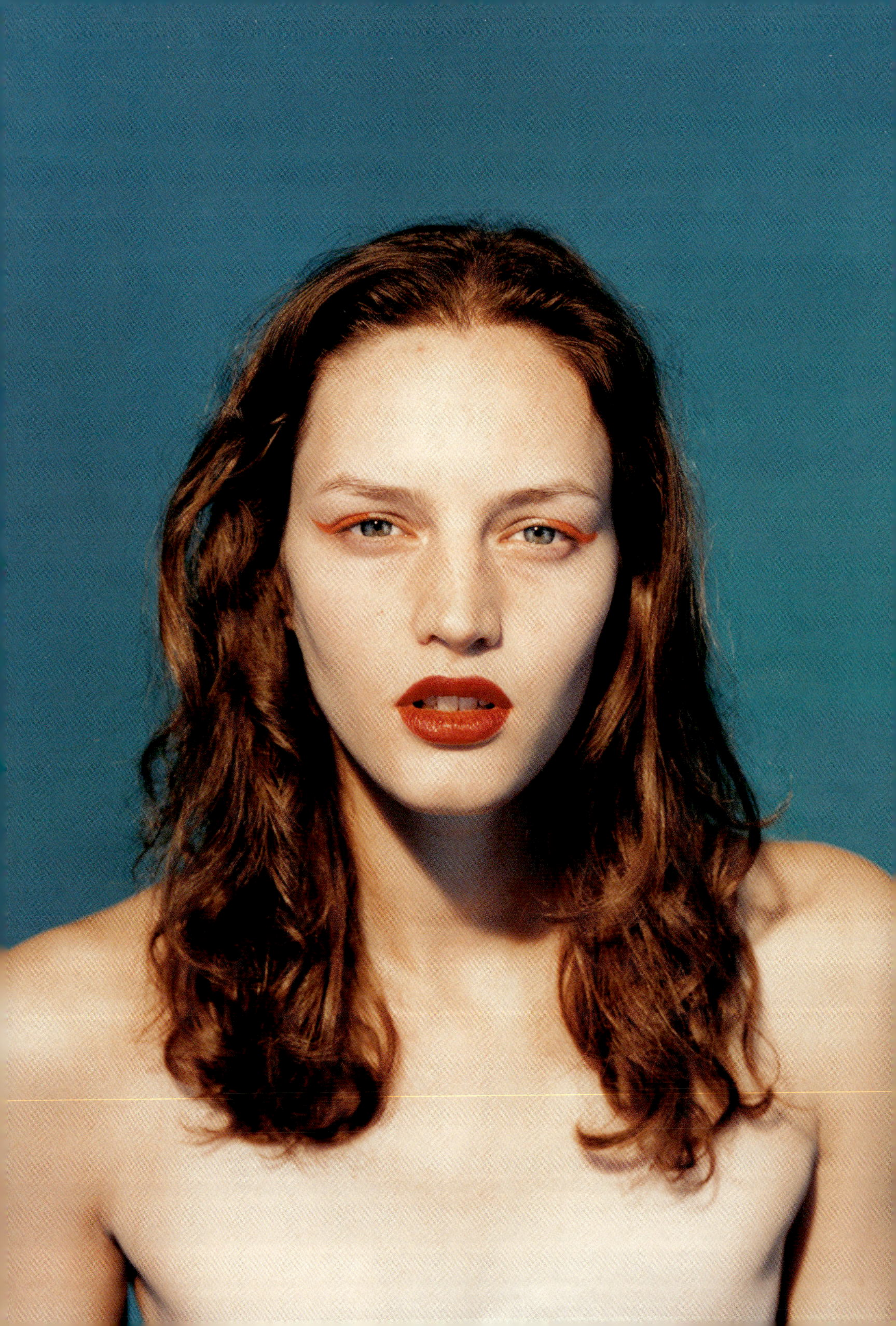

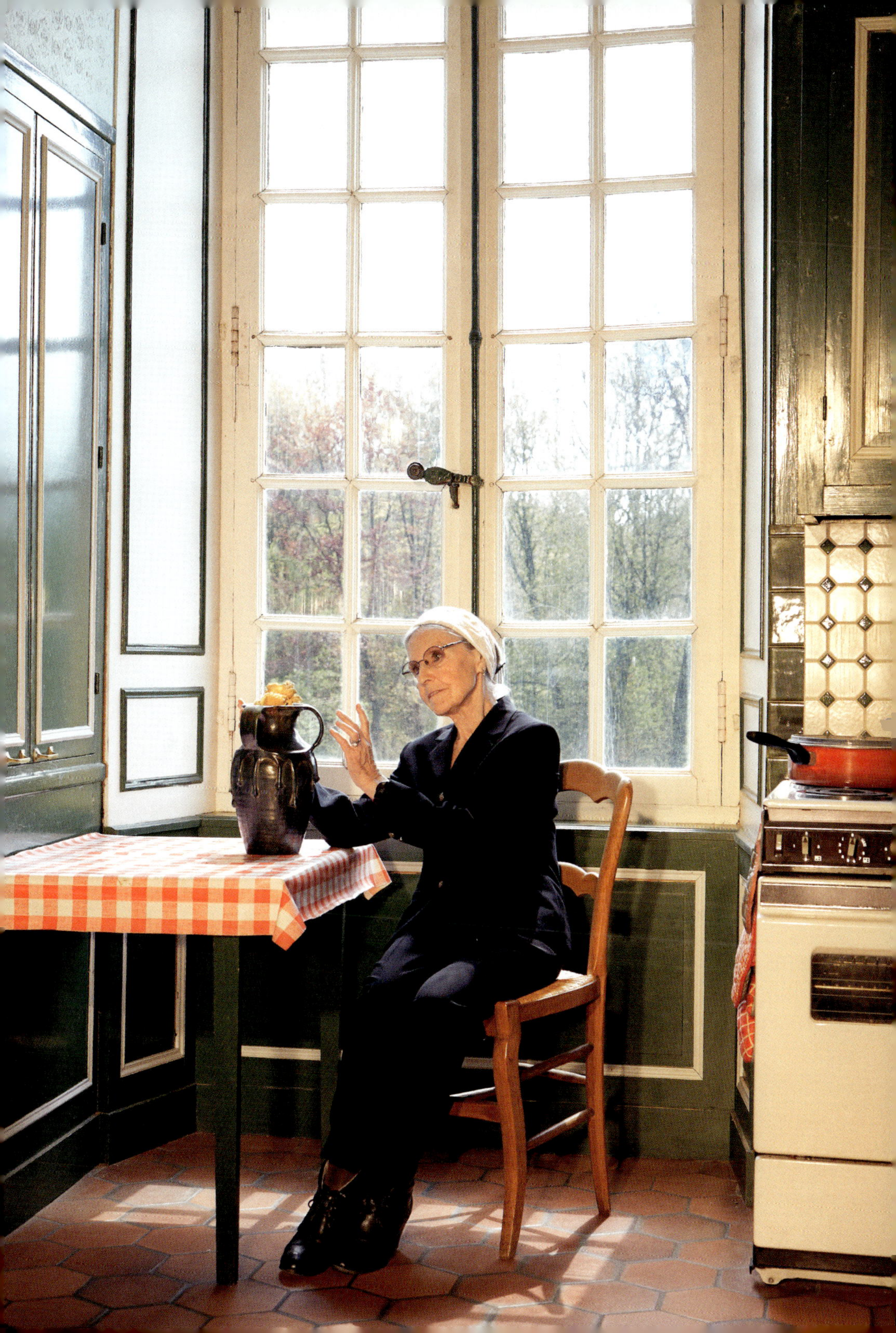

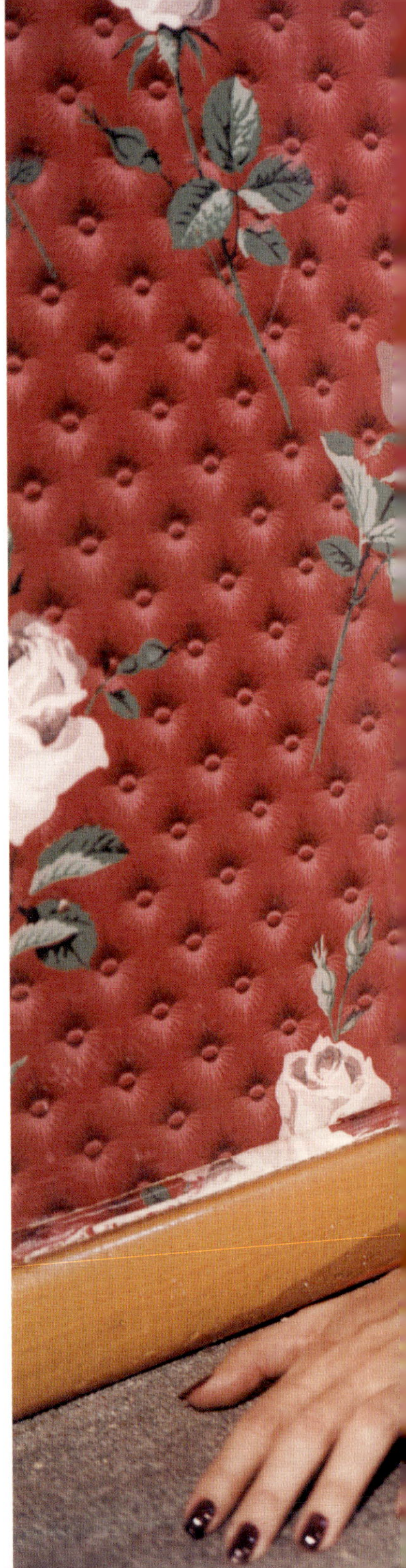

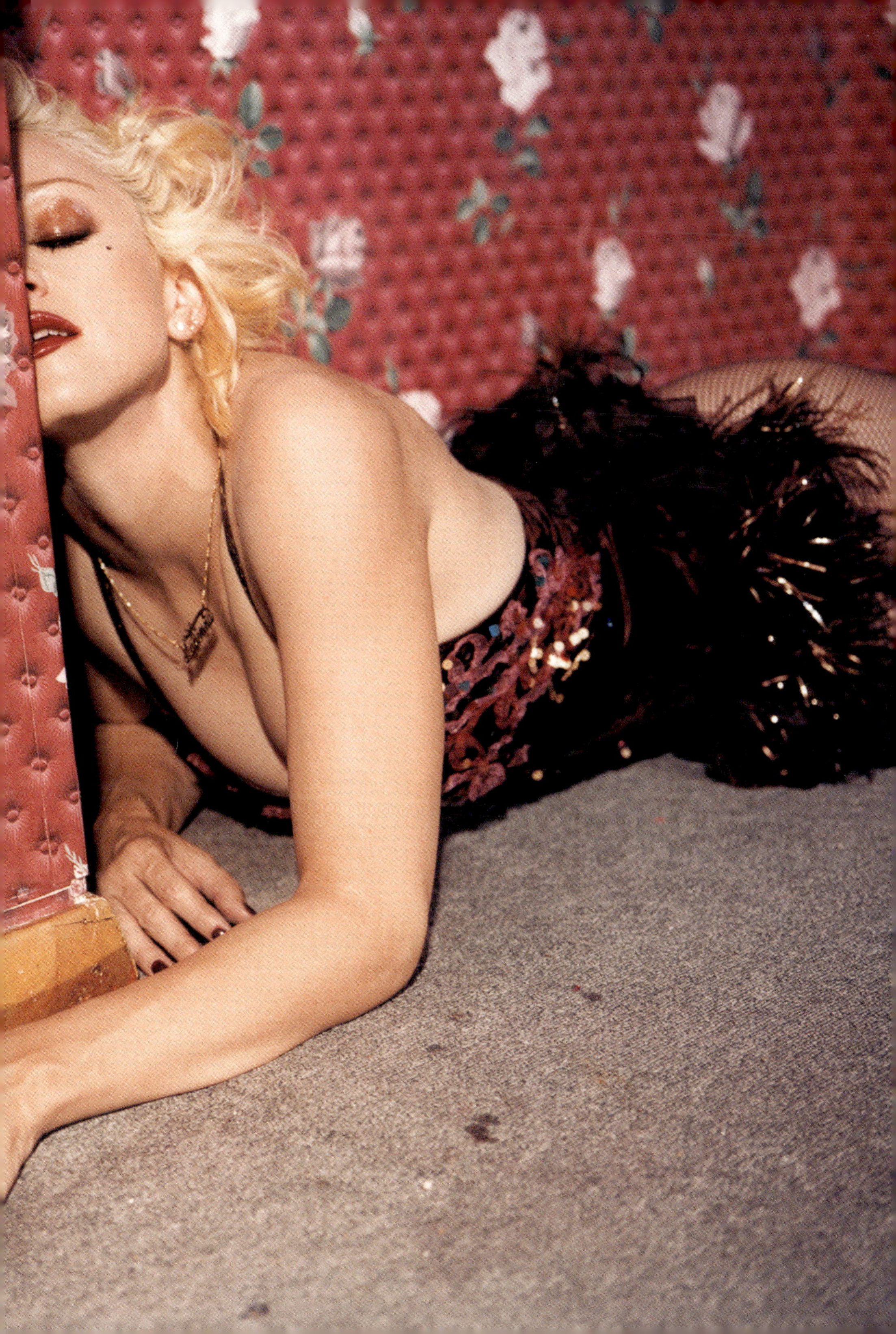

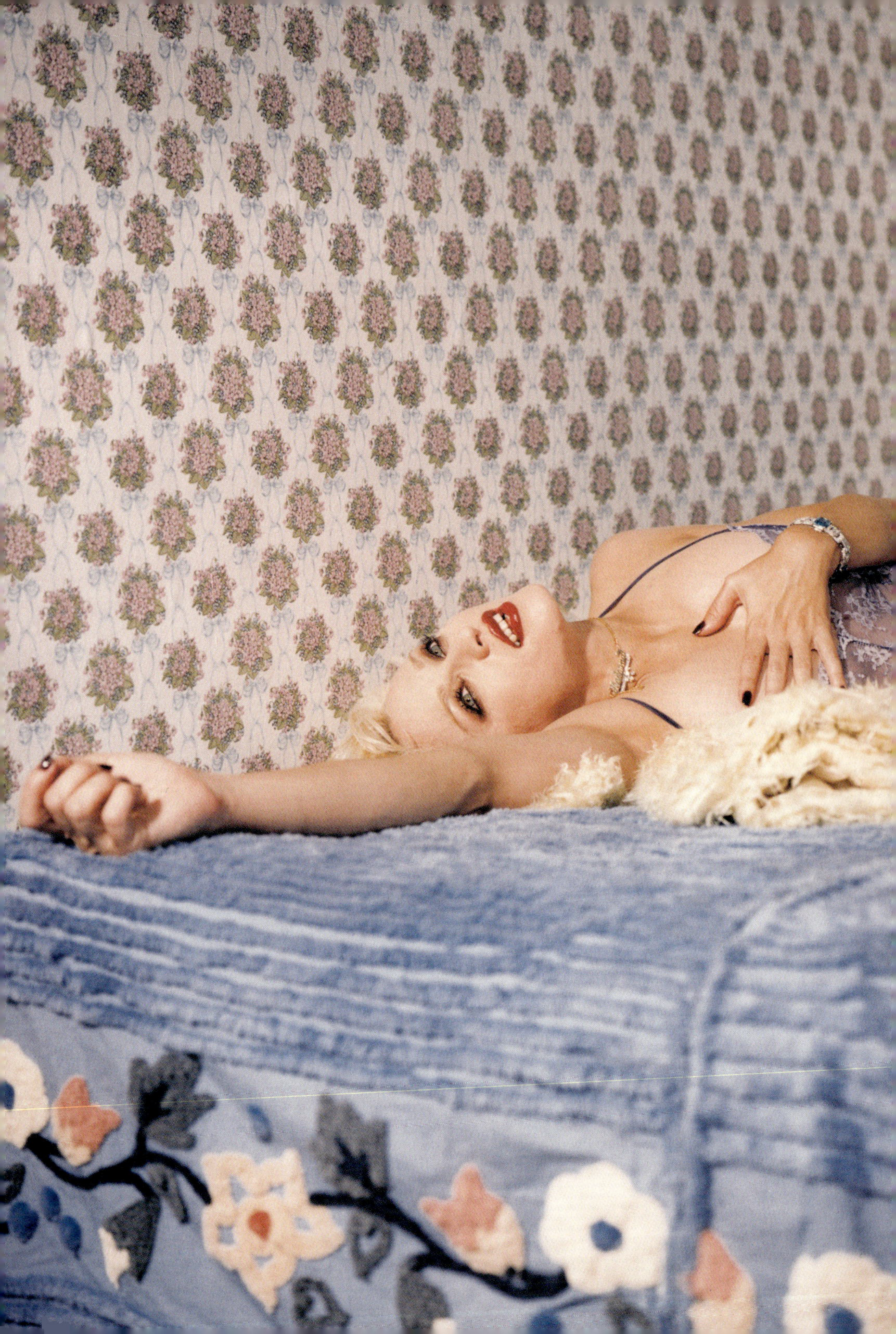

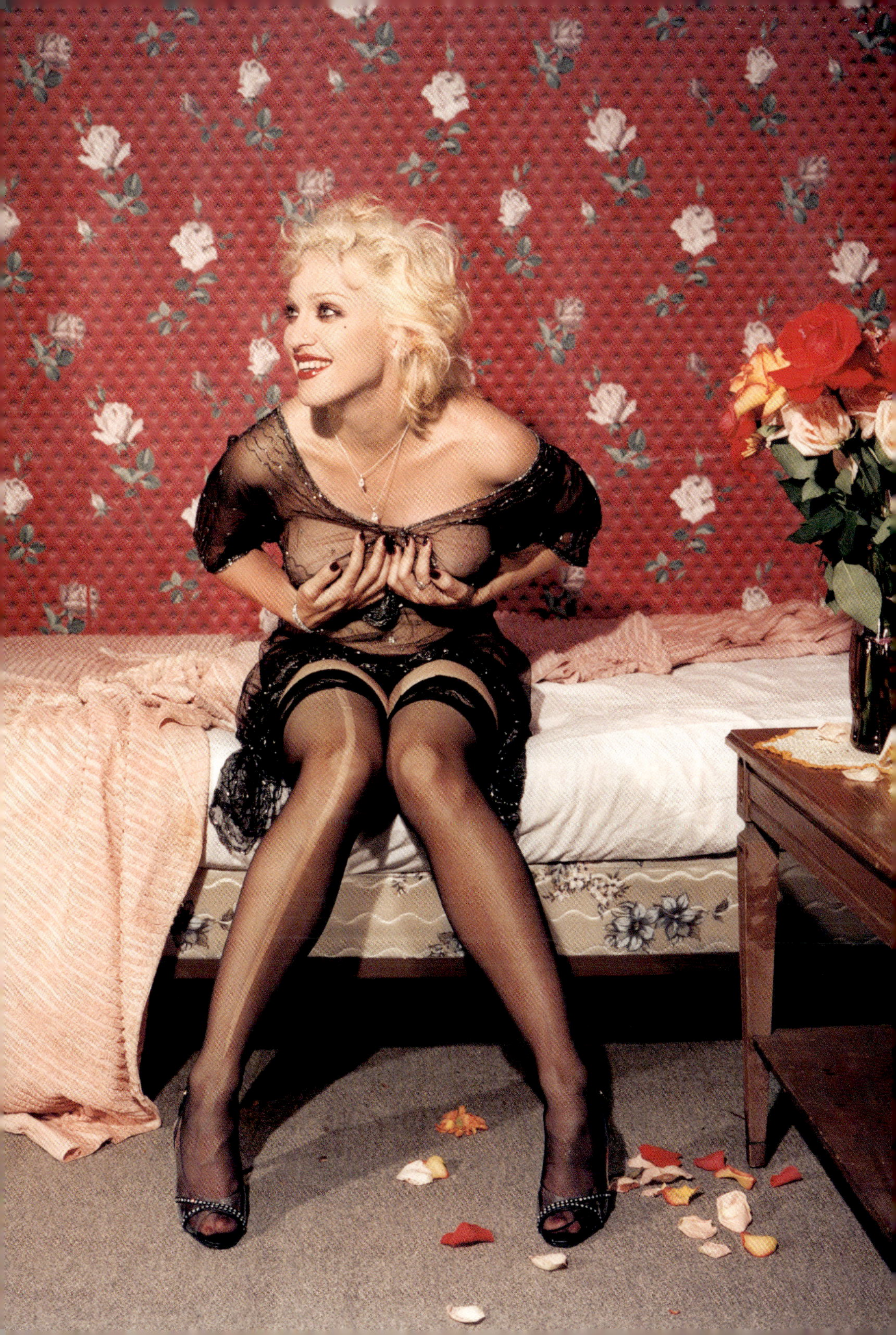

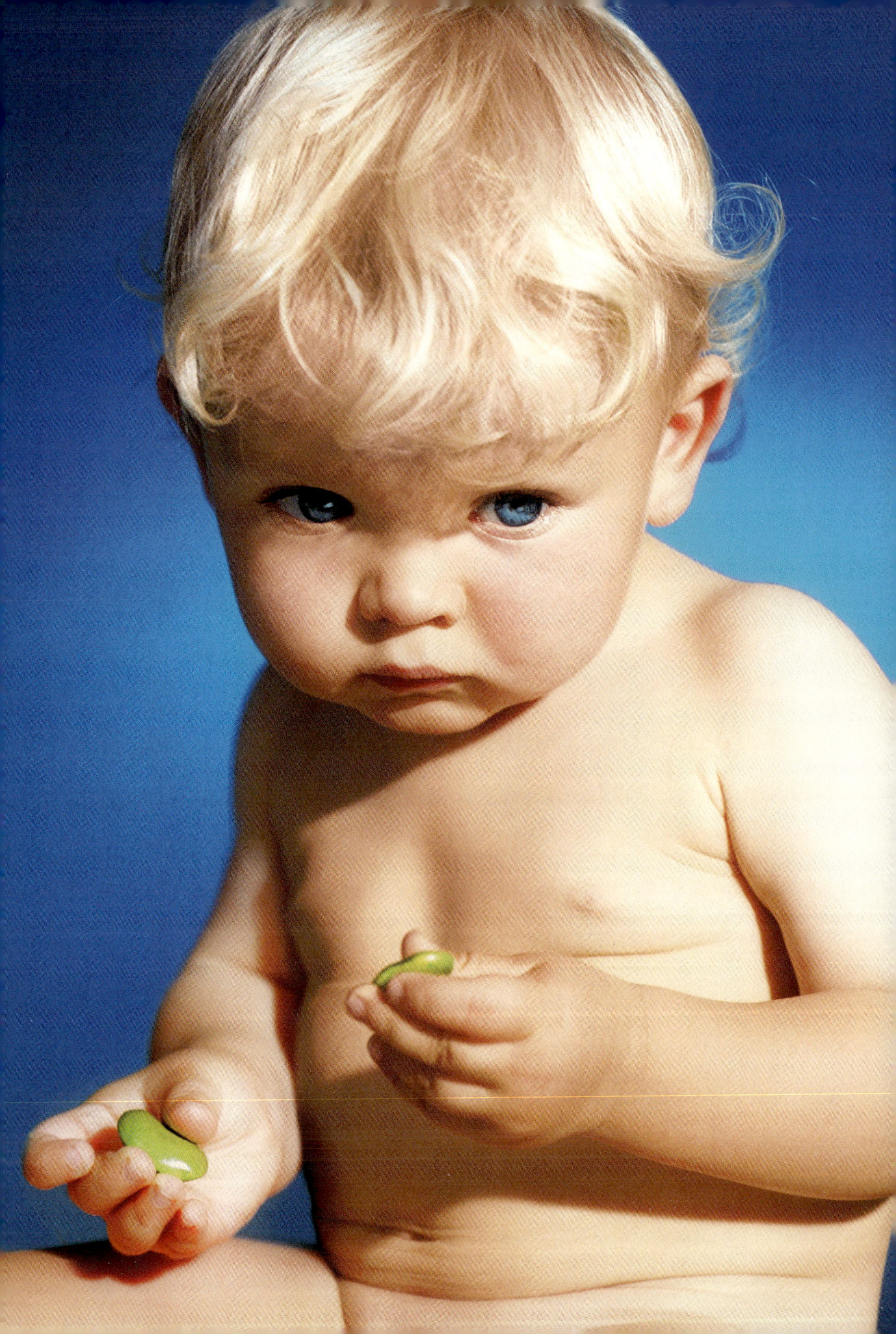

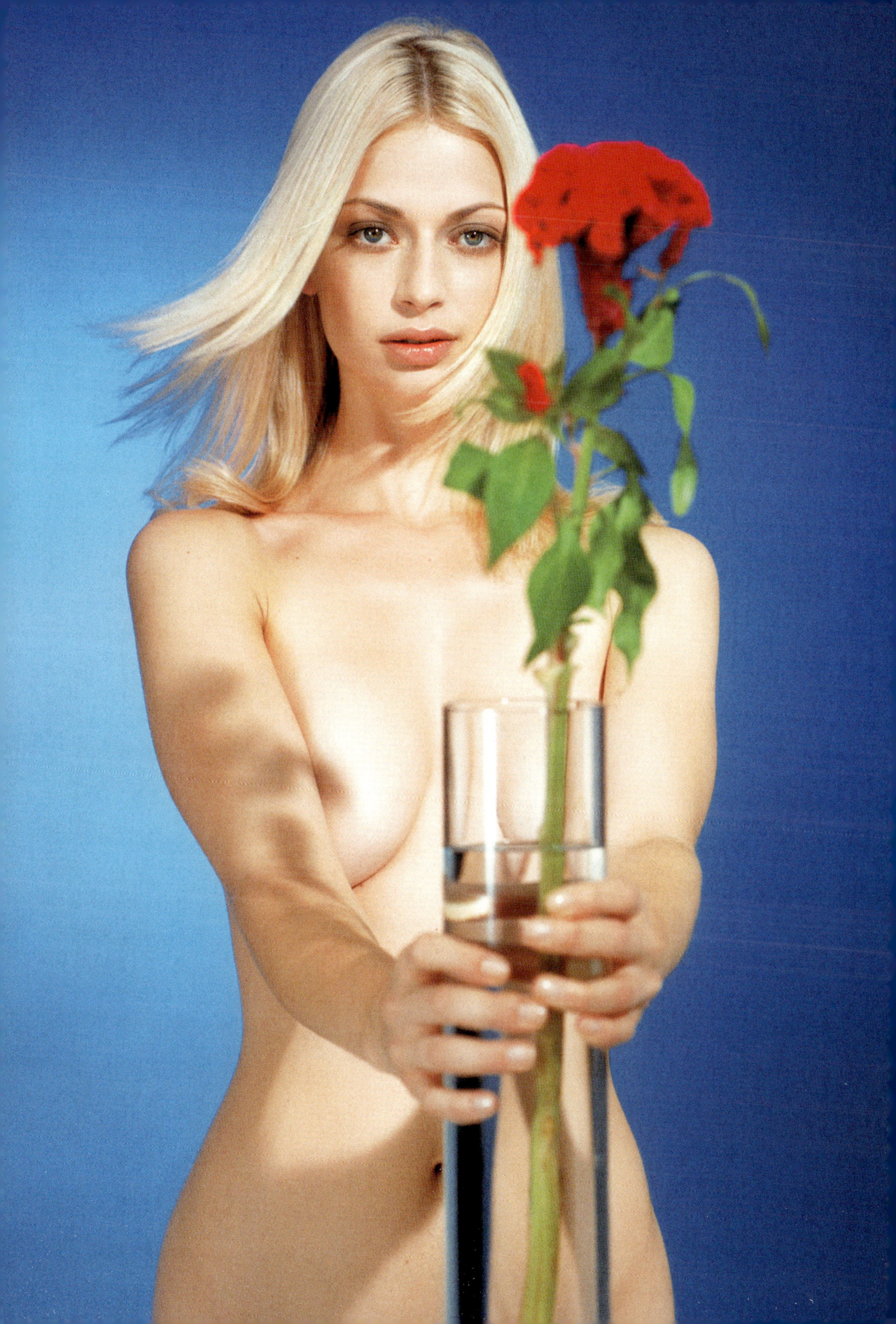

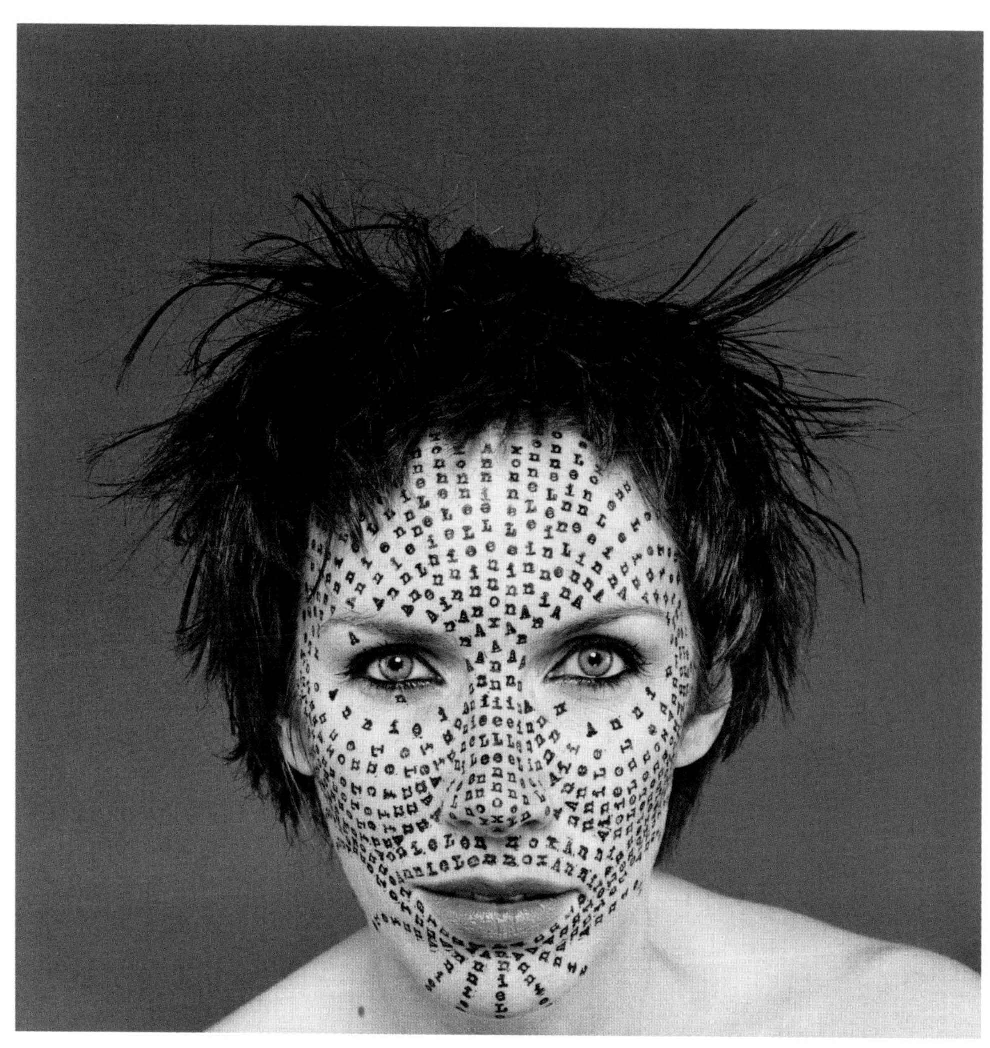

Above — *Annie Lennox, album cover for «Medusa»*, October 1994, London
Opposite page — *Lenny Kravitz III*, June 1991, Paris
Page 192 — *Unexpected views for Christie's*, 1992, Paris
Page 193 — *Serge Gainsbourg et Phify, son garde du corps*, 1982, Paris
Page 194 — *Faye Dunaway in «Arizona Dream»*, May 1991, Douglas, Arizona
Page 195 — *Karen Mulder de dos*, May 1994, Paris
Page 196 — *Milagros, portrait à la bougie*, October 2005, Paris
Page 197 — *Glenn Close dans «Liaisons dangereuses» II*, August 1988, Maisons-Laffitte

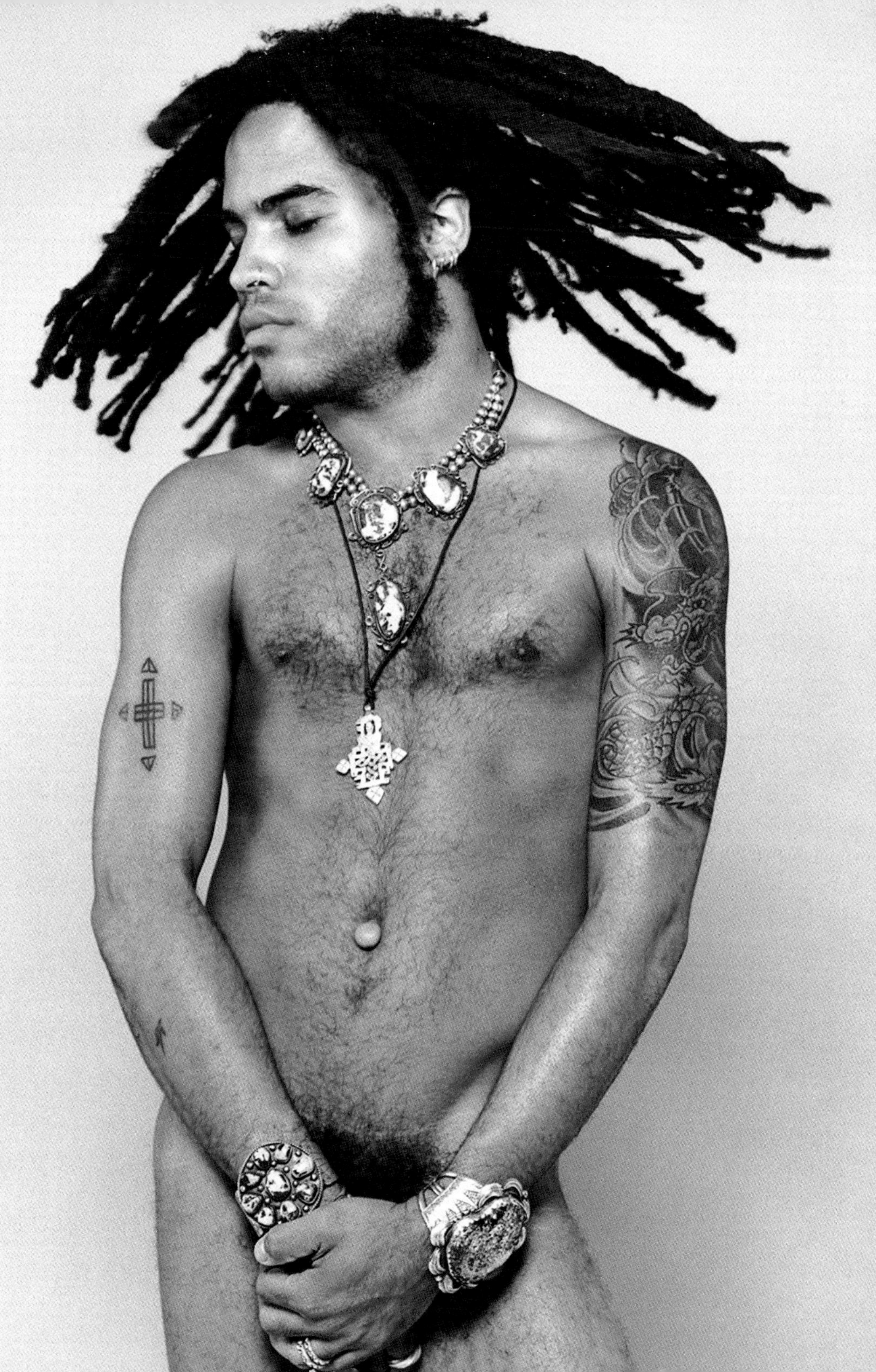

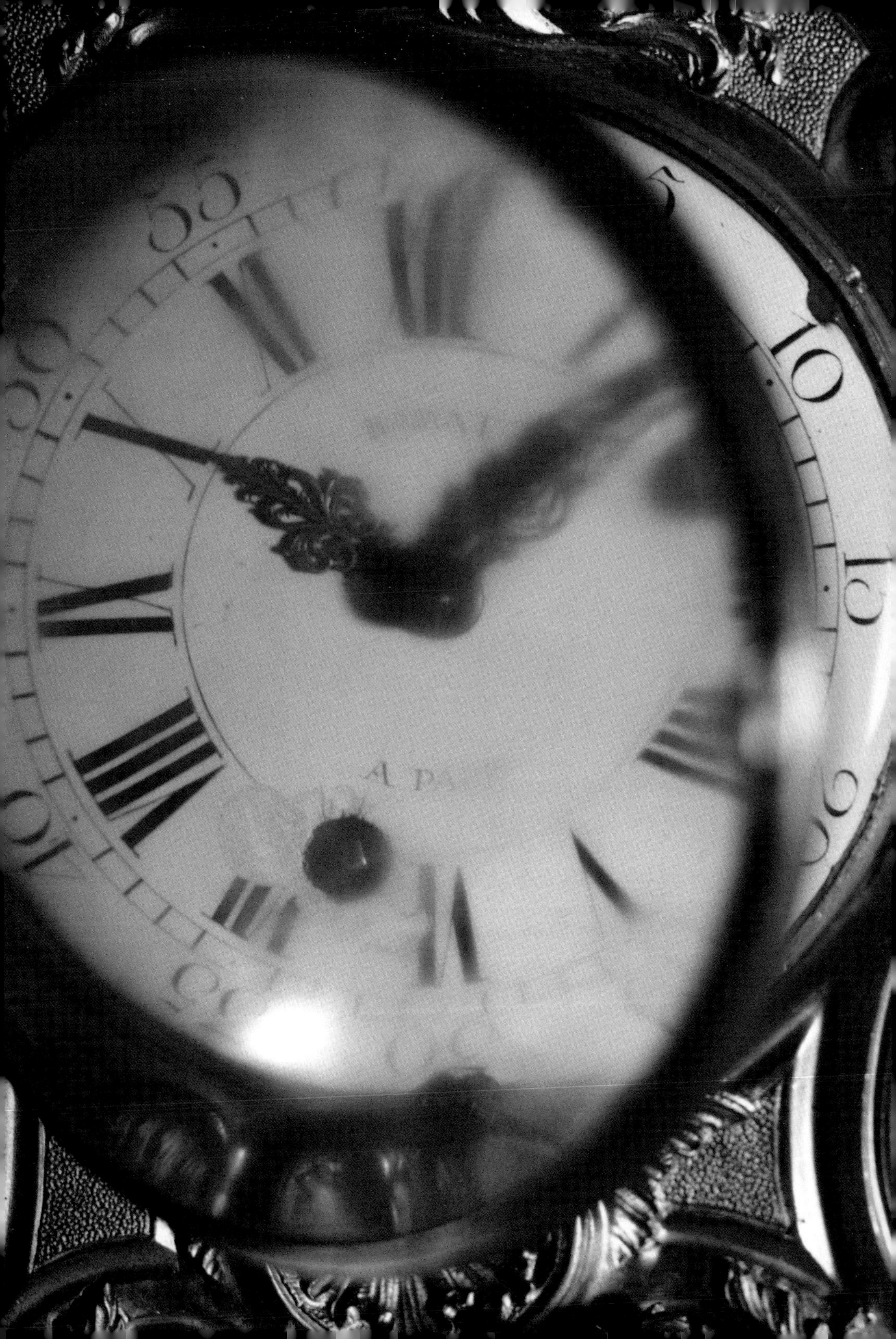

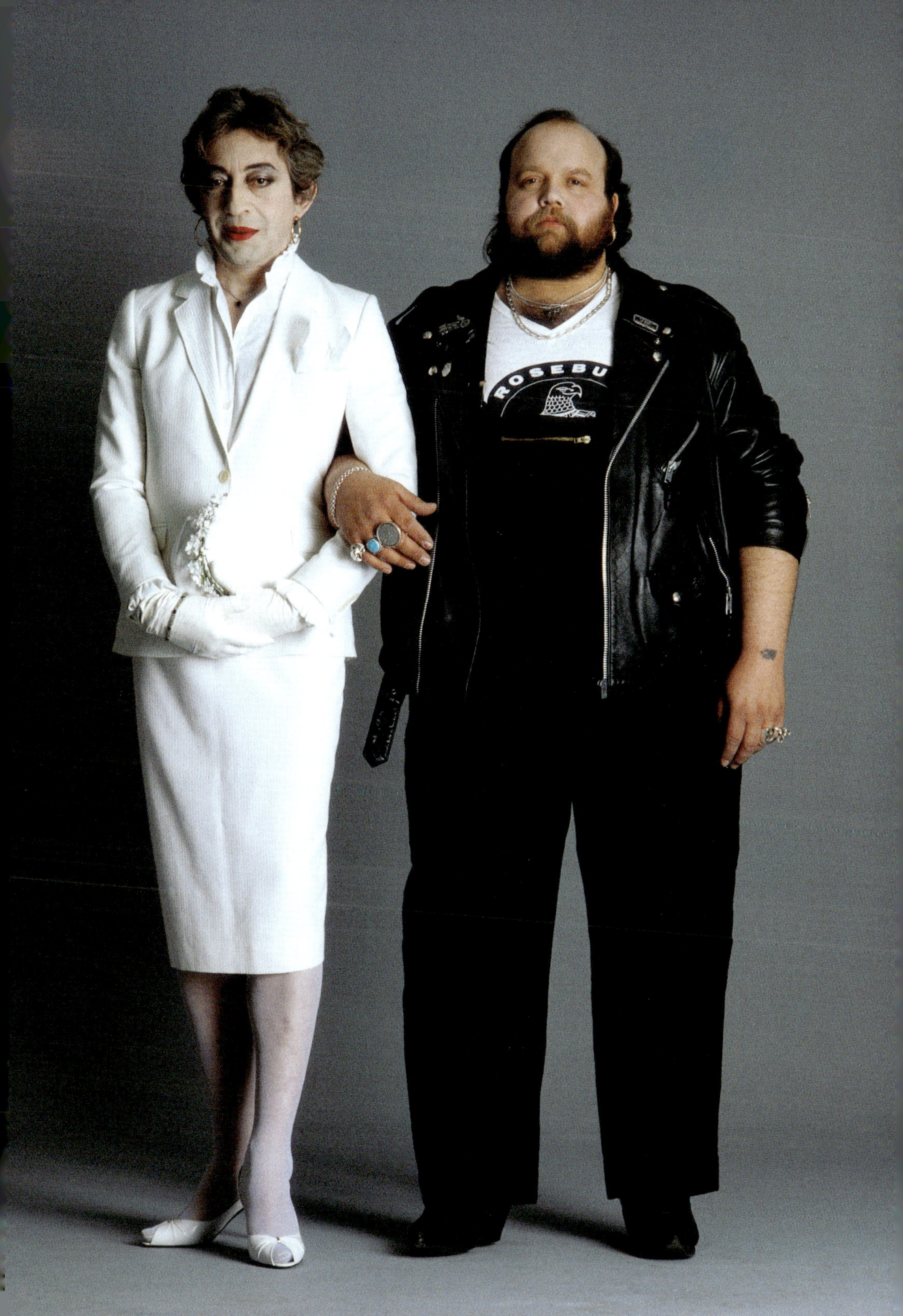
ROSEBU

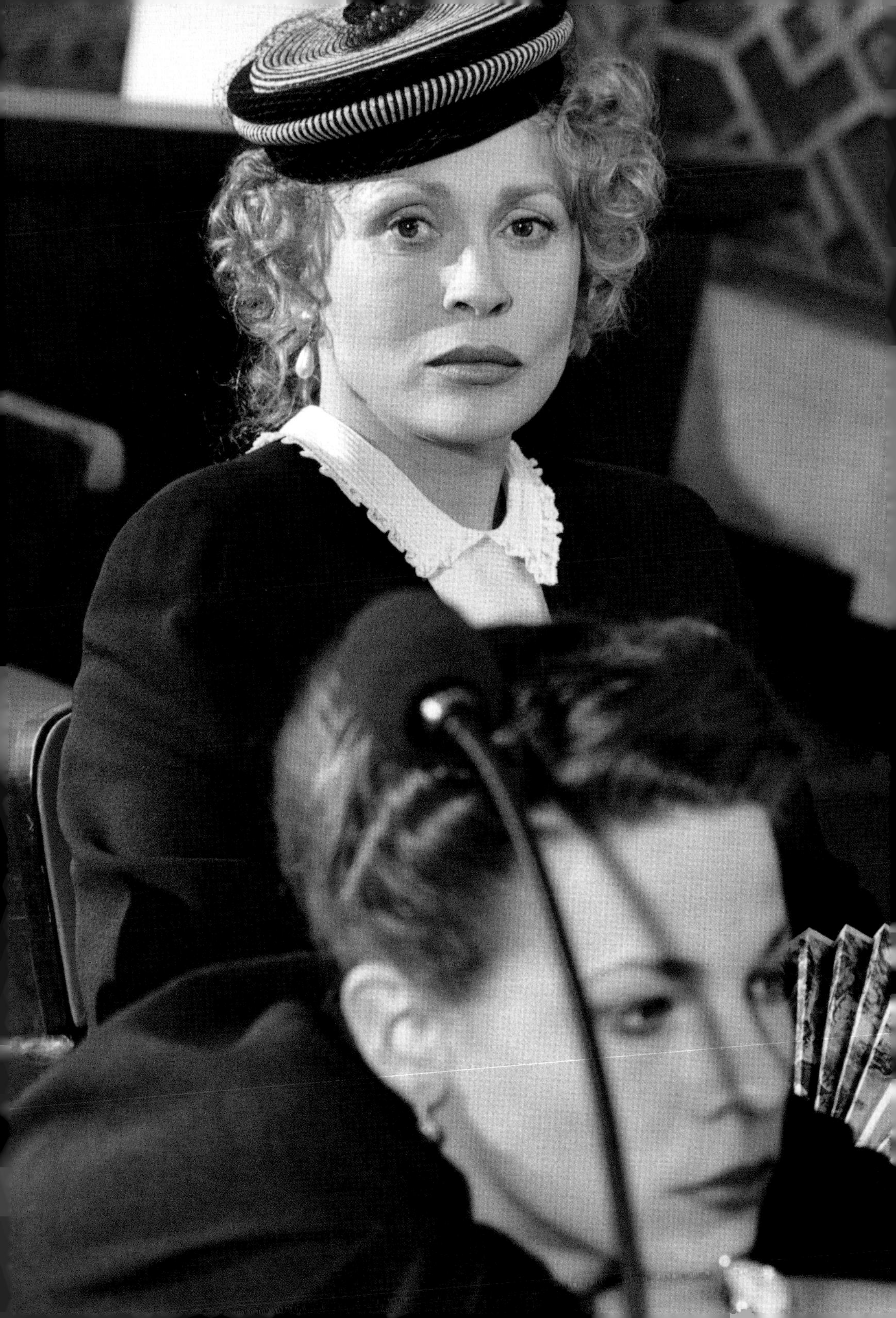

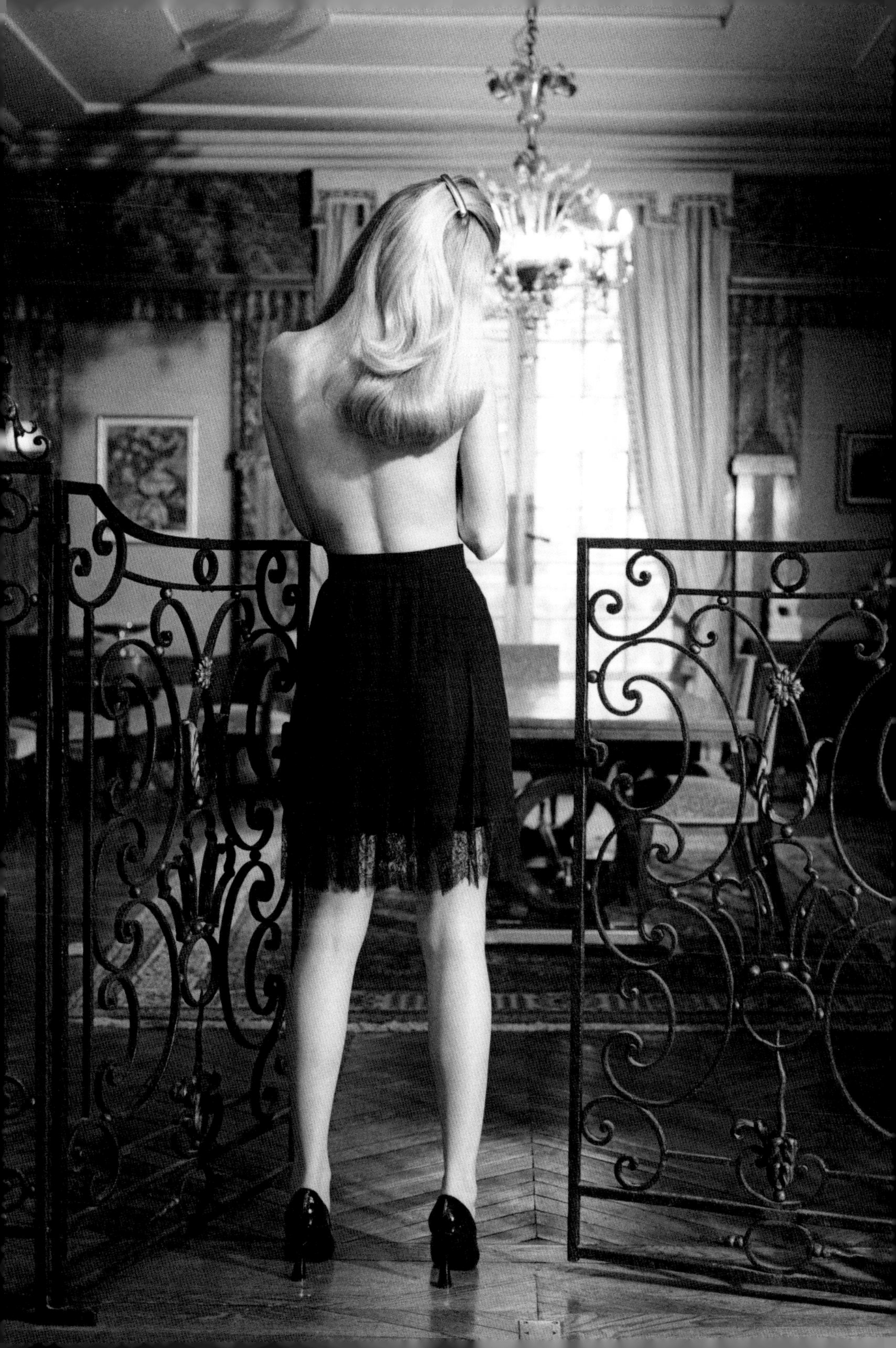

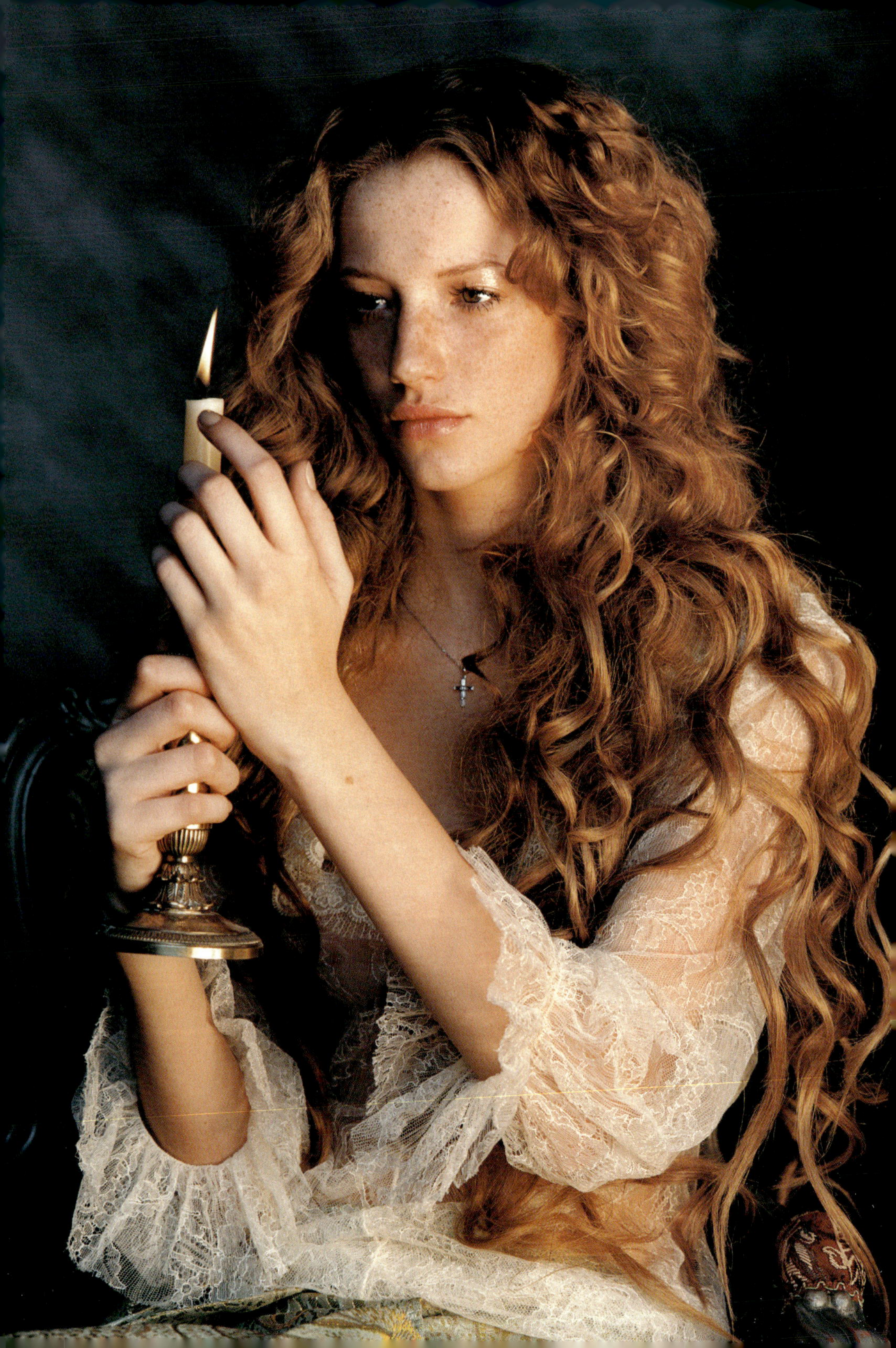

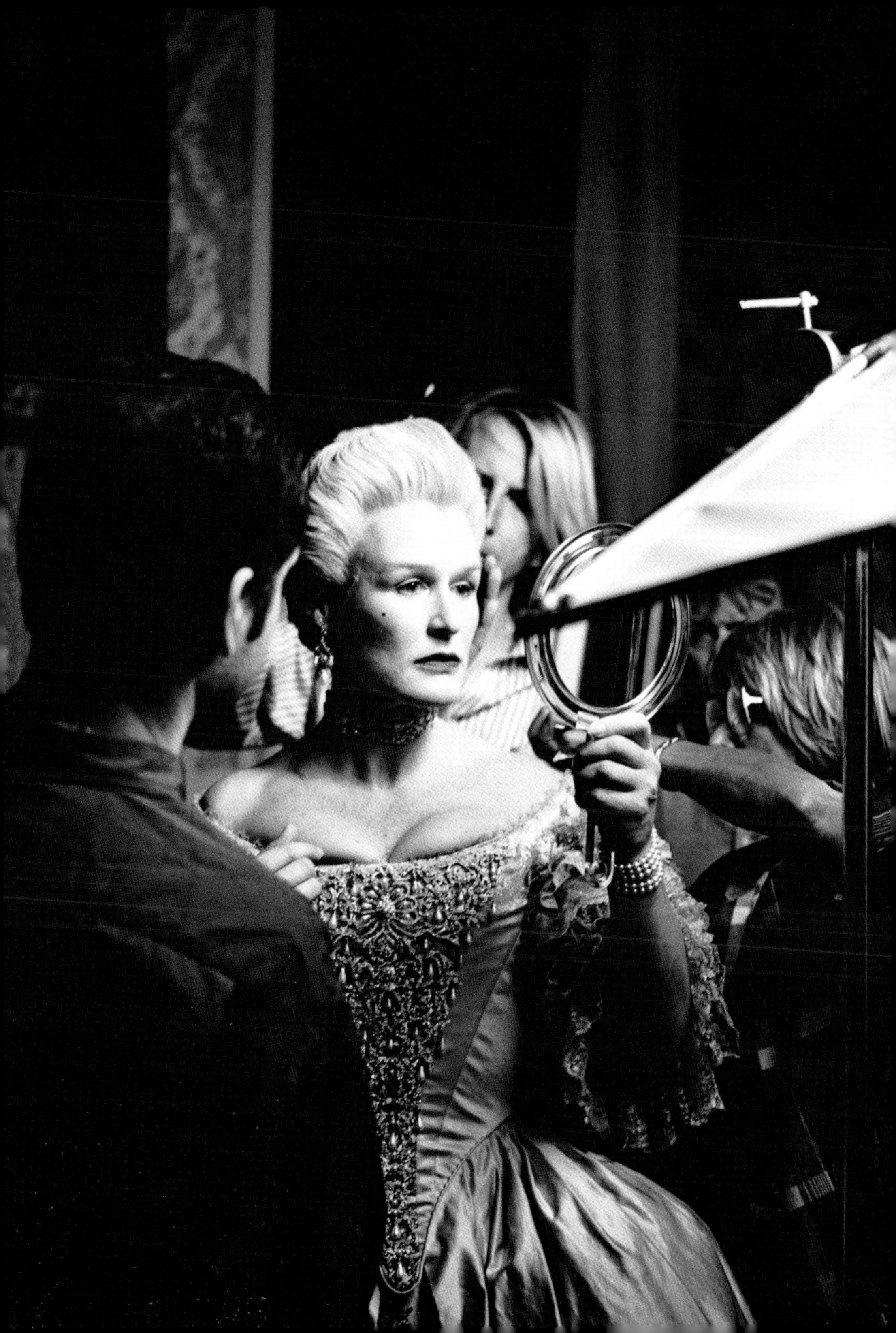

I.N.R.I.

IN COLLABORATION WITH SERGE BRAMLY
1997

With *I.N.R.I.*, we wanted to tell the life of Jesus Christ transposed today in the way frescoes were done on the walls of churches. So we not only had to change register but move to a higher one; to put the narration into the photographs; above all to try and understand that mysterious mechanism by which images become icons.

Nous avons voulu avec *I.N.R.I.*, raconter à la manière d'un cycle de fresques la vie de Jésus transposée de nos jours. Là, il ne s'agissait pas seulement de changer de registre, mais de passer à un registre supérieur; d'introduire la narration dans la photographie; d'essayer surtout d'approcher la mécanique mystérieuse par quoi l'image devient icône.

Mit *I.N.R.I.* wollten wir das Leben Jesu – in die Jetztzeit übertragen – im Stil eines Freskenzyklus erzählen. Dabei mussten wir nicht nur einen neuen Ton anschlagen, sondern auch das Erzählerische in die Fotografie einführen und vor allem versuchen, uns diesem geheimnisvollen Mechanismus anzunähern, der ein Bild zur Ikone werden lässt.

Serge Bramly, in *Rétrospective*, 2004

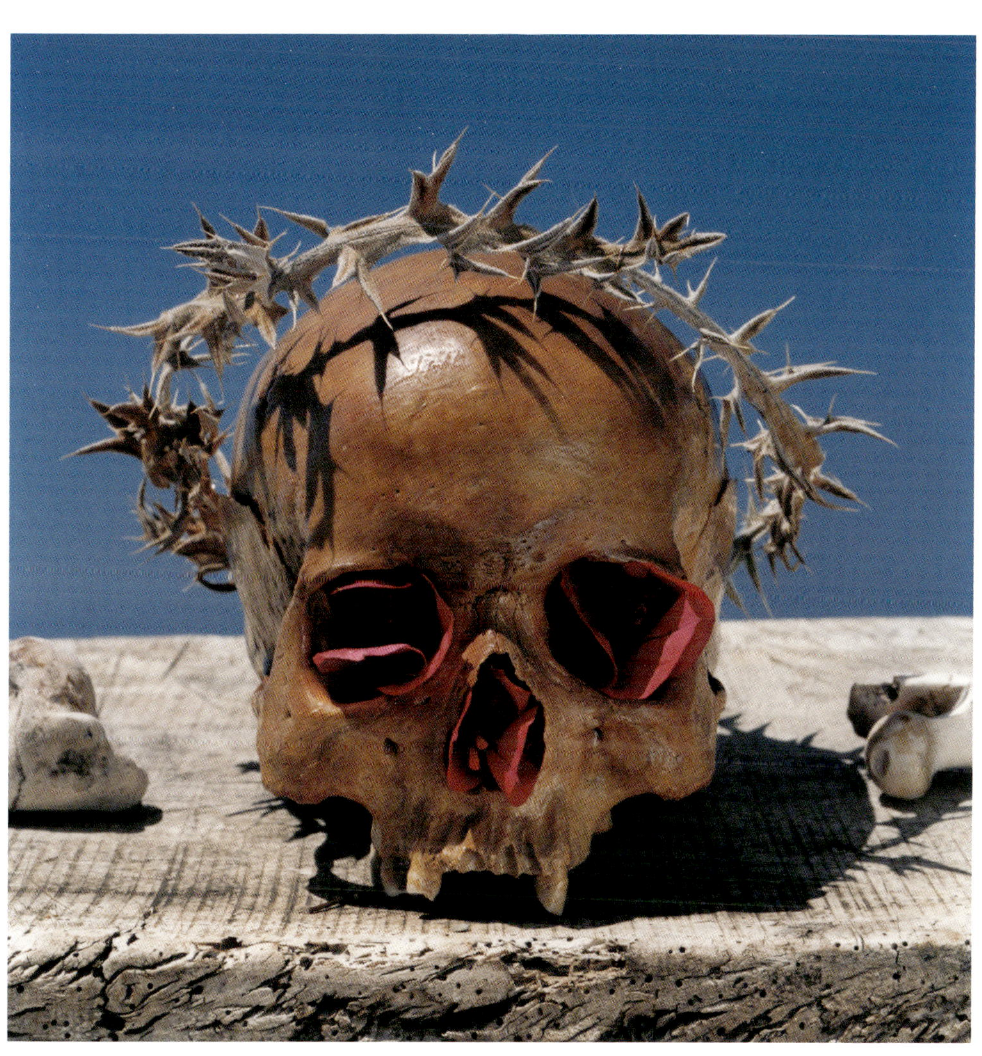

Memento Mori, June 1997, Majorca
Pages 200/201 – *Nativité*, April 1997, Ville-Évrard
Pages 202/203 – *La maison de Nazareth*, April 1997, Ville-Évrard

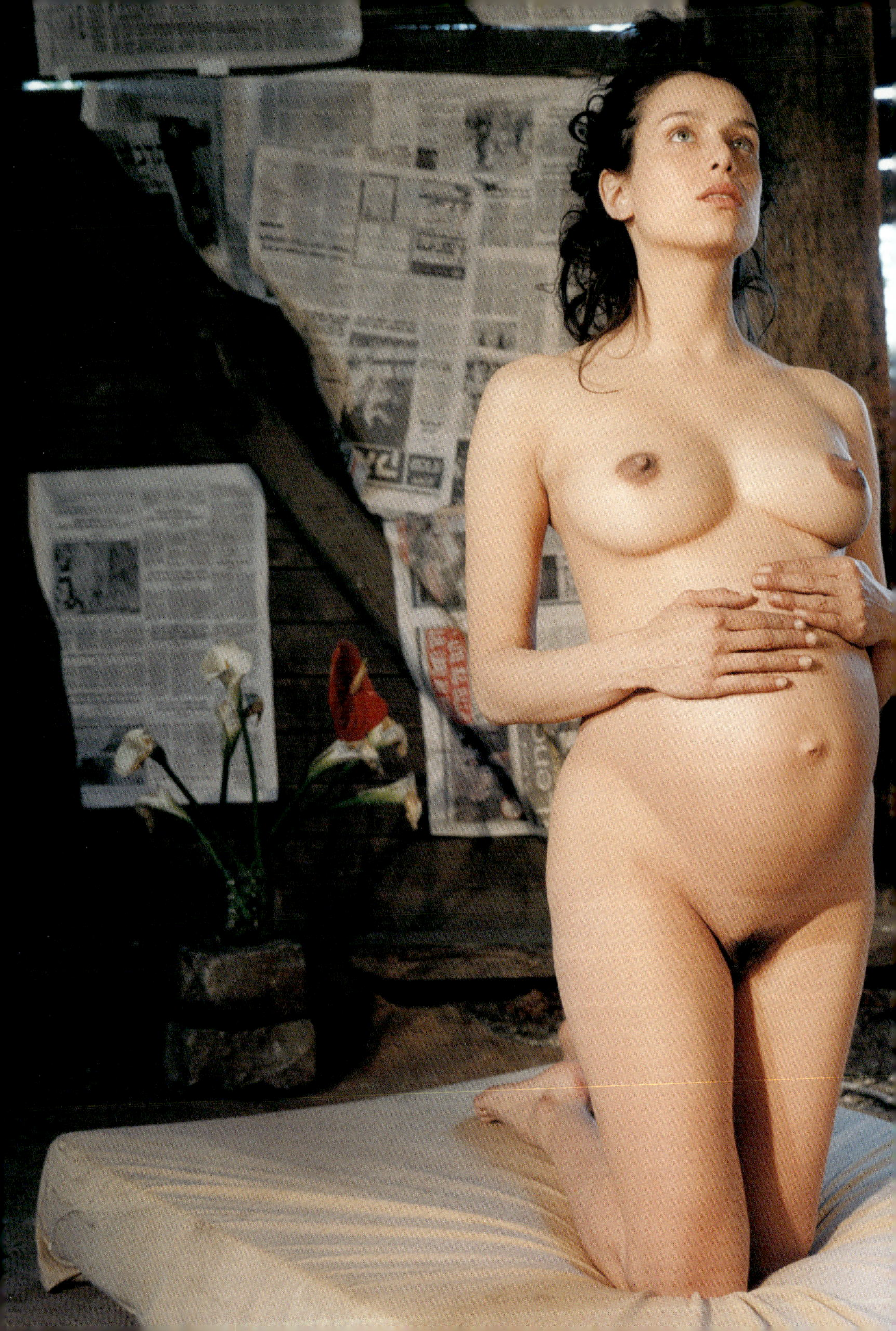

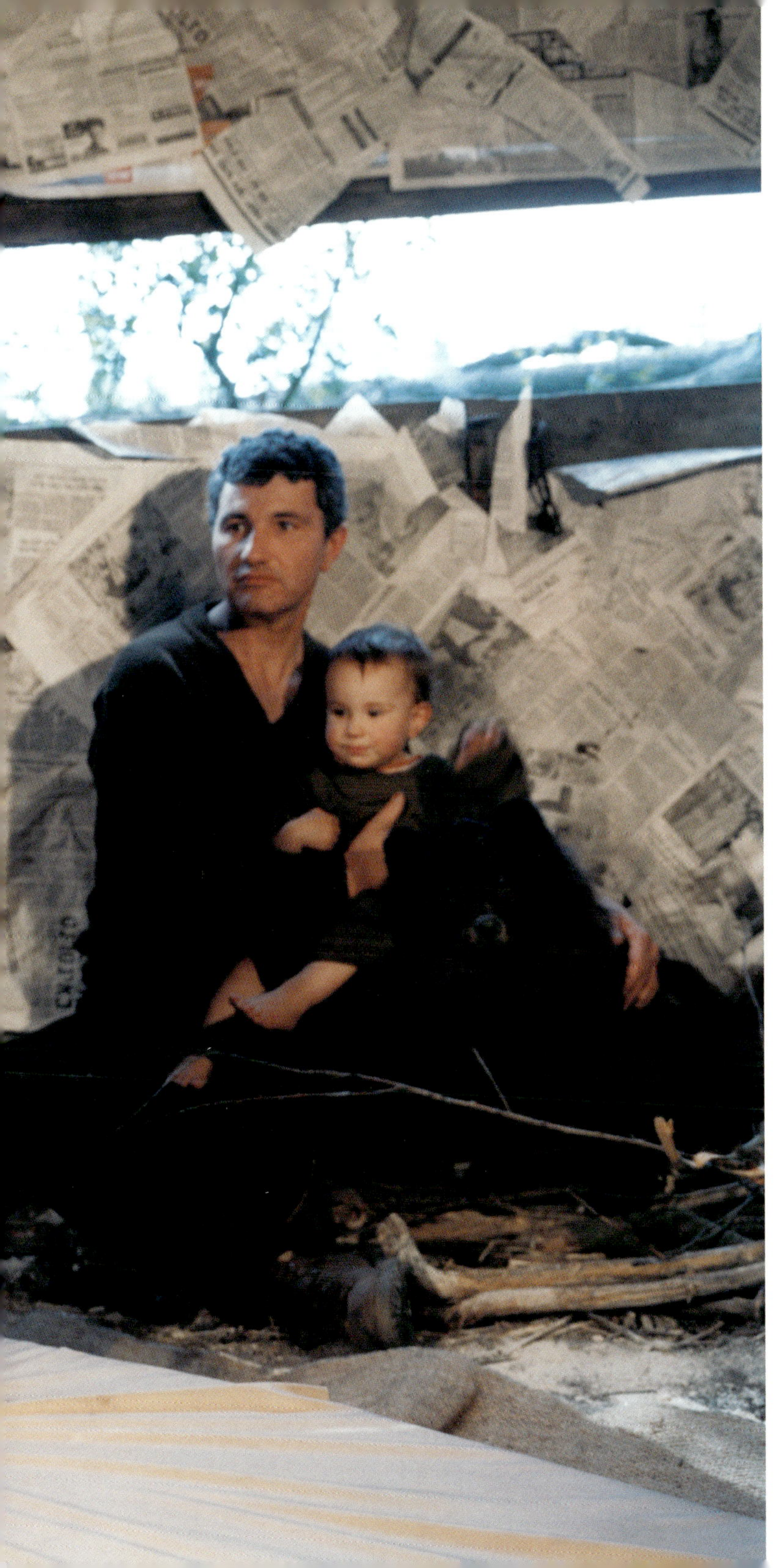

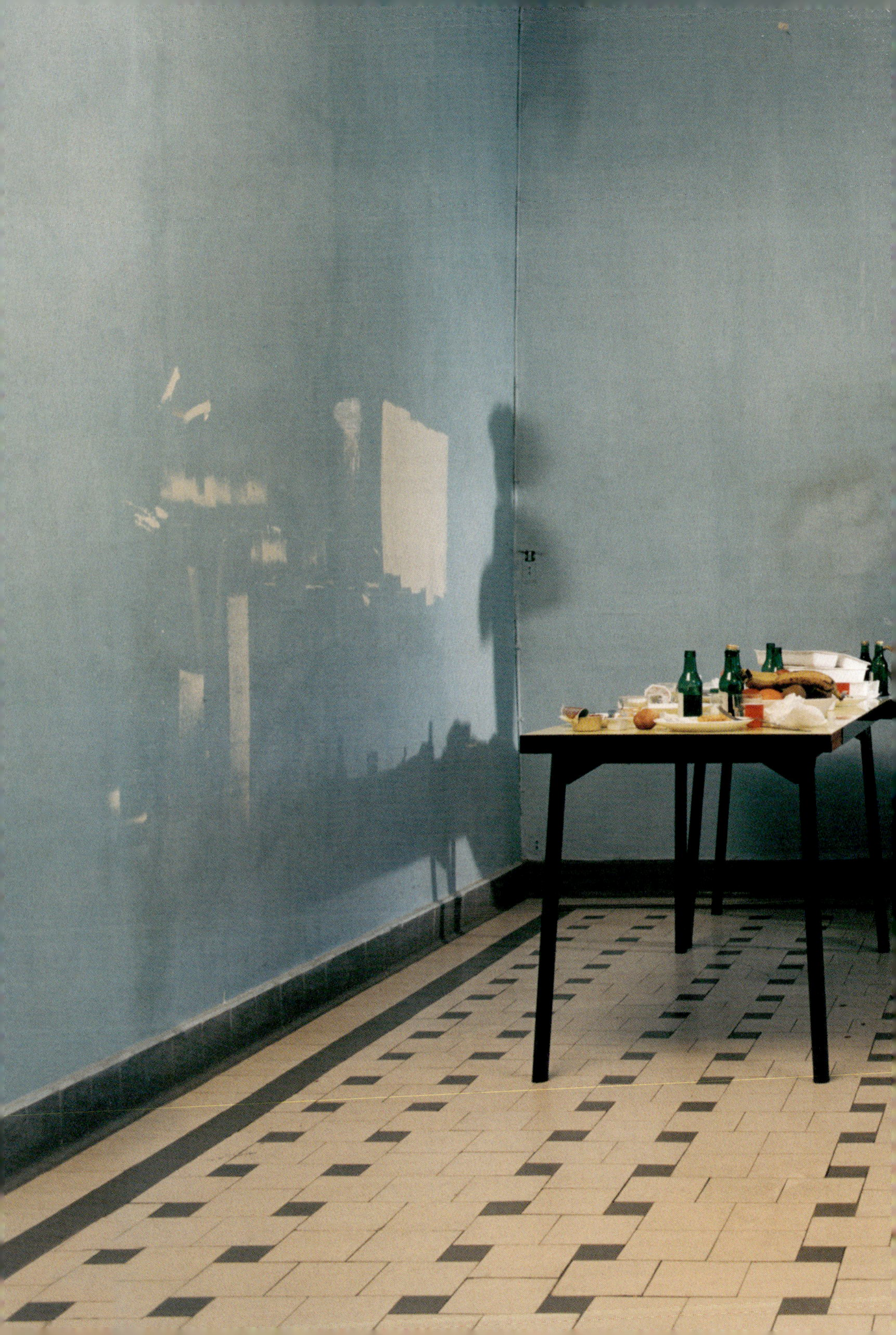

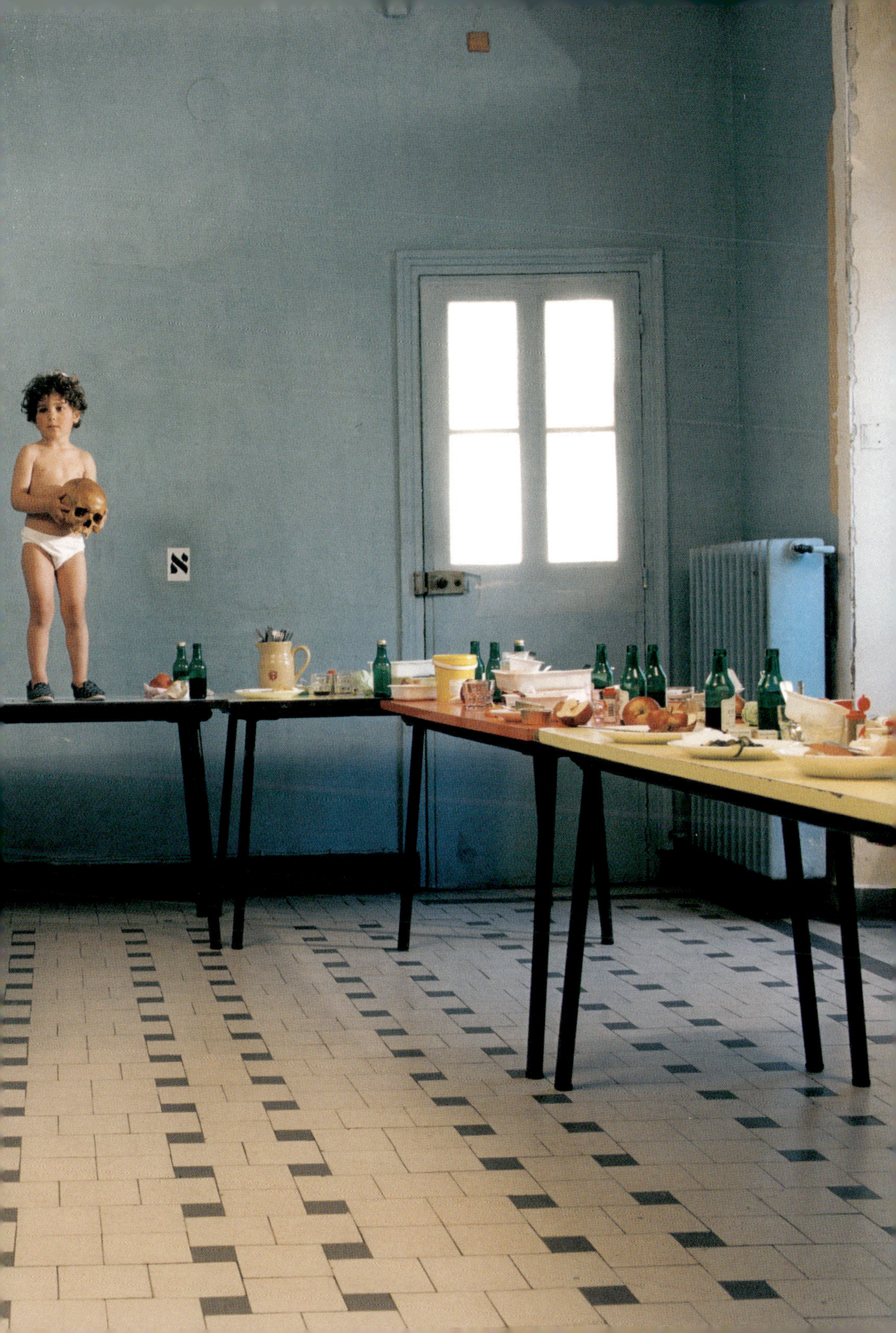

**The source of our project lies in the memory or presentiment
of such images: modern icons. (...)
To recompose such scenes, visions or "apparitions", such was the
goal that we had set ourselves.**

À l'origine de notre projet, il y a le souvenir, ou le pressentiment,
de telles images: des icônes modernes. (...)
Recomposer de telles scènes, visions ou «apparitions», voici le but
que nous nous sommes fixé.

Am Anfang unseres Projekts steht die Erinnerung, oder die Vorahnung
solcher Bilder: moderne Ikonen. (...)
Solche Szenen, Visionen oder „Erscheinungen" neu zu komponieren,
das war es, was wir uns vorgenommen hatten.

Serge Bramly, in *I.N.R.I.*, 1998

Le Festin d'Hérode II, April 1997, Ville-Évrard
Following double page — *La Cène*, May 1997, Ville-Évrard

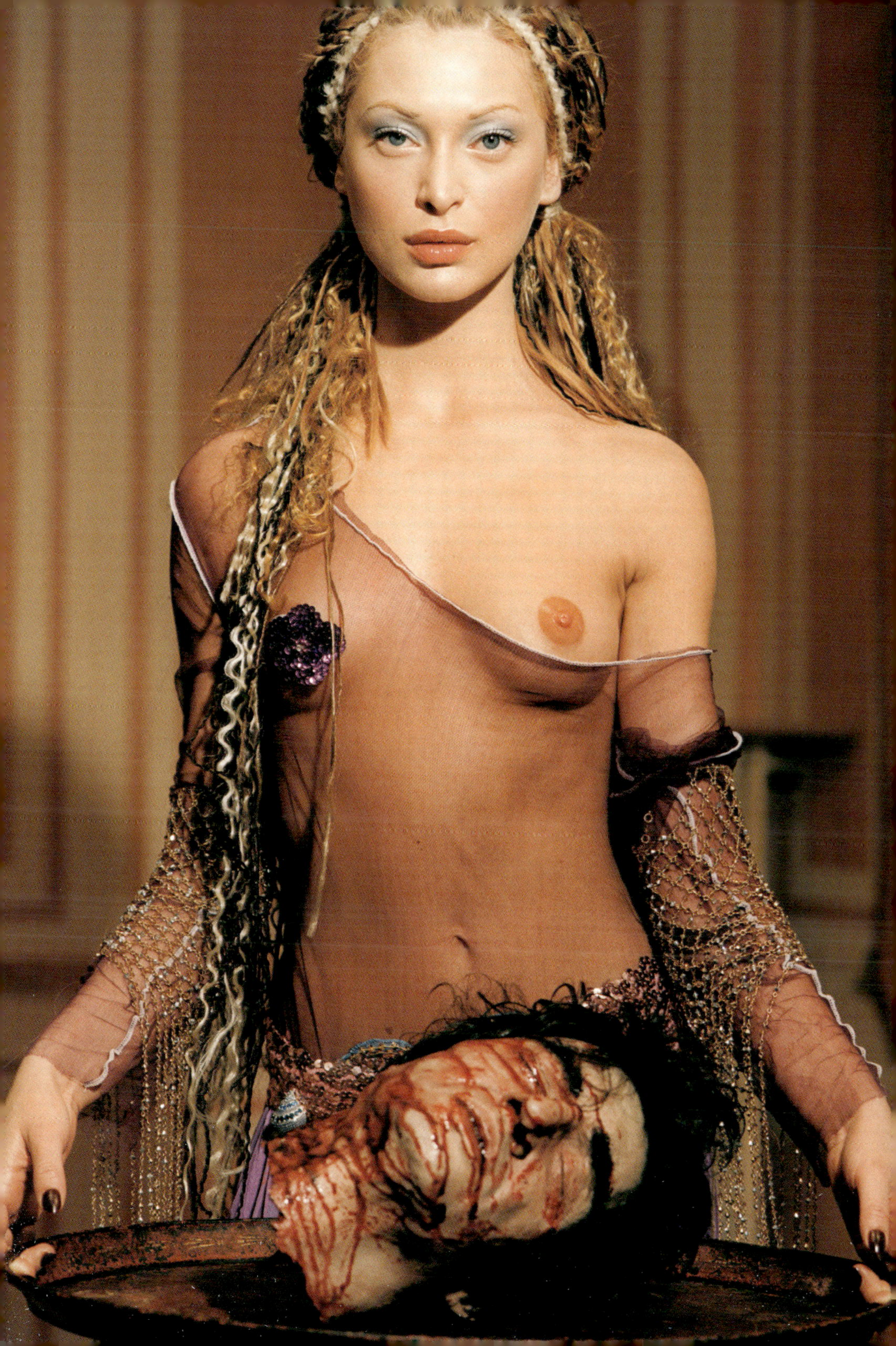

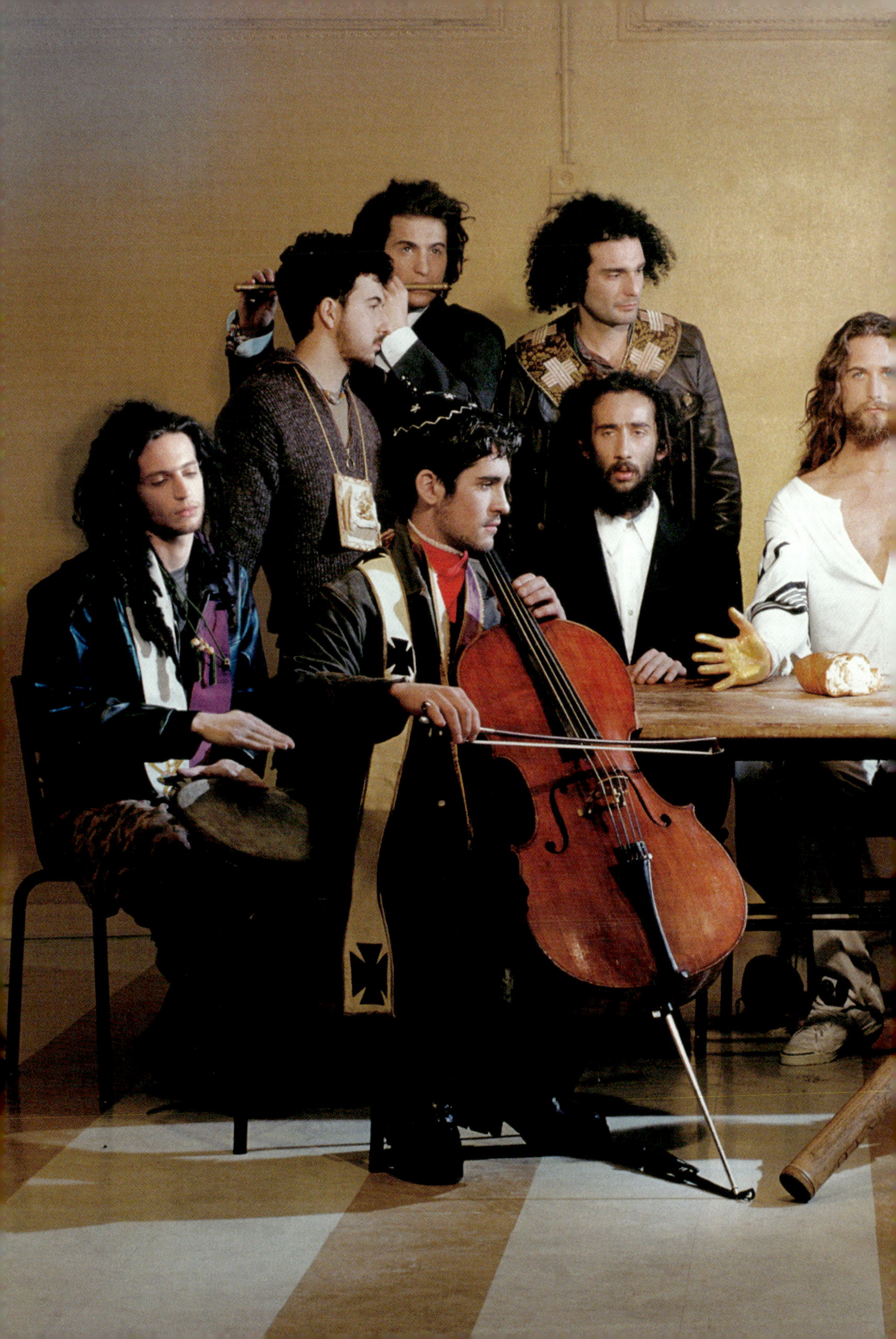

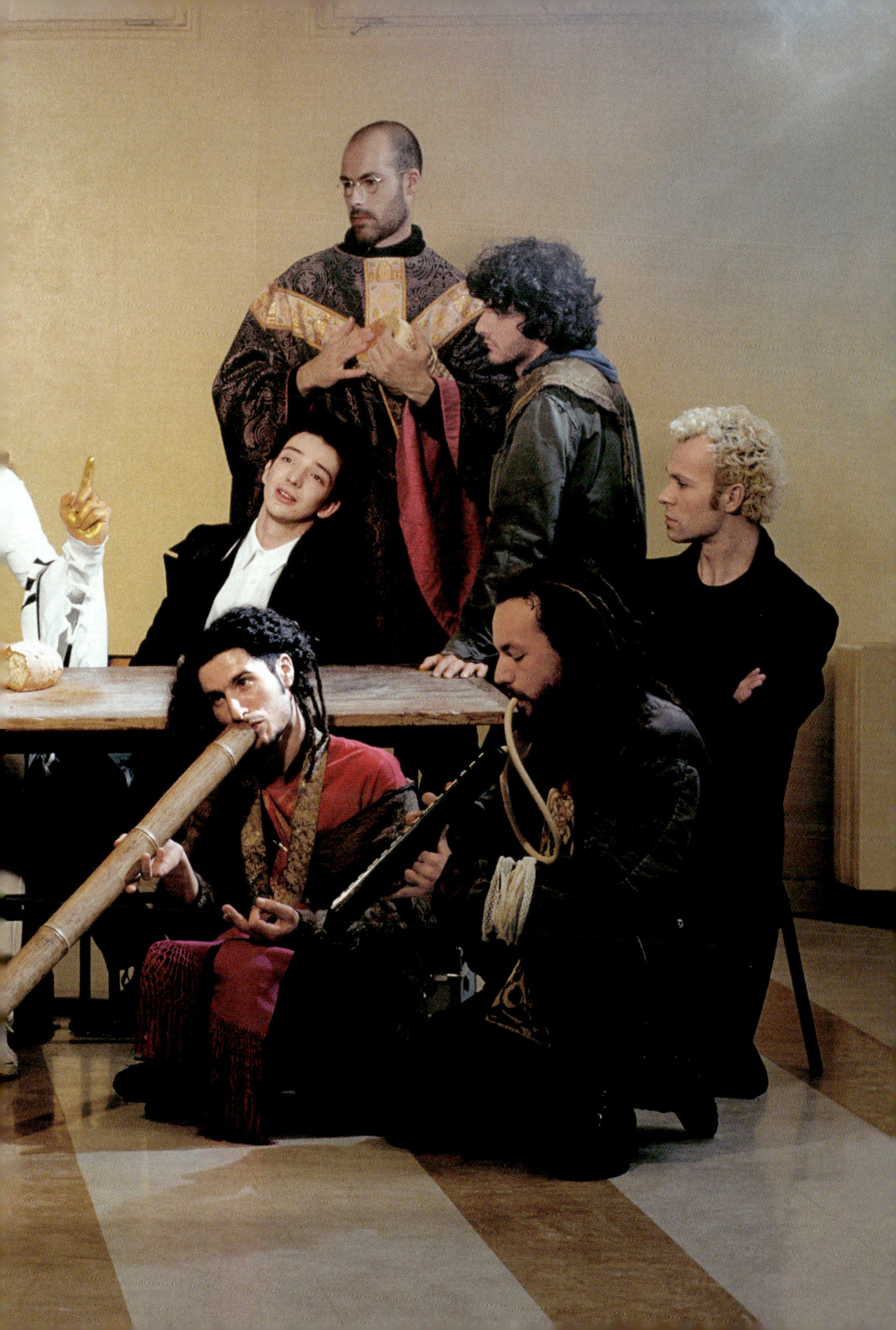

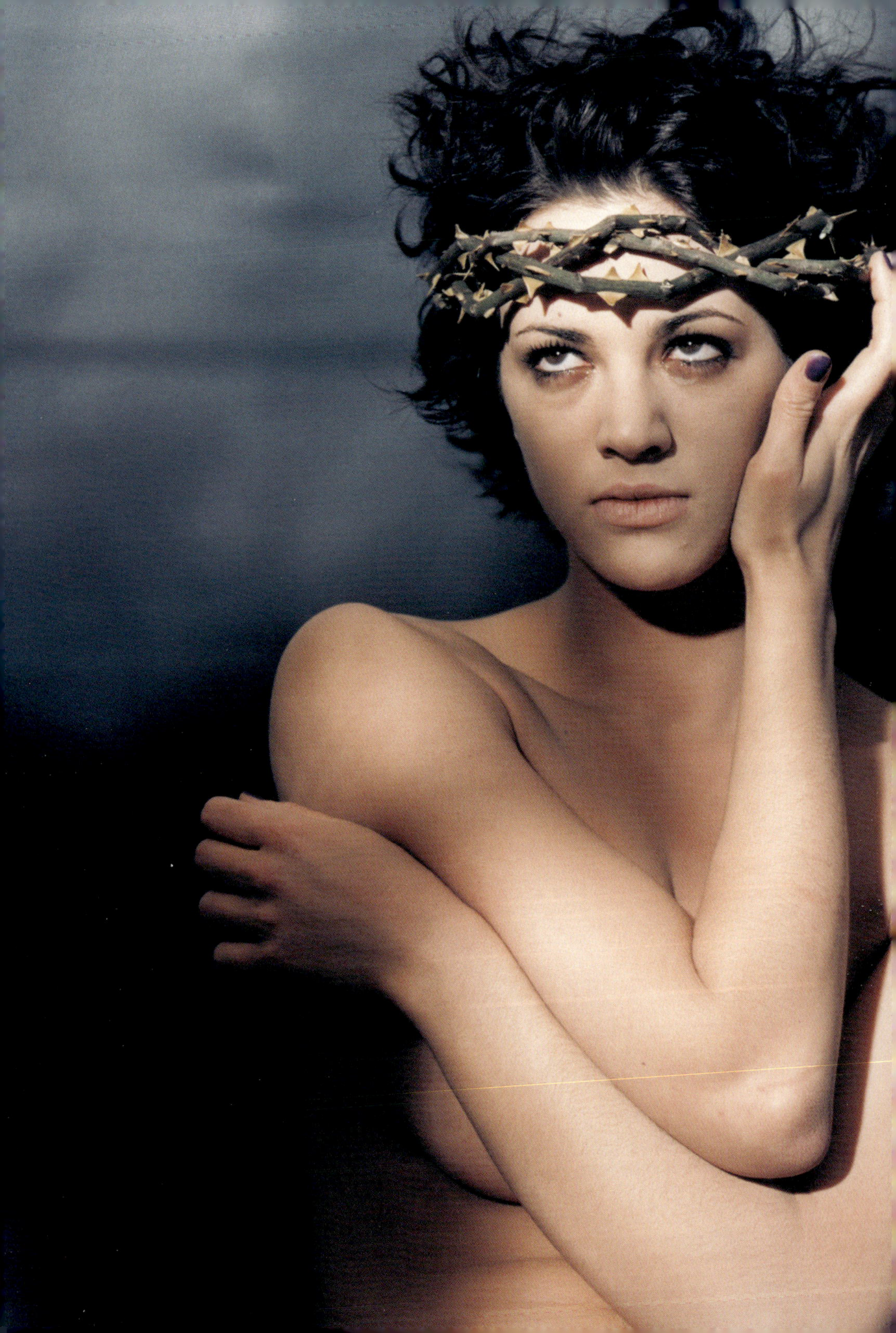

Mater Dolorosa, May 1997, Ville-Évrard

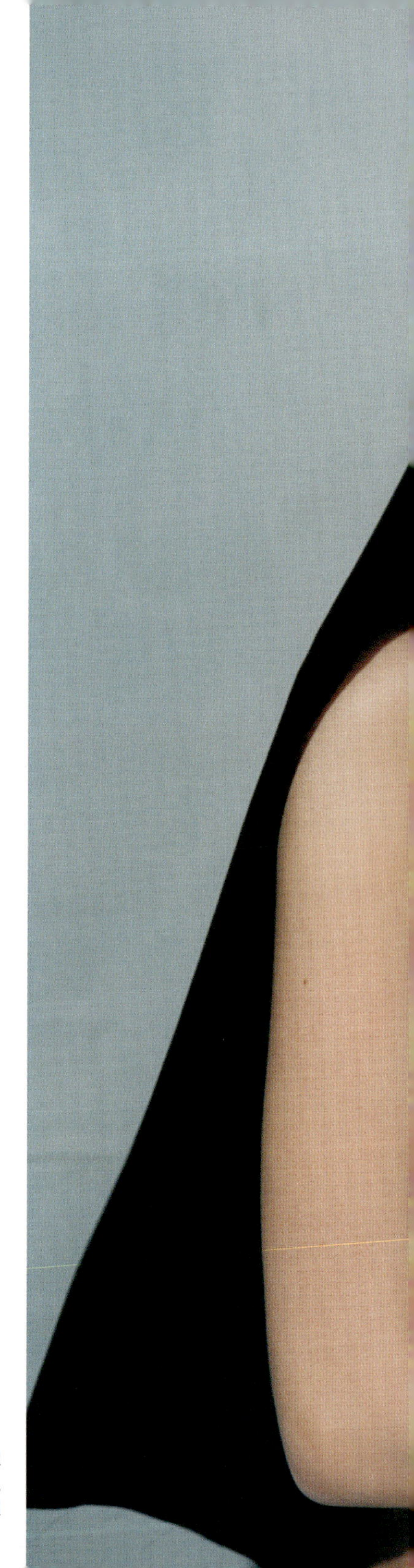

Le Lait miraculeux de la Vierge, March 1997, Ville-Évrard
Following double page — *Crucifixion I, II, III*,
March 1997, Ville-Évrard

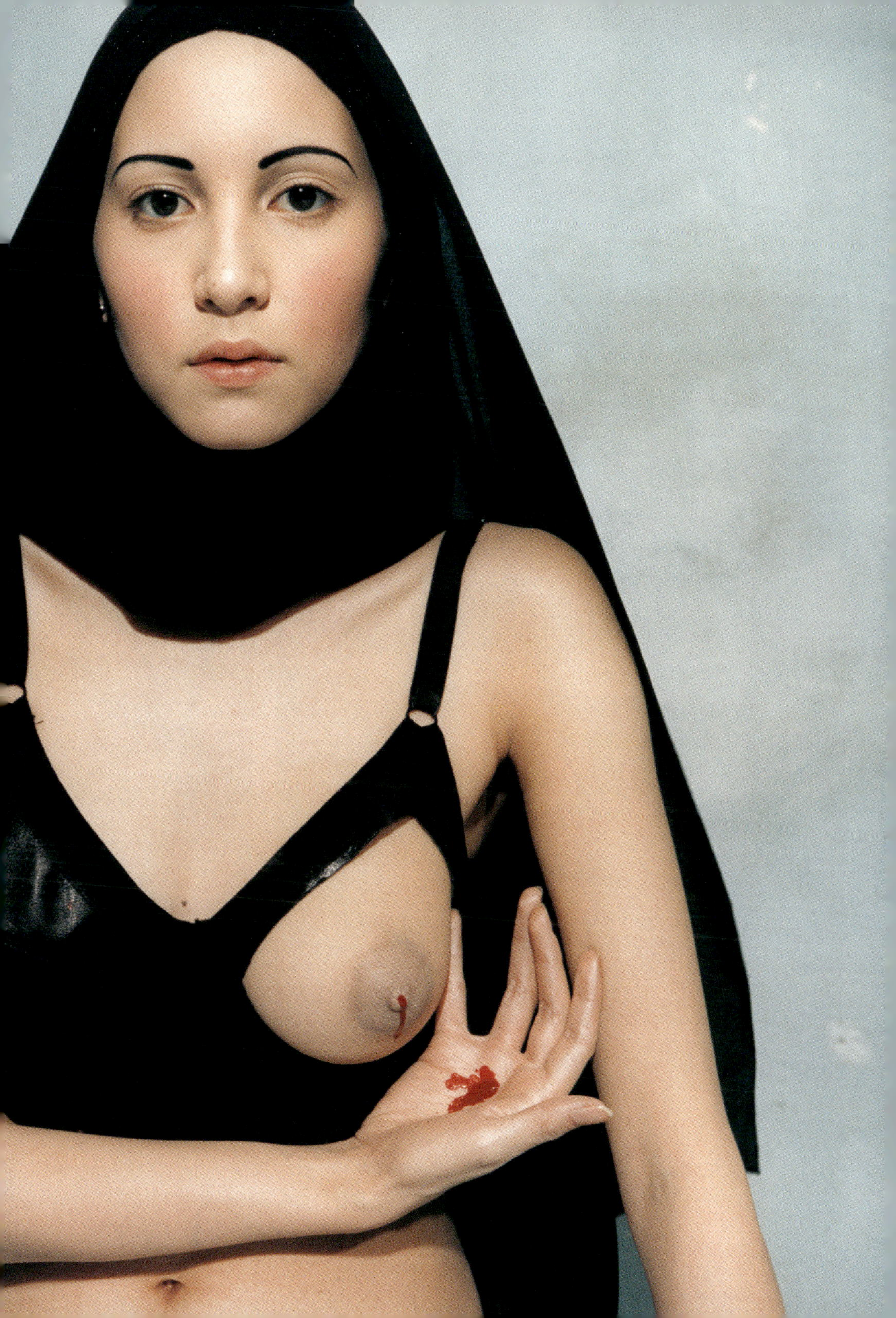

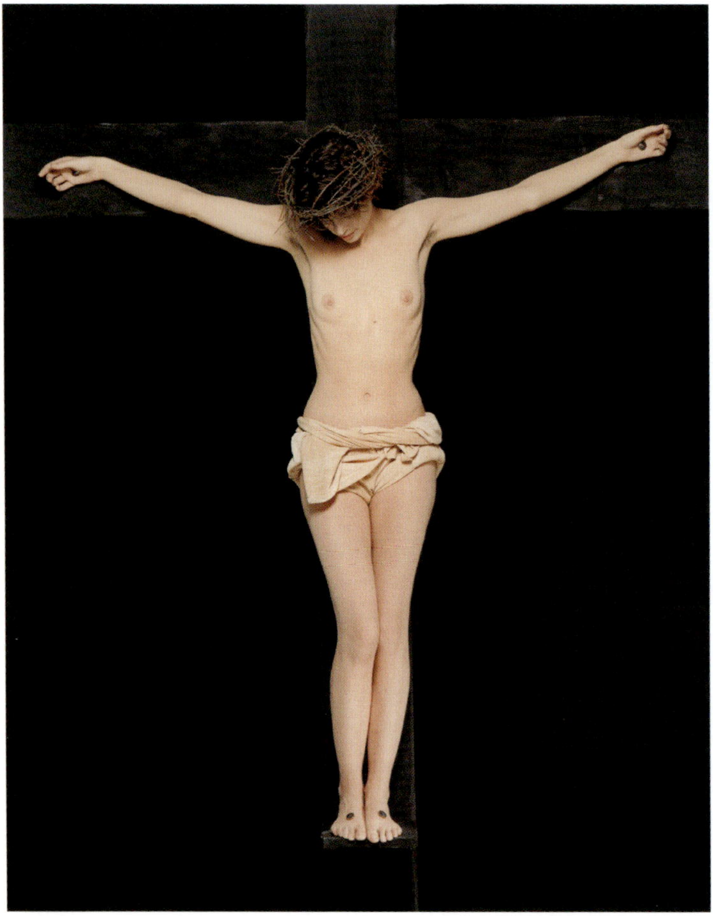

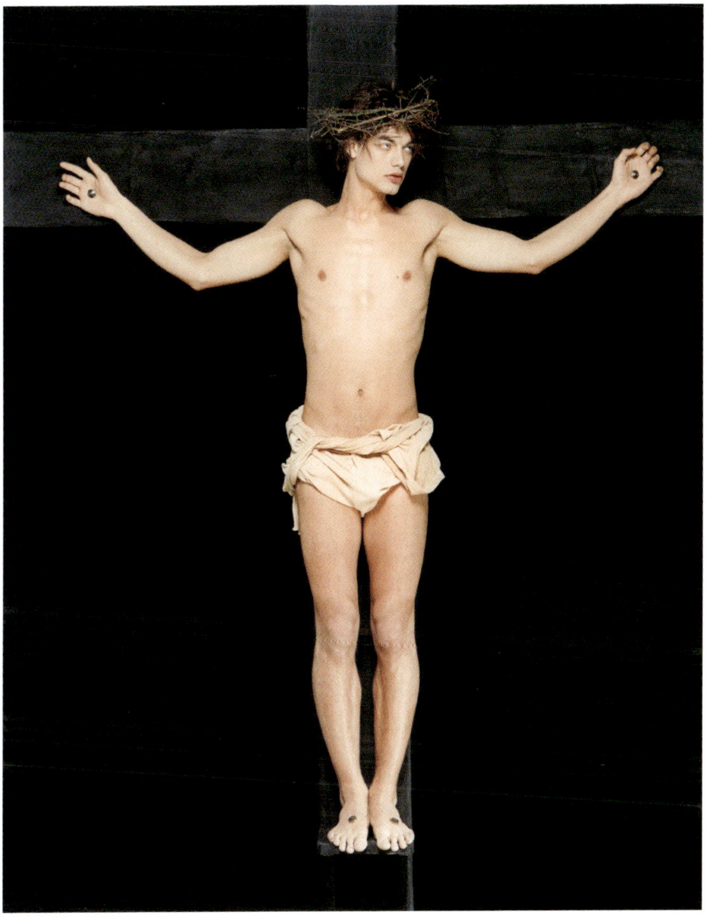

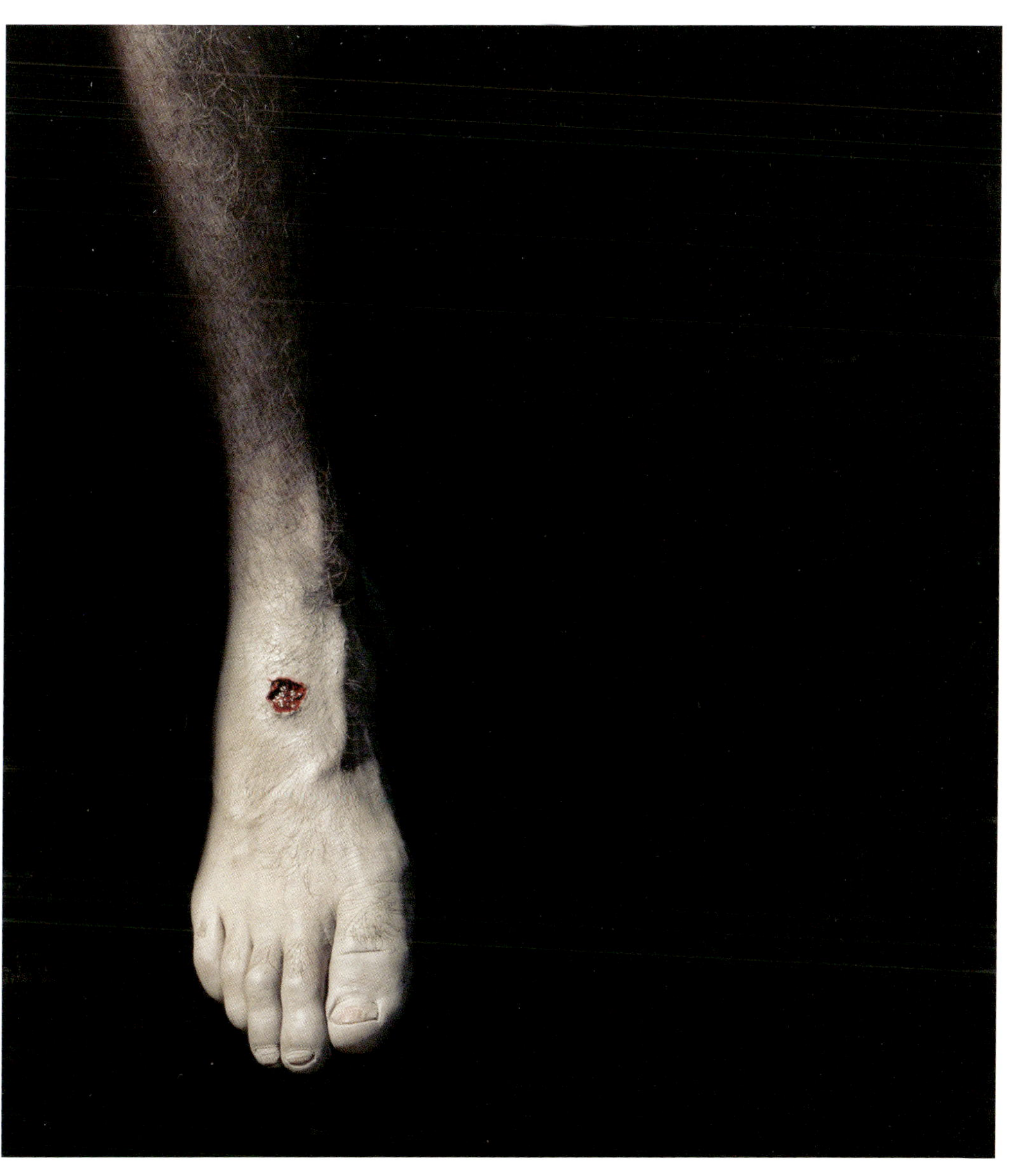

La Mise au tombeau, April 1997, Ville-Évrard   215

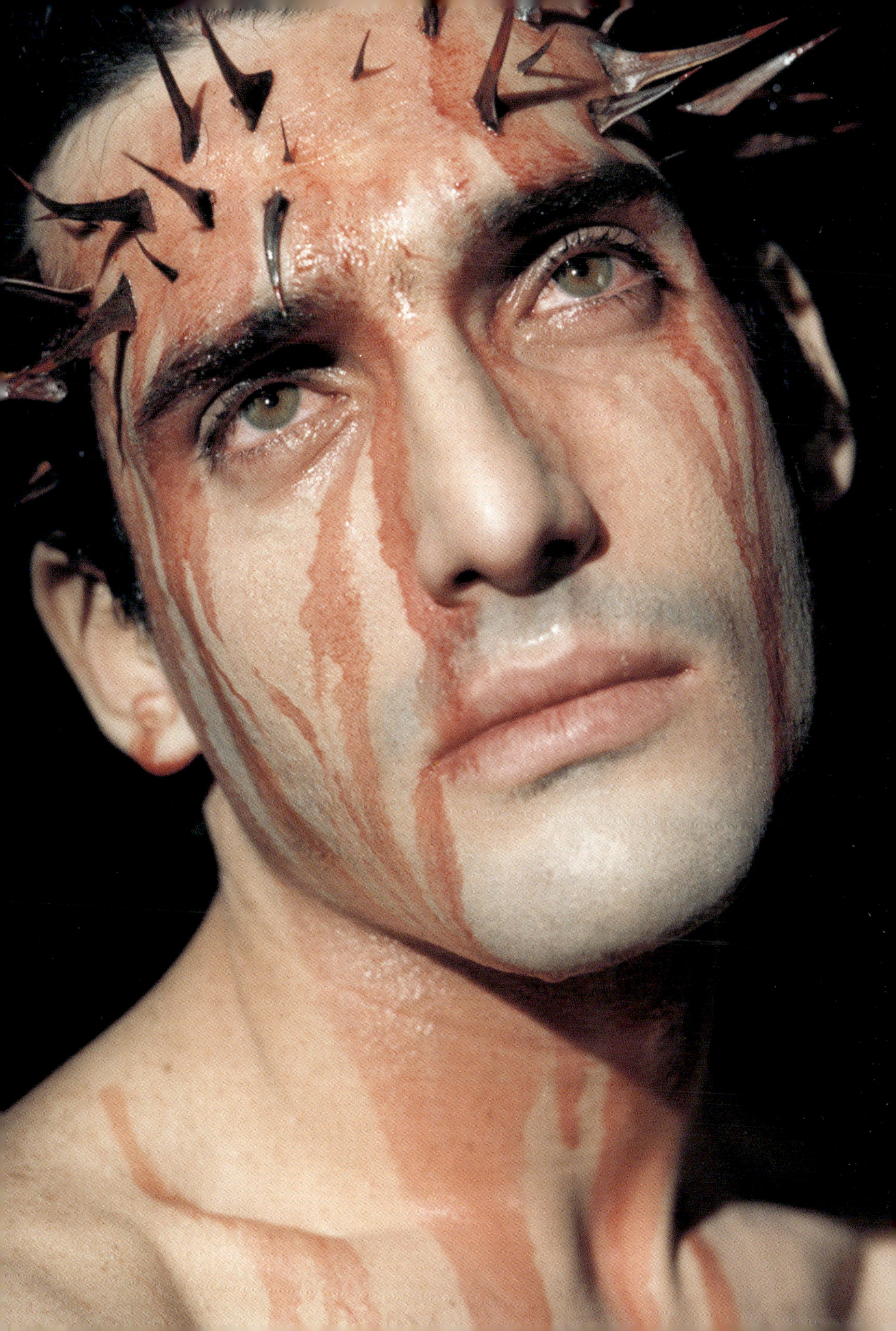

Donna se remaquillant dans son couteau, March 1990, Paris

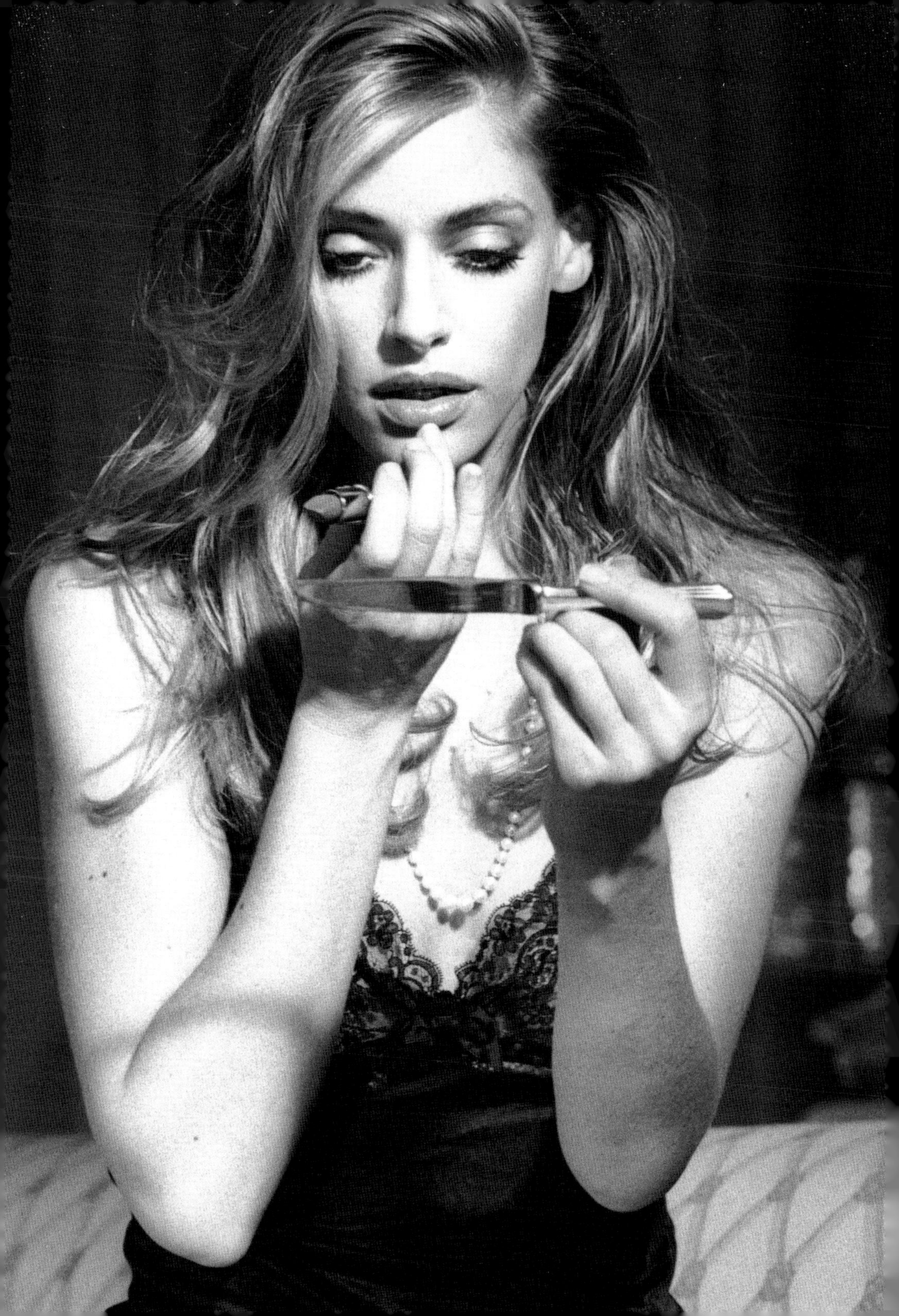

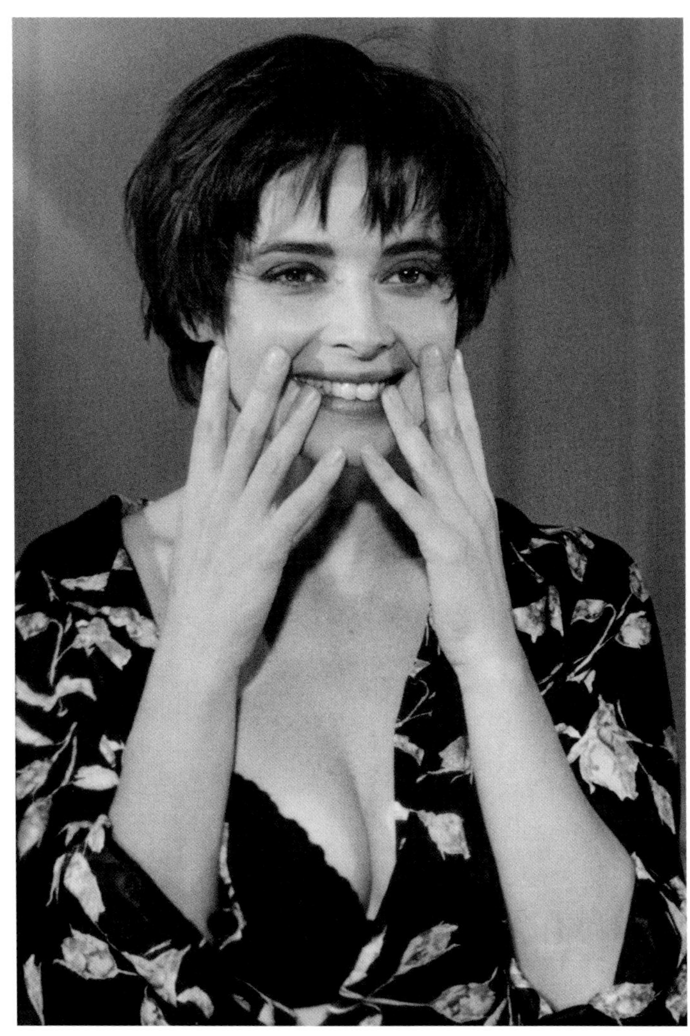

Above — *Isabella Rossellini*, March 1990, Paris
Opposite page — *Cristina en maillot d'Alaïa*, May 1989, Paris

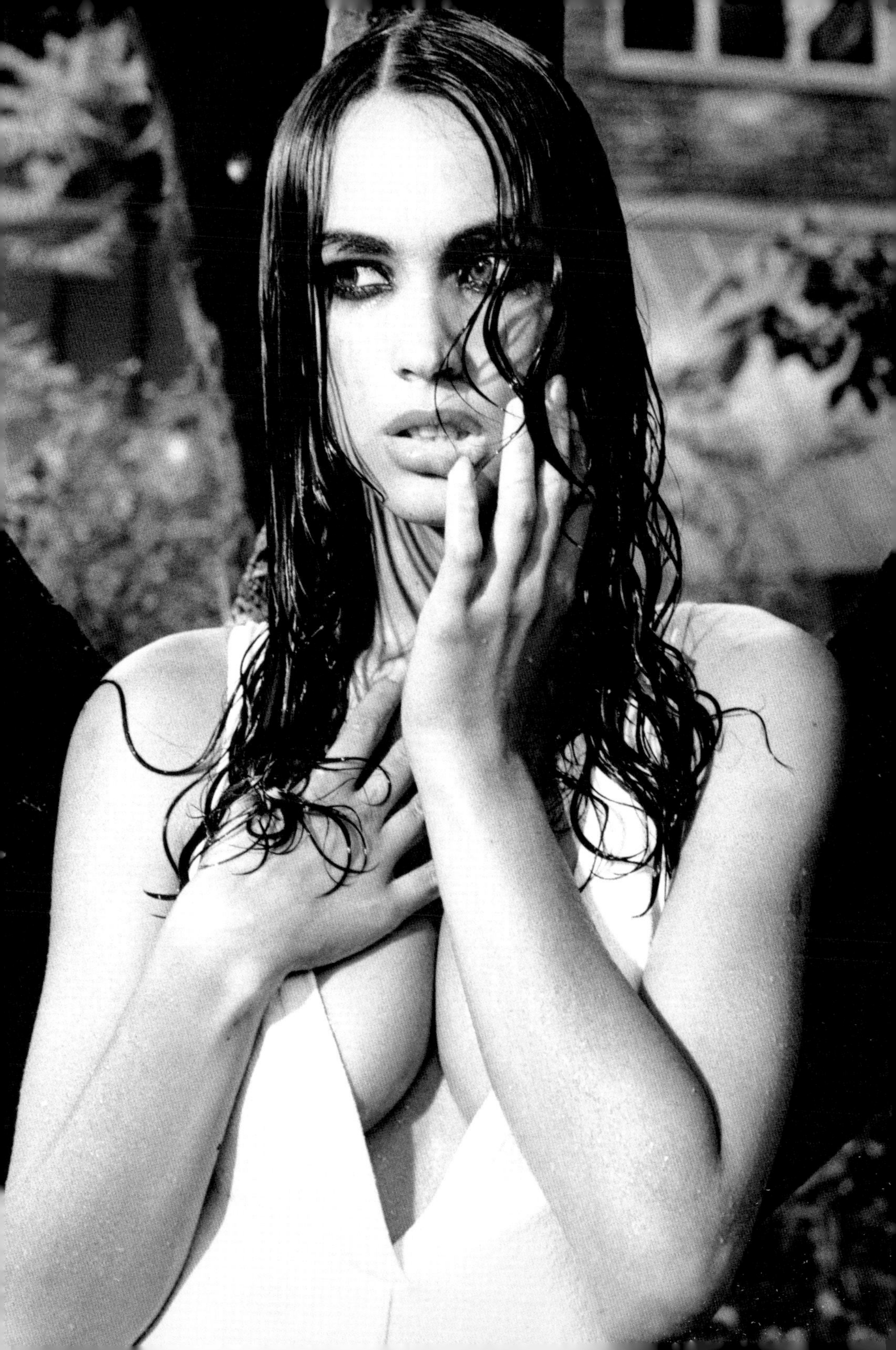

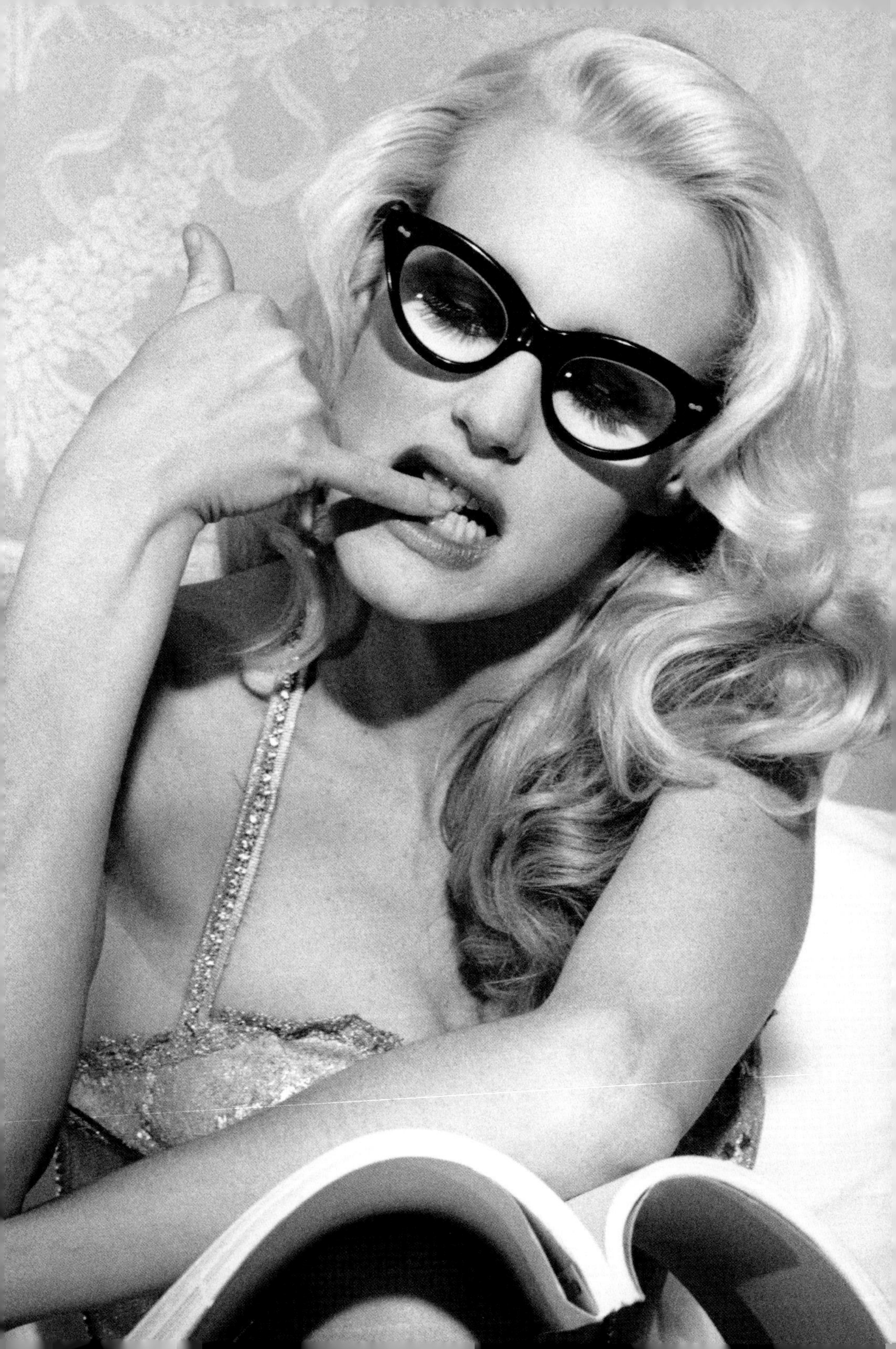

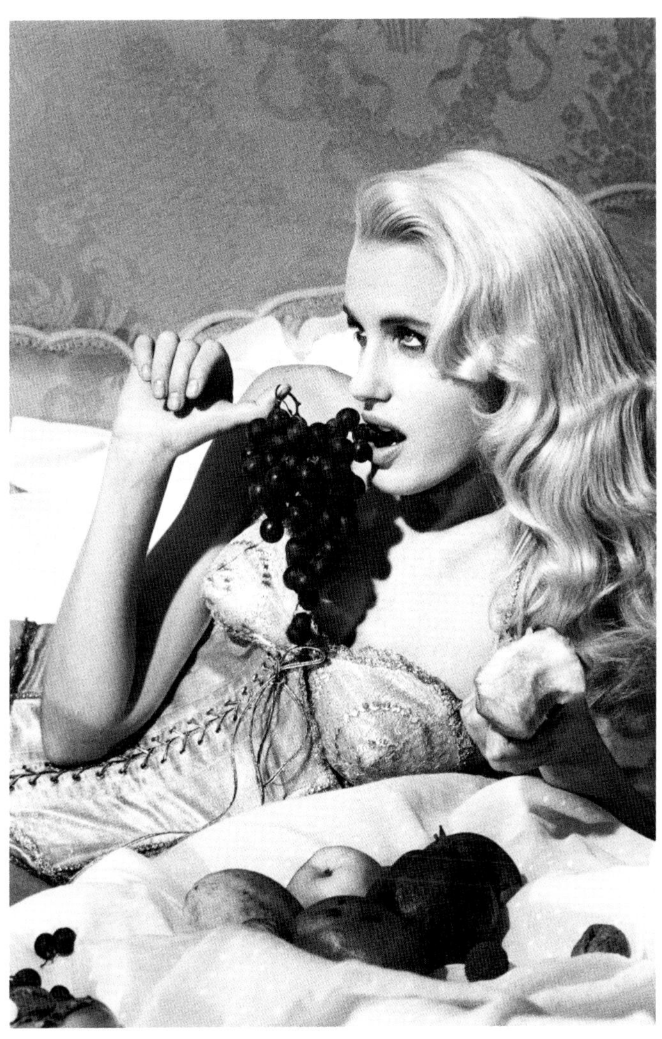

Above – *Daryl Hannah III*, February 1990, Paris
Opposite page – *Daryl Hannah II*, February 1990, Paris

Léah en vanité au vieux moine, pour Anne Valérie Hash, October 2006, Paris
Page 226 — *Inès de la Fressange eating a small turtle*, December 2001, Paris
Page 227 — *Eva Herzigová holding her shoe as a weapon (another version)*, May 2001, Paris
Page 228 — *Fashion picture for «Common Sense»*, January 2011, Paris
Page 229 — *Shu Qi about to drink a goldfish*, March 2006, Paris

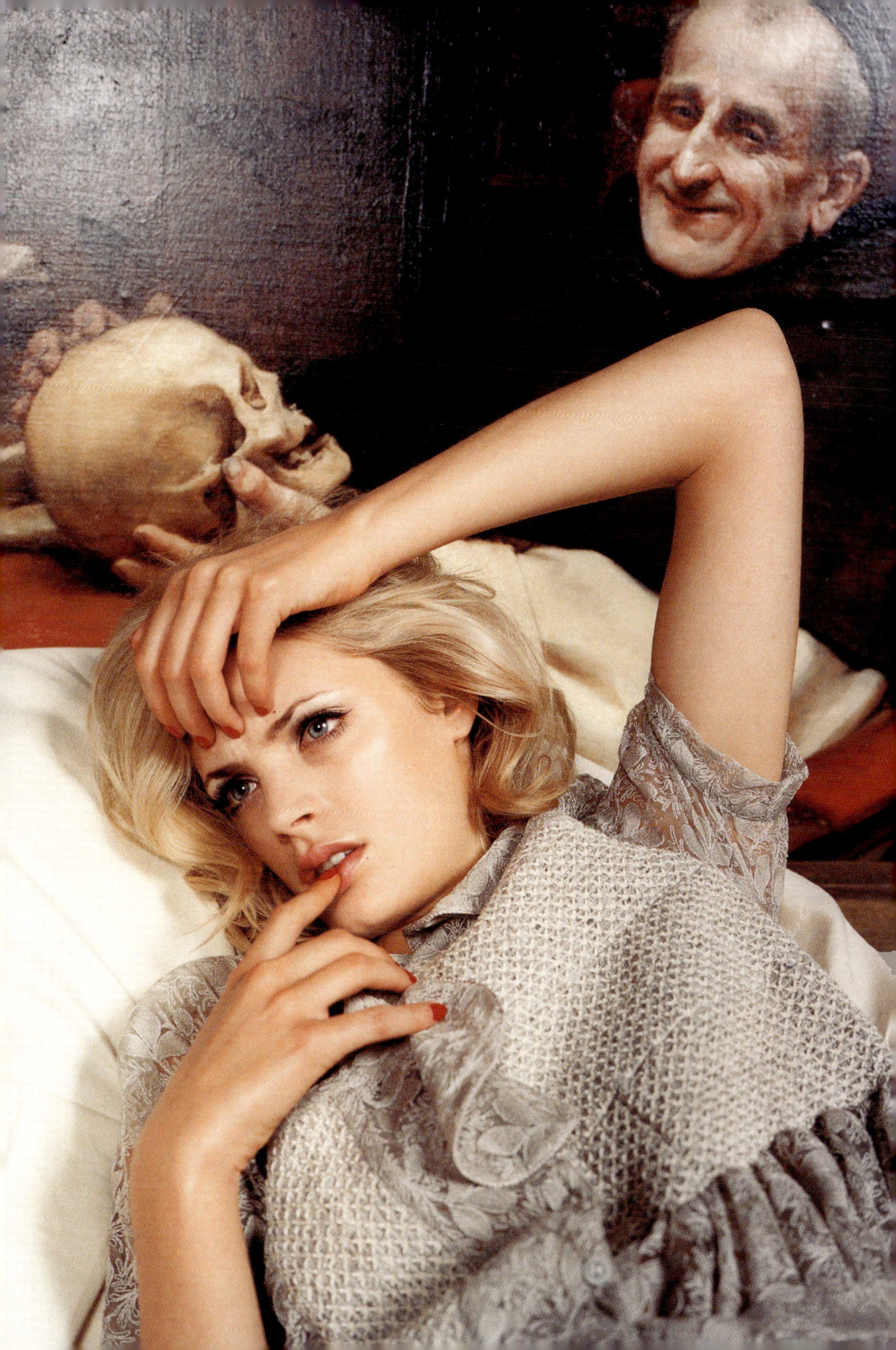

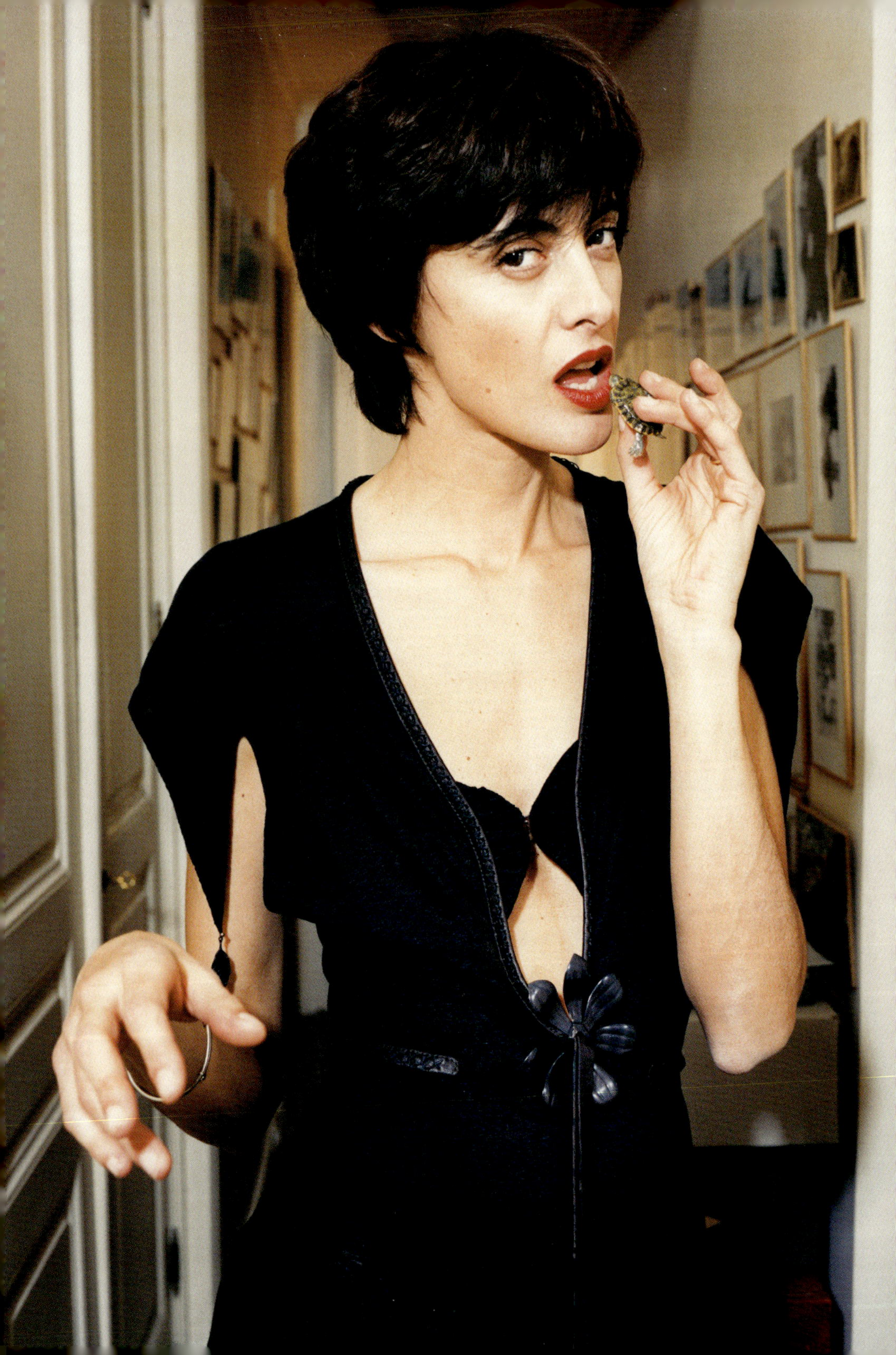

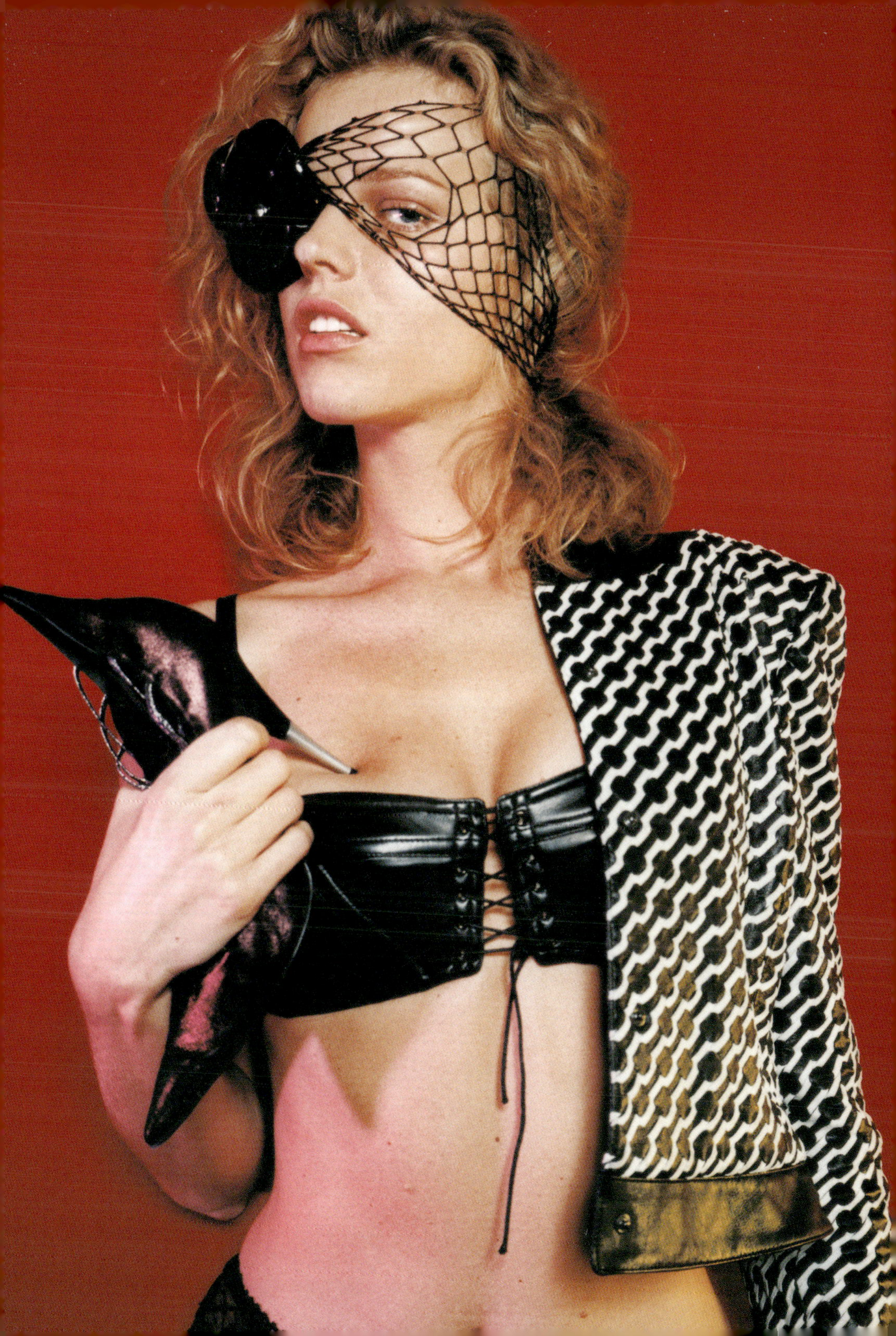

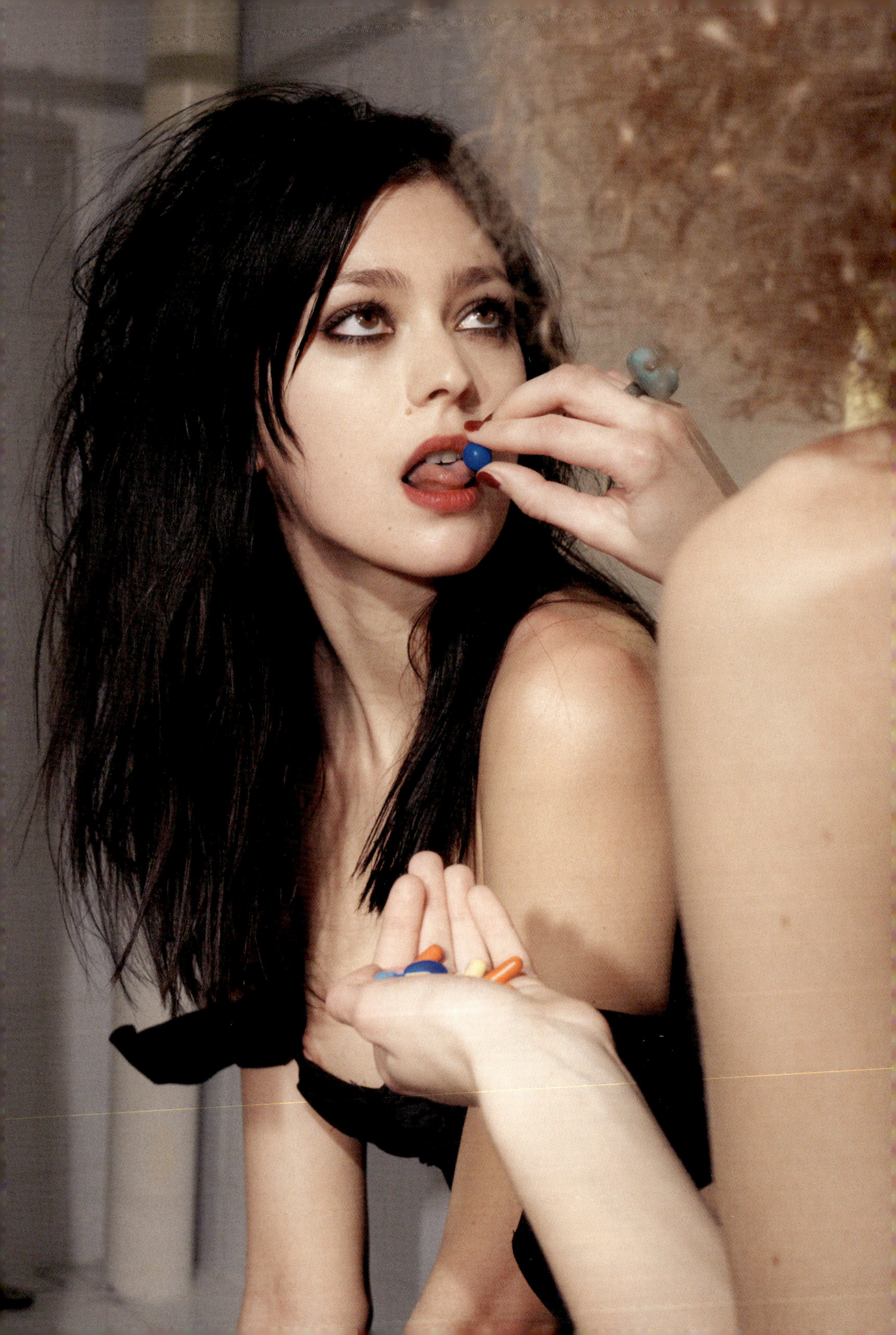

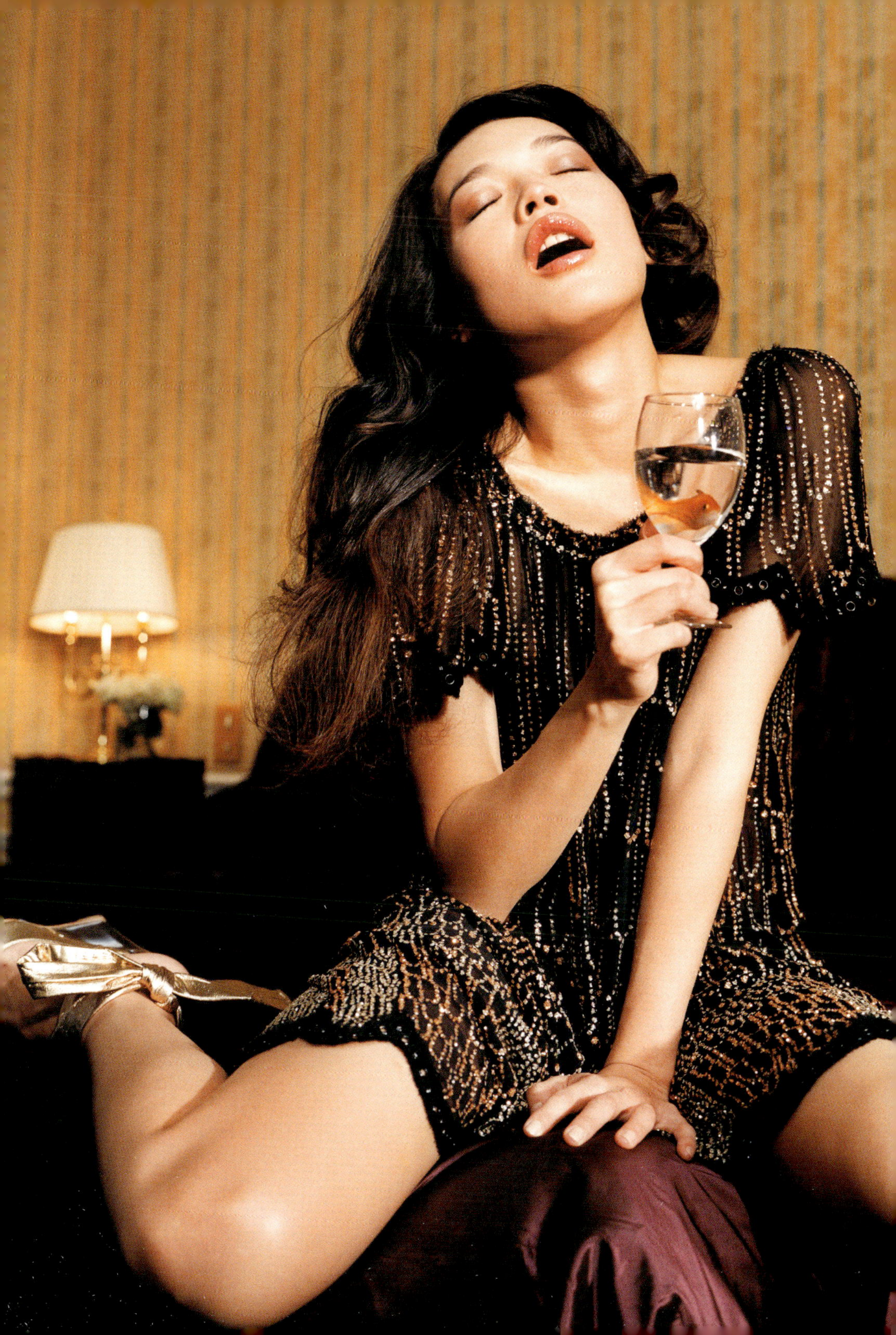

TOKYO ROOM
2007, Tokyo

Two young Japanese women naked in front of a pink curtain on a carpet with brown patterns. (...) They are eating dirty and putting things into each other's mouth. One of them is licking the pulp and seeds of a scarlet fruit off the bust and belly of the other. They have torn it up in their hands and it has stained their fingers and skin. Food and nudity, sex and brutality – all allied to an unflinching gaze and bodies that proudly exhibit themselves.

Deux jeunes Japonaises nues devant un rideau rose et sur une moquette à motifs bruns. (...) Elles mangent salement, elles se donnent à manger. L'une lèche sur le buste et le ventre de l'autre la pulpe et les grains d'un fruit écarlate. Elles l'ont déchiré de leurs mains. Il a sali les doigts et les peaux. Nourriture, nudité, sexe, brutalité – et des regards qui ne cillent pas, et des corps qui n'hésitent pas à s'exhiber.

Zwei junge Japanerinnen, nackt vor einem rosafarbenenen Vorhang auf einem Teppich mit braunem Muster. (...) Sie ferkeln mit dem Essen herum, sie füttern sich gegenseitig. Die eine leckt das Fruchtfleisch und die Kerne einer scharlachroten Frucht von der Brust und vom Bauch der anderen. Sie haben die Frucht mit den Händen aufgerissen und damit ihre Finger und Haut beschmiert. Nahrung und Nacktheit, Sex und Brutalität – und Augen, die nicht blinzeln, und Körper, die sich hemmungslos zur Schau stellen.

Philippe Dagen, in *Can you find happiness*, 2008

Tokyo Room III, Tomo and Madoka, September 2007, Tokyo
Pages 232/233 — *Tokyo Room I, Madoka*, September 2007, Tokyo
Page 234 — *Tokyo Room IV, Tomo and Madoka*, September 2007, Tokyo
Page 235 — *Tokyo Room V, Madoka and Tomo*, September 2007, Tokyo

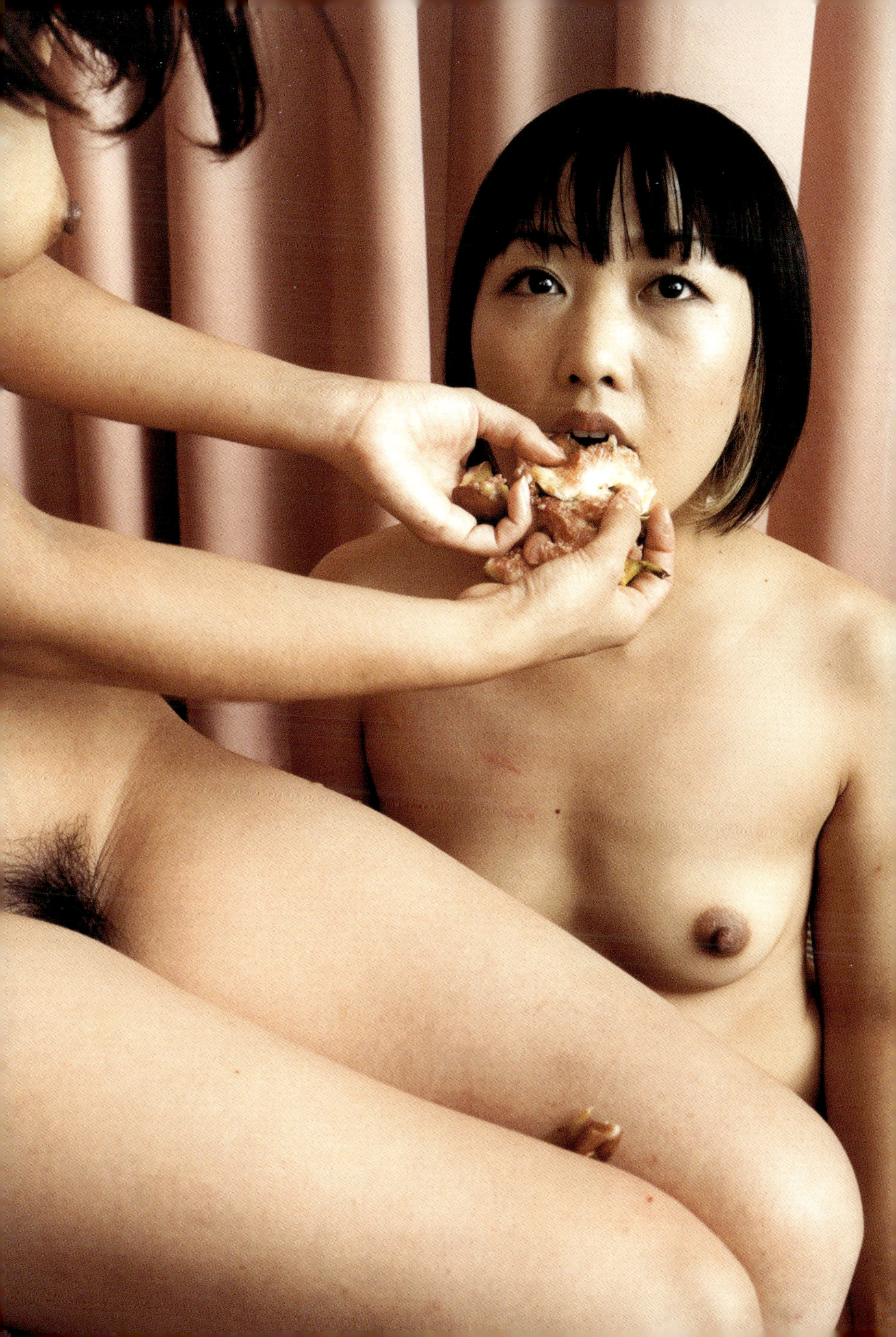

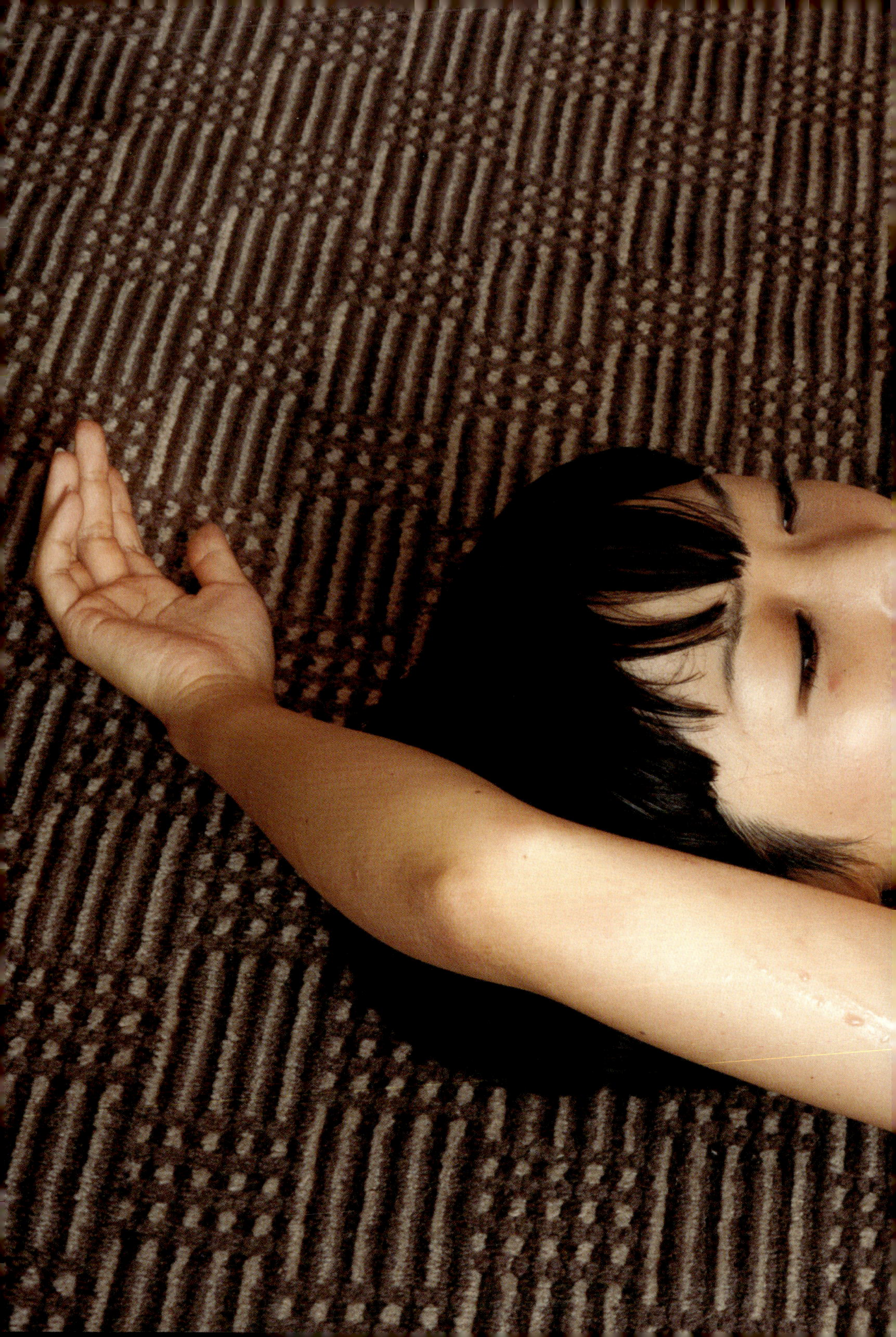

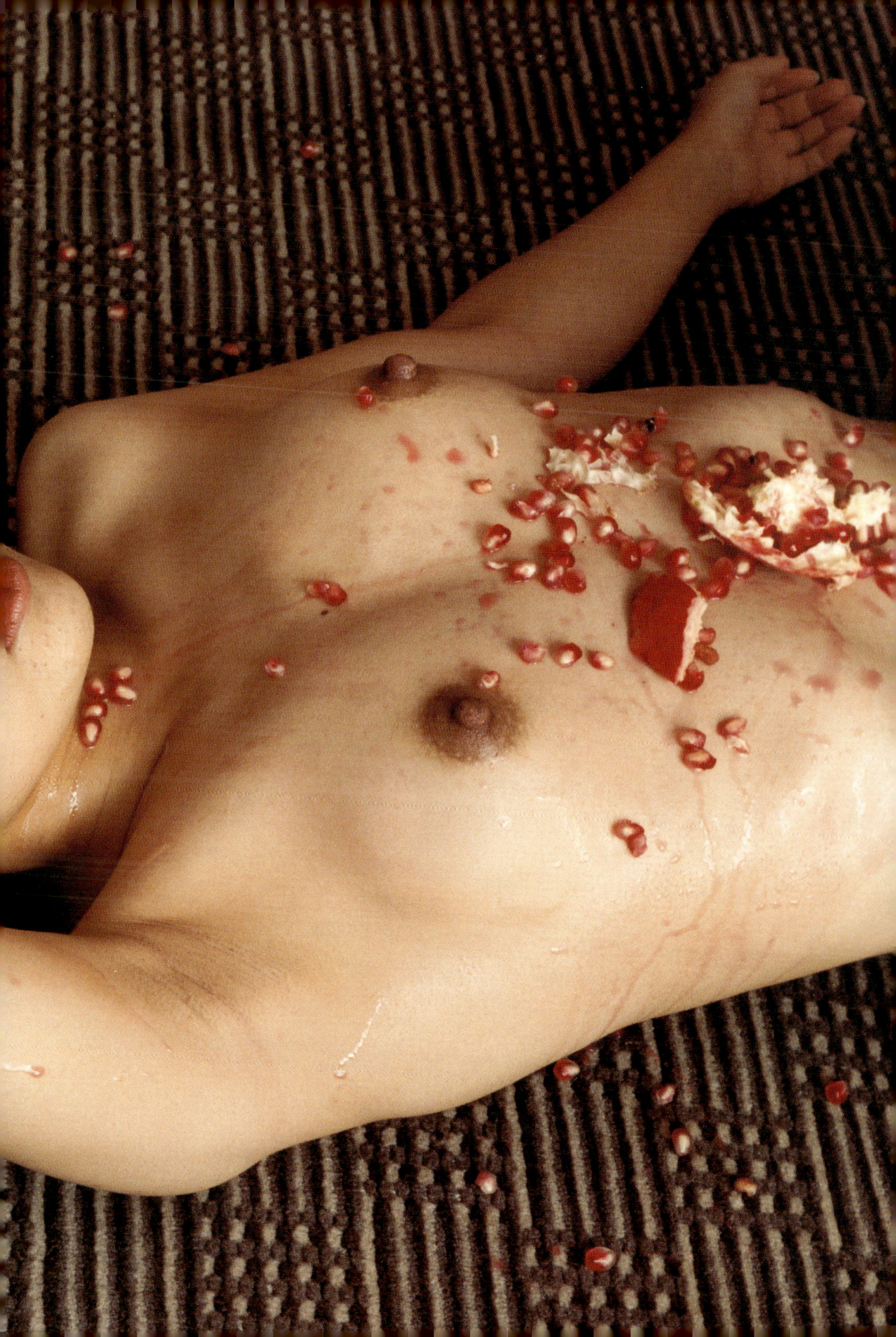

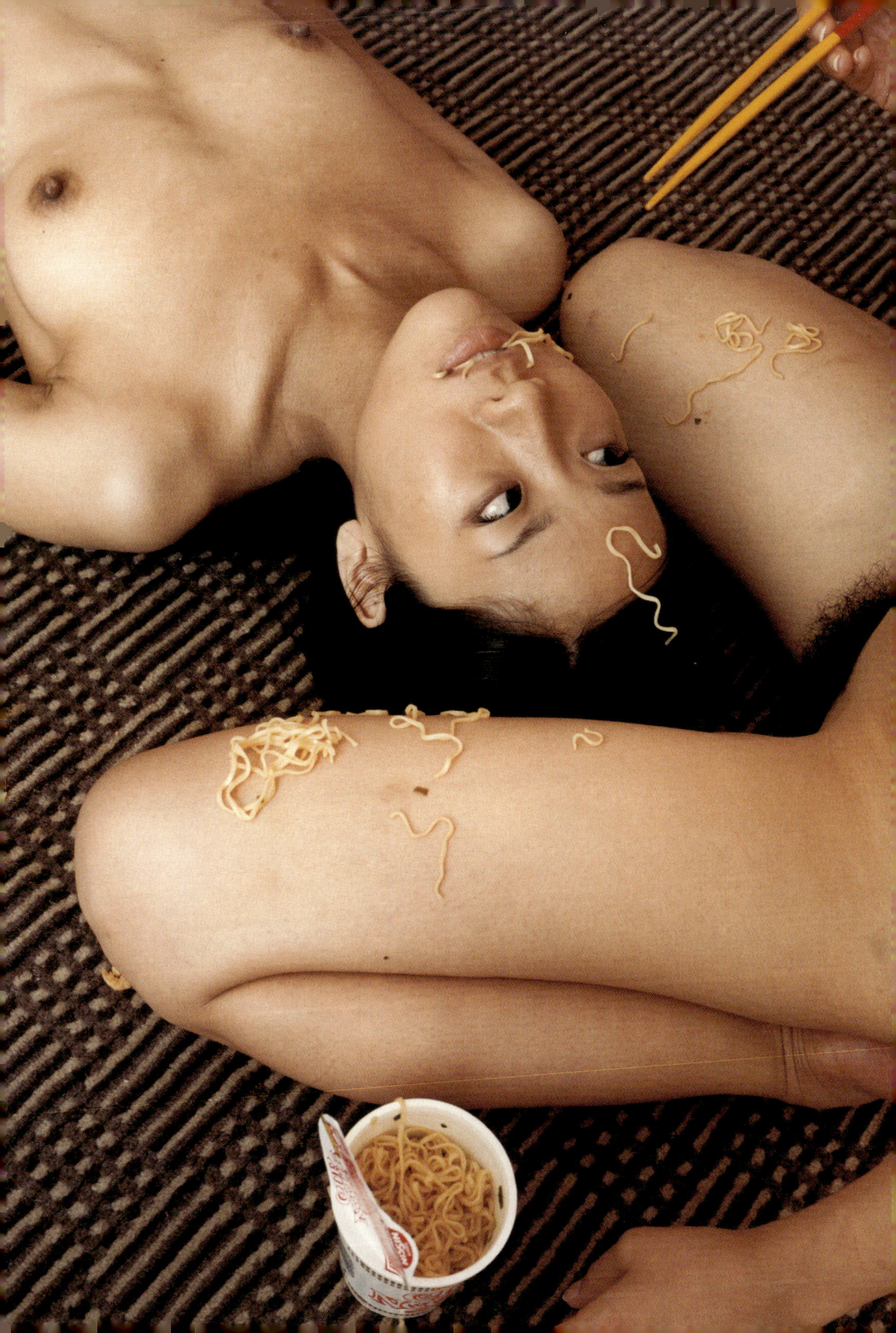

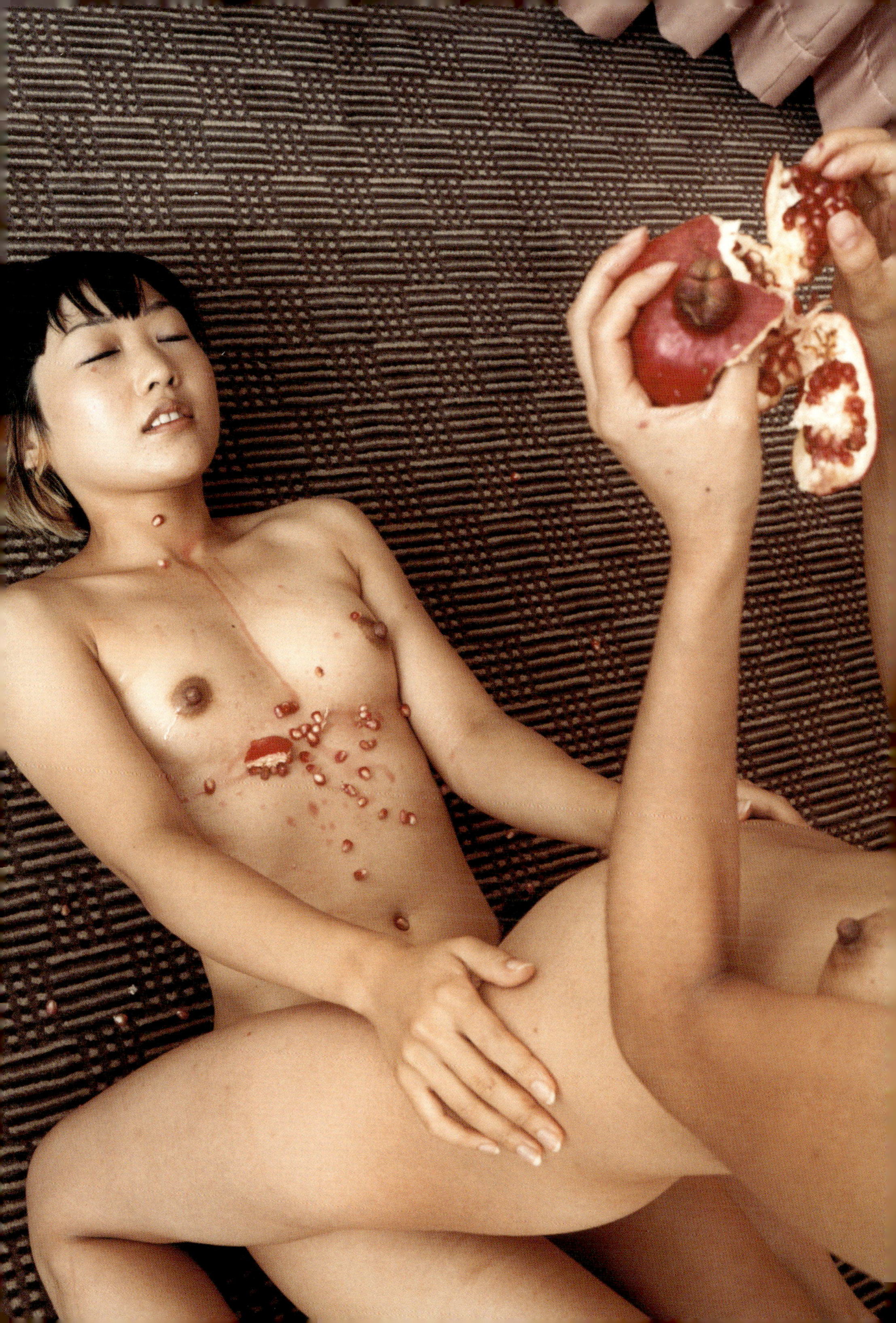

X'MAS
IN COLLABORATION WITH SERGE BRAMLY
1999, Paris

X'Mas II – Confidence Trick, June 2000, Paris

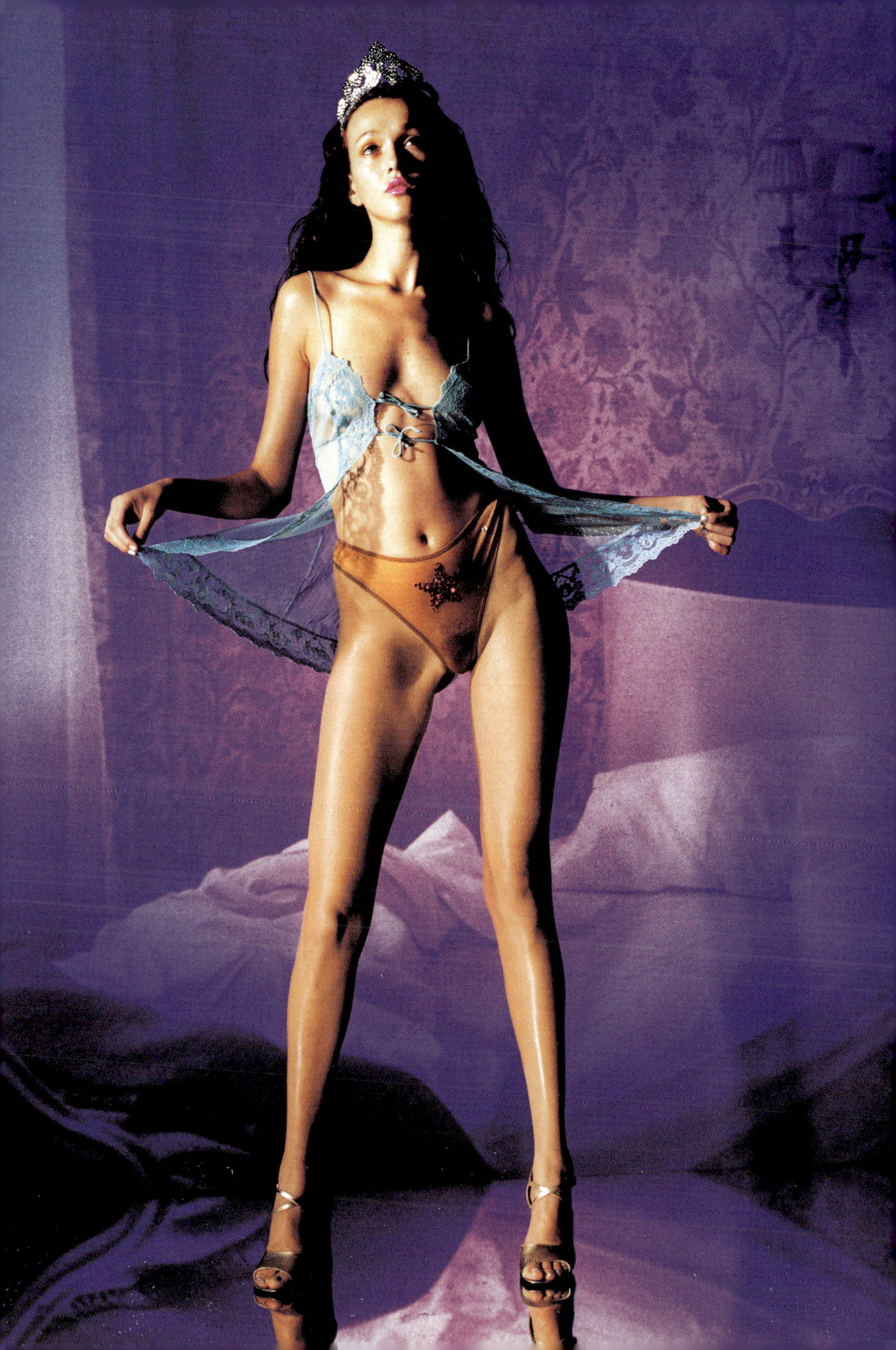

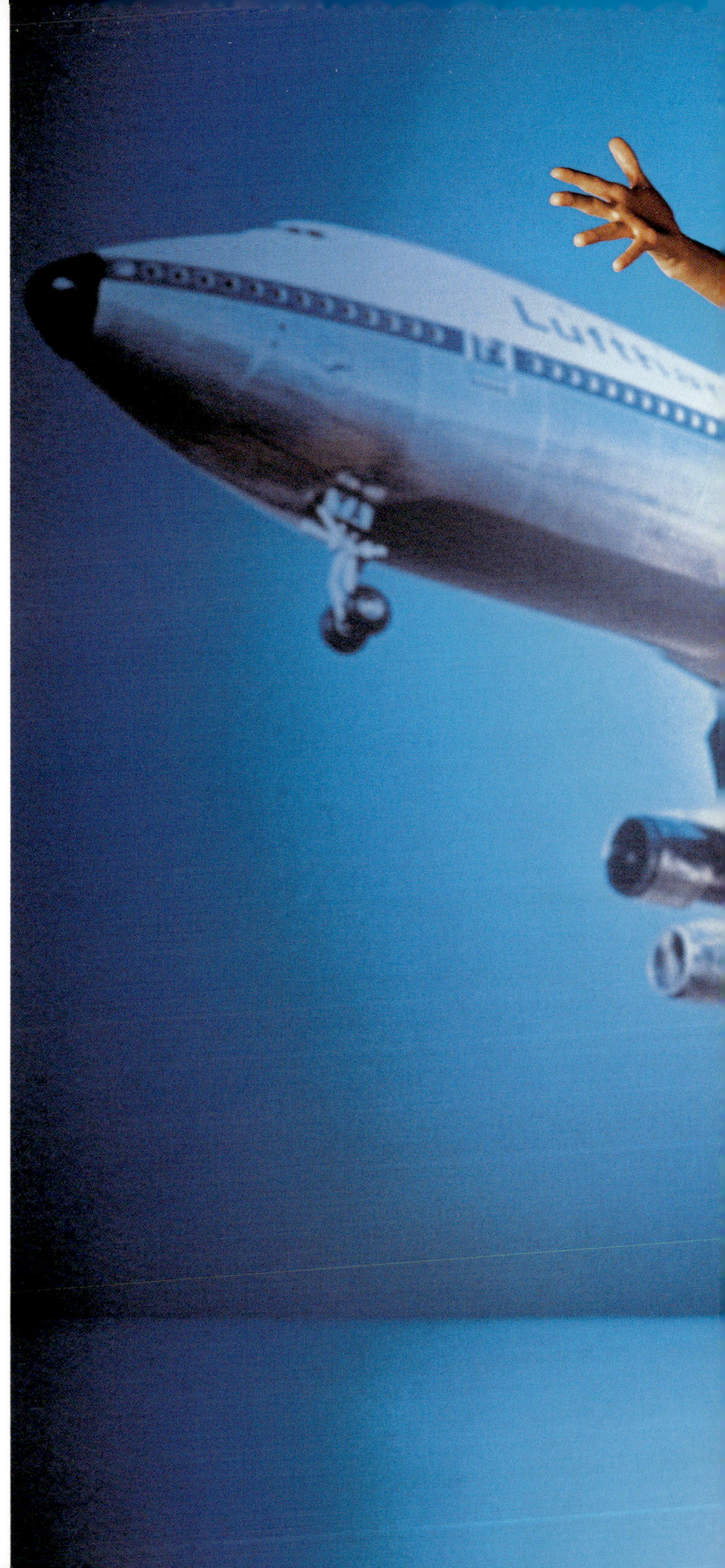

X'Mas II –
Flying Lufthansa,
June 2000, Paris

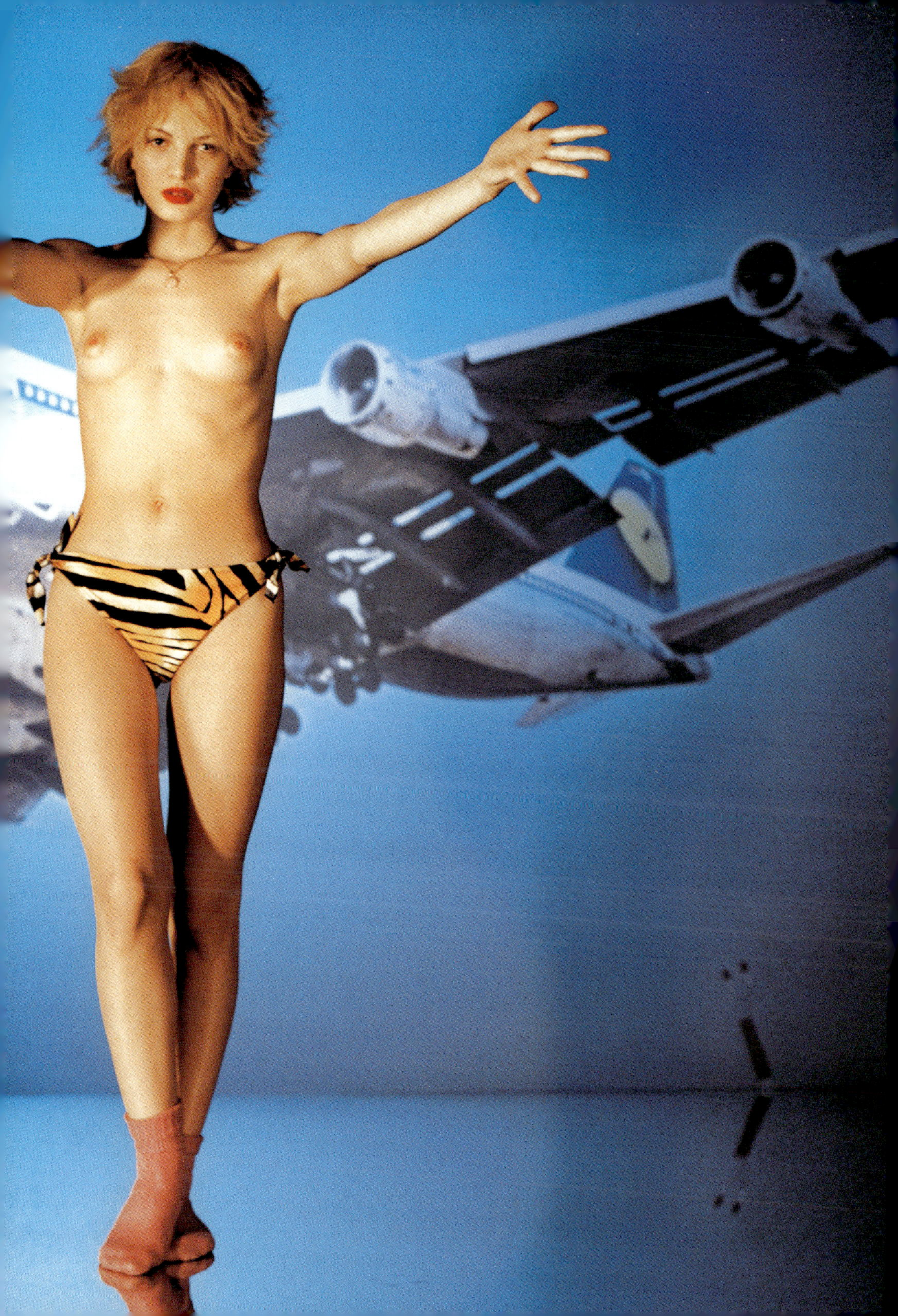

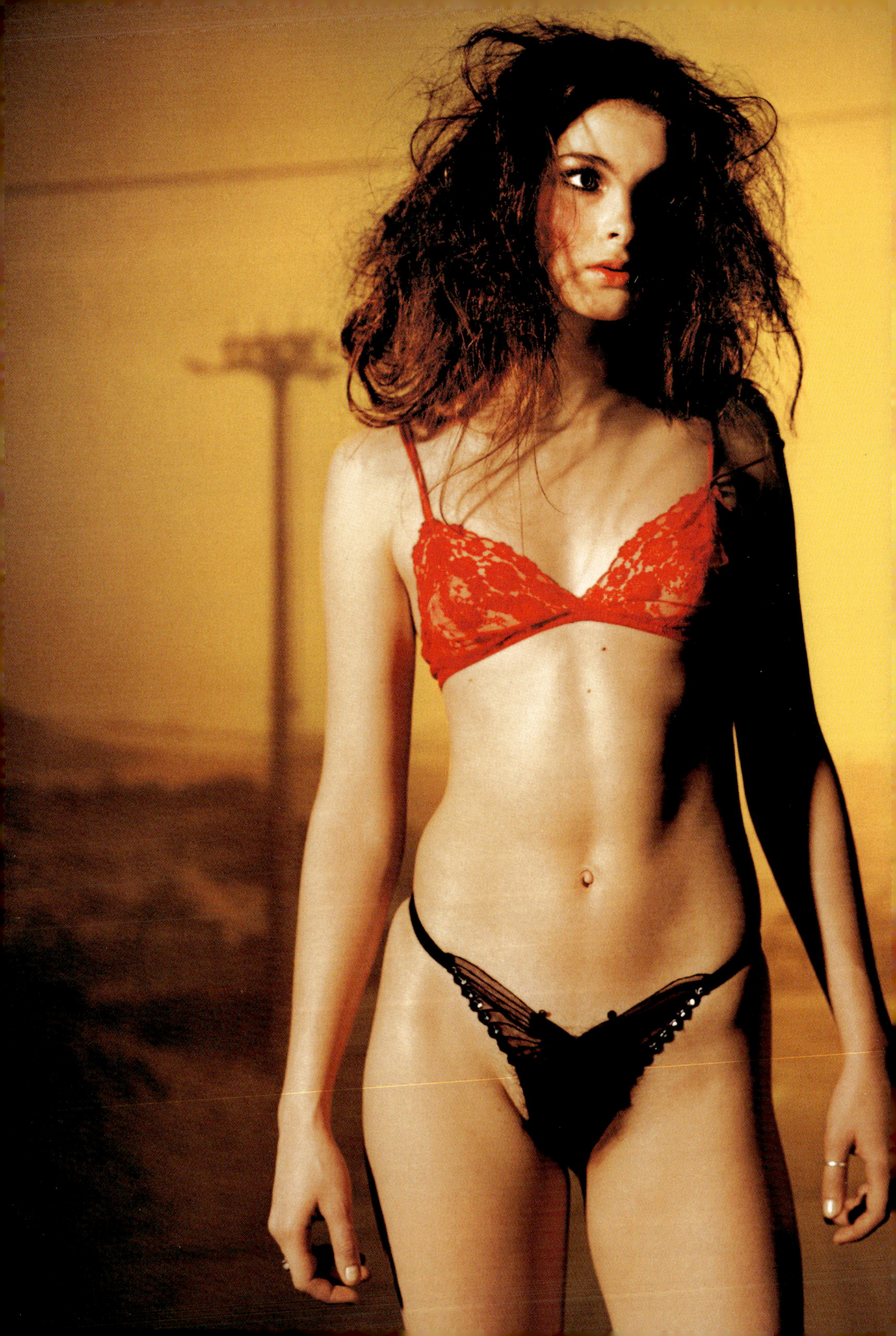

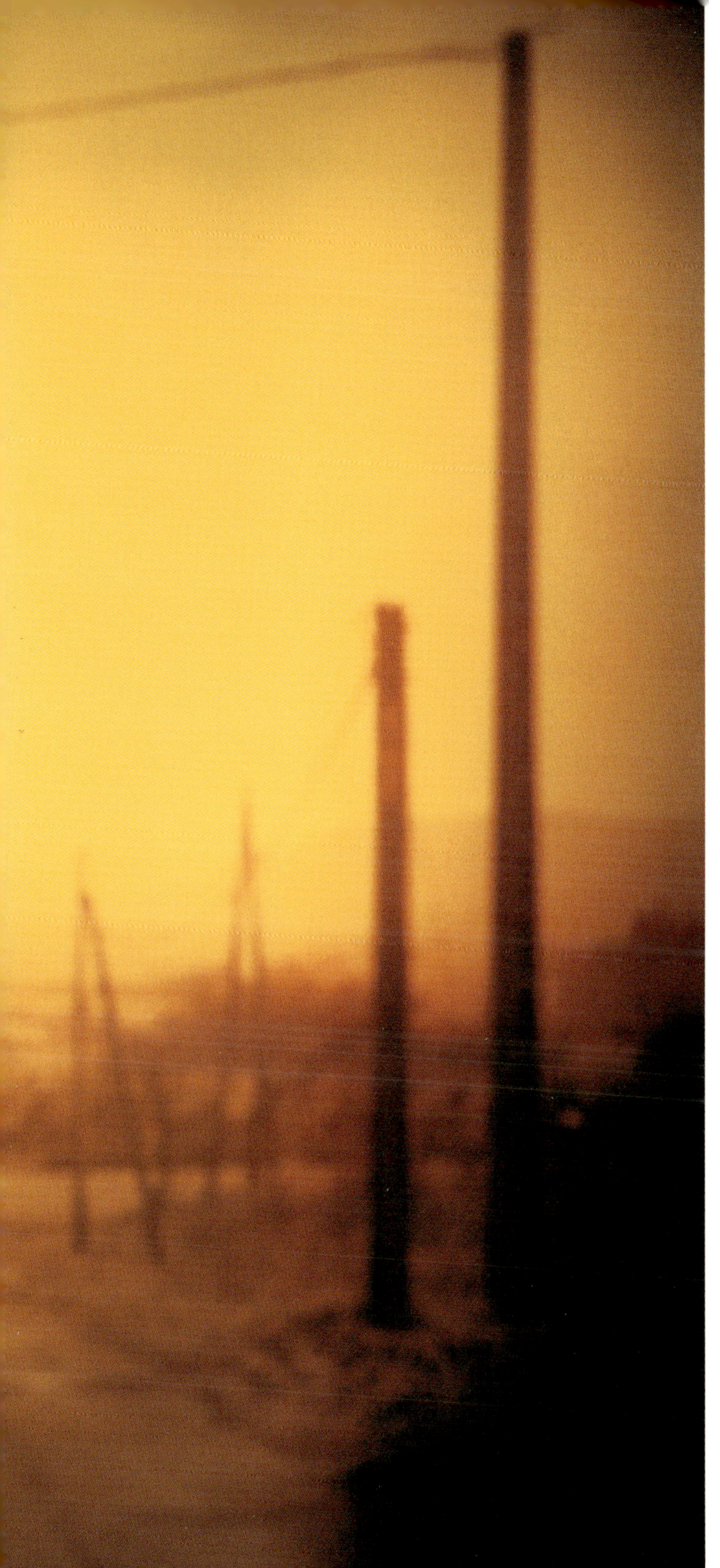

X'Mas II – Corsican Road,
March 2000, Paris   241

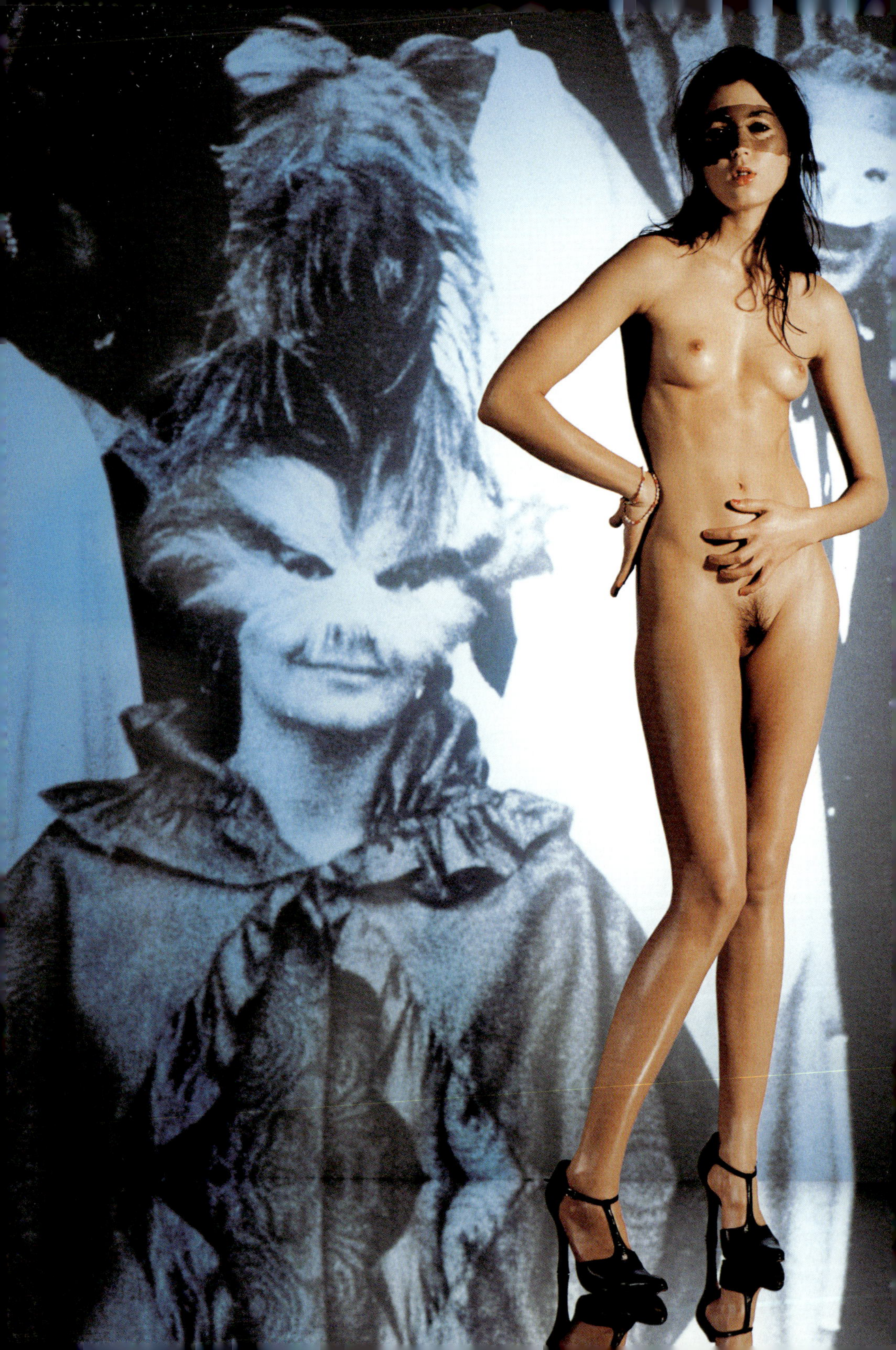

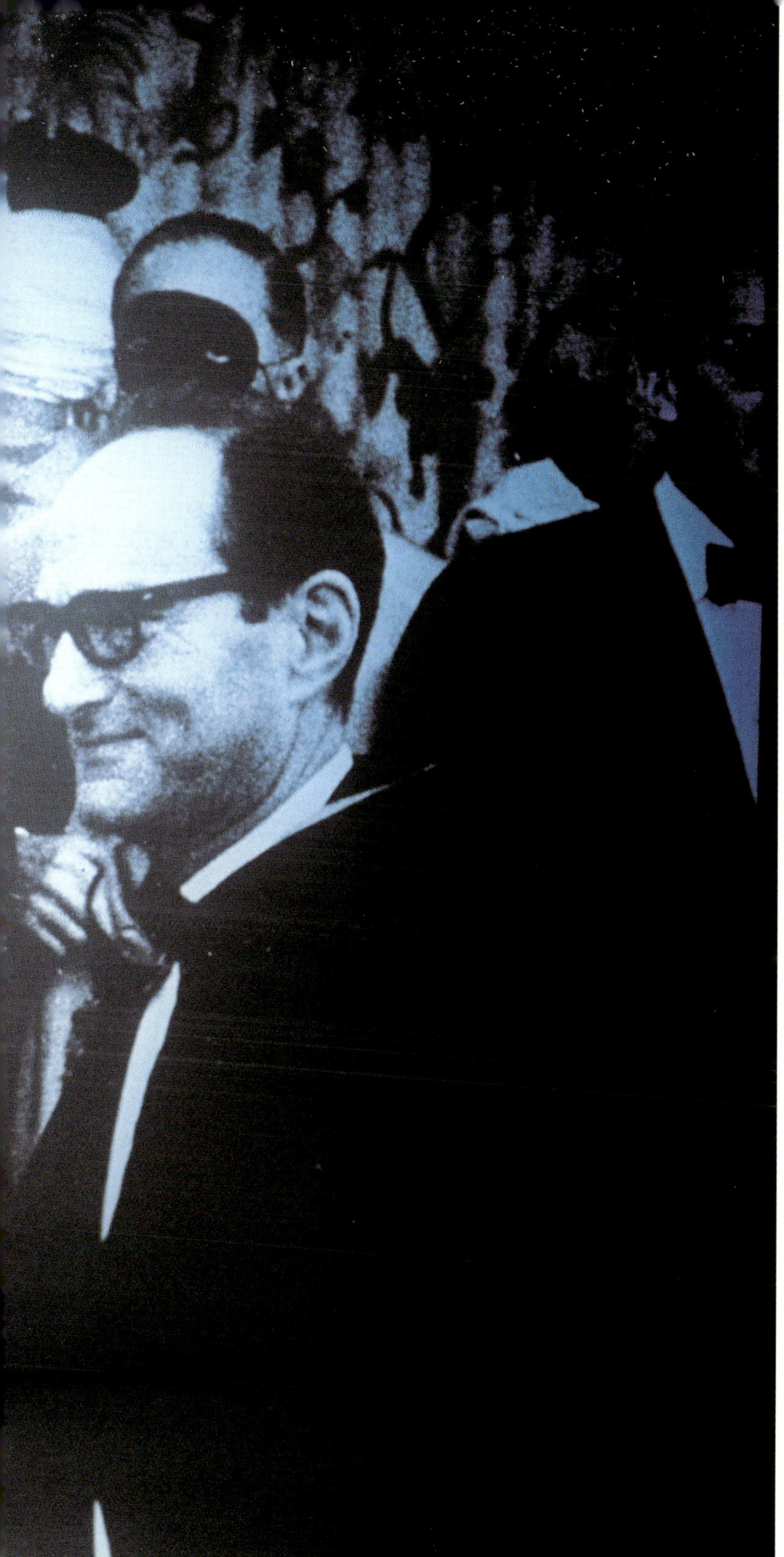

*X'Mas II – Mum
and Dad*, March
2000, Paris

243

Her art seems at first all exuberance and provocation, sensuality
and eroticism; then, when you study it more carefully, you discover
that it is made up of modesty, refinement and a kind of absolute;
that above all, it expresses a love of one's fellow humans, first and
foremost of women, allowing them to be stronger, to exist.

Son art est, en apparence, fait d'exubérance et de provocation, de
sensualité et d'érotisme. Et puis, quand on étudie un peu mieux
son travail, on découvre qu'il est fait de pudeur, de raffinement
et d'absolu; qu'il est avant tout expression d'un amour de l'autre,
et d'abord des femmes, pour leur permettre de s'affirmer, d'exister.

Ihre Kunst besteht – scheinbar – aus Übermut und Provokation,
Sinnlichkeit und Erotik. Betrachtet man ihre Arbeit dann aber ein
wenig genauer, stellt man fest, dass sie von Feingefühl, Subtilität und
etwas Absolutem getragen wird. Und dass sie in erster Linie Ausdruck
der Liebe zum Anderen und insbesondere zu Frauen ist und ihnen
ermöglichen will, sich zu behaupten, zu existieren.

Jacques Attali, in *Reporters sans frontières*, 2008

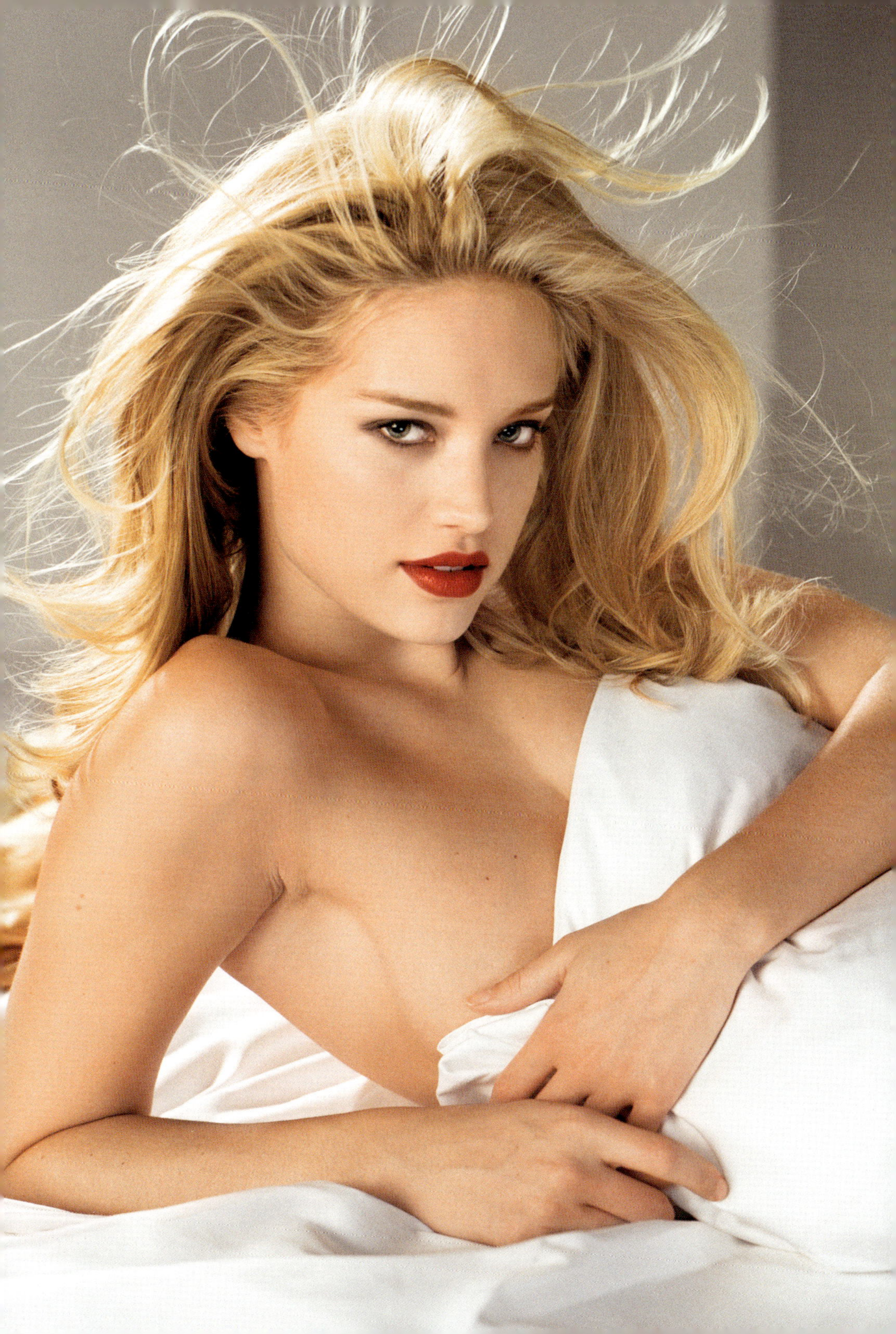

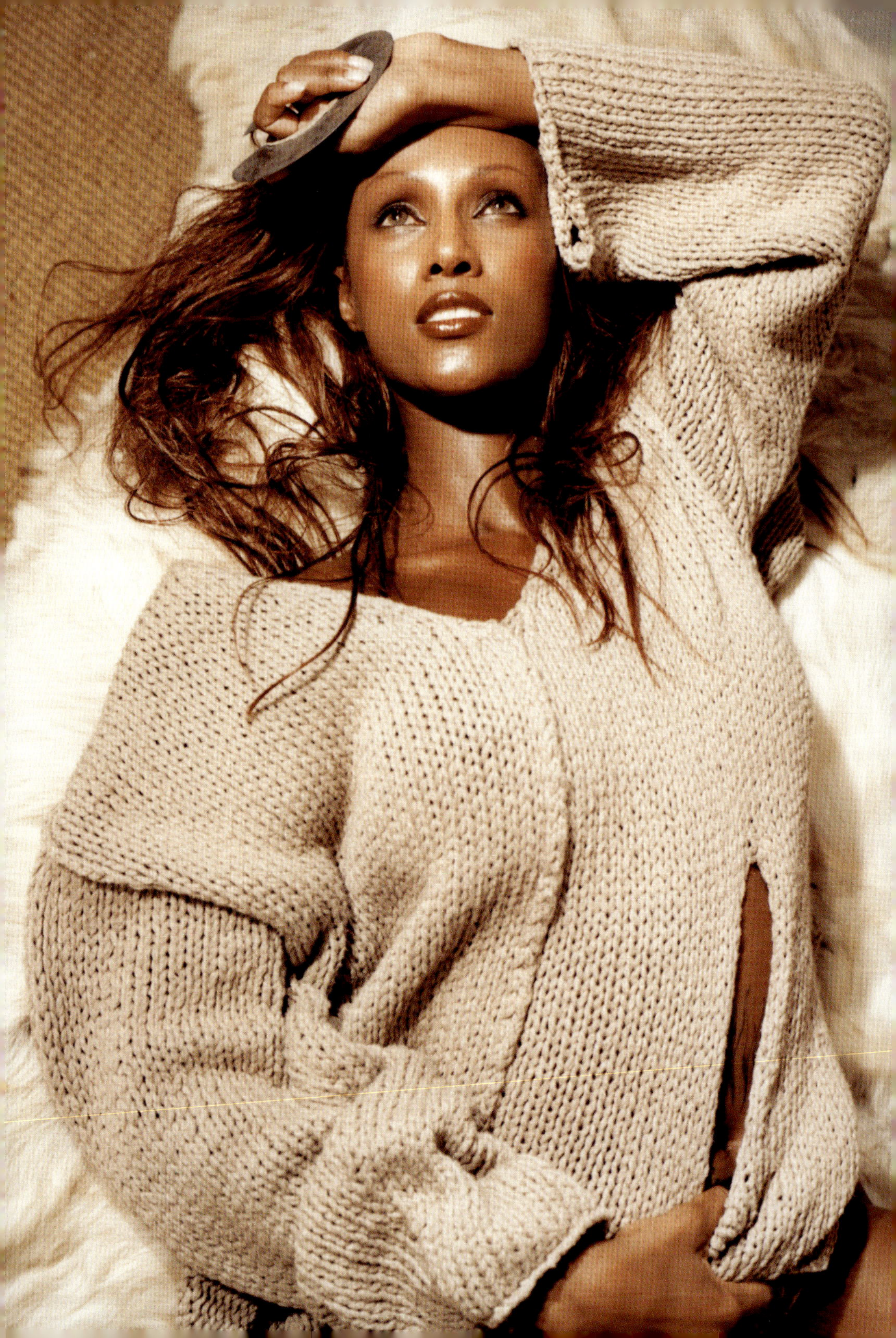

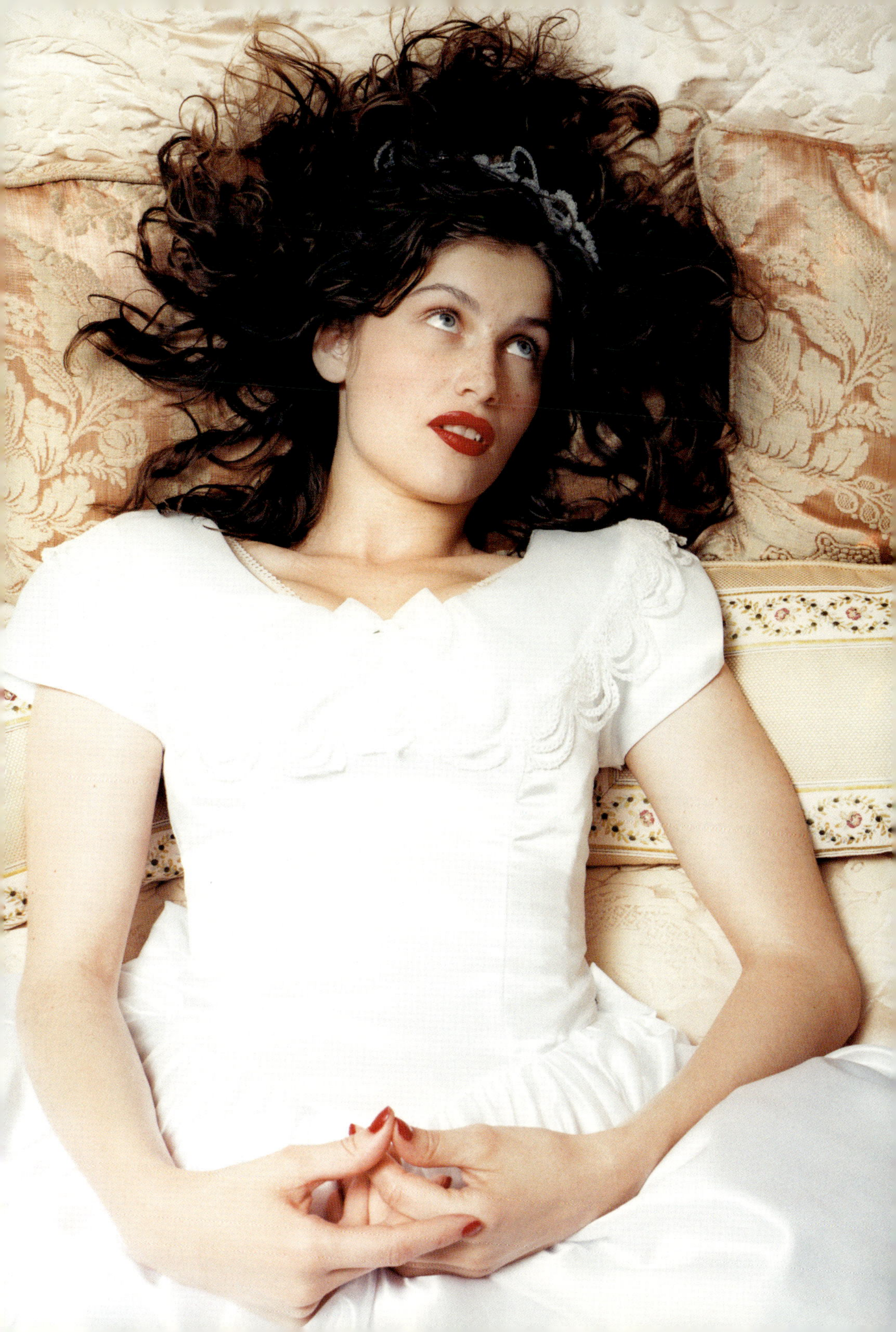

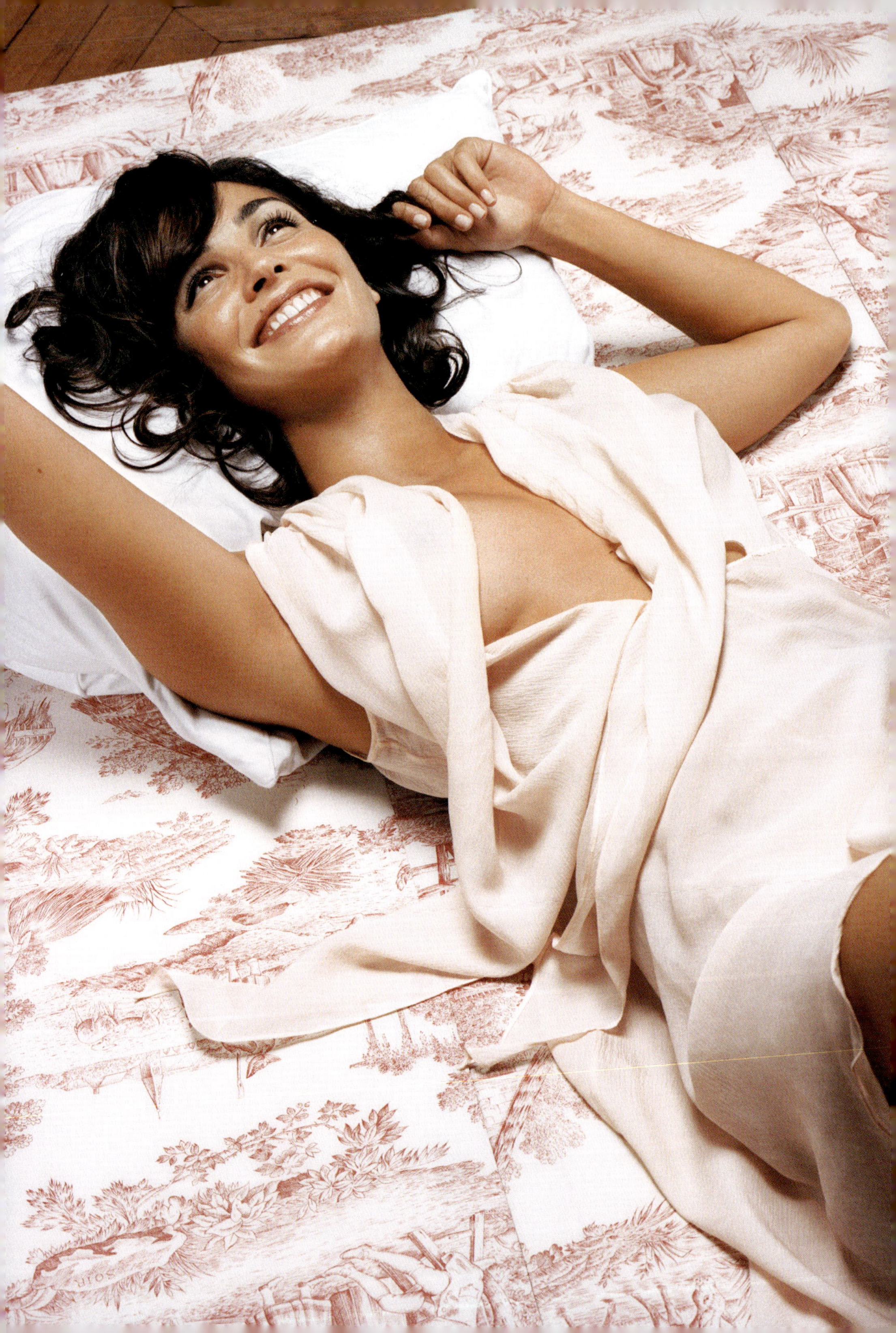

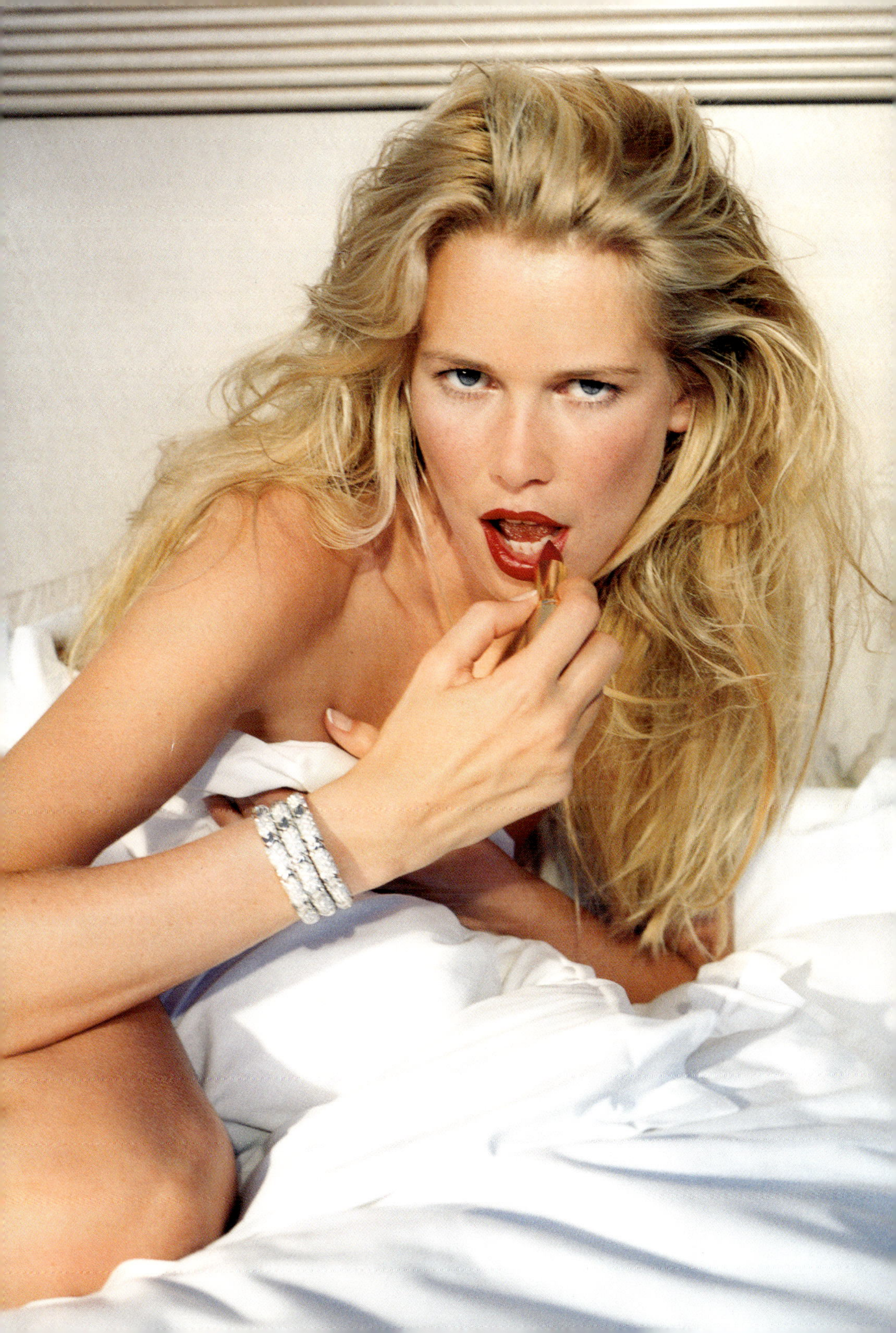

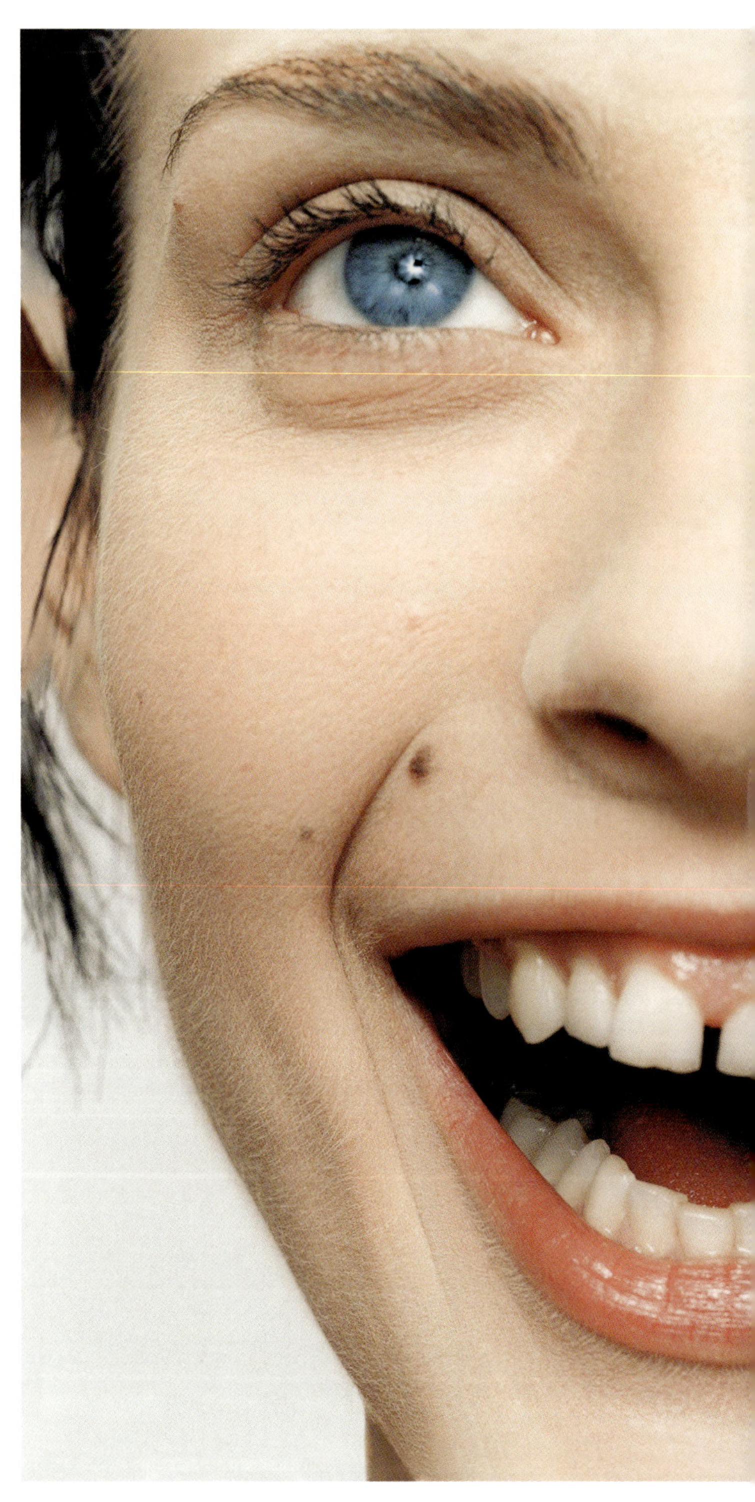

Pages 250–255 —
Pieces of Camellia 1, 5, 6,
June 2000, Paris

250

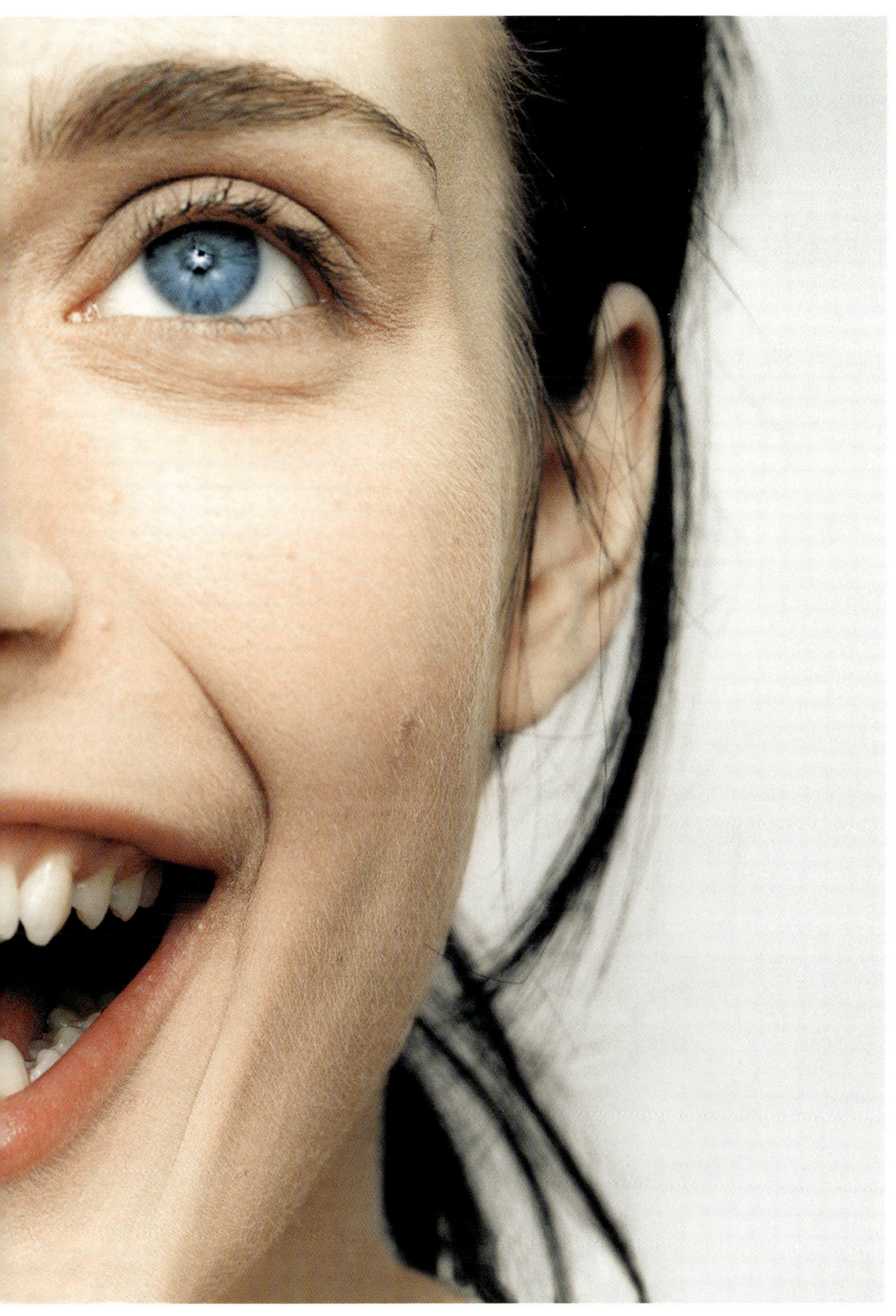

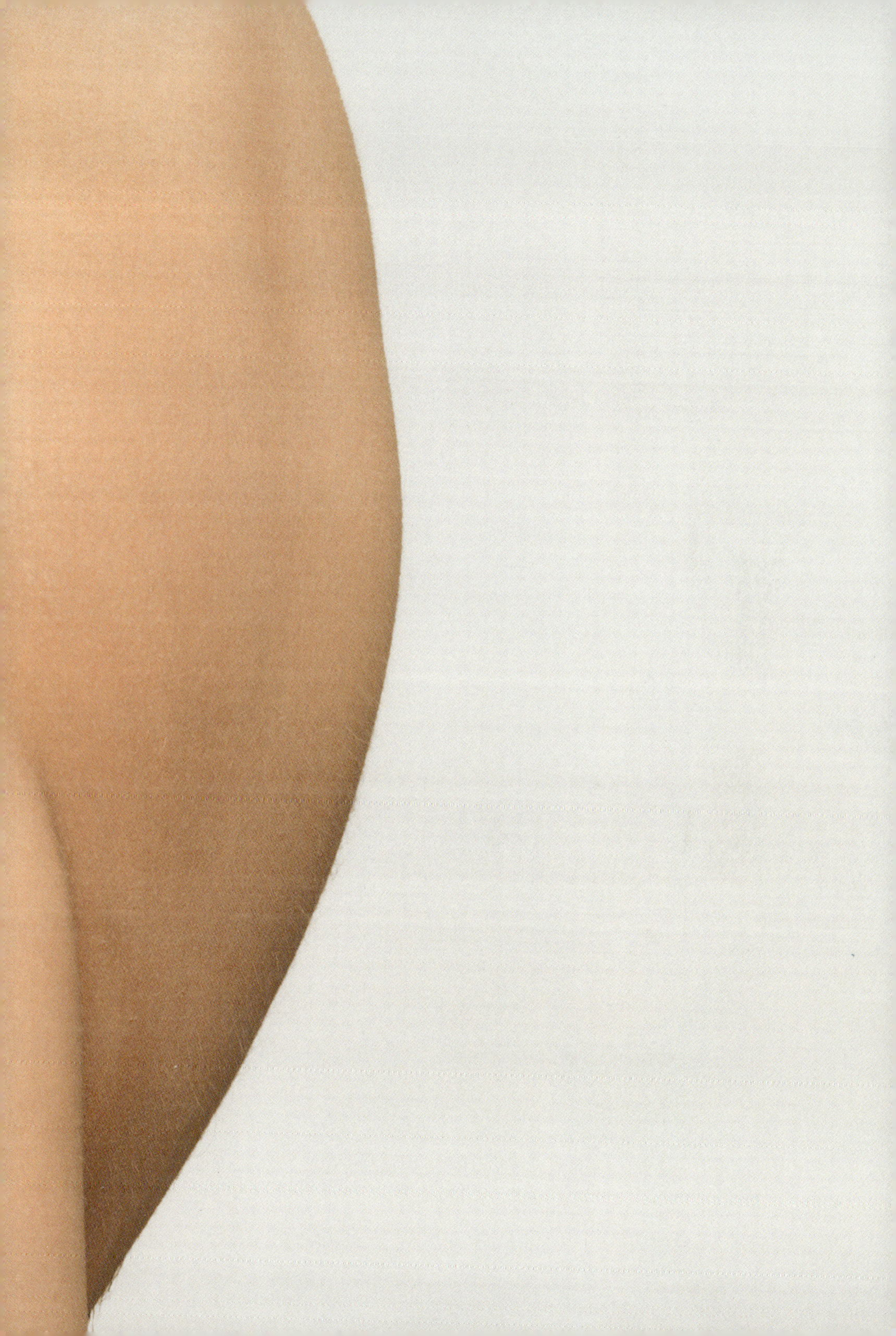

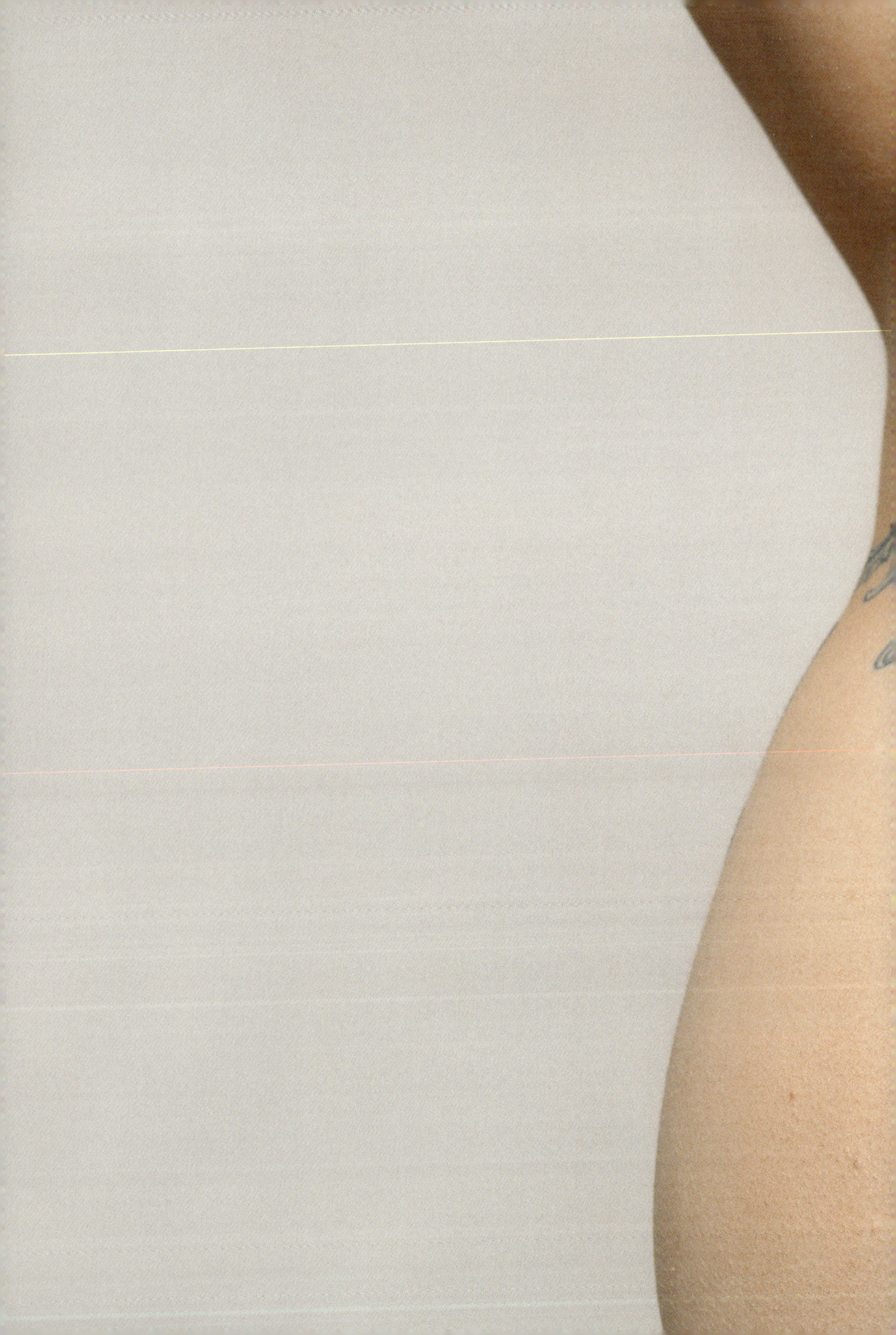

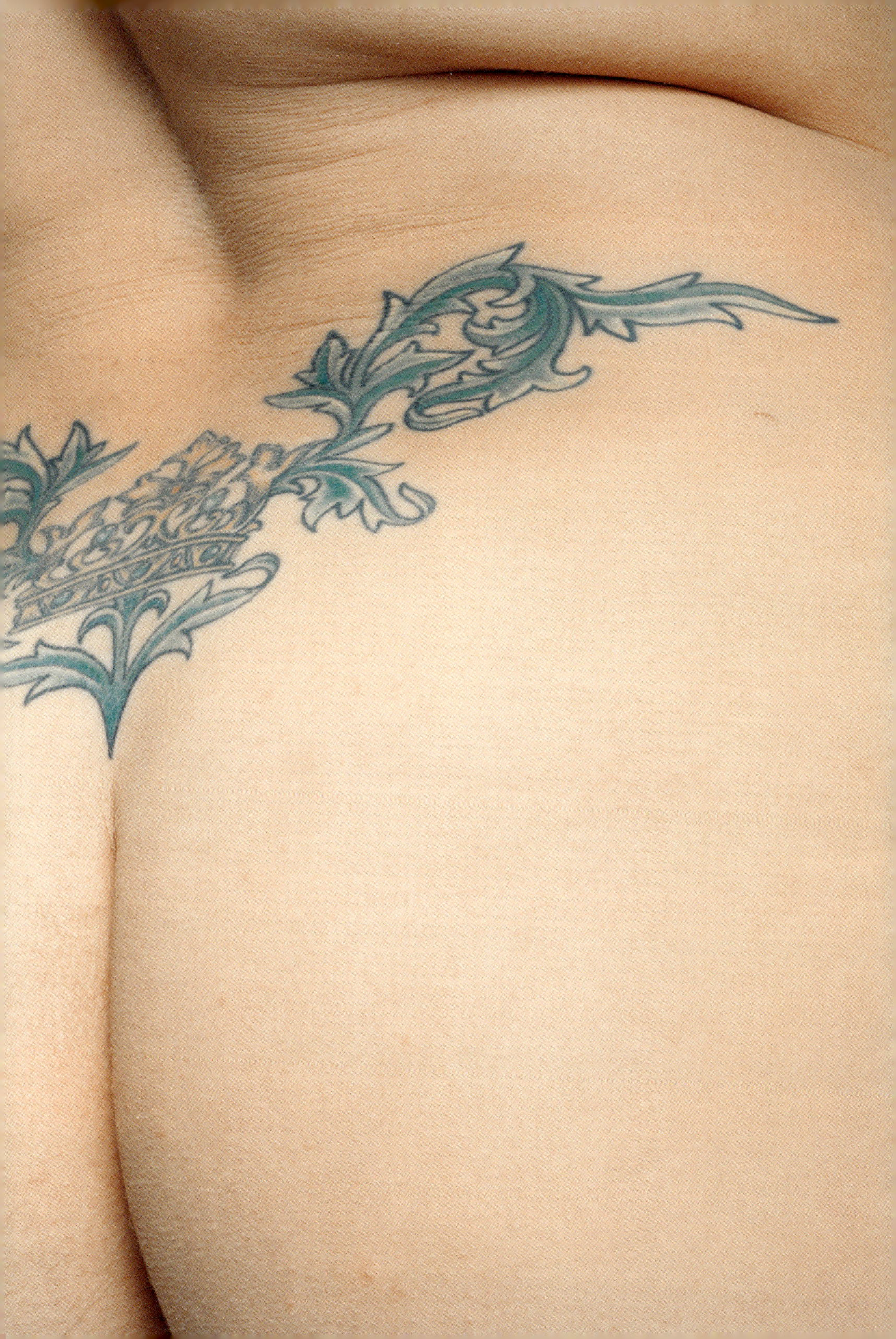

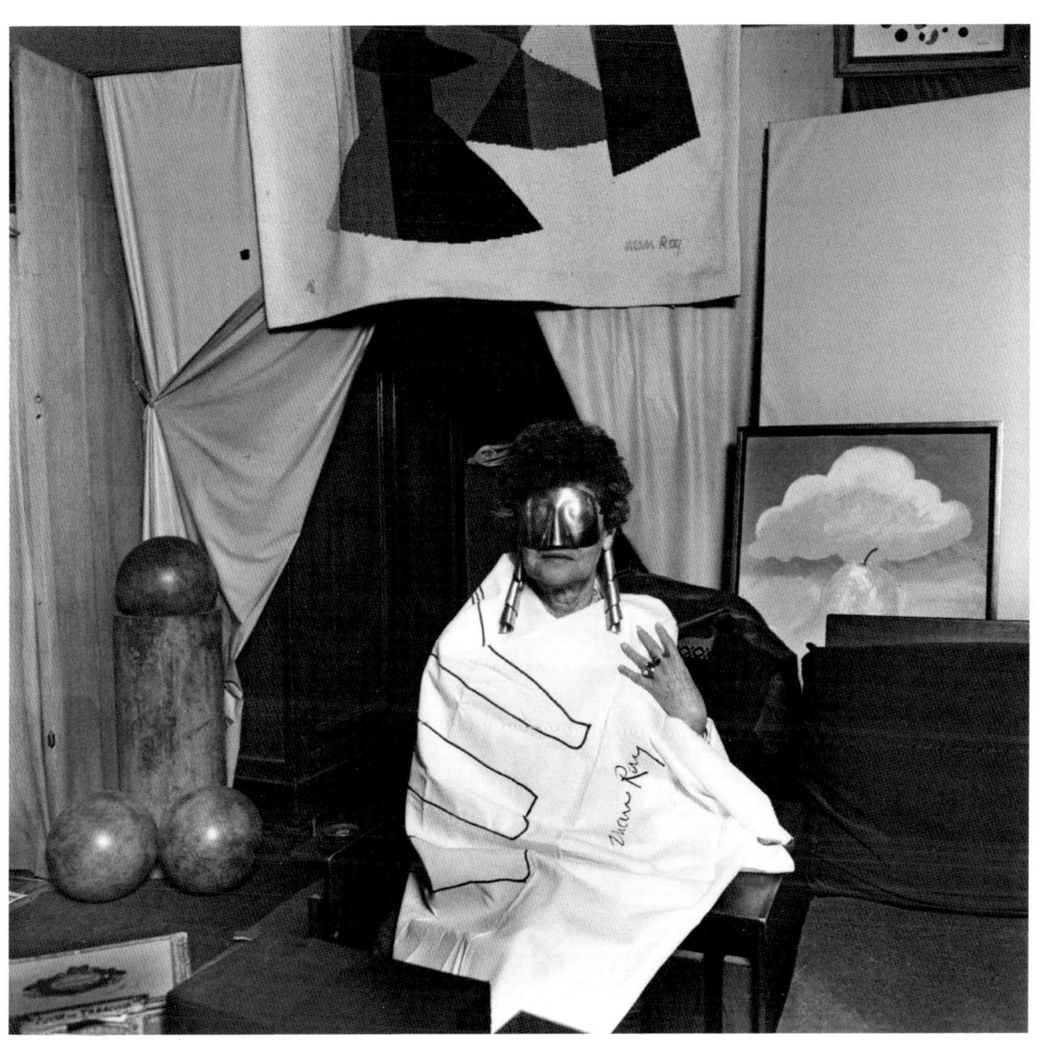

Juliet dans l'atelier de Man Ray, May 1981, Paris

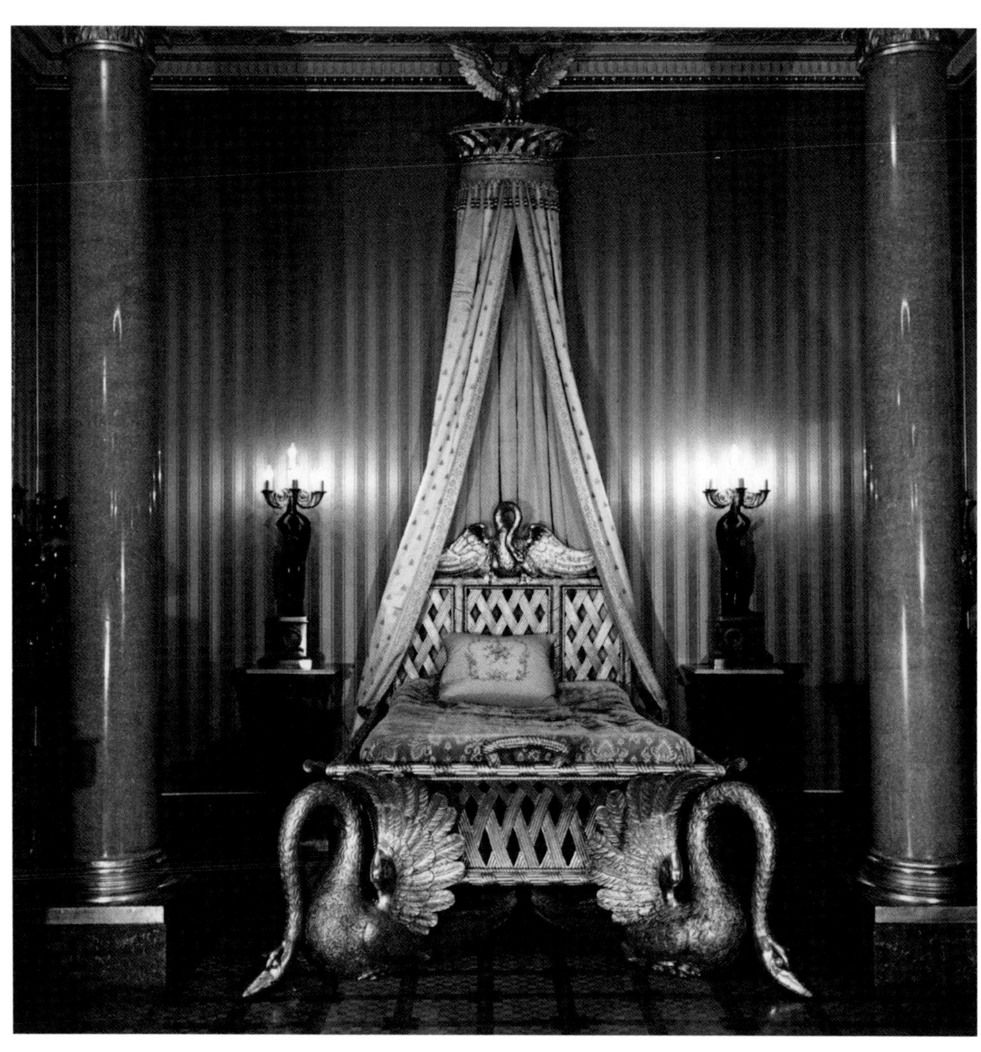

 Un lit chez la princesse Gloria von Thurn und Taxis, December 1987, Regensburg

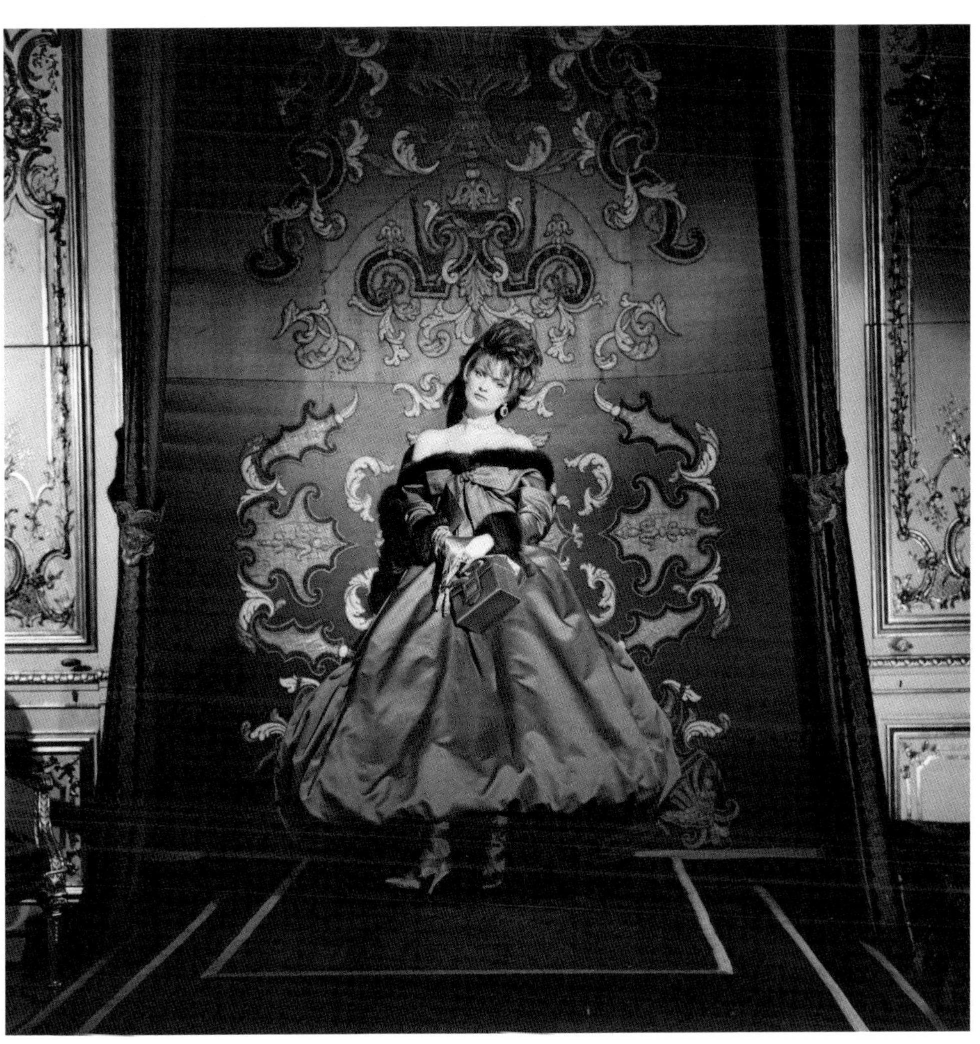

La princesse Gloria von Thurn und Taxis chez elle, December 1987, Regensburg
259

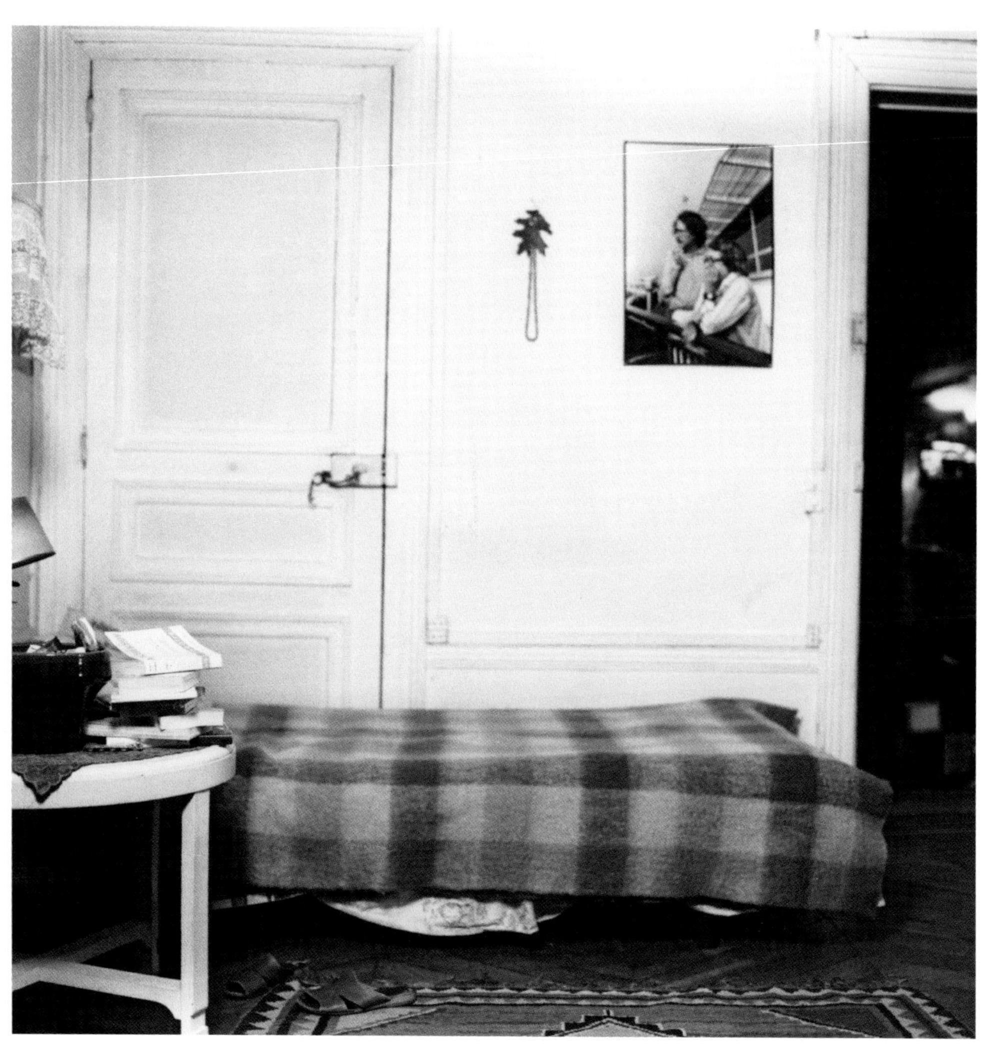

Le lit de Marguerite Duras, January 1985, Paris

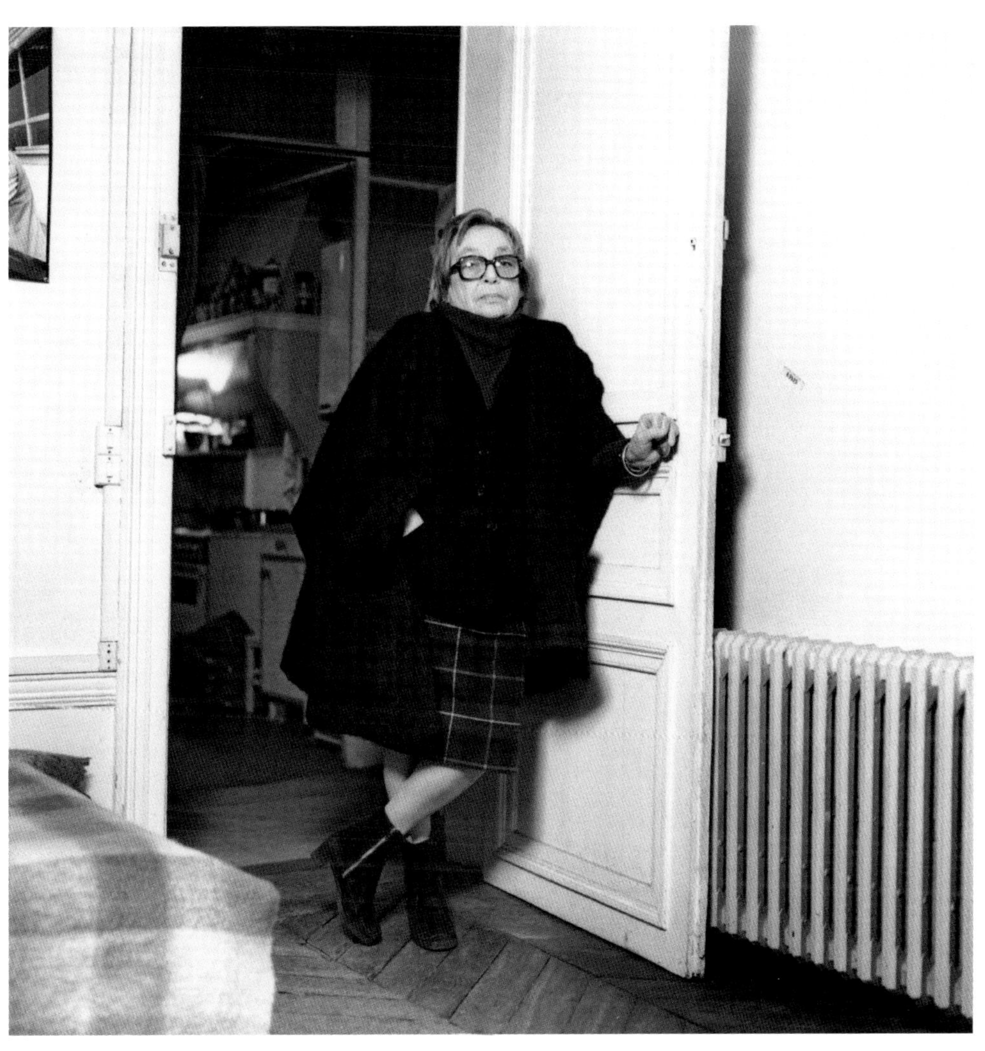

Marguerite Duras chez elle, January 1985, Paris

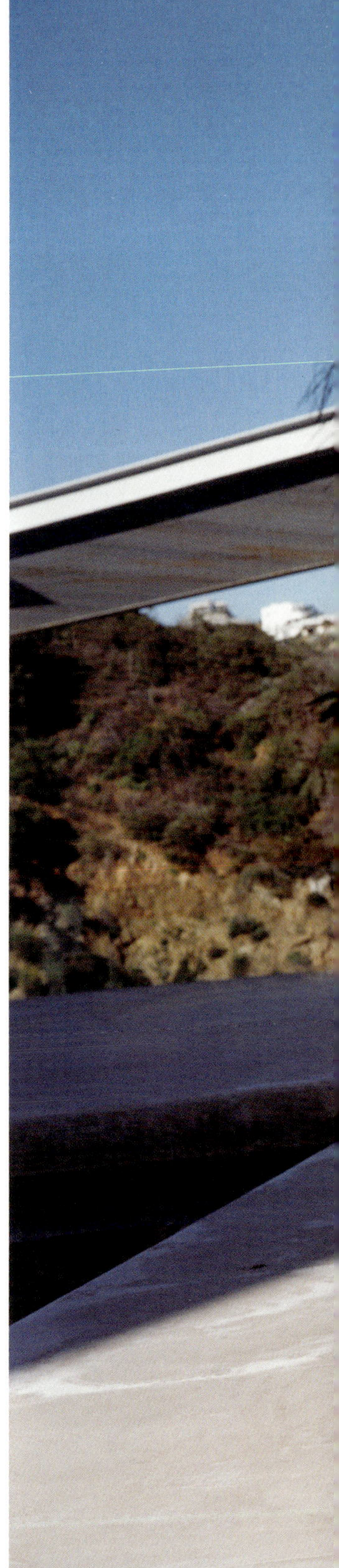

Elizabeth Berkley stuck in bamboo bushes,
March 1995, Los Angeles
Page 264 — *Parker Posey*, February 1994, Los Angeles
Page 265 — *Monique walking in a red latex dress at dawn on
Hollywood Boulevard*, February 1994, Los Angeles
Pages 266/267 — *Kate Winslet*, September 2010, Paris

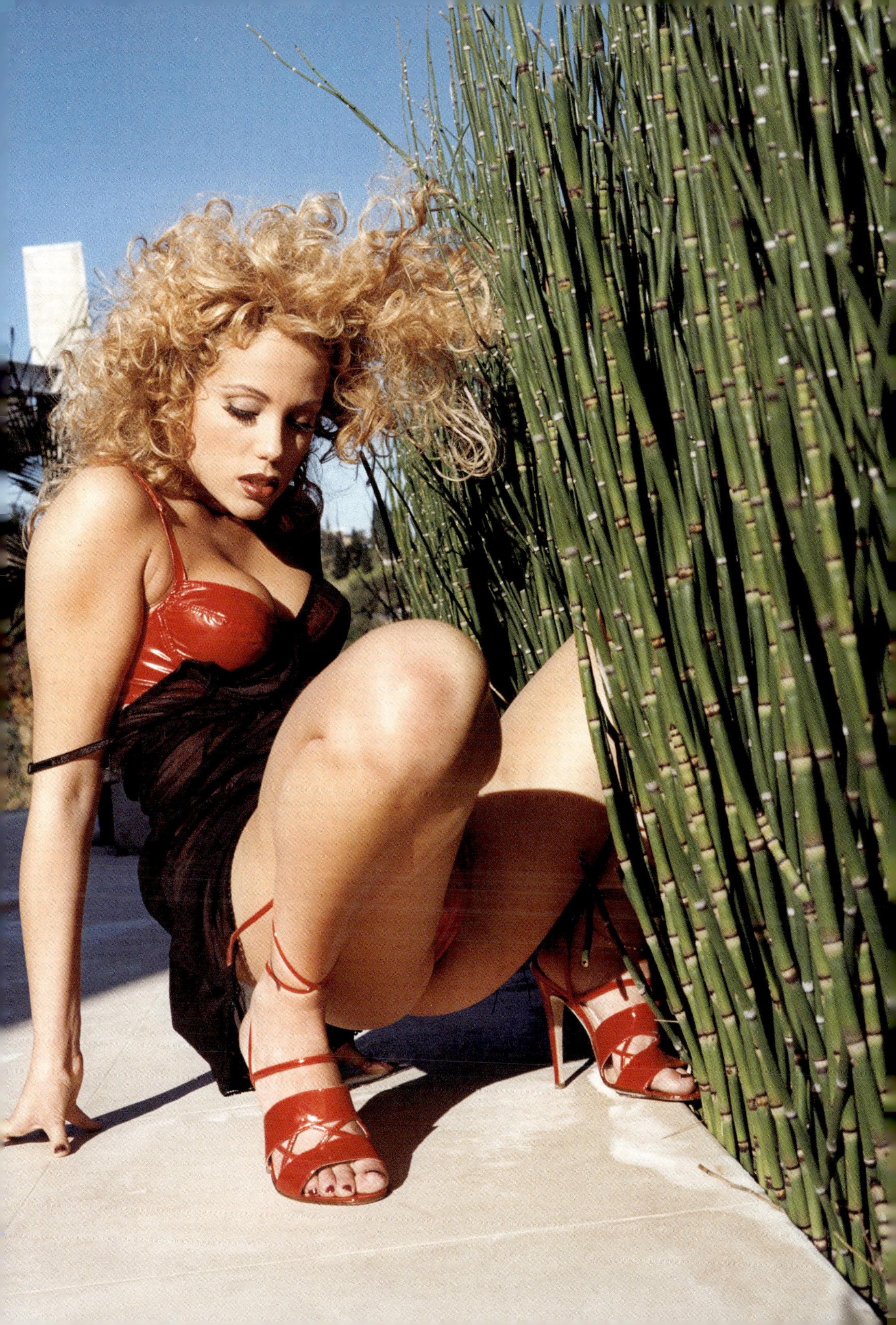

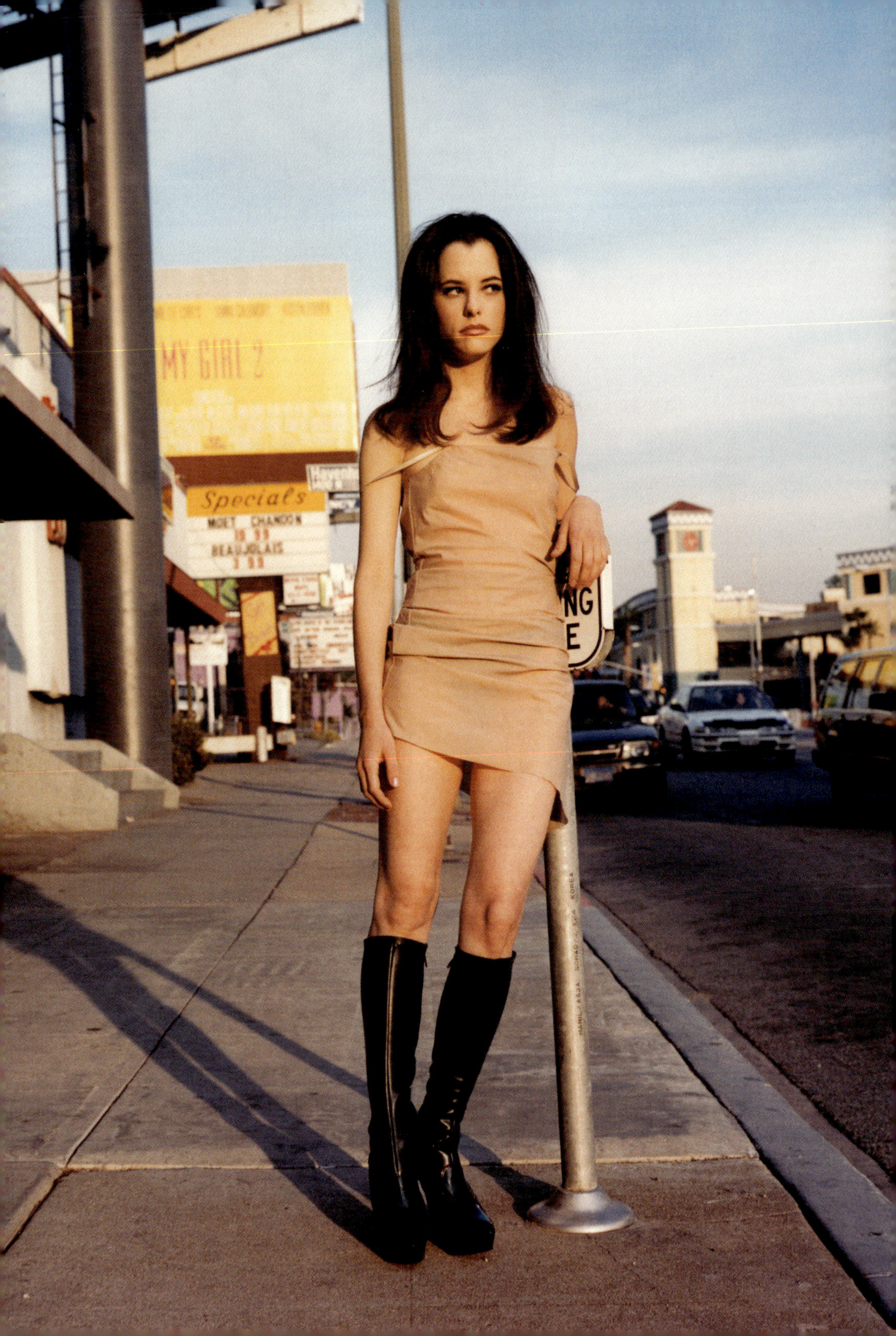
MY GIRL 2
Specials
MOET CHANDON
BEAUJOLAIS
MANILA R.S.A. SCHAO PER C.A. KOREA

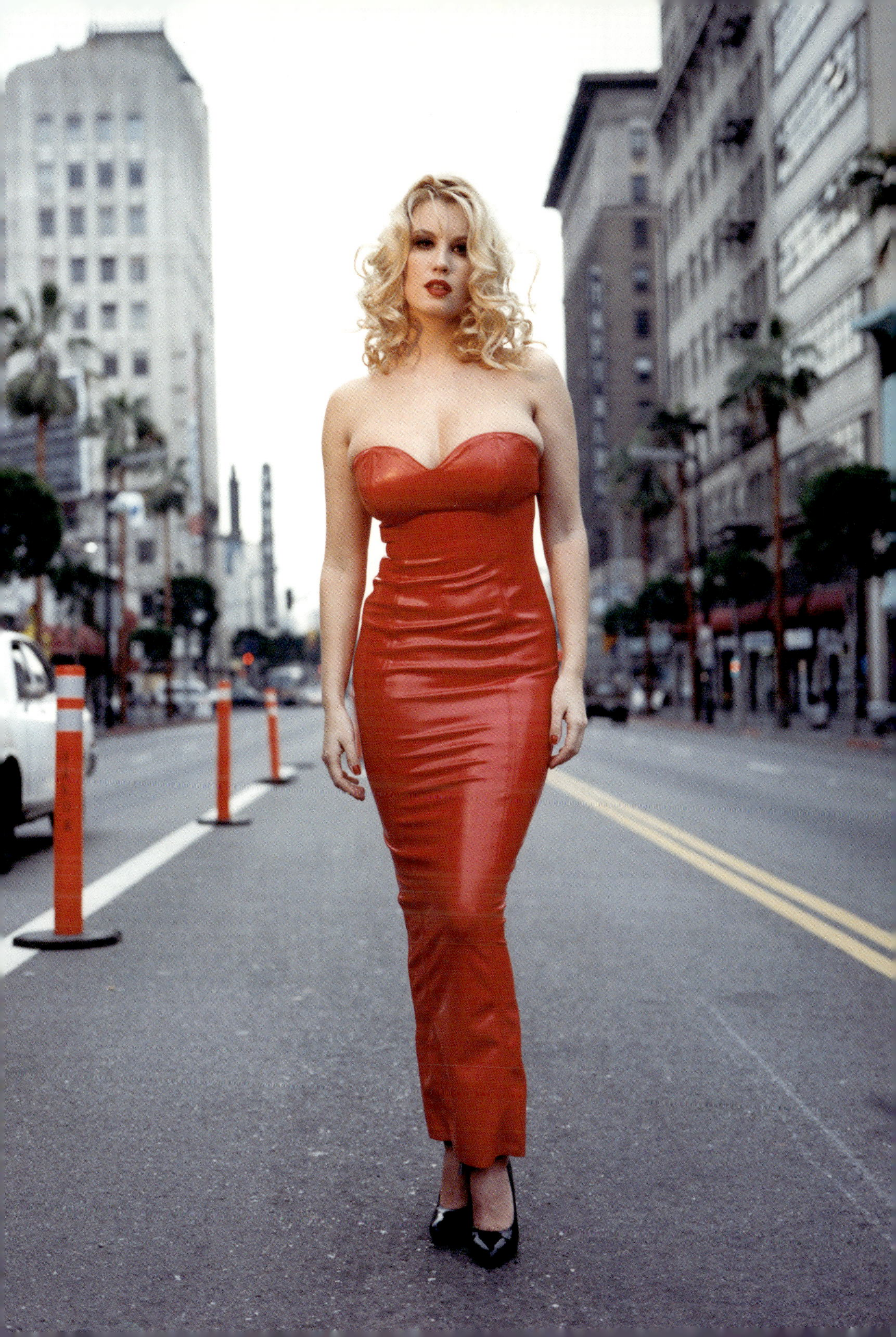

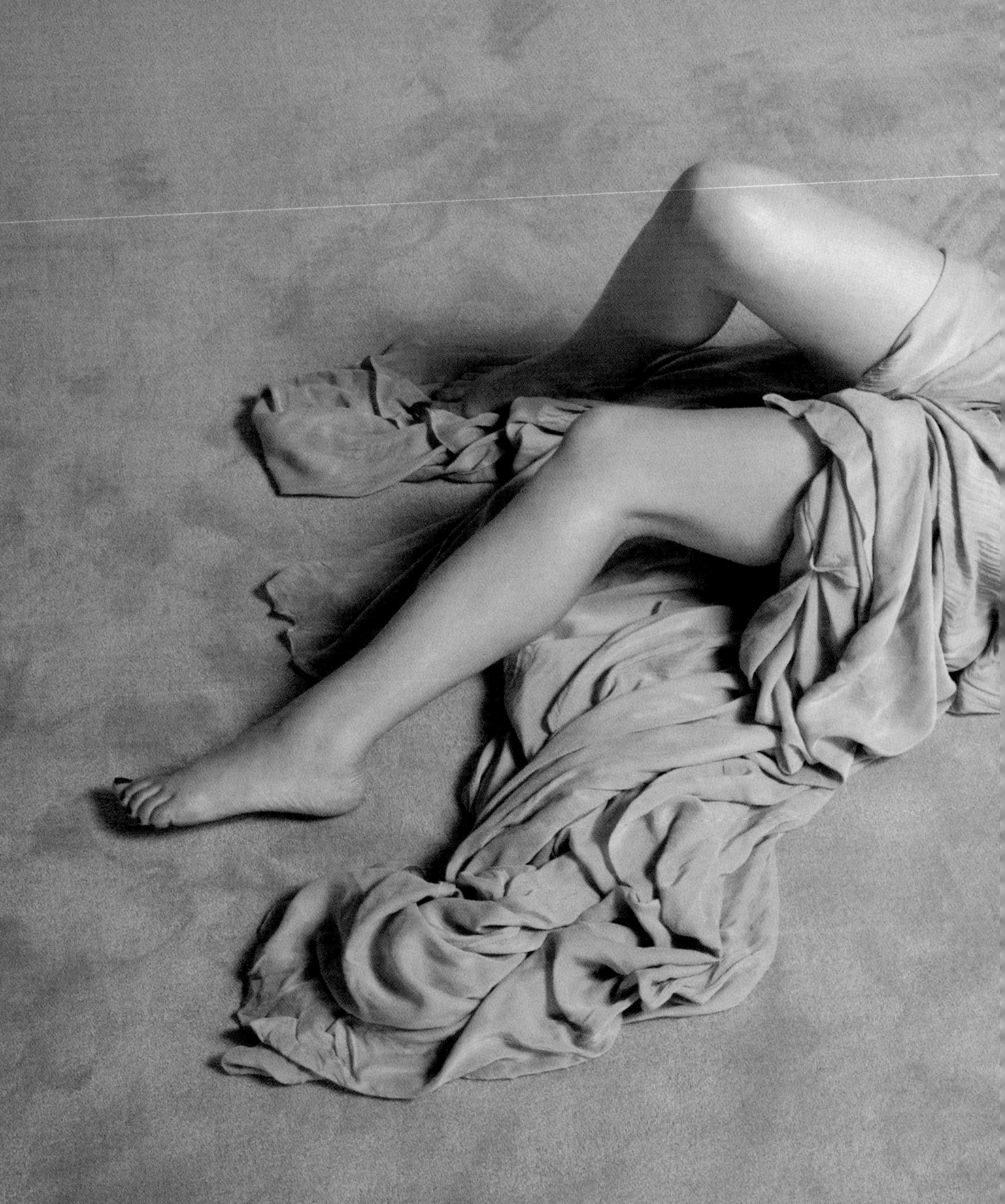

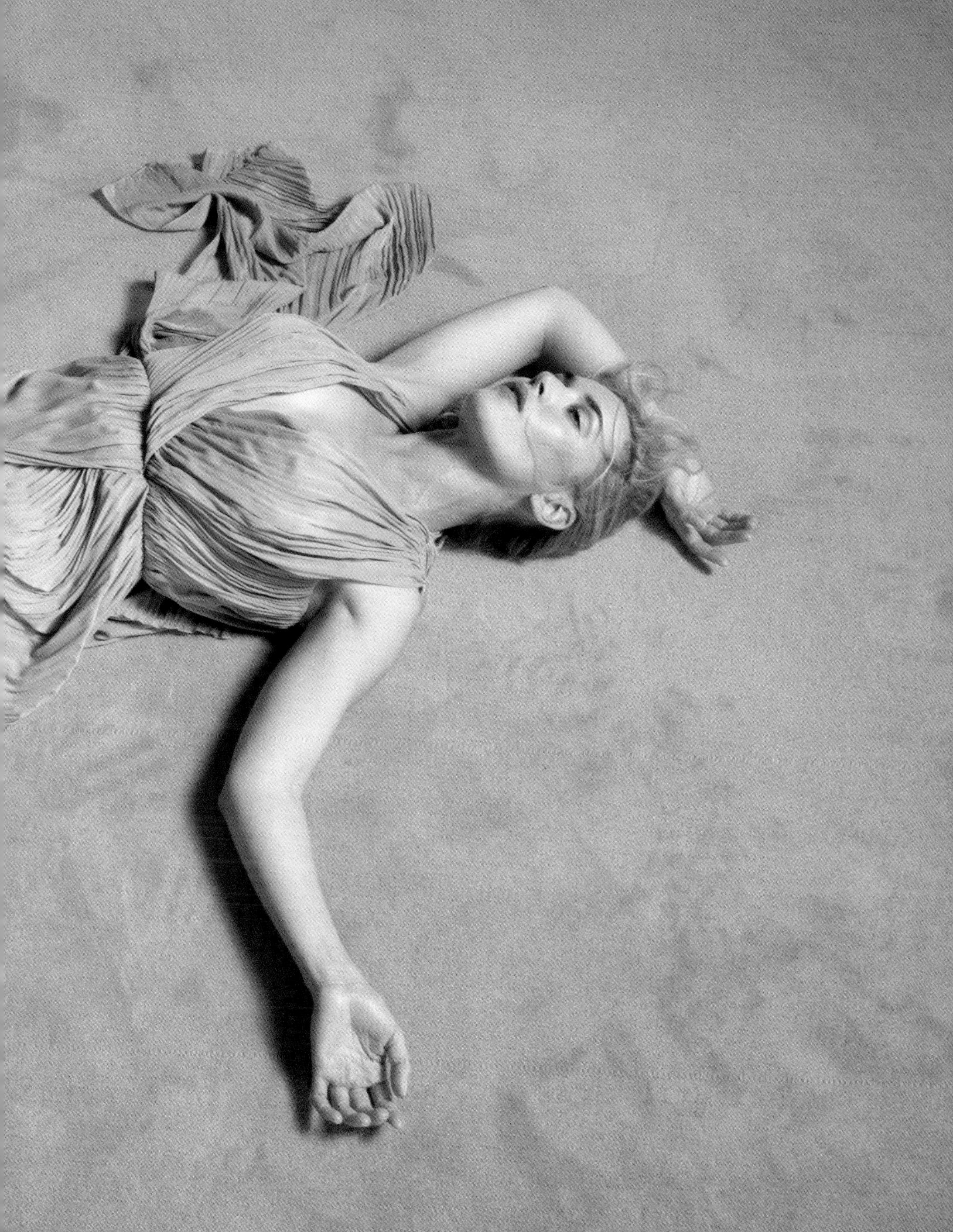

Heather Graham in a strange mood, crushing a Tab can, November 1996, Los Angeles
Page 270 — *Reese Witherspoon hiding in the garden II*, November 1996, Los Angeles
Page 271 — *Joey Adams washing her underpants*, November 1996, Los Angeles

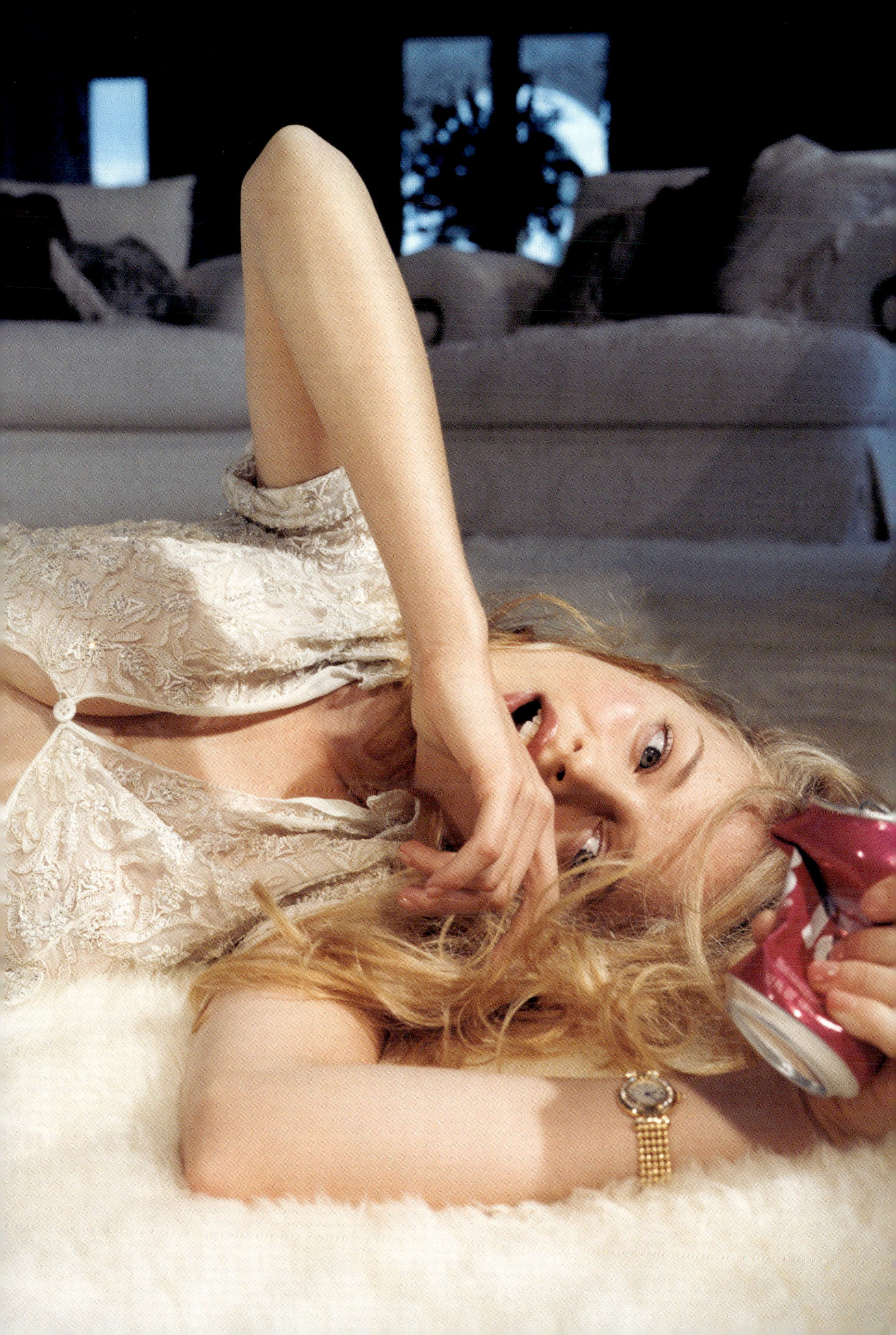

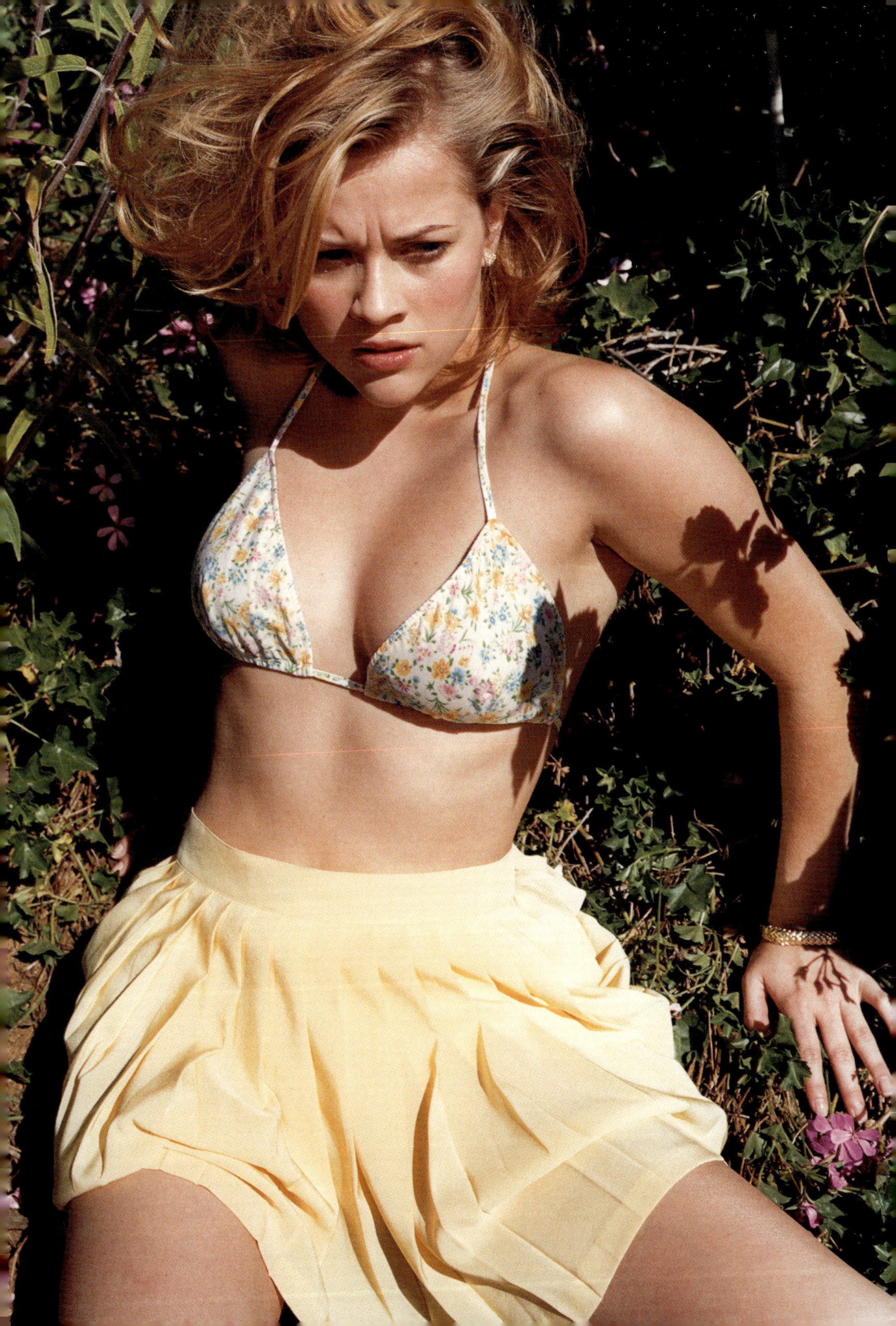

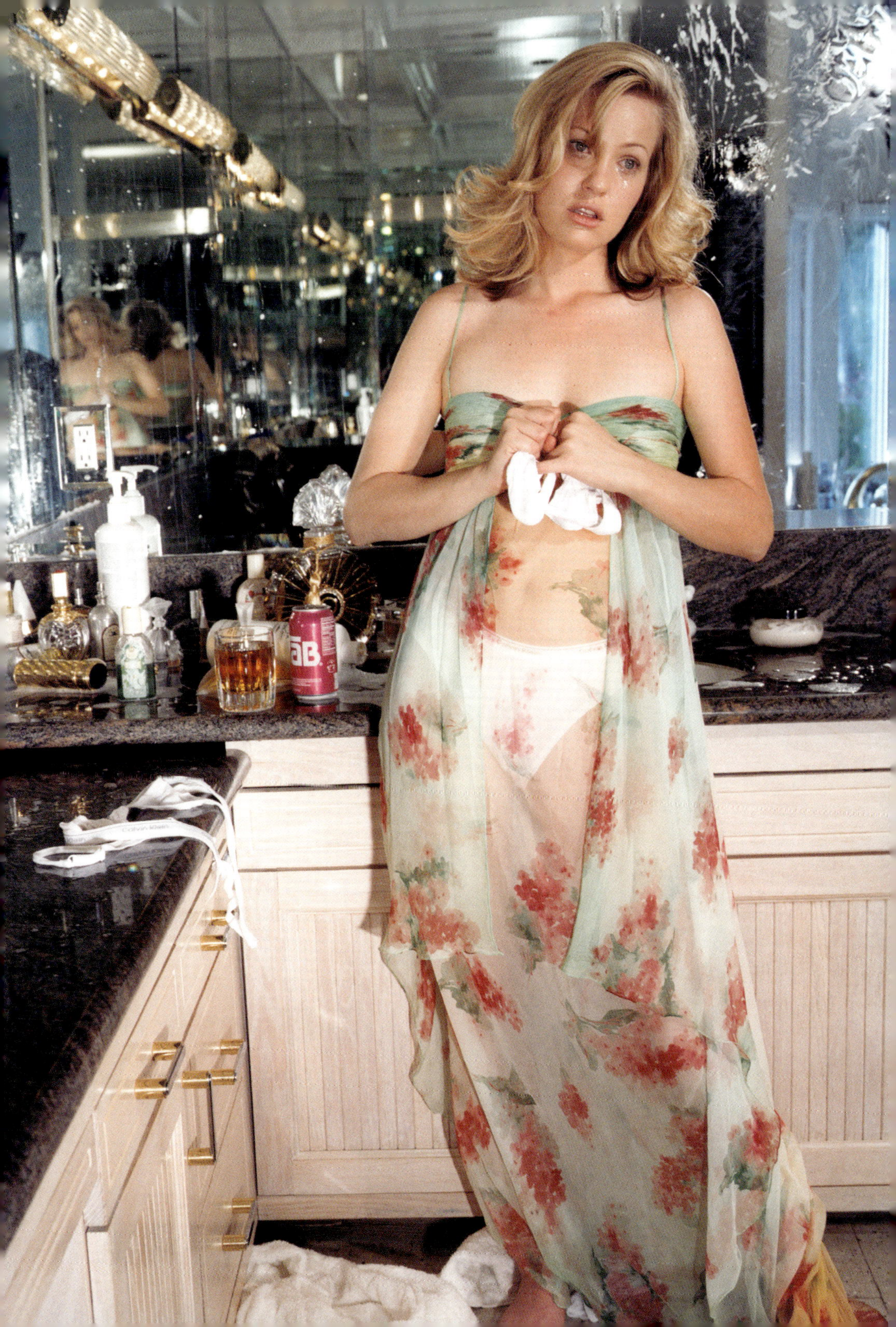

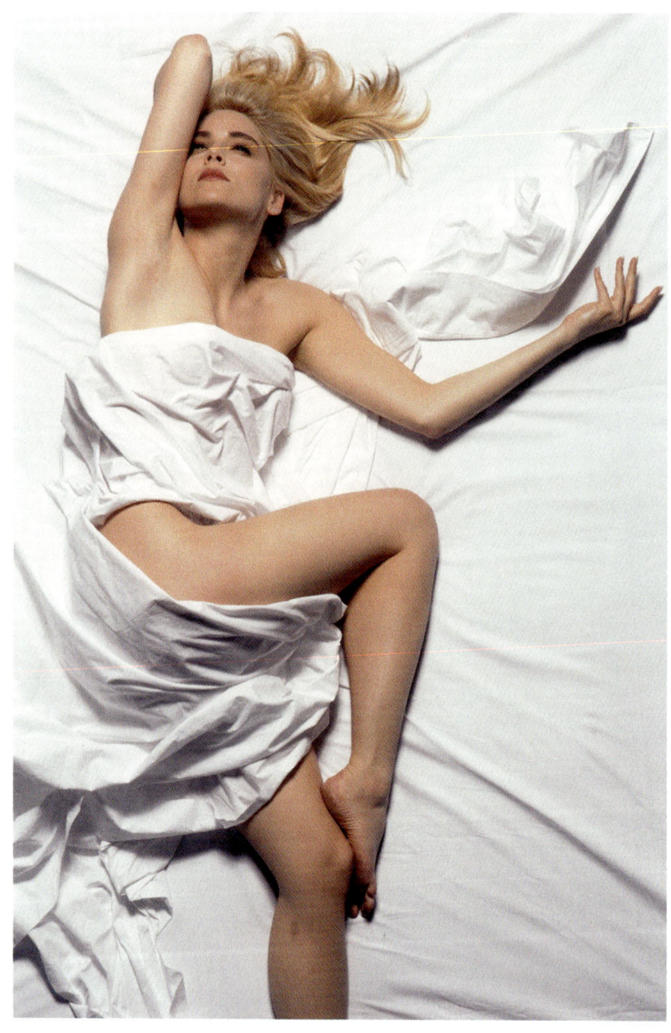

Above — *Sharon Stone for the poster of «Basic Instinct»*, July 1991, Los Angeles
Opposite page — *Close-up of Anne Pedersen doing a strange bubble*, February 1996, Paris
Page 274 — *Jaimie Richard*, October 1994, New York
Page 275 — *Daryl Hannah fait des bulles de savon*, April 1991, Los Angeles
Pages 276/277 — *Monica Bellucci in the Moroccan desert*, December 2001, Morocco

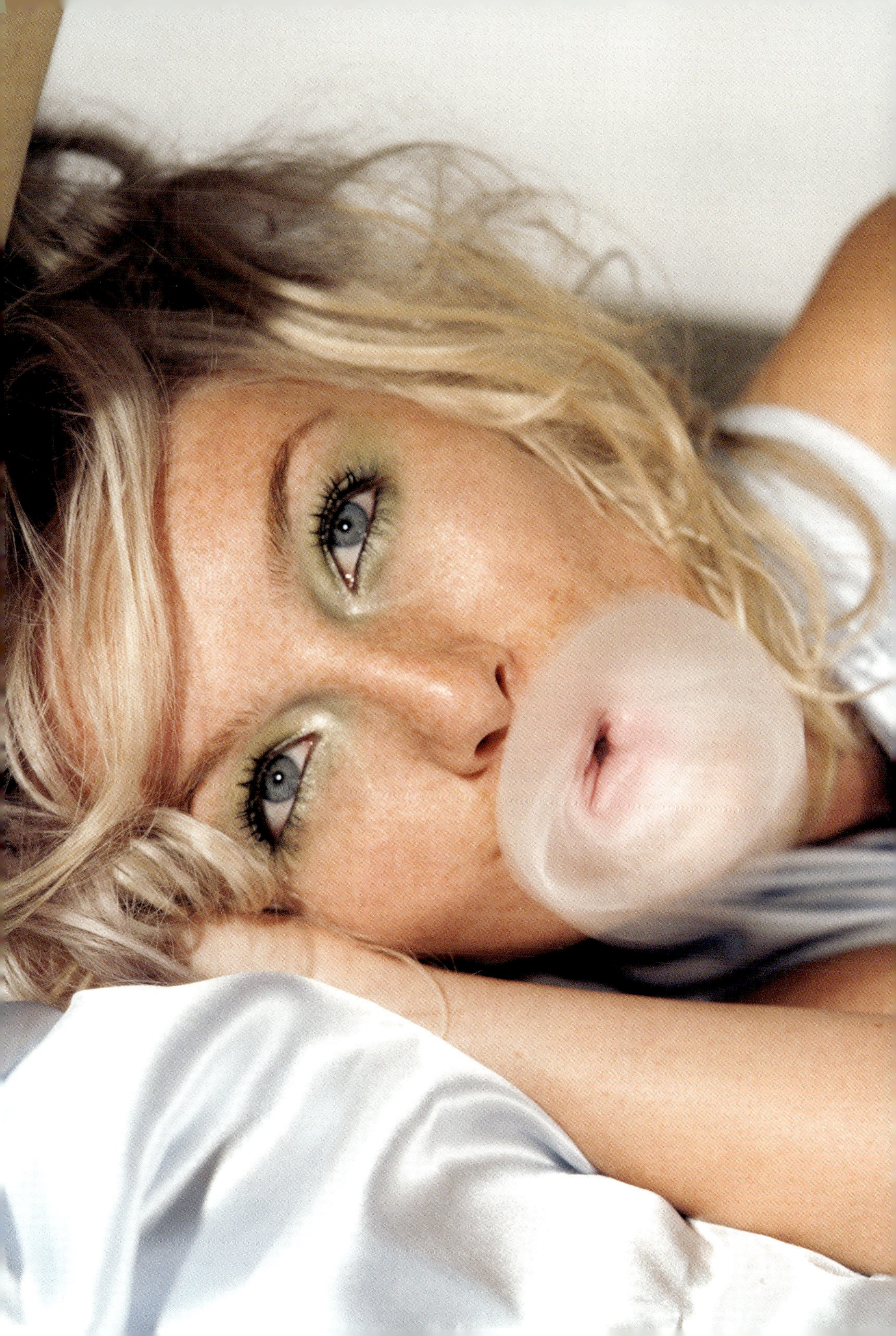

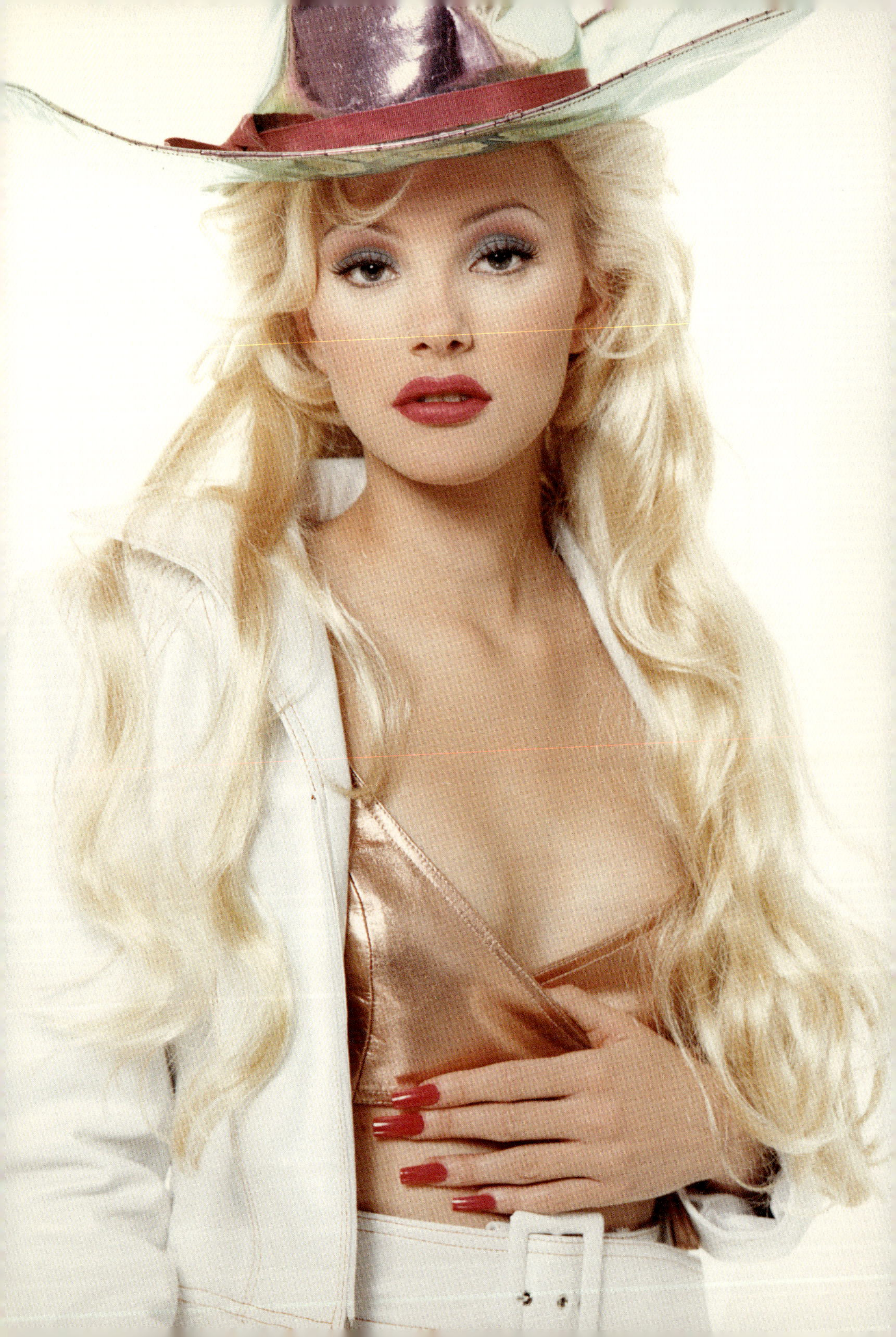

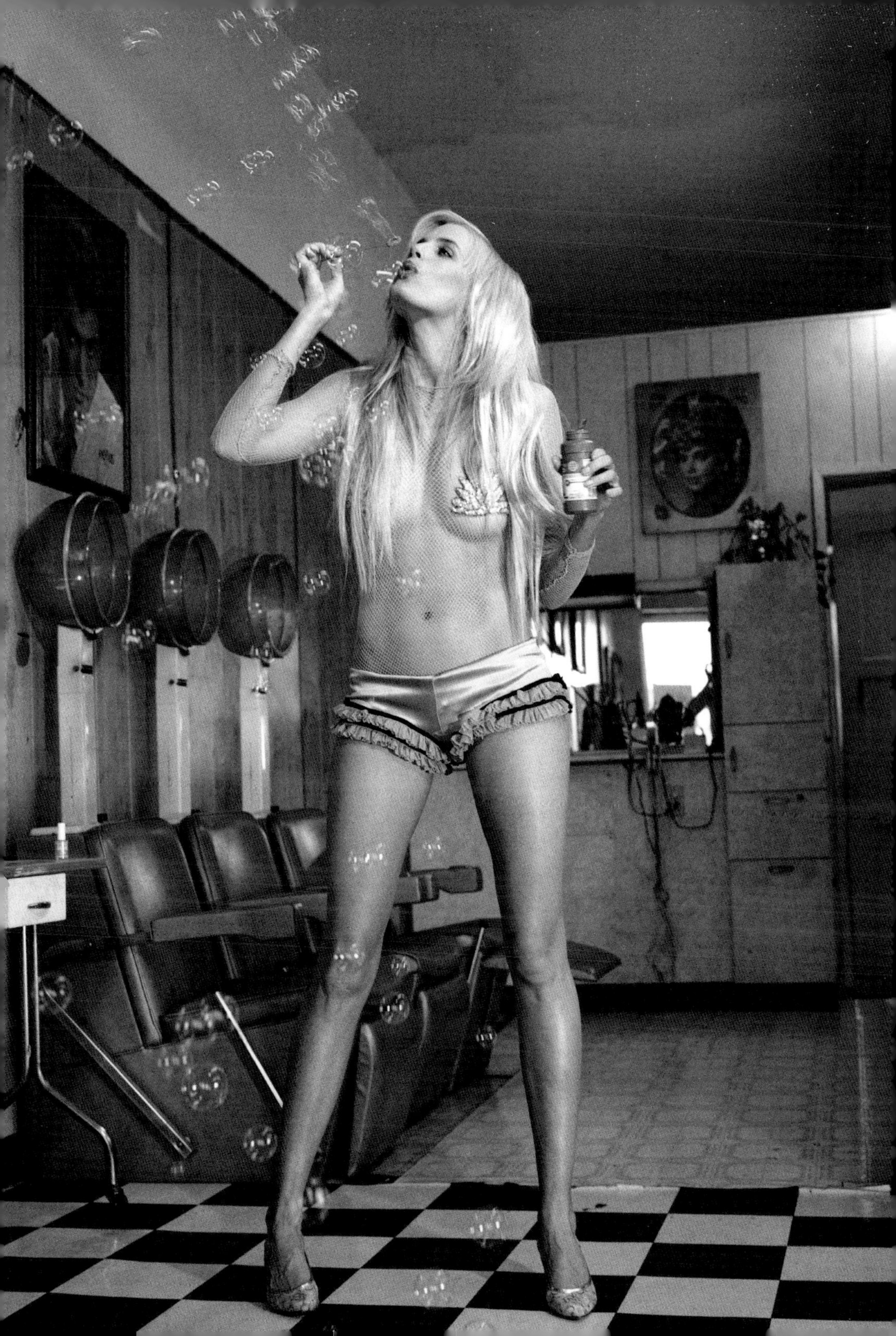

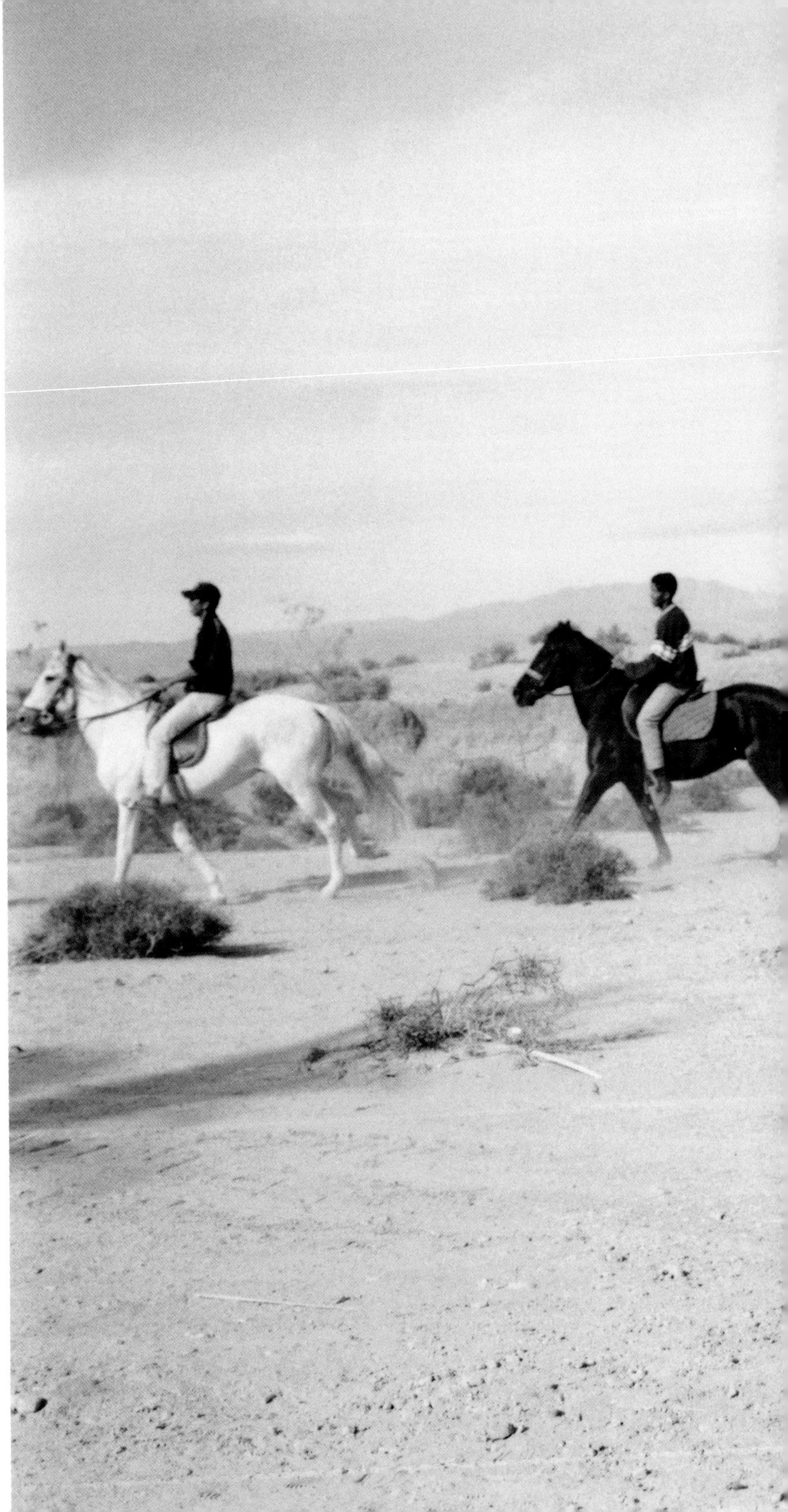

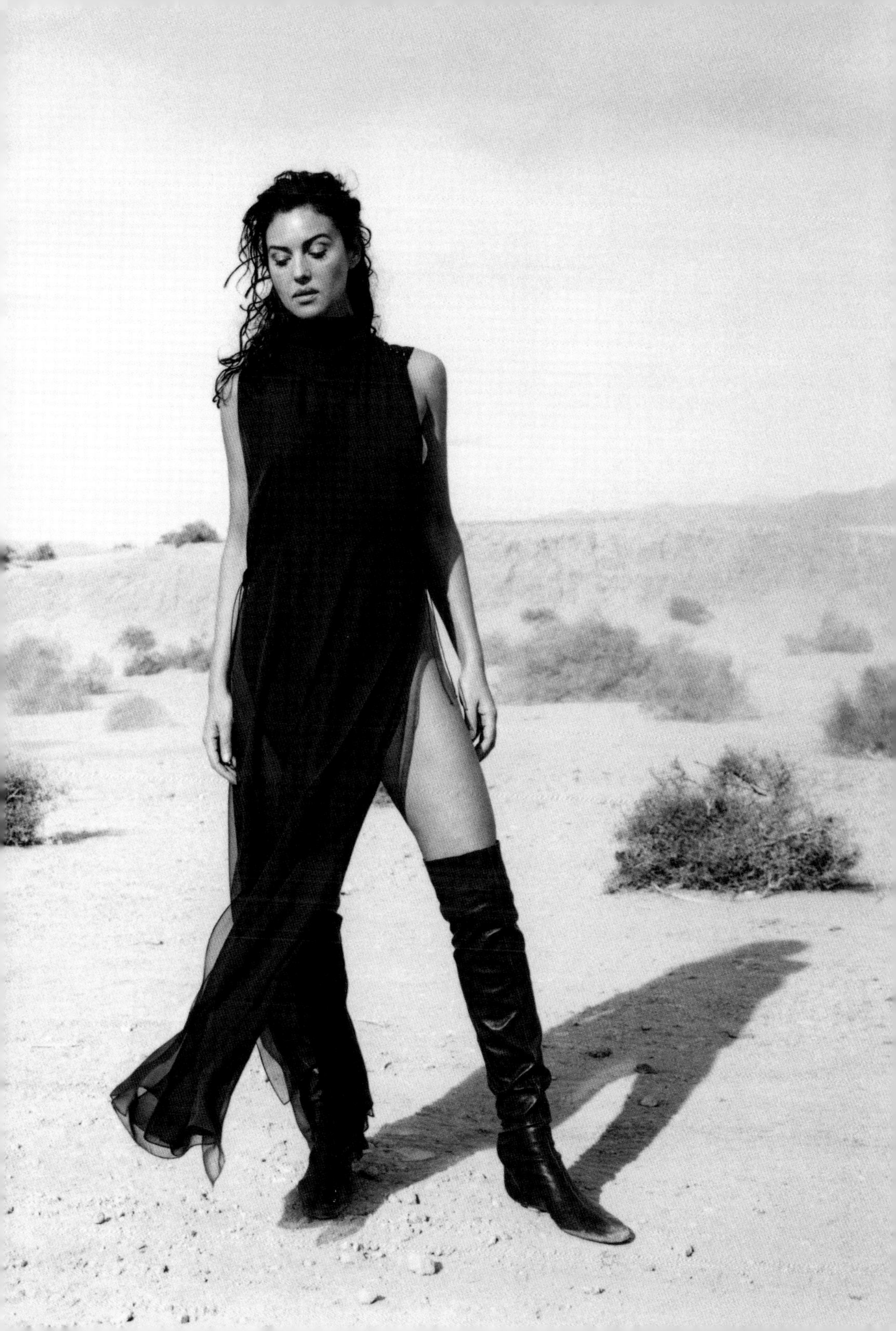

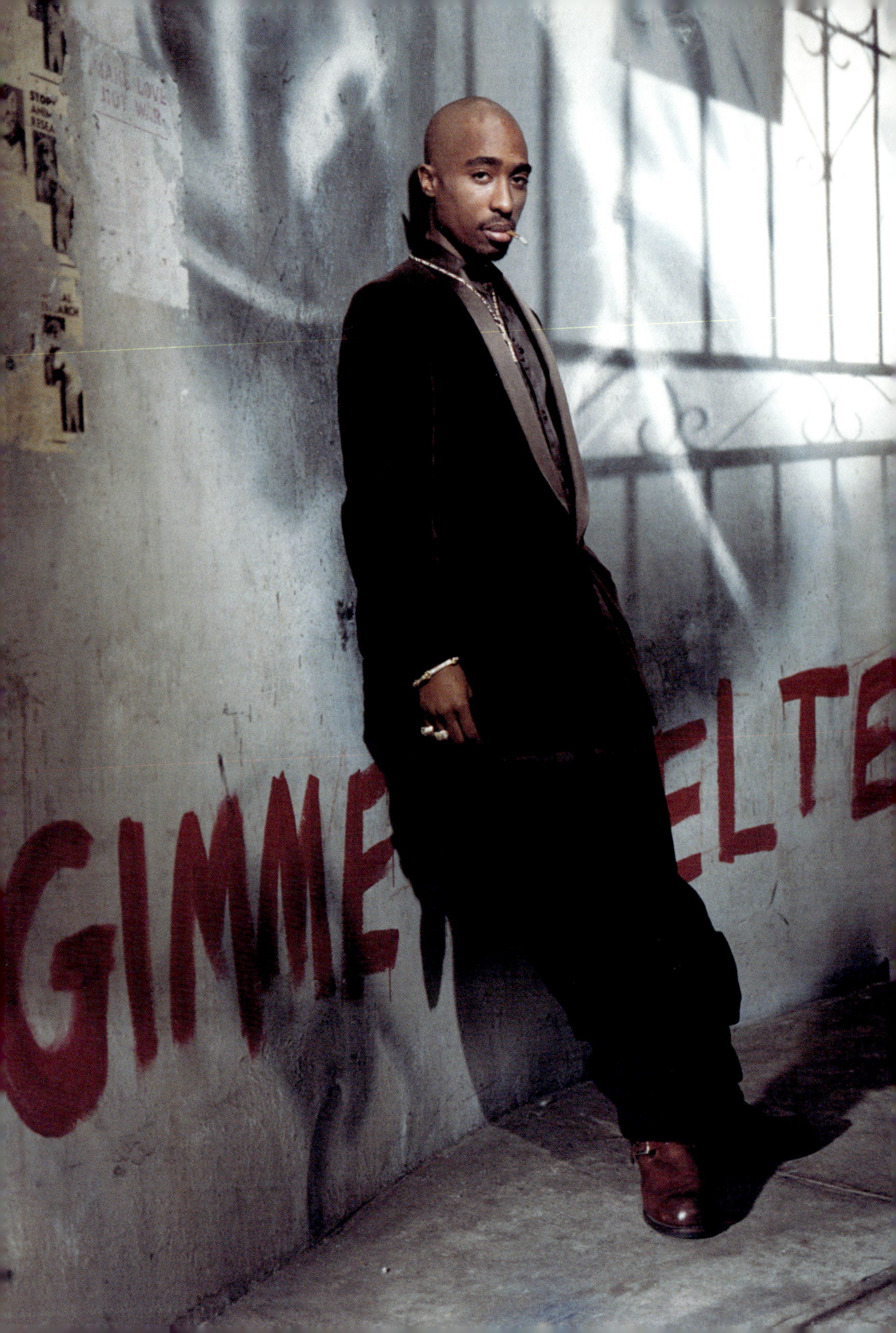

MAKE LOVE
NOT WAR.
STOP AND
RESEA
GIMME SHELTER

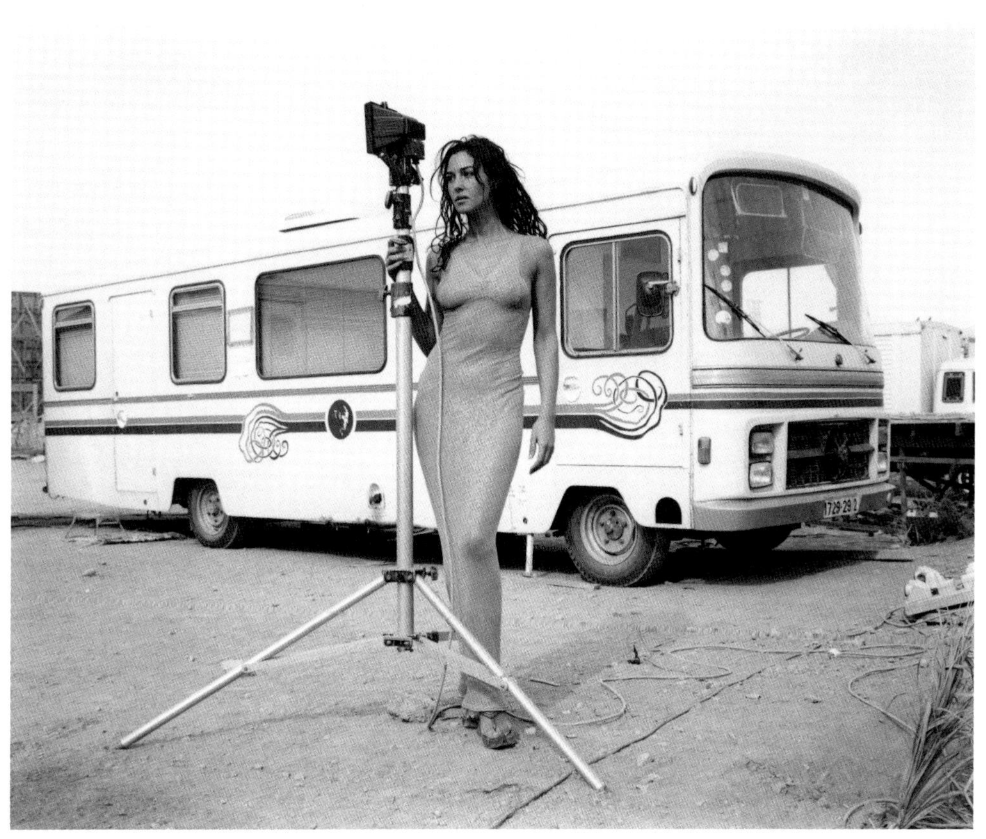

Above — *Monica Bellucci in the Moroccan desert II*, December 2001, Morocco
Opposite page — *«Gimme Shelter» with Tupac Shakur*, April 1994, Los Angeles

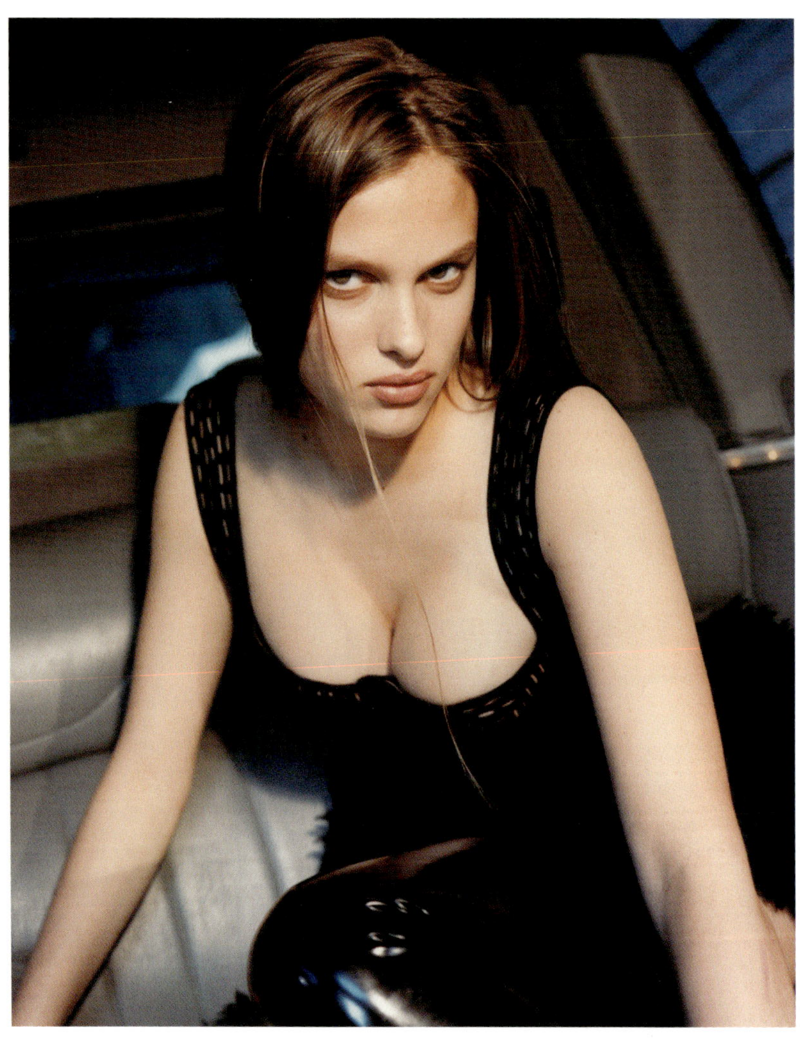

Above — *Vinessa Shaw in an Alaïa dress, sitting in a limousine, age 15*, February 1994, Los Angeles
Opposite page — *Angelina Jolie playing «Valley of the Dolls»*, February 1994, Los Angeles
Pages 282/283— *Julie Strain on the terrace at the Château Marmont*, February 1994, Los Angeles
Pages 284/285 — *Sherilyn Fenn allongée sur un bar quelque part sur une route*, April 1991, Los Angeles
Page 286 — *Portrait de Sherilyn Fenn couchée sur un bar*, April 1991, Los Angeles
Page 287 — *Liv Tyler smoking and ironing at the Chelsea Hotel II*, October 1995, New York

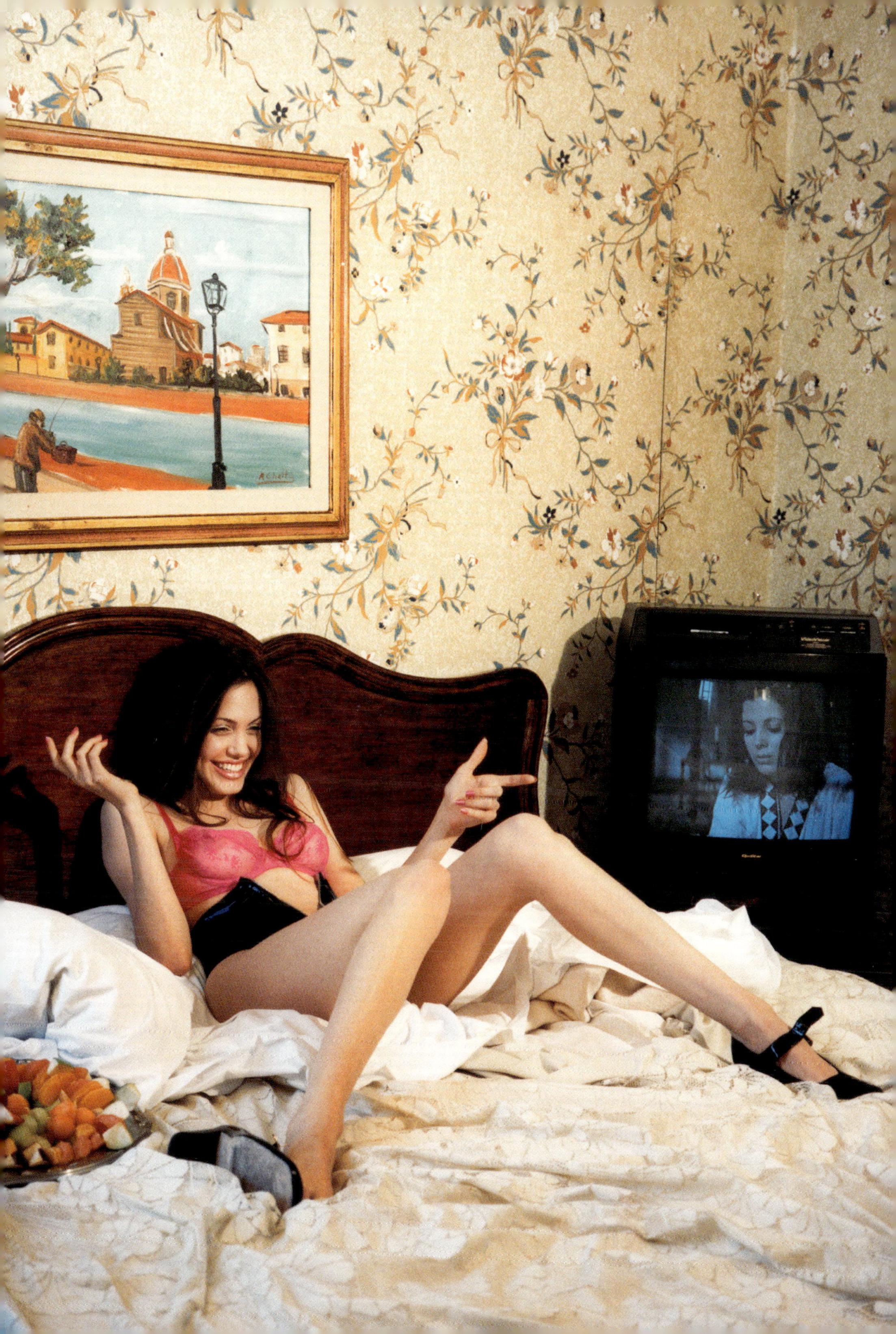

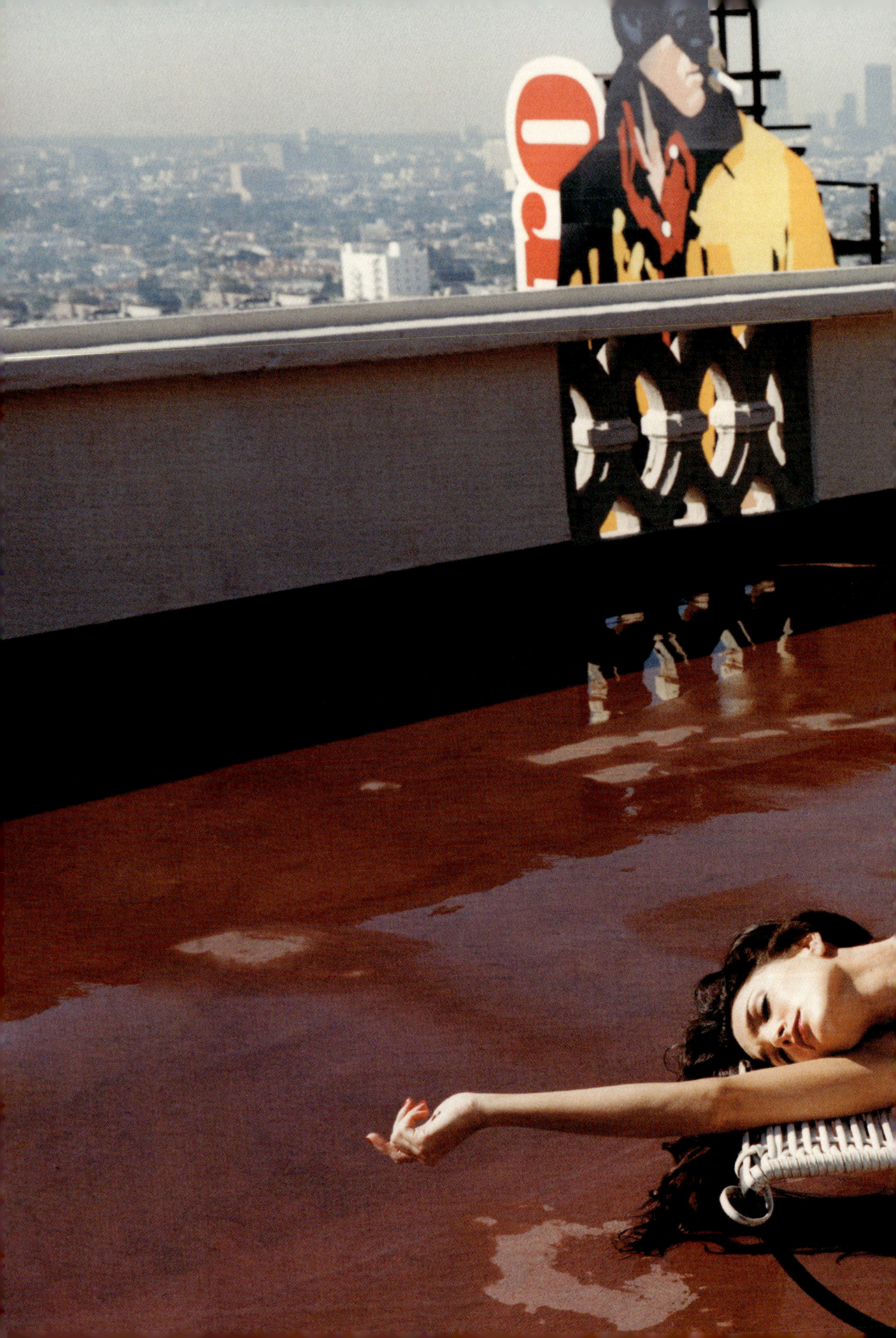

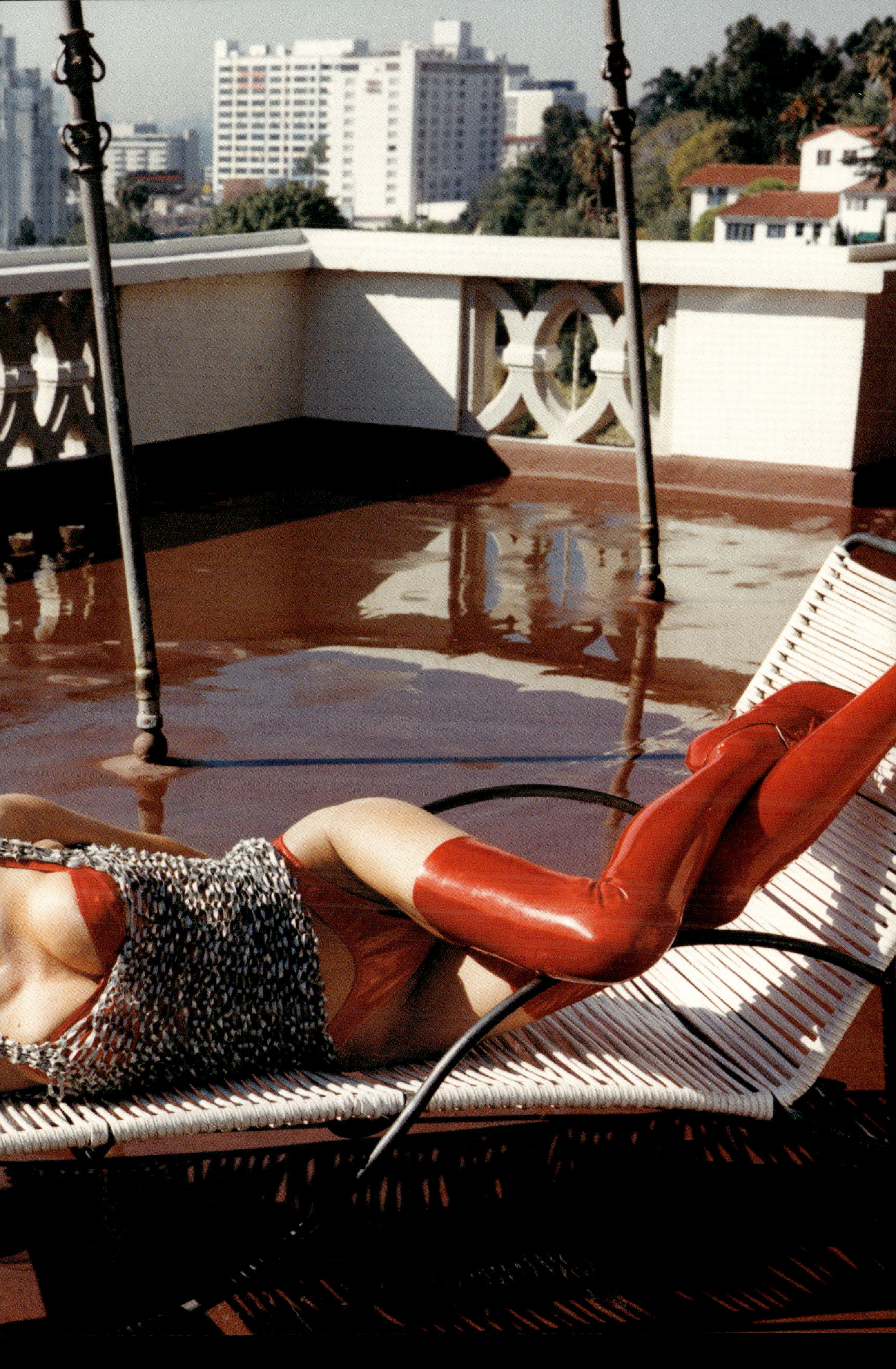

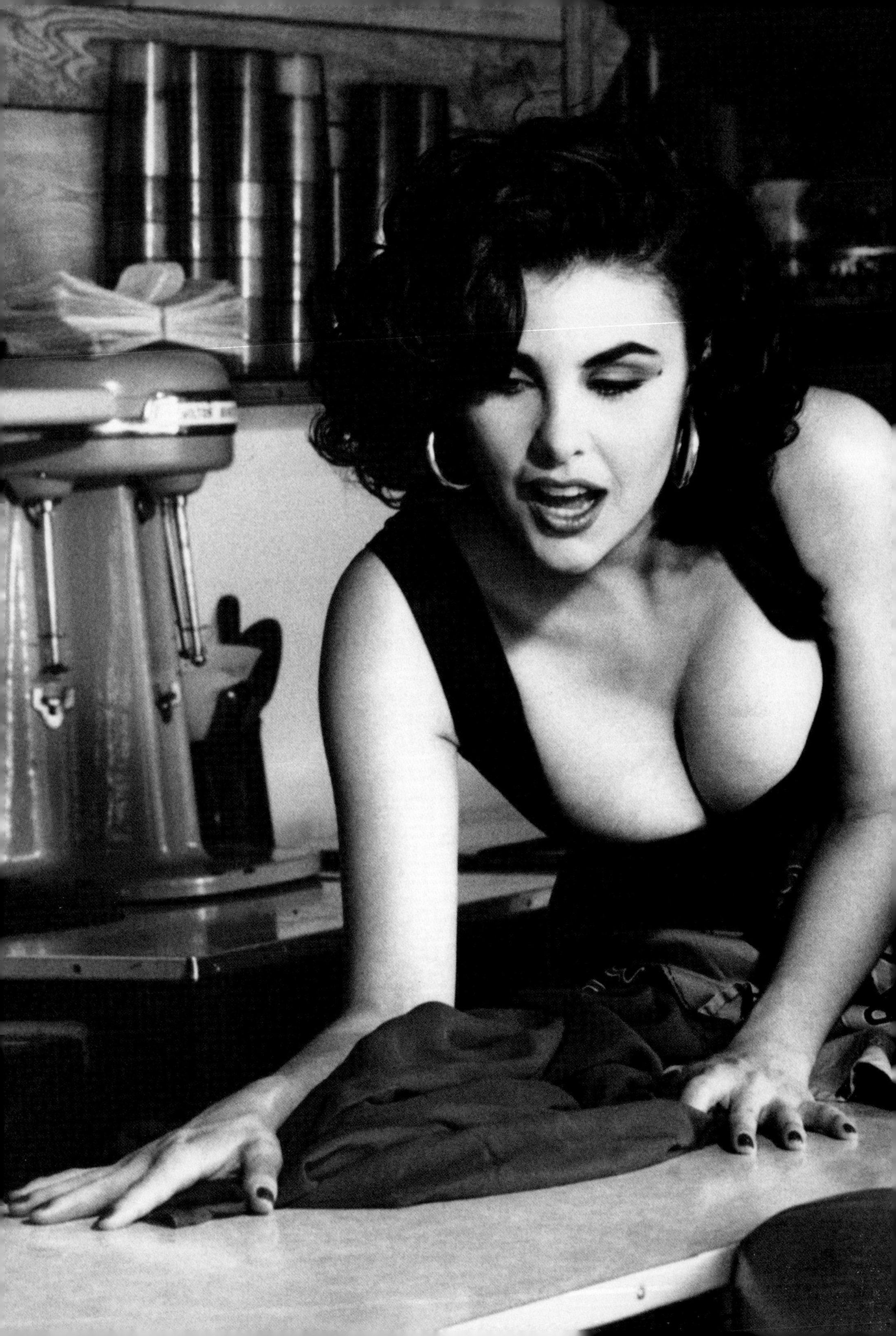

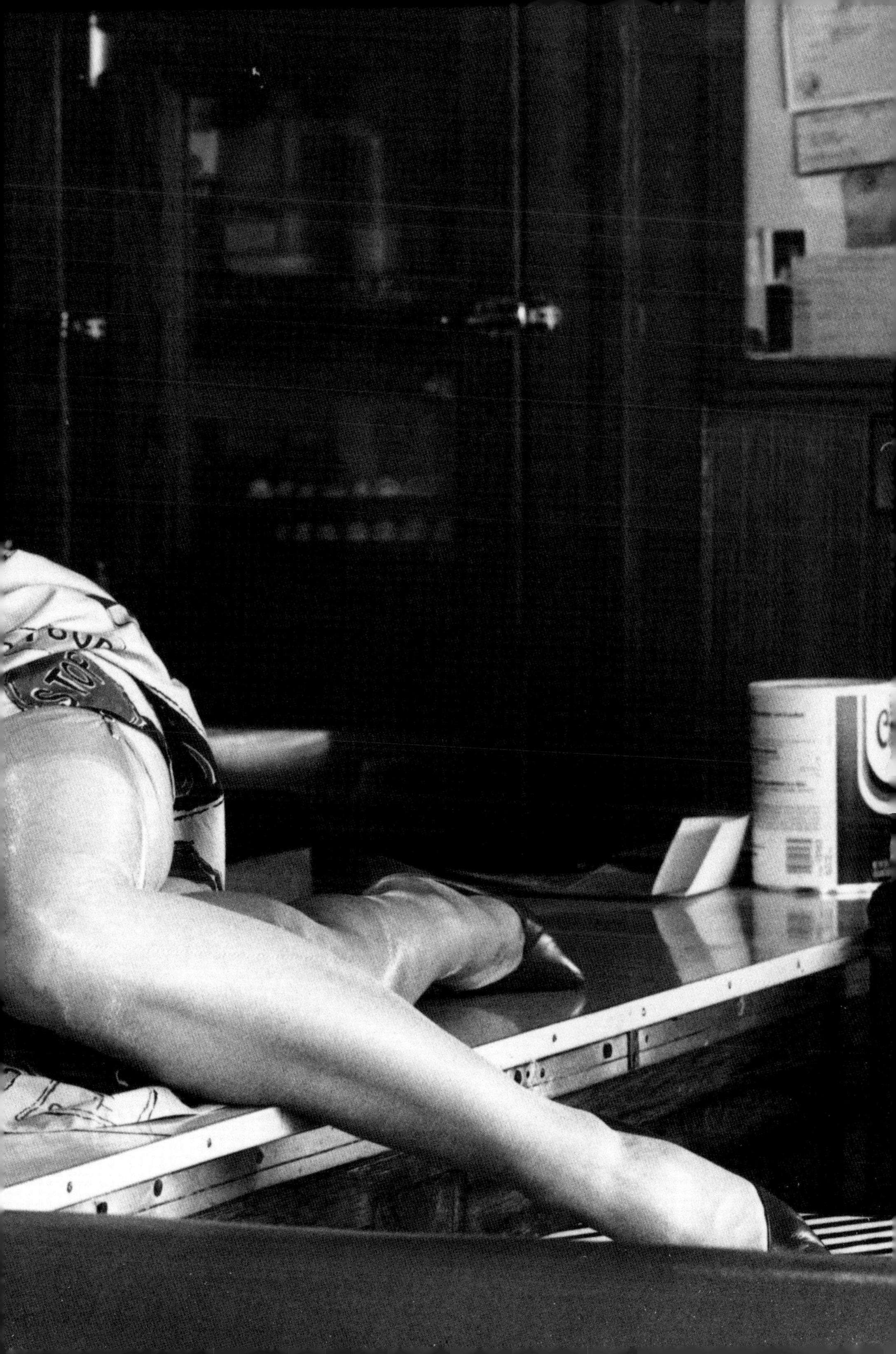

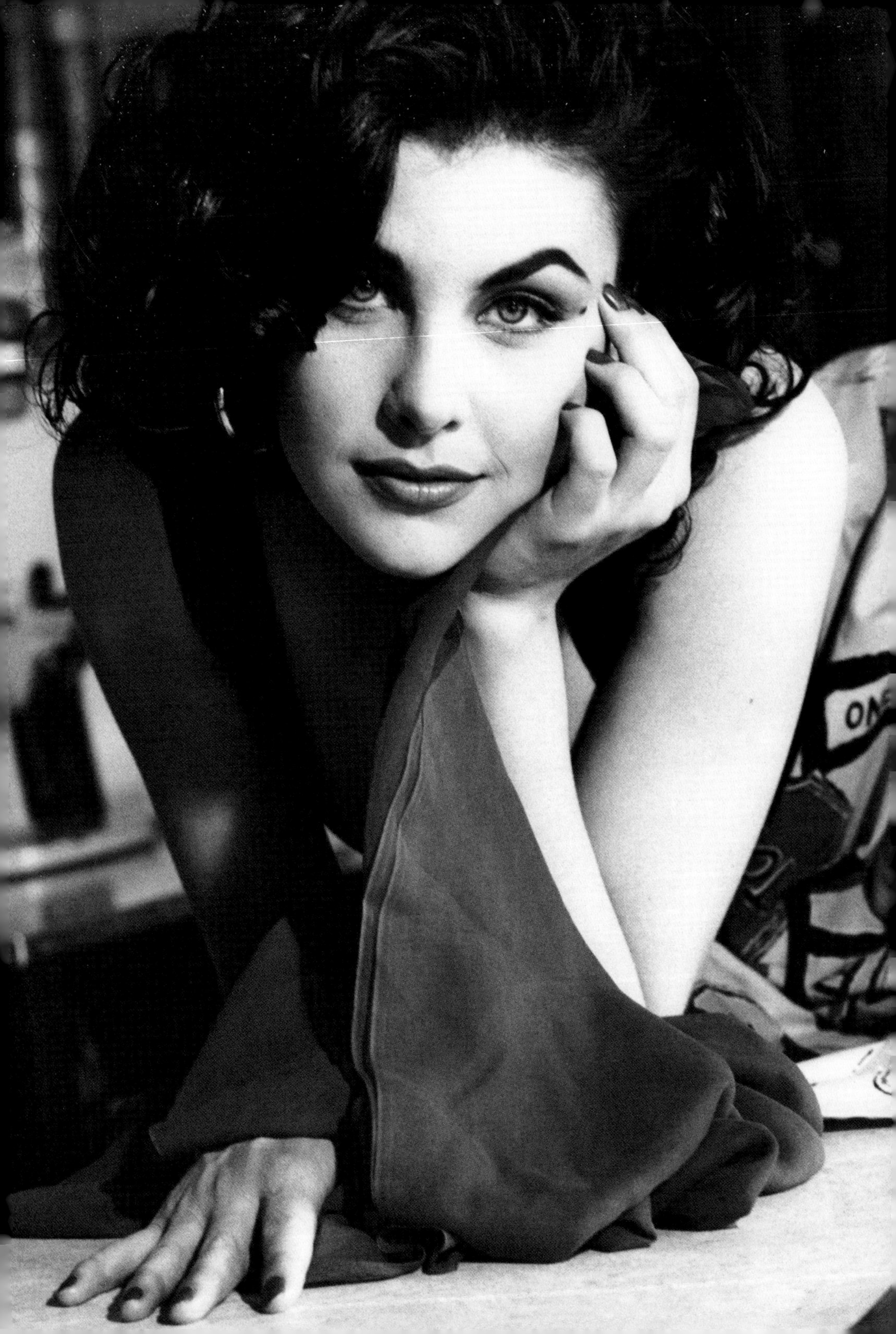

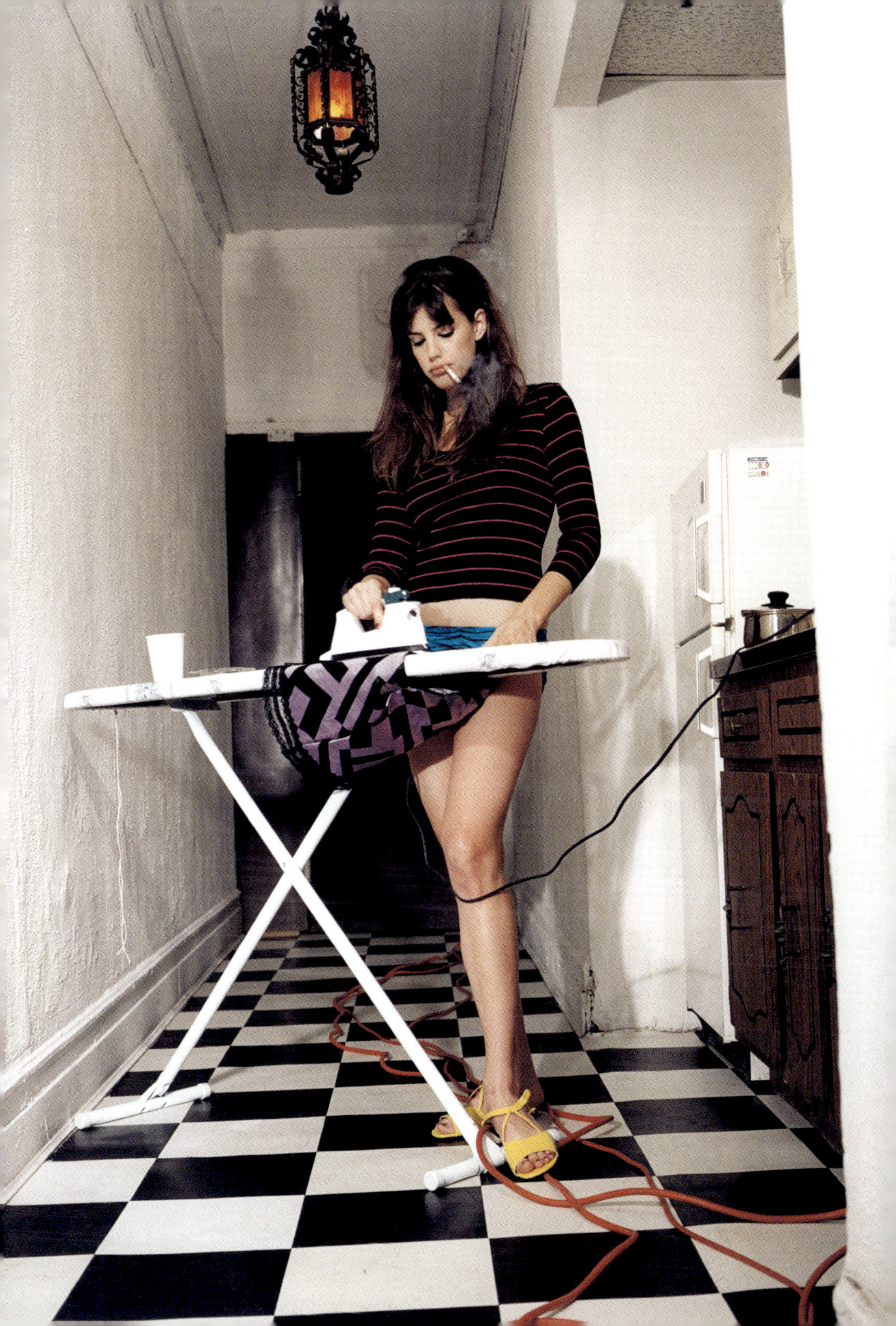

When I listen to her and look at the work-prints, it seems to me
that the analysis of her work is incomplete – that one word is
missing. Because there is something in this very singular art
about happening, ceremony, the sacred and the profane. As time
passes and changes it, her intimate oeuvre ultimately belongs less
to photography than to performance.(...)
The two arts combine themselves admirably: performances
to make pictures from, photographs to enhance those magical
moments – black or white magic, depending on the day.

À l'écouter, à regarder les tirages de travail, il m'apparaît que l'analyse de son travail n'est pas achevée – qu'il lui manque un mot. Car,
en cet art si singulier, il entre du happening, de la cérémonie, du
sacré, de la profanation. À mesure que le temps passe et la change,
son œuvre intime relève moins de la photographie et davantage de
la performance. (...)
Les deux arts font admirablement la paire, des performances pour
en faire des photographies, des photographies pour magnifier ces
instants de magie – magie blanche ou magie noire selon les jours.

Während ich ihr zuhöre und ihre Abzüge betrachte, wird mir klar, dass
die Analyse ihres Werkes nicht abgeschlossen ist – dass noch ein Begriff
fehlt. Denn in diese so einzigartige Kunst fließen auch das Happening,
die Zeremonie, das Heilige und das Profane mit ein. Je mehr Zeit ver-
geht und ihr Werk verändert, desto weniger hat es mit Fotografie und
umso mehr mit Performance zu tun. (...)
Die beiden Künste passen ausgesprochen gut zueinander, die
Performances werden zu Fotografien, und die Fotografie steigert diese
magischen Momente – weiße oder schwarze Magie, das hängt vom
jeweiligen Tag ab.

Philippe Dagen, in *Can you find happiness*, 2008

Stella Lucia for "Dazed", Studio, April 2017, Paris
Page 290 — *Asia Argento, threatening with a knife*, December 1996, Paris
Page 291 — *Caterina Murino*, January 2011, Paris

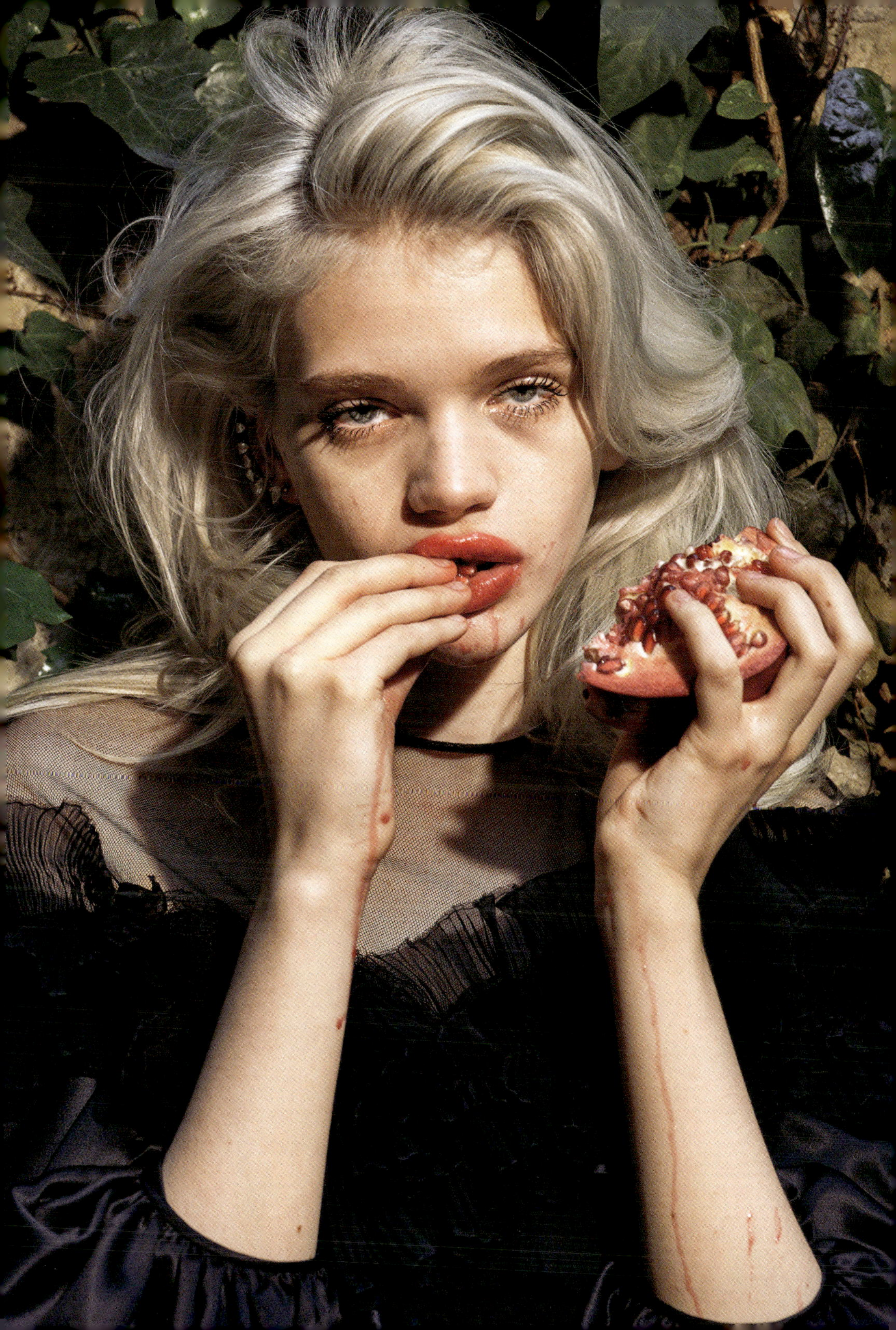

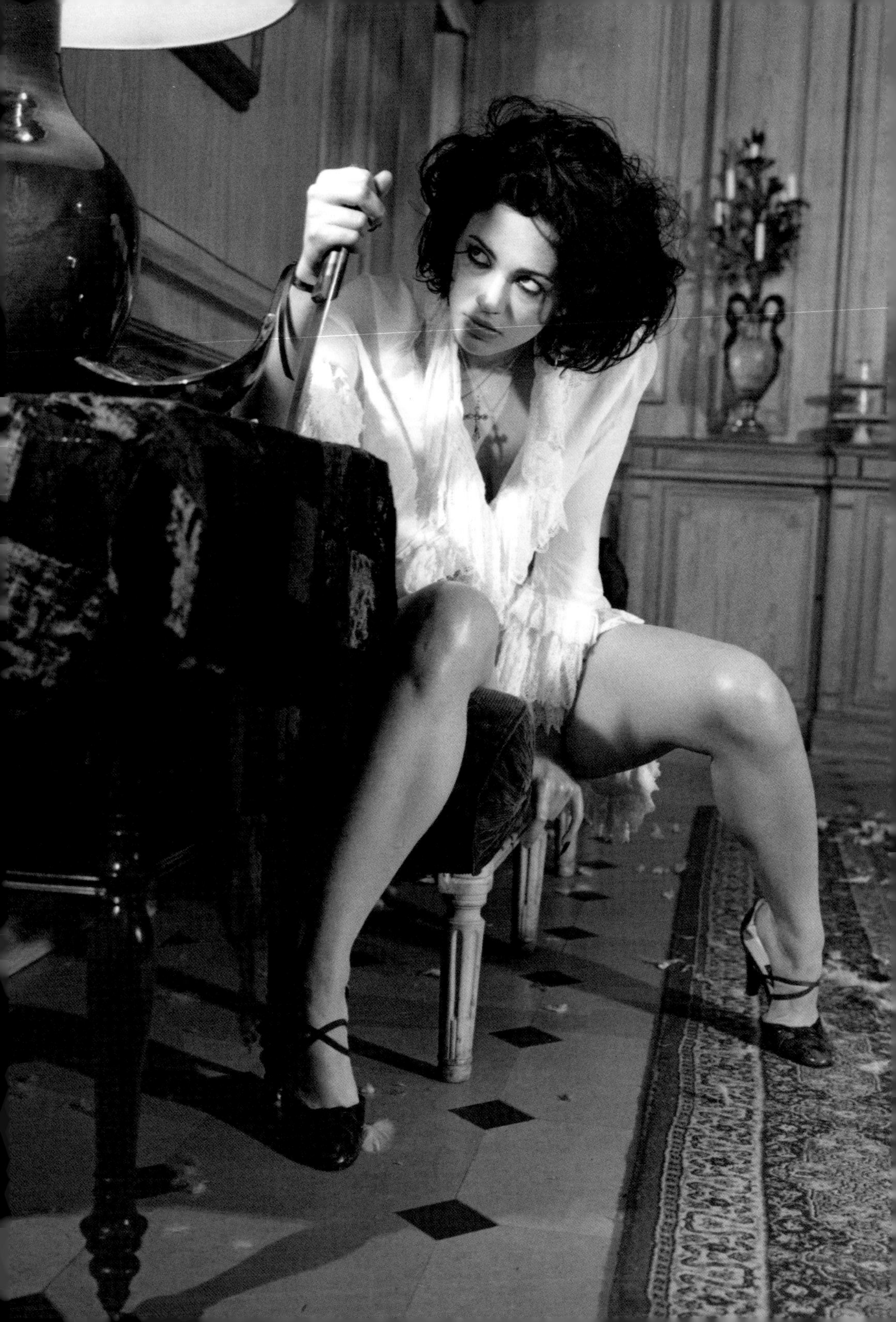

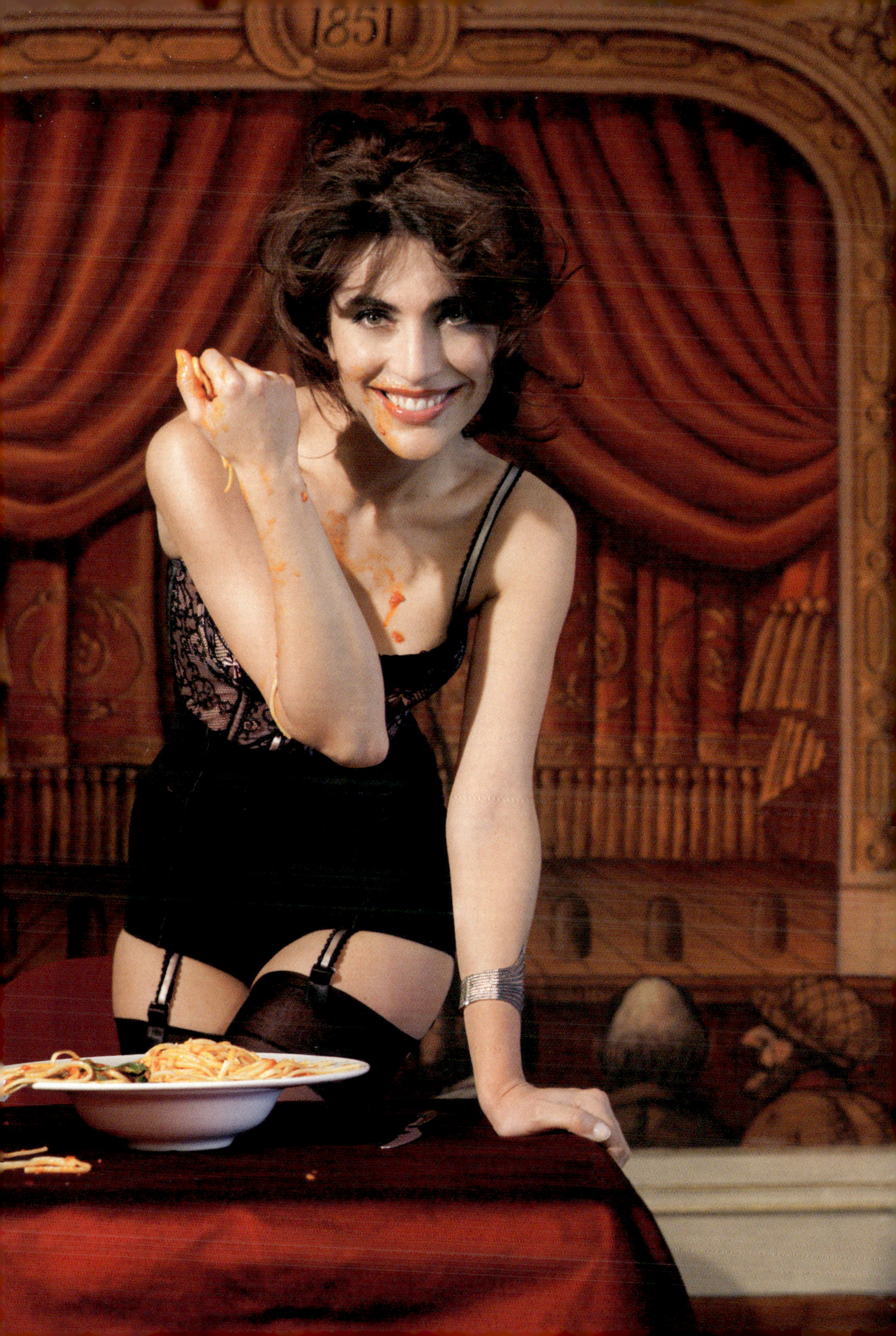

1851

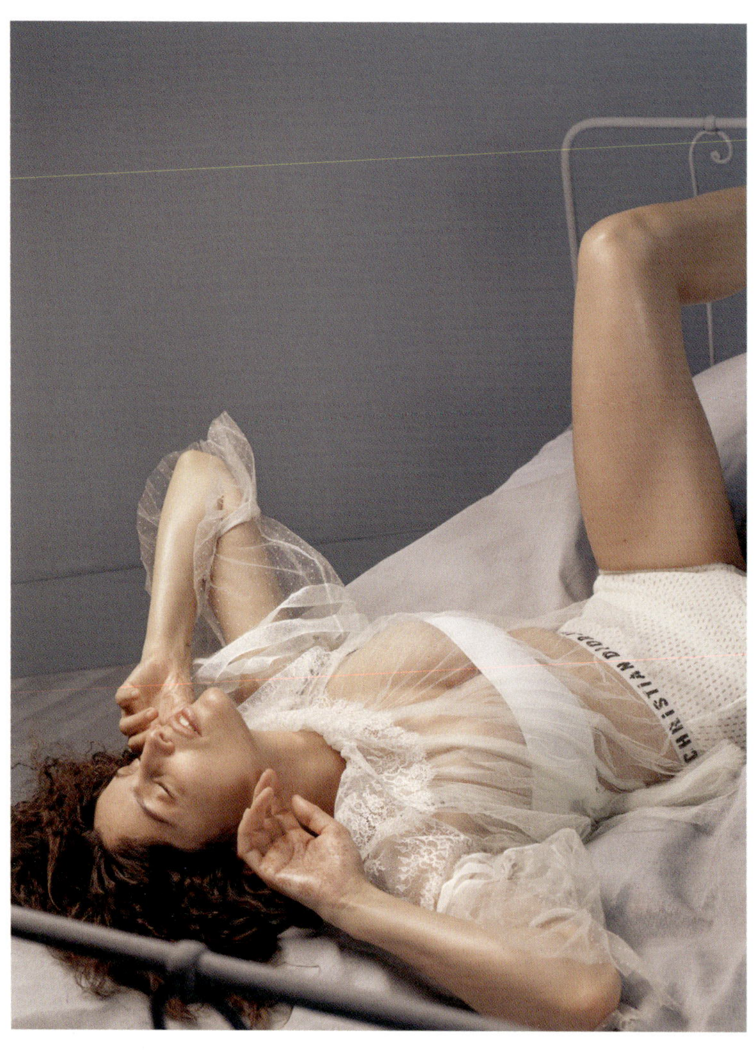

Above — *Laetitia Casta for «Dior Magazine» #18*, December 2016, Paris
Opposite page — *Vanessa Paradis, le laçage de corset*, February 2004, Amsterdam

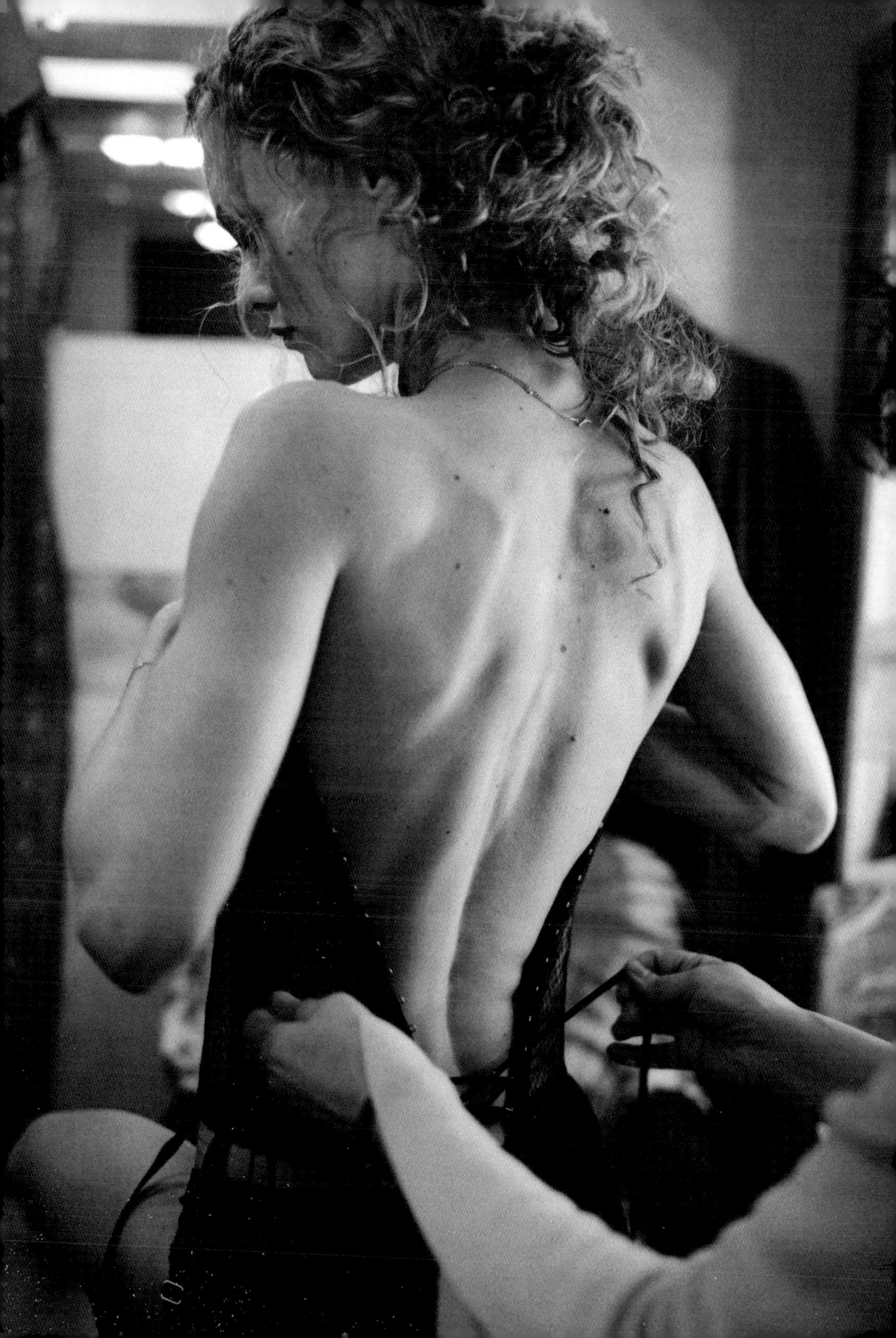

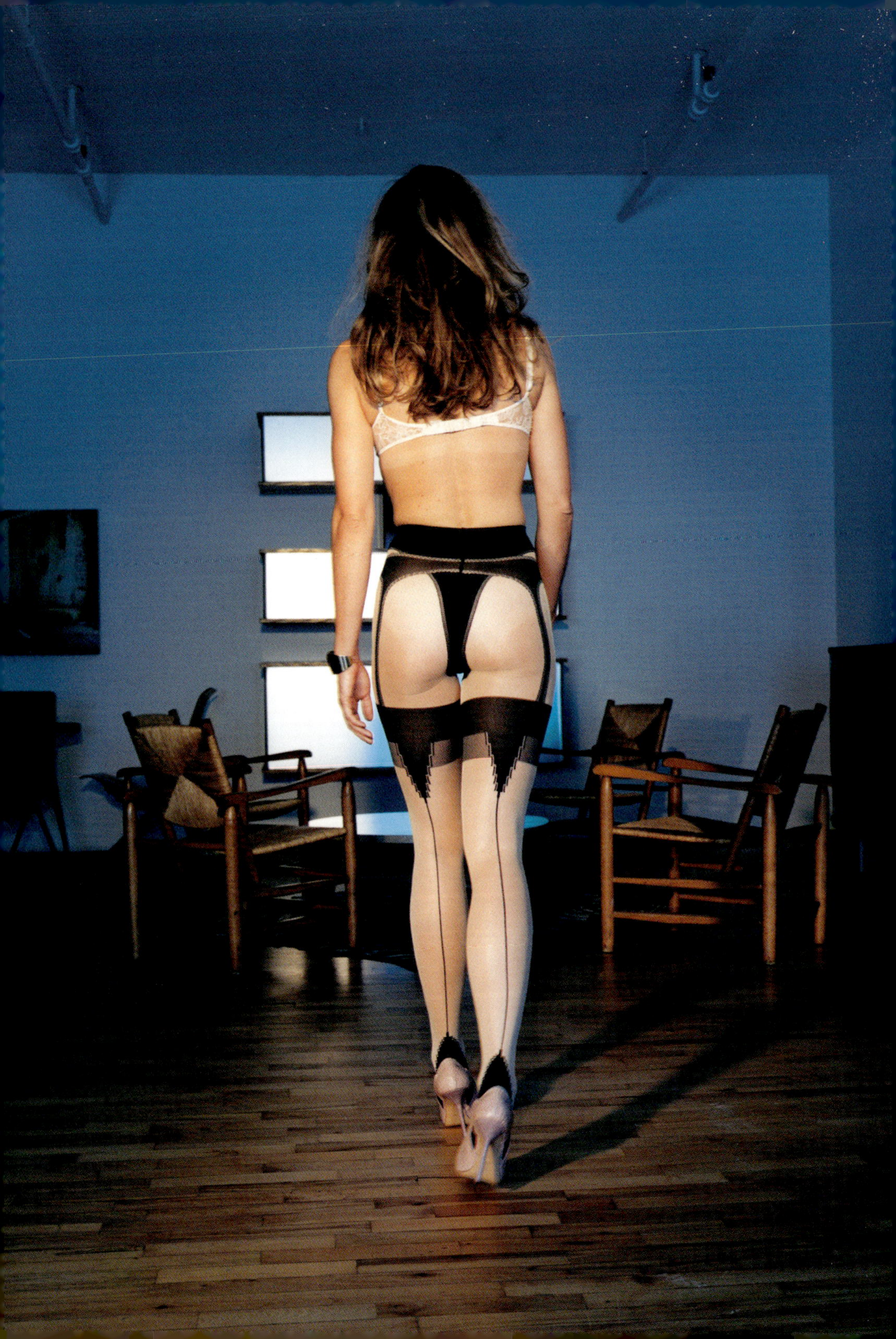

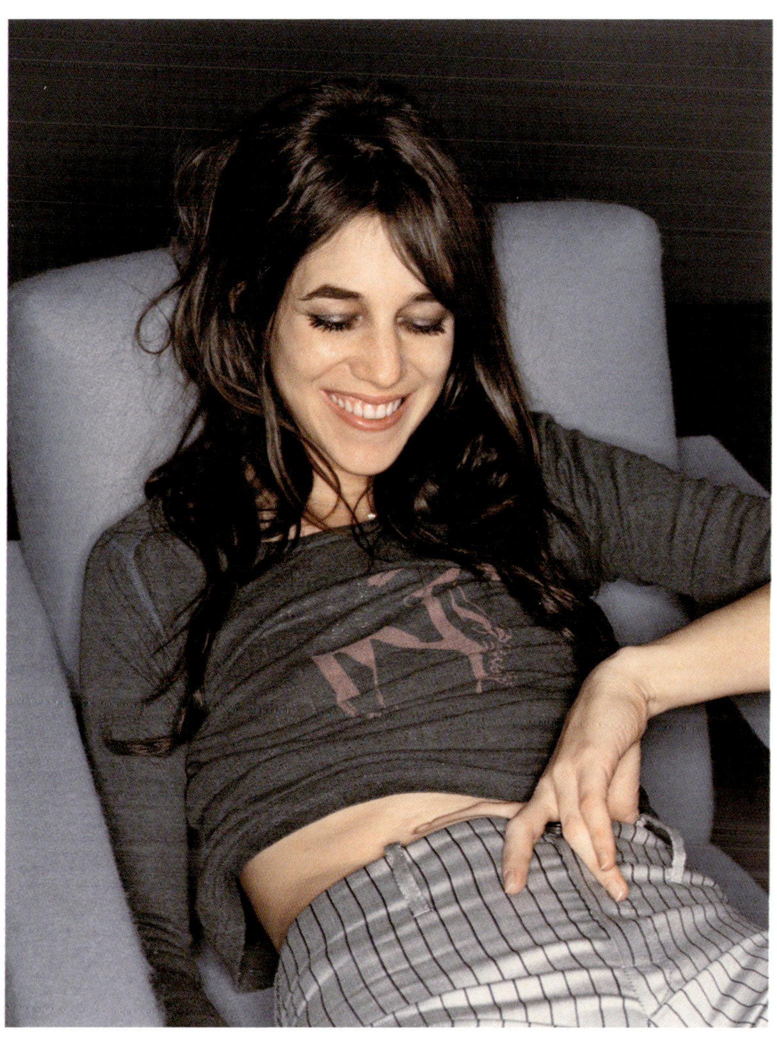

Above — *Charlotte Gainsbourg*, December 2007, Paris
Opposite page — *Cordula de dos traversant la pièce*, May 2000, New York
Page 296— *Angela me fait une confiance aveugle*, September 2007, Tokyo
Page 297 — *Black Magic with Asia Argento*, December 1996, Paris

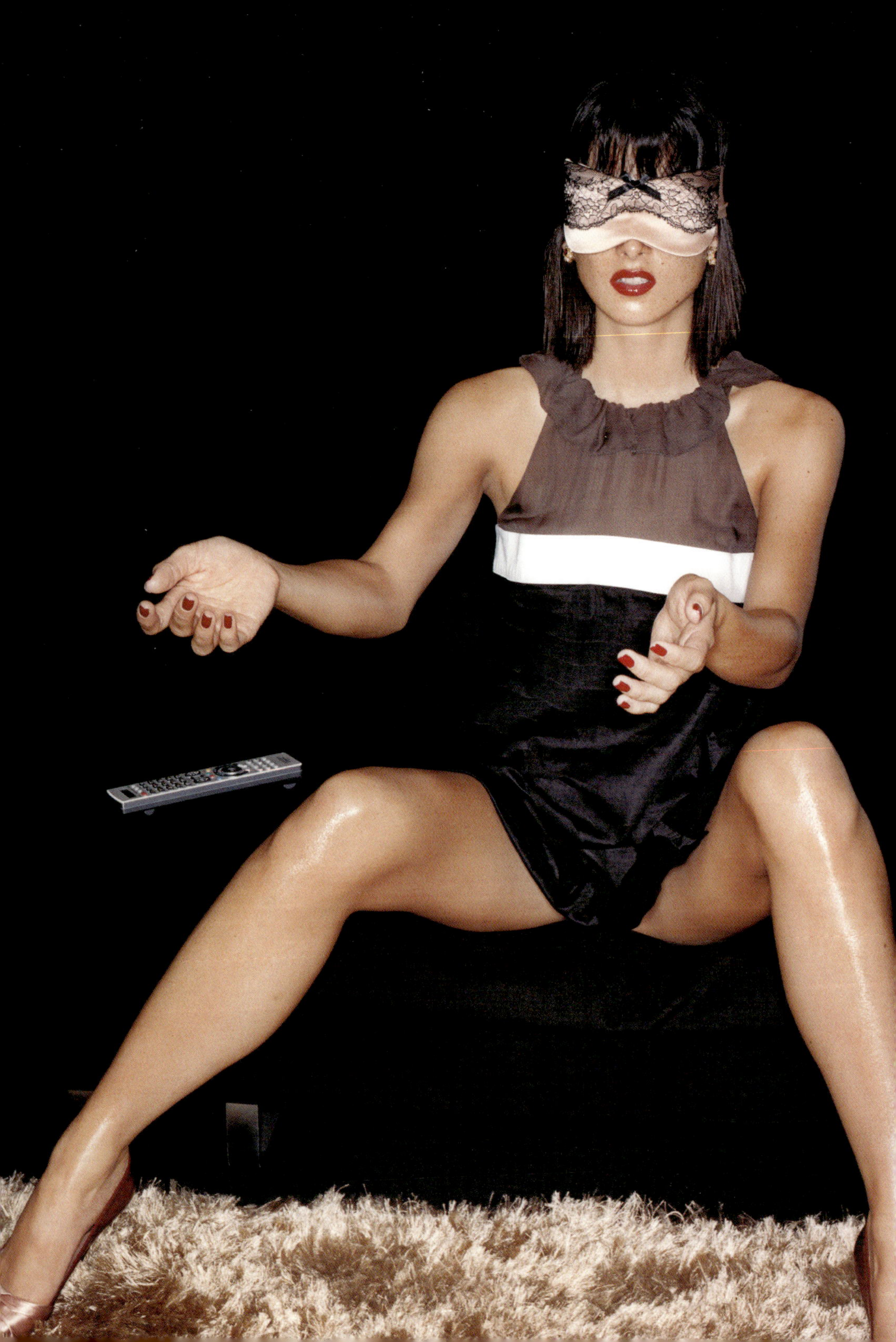

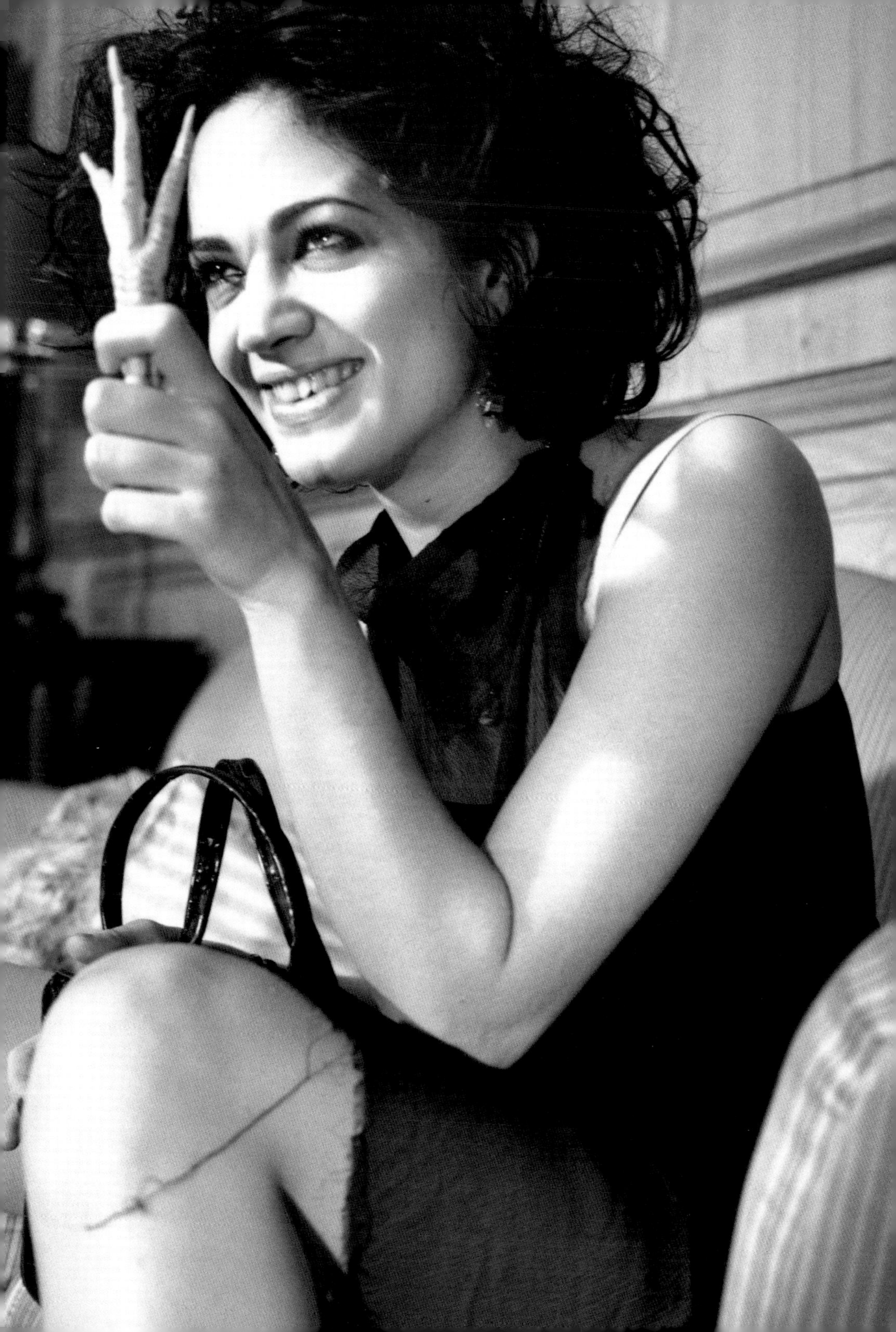

SHANGHAI
IN COLLABORATION WITH SERGE BRAMLY
2002, Shanghai

We approached the women of Shanghai in all their diversity, as one puts together the pieces of a puzzle. It was a fragmentary approach, without any expectation, case-by-case, individual, driven by the momentum. There would always be time enough to find its meaning afterwards.

Nous abordions les femmes de Shanghai dans leur diversité, comme on assemble les pièces d'un puzzle. C'était une approche fragmentaire, sans *a priori*, au cas par cas, individuelle et momentanée, dont il serait toujours temps ensuite de tirer un sens.

Wir näherten uns den Frauen in Shanghai in all ihrer Vielfalt, so wie man die Teile eines Puzzles zusammensetzt. Unsere Herangehensweise war ausschnitthaft, unvoreingenommen, von Fall zu Fall verschieden, individuell und spontan – später würde immer noch Zeit sein, ihren Sinn zu ergründen.

Serge Bramly, Paris, 2015

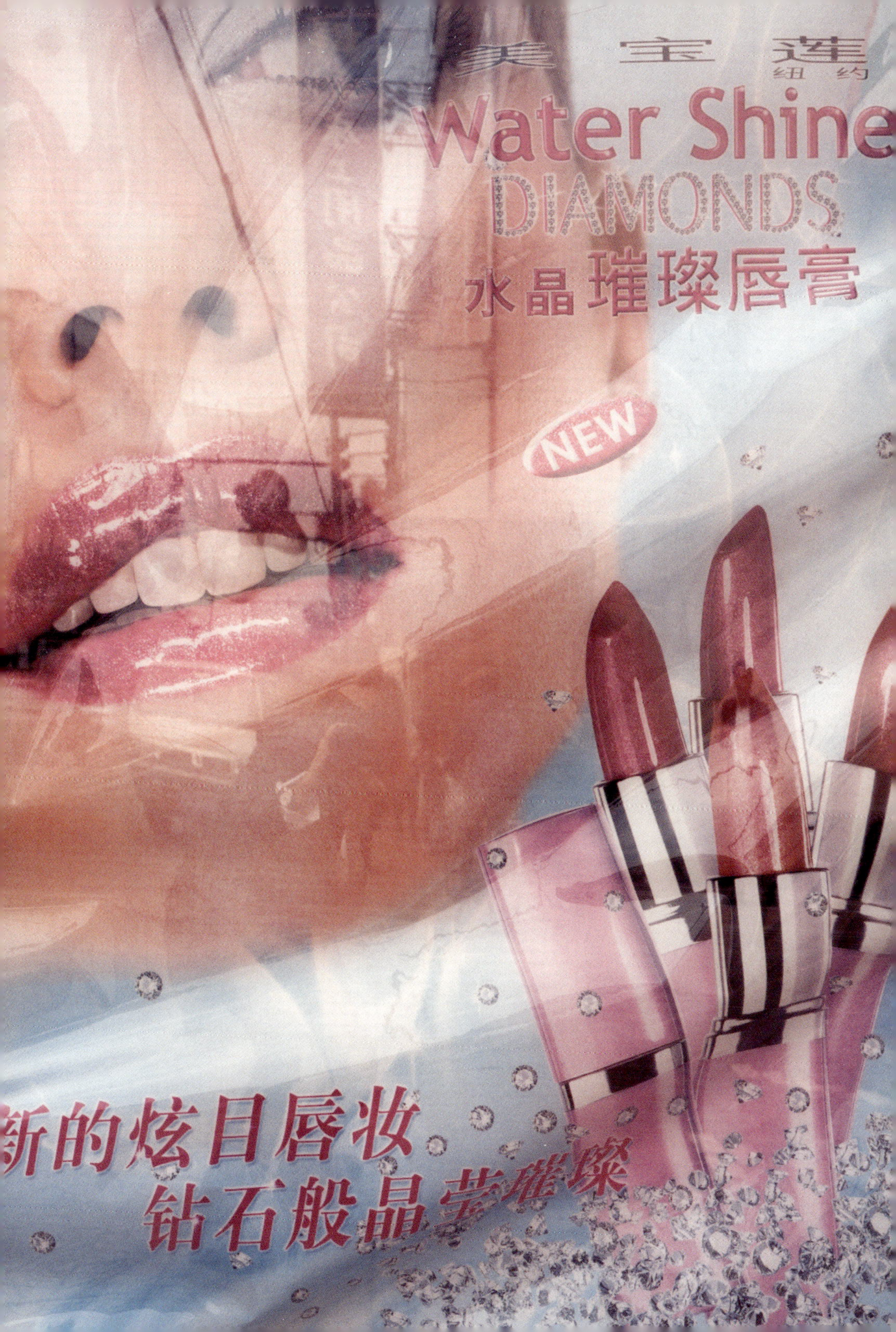

美宝莲 纽约
Water Shine
DIAMONDS
水晶璀璨唇膏
NEW
新的炫目唇妆
钻石般晶莹璀璨

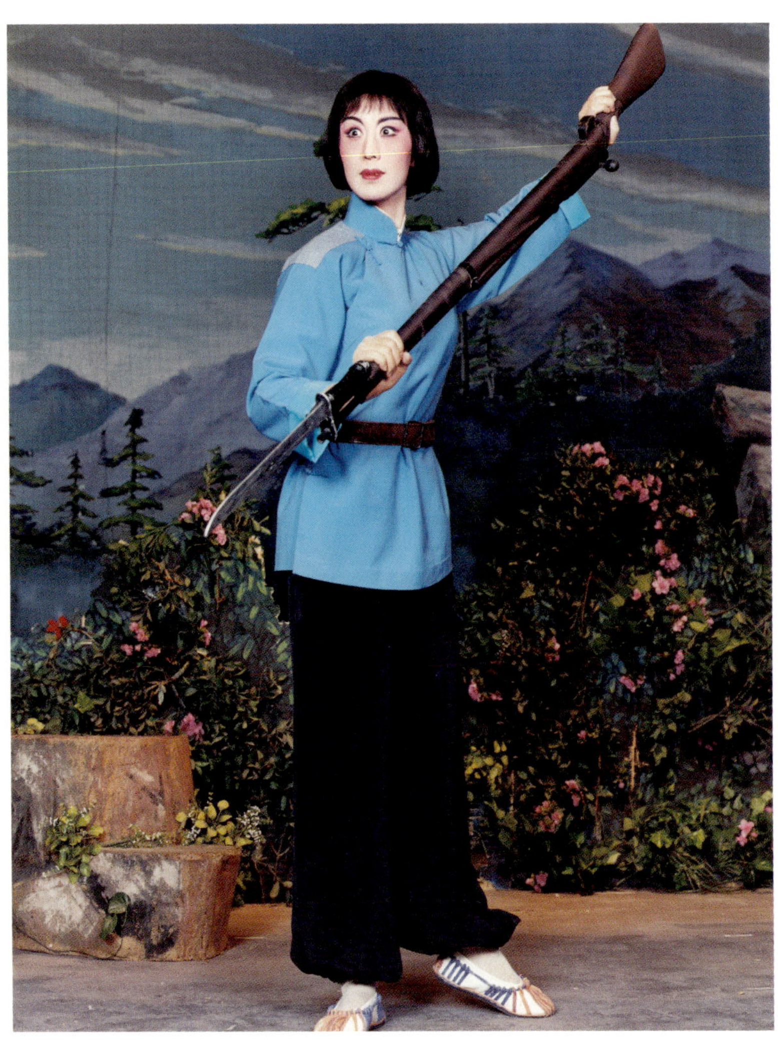

Above — *Shi Min, jouant le rôle d'une héroïne révolutionnaire dans la pièce Du Juan Shan, au théâtre Yi Fu*, October 2002, Shanghai
Opposite page — *Tian Yuan devant une baie vitrée surplombant le fleuve*, November 2002, Shanghai

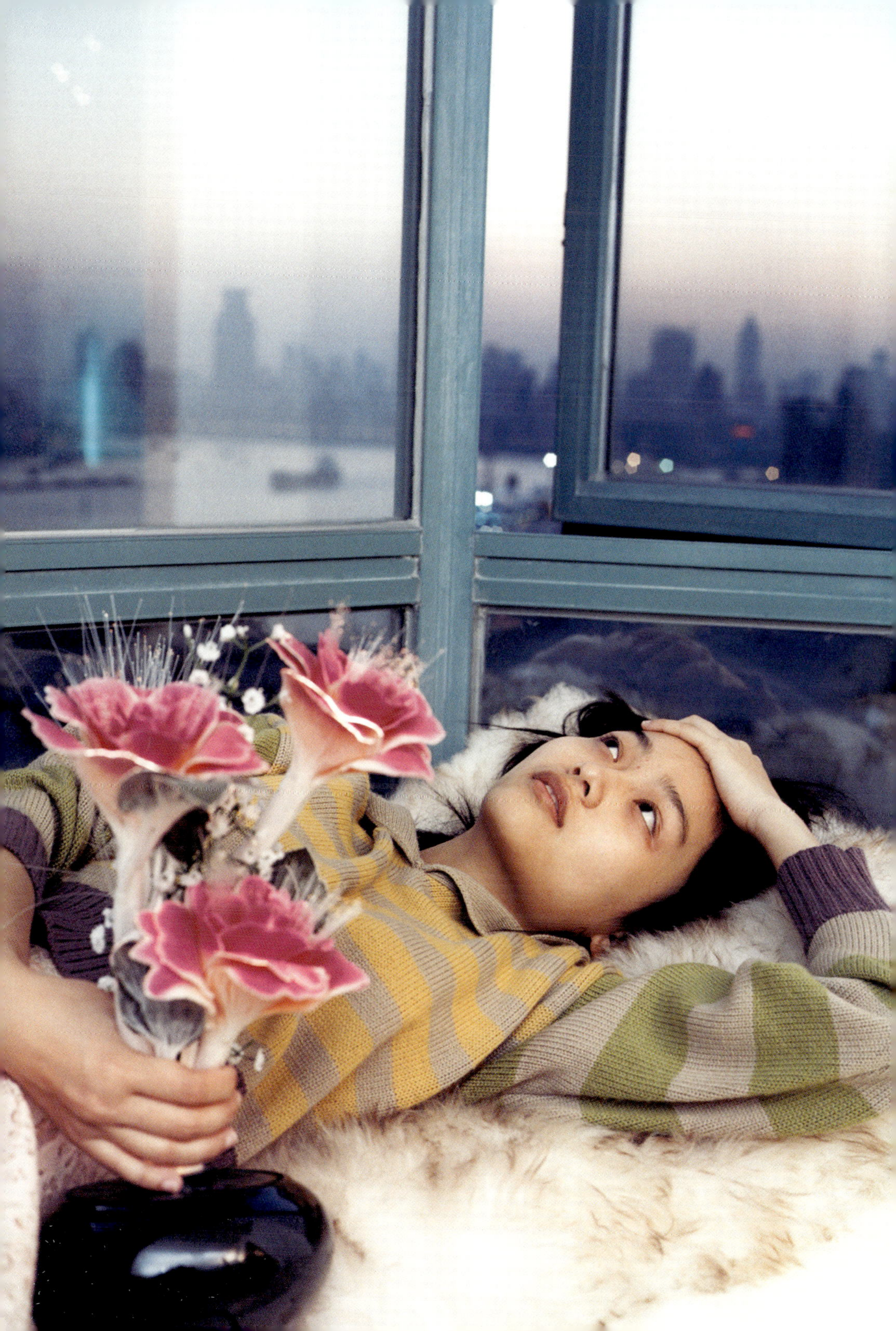

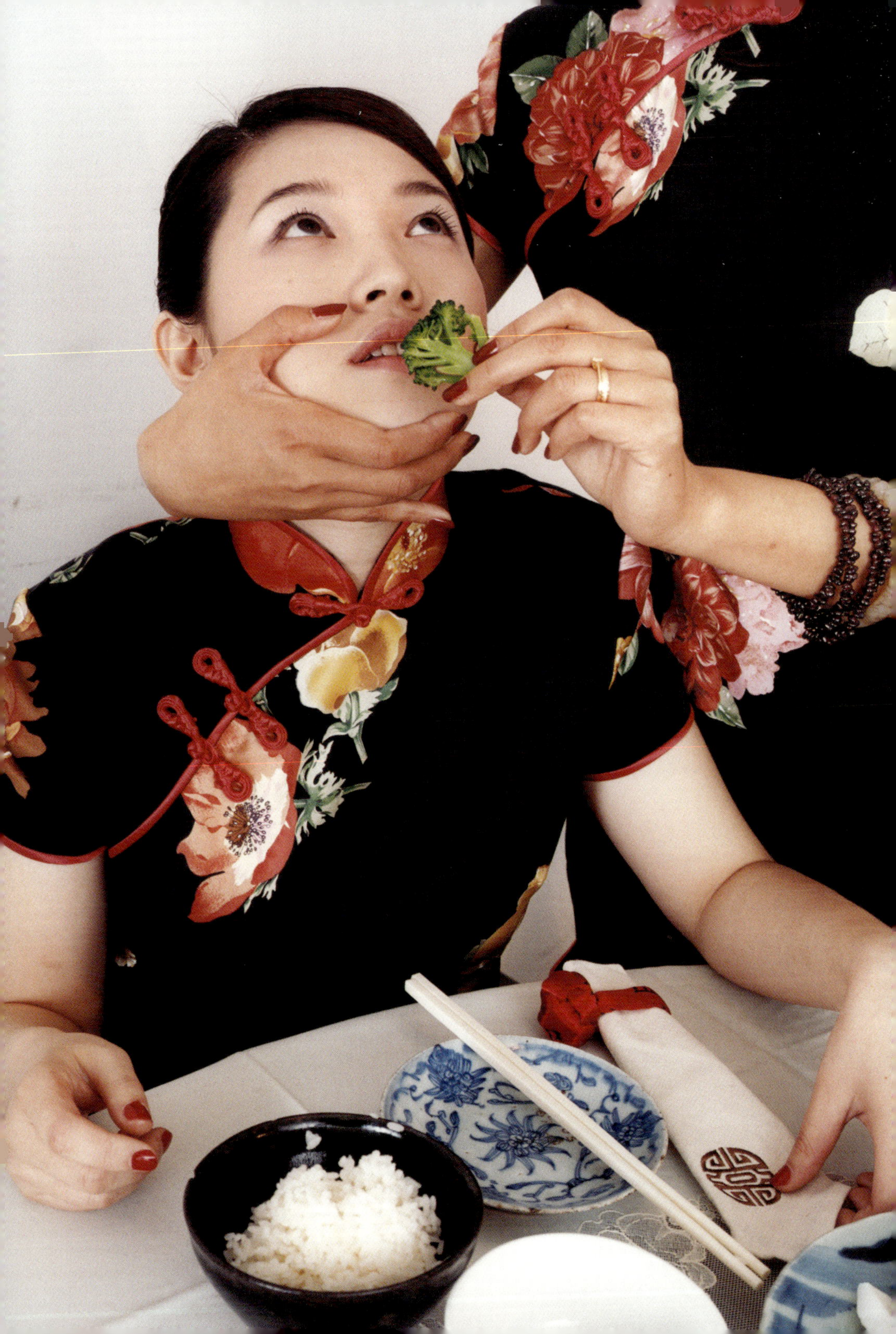

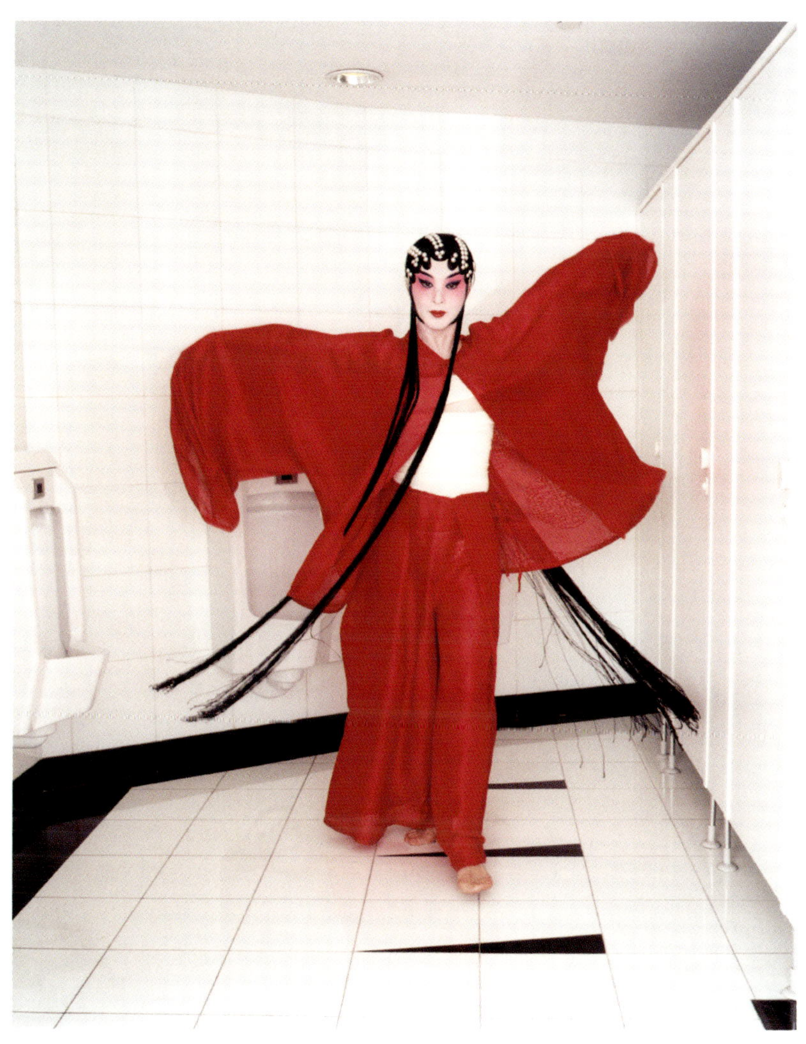

Above — *Jin Xing dans les toilettes de chez Maxim's au grand théâtre de Shanghai*, April 2002, Shanghai
Opposite page — *Le repas de Kelly dans une maison d'hôtes I*, April 2002, Shanghai
Page 304 — *What's on a man's mind*, November 2002, Shanghai
Page 305 — *Wu Pei Yi, assise dans un décor panthère avec une blouse à fleurs*, October 2002, Shanghai

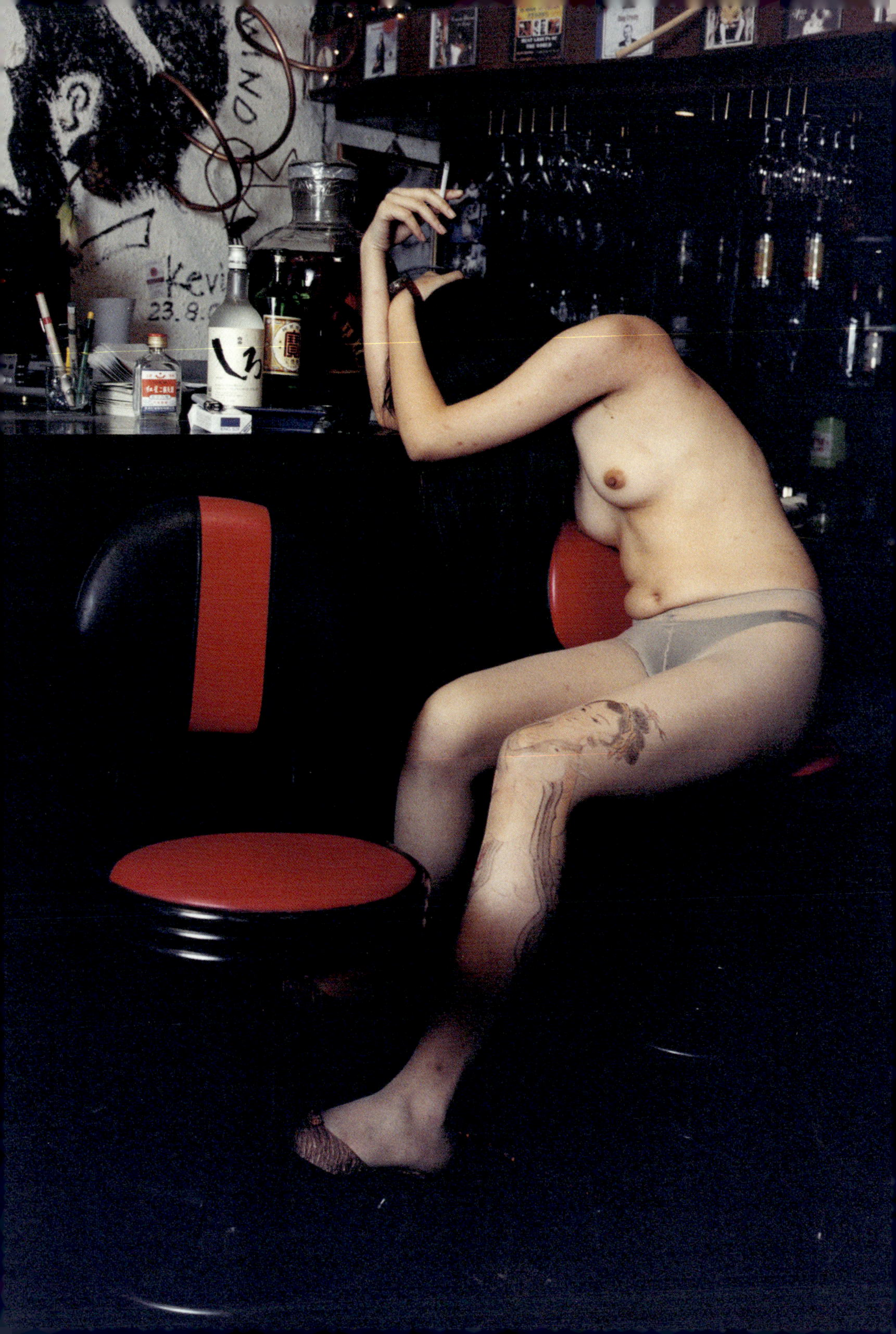

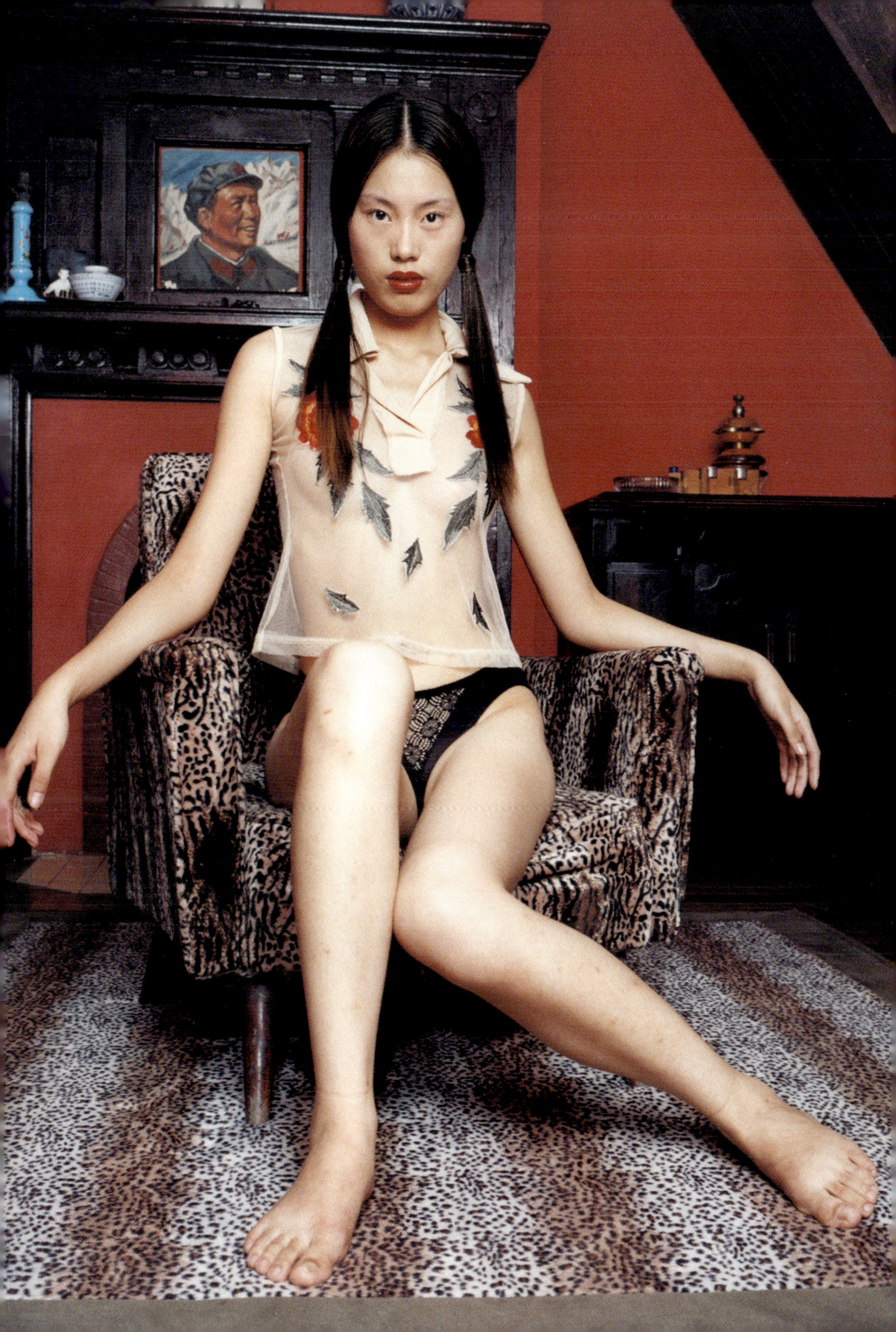

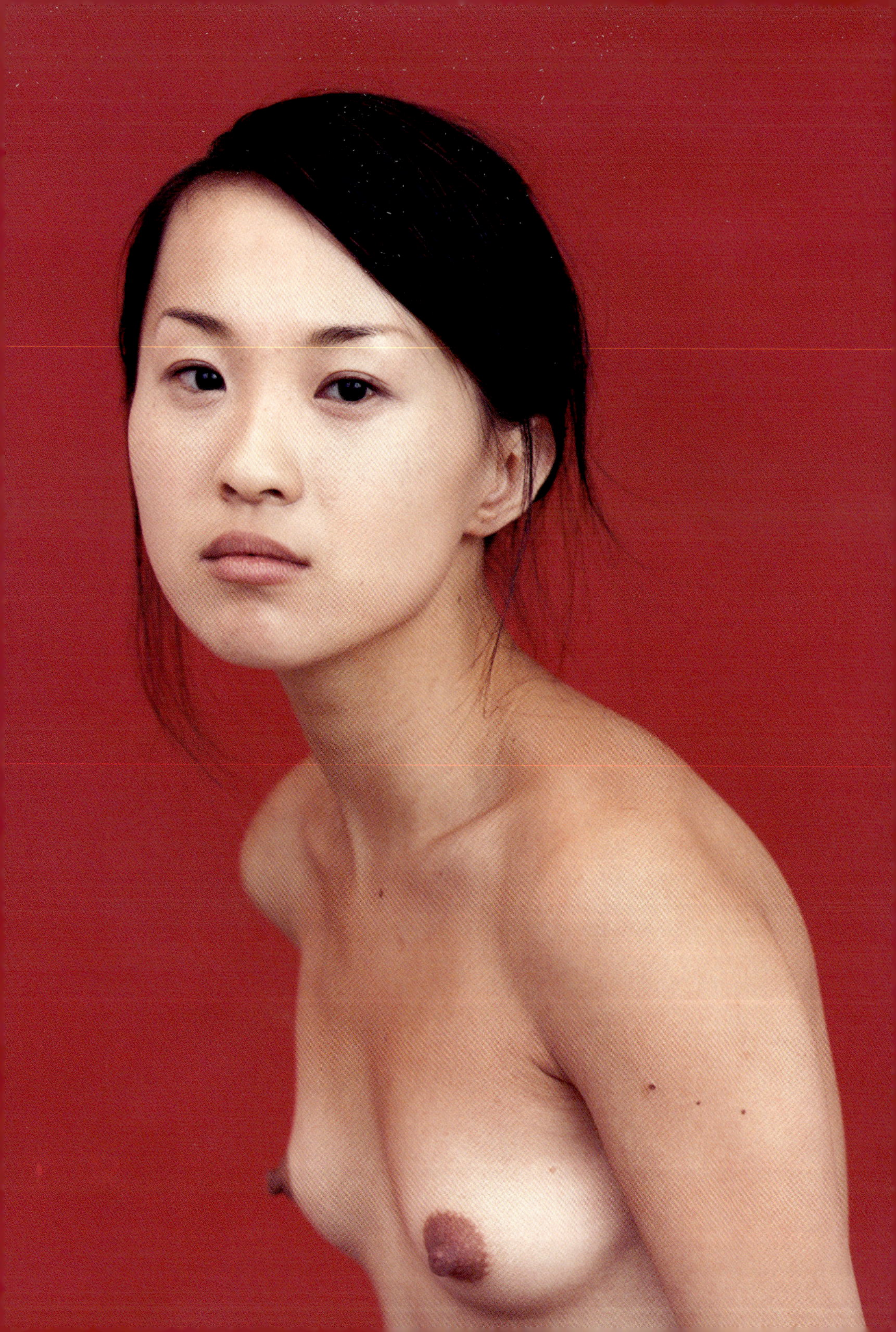

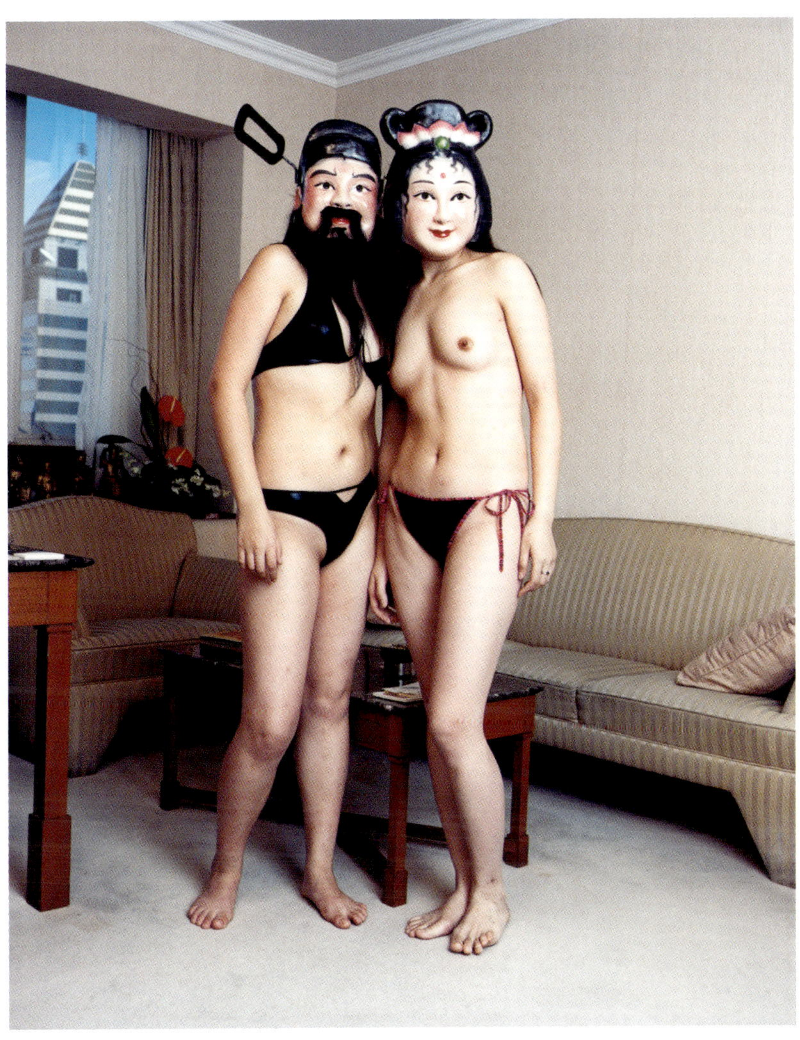

Above — *Masques d'opéra photographiés sur deux amies*, November 2002, Shanghai
Opposite page — *Ginger*, November 2002, Shanghai

Guan Xin, abbesse supérieure du monastère de Chen Xiang Ge, membre du conseil de l'Association bouddhiste de Chine, October 2002, Shanghai
Following double page — *Sara Stroller, intérieur nuit, se contemple dans le miroir*, March 2006, Paris
Page 312 — *Sara, close-up*, March 2006, Paris
Page 313 — *Sara Stroller en «Kiki de Montparnasse» se cache avec une fleur noire*, March 2006, Paris
Pages 314/315 — *Kiki nue, couchée dans mon lit*, March 2006, Paris

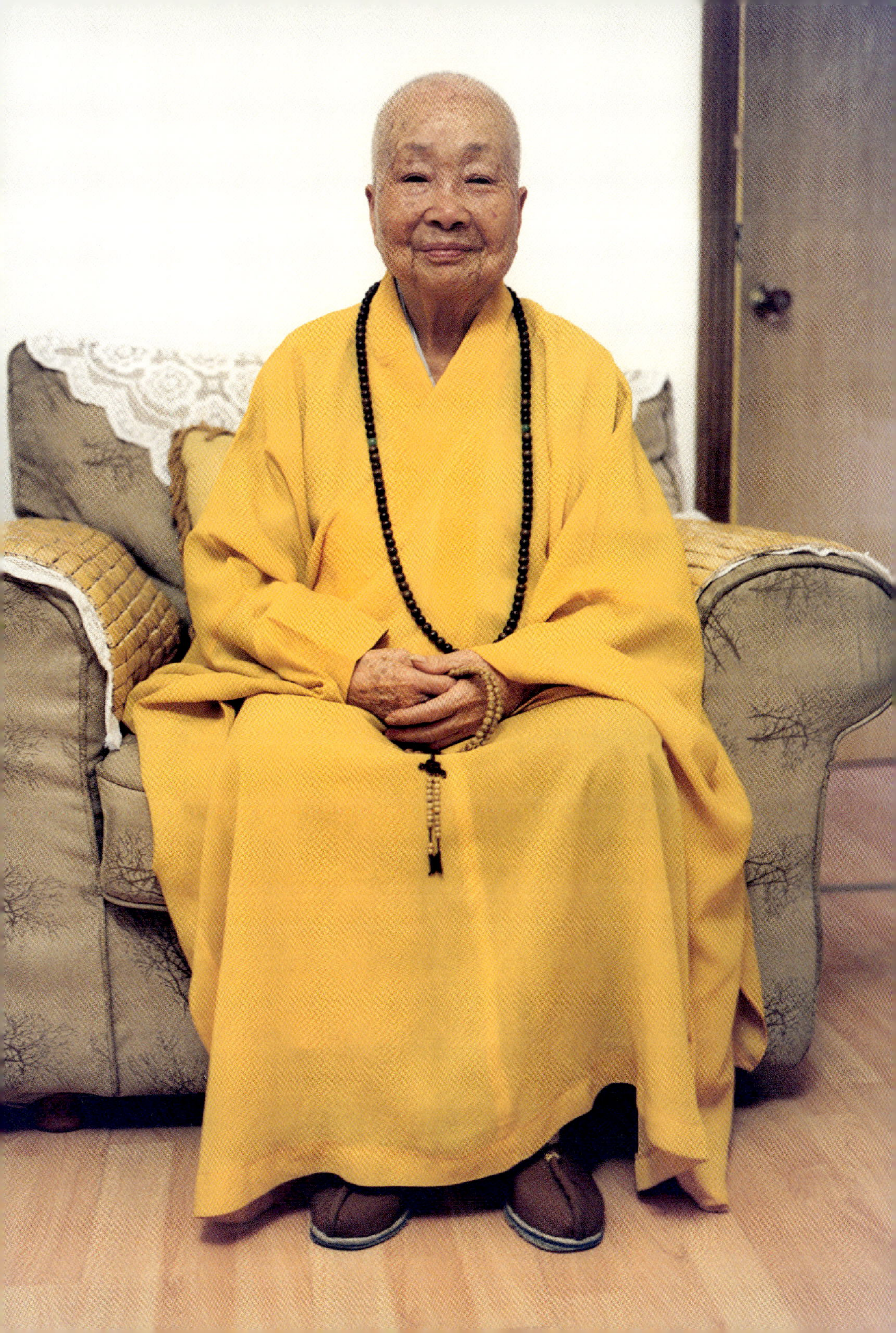

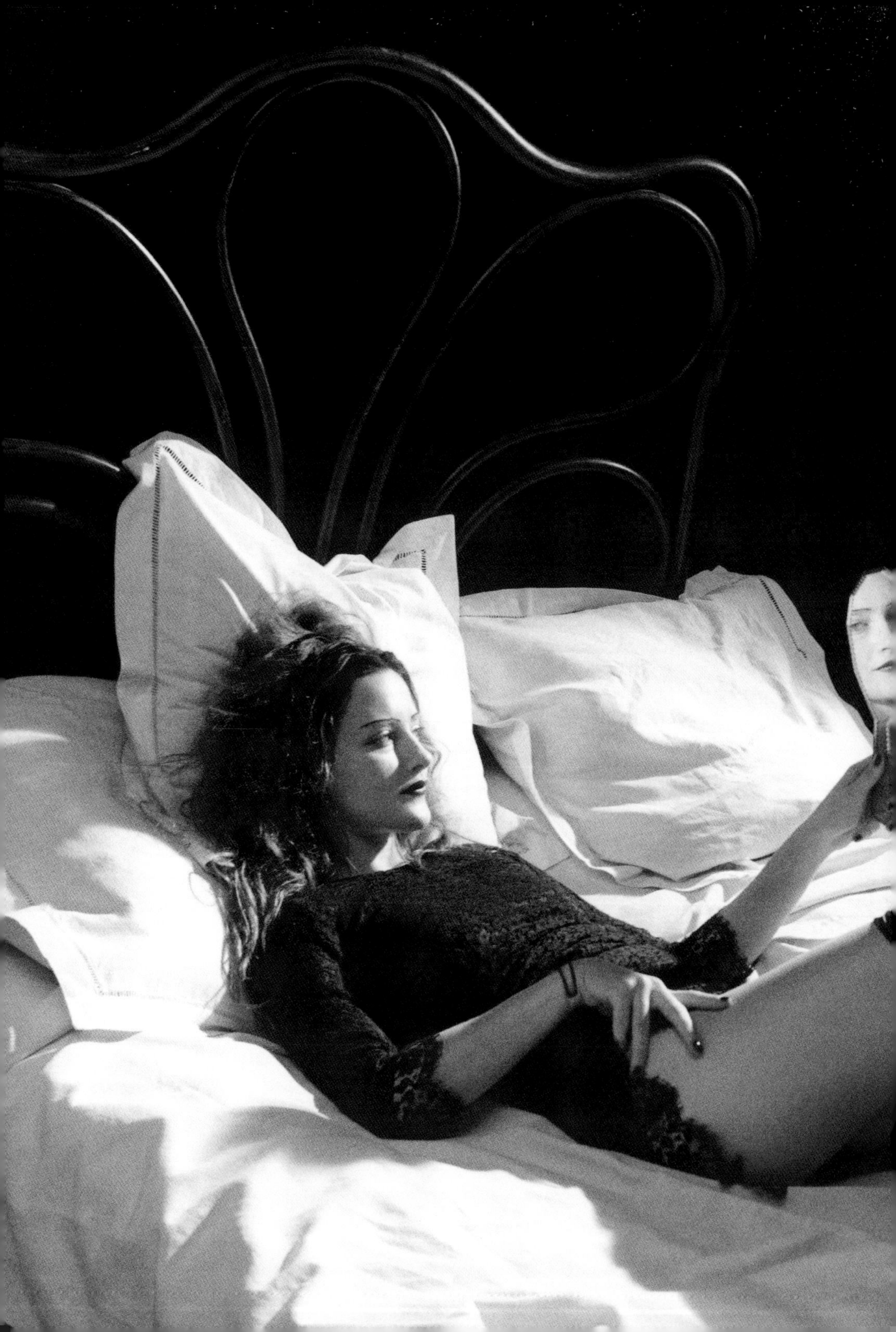

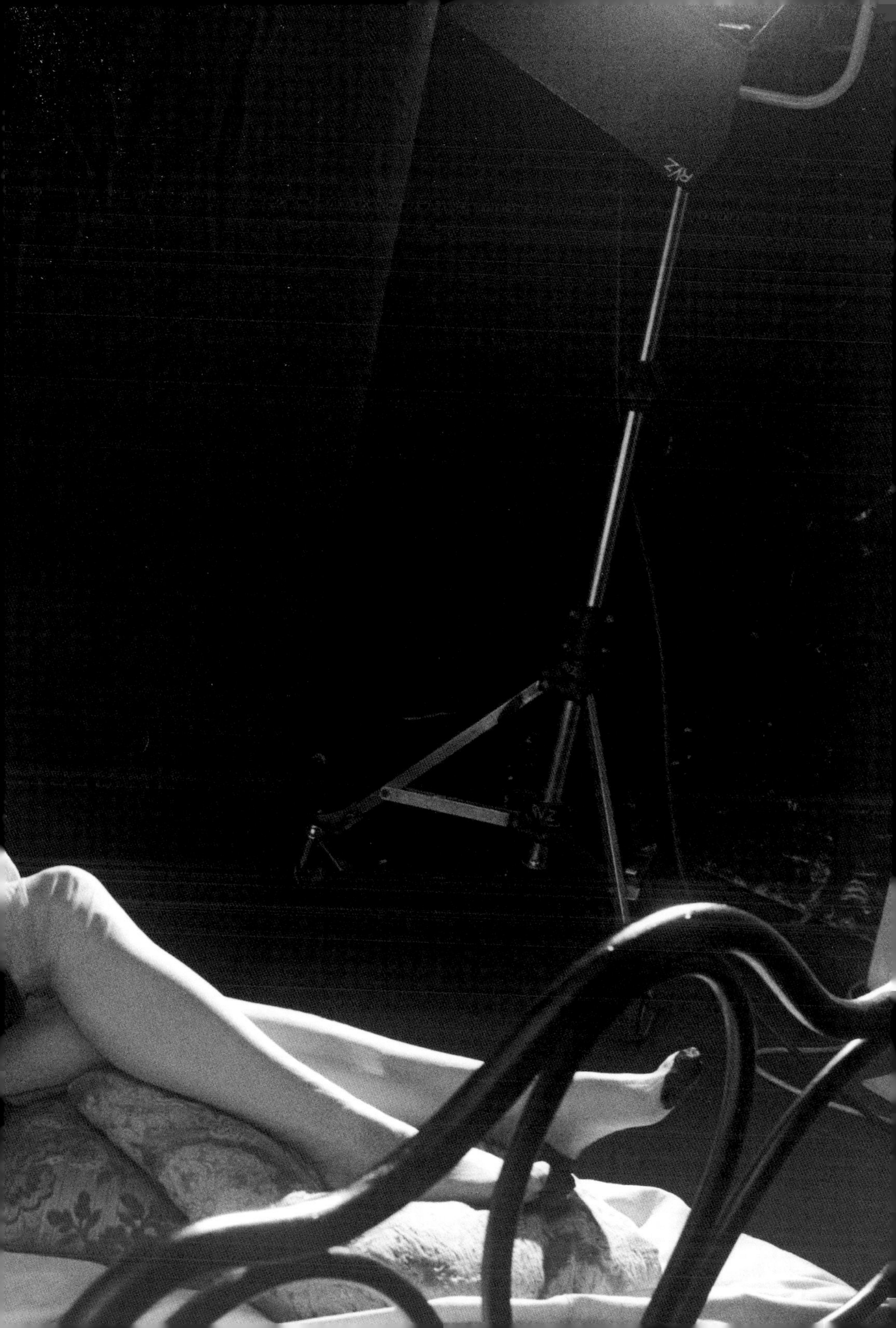

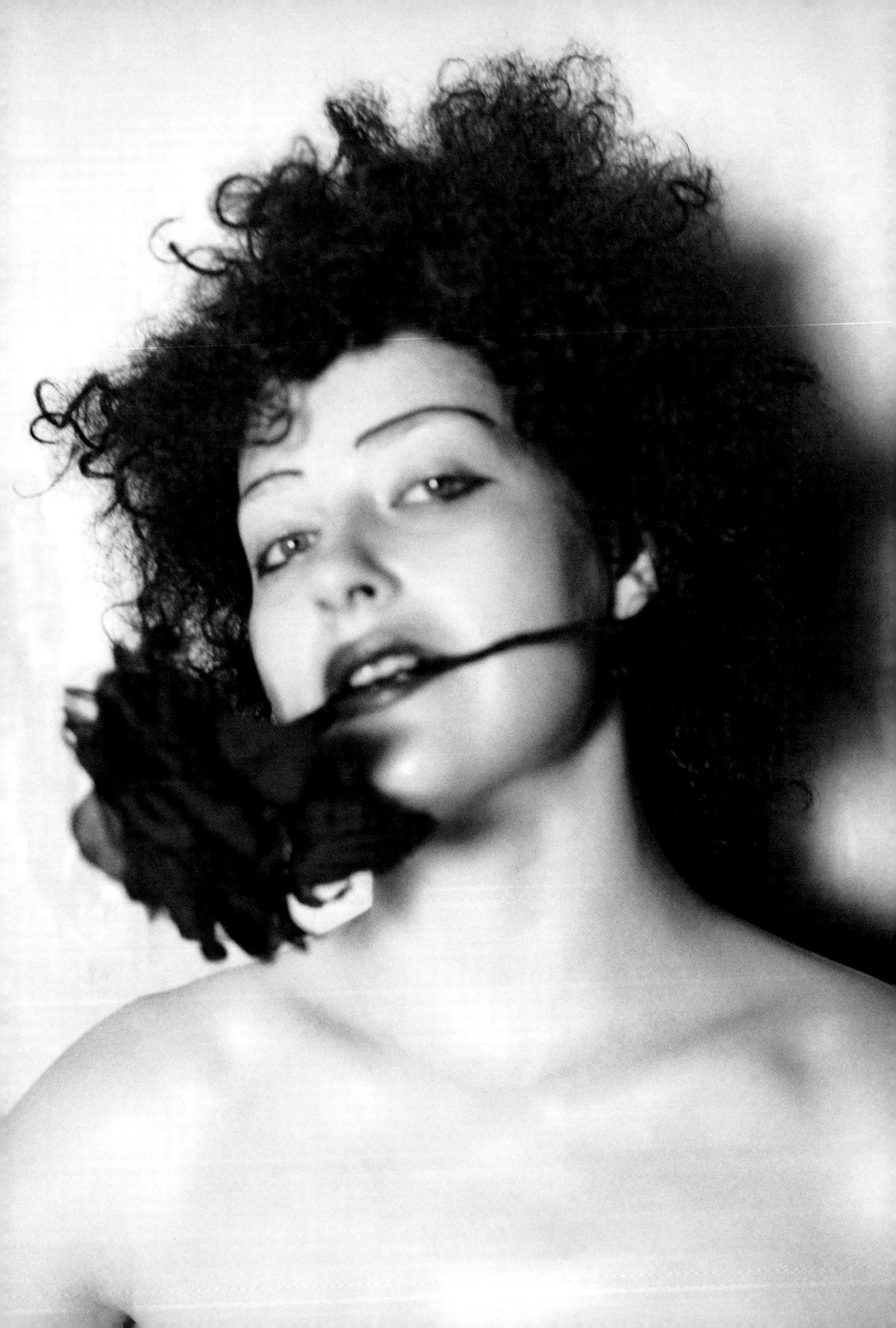

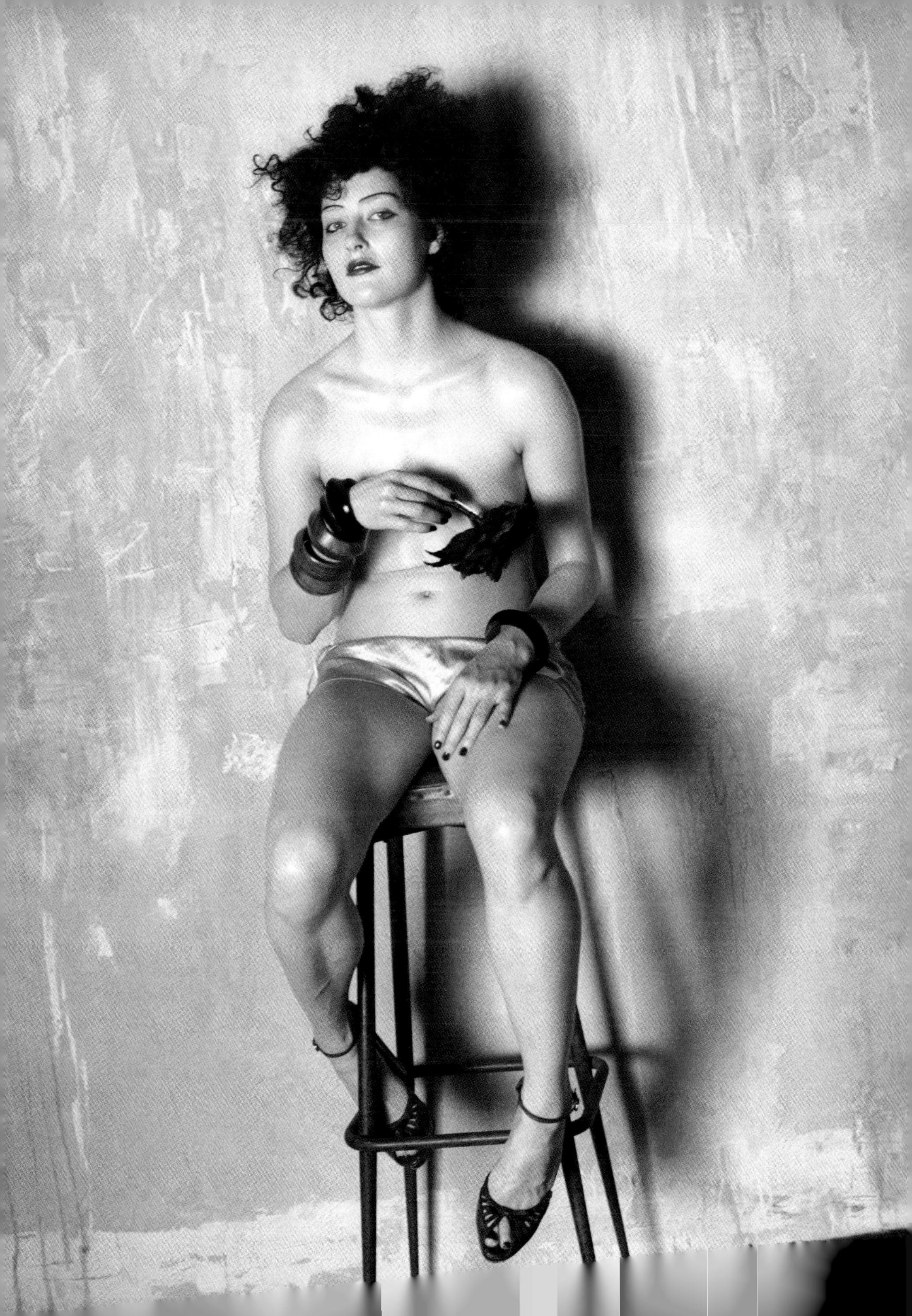

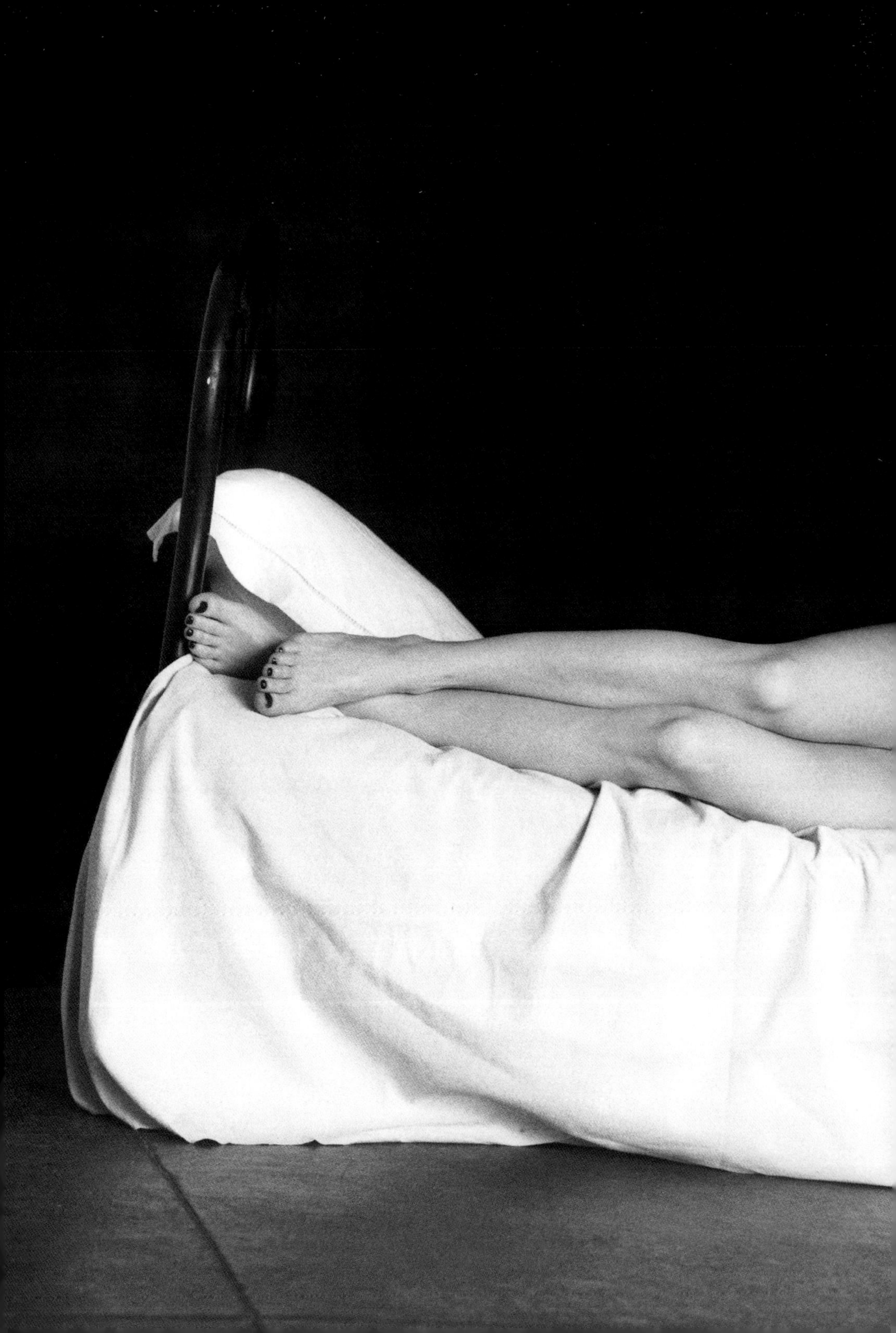

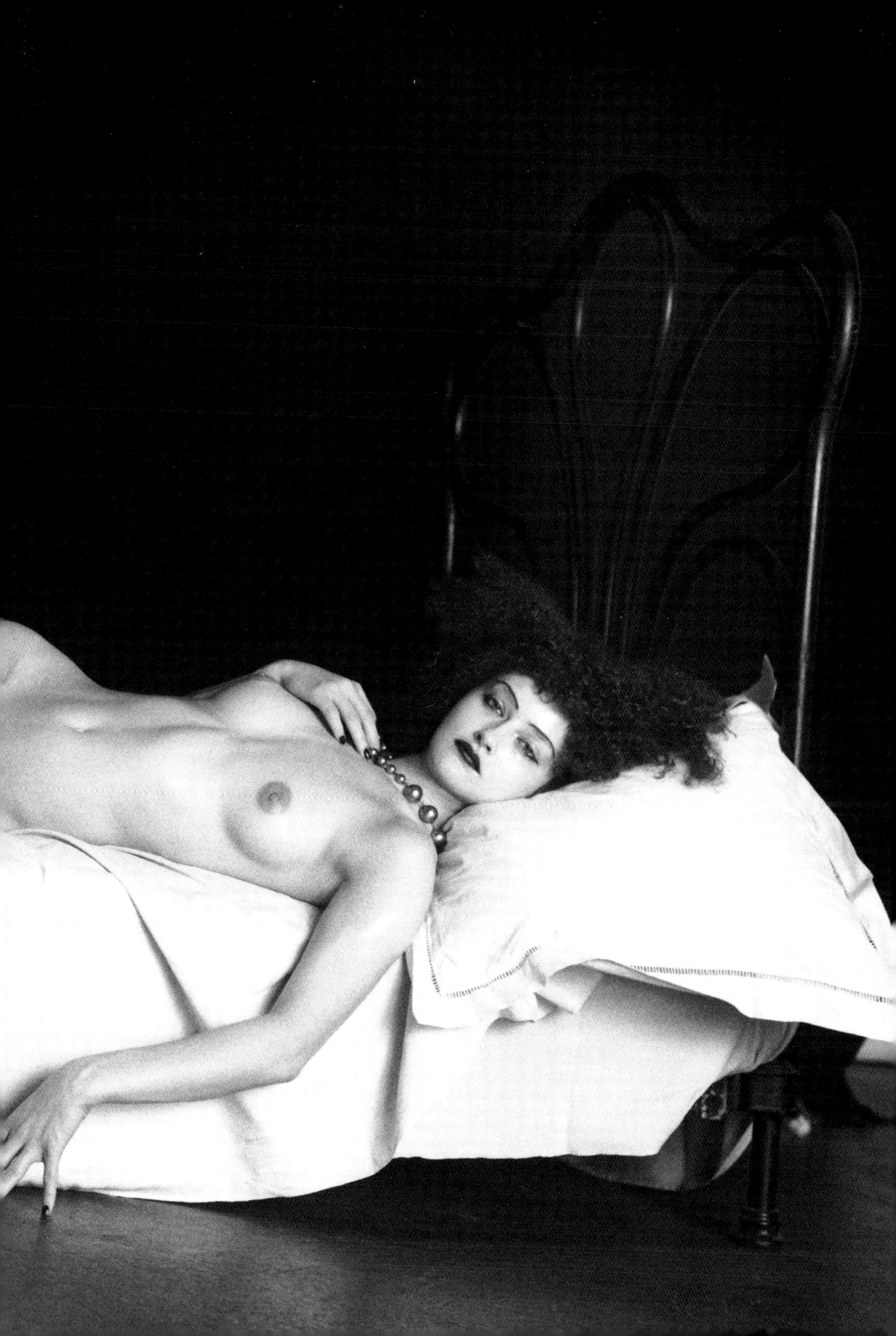

MORCEAUX CHOISIS
2001, Paris

(...) no trace of negligence, girls with perfect bodies, an elegant, pearly light. But the half-glances, the shoes, the very poses make of *Morceaux choisis* the most critical reflection on pornography in art today, because it shows that, even in the exercise of an uninhibited realism, nothing is simple – nothing is certain. Even ecstasy itself may be only a pose.

(...) aucune négligence, des filles aux corps parfaits, une lumière élégamment nacrée. Mais les regards en coin, les chaussures, les poses même font de *Morceaux choisis*, dans l'art actuel, la réflexion la plus critique sur la pornographie parce qu'elle montre que, jusque dans ces exercices d'un réalisme sans interdit, rien n'est simple – rien n'est sûr. L'extase elle-même peut n'être qu'une pose.

(...) keinerlei Makel, Mädchen mit perfekten Körpern, ein elegantes perlmuttfarbenes Licht. Aber durch die Blicke aus den Augenwinkeln, die Schuhe und die Posen selbst wird *Morceaux choisis* in der aktuellen Kunst zu einer äußerst kritischen Reflexion über Pornografie, denn sie zeigt, dass selbst in diesen Übungsstücken eines tabulosen Realismus nichts einfach und nichts sicher ist. Selbst die Ekstase könnte nur eine Pose sein.

Philippe Dagen, in *Can you find happiness*, 2008

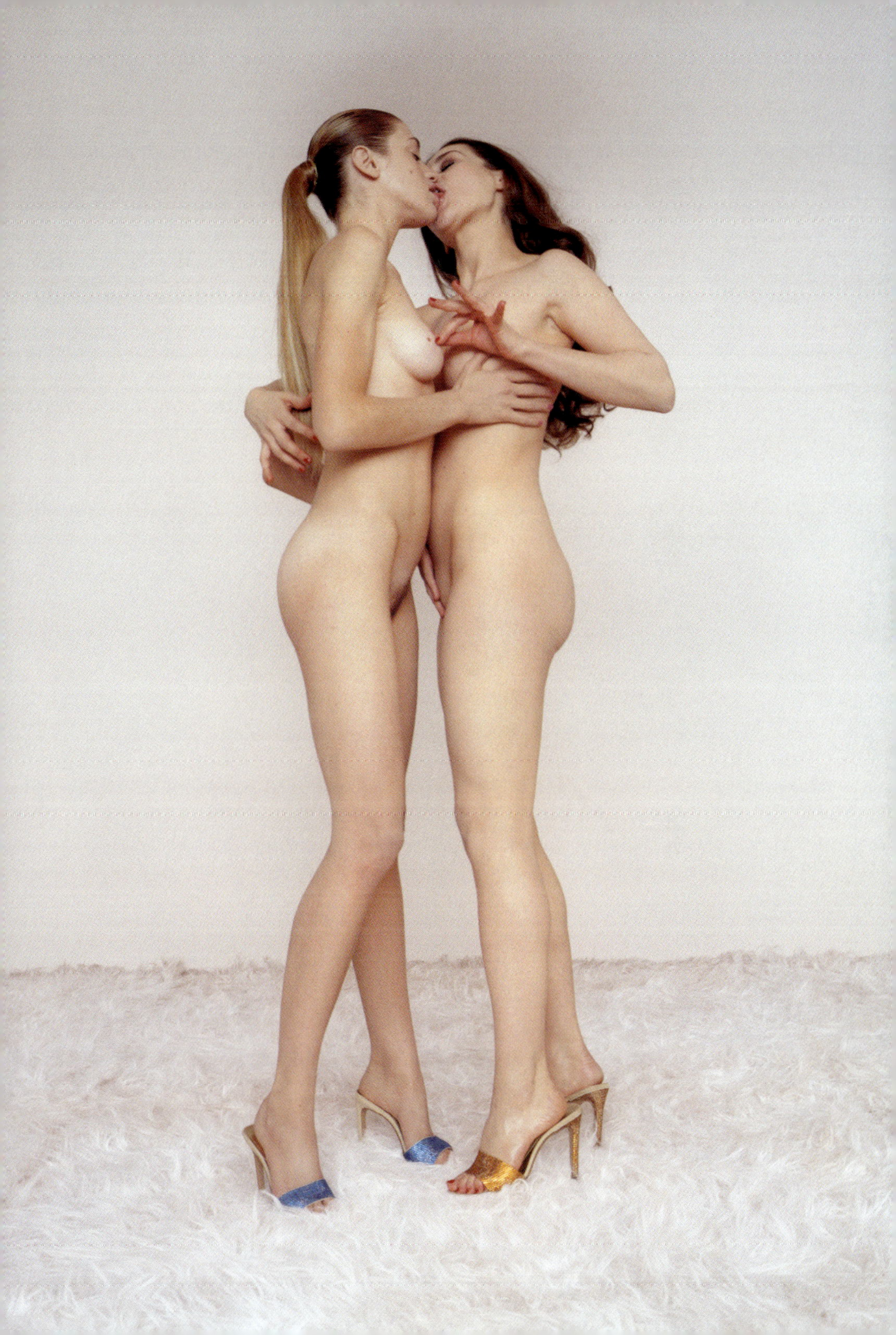

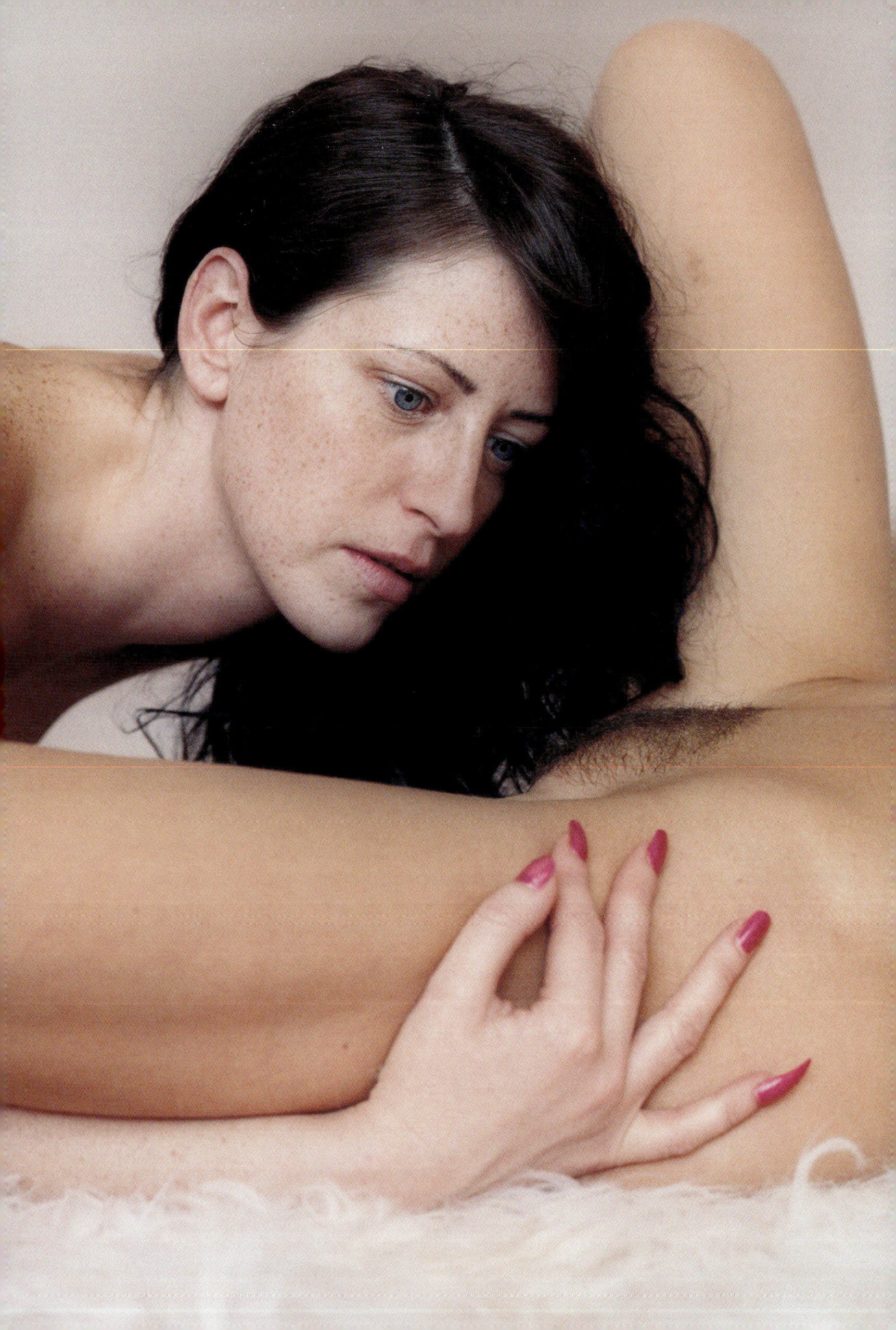

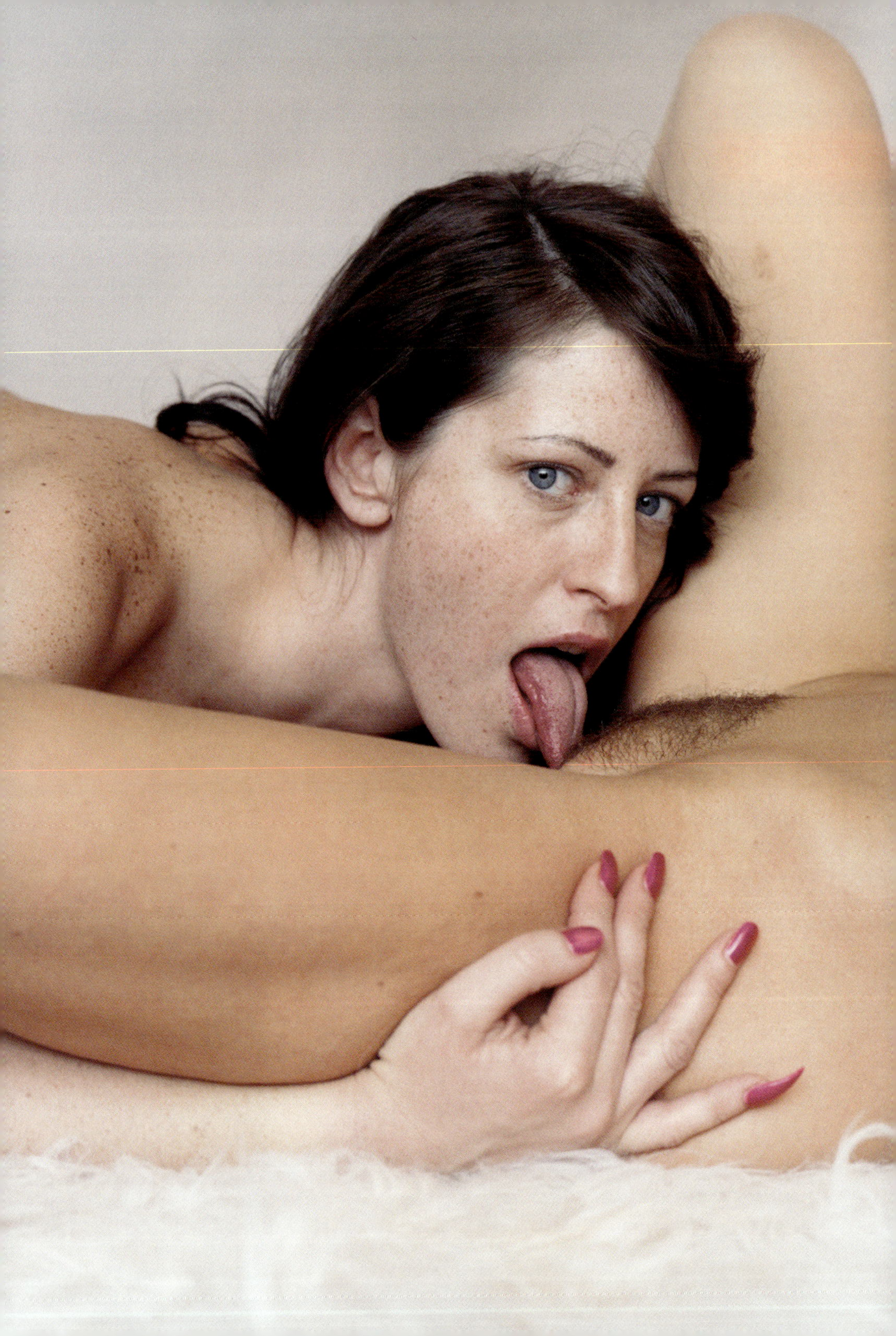

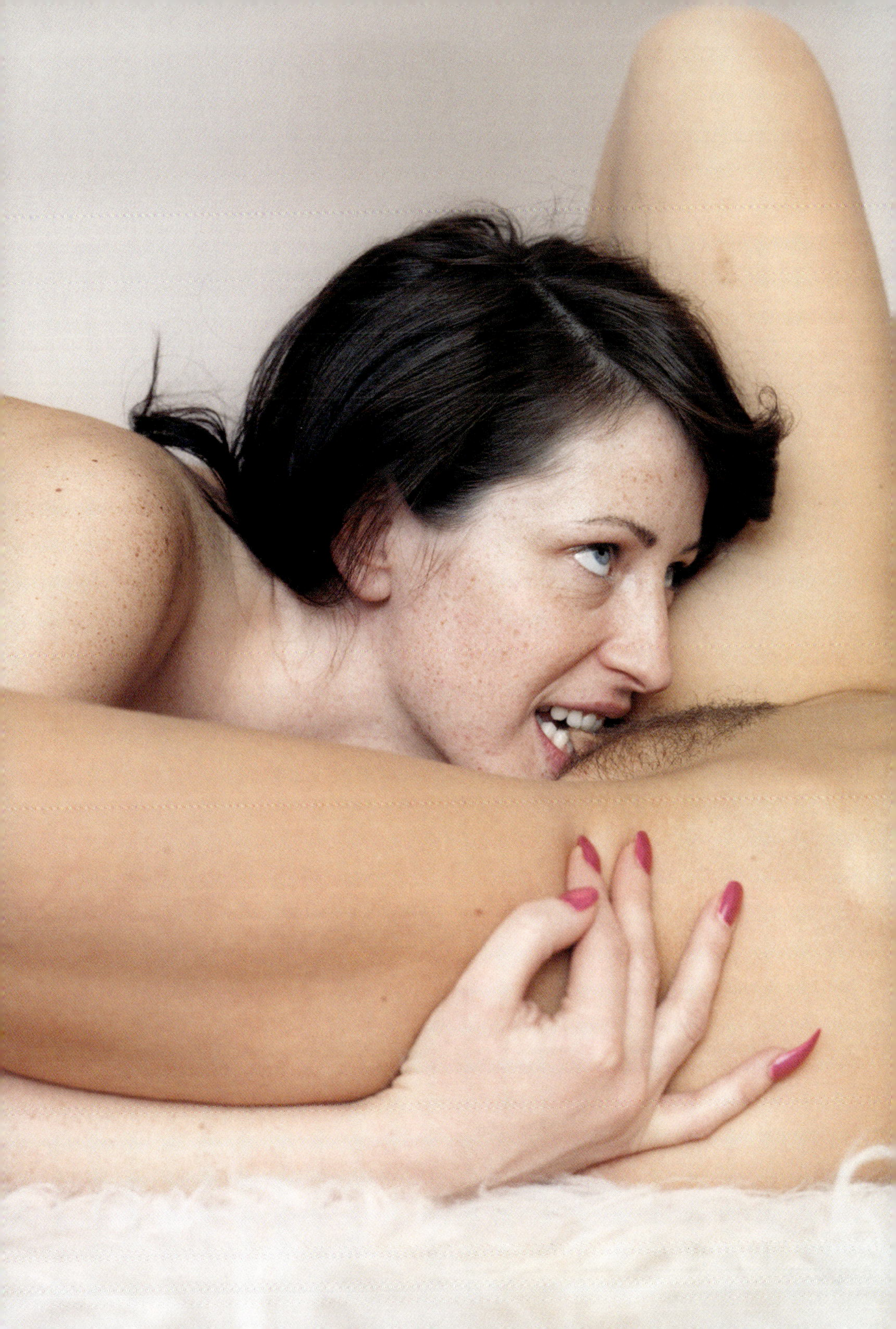

MC20, January 2001, Paris
Pages 324/325 — *Lauren Hutton*, June 1986, Paris
Pages 326/327 — *Emmanuelle Béart dans les feuilles*, July 1989, Luberon
Pages 328/329 — *Juliette Binoche*, October 1987, Paris

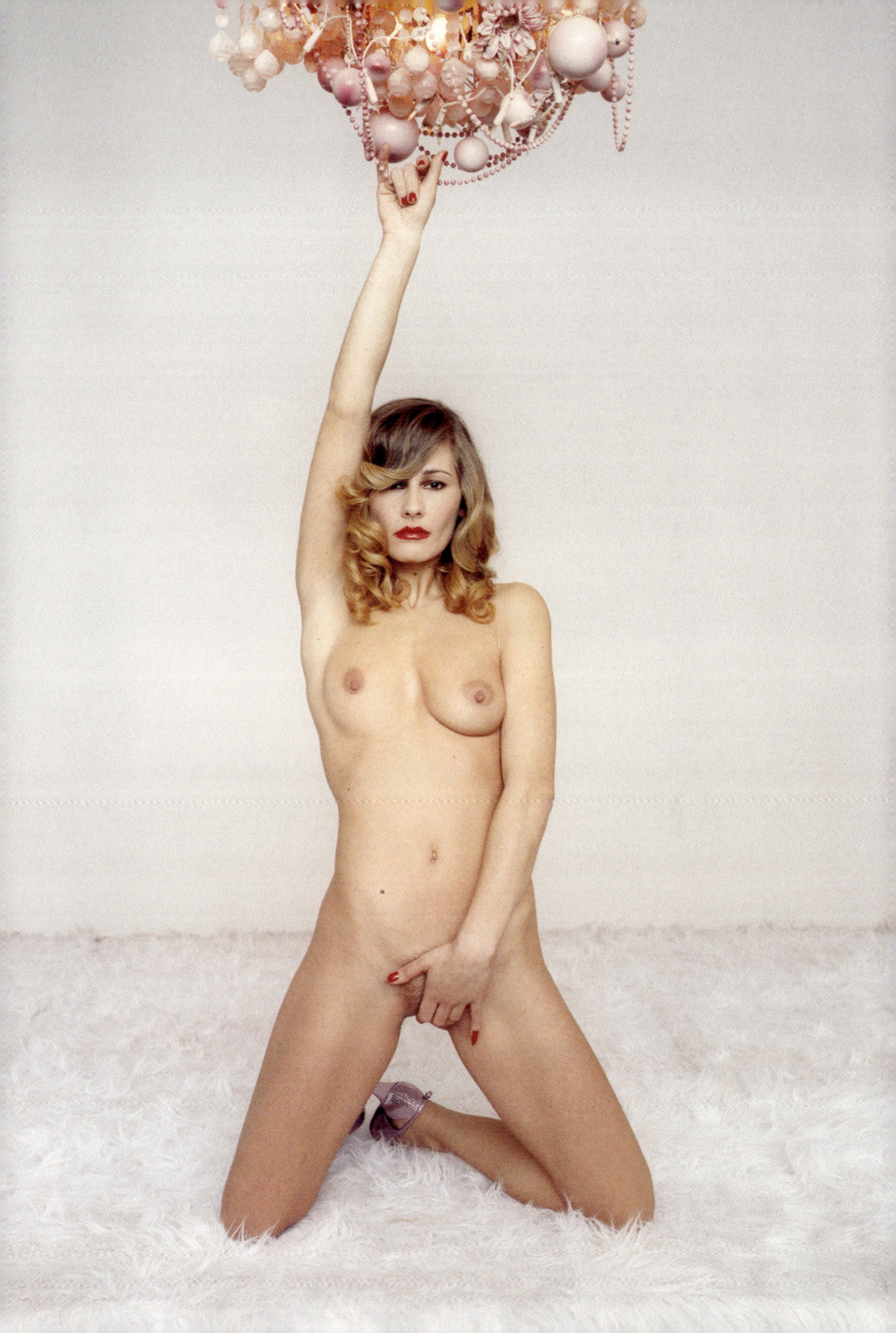

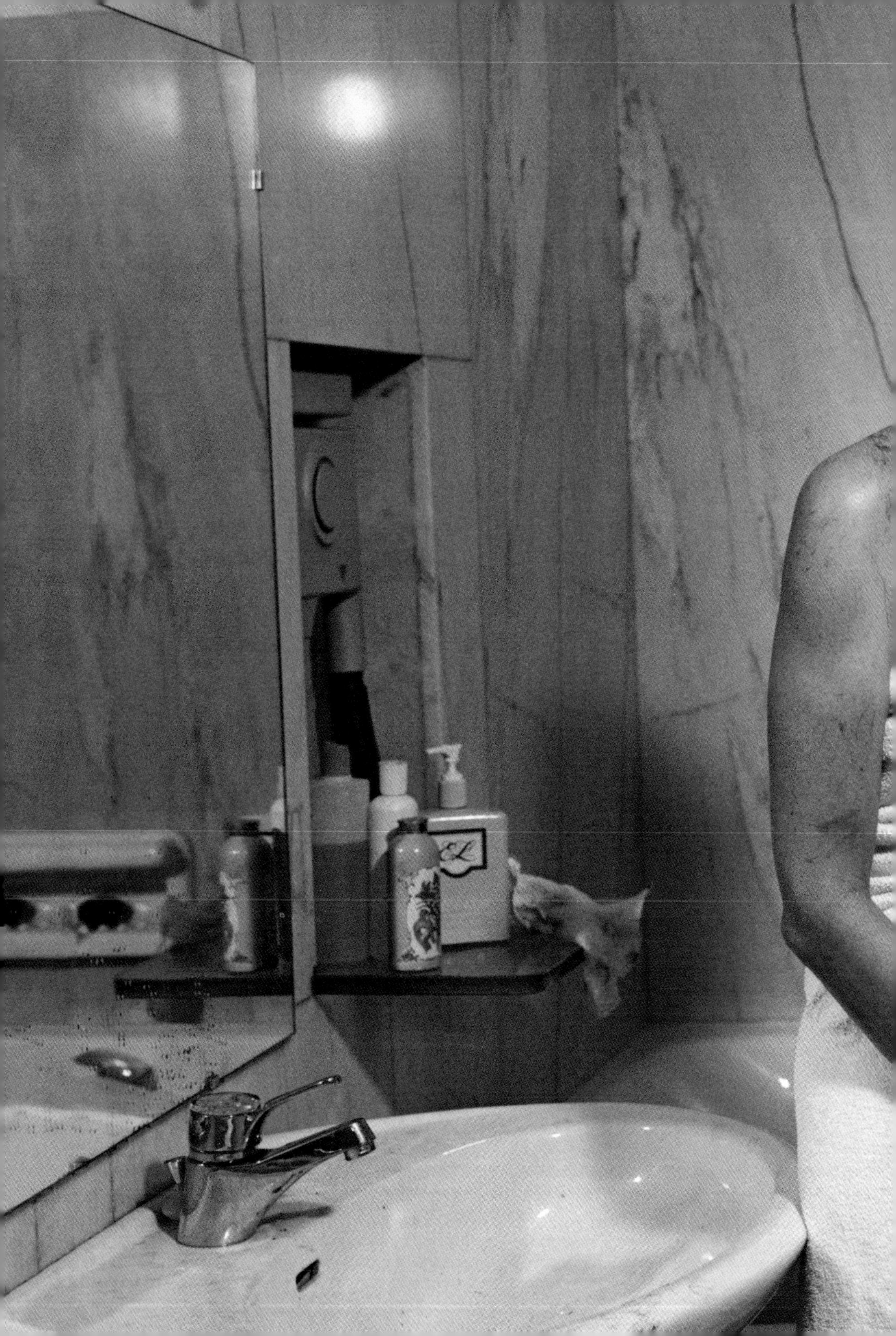

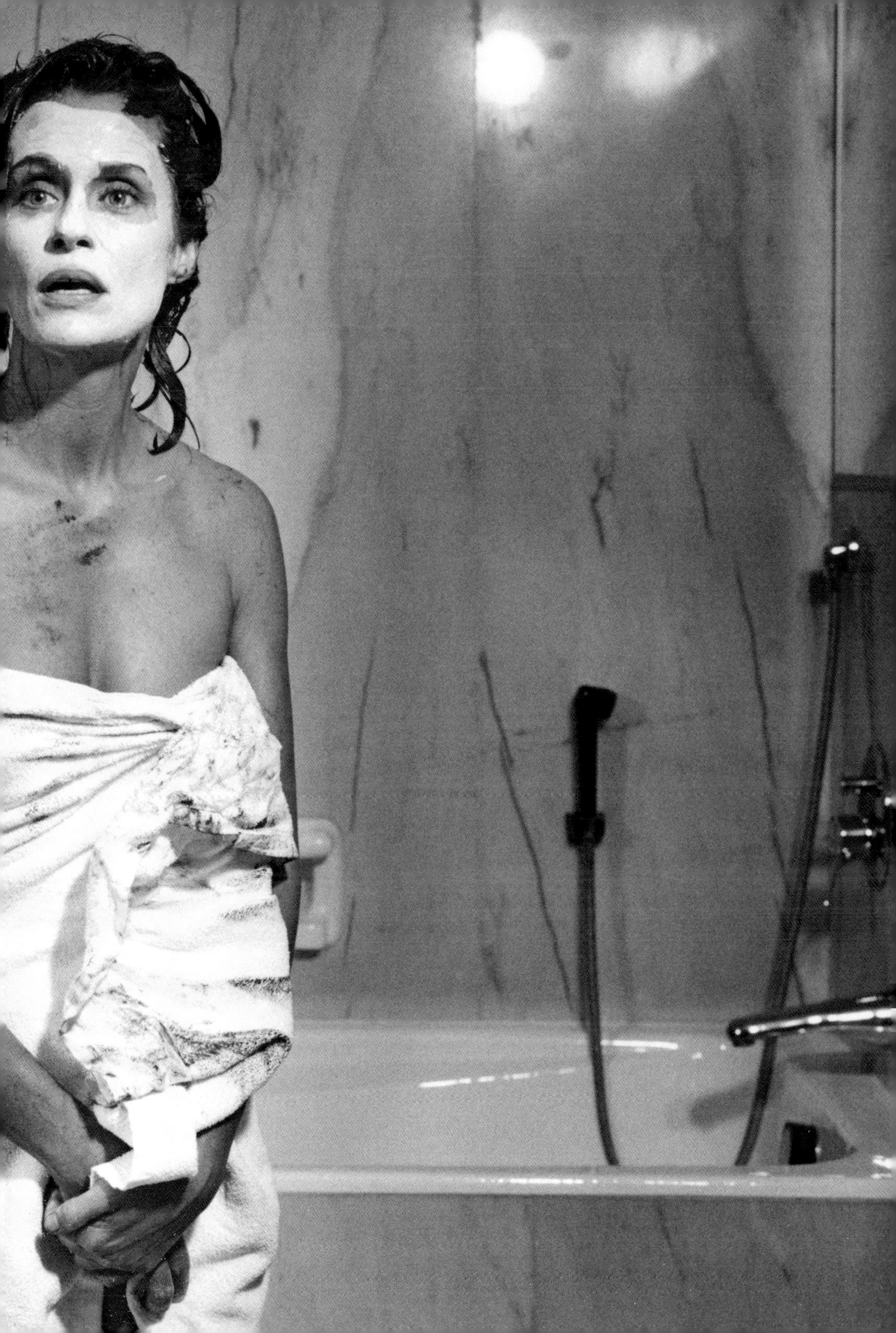

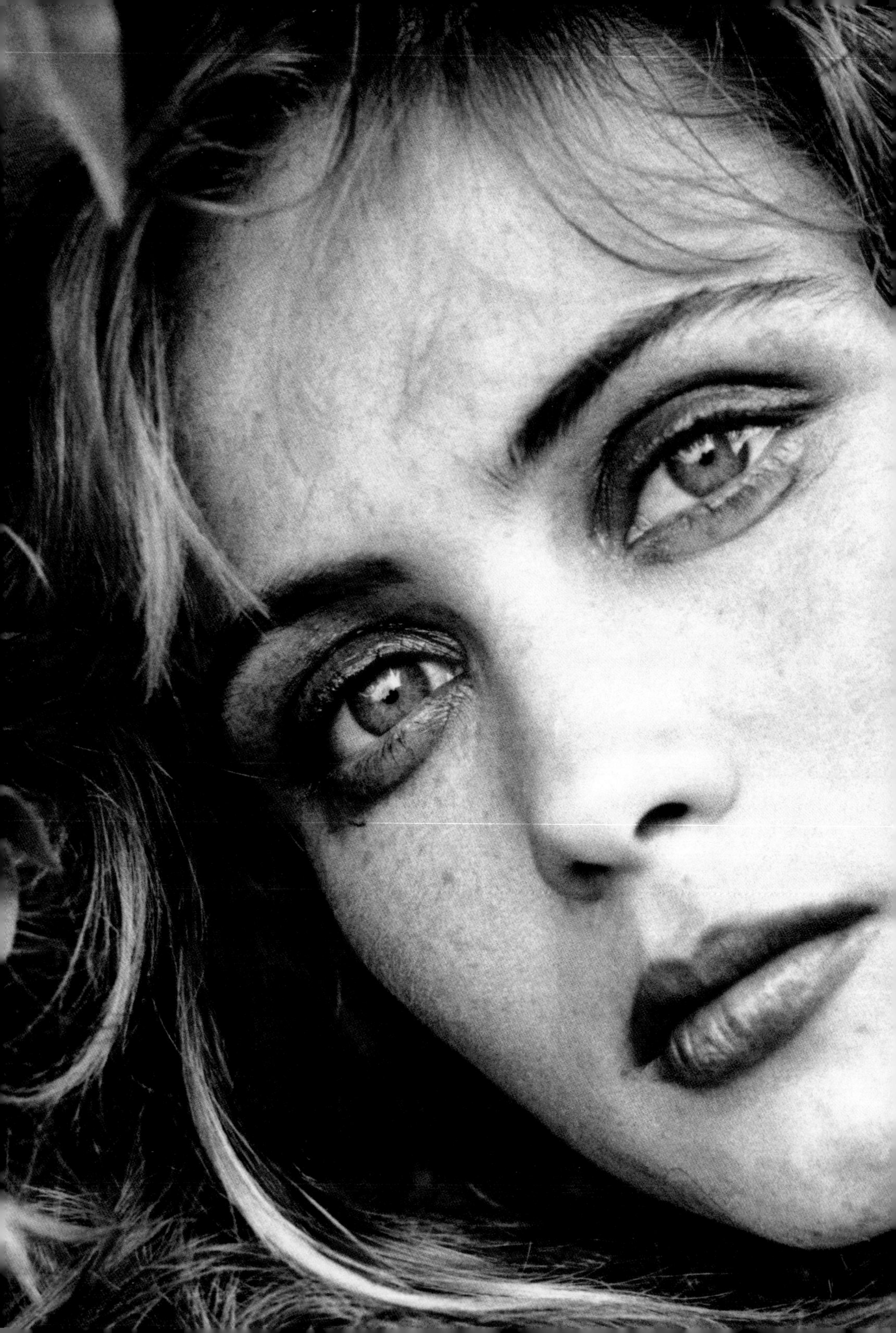

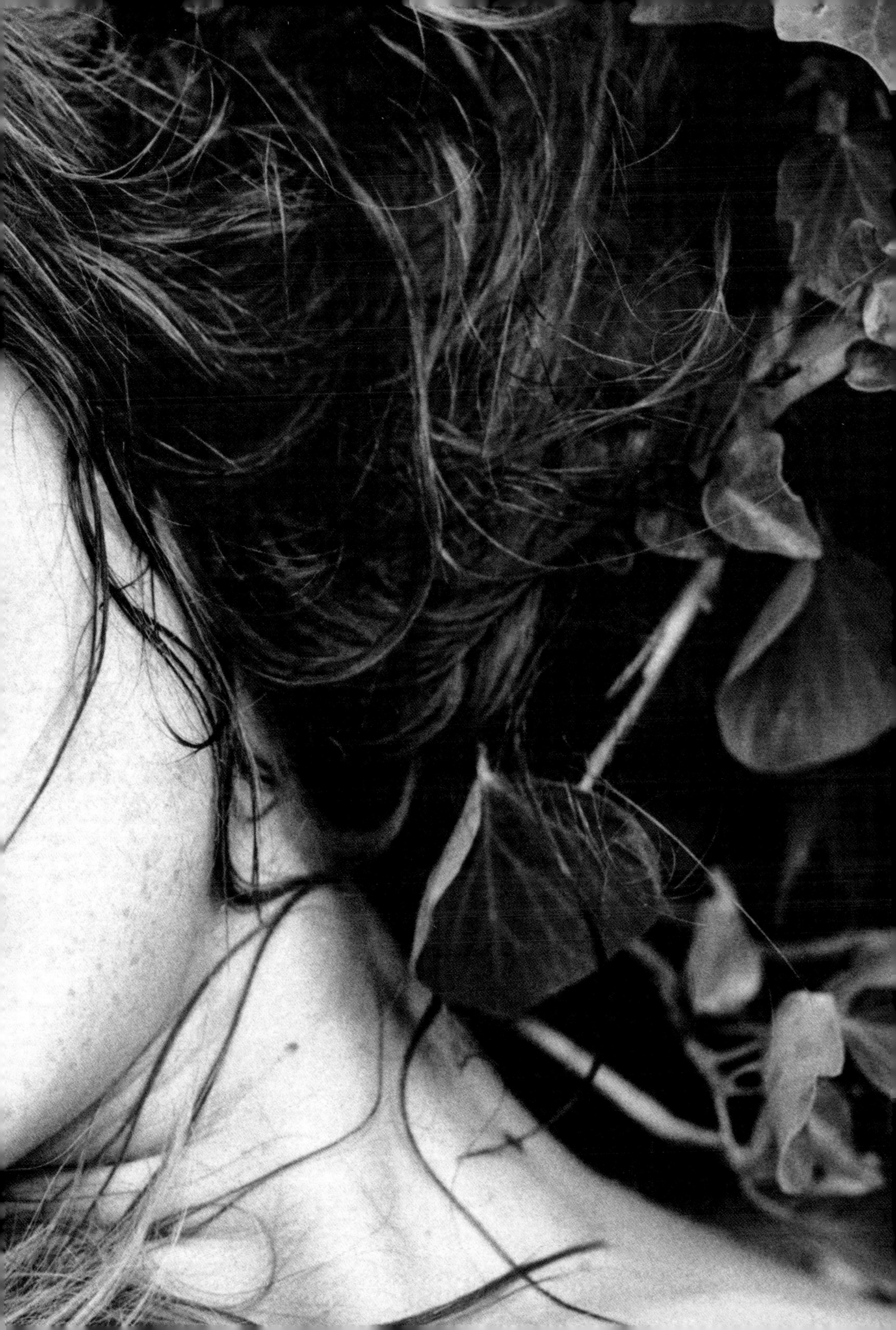

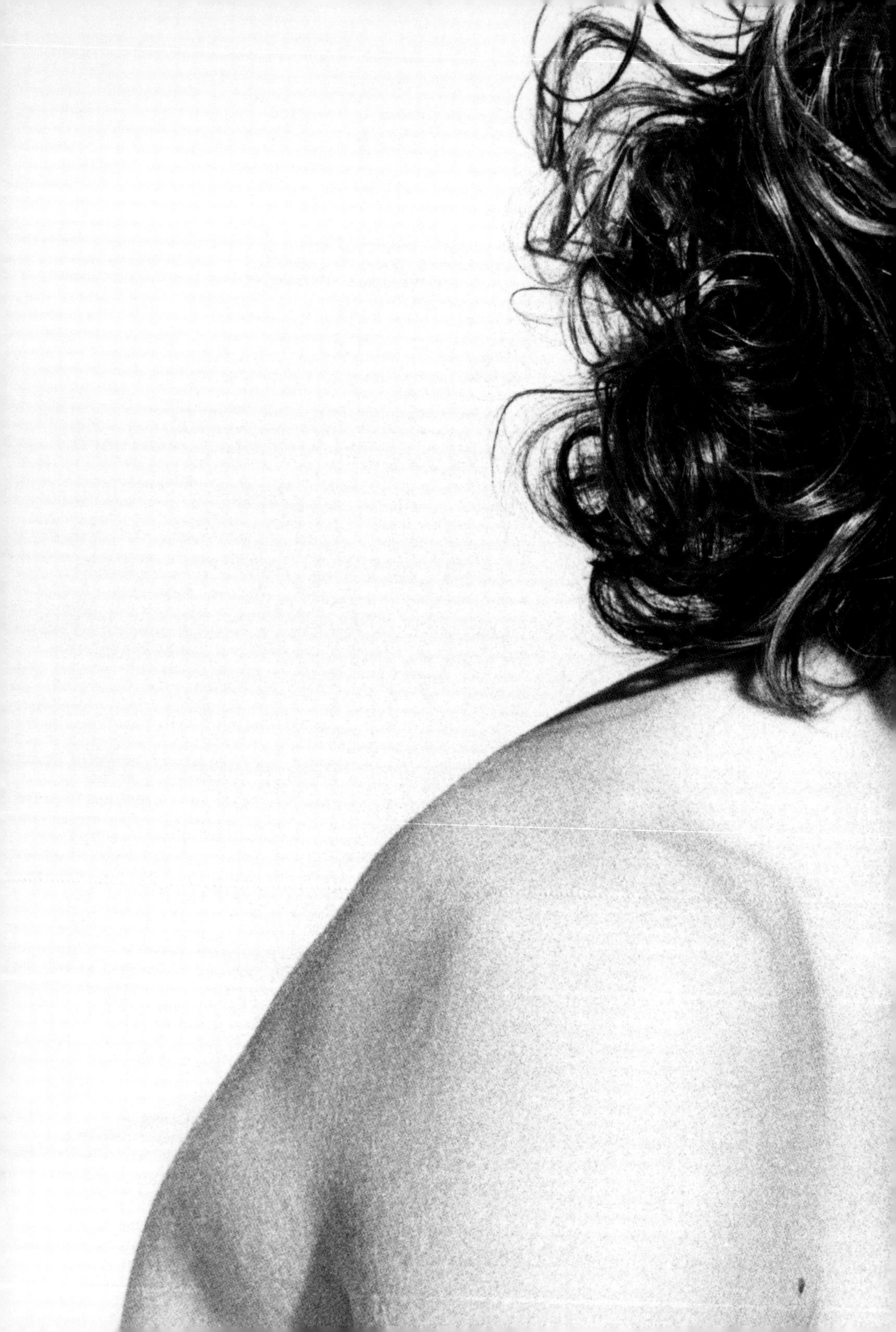

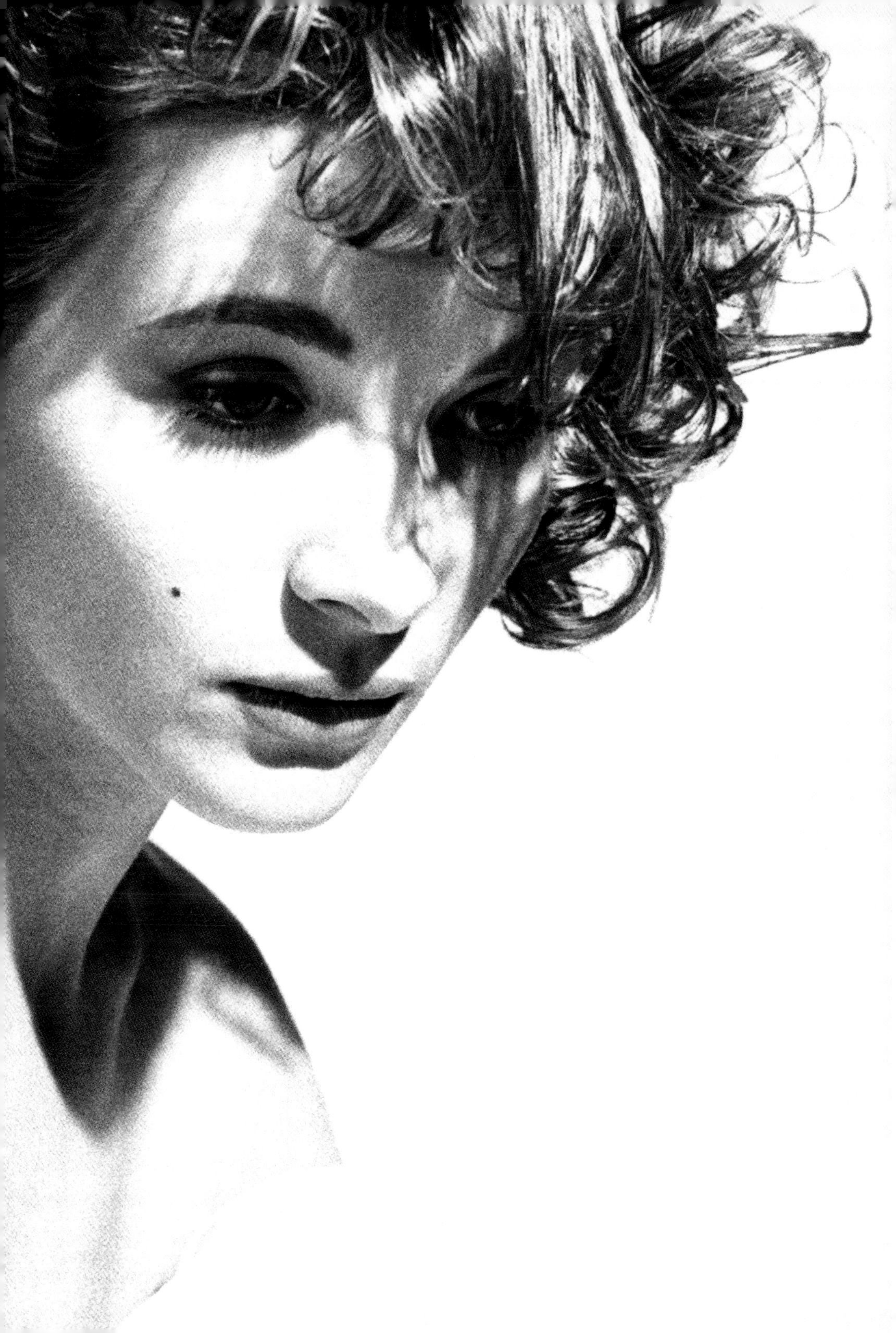

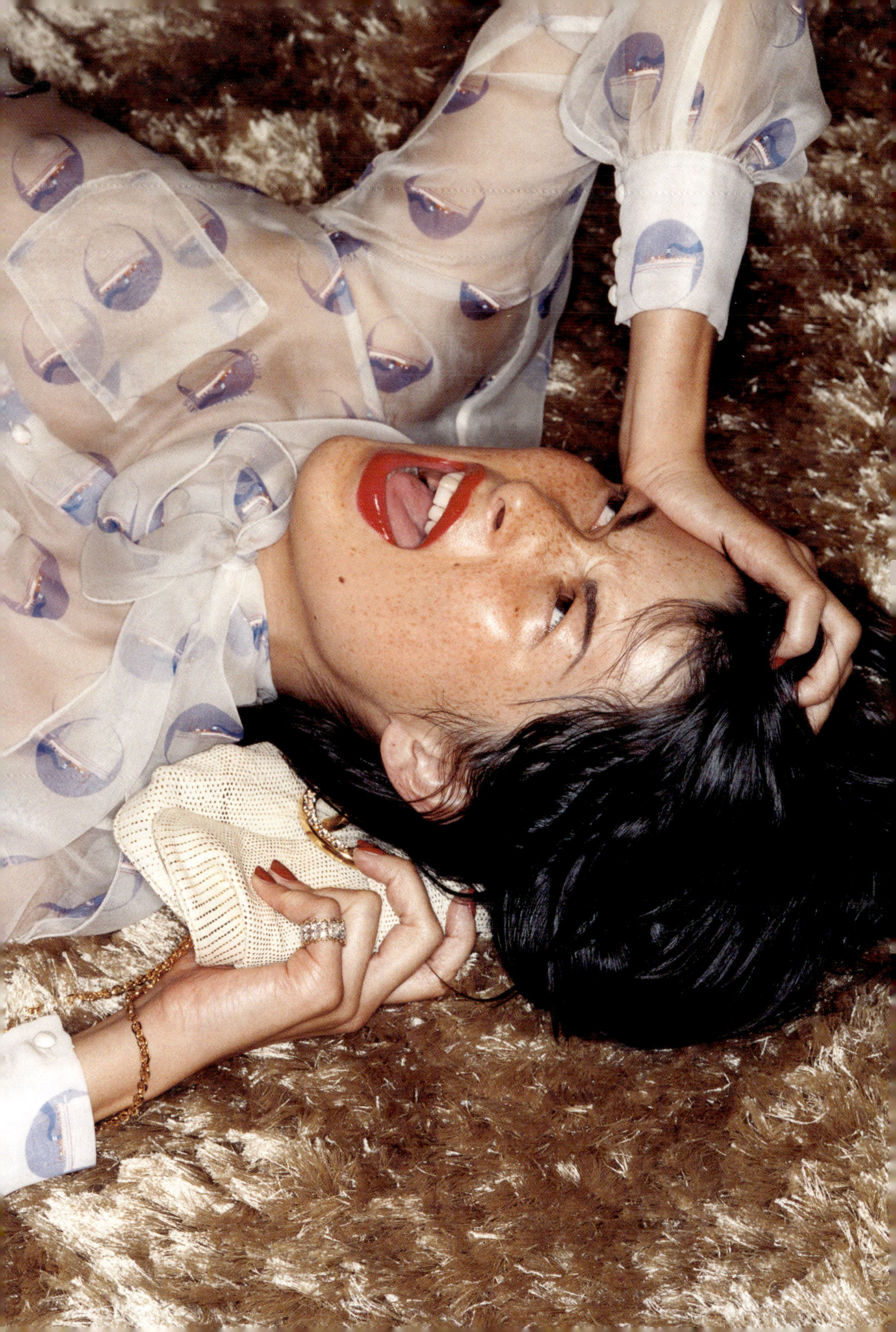

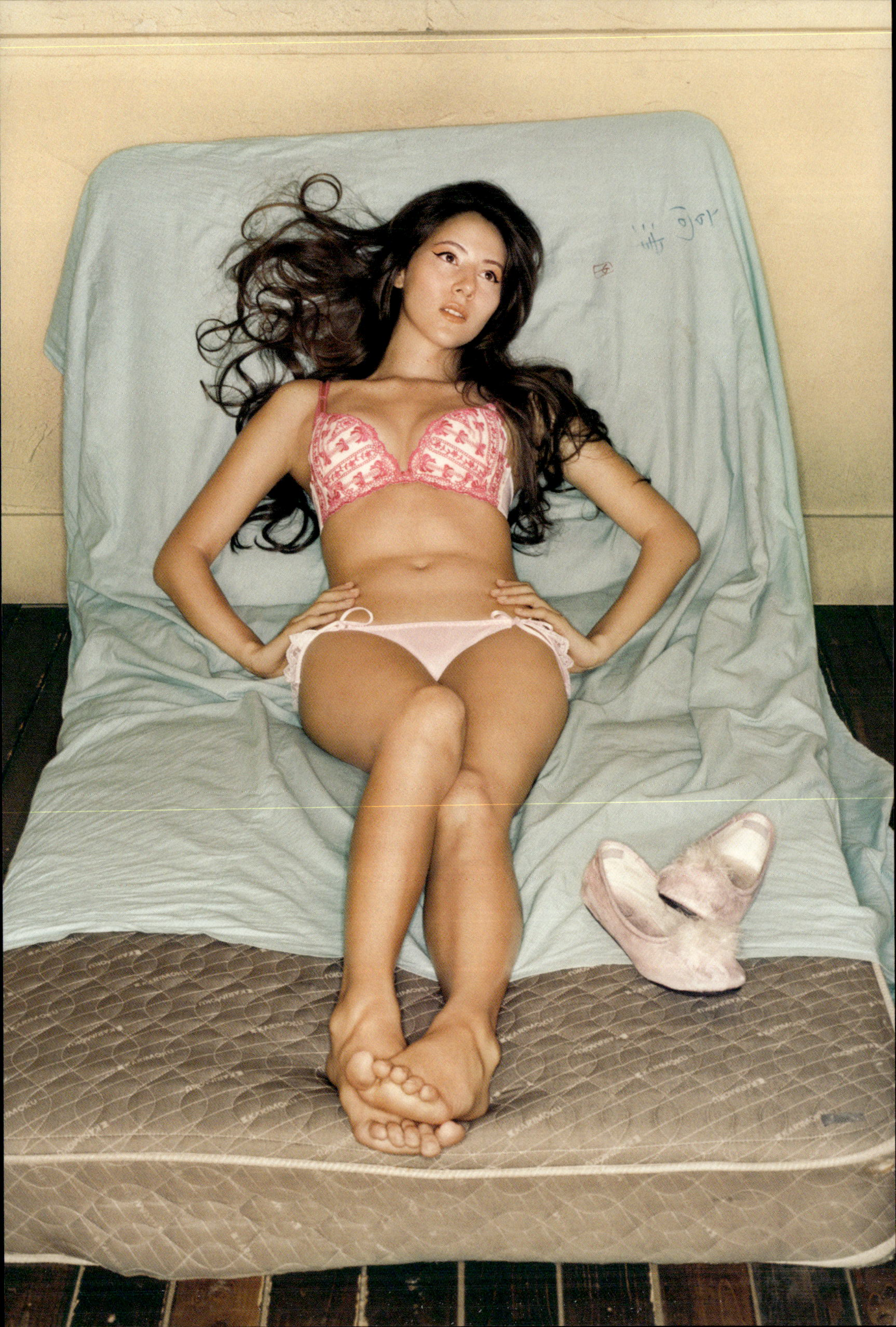

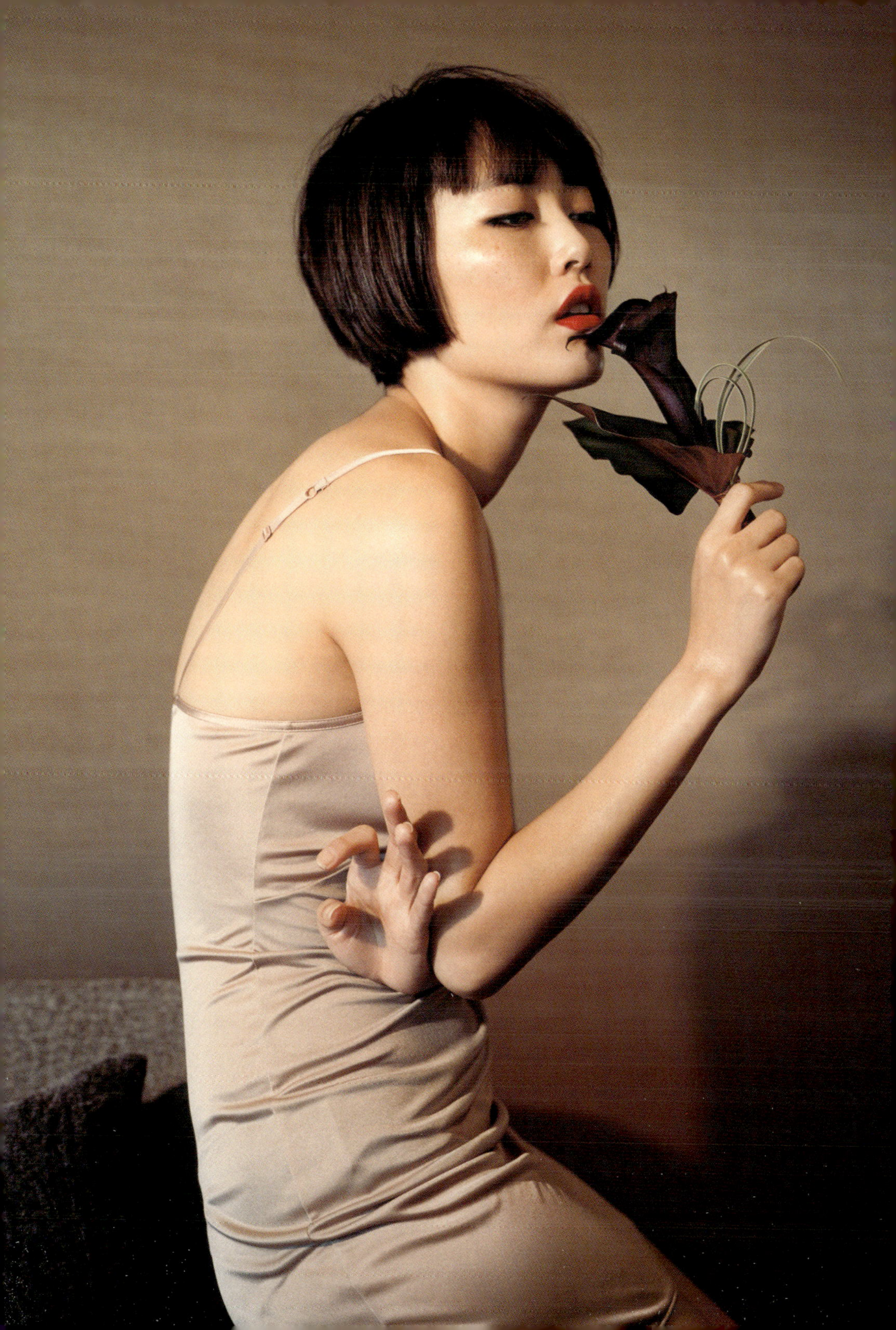

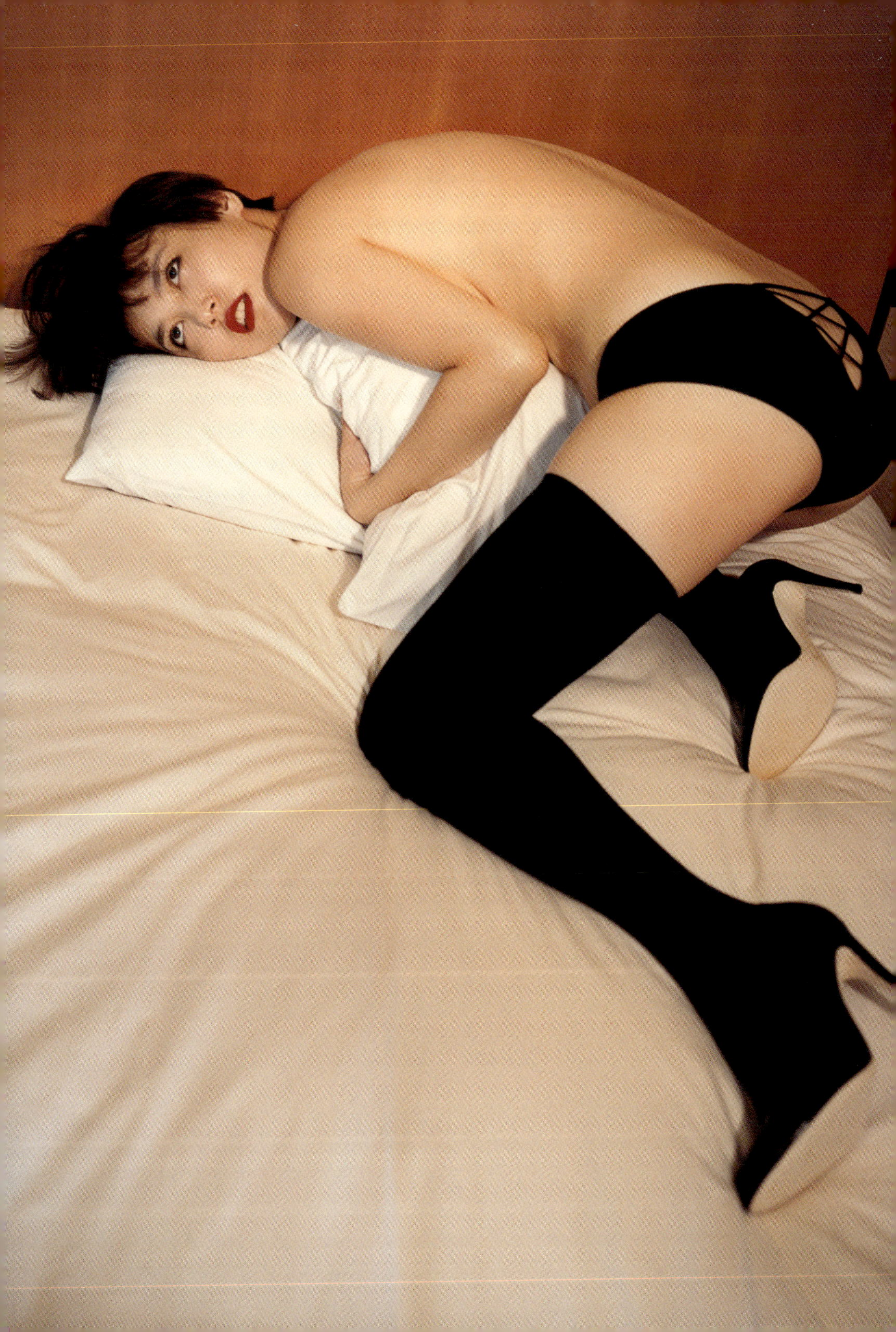

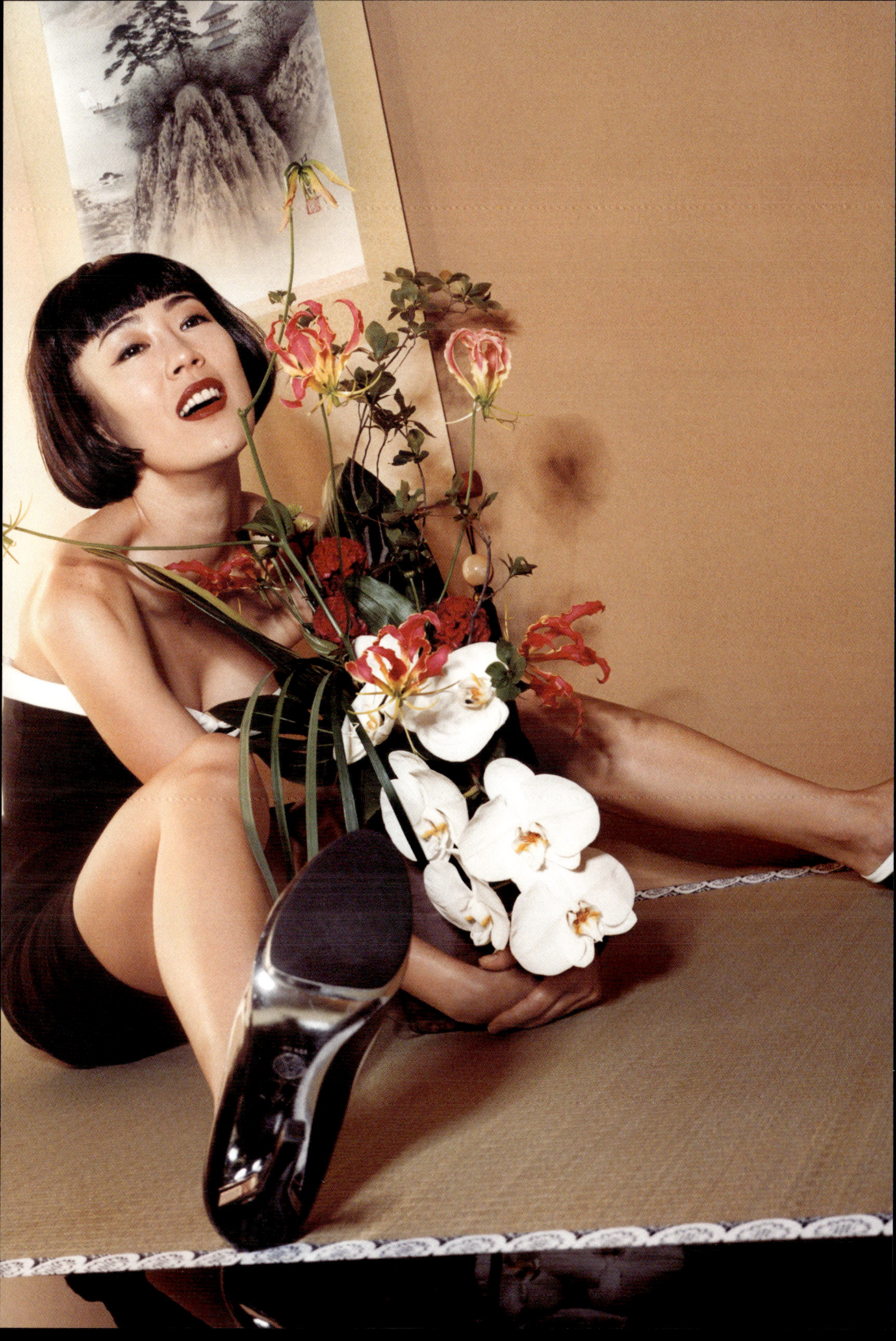

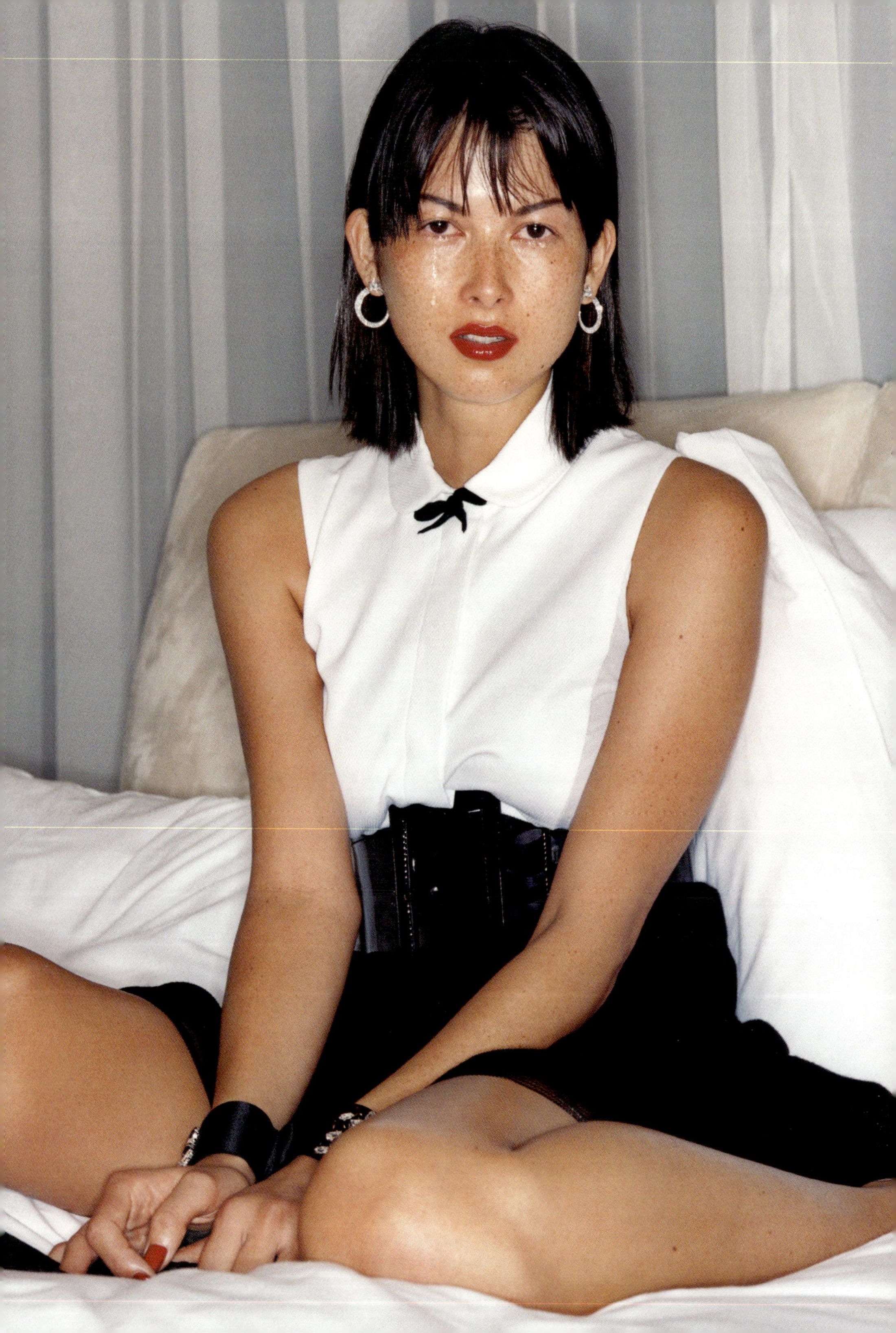

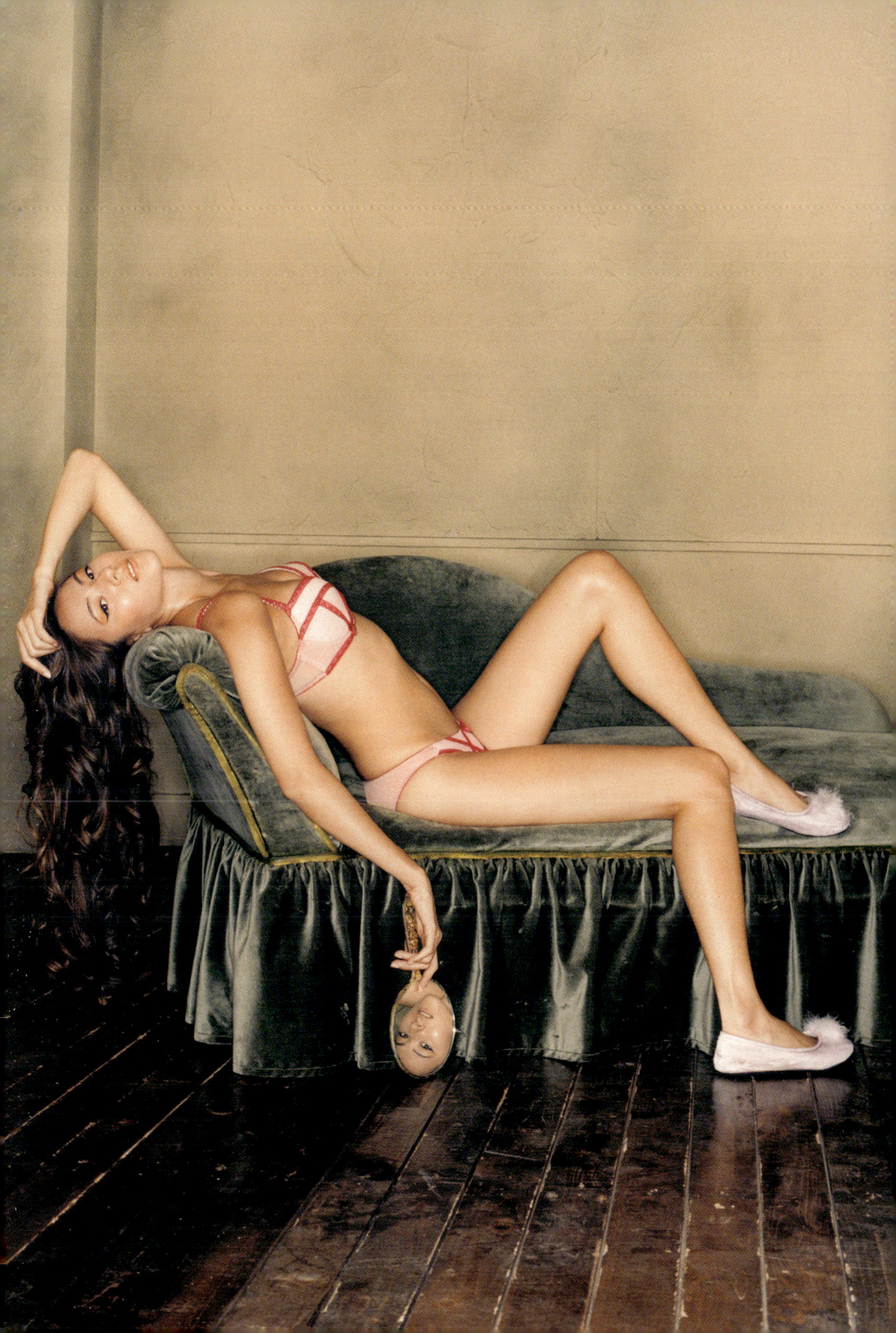

Jessica, portrait au chat, September 2007, Tokyo

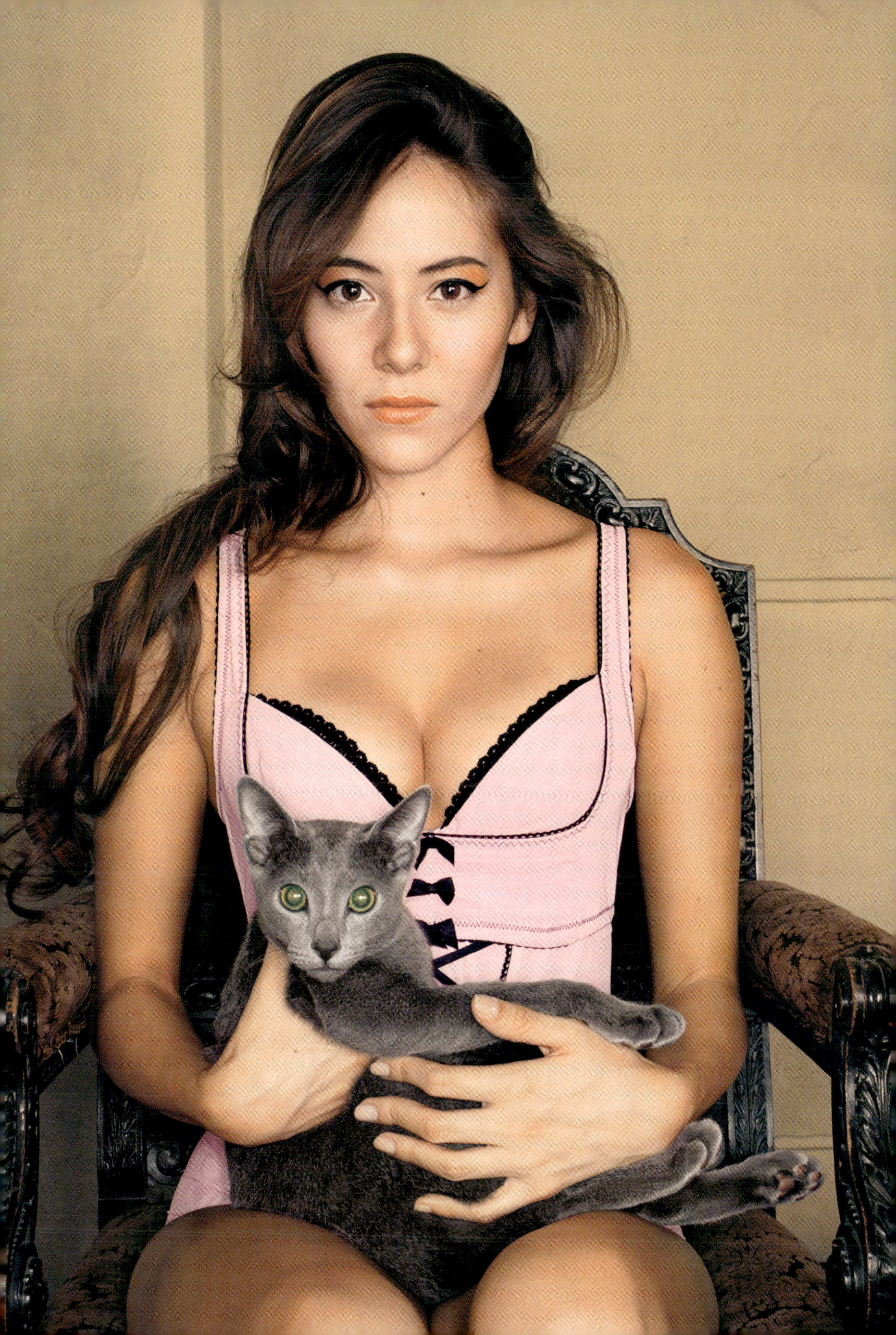

Opposite page, pages 342/343, 344, 345 — *Laurence Treil pour «Playboy»*,
December 1991, Fontainebleau
Pages 346/347— *In bed with Claudia Schiffer VII*, May 2000, Cannes

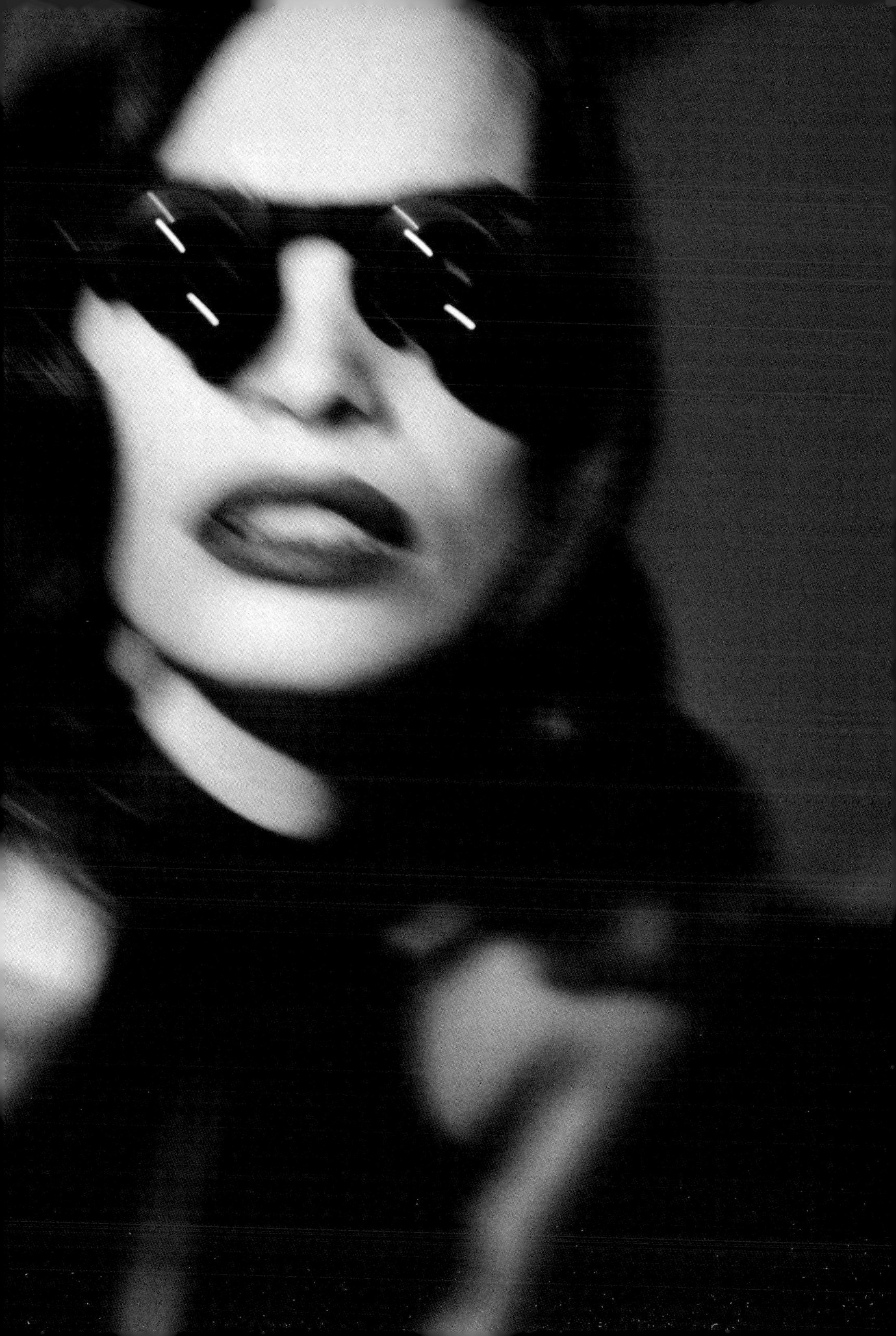

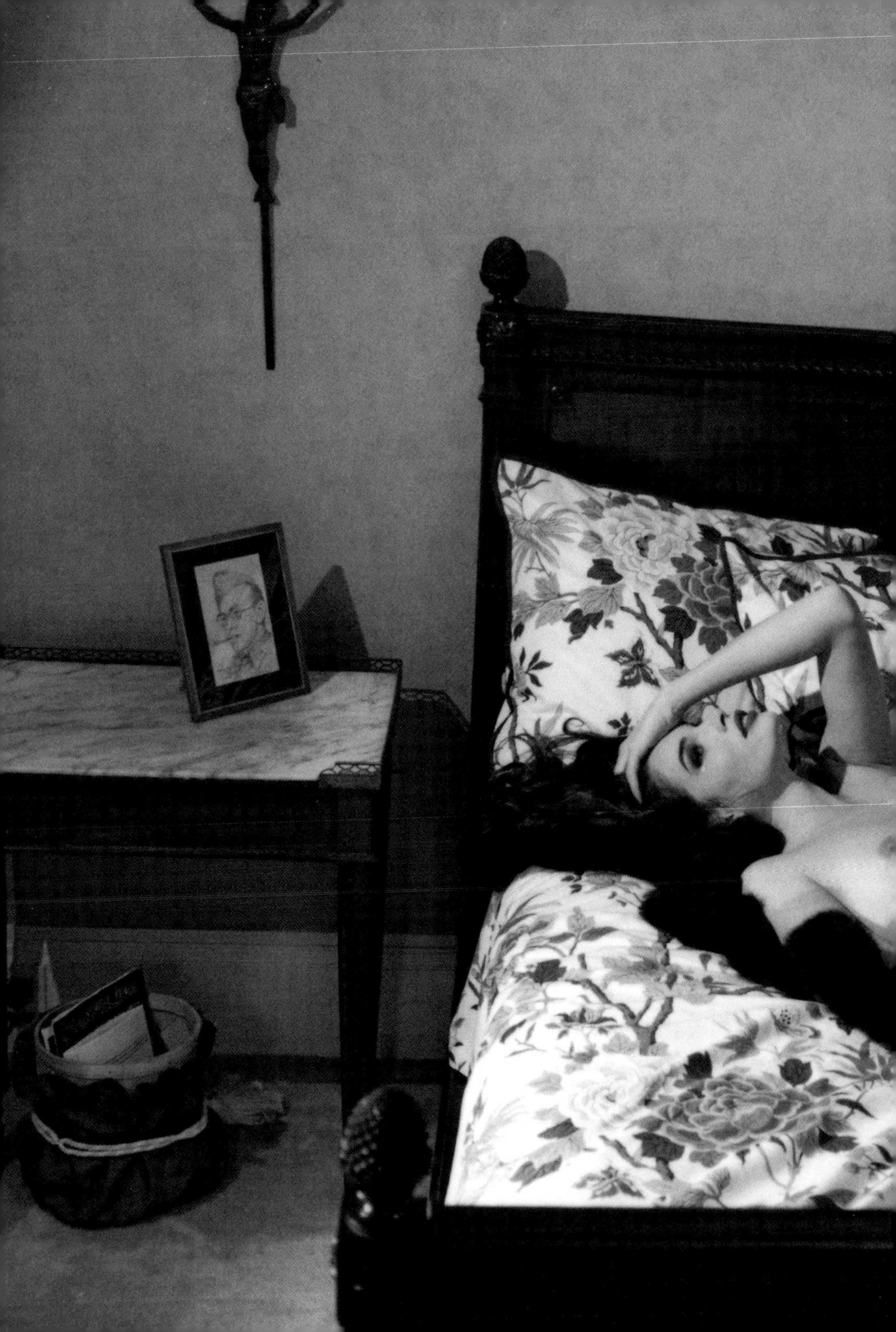

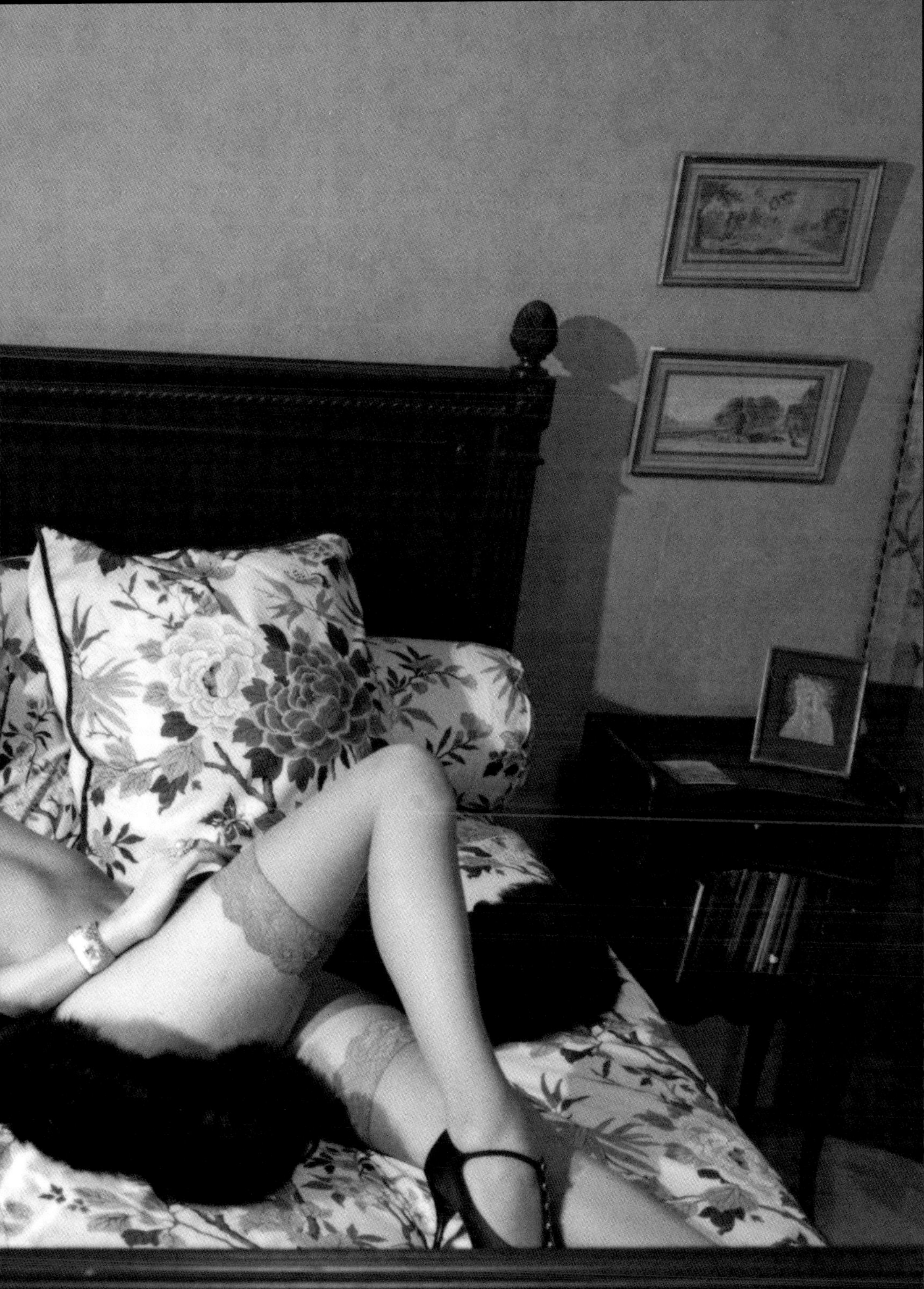

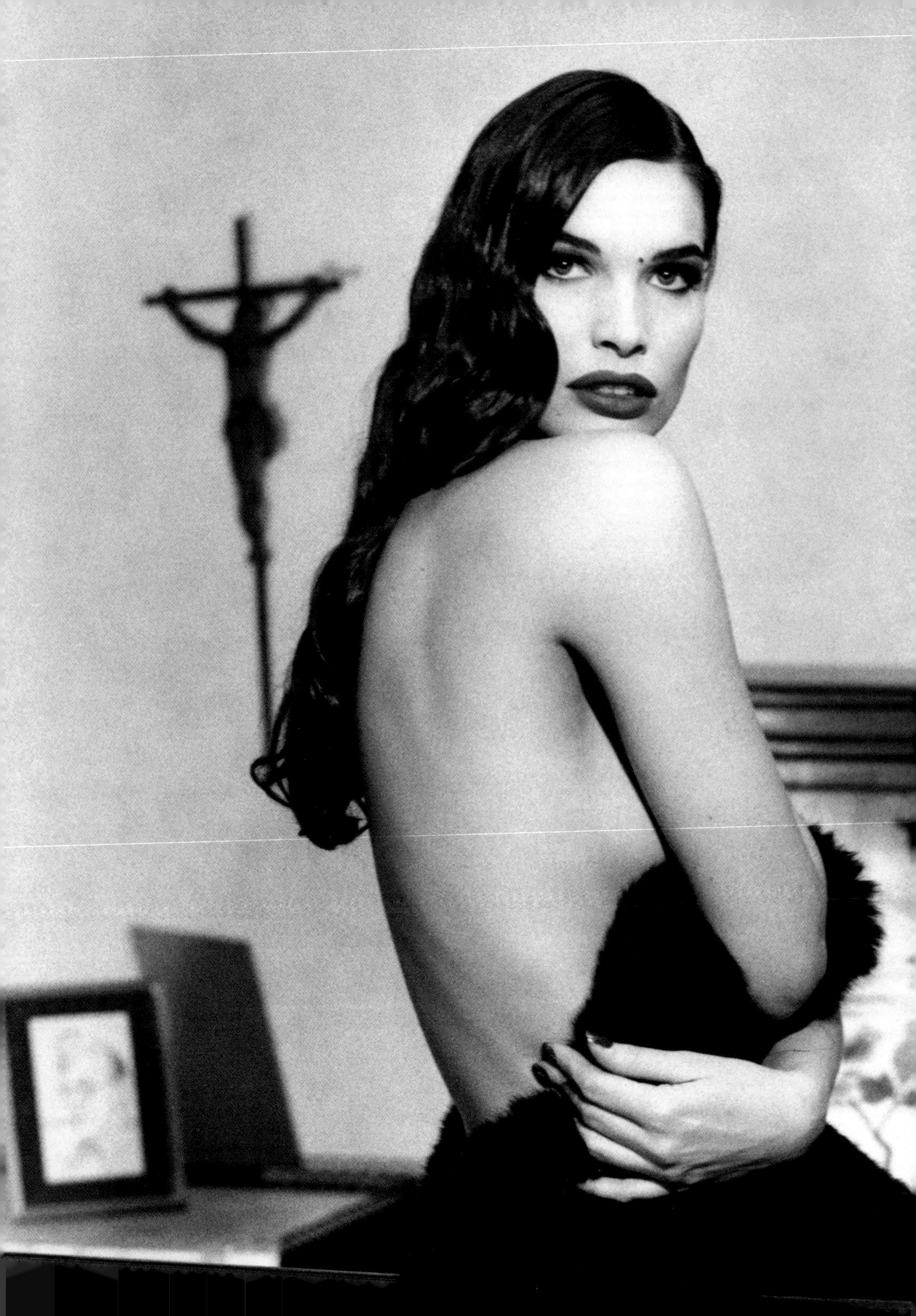

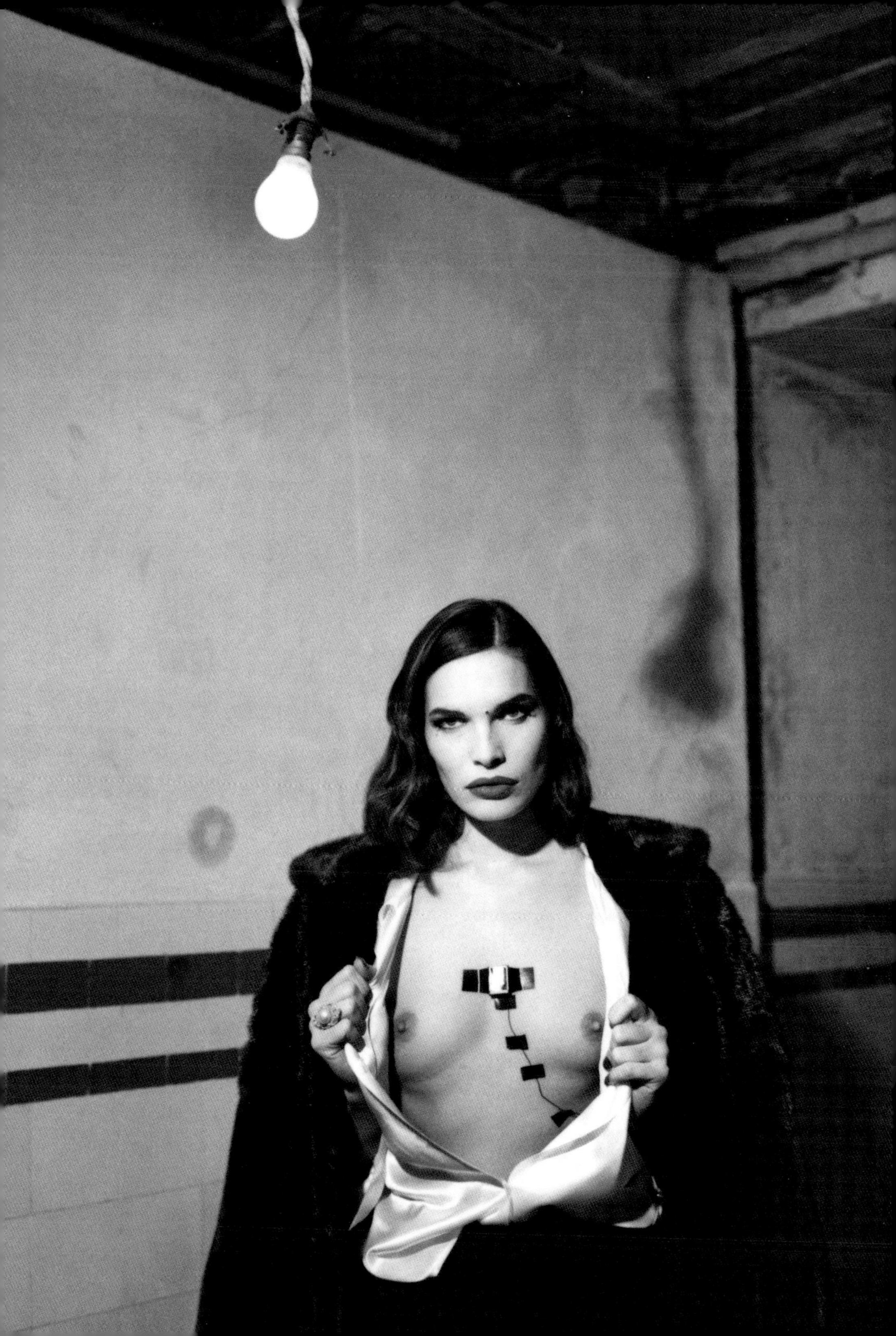

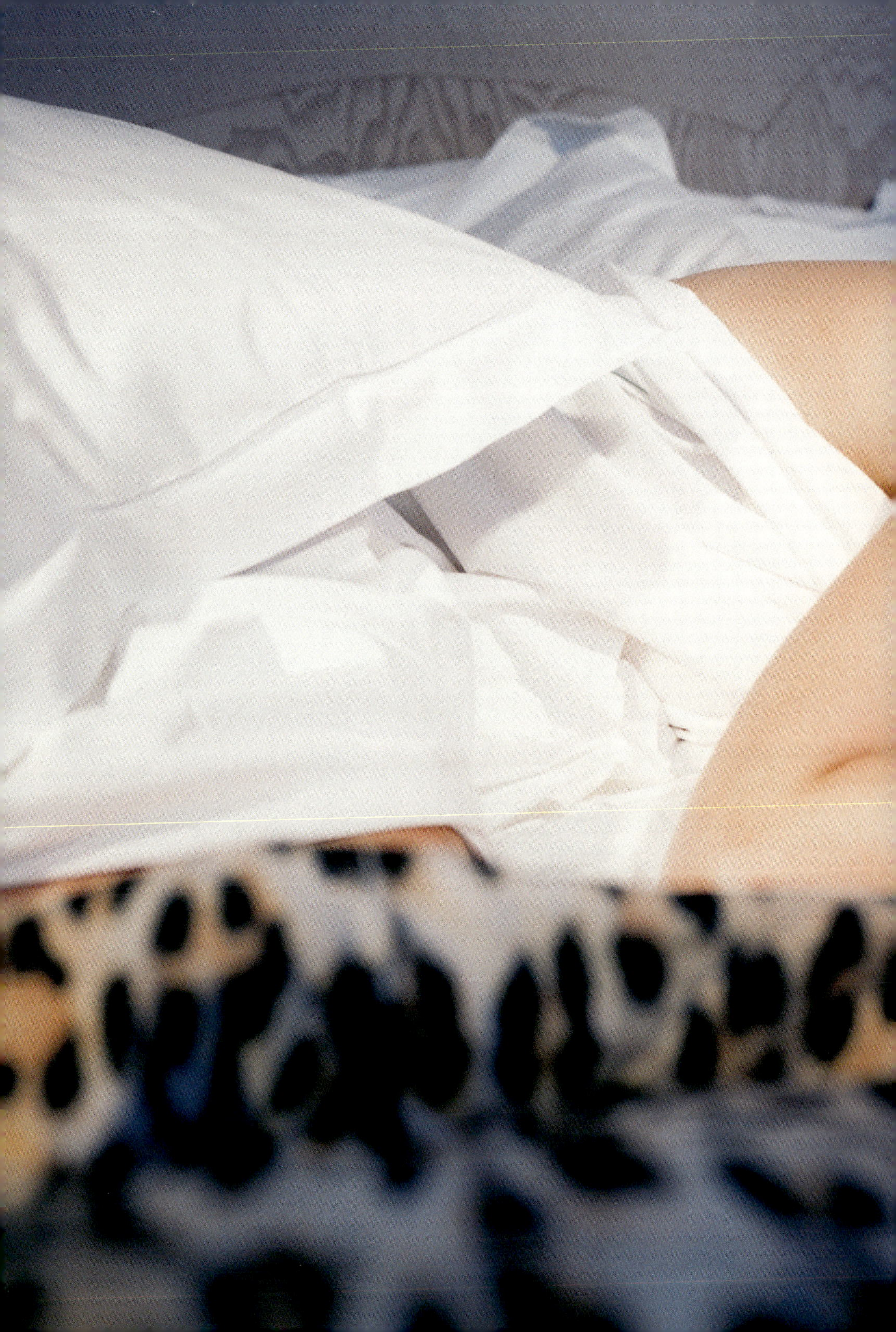

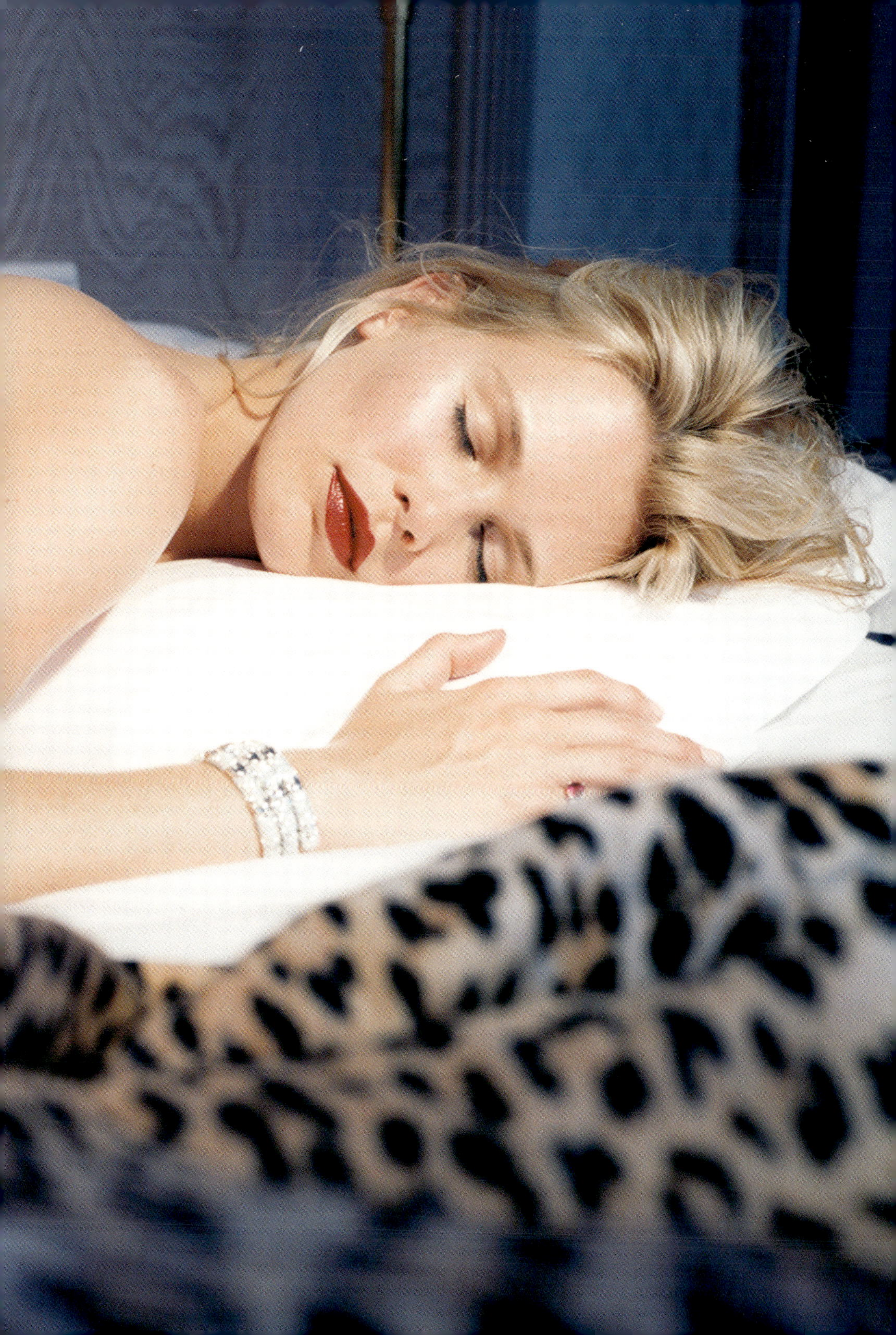

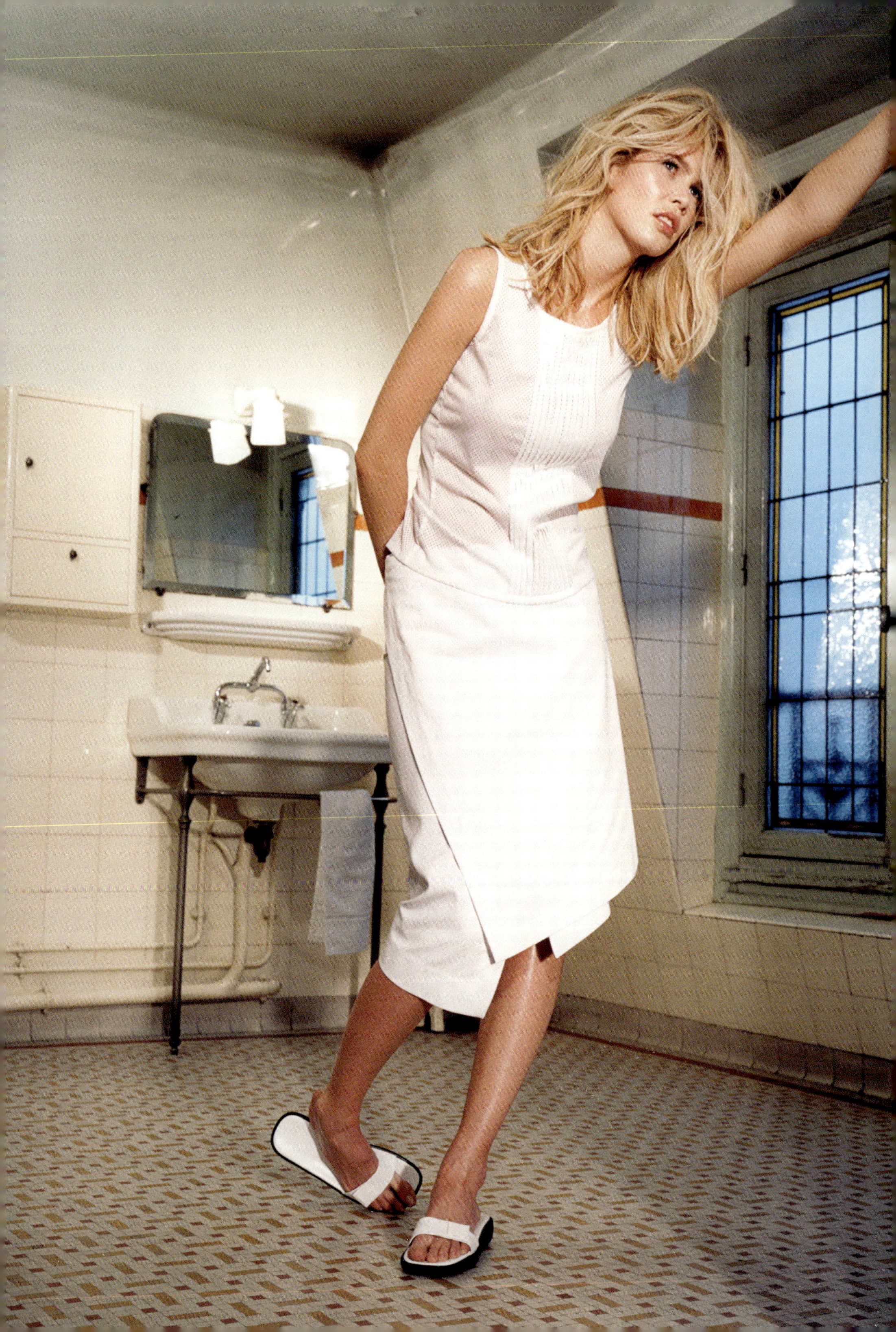

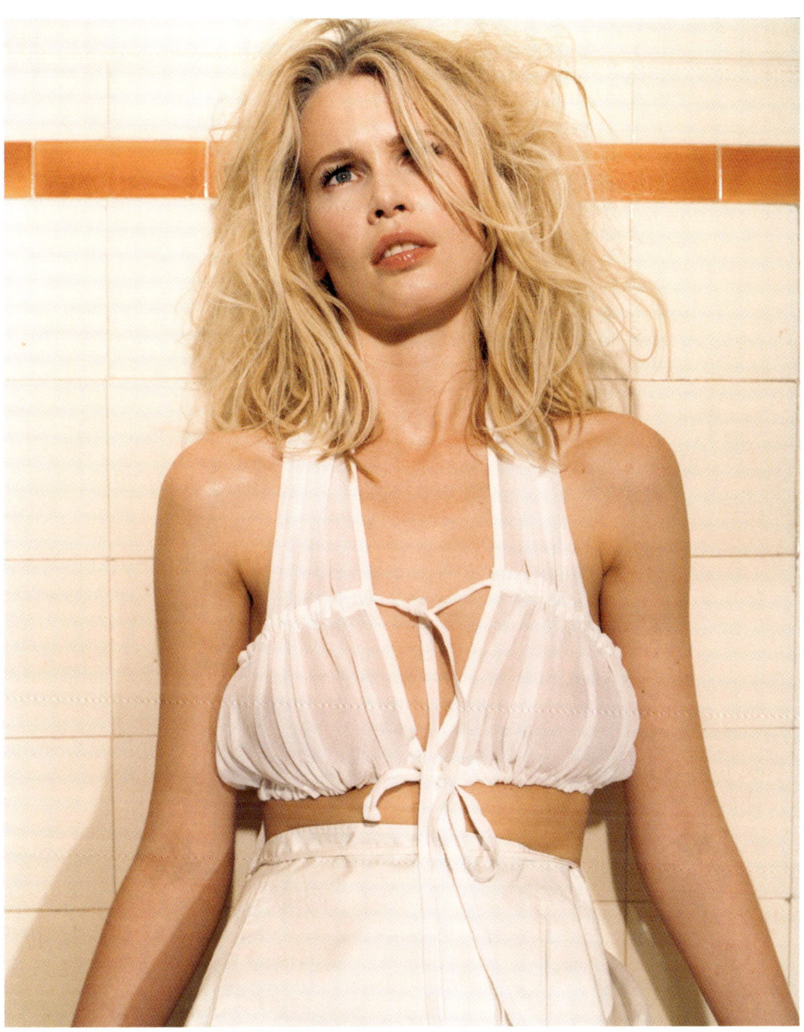

Above — *Portrait de Claudia ailleurs, aux carrelages blancs*, March 1999, Paris
Opposite page — *Claudia Schiffer dans la salle de bains du Terminus Est*, March 1999, Paris

HÉROÏNES

2005, Paris

Tulle, voile, satin, laces and pleats, pearls and spangles: expensive dresses, haute couture, or so you might think, but as if unearthed from some trunk found in the attic. They are crumpled, tired, they seem to have been flung on any old how – though in fact with all the talent and reinterpretation by Jean Colonna – so that some of these "heroines" look like little girls caught dressing up in their mothers' clothes.

Tulle, voile, satin, dentelles et plissés, perles et paillettes laissent penser qu'on a affaire à des robes de prix, des robes de haute couture, mais qu'on aurait exhumées d'une malle trouvée au grenier. Elles sont froissées, quelque peu défraîchies, enfilées apparemment n'importe comment – mais en fait selon tout l'art de leur réinterprétation par Jean Colonna –, ce qui donne à certaines des «héroïnes» l'air de fillettes surprises en train de jouer avec les habits de leurs aînées.

Tüll, Schleier, Satin, Spitzen und Plissee, Perlen und Pailletten verweisen auf kostbare Kleider, auf Haute-Couture-Stücke, die man jedoch in einem Koffer auf dem Dachboden wiedergefunden hat. Sie sind zerknittert, ein wenig verschlissen und scheinbar achtlos übergeworfen – in Wirklichkeit jedoch äußerst kunstvoll neu interpretiert durch Jean Colonna –, wodurch manche dieser „Heldinnen" aussehen wie kleine Mädchen, die man beim Spielen in den abgelegten Kleidern ihrer Mütter ertappt hat.

Catherine Millet, in *Héroïnes*, 2006

Veroushka Knoge, étude, February 2005, Paris
Page 352 — *Nataša Vojnović, étude*, March 2005, Paris
Page 353 — *Renée Dorski, étude*, March 2005, Paris
Page 354 — *Lydia Hurst, étude n° 2*, March 2005, Paris
Page 355 — *Dita Von Teese, étude*, March 2005, Paris
Page 356 — *Tilda Swinton, étude*, June 2005, Paris
Page 357 — *Irina Lăzăreanu, étude*, February 2005, Paris
Page 358 — *Milla Jovovich, étude n° 2*, March 2005, Paris
Page 359 — *Milla Jovovich, étude*, March 2005, Paris

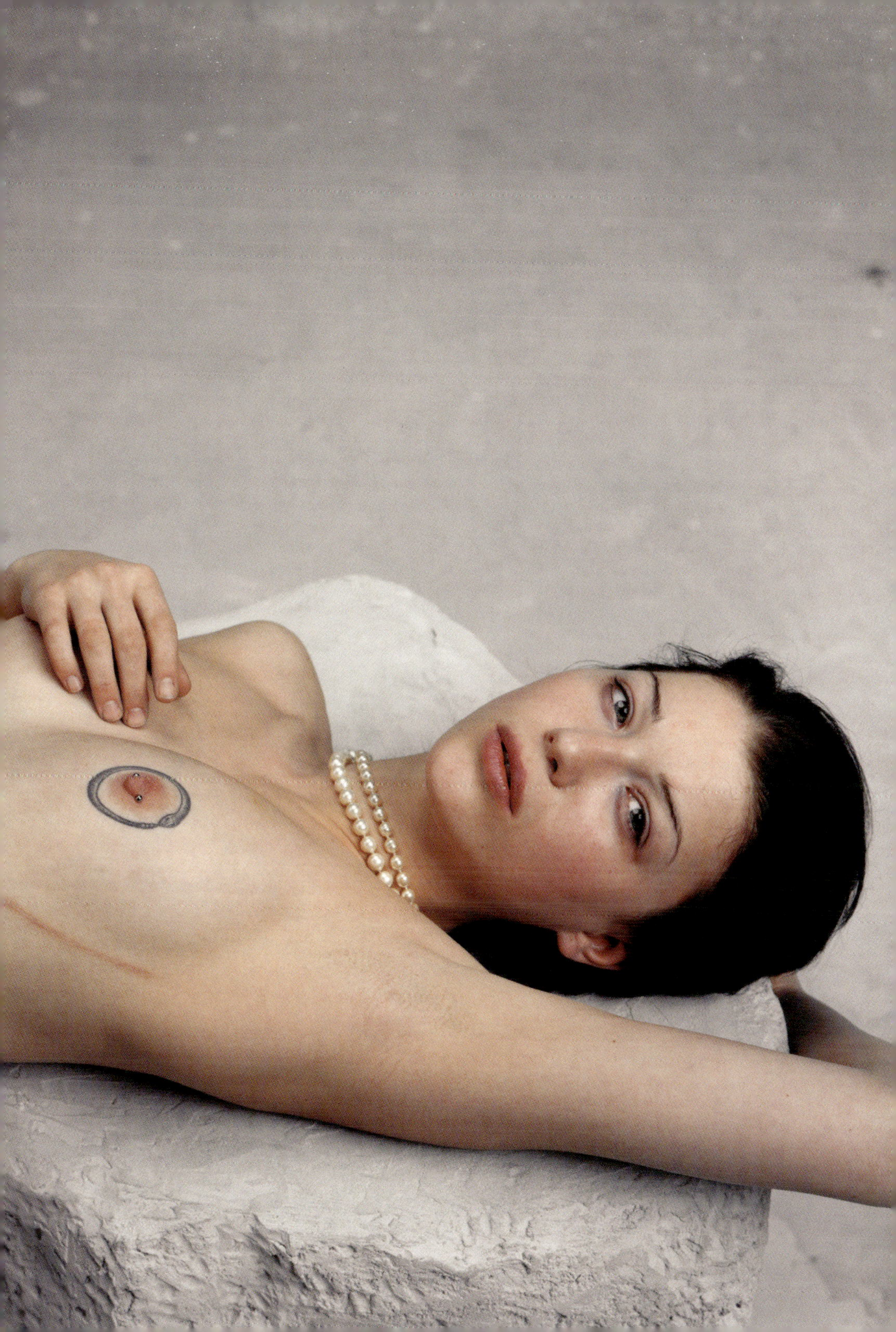

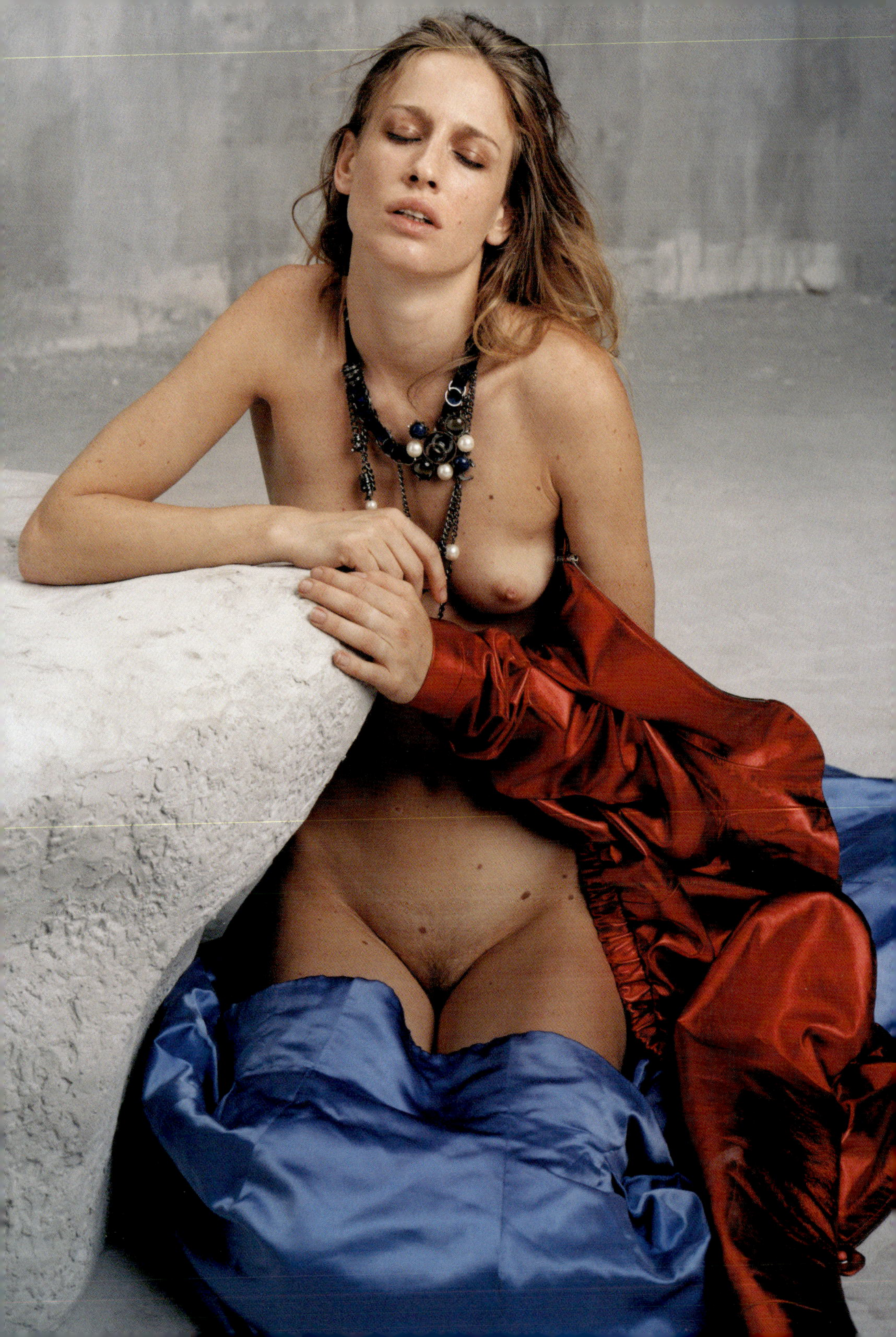

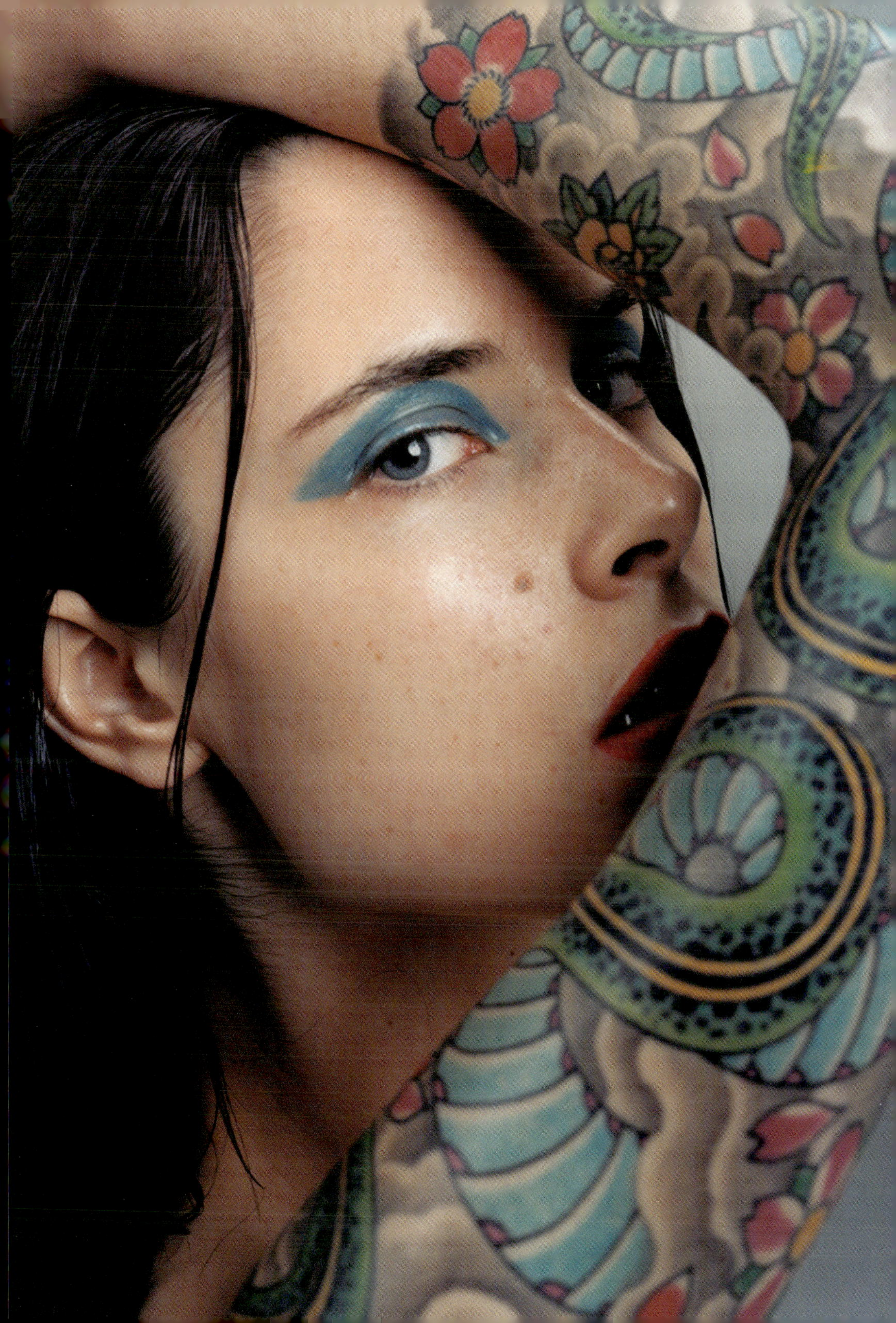

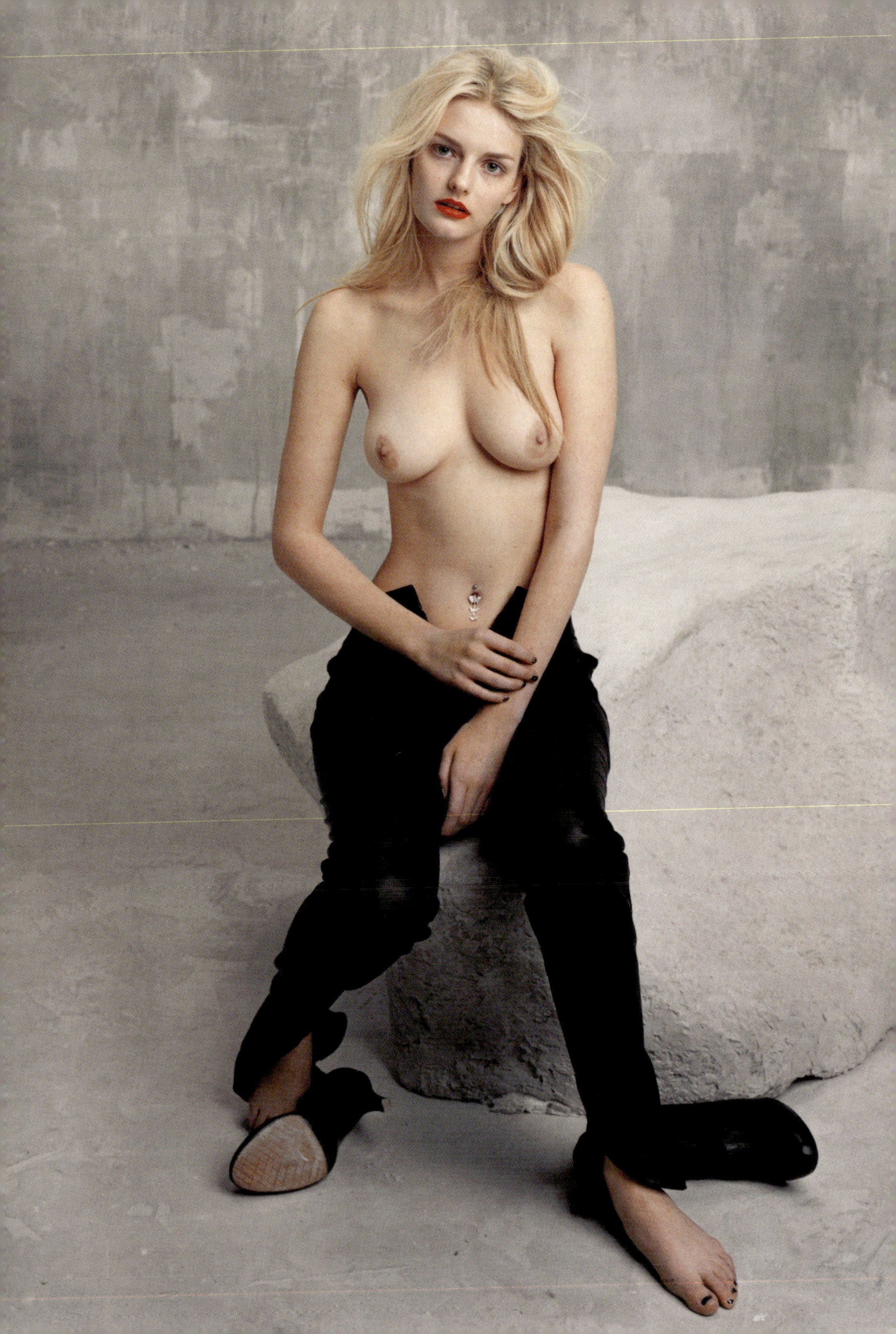

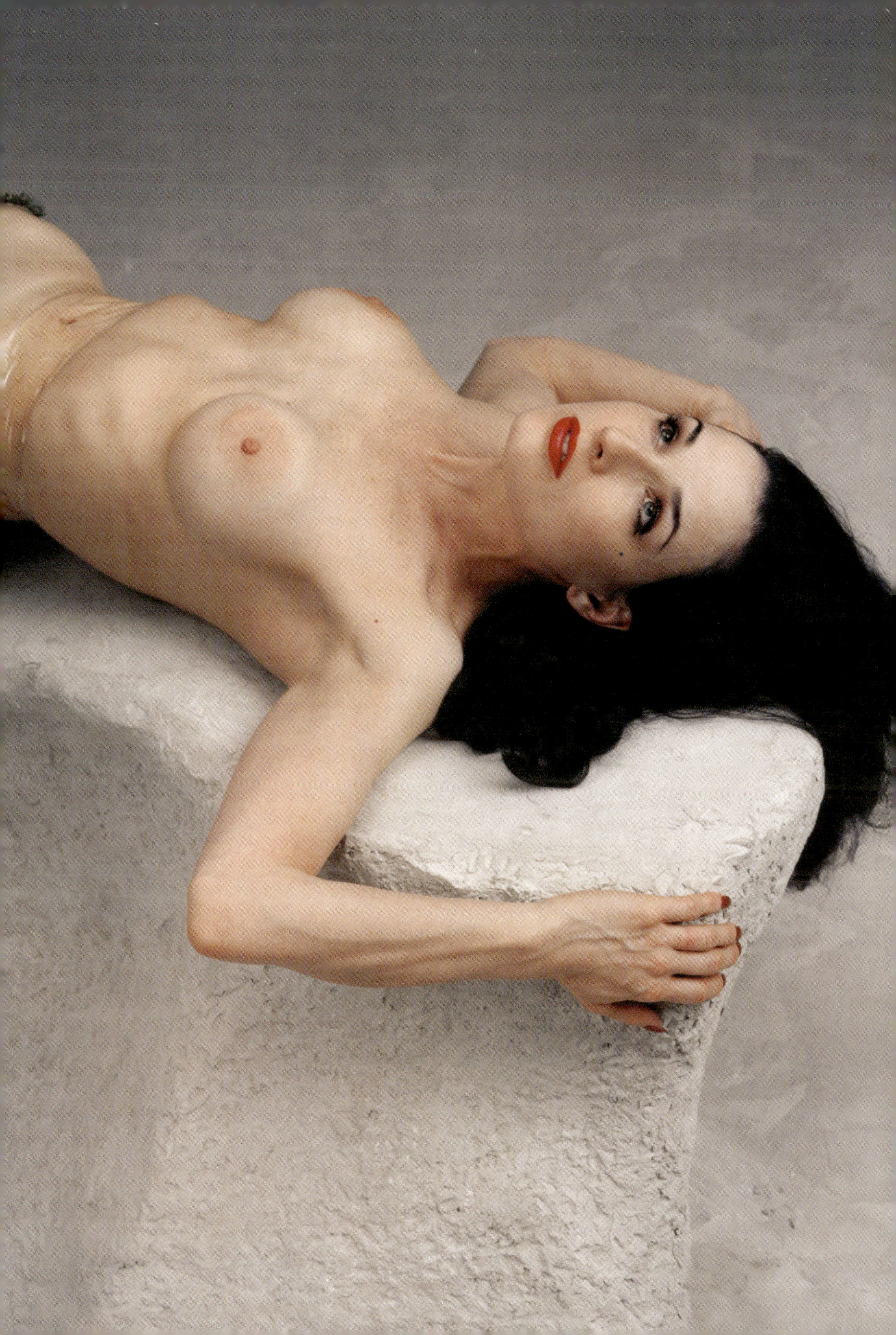

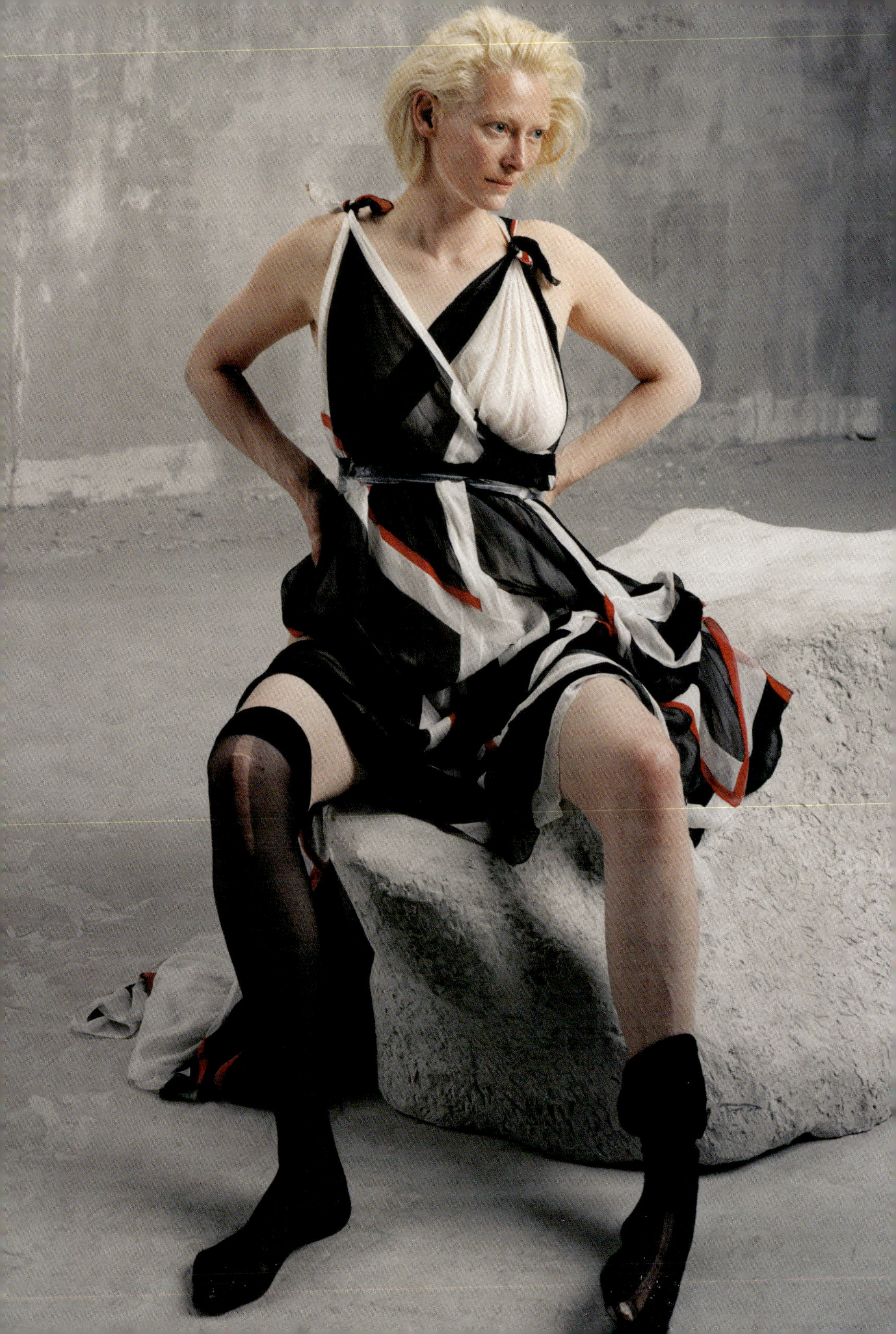

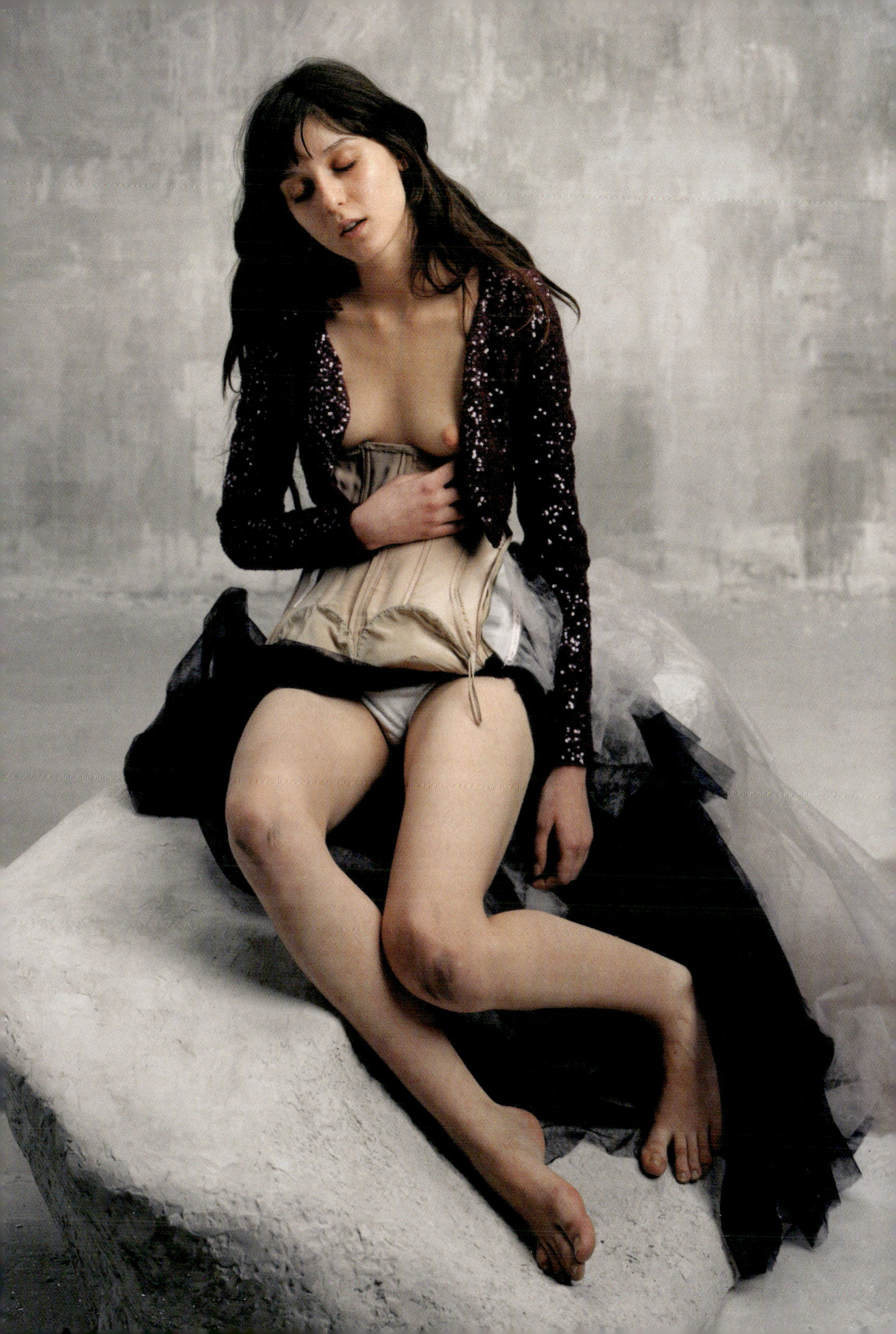

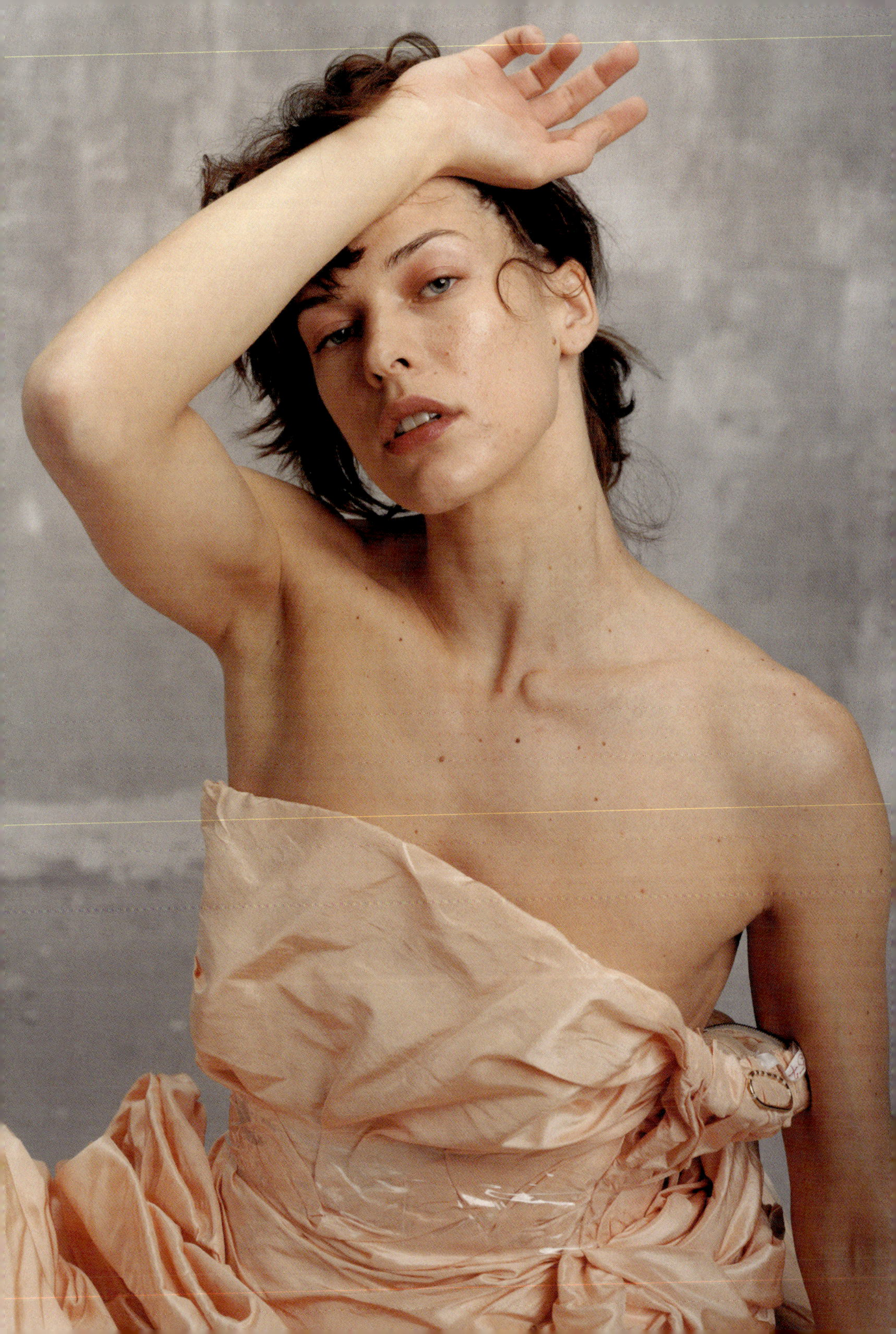

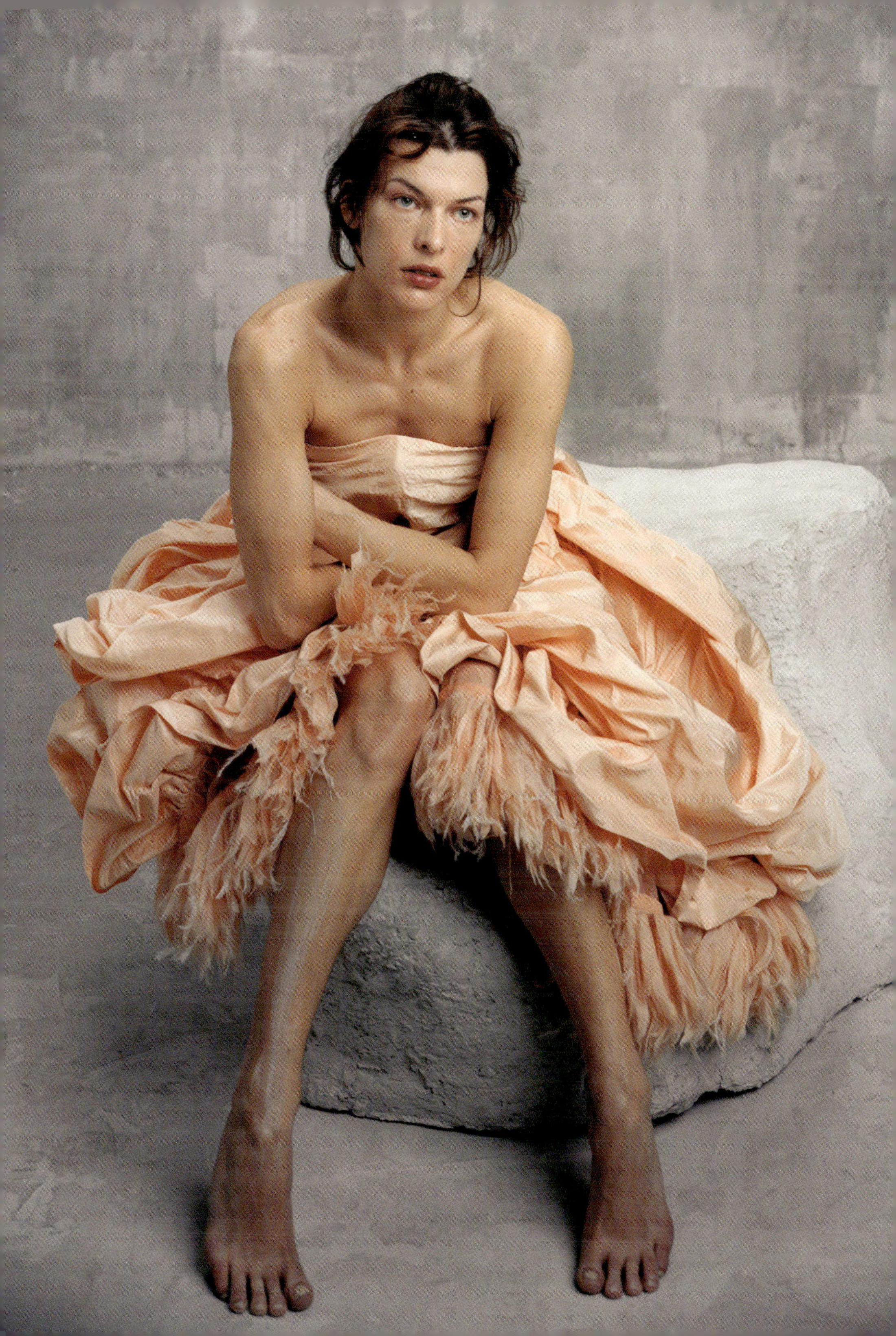

Charlotte Rampling, September 1985, Paris

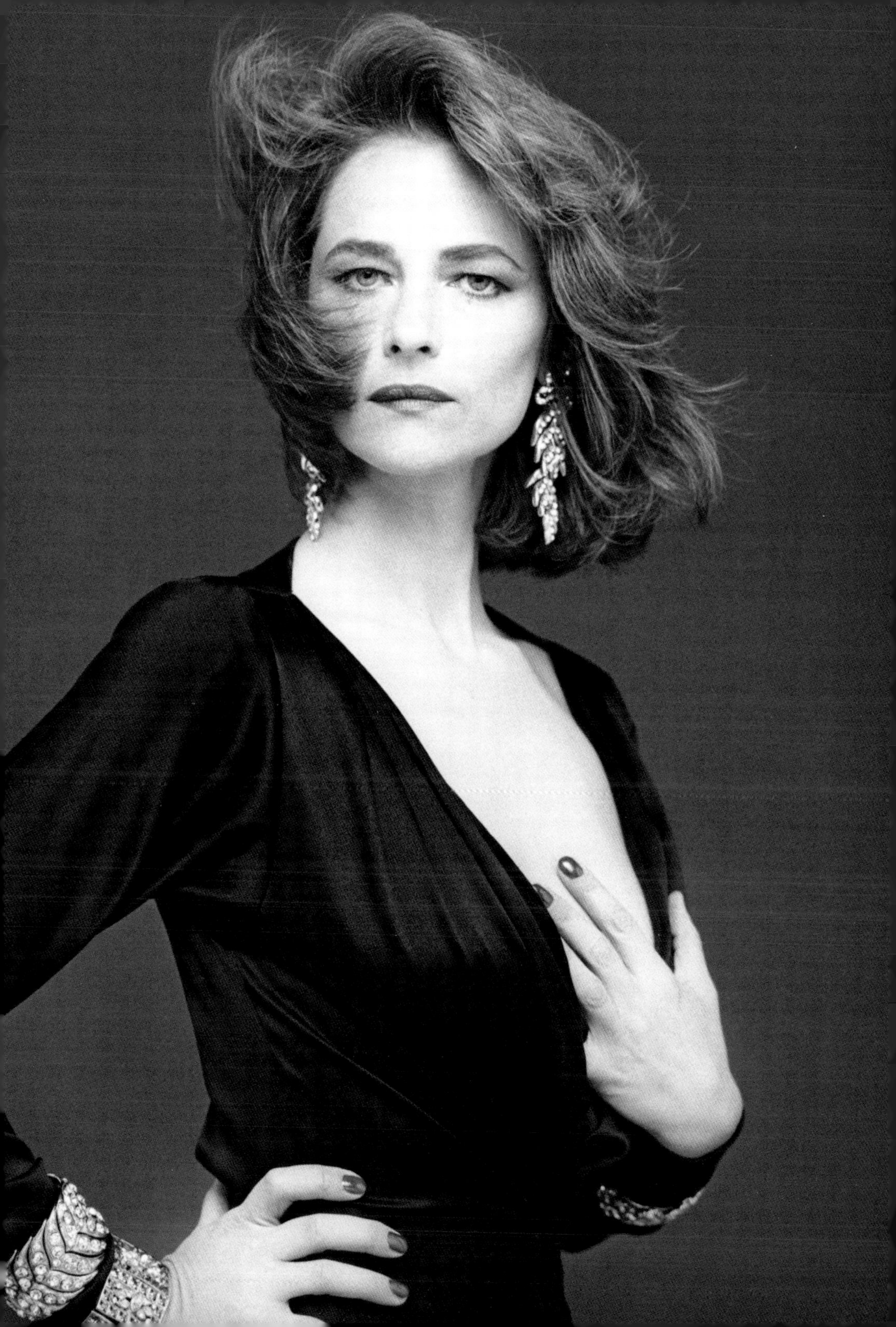

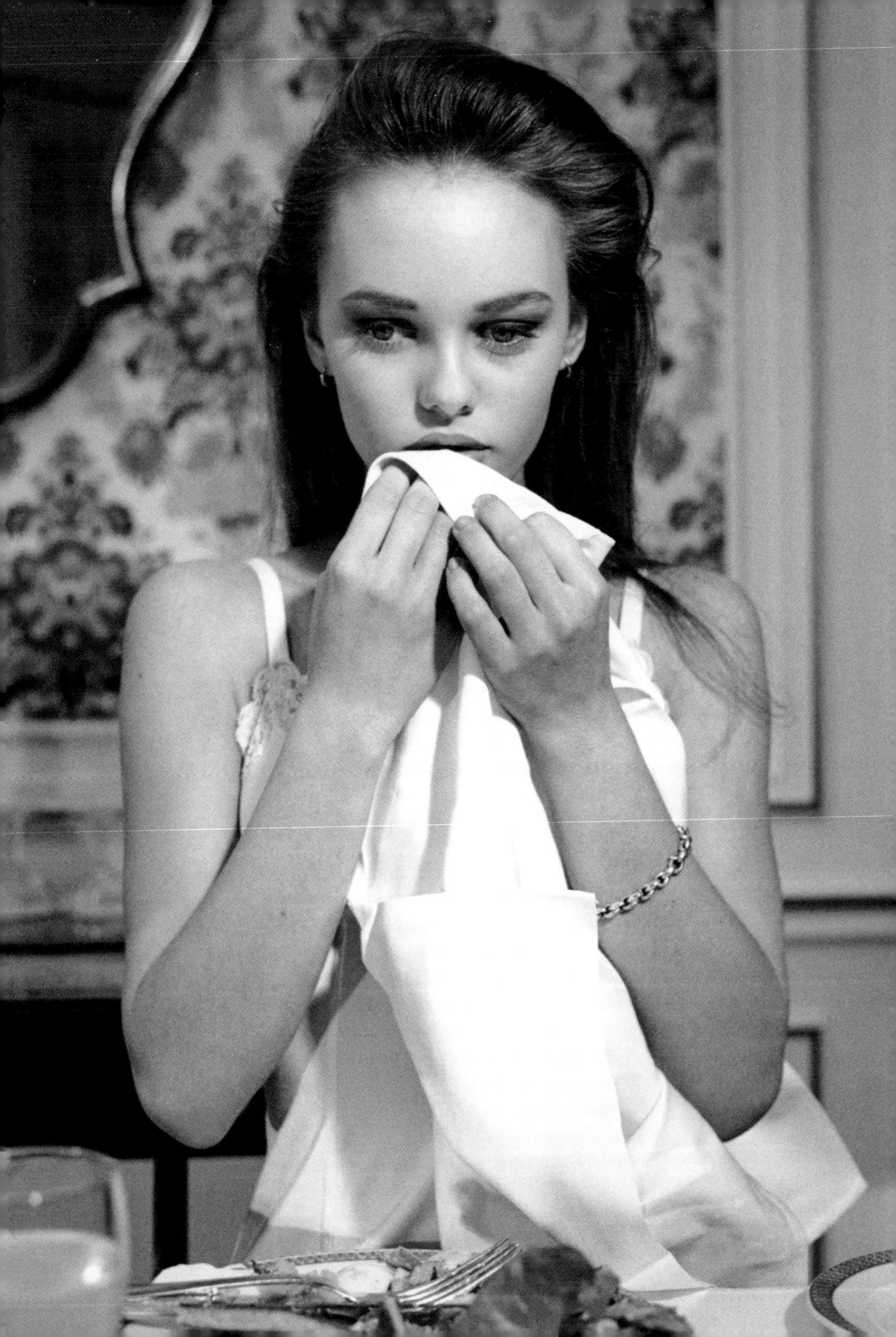

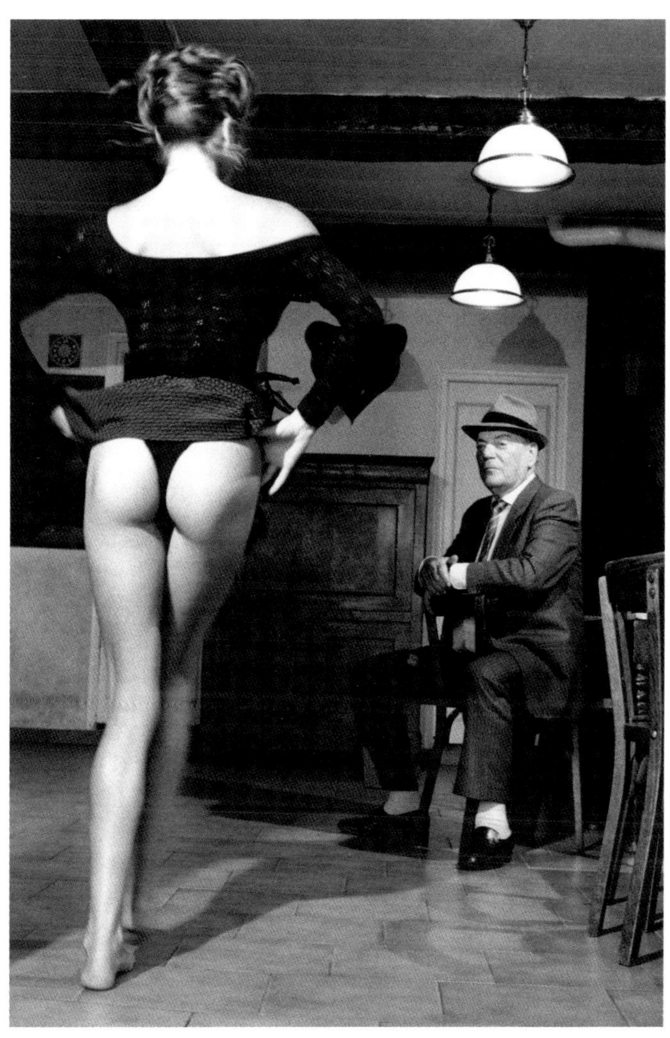

Above — *Eddie Constantine regardant Ebby*, September 1991, Saint-Tropez
Opposite page — *Vanessa Paradis à l'hôtel Normandy II, les yeux baissés*, December 1989, Deauville

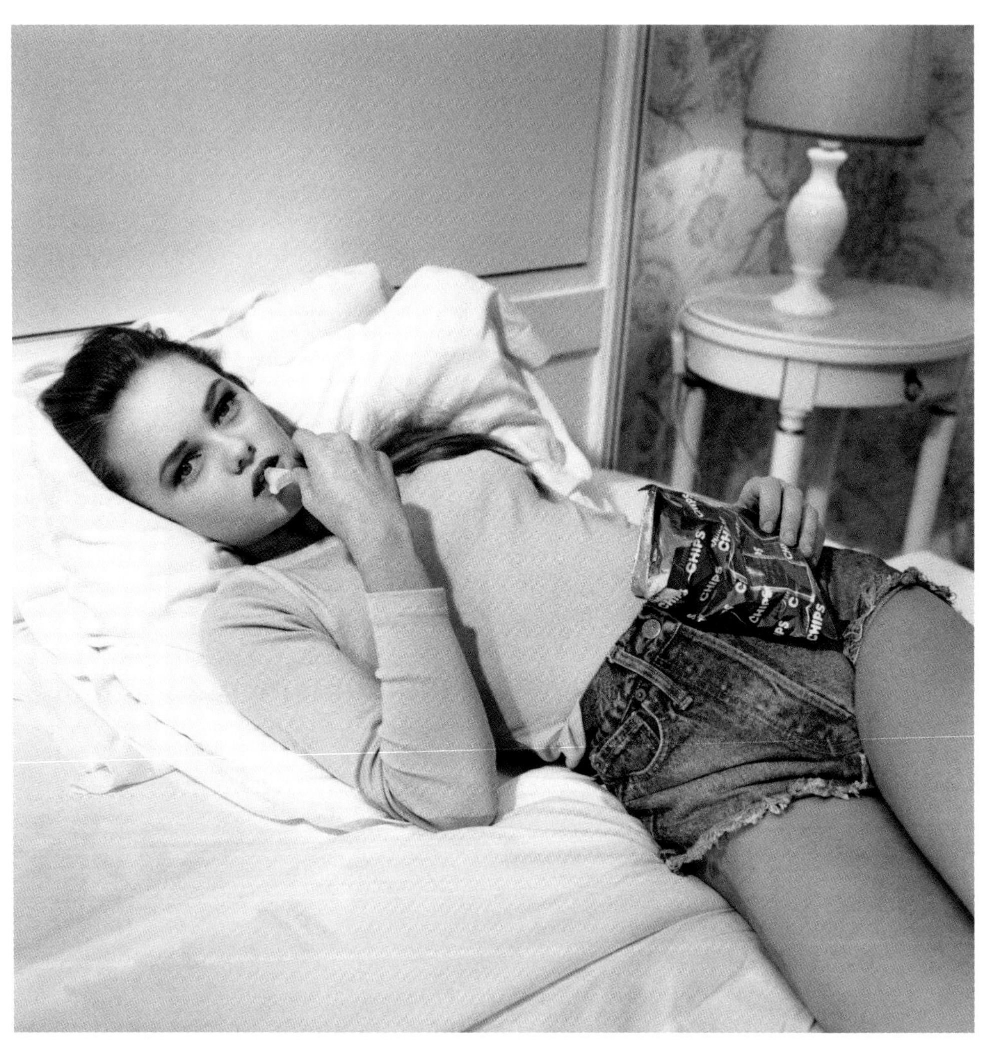

Above — *Vanessa Paradis à l'hôtel Normandy I*, December 1989, Deauville
Opposite page — *Roman Polanski*, 1981, Paris

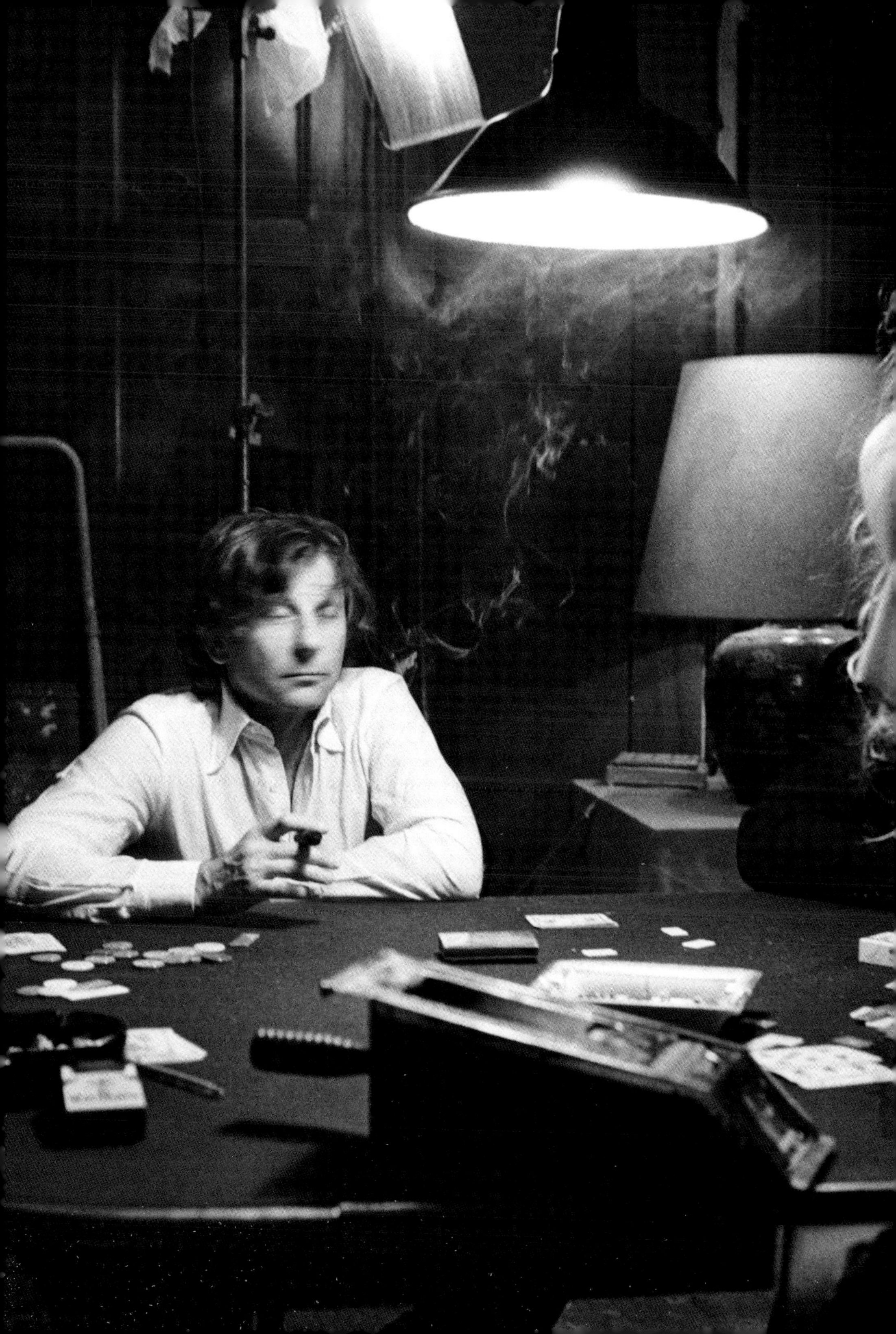

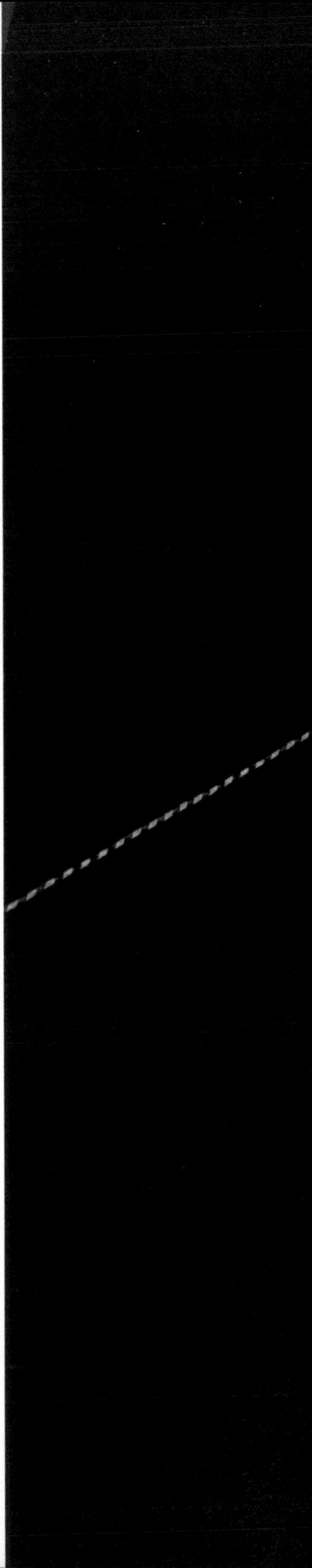

Paloma Picasso rouge et noire avec les pinceaux de son père I,
March 1996, Paris

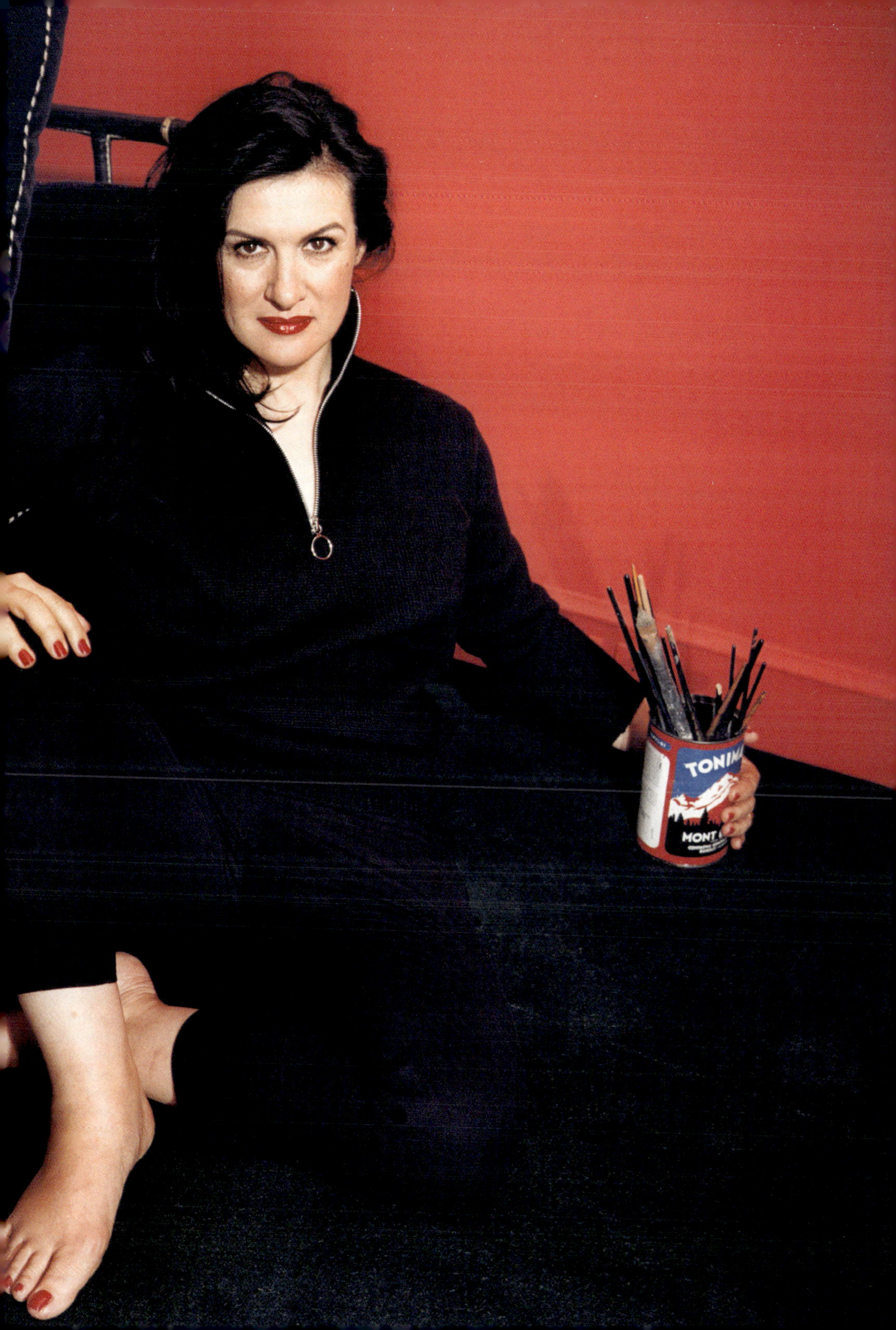

TONIM
MONT

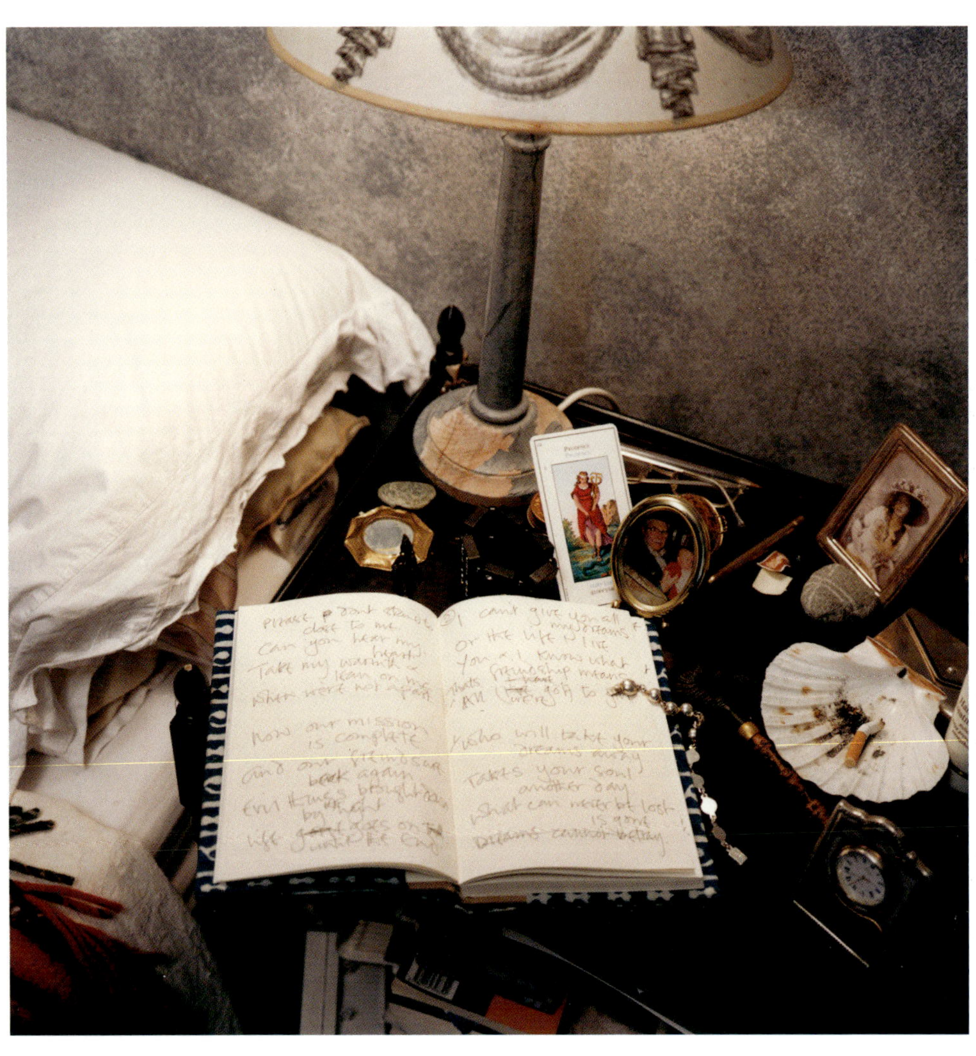

Above — *Marianne Faithfull's nightstand*, April 1995, Dublin
Opposite page — *Marianne Faithfull sitting in her bathroom*, April 1995, Dublin

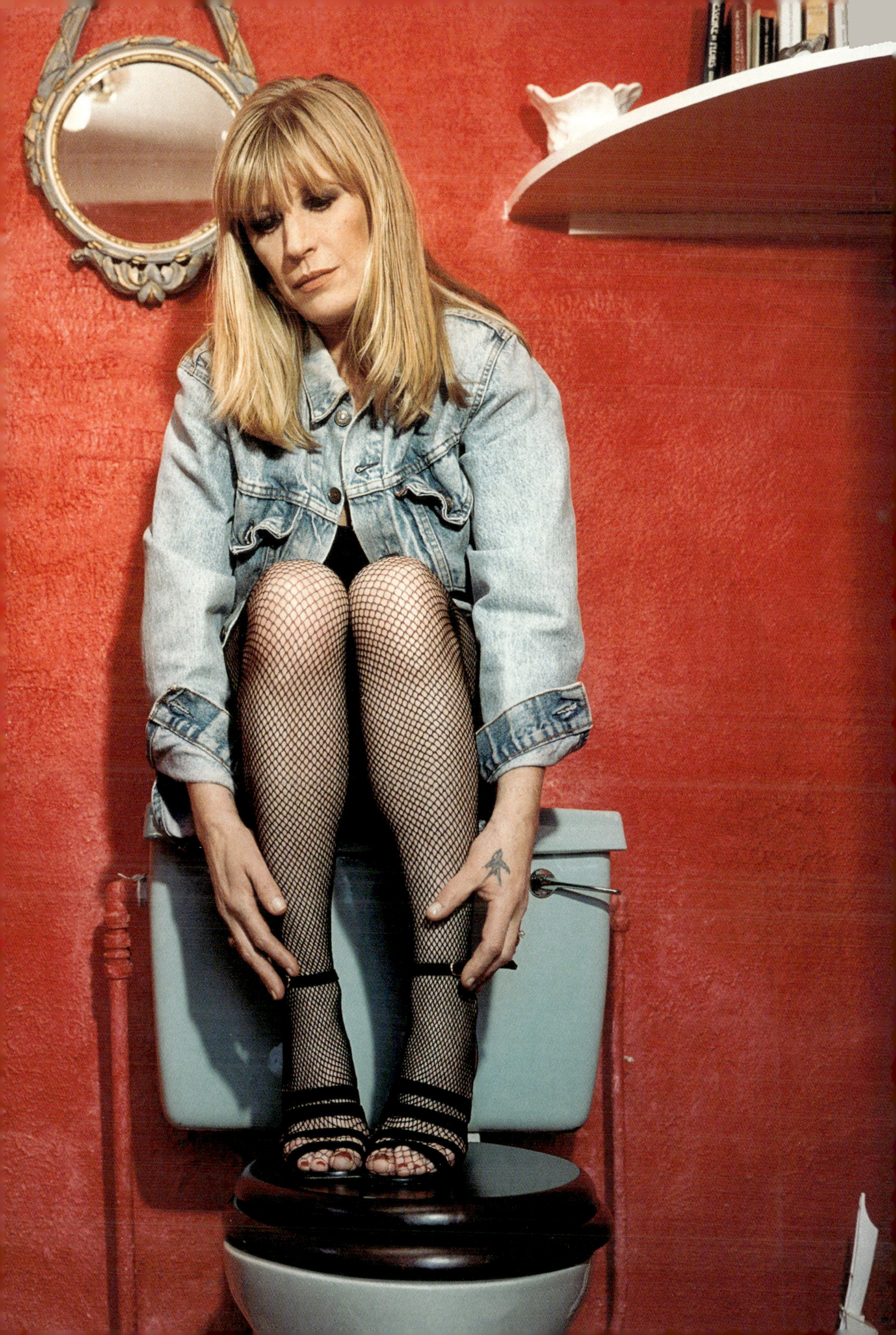

Karolína Kurková, December 2001, Paris
Page 372 — *Fashion with Karolína*, December 2001, Paris
Page 373 — *Karolína Kurková in my studio holding her foot*, December 2001, Paris
Page 374 — *Karolína de dos dans mon studio*, December 2001, Paris
Page 375 — *Karolína Kurková pensive derrière la verrière de mon bureau*, December 2001, Paris
Pages 376/377 — *Loulou de la Falaise (unpublished picture)*, 1983, Paris

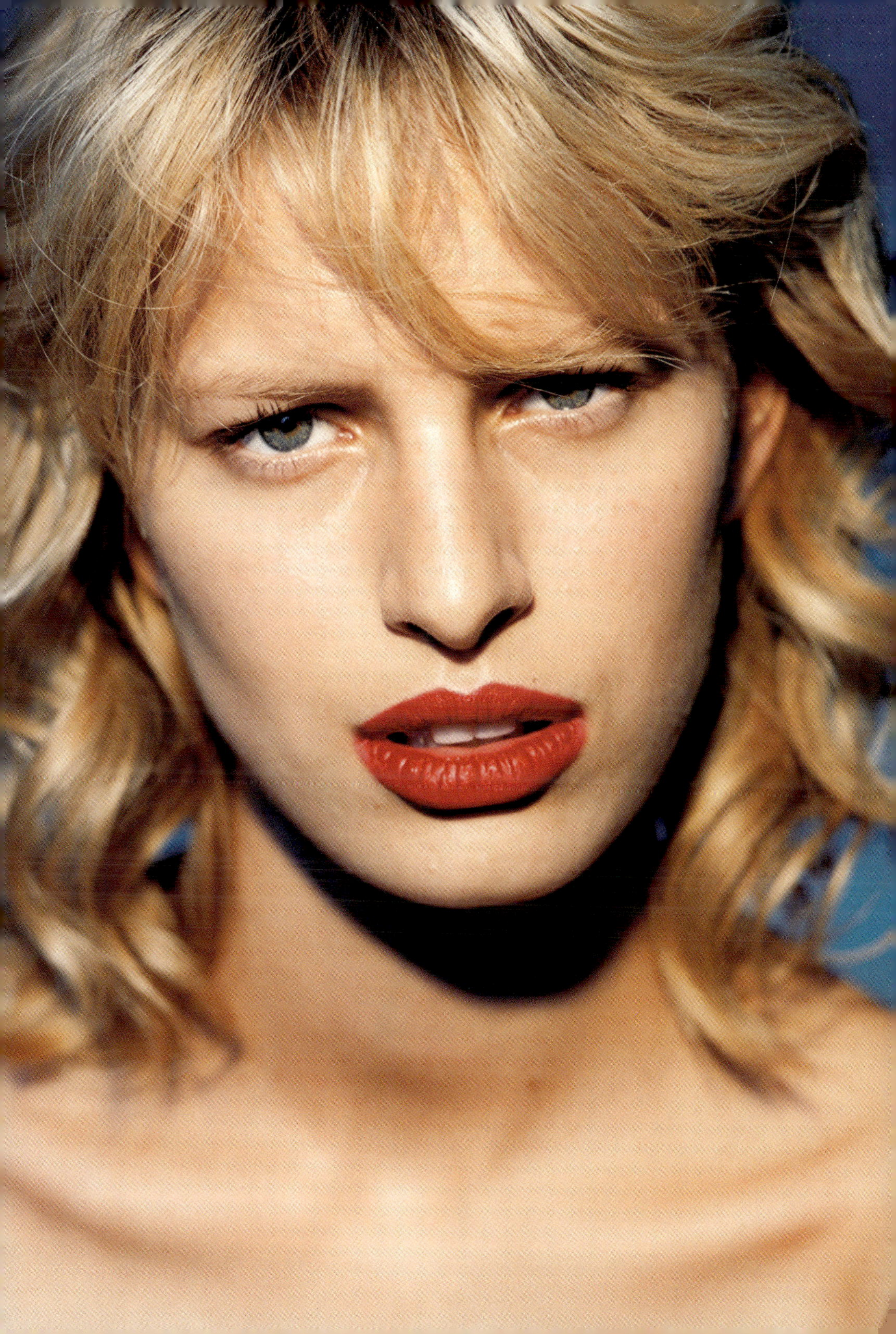

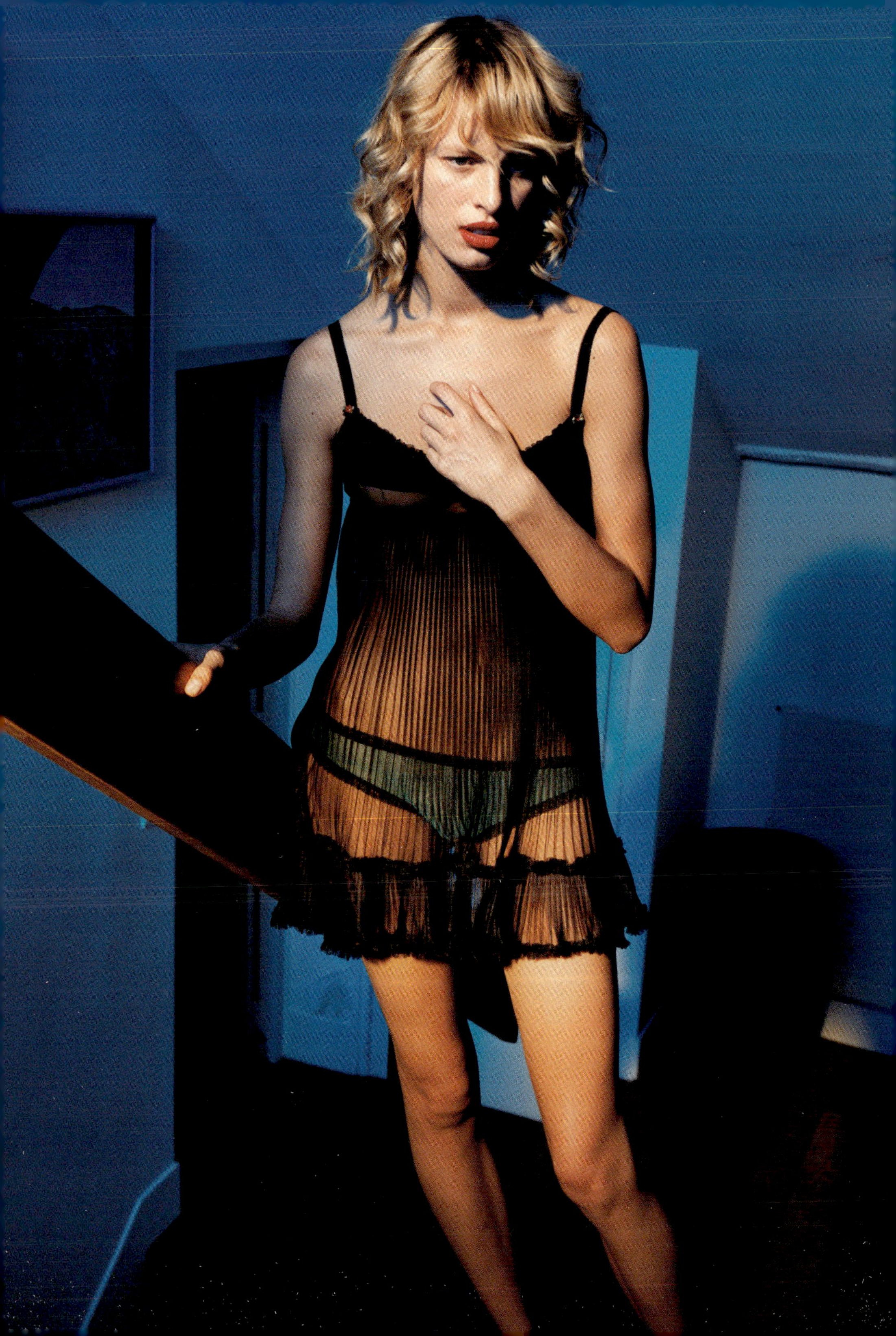

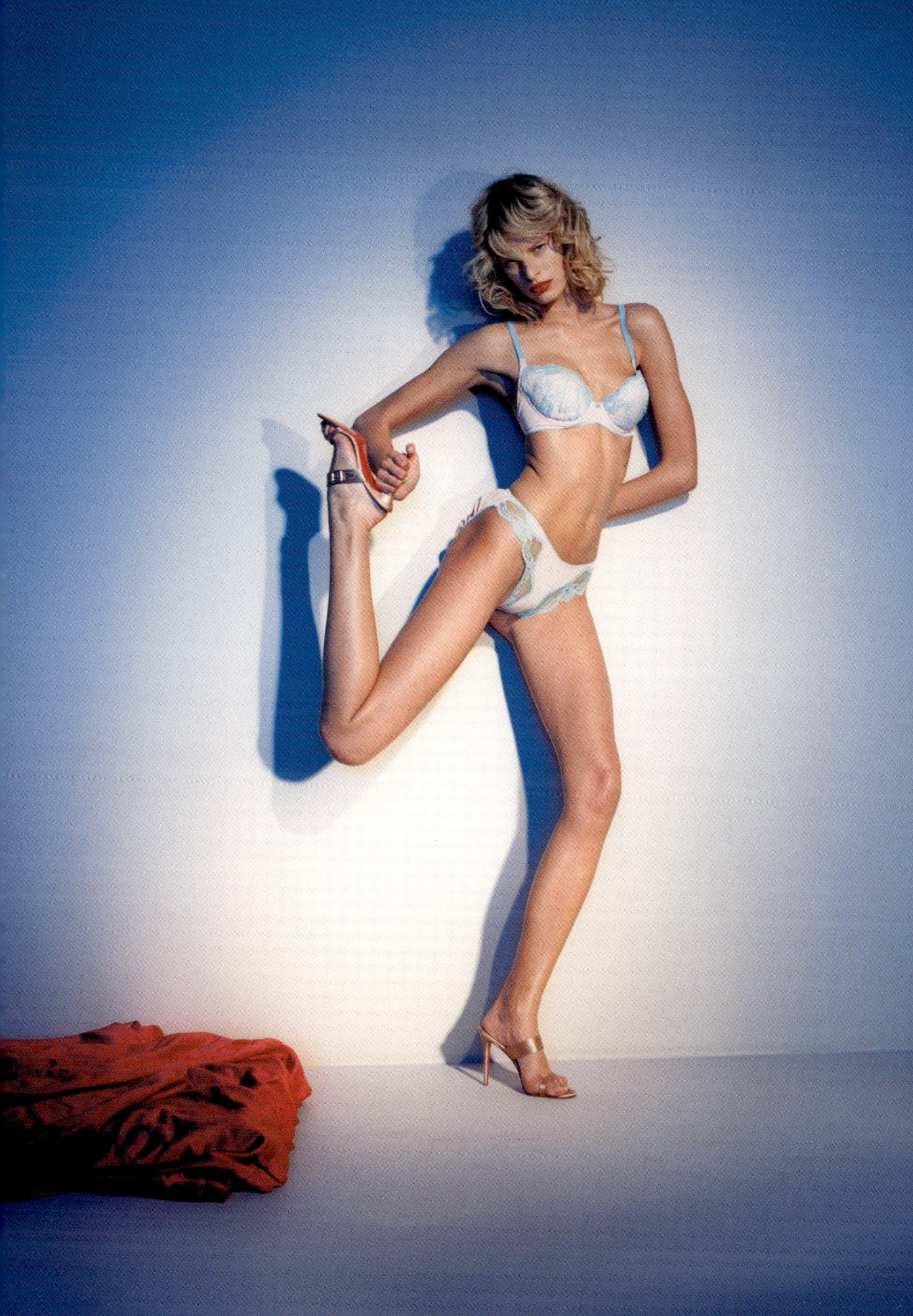

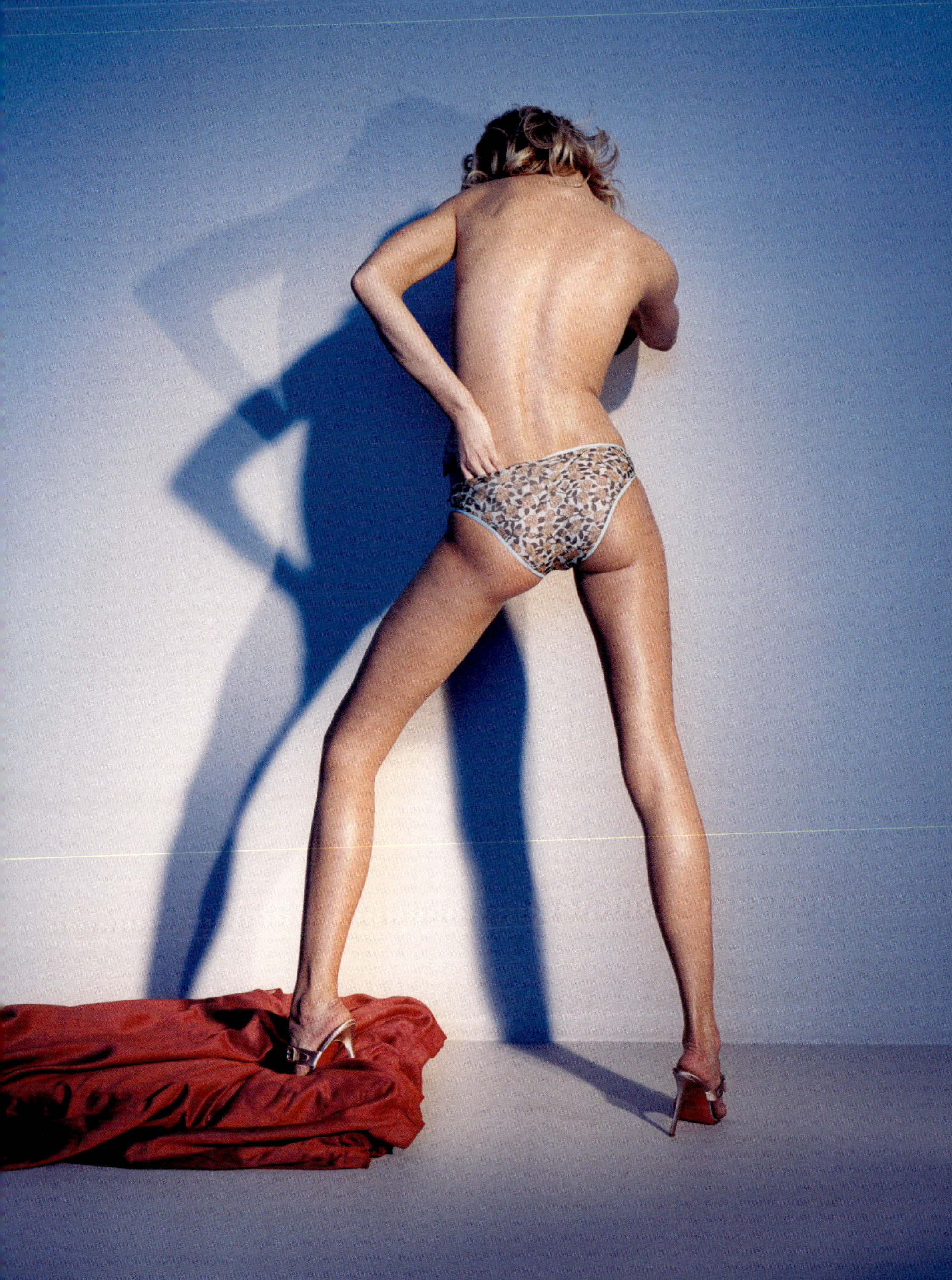

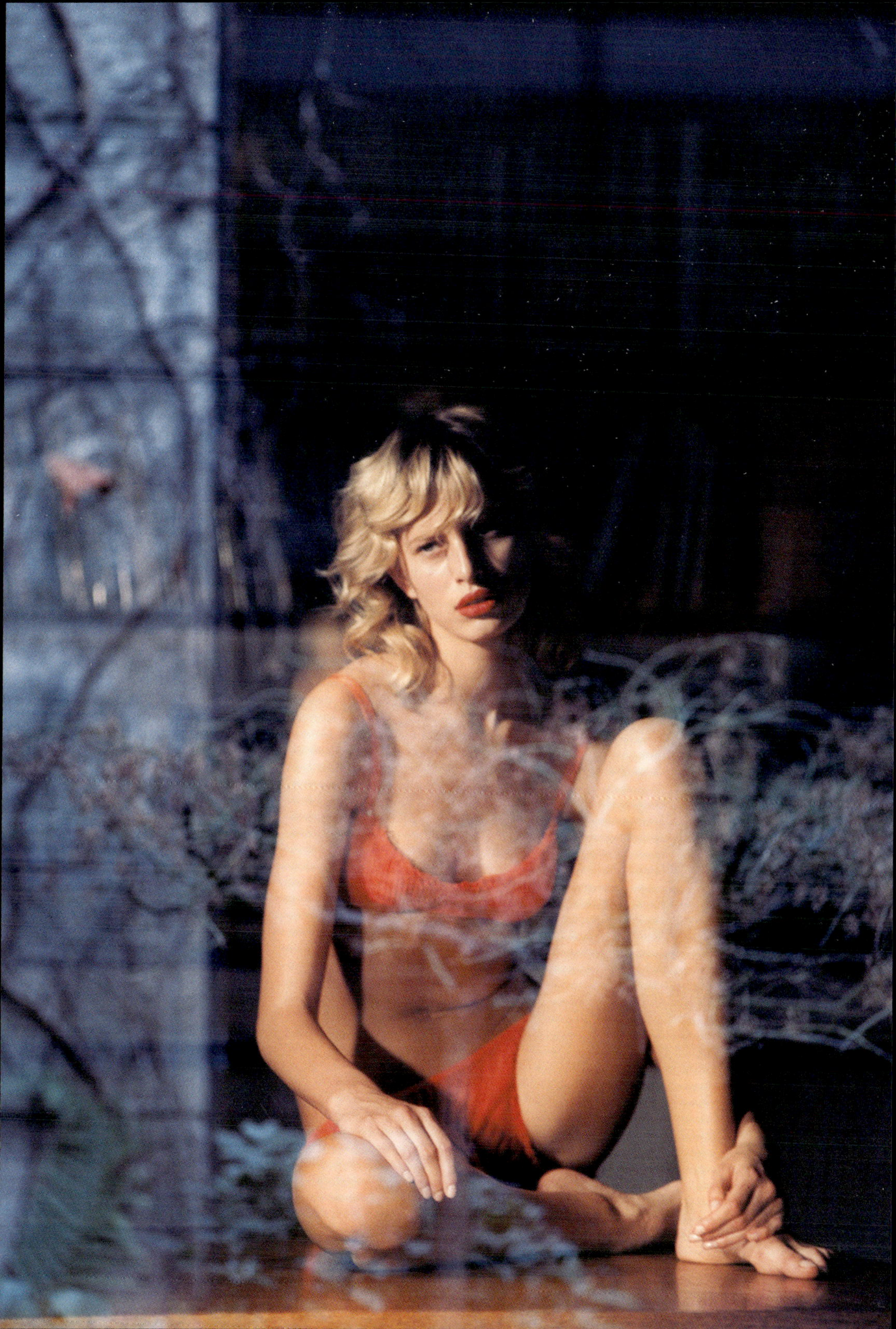

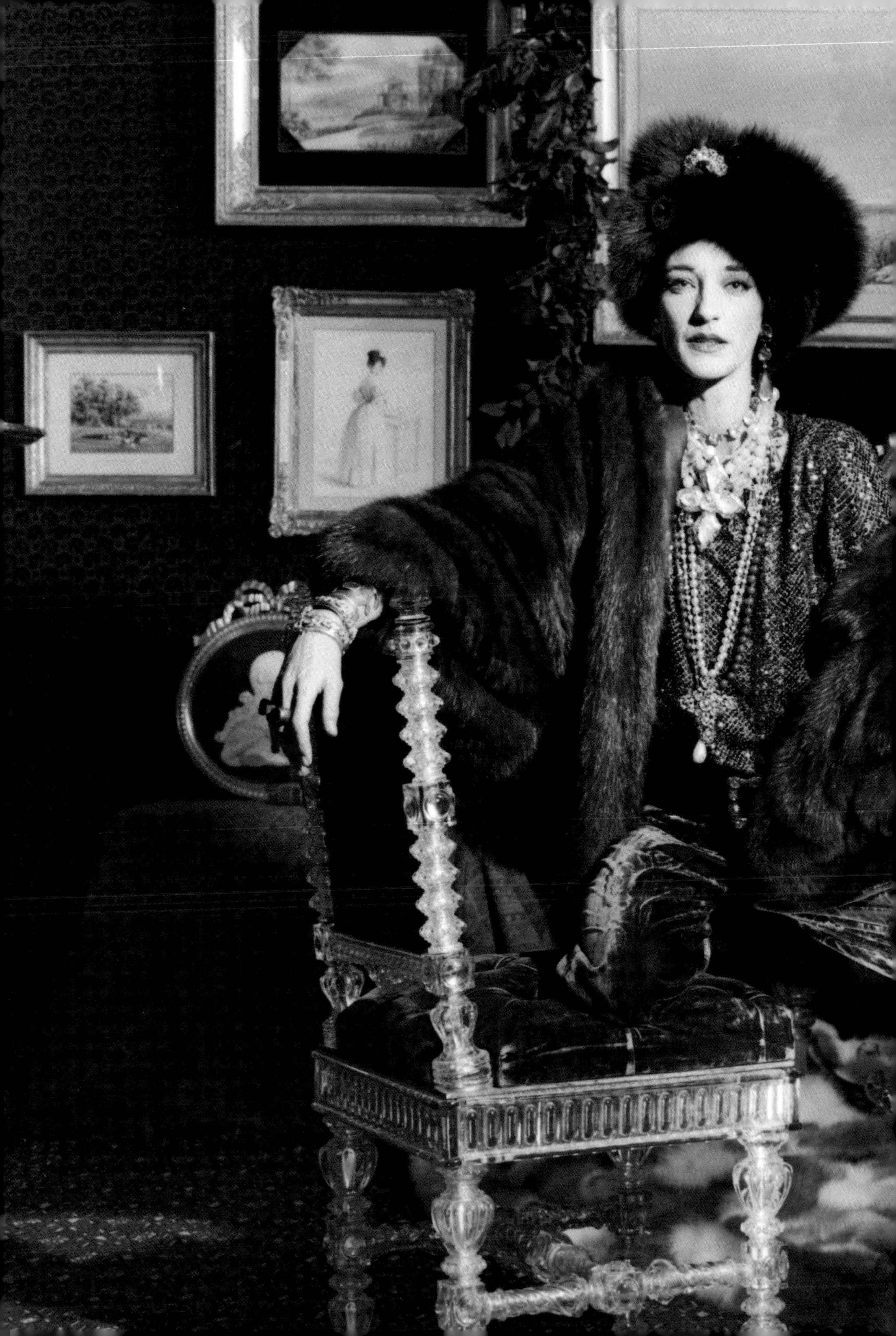

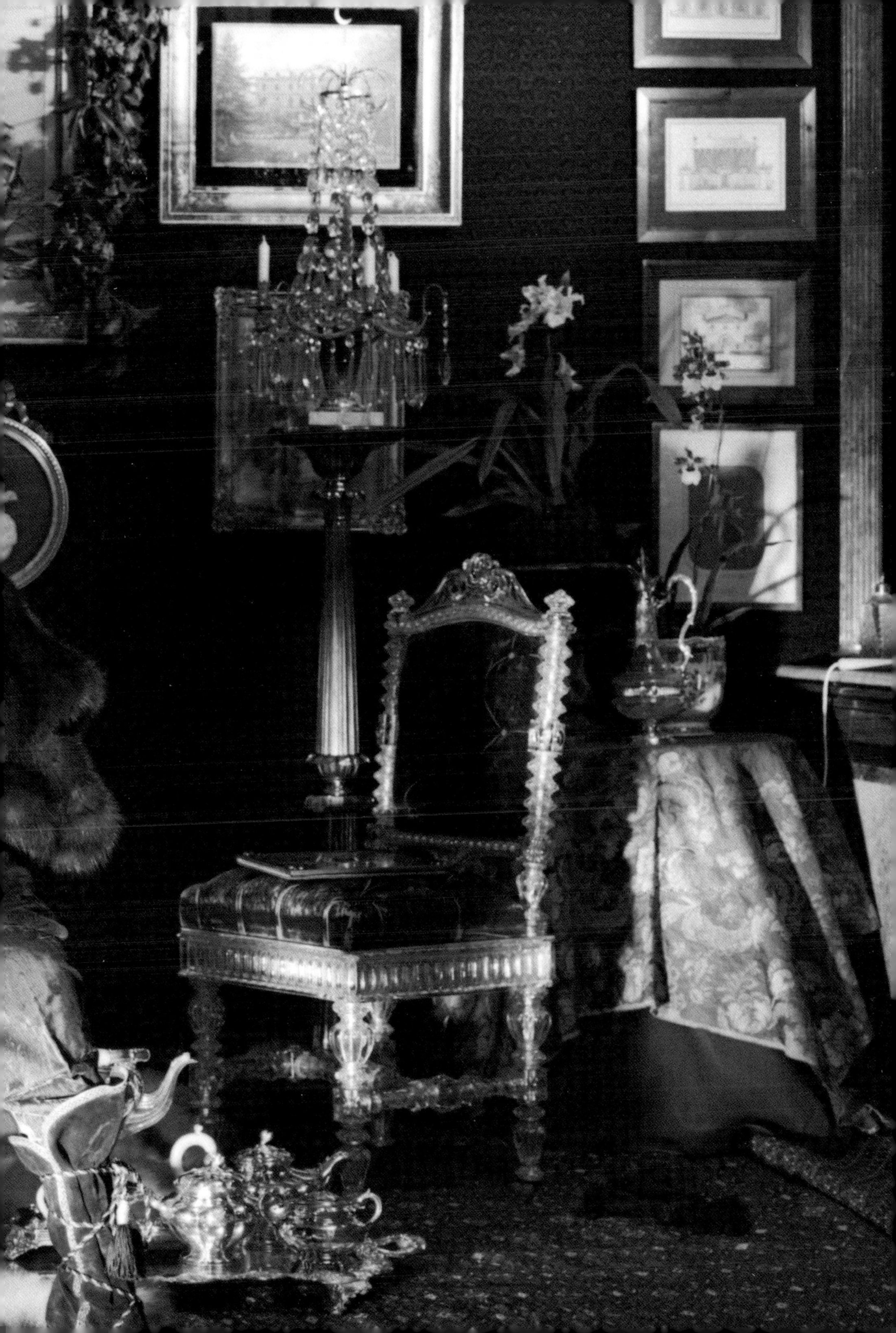

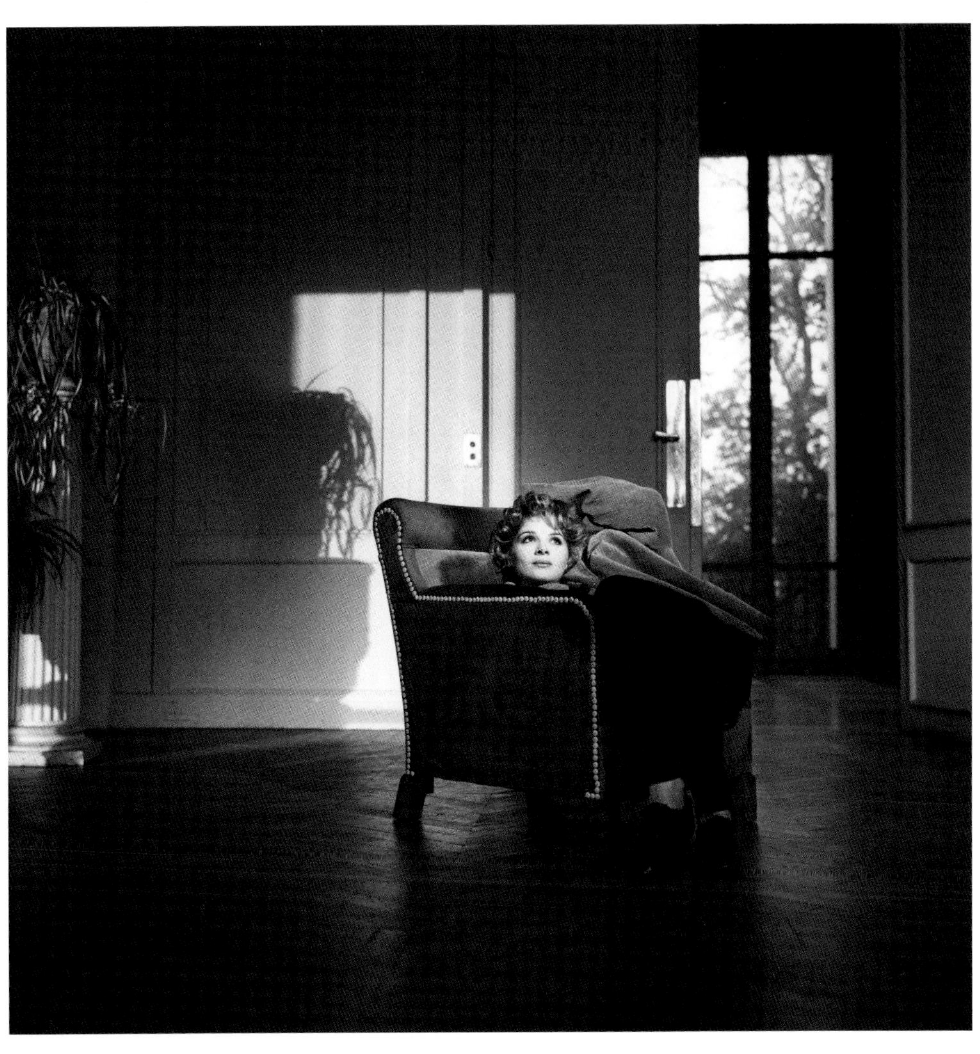

 Juliette Binoche au bord des larmes, October 1987, Paris

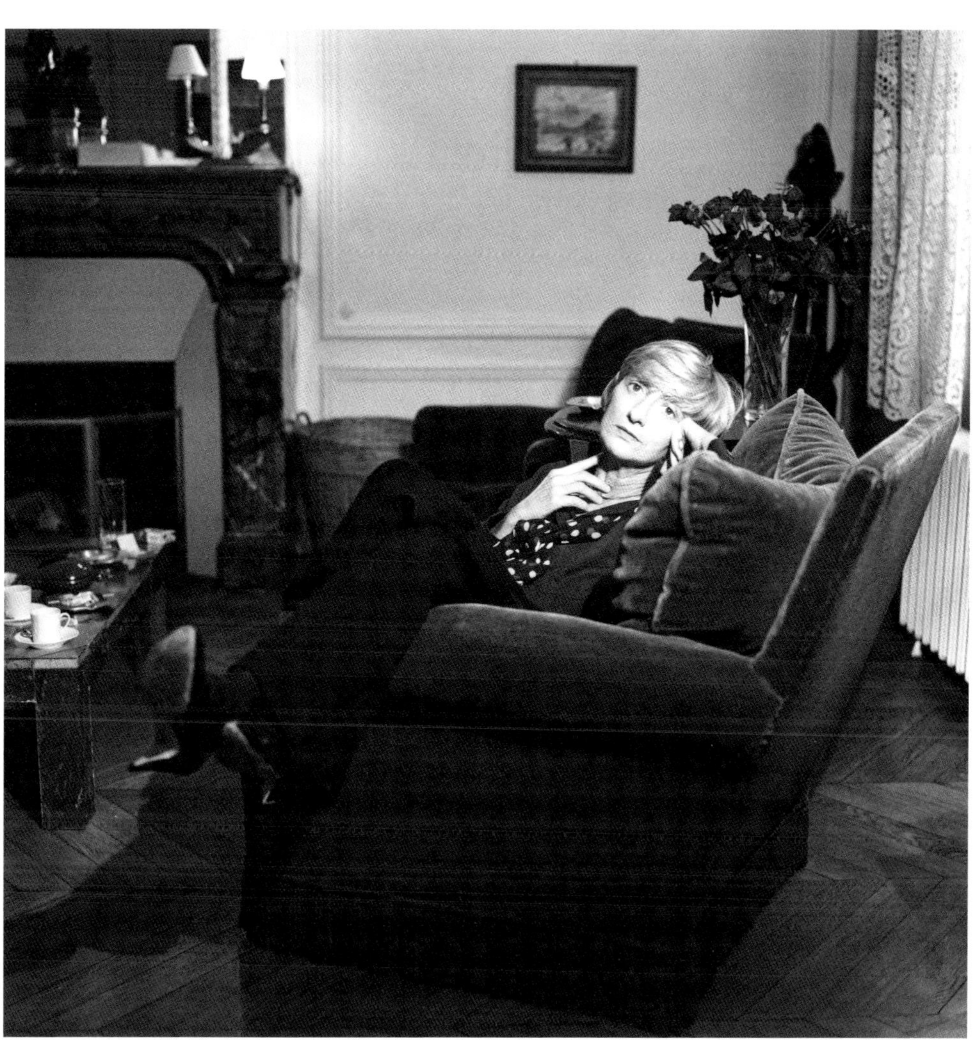

Françoise Sagan, October 1985, Paris

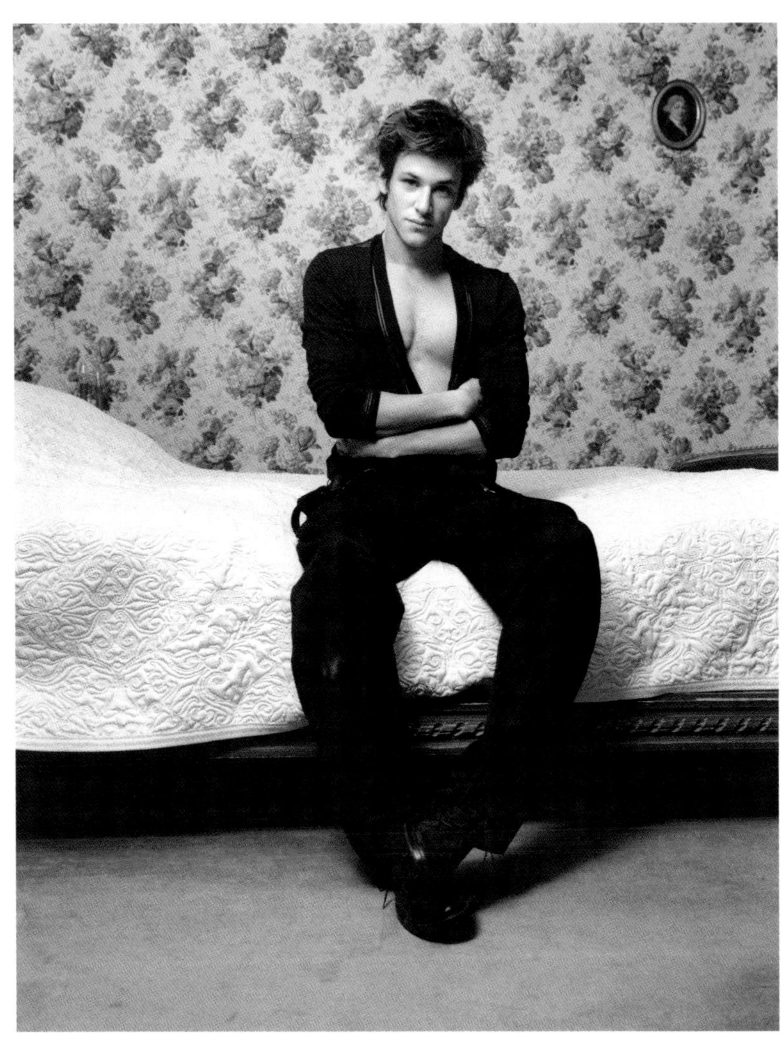

Above — *Gaspard Ulliel*, December 2006, Paris
Opposite page — *Loulou de la Falaise*, June 1986, Paris
Page 382 — *Nastassja Kinski dans un fauteuil*, July 1991, Paris
Page 383 — *Jean-Marc Mormeck, champion du monde de boxe pour SOS Racisme*, March 2015, Paris

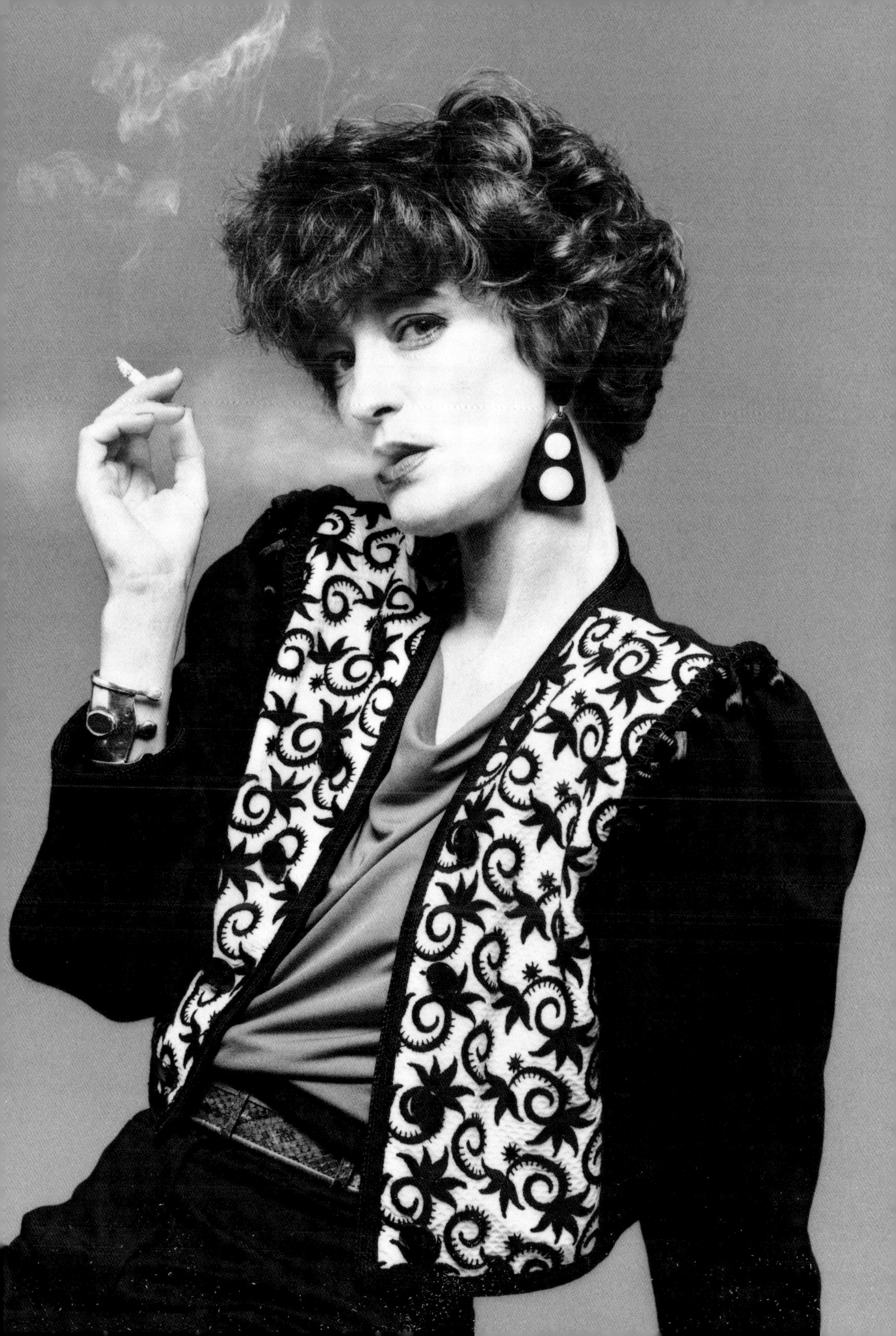

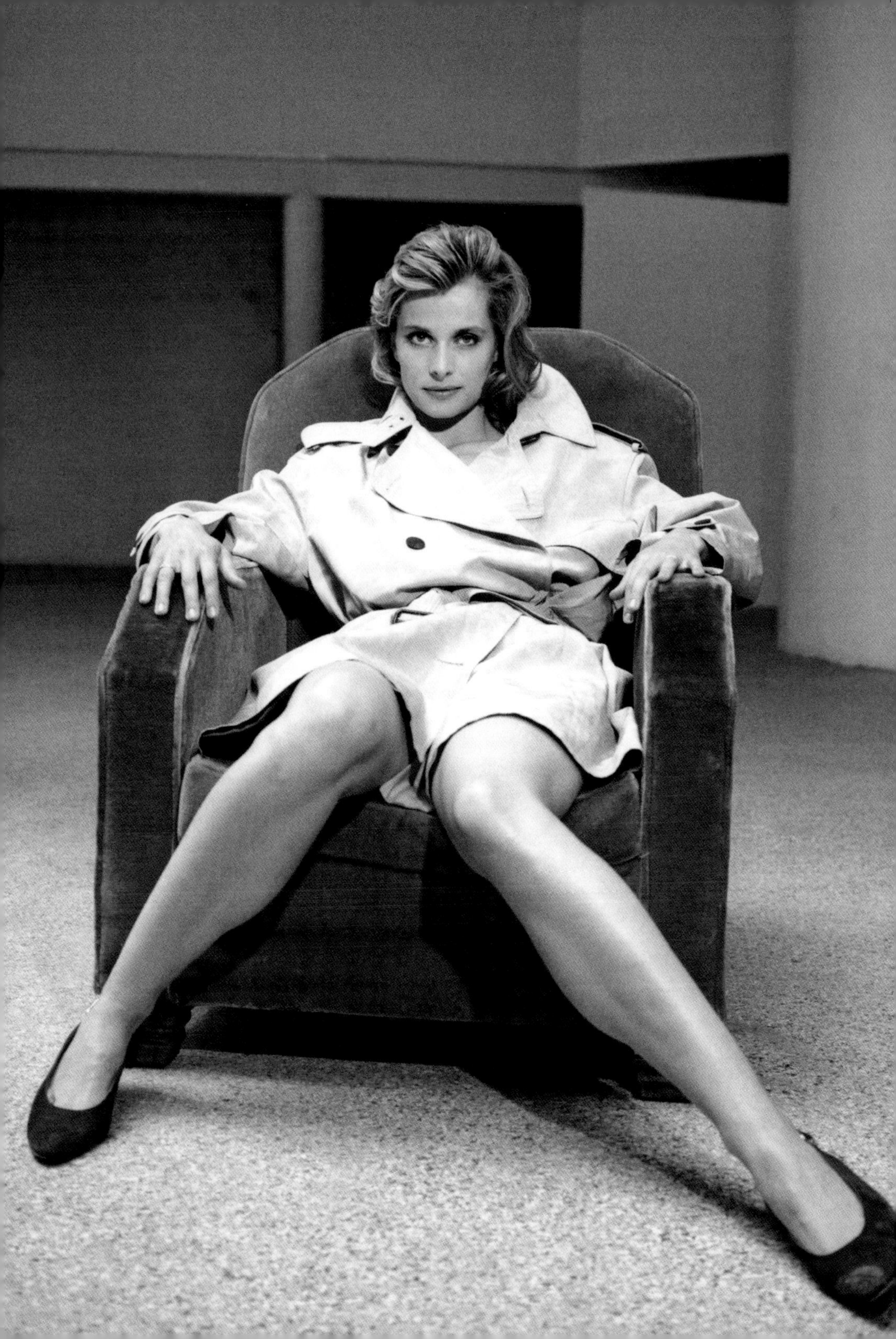

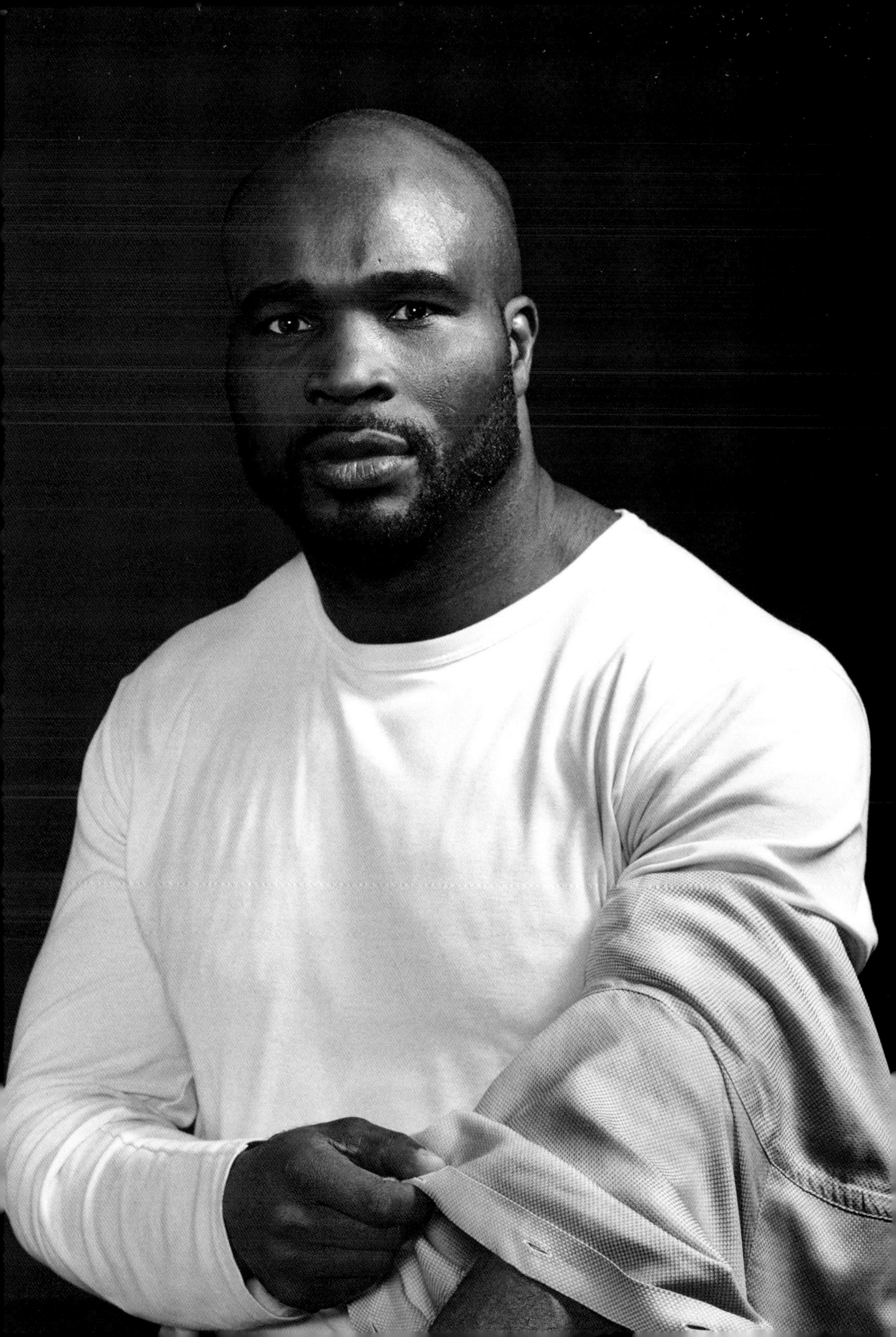

THE BOOK OF OLGA
2006, Paris

**The paradoxical art of Bettina Rheims brings us close to the most
exultant excesses, those of colour, exhibitionism and voyeurism.
By doing so it transports us to a place where eroticism is at one
with humour and the most profound humanity. It is particularly
well-served here.**

L'art paradoxal de Bettina Rheims, qui nous laisse approcher des
excès les plus jubilatoires, ceux de la couleur, ceux de l'exhibition-
nisme et du voyeurisme, pour mieux nous faire basculer ailleurs,
là où l'érotisme rejoint l'humour et la profonde humanité, est ici
particulièrement bien servi.

Hier wird das Paradoxe an der Kunst von Bettina Rheims deutlich.
Sie lässt uns teilhaben an all diesen Ausschweifungen, diesem Fest der
Farben, dem Exhibitionismus und dem Voyeurismus, um uns letztend-
lich nur umso entschiedener in ein Universum zu befördern, in dem
sich Erotik, Humor und tiefe Menschlichkeit miteinander verbinden.

Catherine Millet, in *The Book of Olga*, 2008

Olga, Chapter III, number four, November 2007, Paris
Page 386 — *Olga, Chapter II, number one,* January 2007, Paris
Page 387 — *Olga, Chapter II, number five,* January 2007, Paris
Pages 388/389 — *Olga, Chapter I, number two,* September 2006, Deauville
Page 390 — *Olga, Chapter III, number five,* November 2007, Paris
Page 391 — *Olga, Chapter II, number six,* January 2007, Paris

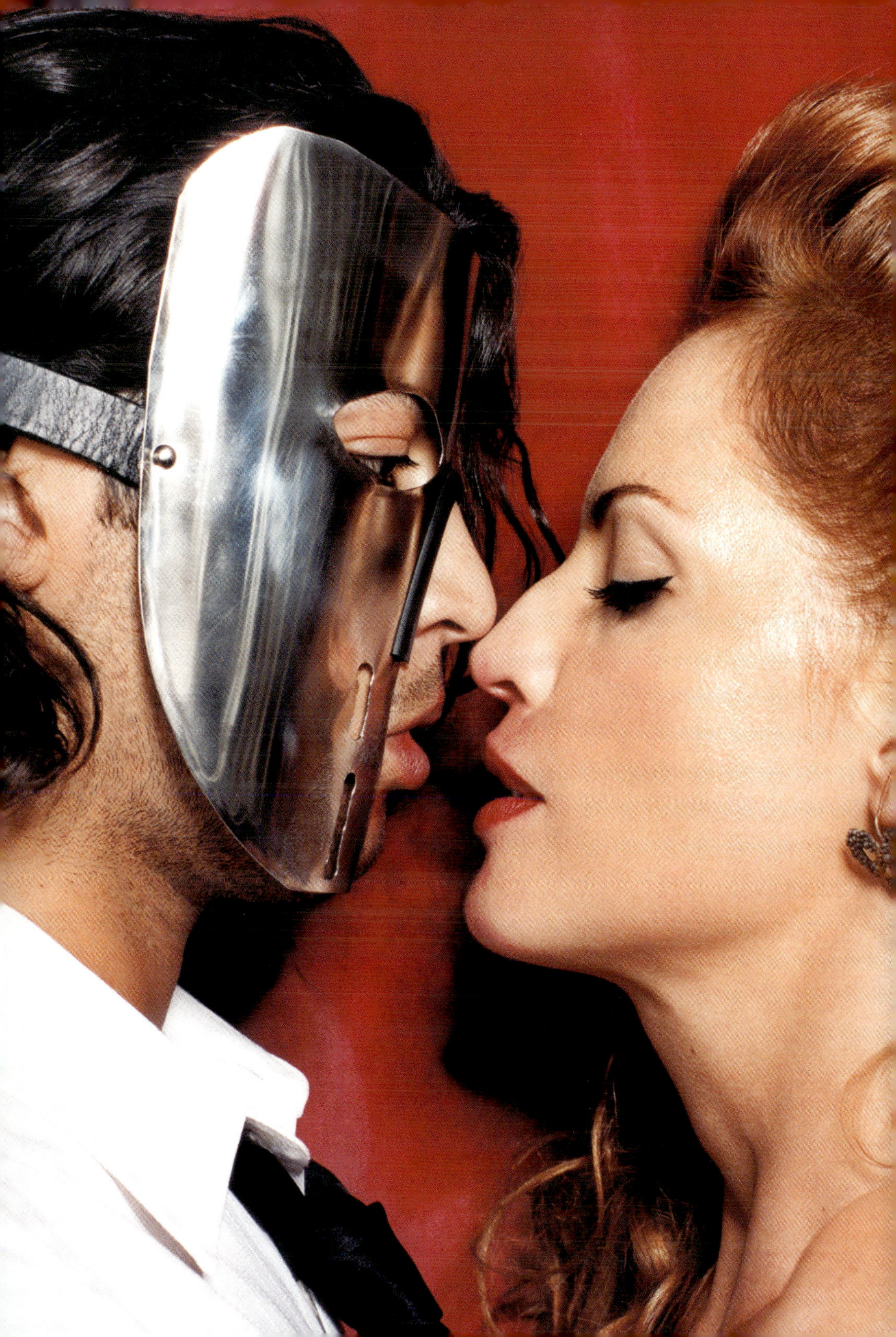

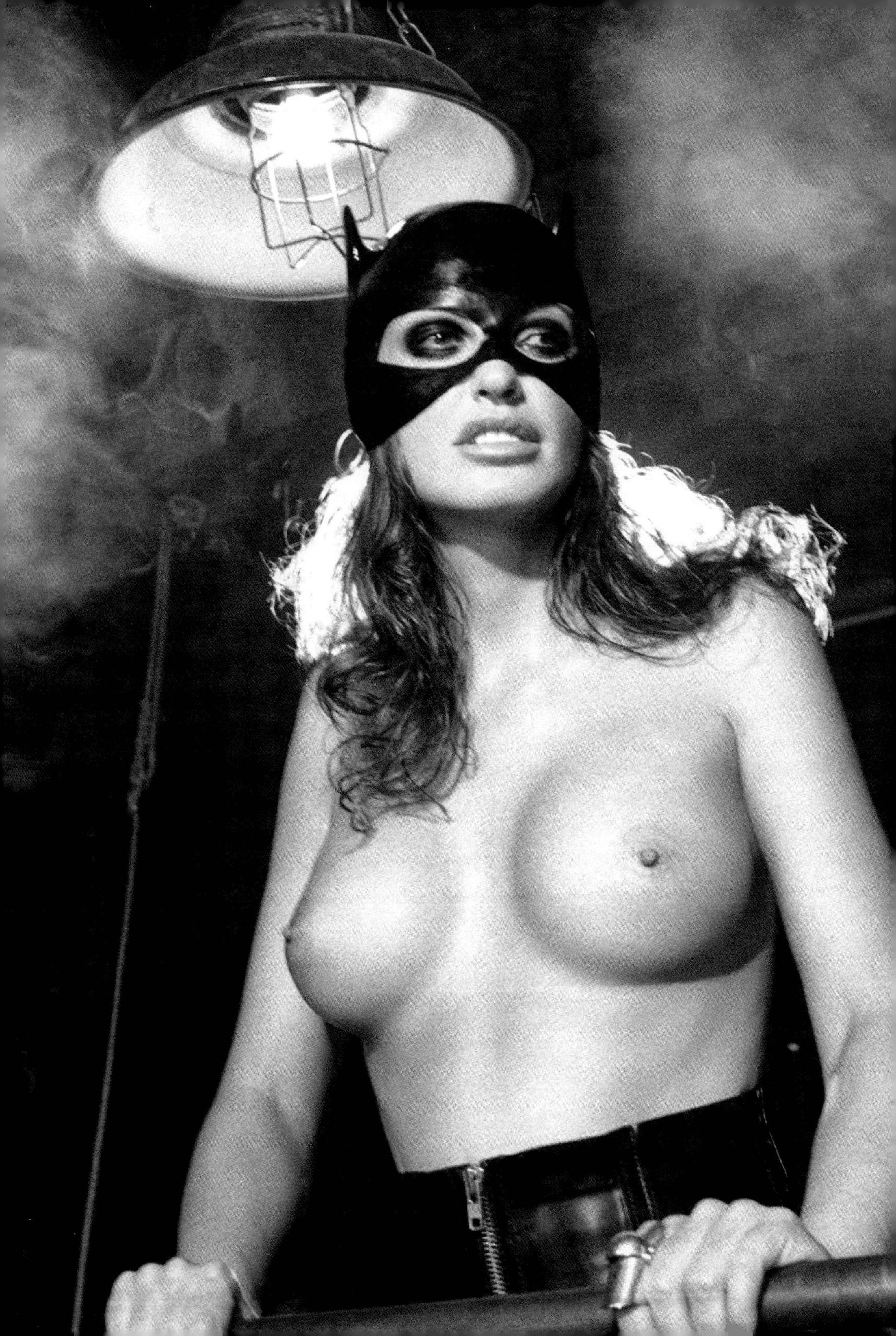

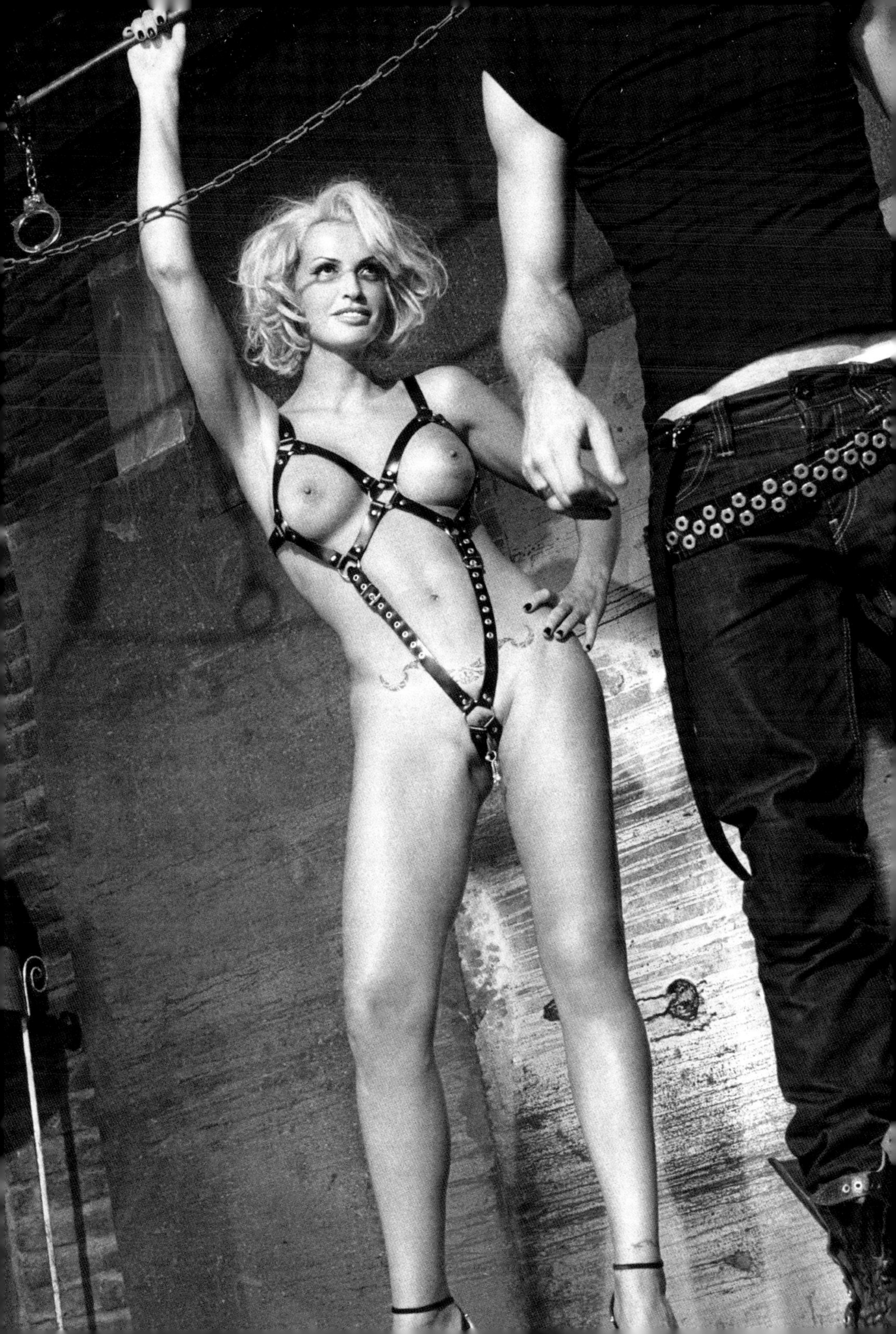

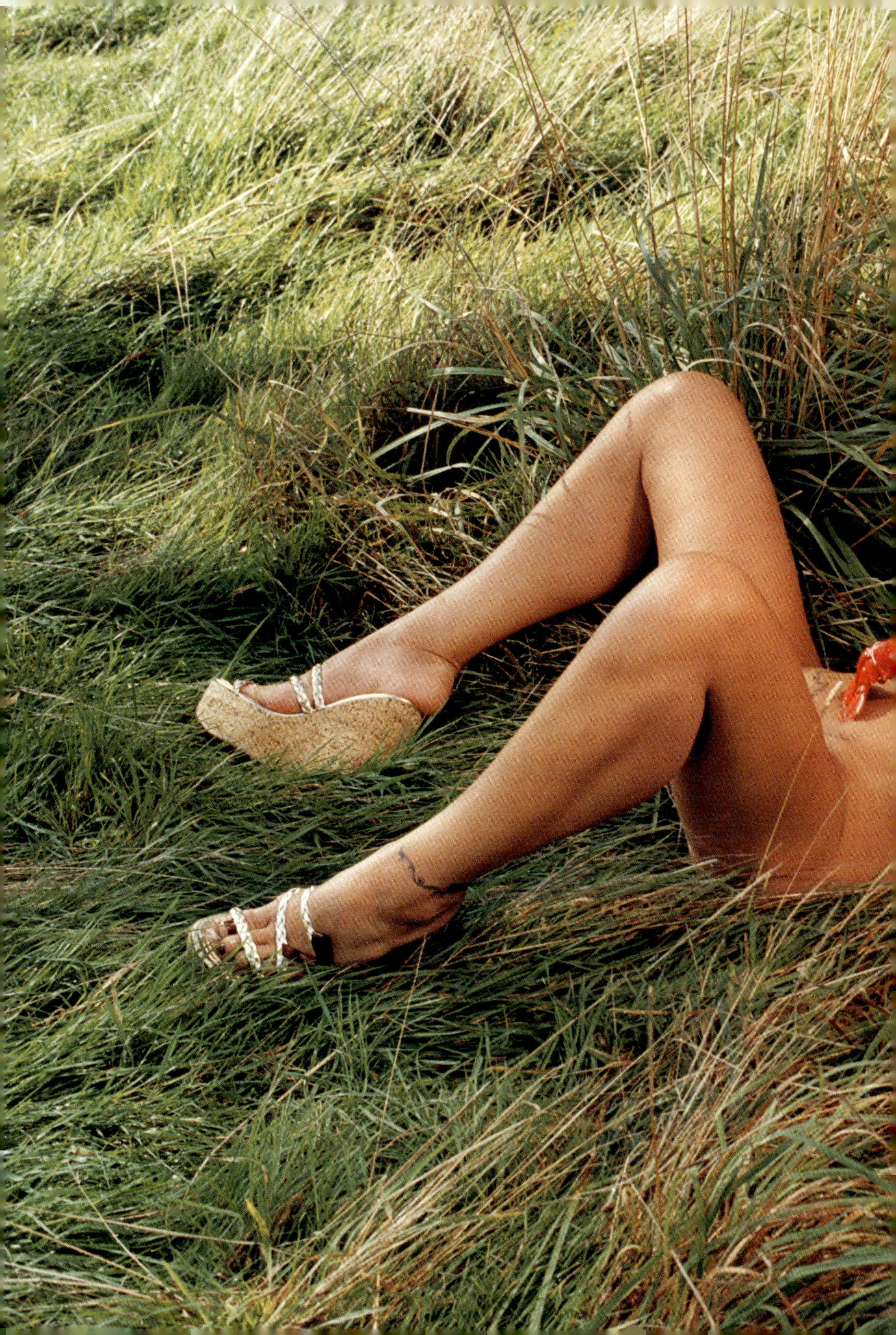

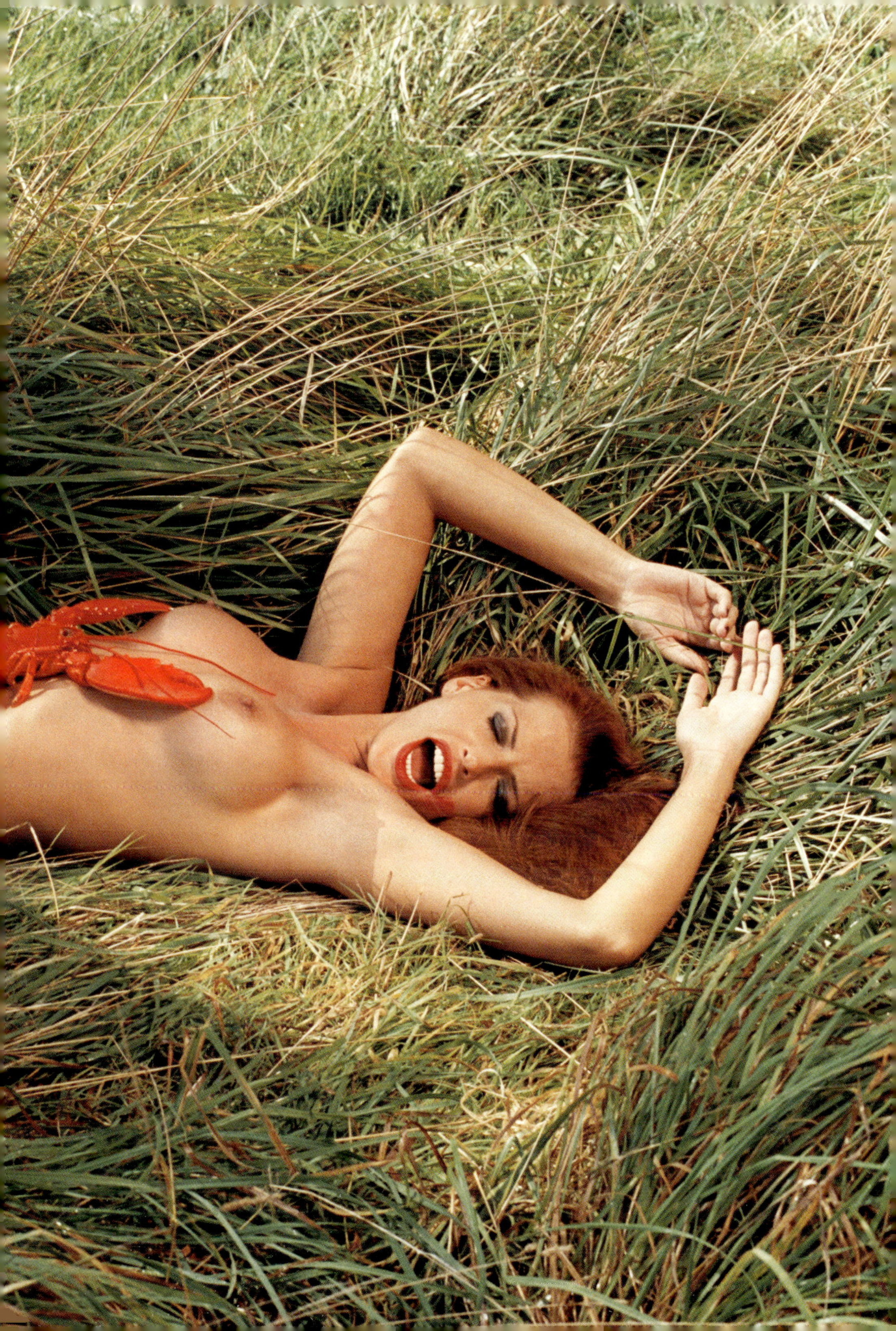

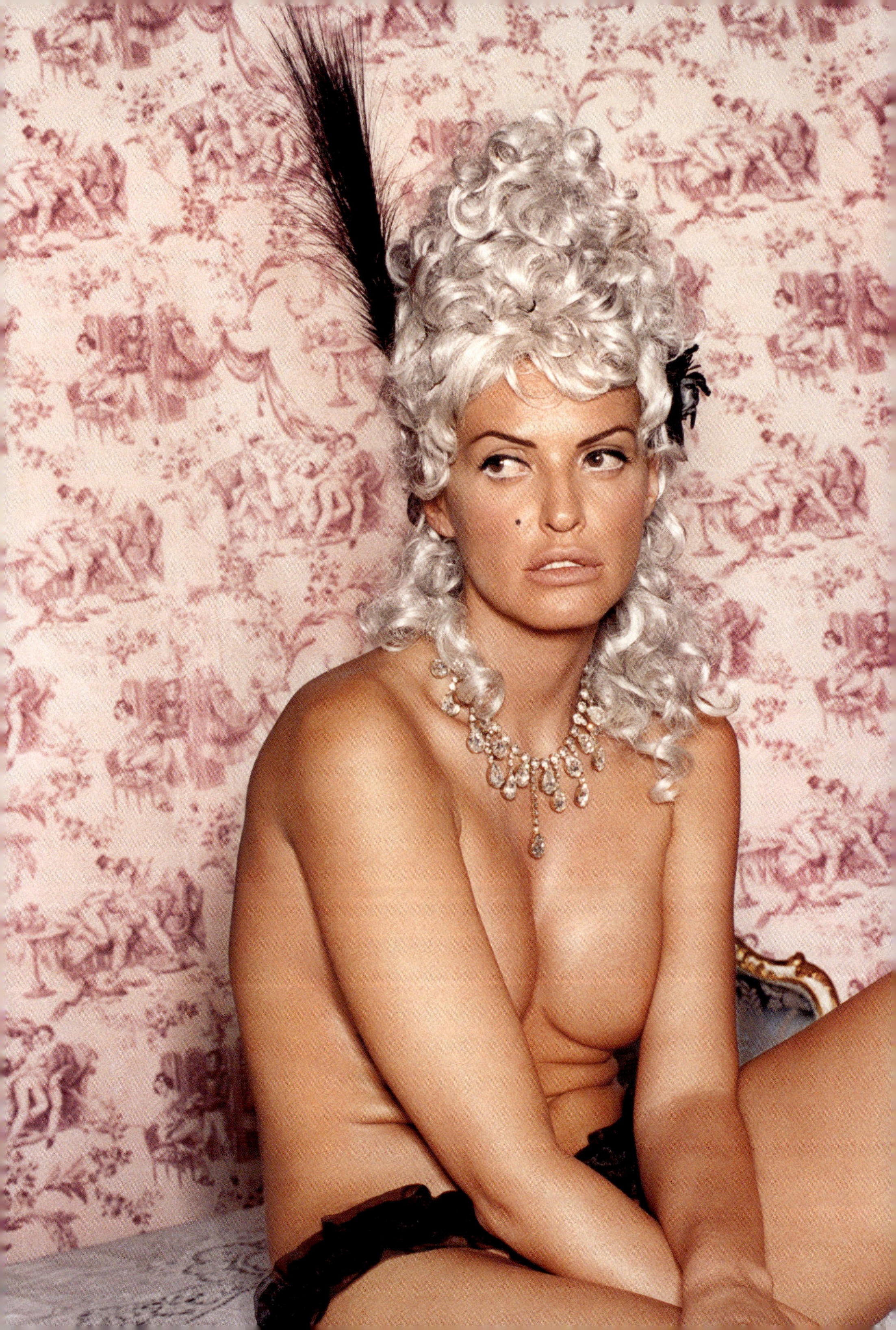

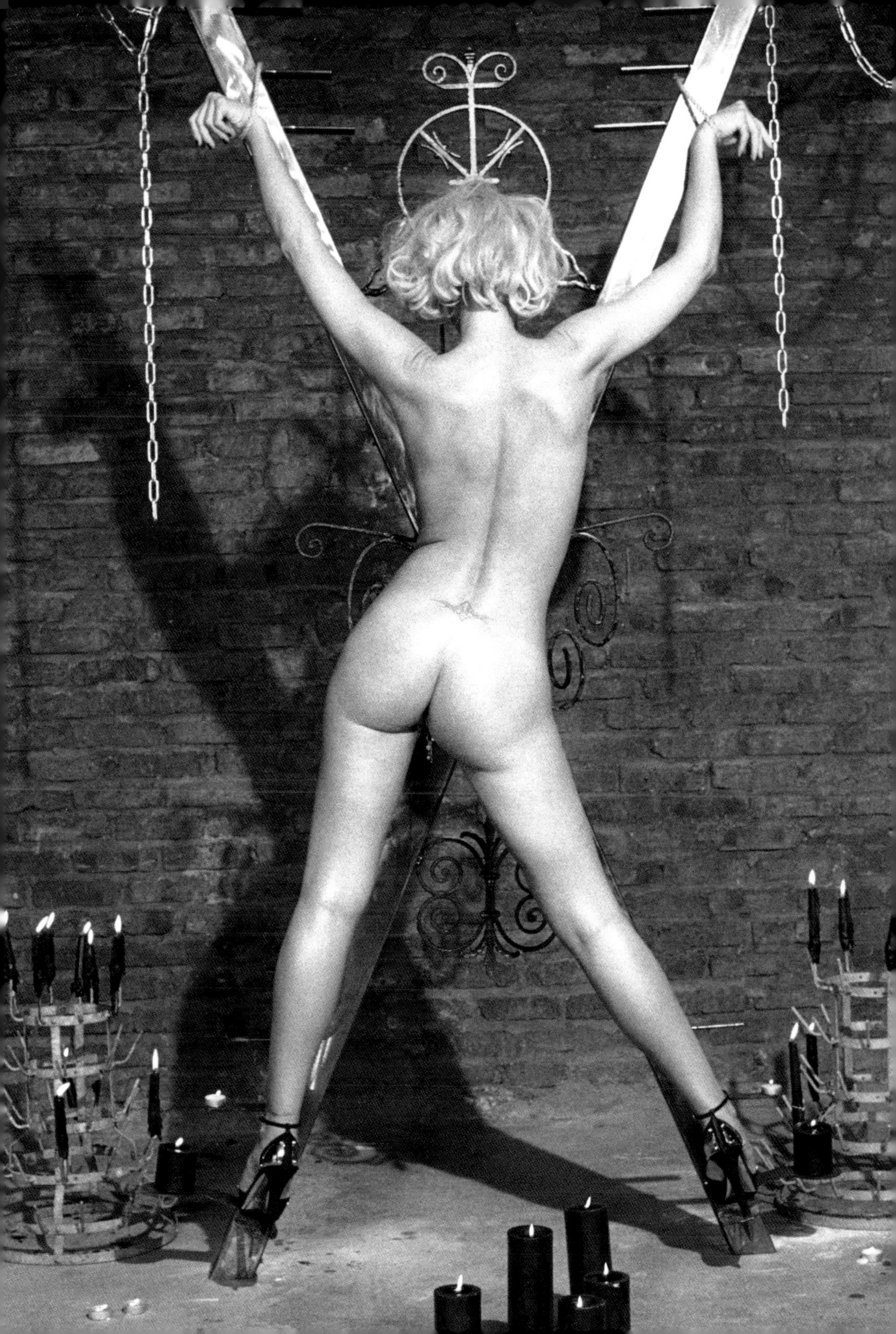

THE STORY OF IRINA

2008, Marlborough

"Here is one of the poems in my journal
(...) will send more along the way!"

Lost in the shadows of our thoughts
We were often wrong
Wild, and strong were our words
We blame it on each other
And in an hour we laughed and called it a song

«Voici l'un des poèmes de mon journal.
(...) d'autres viendront plus tard!»

Perdus dans les ombres de nos pensées
Nous avions souvent tort
Nos paroles étaient dures et fortes
Nous nous fîmes des reproches
Pour en rire aussitôt et en faire une chanson

„Hier ist eins der Gedichte aus meinem Tagebuch.
(...) sende später mehr!"

Verloren in den Schatten unserer Gedanken
Haben wir uns oft geirrt
Wild und stark waren unsere Worte
Wir geben uns gegenseitig die Schuld
Und eine Stunde später lachten wir und machten
daraus einen Song

Irina, January 2015

Opposite page and following pages — *The story of Irina Lăzăreanu at Pete Doherty's house,*
May 2008, Marlborough, Wiltshire

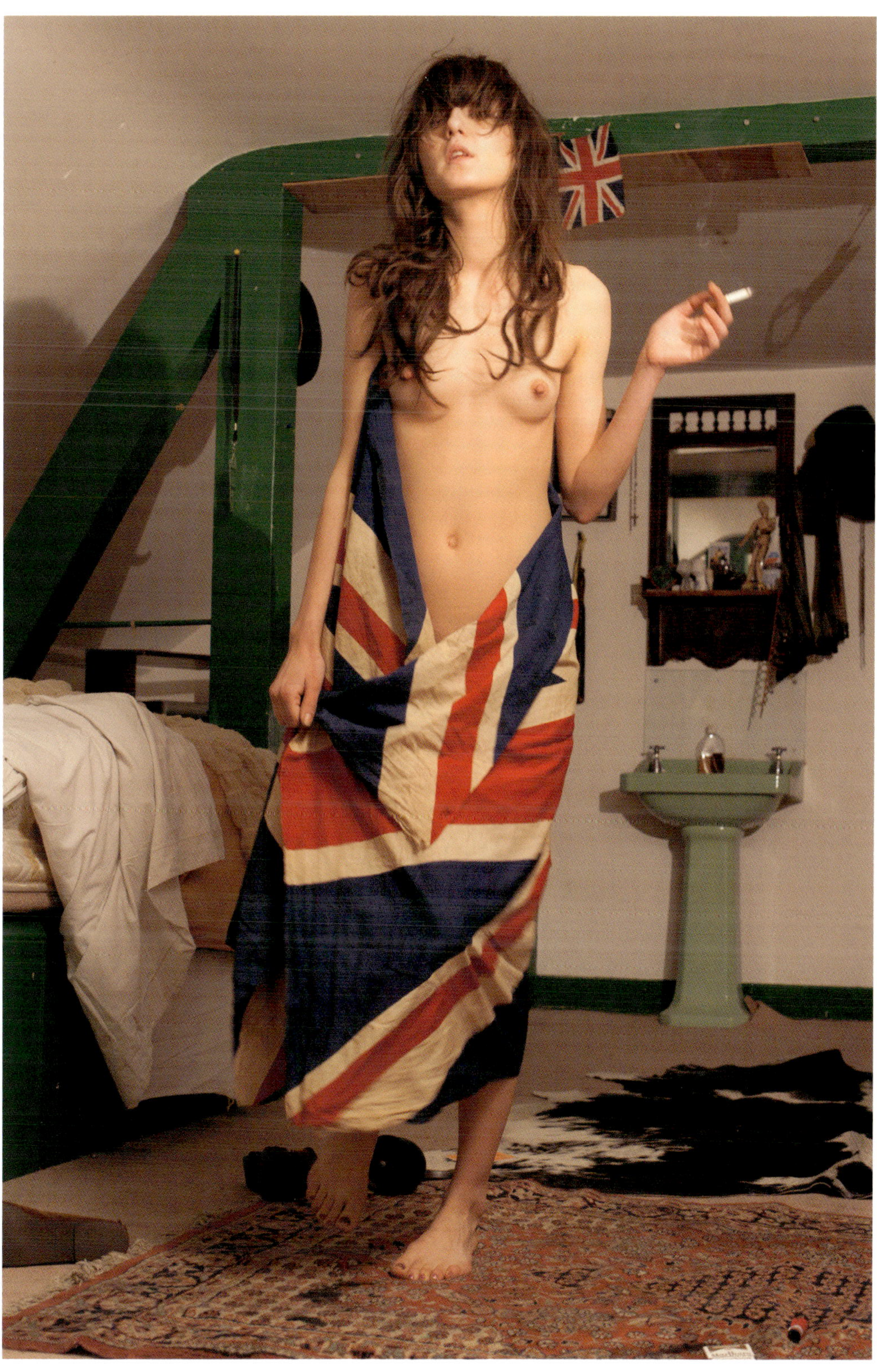

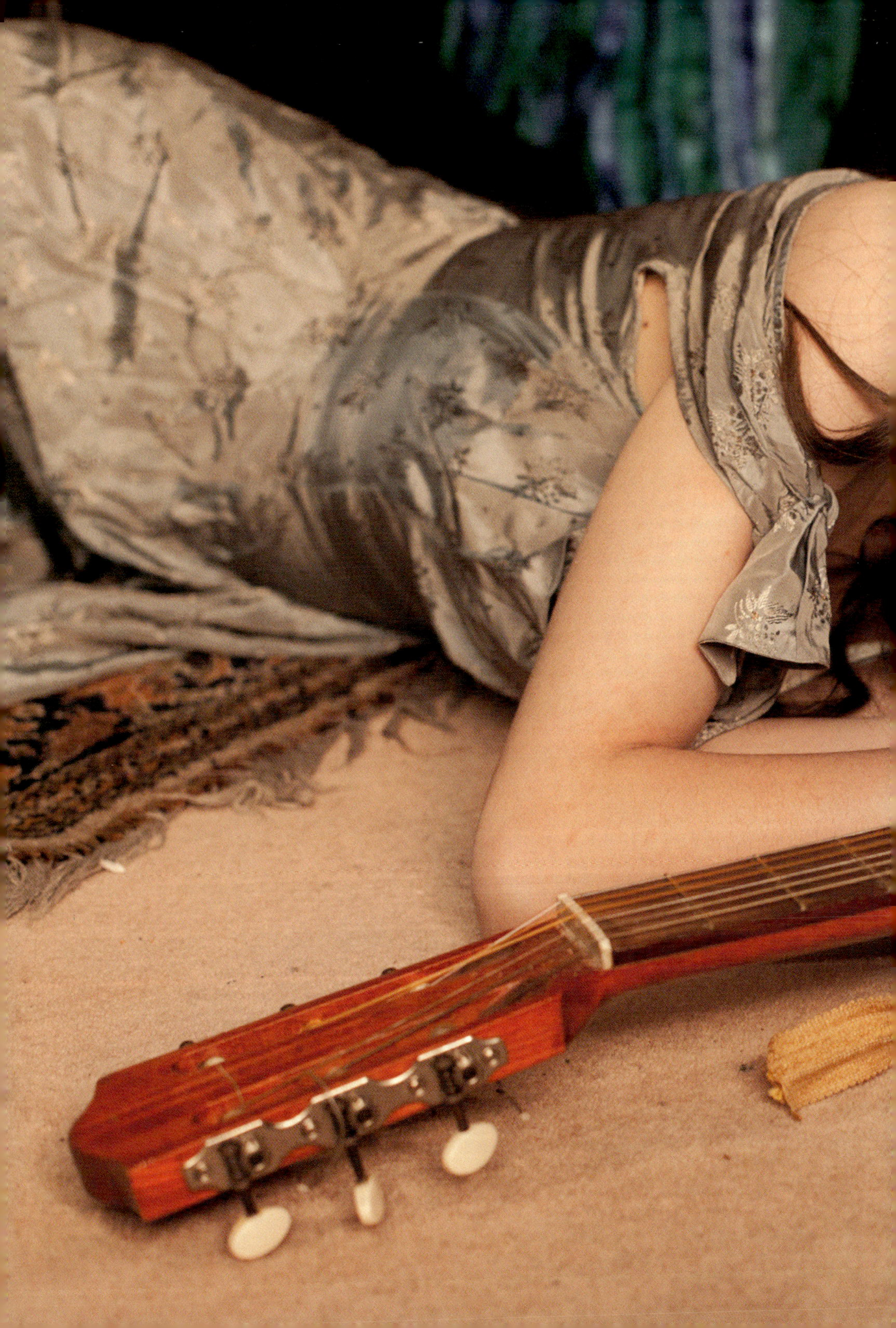

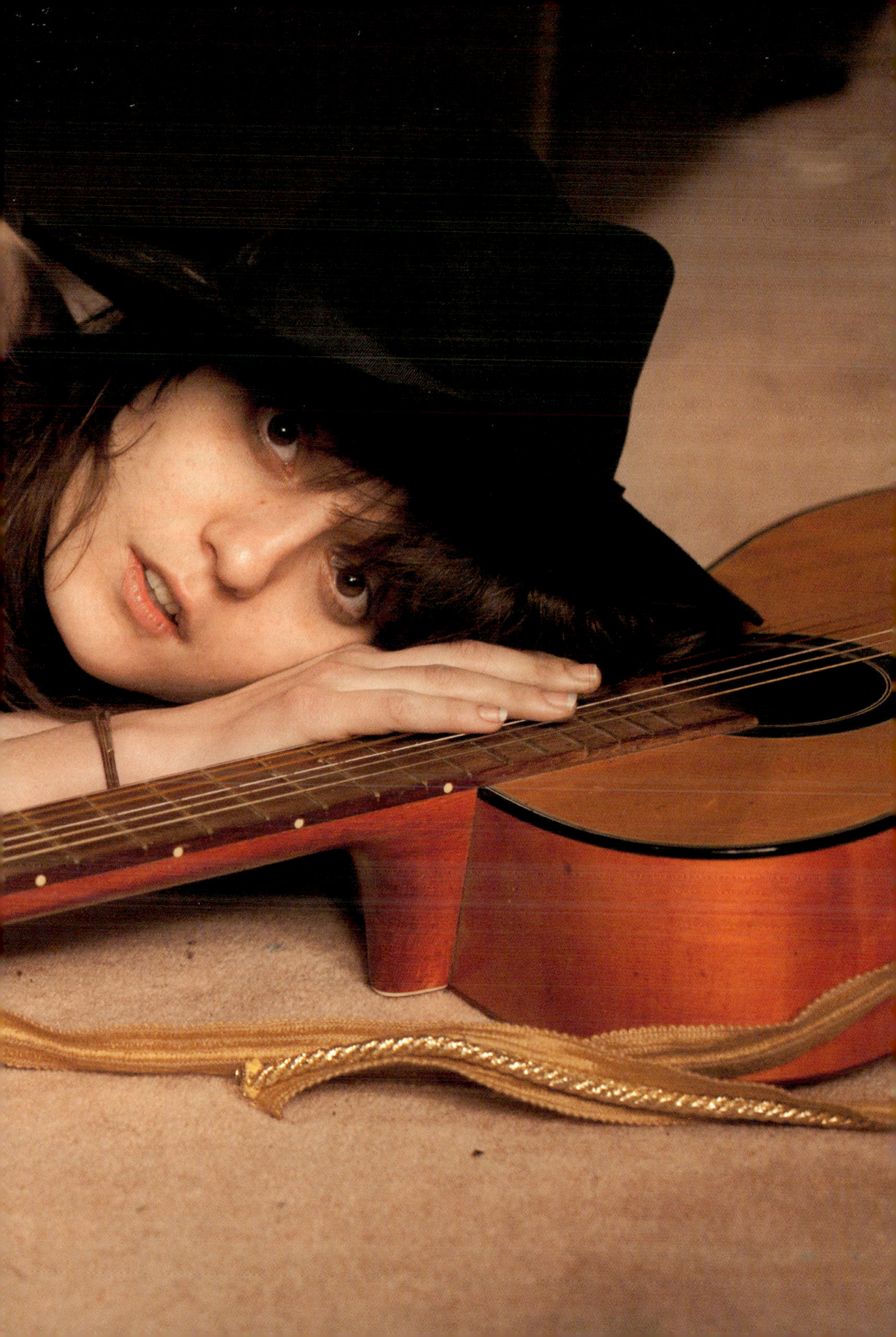

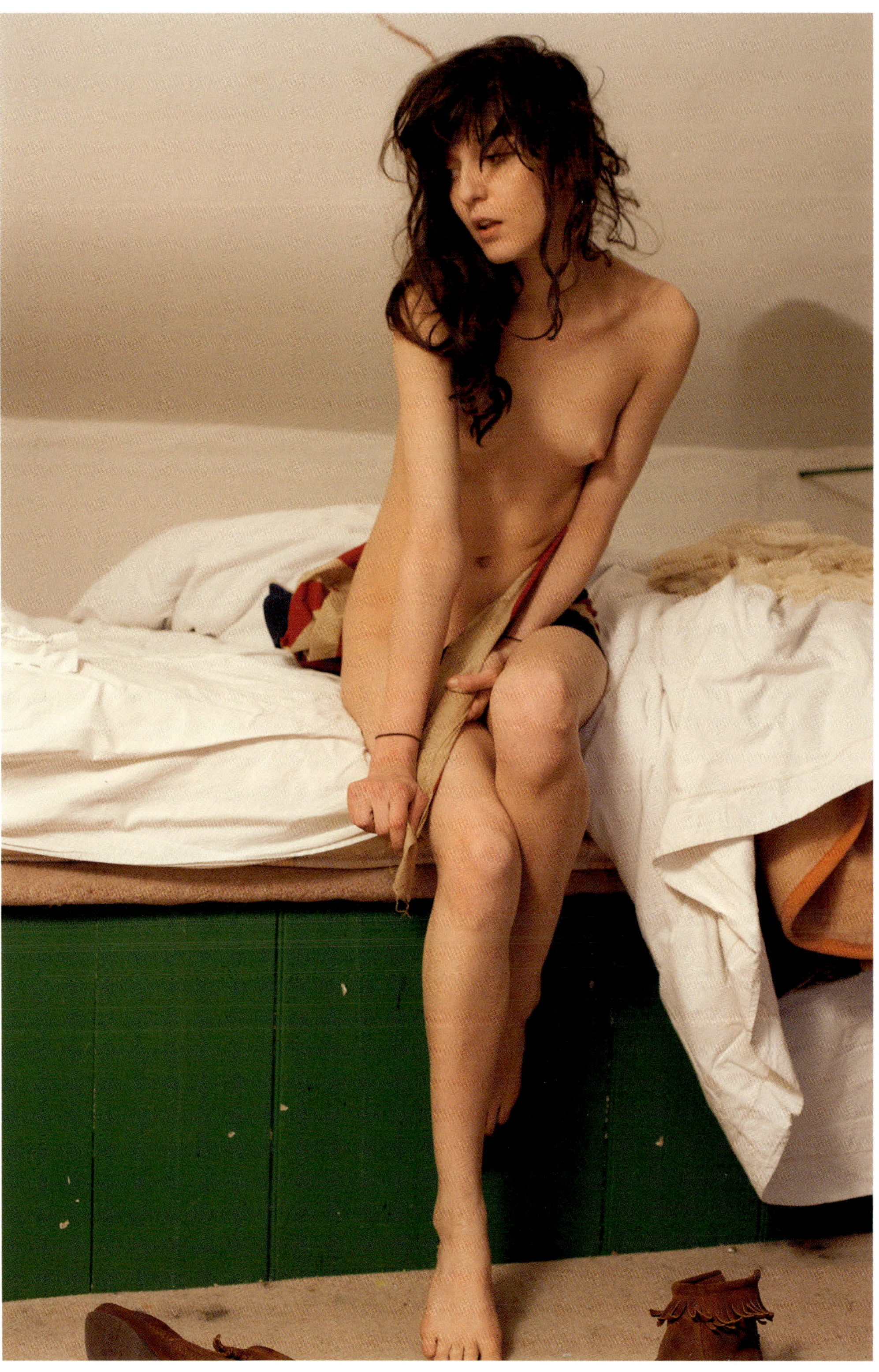

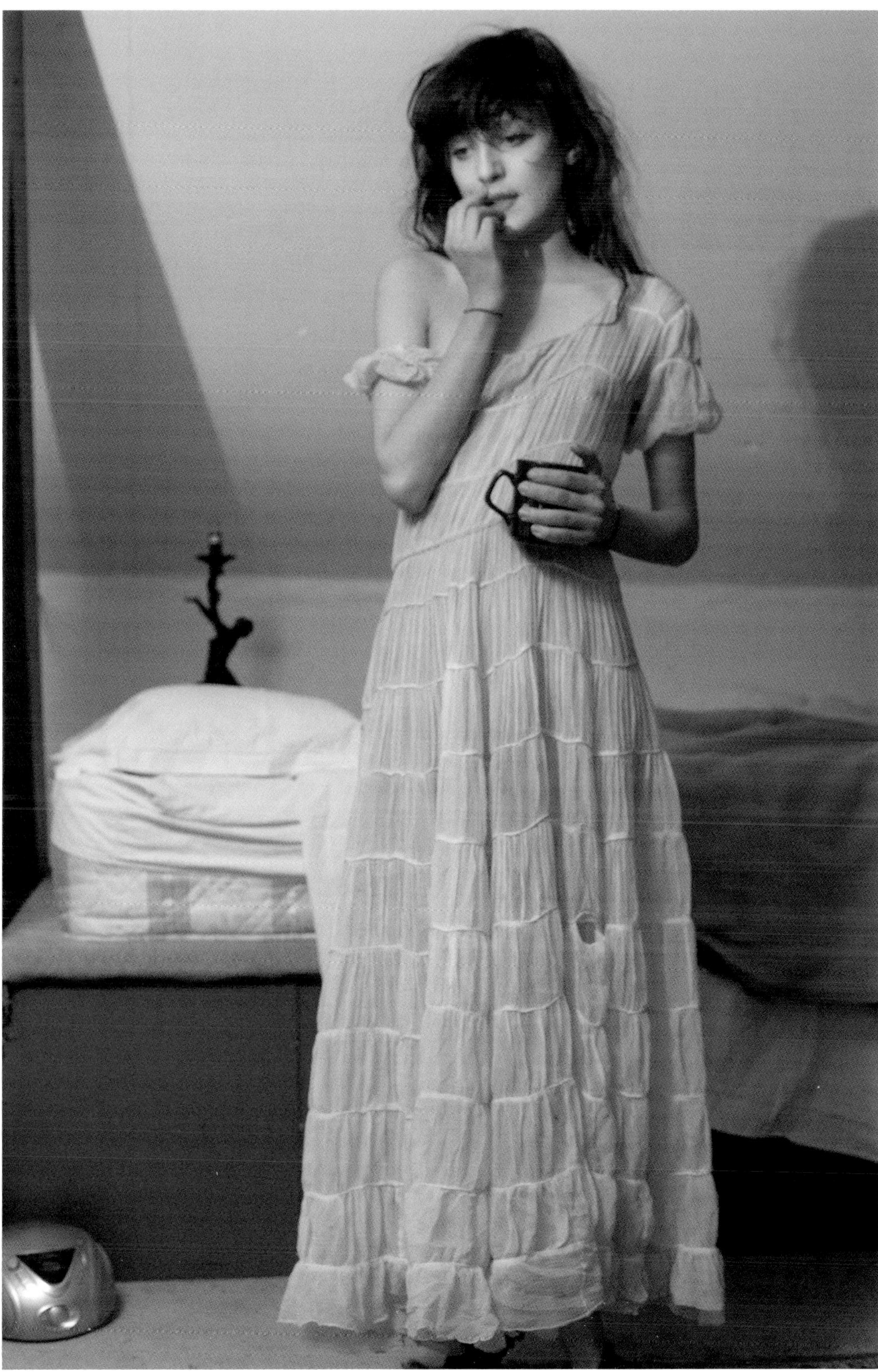

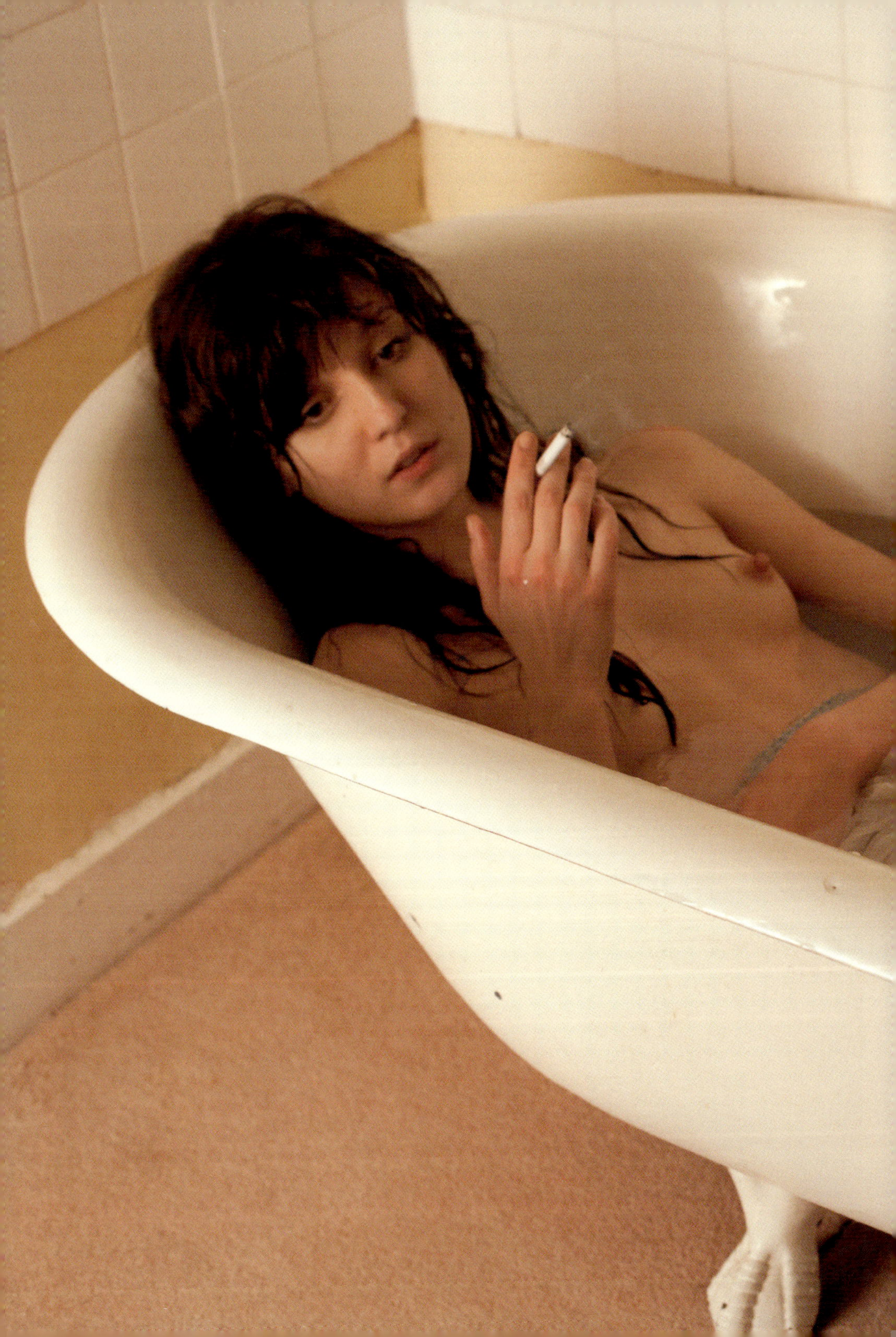

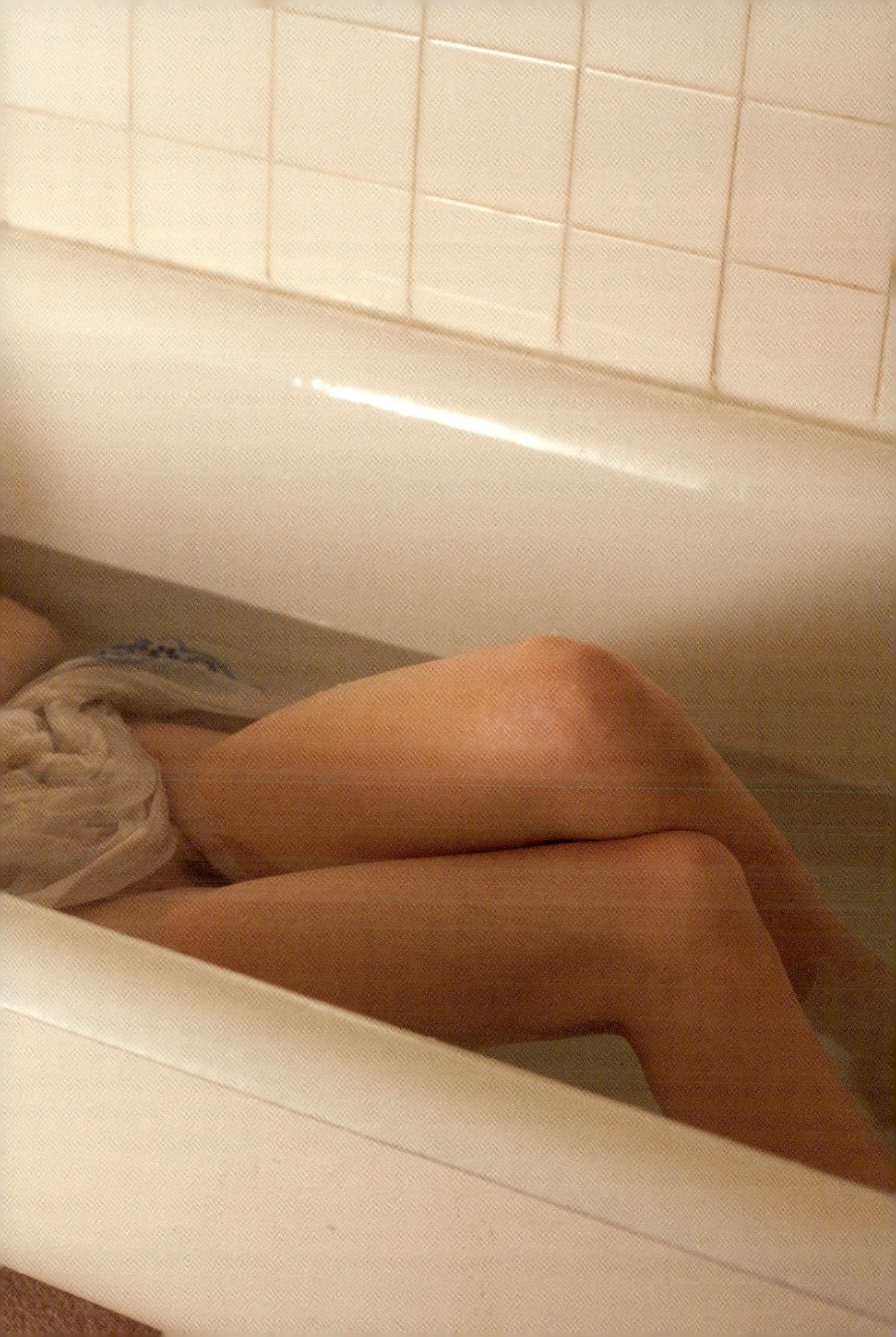

JUST LIKE A WOMAN
IN COLLABORATION WITH SERGE BRAMLY
2008, Paris

Alison II, January 2008, Paris
Page 402 — *Dovile*, January 2008, Paris
Page 403 — *Ugne*, January 2008, Paris

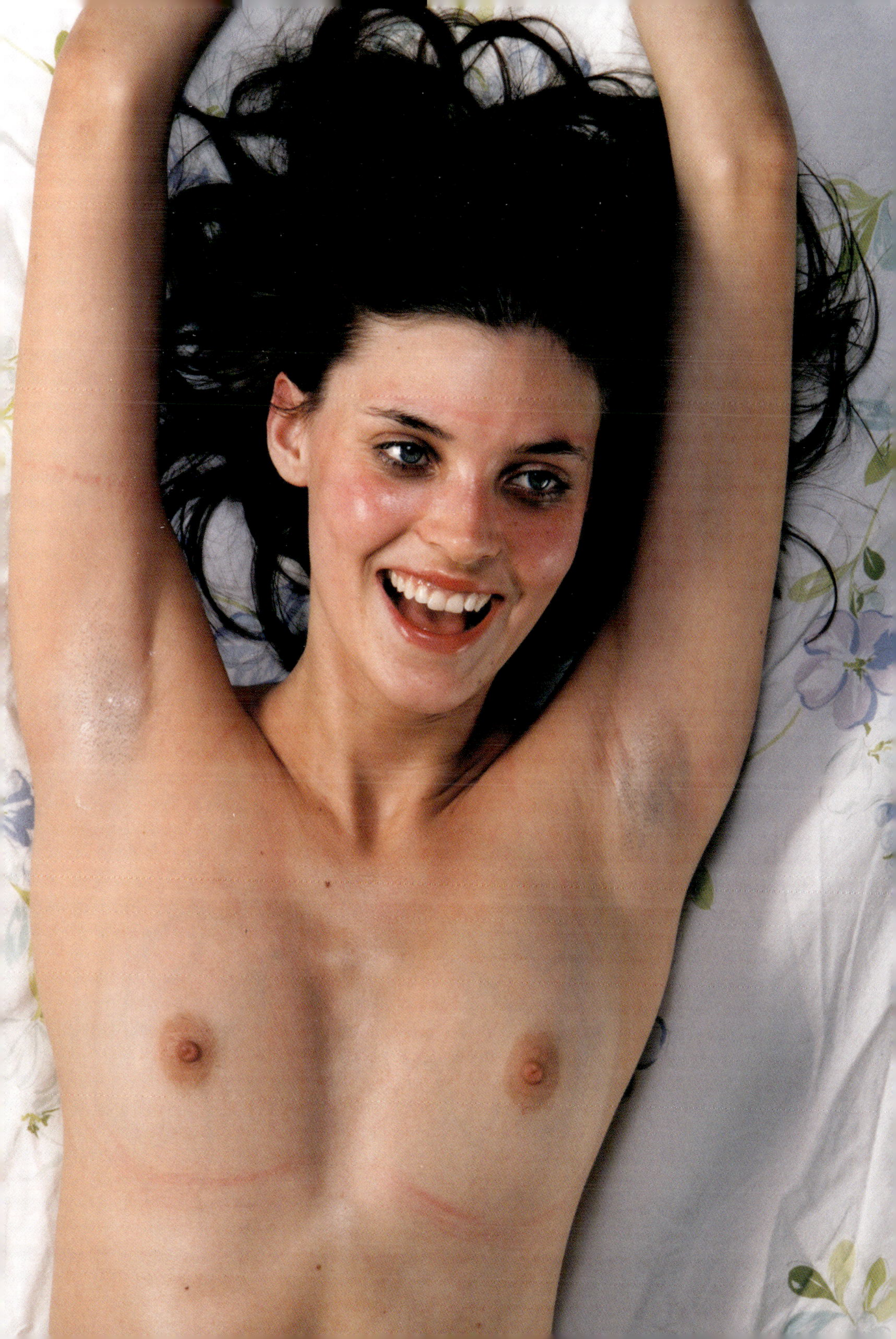

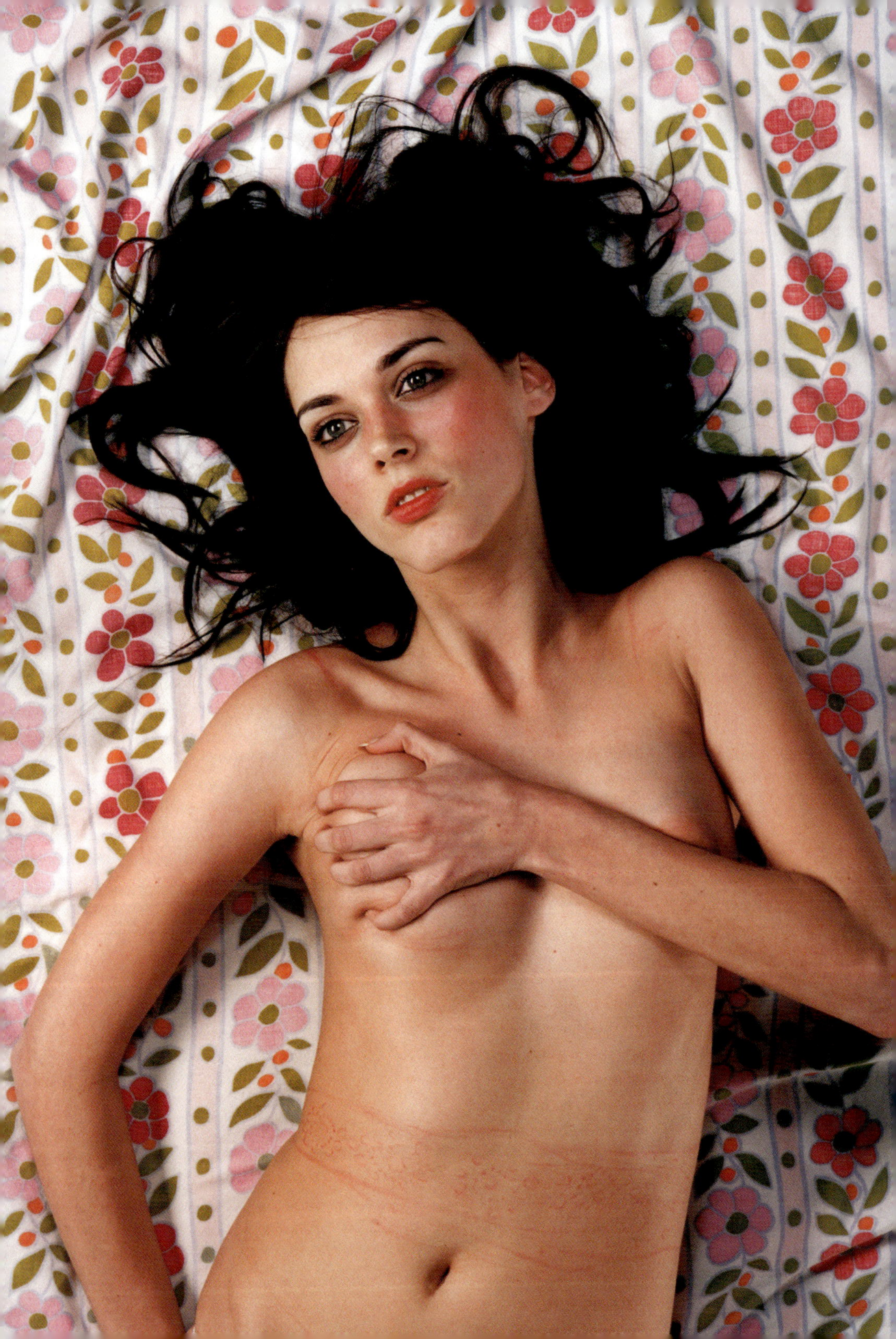

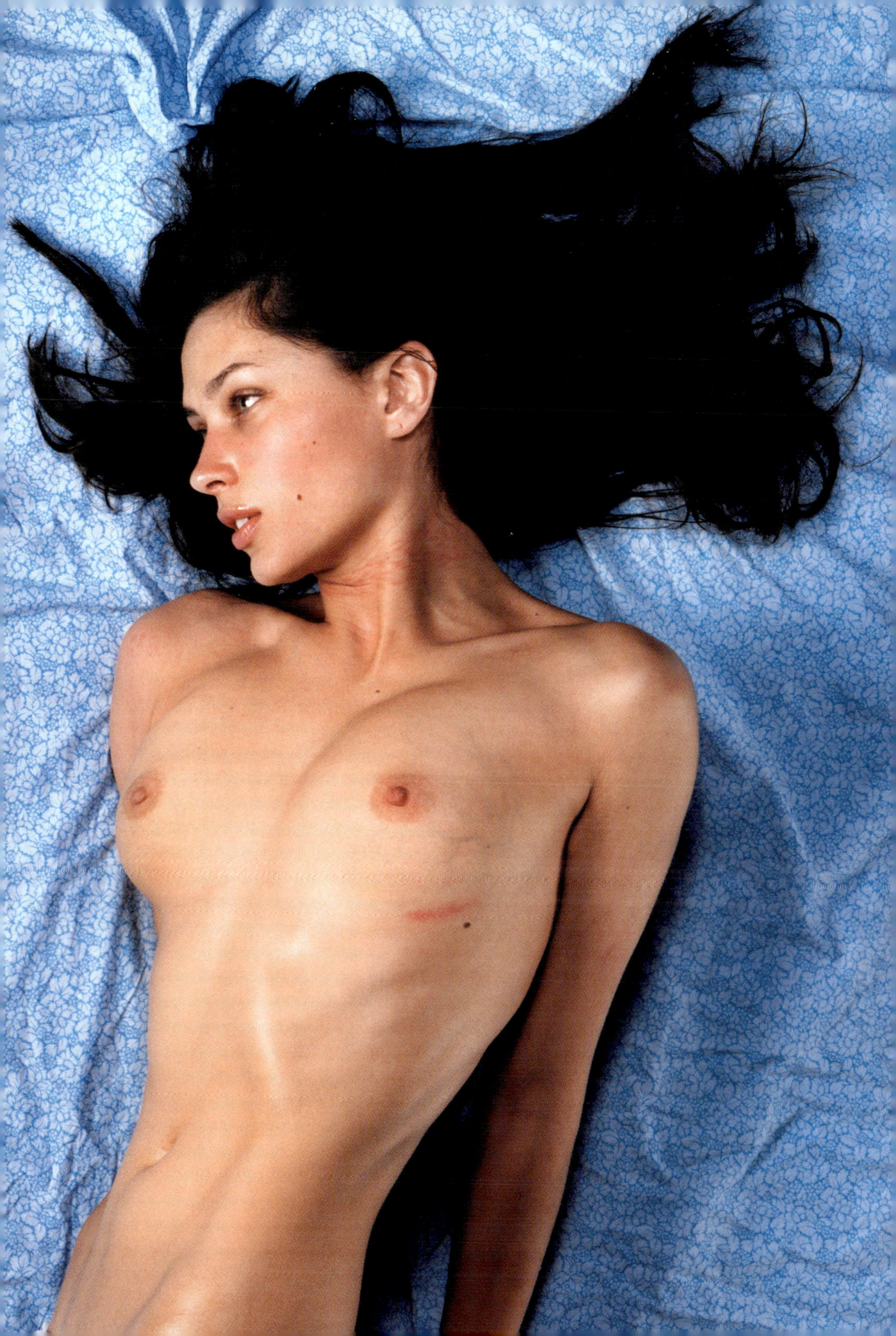

Lara, January 2008, Paris
Page 406 — *Magdalena*, January 2008, Paris
Page 407 — *Anne-Sophie*, January 2008, Paris

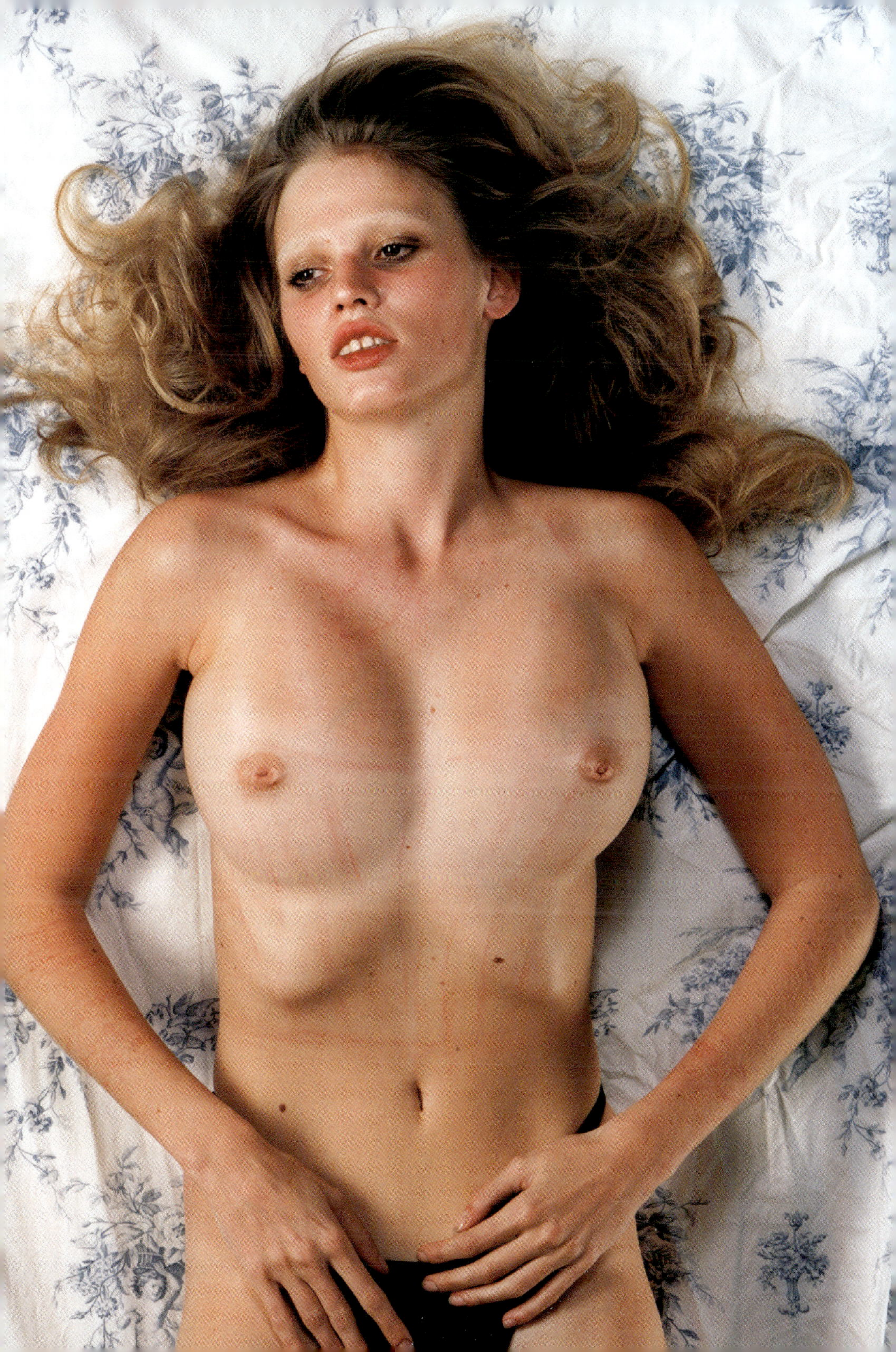

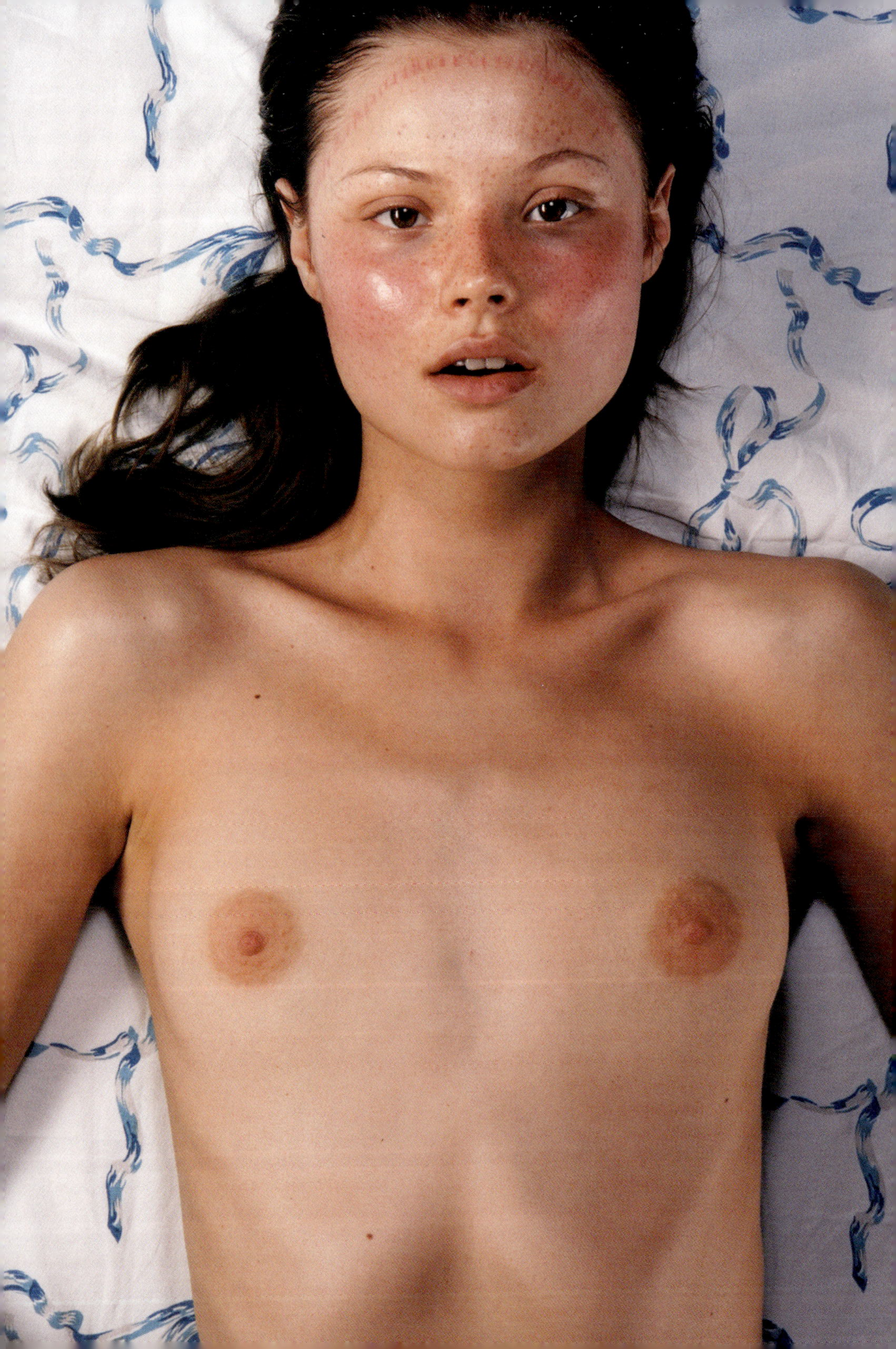

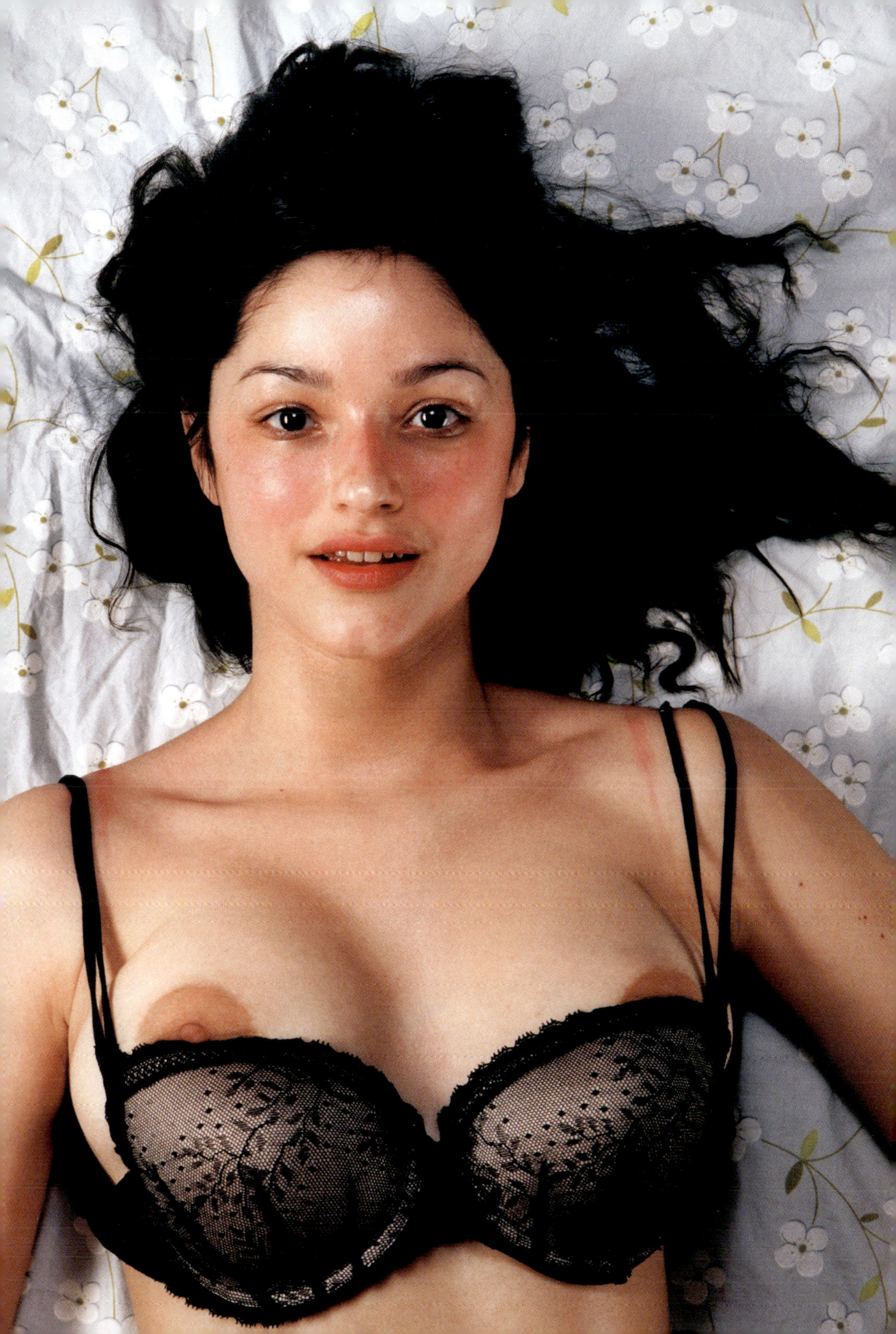

ROSE, C'EST PARIS
IN COLLABORATION WITH SERGE BRAMLY
2009, Paris

It seemed clear to us that Paris, like Marcel Duchamp, formulated enigmas as attractive as they were devoid of solution. Duchamp invented his own double: Rrose Sélavy. We therefore made this *cadavre exquis* into our equation and starting point: Rose + Paris = the archives of our memories.

Il nous semblait évident que Paris, tout comme Marcel Duchamp, formulait des énigmes aussi attirantes que dépourvues de solution. L'artiste s'était inventé un double: Rrose Sélavy. Nous avons posé alors cette équation de départ, en forme de *cadavre exquis*: Rose + Paris = les archives de notre mémoire.

Für uns war es offensichtlich, dass Paris – genau wie Marcel Duchamp – ebenso verlockende wie unlösbare Rätsel aufgab. Der Künstler hatte sich eine zweite Persönlichkeit zugelegt: Rrose Sélavy. Wir sind also von dieser Gleichung in Form eines *Cadavre exquis* ausgegangen: Rose + Paris = die Archive unserer Erinnerung.

Serge Bramly, Paris, 2015

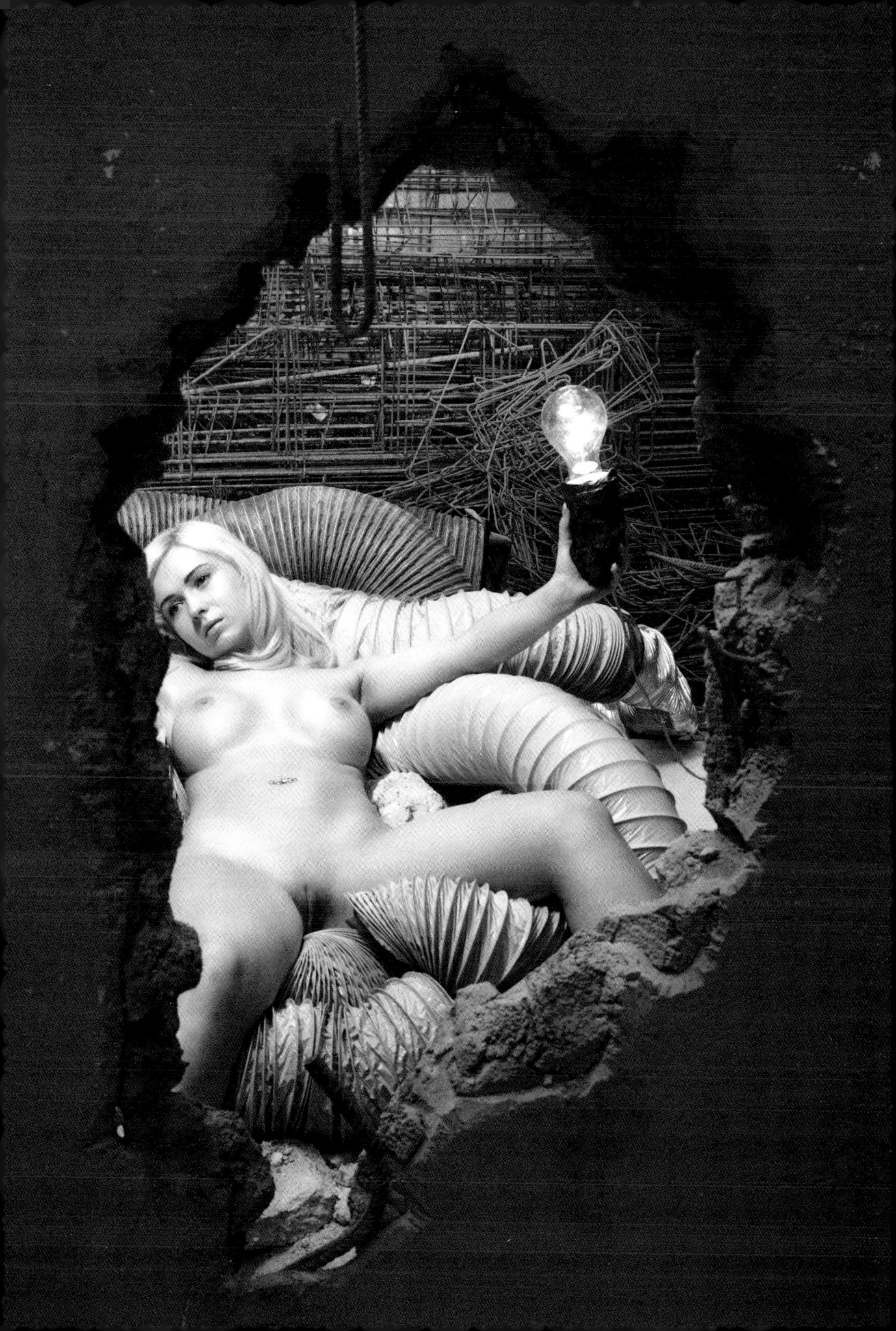

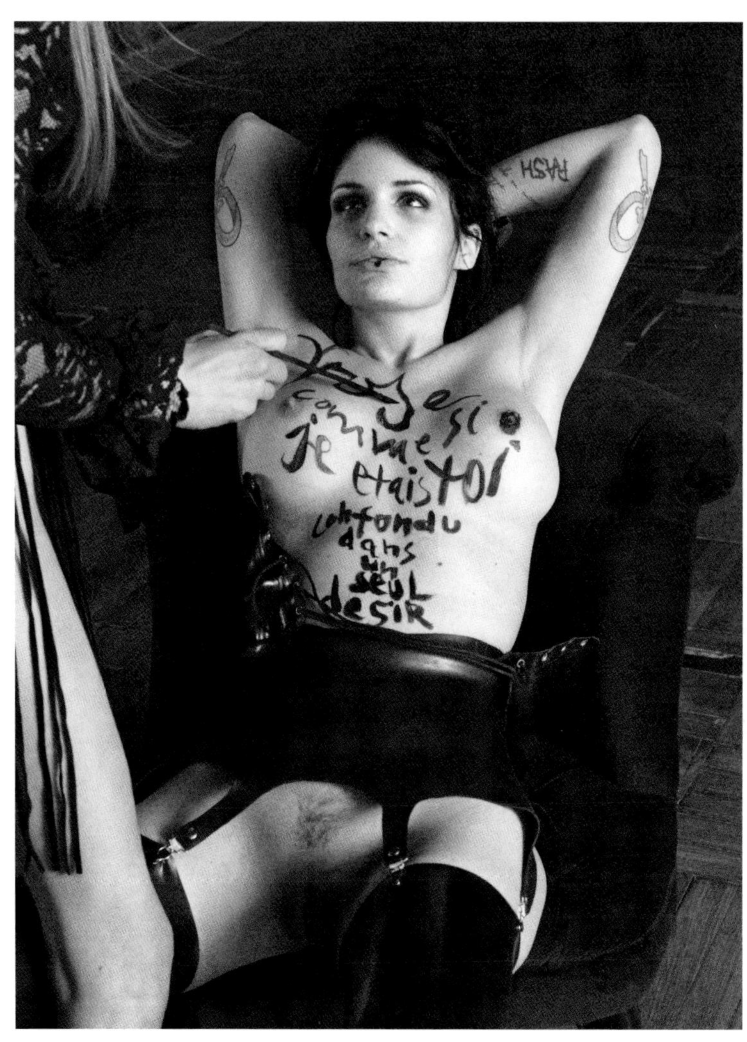

Above — *Confondu dans un seul désir*, February 2009, Showroom Anne Valérie Hash, Paris
Opposite page — *La mort mise à mort*, November 2008, Bibliothèque de l'Arsenal, Paris
Pages 412/413 — *La relève du matin*, December 2008, Rue de Bourgogne, Paris
Page 414 — *Le dompteur de vanités*, December 2008, Avenue des Tilleuls, Paris
Page 415 — *Causes perdues*, February 2009, Showroom Anne Valérie Hash, Paris
Pages 416/417 — *La mort de l'oiseau*, March 2009, Musée de la vie romantique, Paris
Pages 418/419 — *Pierres de rêves*, February 2009, Hôtel Rotary, Paris
Page 420 — *Le phénomène de l'osmose*, November 2008, Rue de l'Université, Paris
Page 421 — *Les muses inquiétantes*, February 2009, Hôtel Rotary, Paris

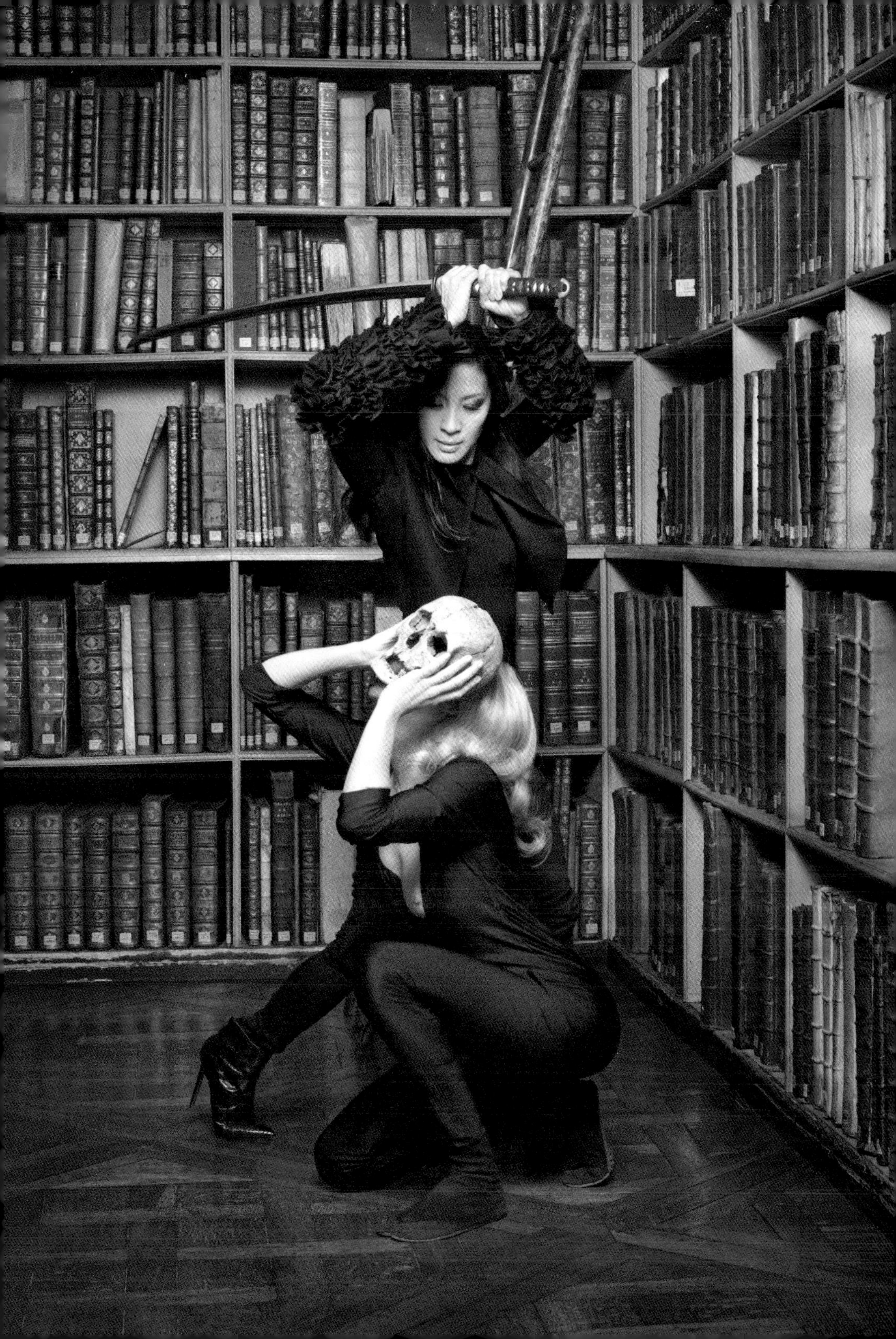

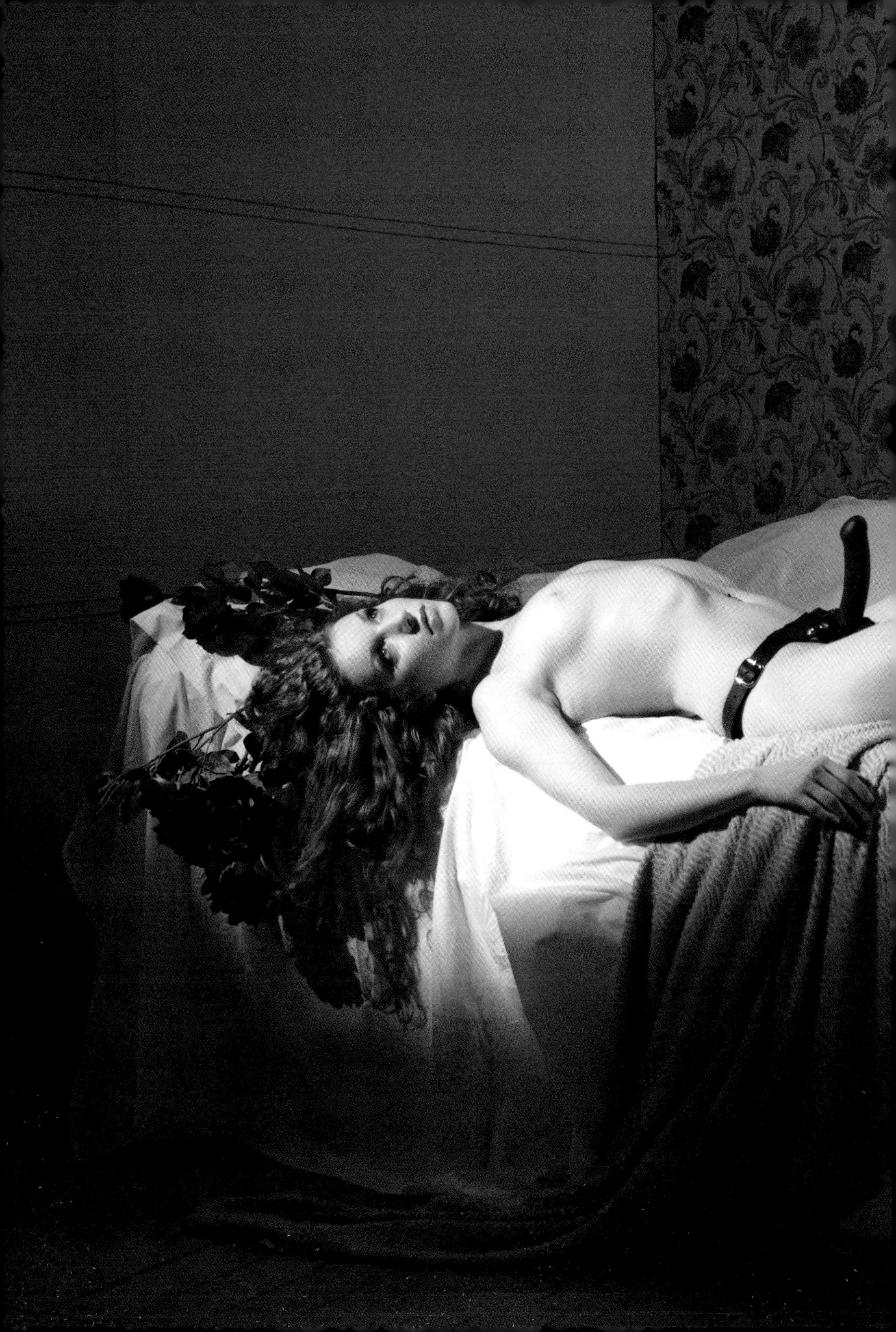

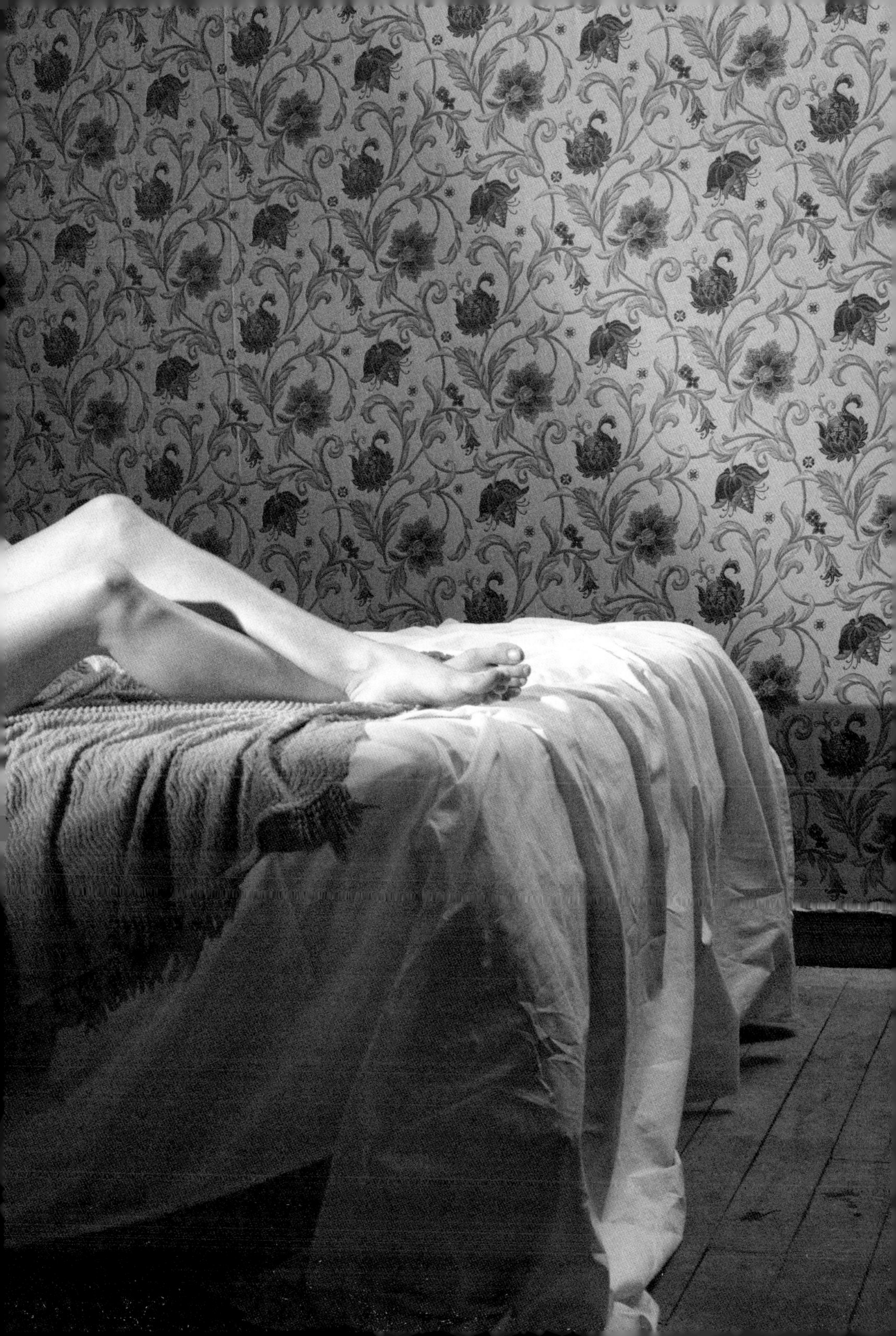

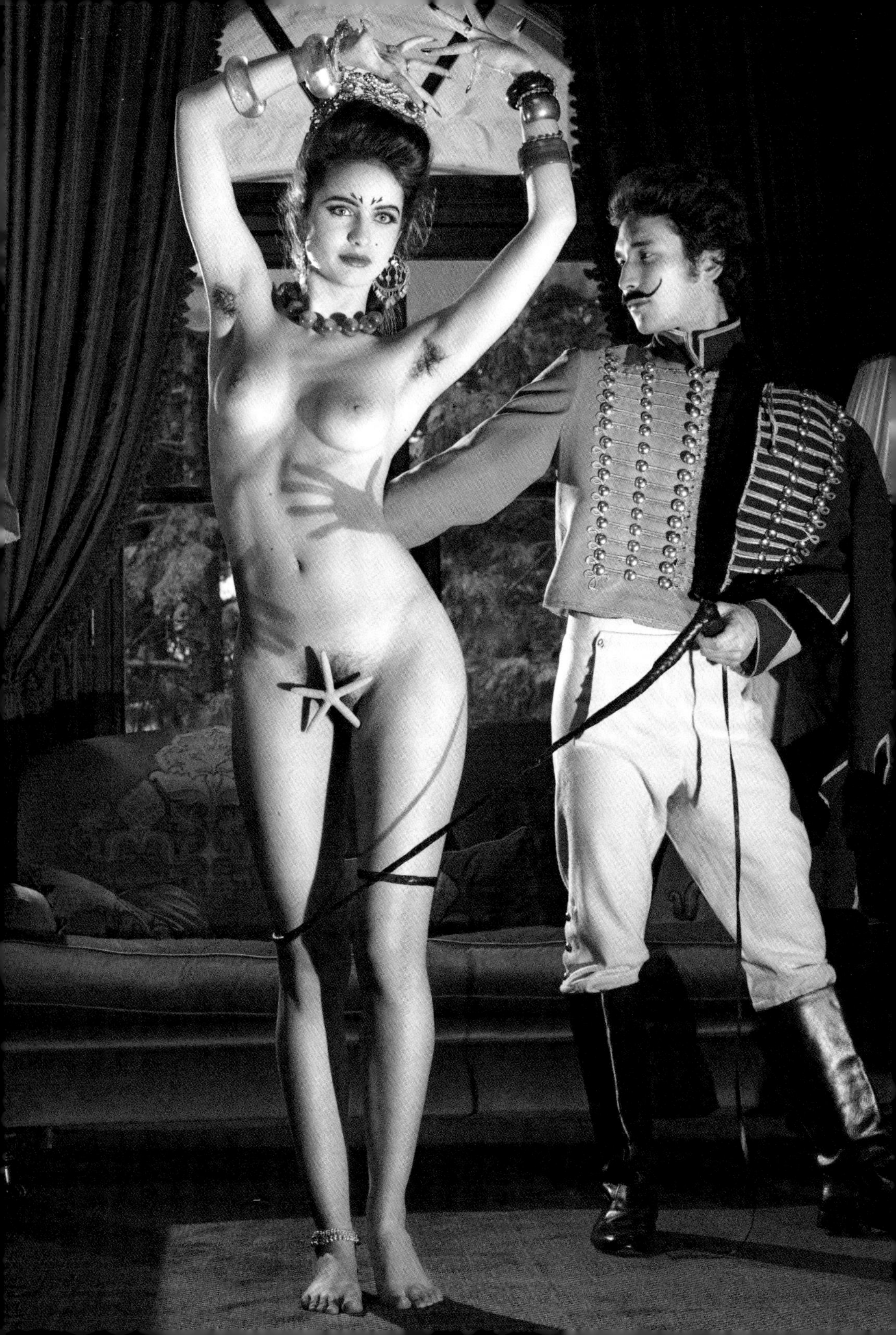

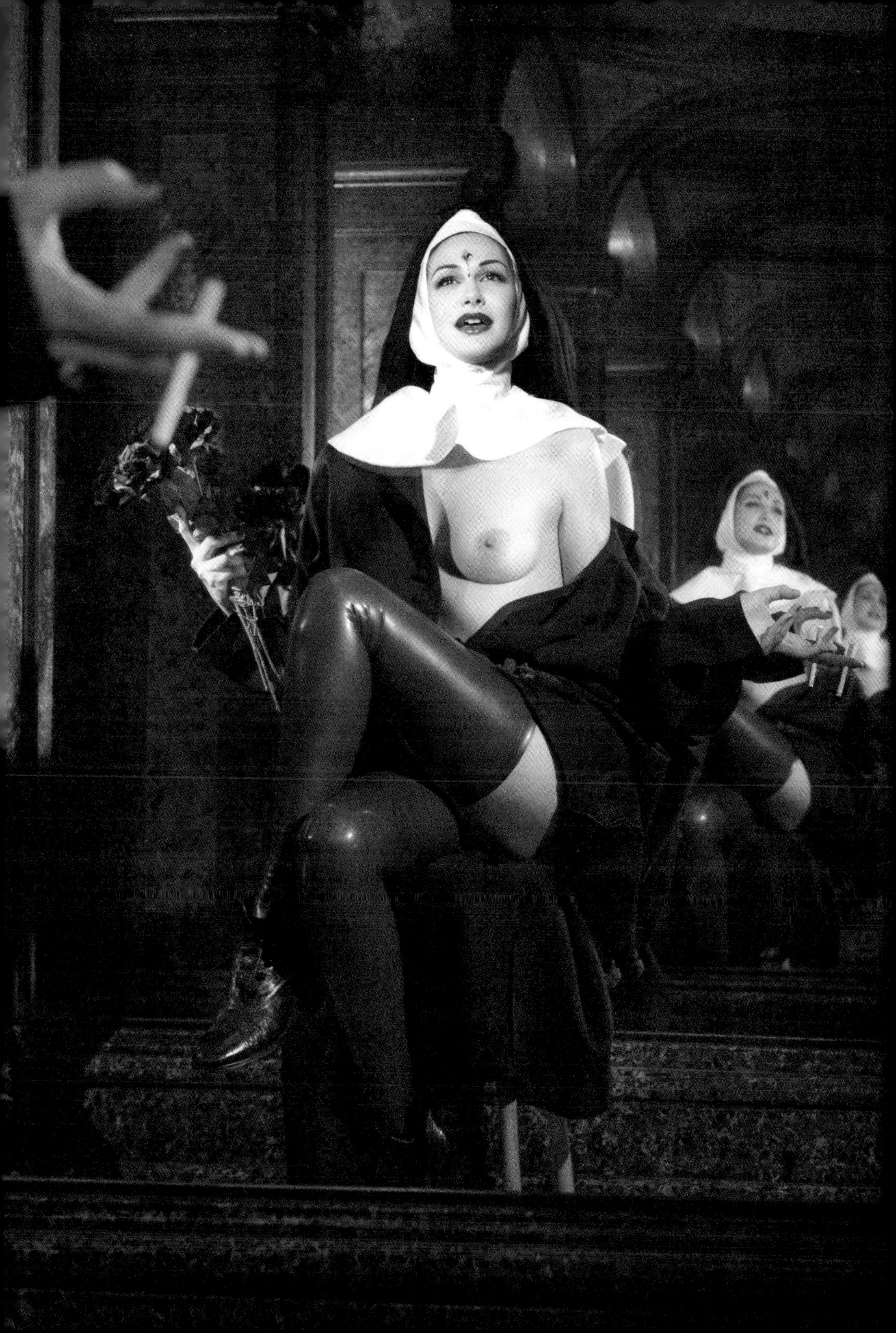

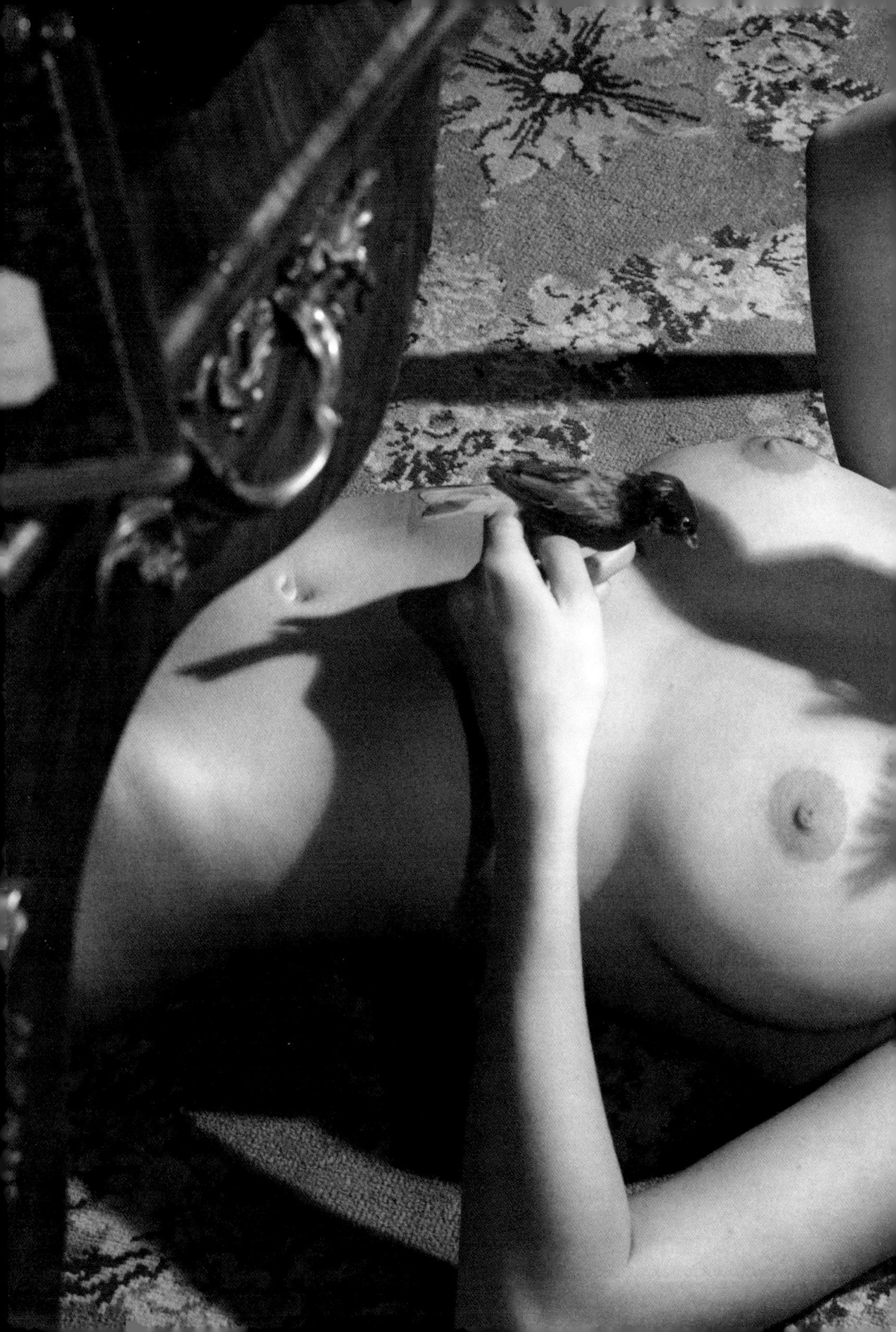

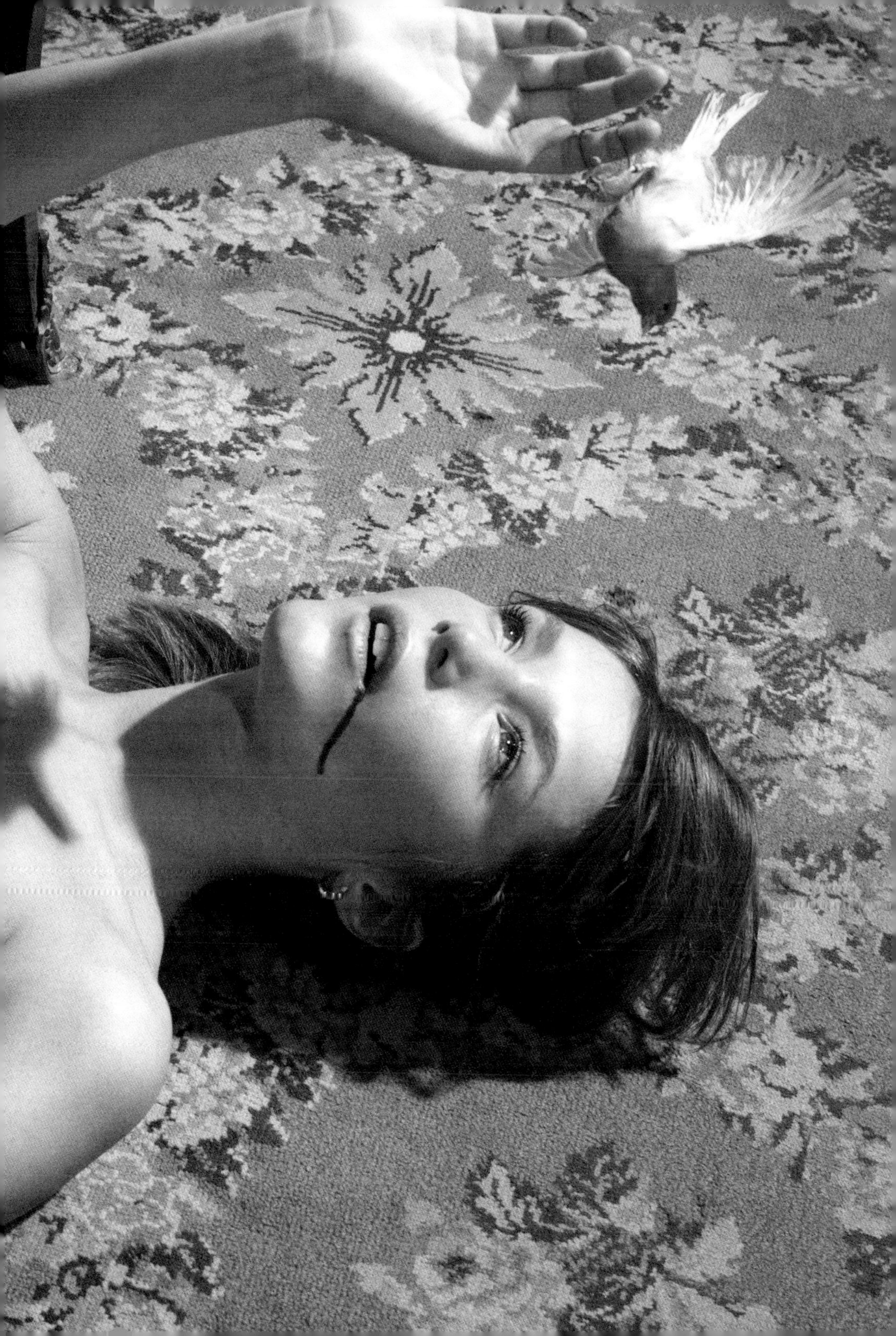

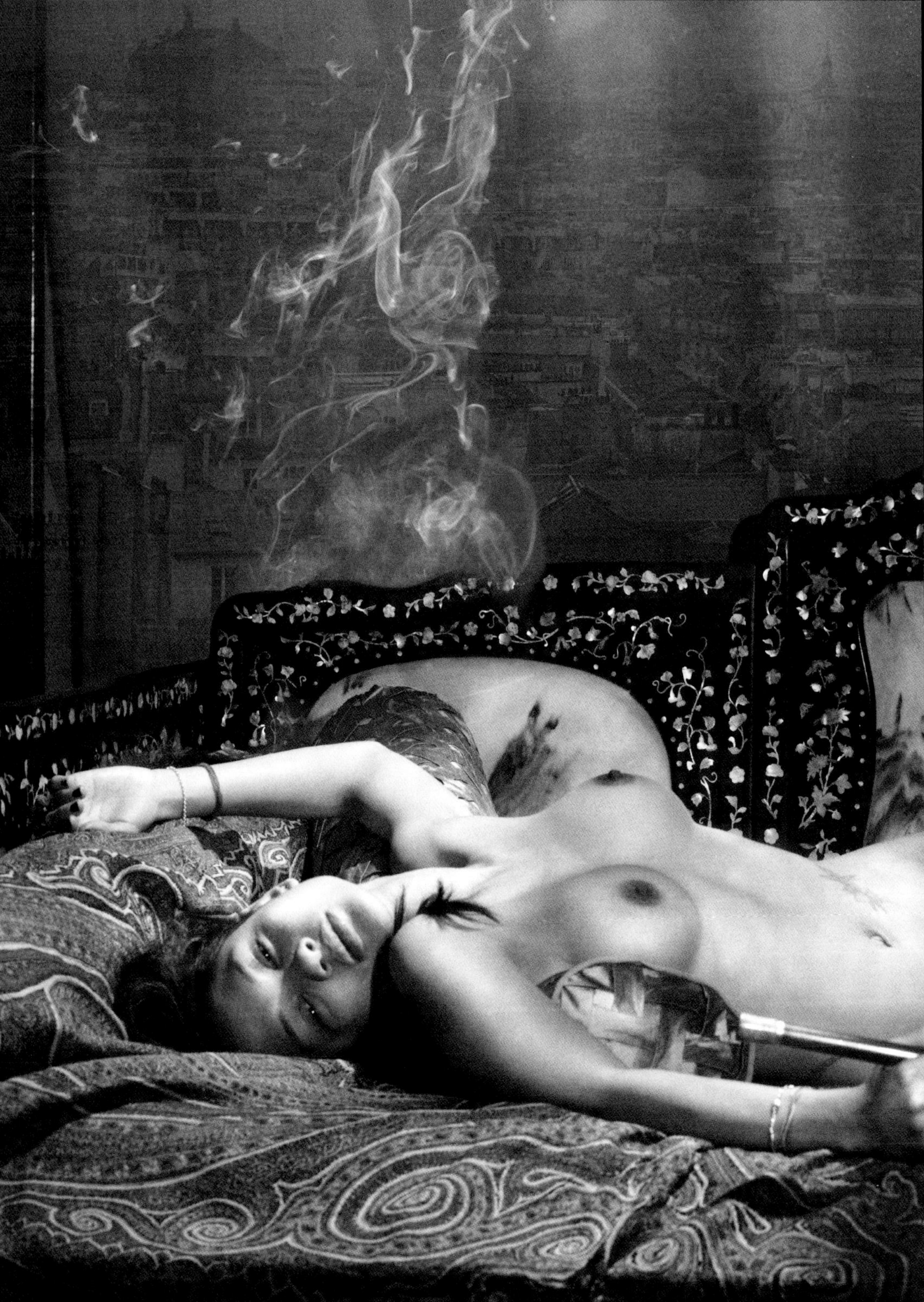

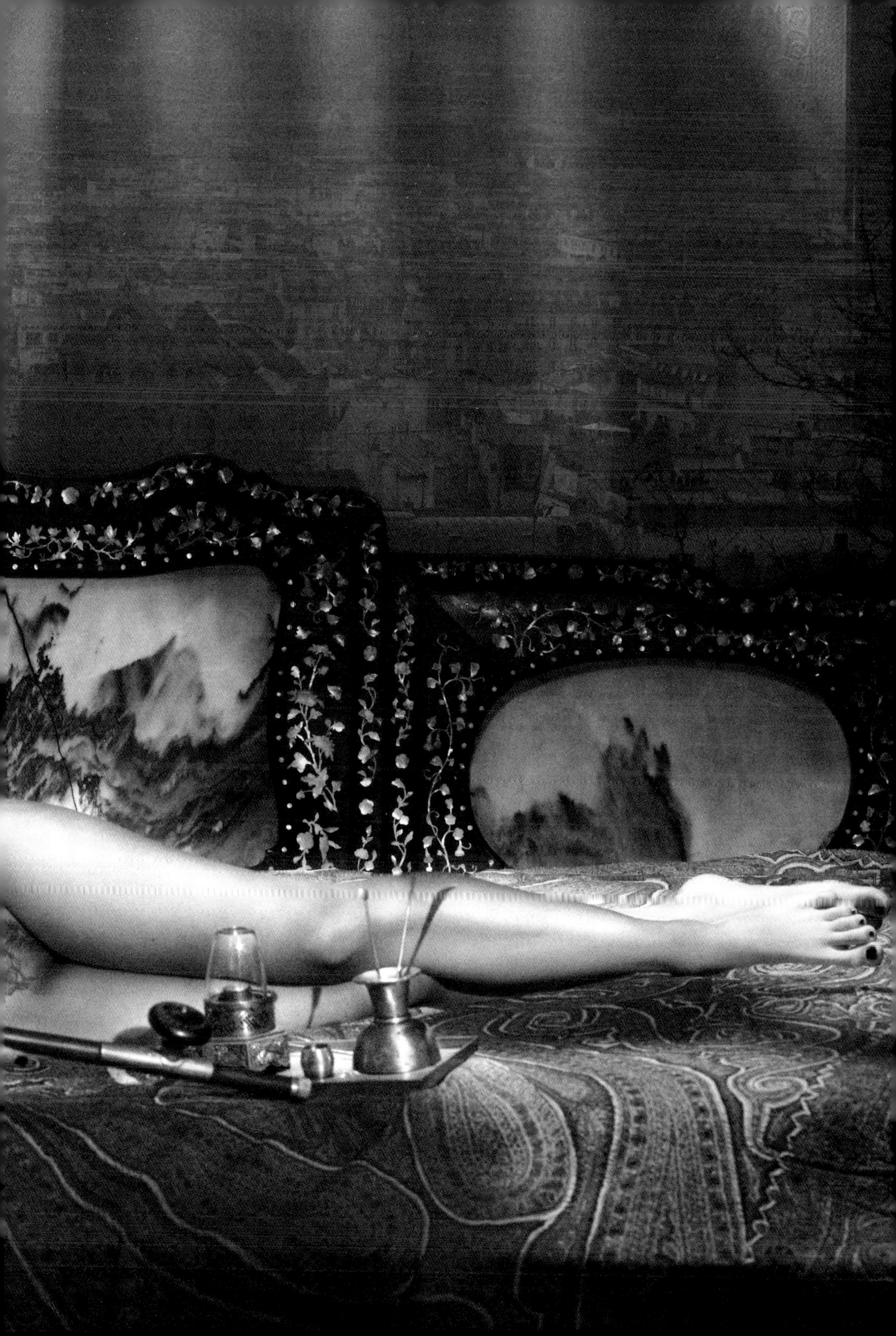

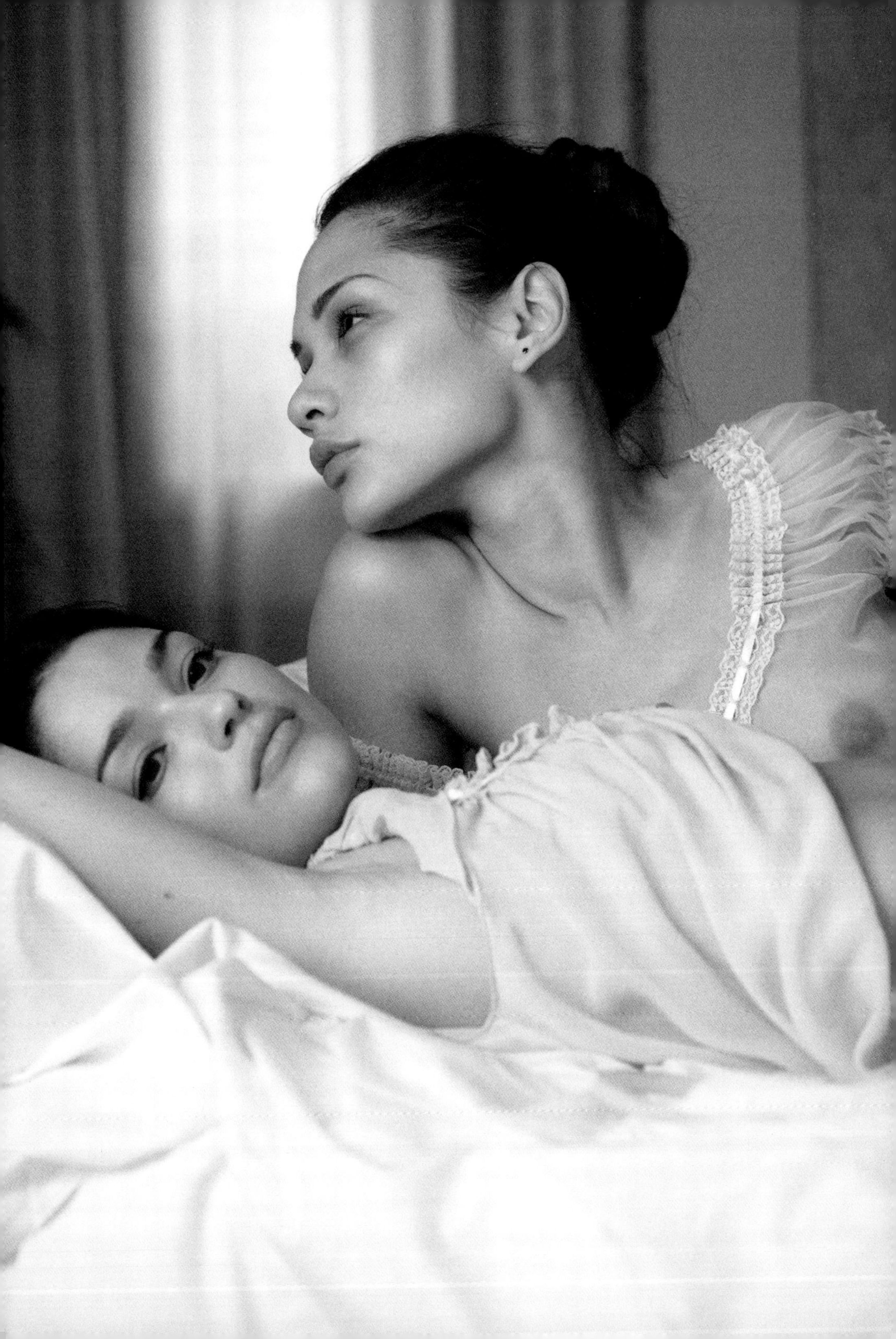

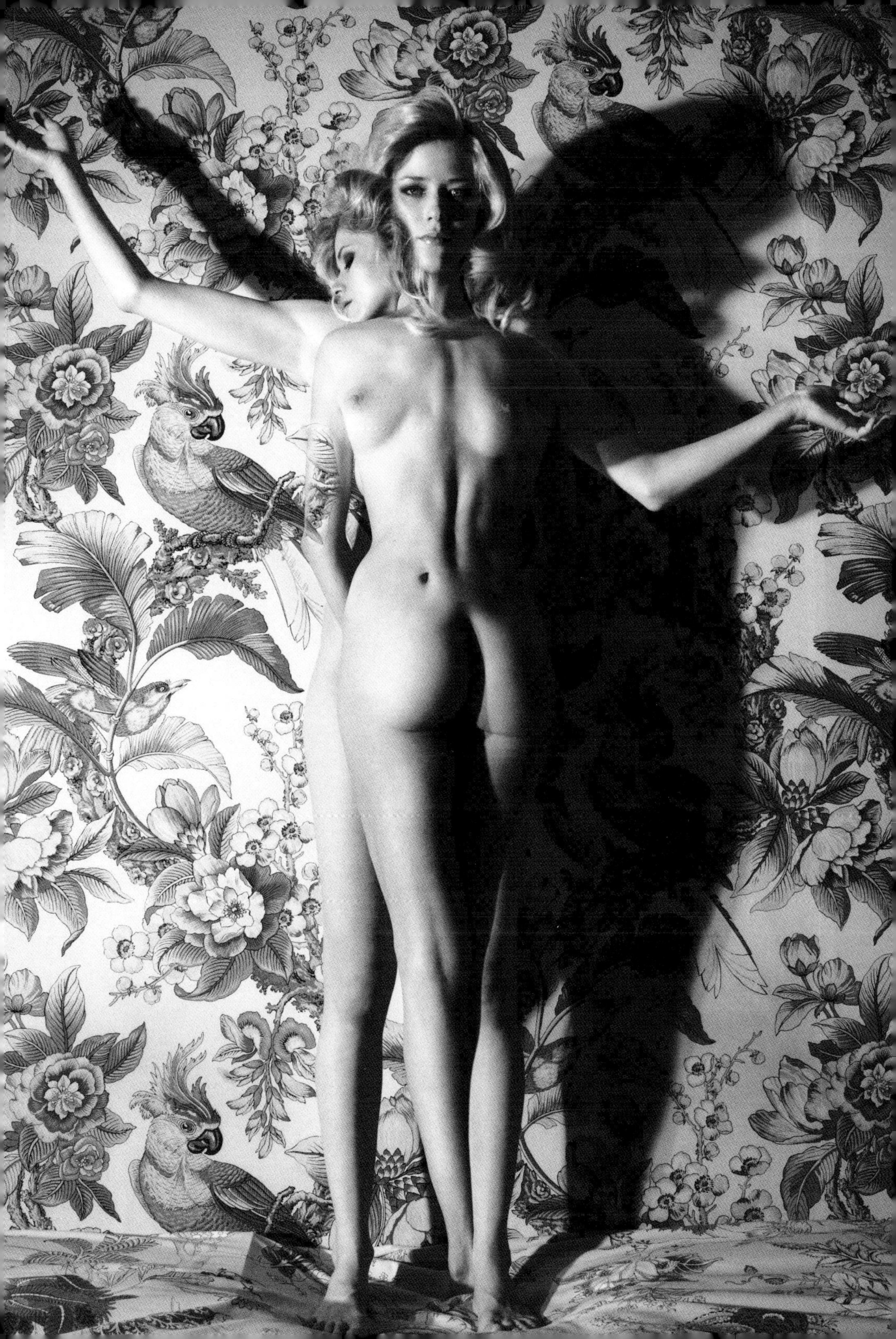

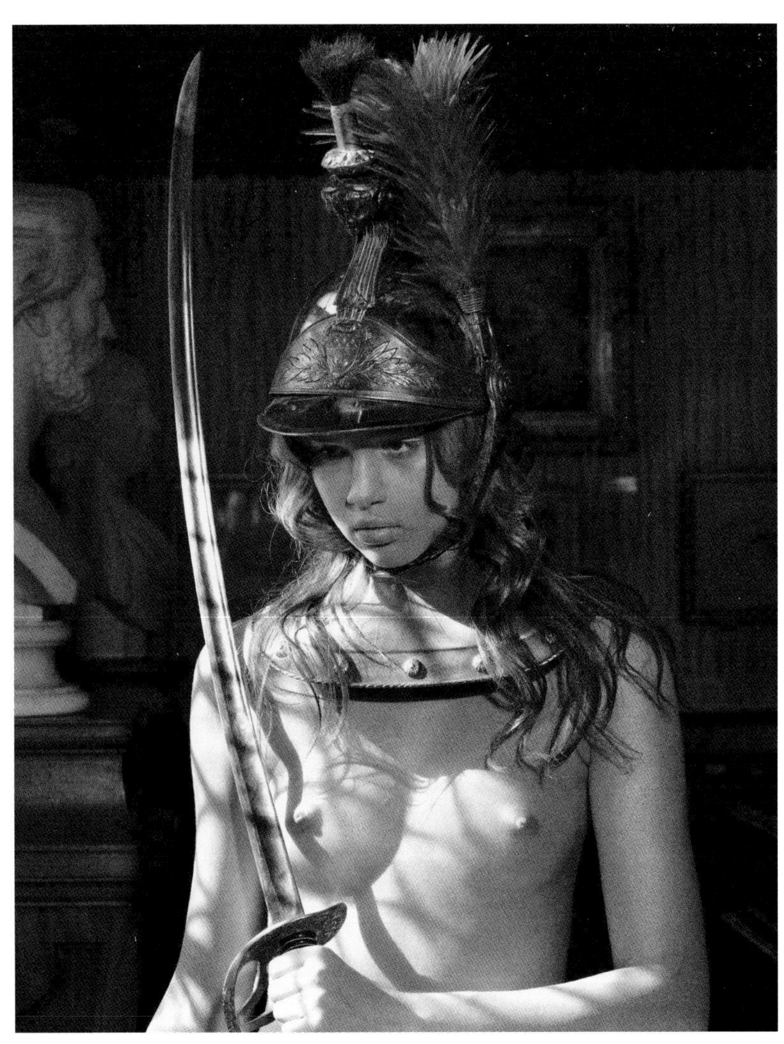

Above — *La fille au casque d'or*, March 2009, Musée de la vie romantique, Paris
Opposite page —*Paris diadème, avec Audrey Marnay*, March 2009, Observatoire de Paris, Paris
Page 424 — *Bouquet de fleurs sur une jonque*, September 2002, Shanghai
Page 425 — *Charlotte Rampling forever avec des bretelles rouges*, February 2006, Paris
Page 426 — *Russian Tatler*, February 2011, Paris
Page 427 — *La joueuse de tennis Tatiana Golovin avec un pack de lait*, December 2004, Paris

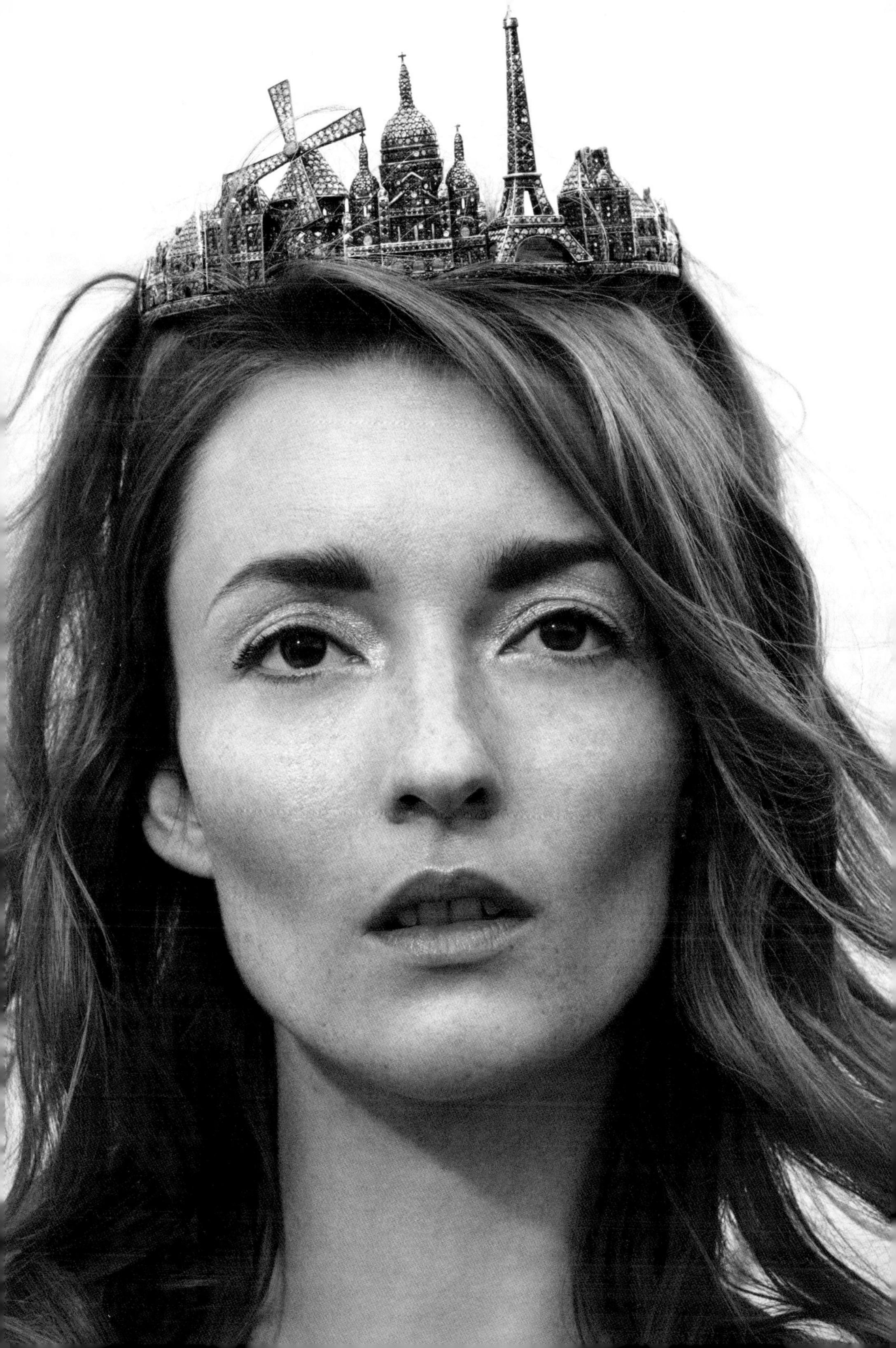

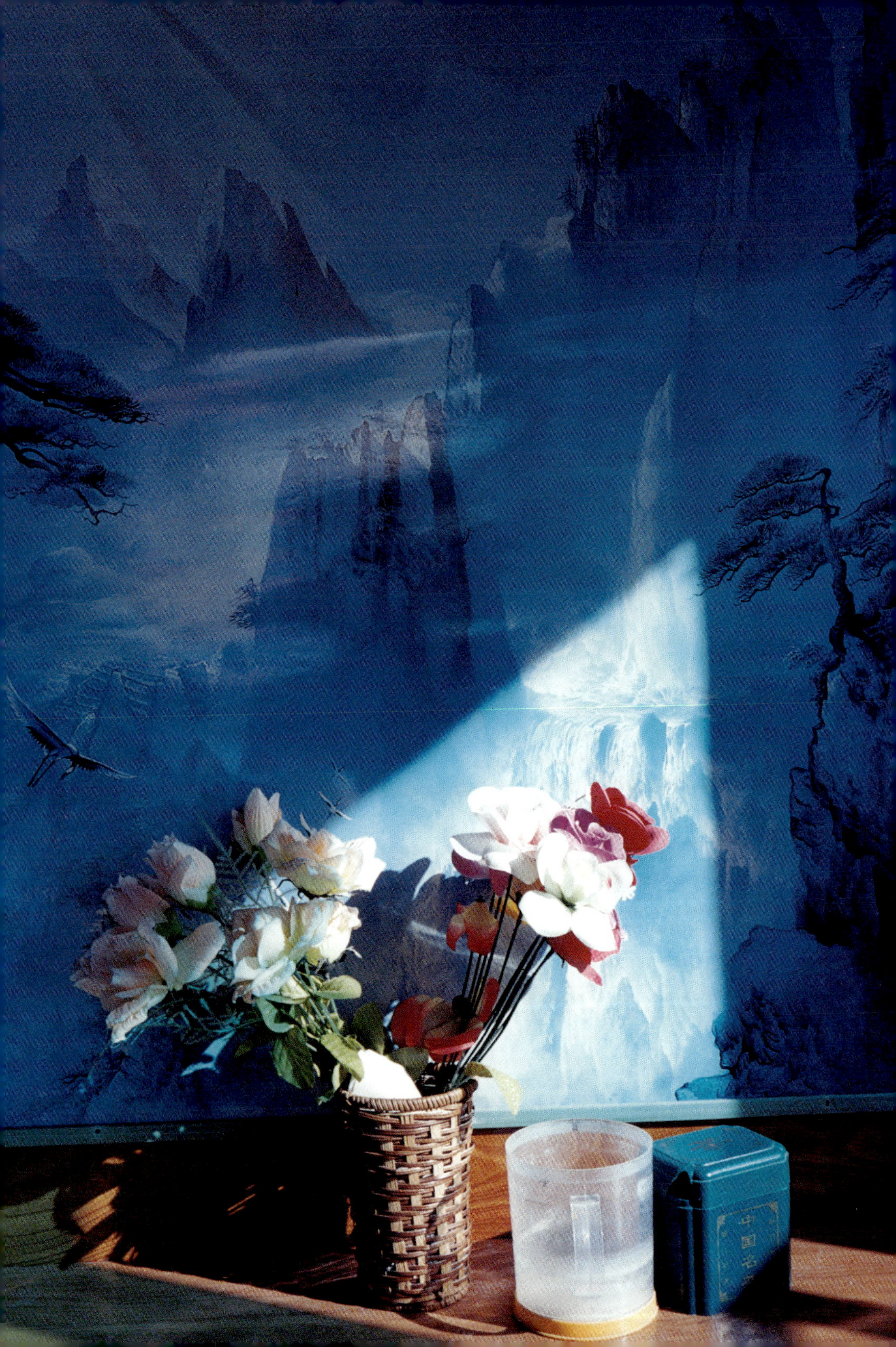

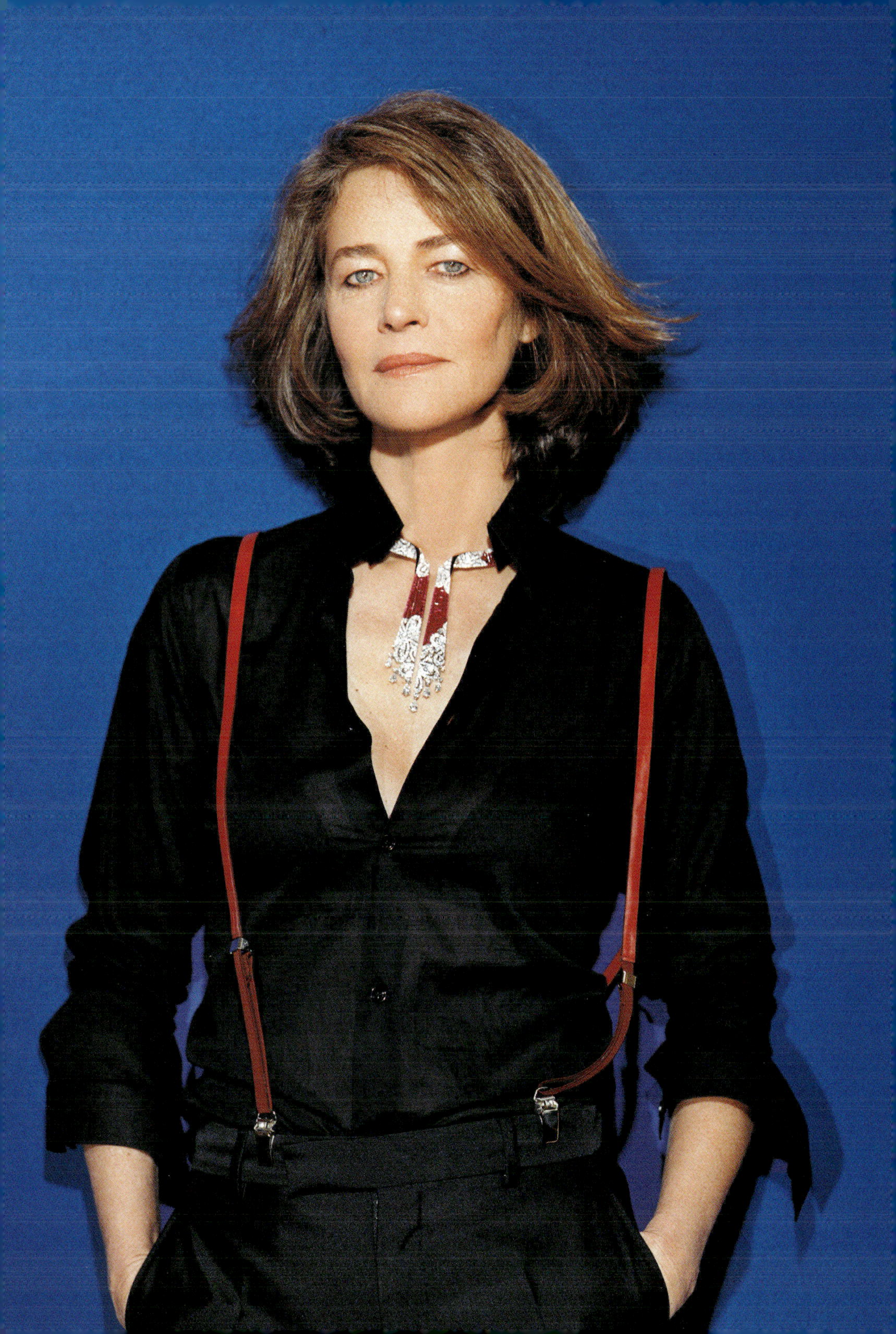

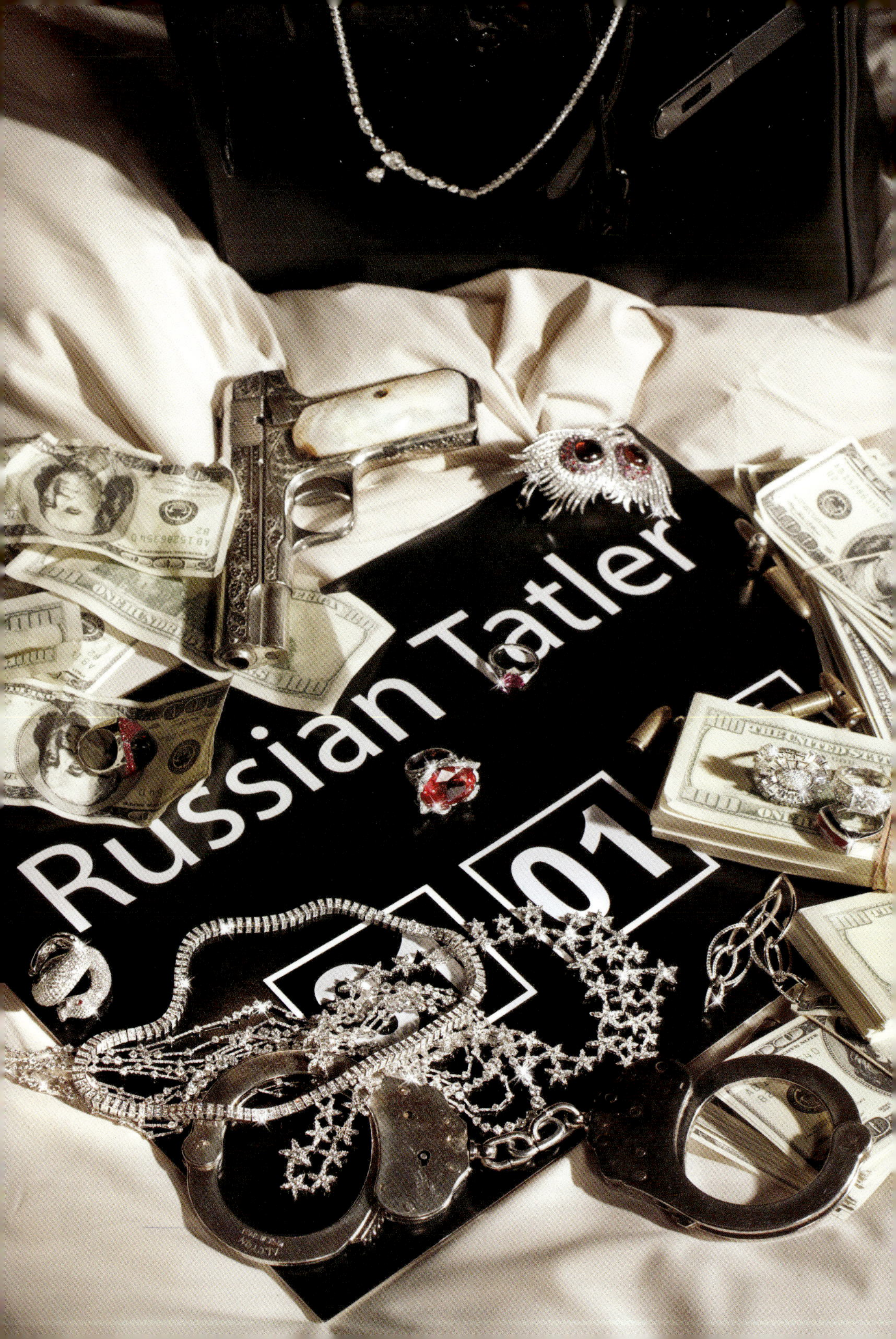

Russian Tatler
01

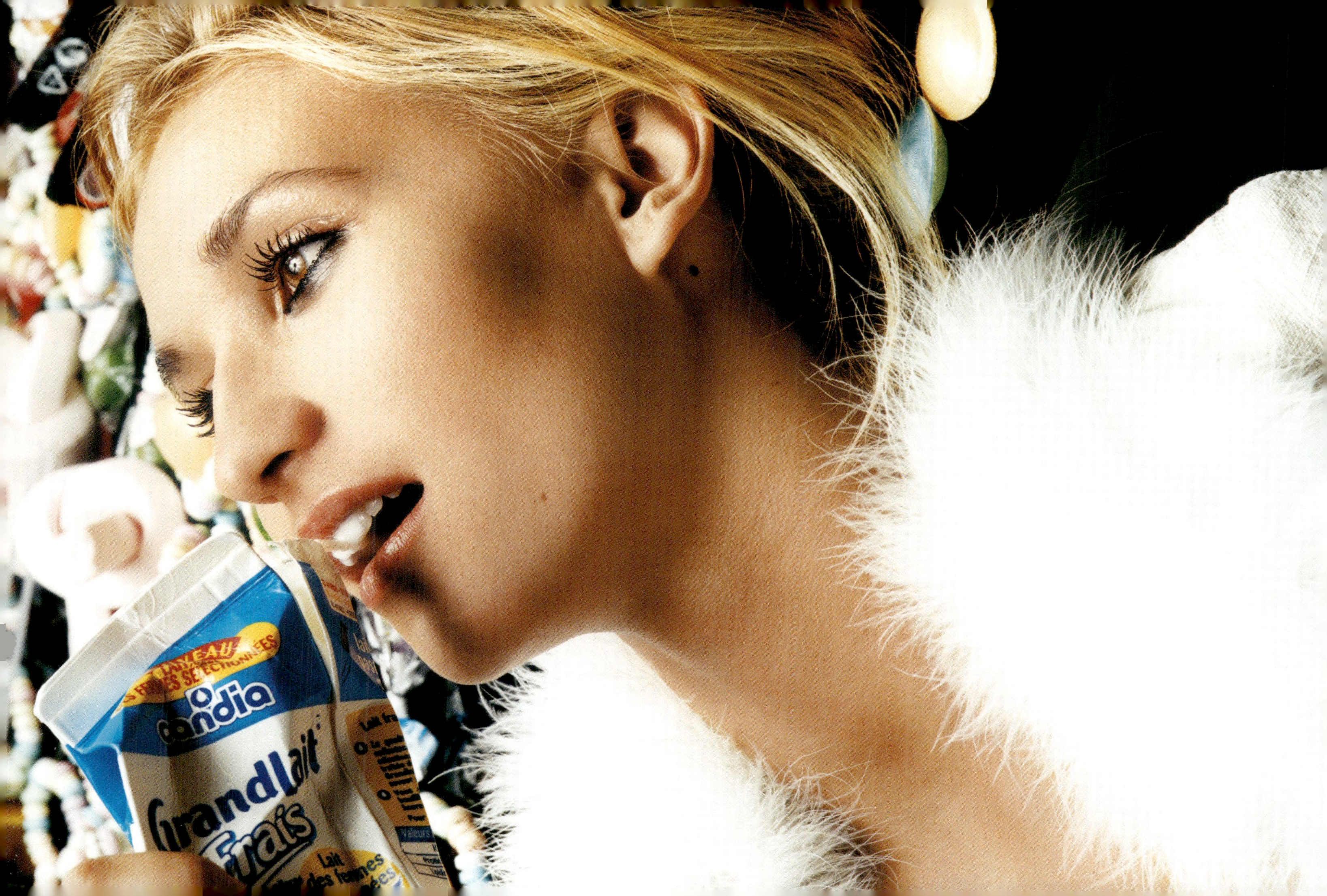
Candia
Grandlait
Grand frais
LES FERMES SÉLECTIONNÉES

Detail of Paz, March 2015, Paris
Following double page—*Paz de la Huerta turned my studio into a garden, for «AIE Magazine»*, March 2015, Paris

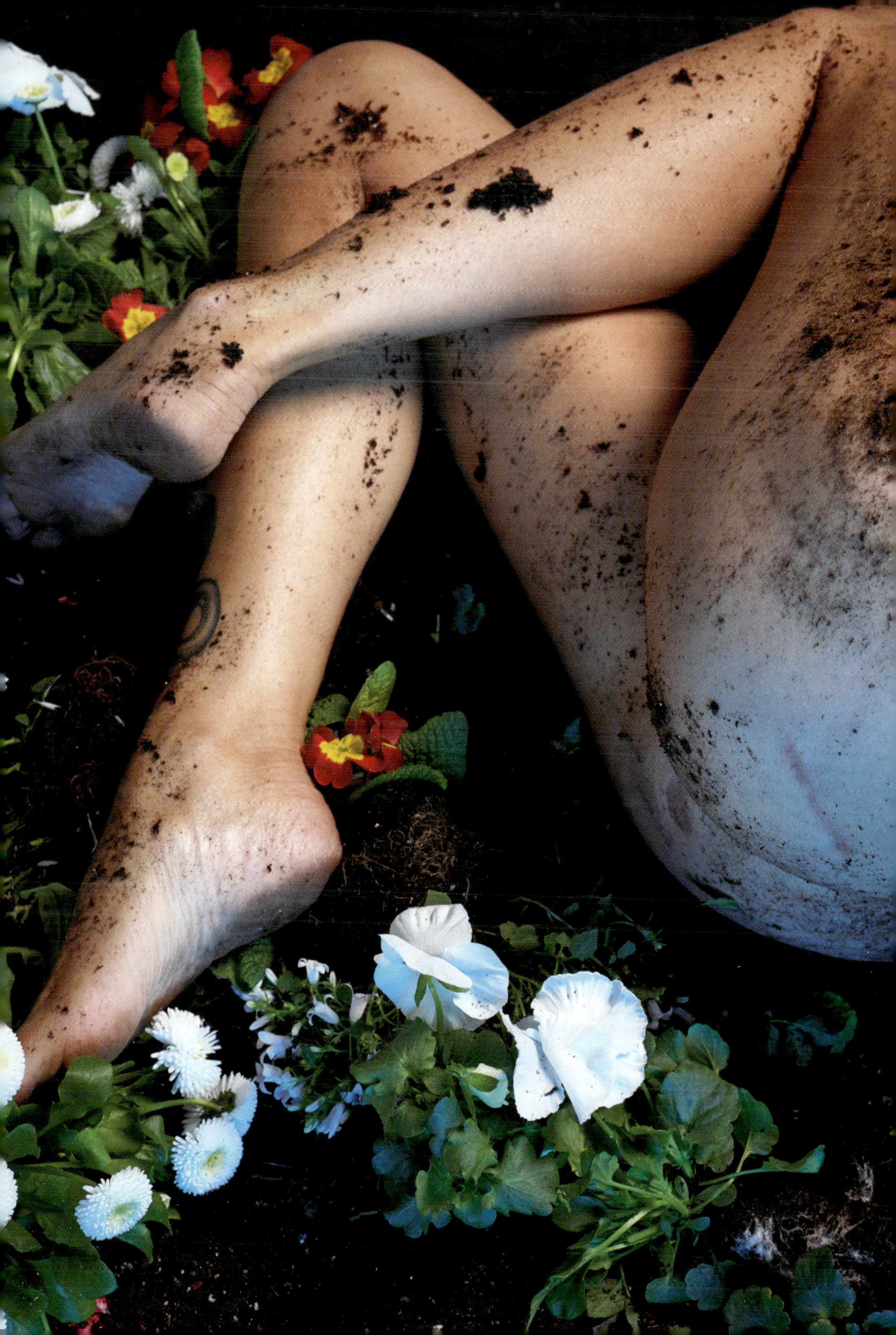

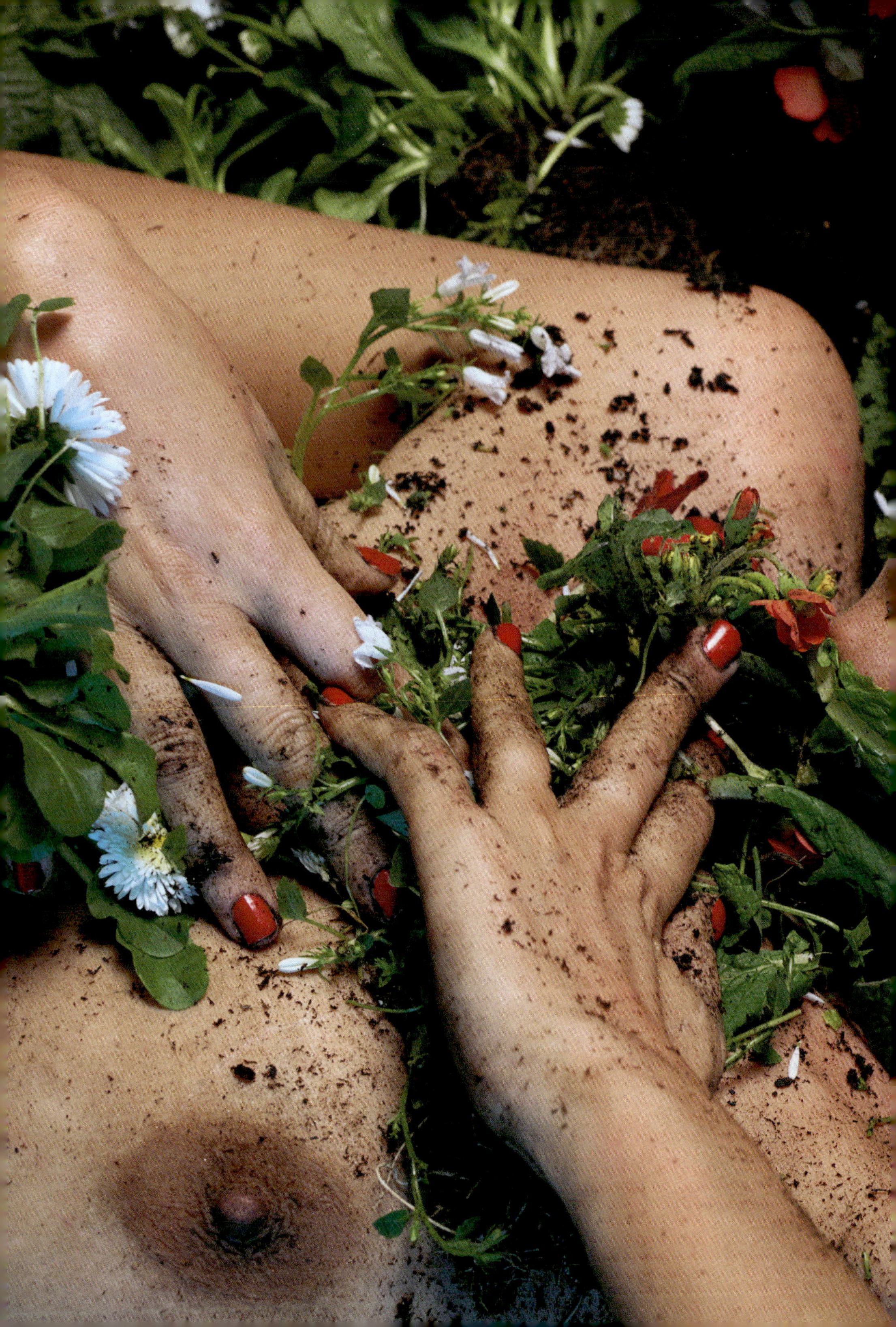

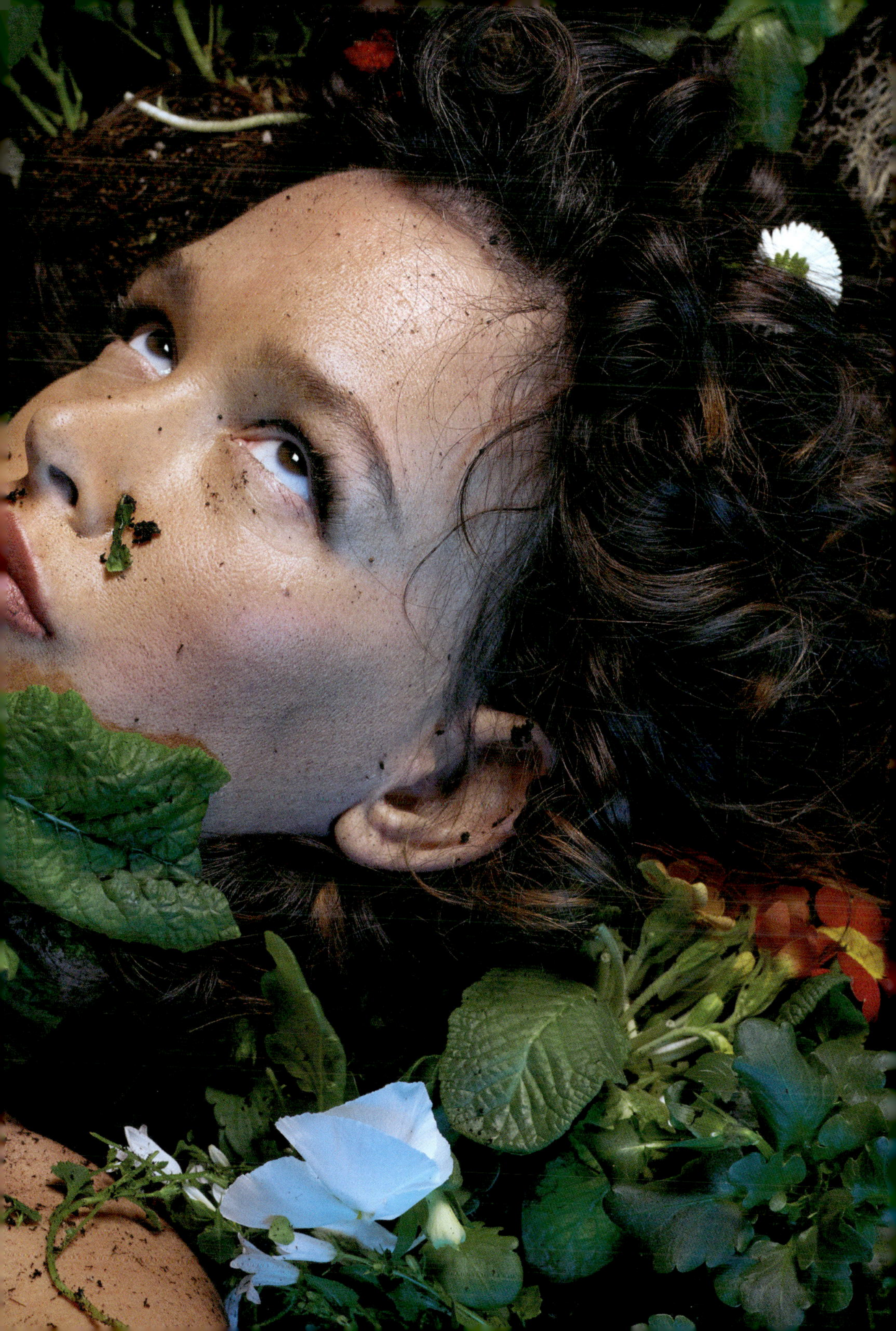

GENDER STUDIES

2011, Paris

I'm me. I have a beard and I wear lipstick. It's quite simple.
Je suis moi. Je mets du rouge à lèvres en ayant de la barbe… tout simplement.
Ich bin ich. Ich trage Lippenstift und habe einen Bart, ganz einfach.

Oh Jack! What a pretty name … for a girl.
Oh Jack! Quel joli nom… pour une fille.
Oh Jack! Das ist ja ein schöner Name… für ein Mädchen.

I'm a boy with a different idea of what is masculine and feminine. I don't like the definitions and I don't live by them.
Je suis un garçon, qui a une conception différente du féminin et du masculin. Je n'aime pas les définitions habituelles et elles n'influencent pas ma vie.
Ich bin ein Junge mit einer anderen Vorstellung von dem, was männlich ist und was weiblich. Ich mag solche Definitionen nicht und richte mein Leben auch nicht nach ihnen aus.

Well, you cannot ask for a transsexual to look like a man. She is fighting all her life to not look like that.
On ne peut pas demander à un transsexuel d'avoir l'air d'un homme. Elle se bat toute sa vie pour s'en éloigner.
Also, du kannst von einer Transsexuellen nicht verlangen, wie ein Mann auszusehen. Sie kämpft ja ihr Leben lang dagegen an, so auszusehen.

It's a weird psychological war between femininity and masculinity for me and I was always in that in-between.
Pour moi, il y a une guerre psychologique bizarre entre féminité et masculinité, et j'ai toujours été dans cet entre-deux.
Für mich gibt es einen merkwürdigen Psychokrieg zwischen Weiblichkeit und Männlichkeit, und ich stand immer irgendwo zwischen den Fronten.

Extracts from Frédéric Sanchez's sound piece, 2011

Alexandre S. III, June 2011, Paris
Page 434 — *Simon K. I*, June 2011, Paris
Page 435 — *Dafné C.*, June 2011, Paris

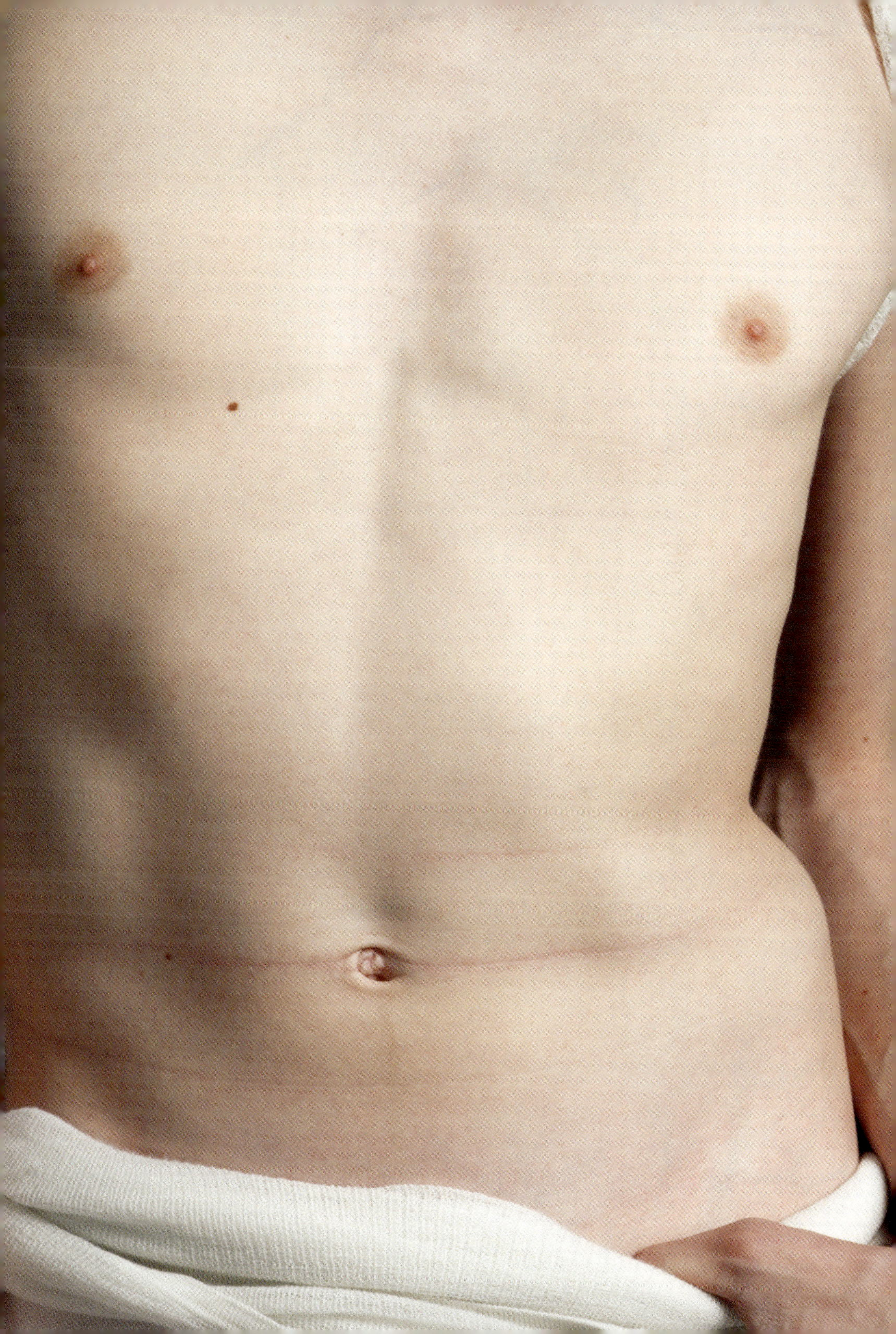

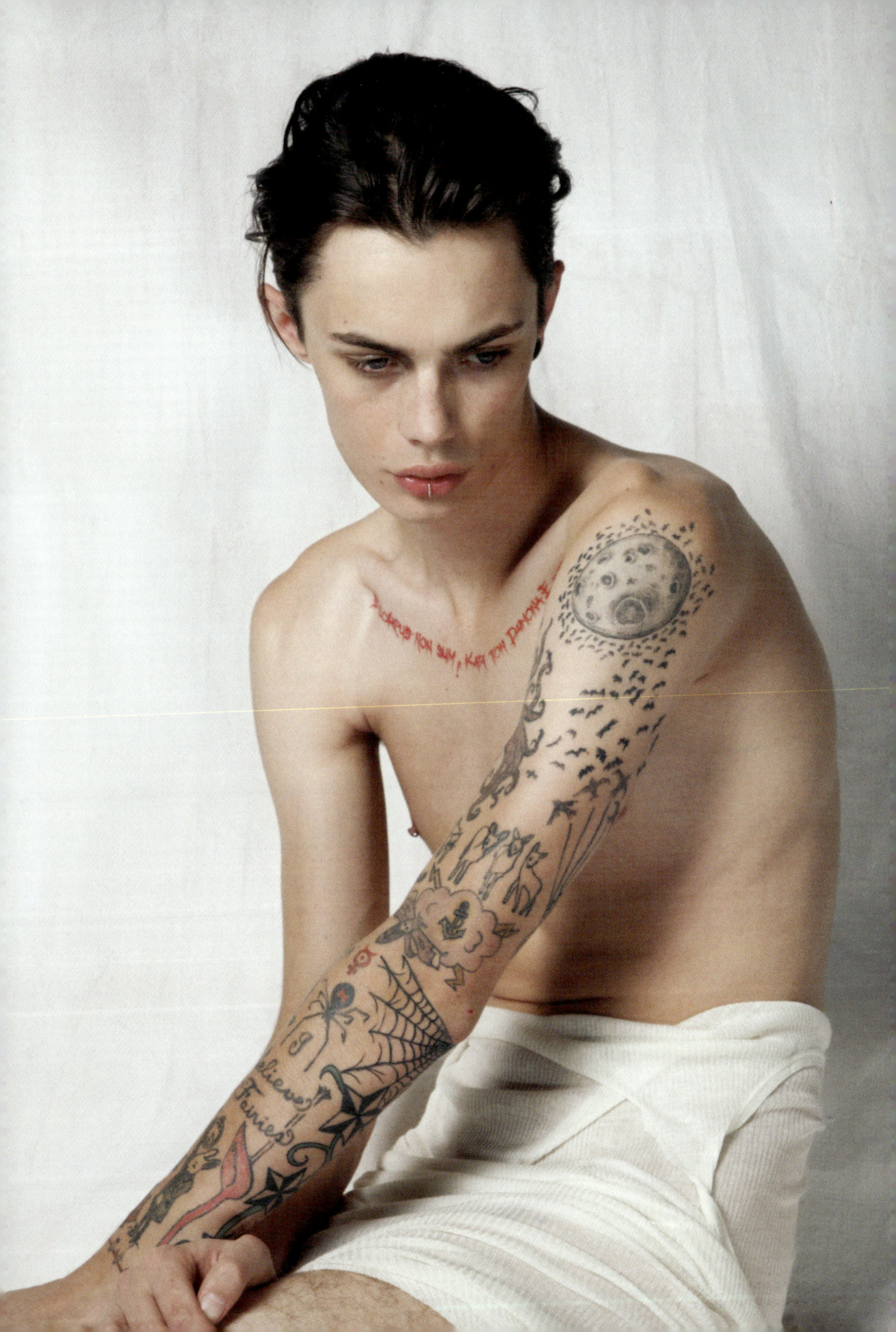

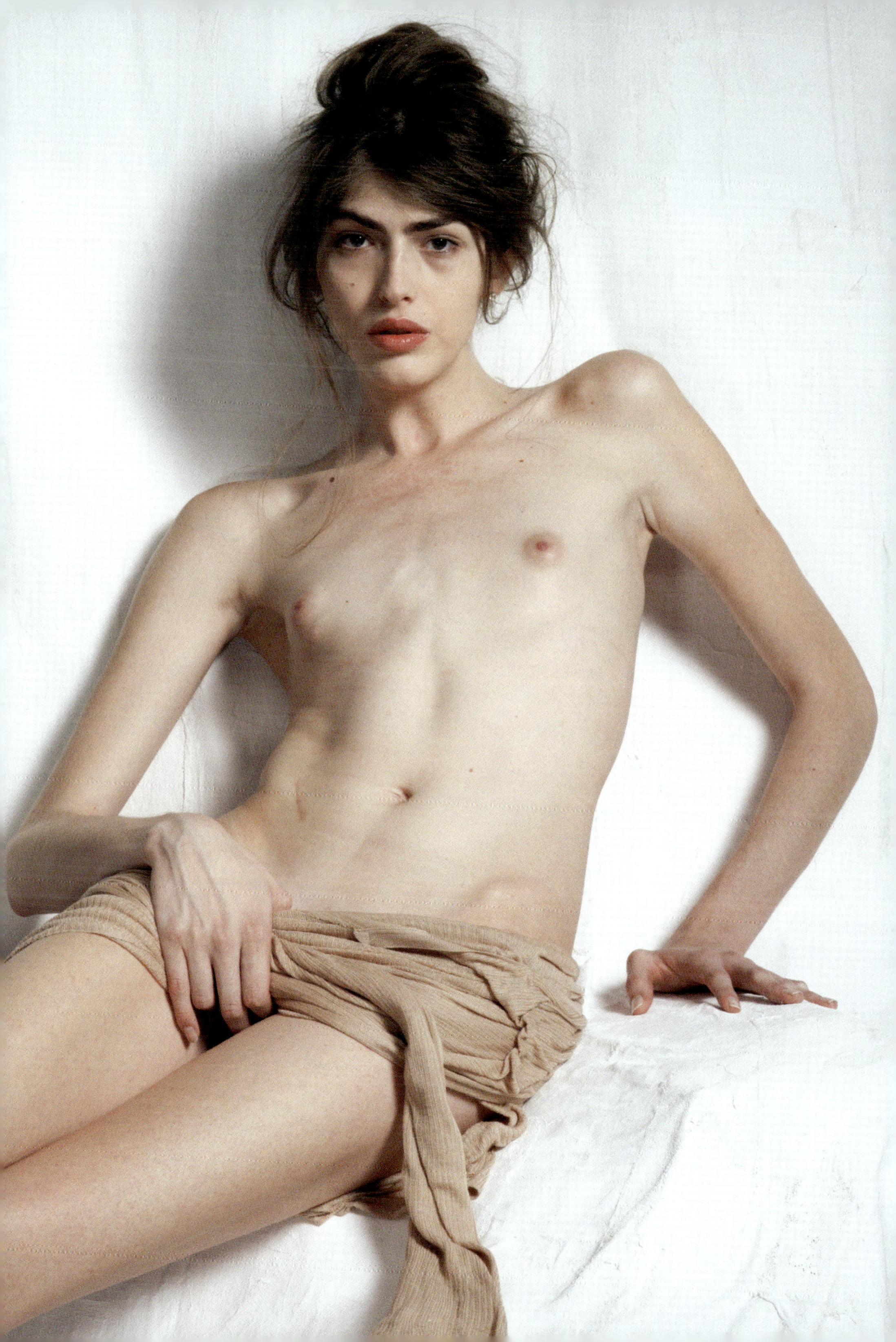

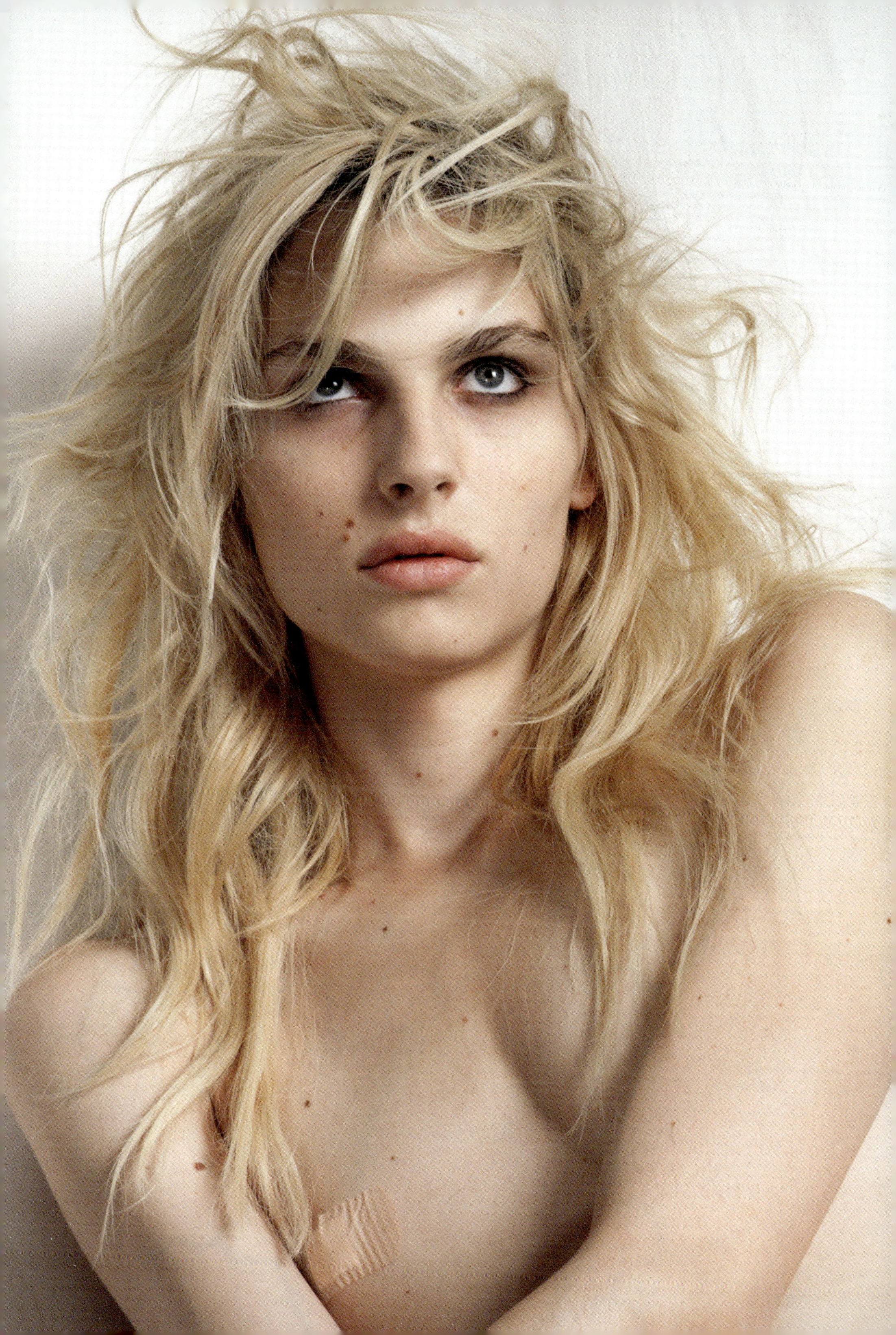

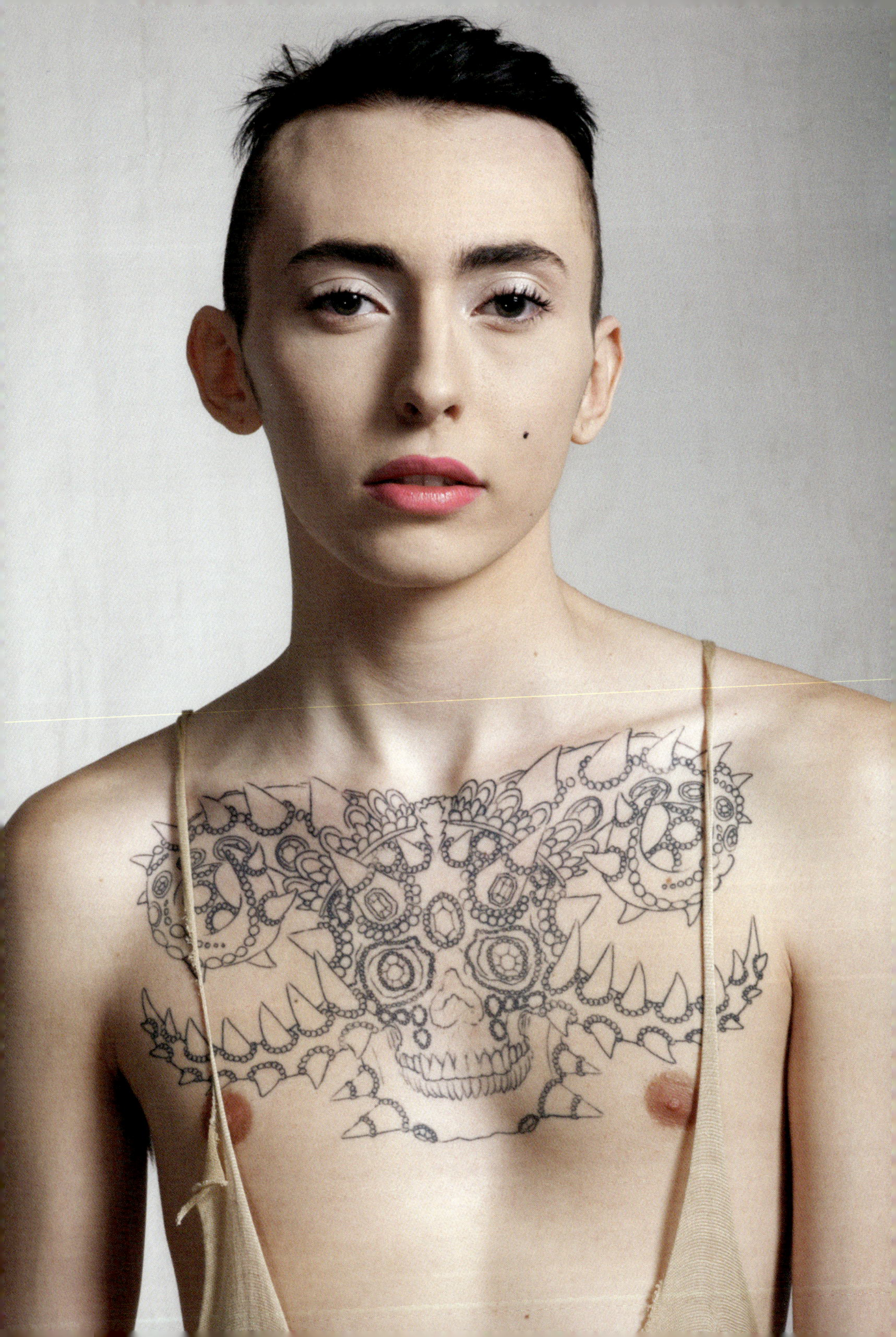

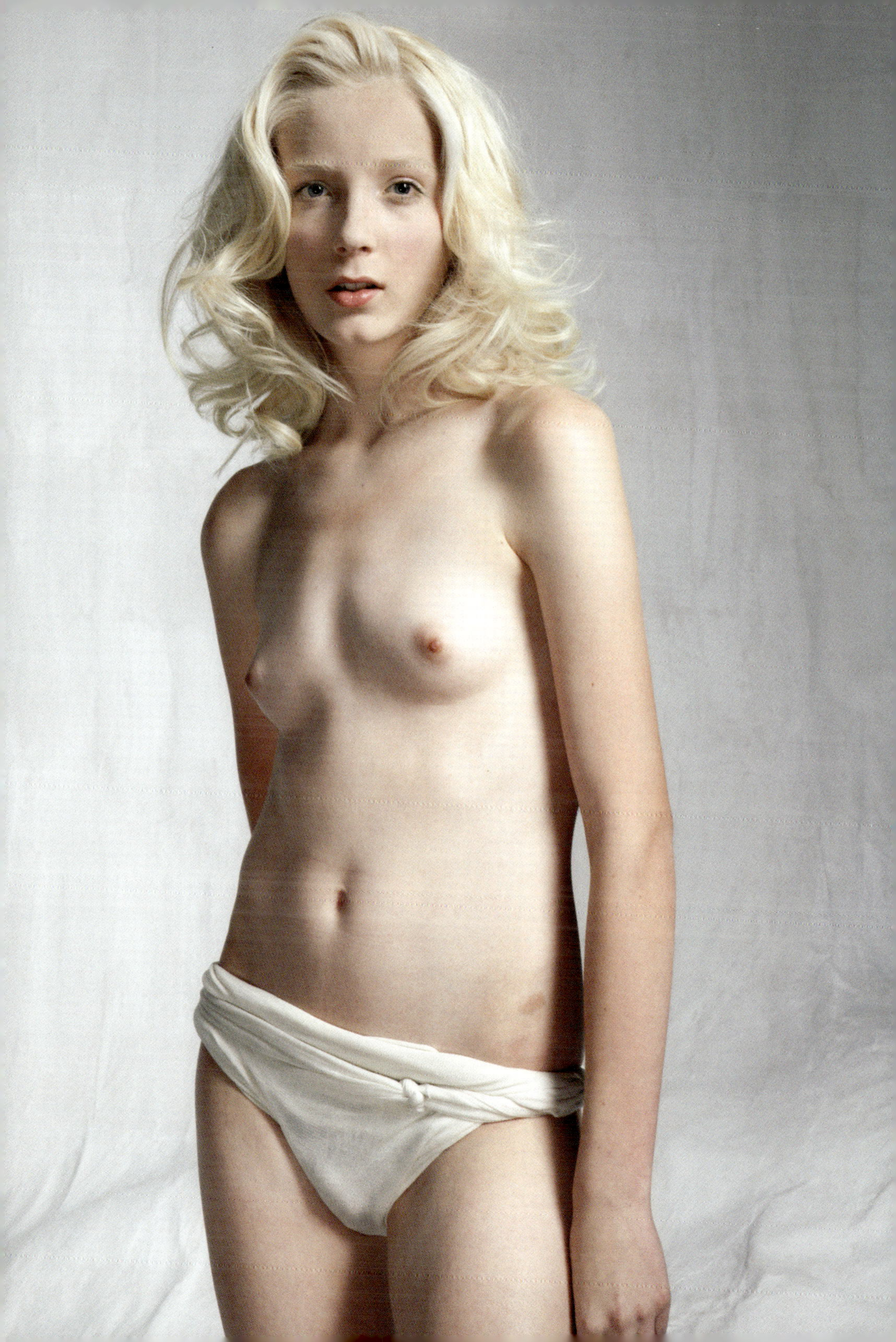

BONKERS!
A FORTNIGHT IN LONDON
2013, London

"It" girls, that we managed to stop momentarily in their frantic maelstrom (...)
Wonderful frivolous girls, dancing on the ruins of our burning world, playing with their constantly changing character, bravely reminding us that life is only a game.

Des «It girls», qu'on a réussi à stopper un moment de leur course frénétique (...)
Divines et frivoles, dansant sur les ruines de notre pauvre monde en crise. Elles jouent, se transforment et se réinventent pour nous rappeler, avec courage, que la vie n'est qu'un jeu.

„It-Girls", die wir einen Augenblick lang in ihrem besessenen Lauf anhalten konnten (...)
Göttlich und frivol tanzen sie auf den Ruinen unserer armen, krisengeschüttelten Welt. Sie spielen, verwandeln sich und erfinden sich neu, um uns mutig daran zu erinnern, dass das Leben nur ein Spiel ist.

Bettina Rheims, in *Bonkers*, 2014

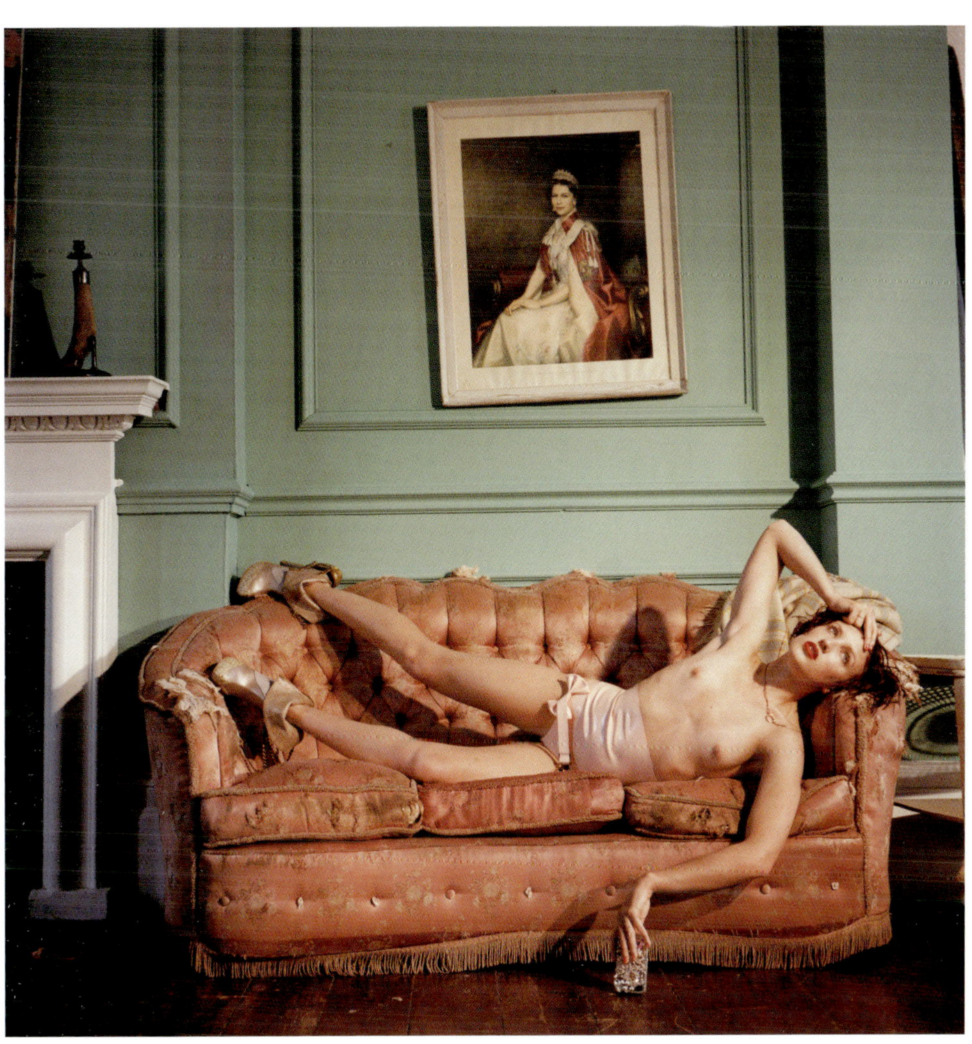

Georgie Bee wearing her own amazing shoes, June 2013, London
Page 442 – *Harriet Verney Sweet Queenie daydreaming*, June 2013, London
Page 443 – *Amber Le Bon has lost ... her car keys*, June 2013, London

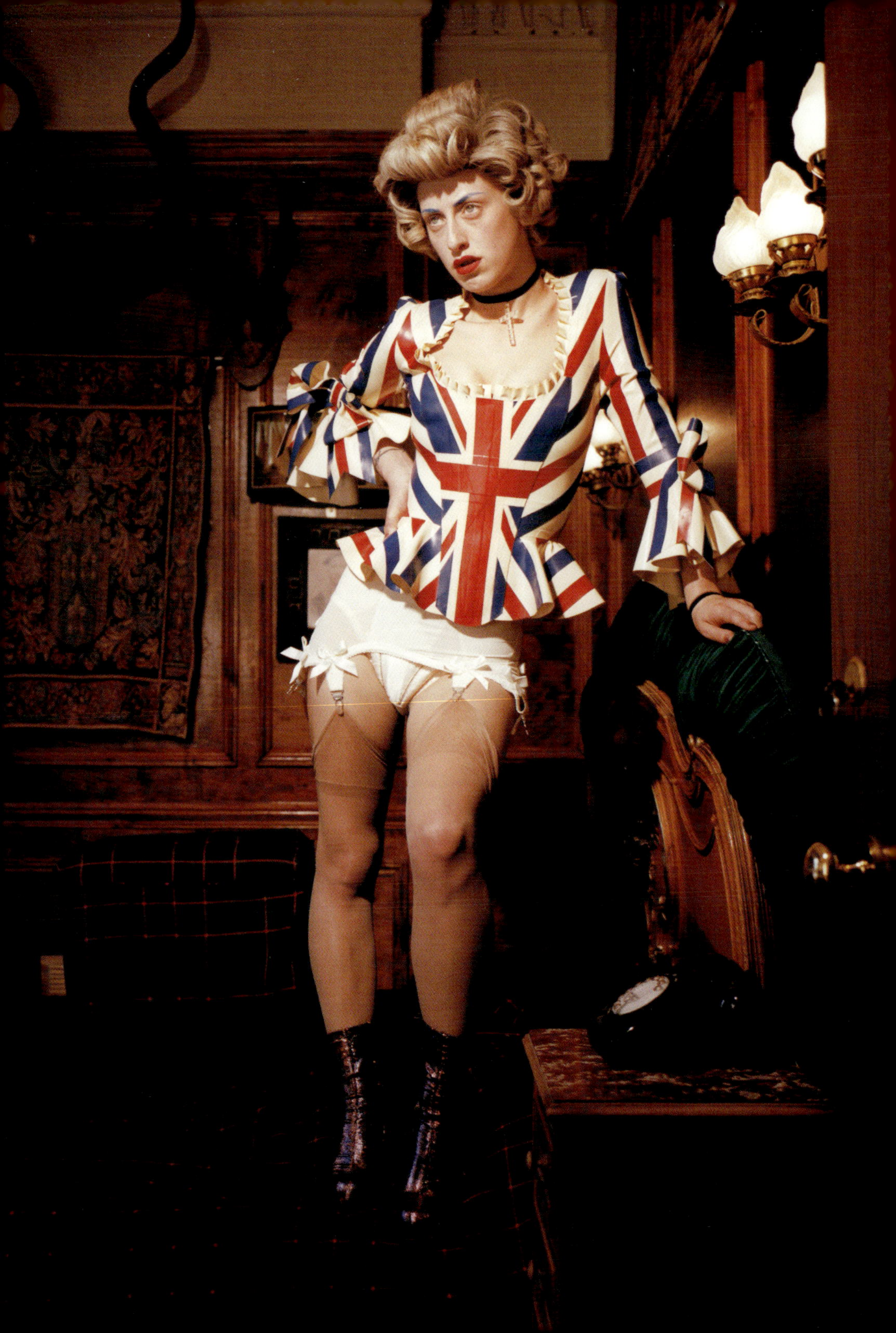

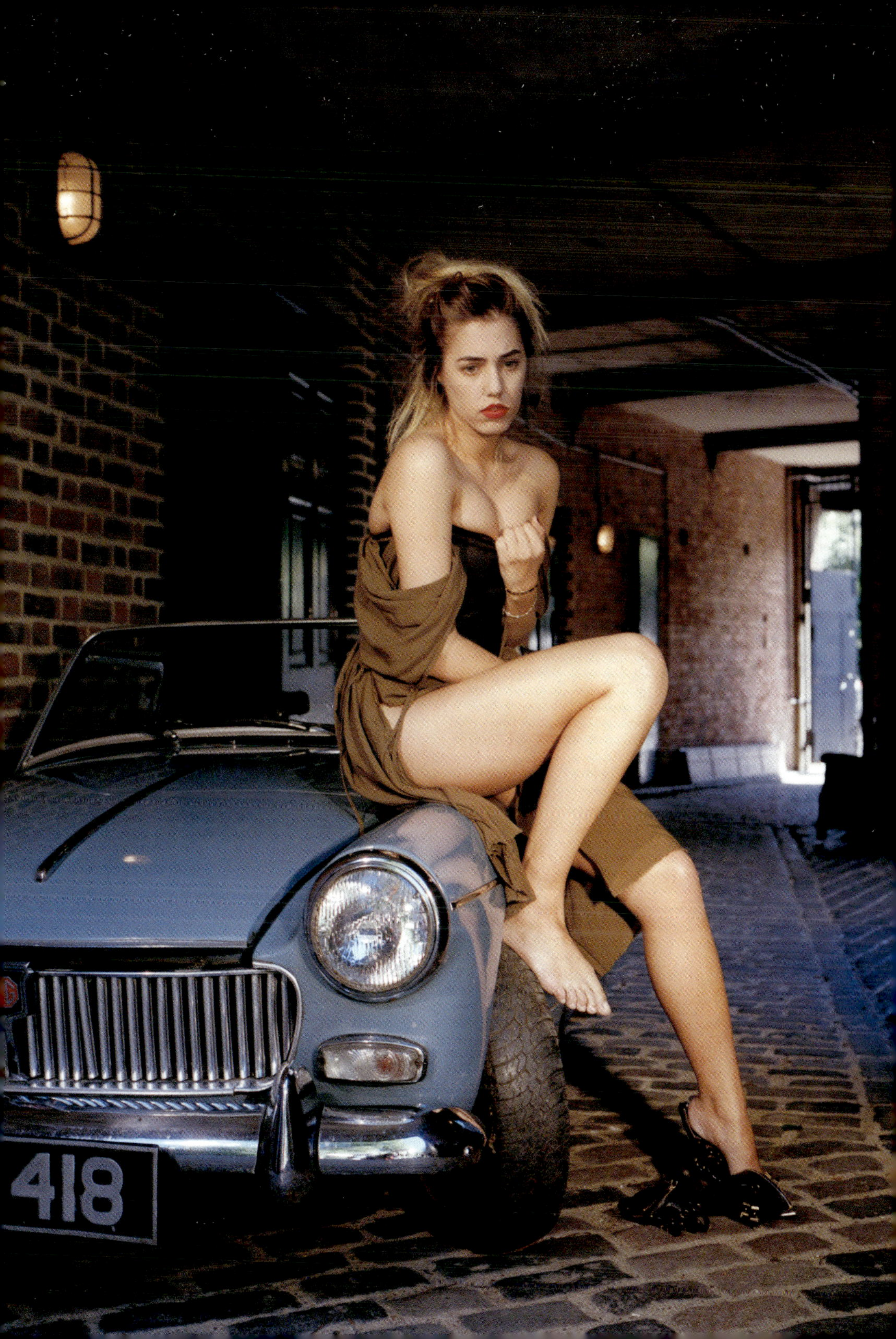

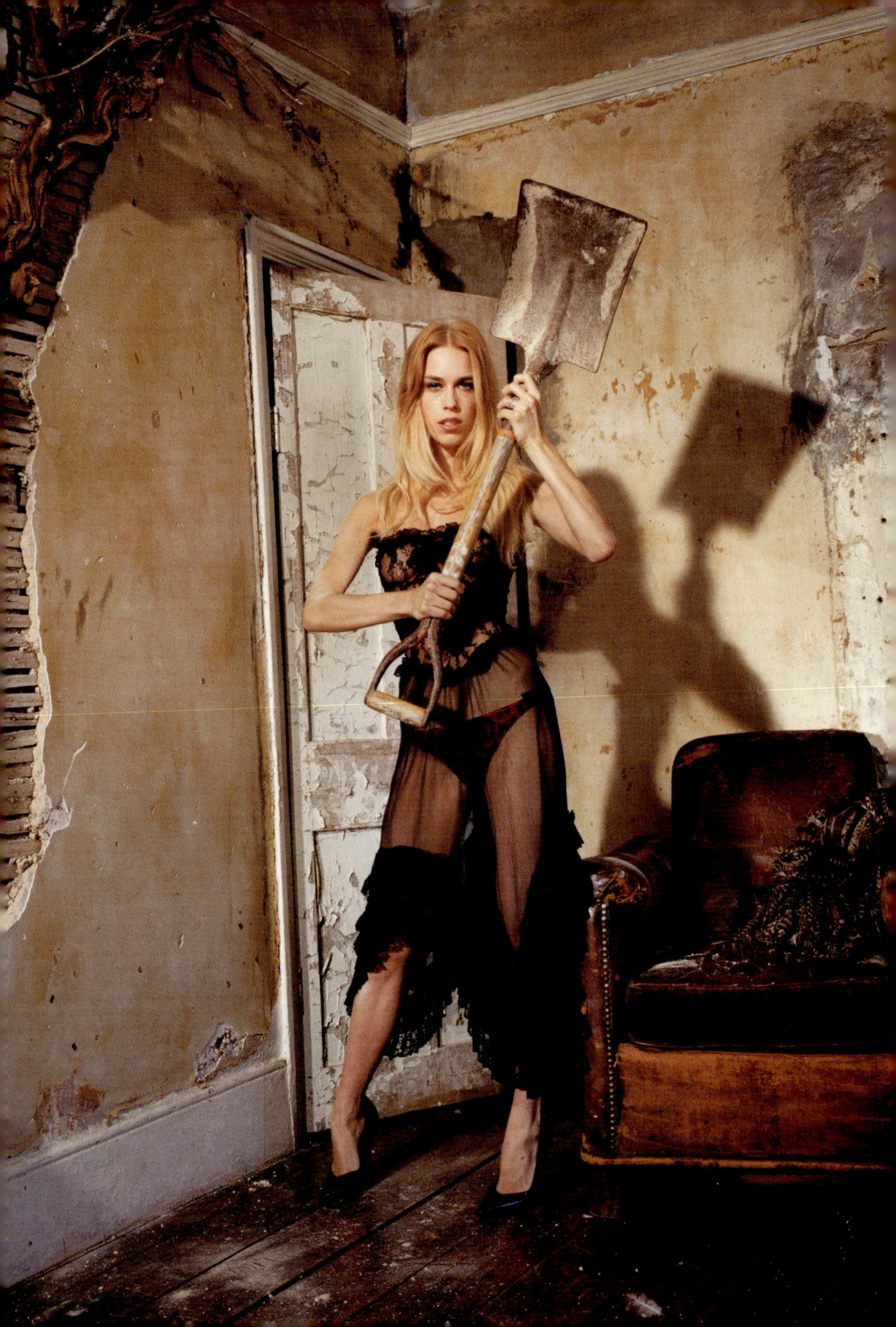

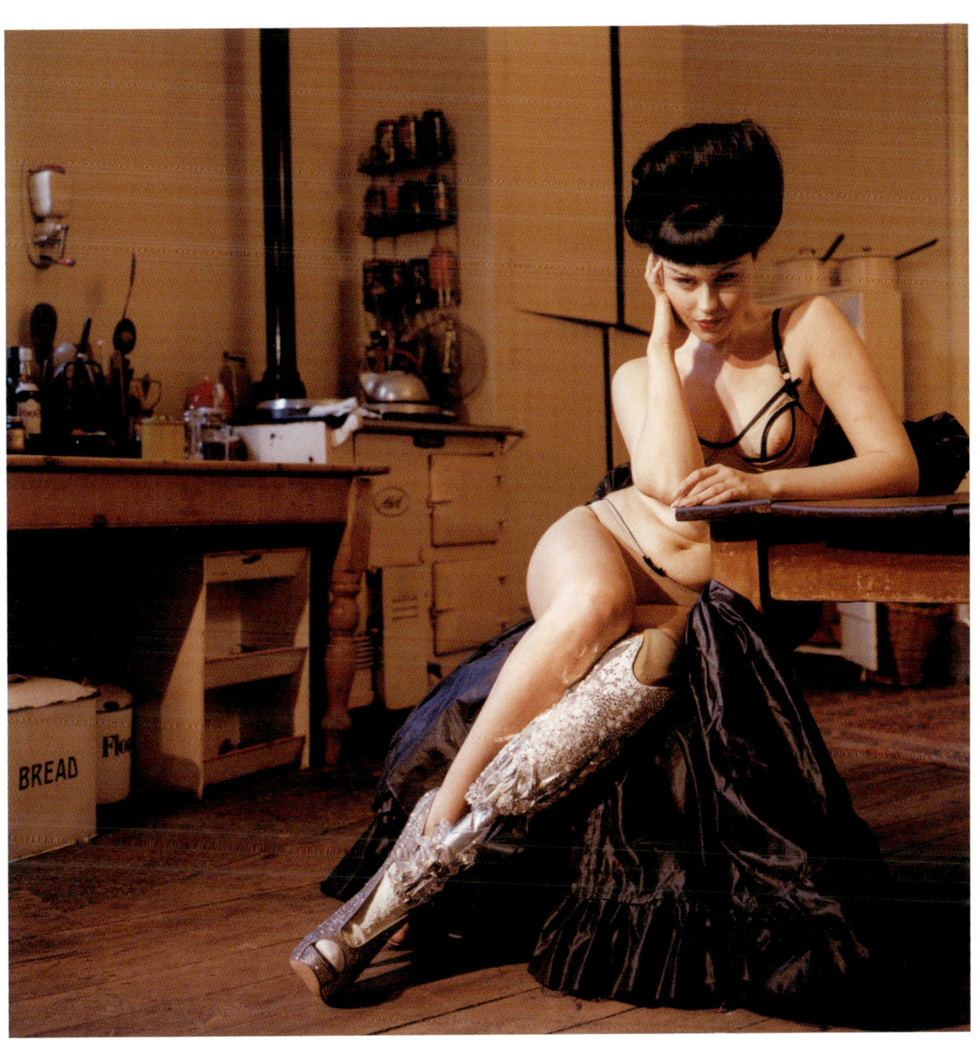

Above — *Viktoria Modesta, bionic girl with a crystal leg,* June 2013, London
Opposite page — *Mary Charteris knocking on heaven's door,* June 2013, London
Page 446 — *Arabella Drummond, Pirate and Fire Artist,* June 2013, London
Page 447 — *Dioni Tabbers, Miss Wilde,* June 2013, London

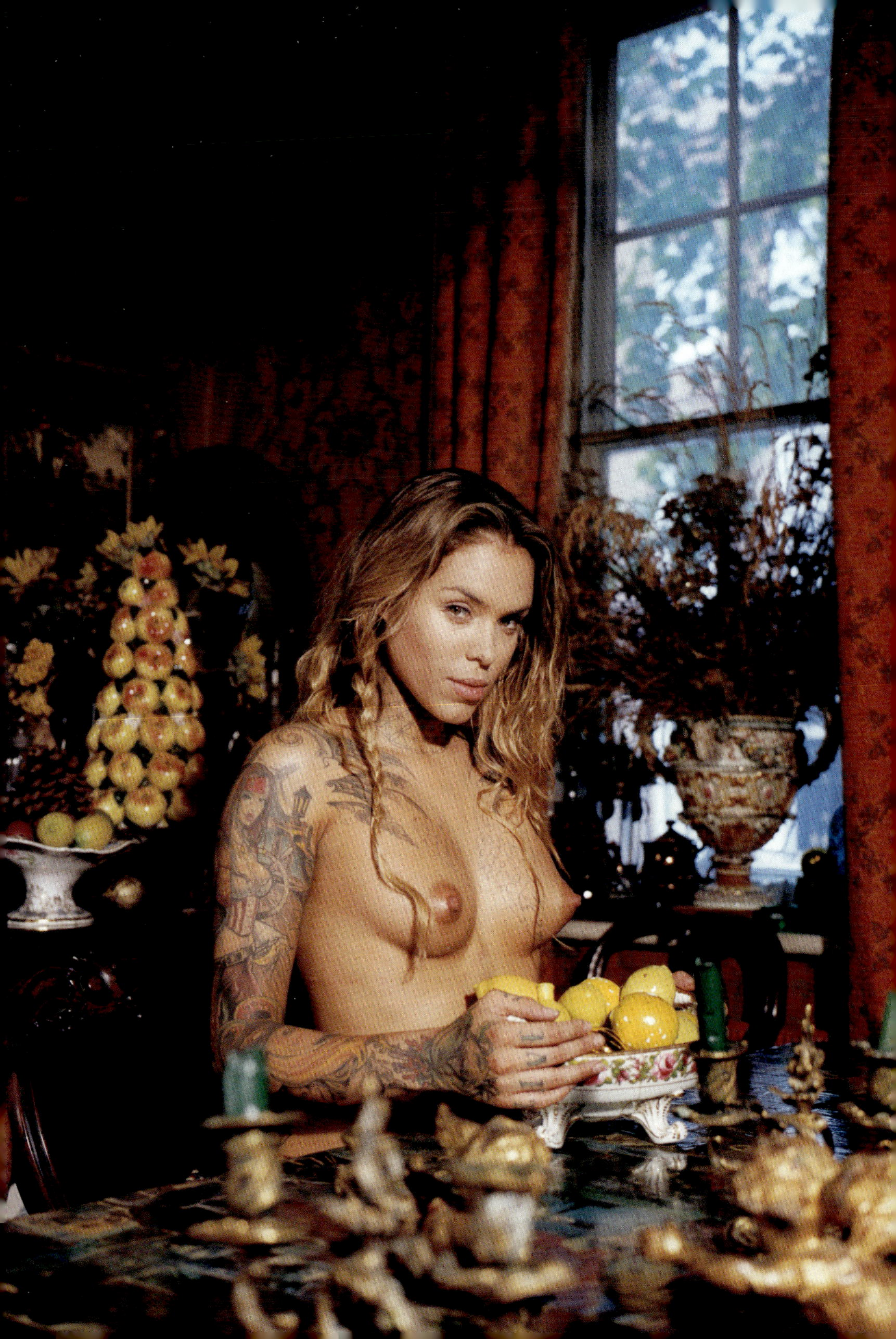

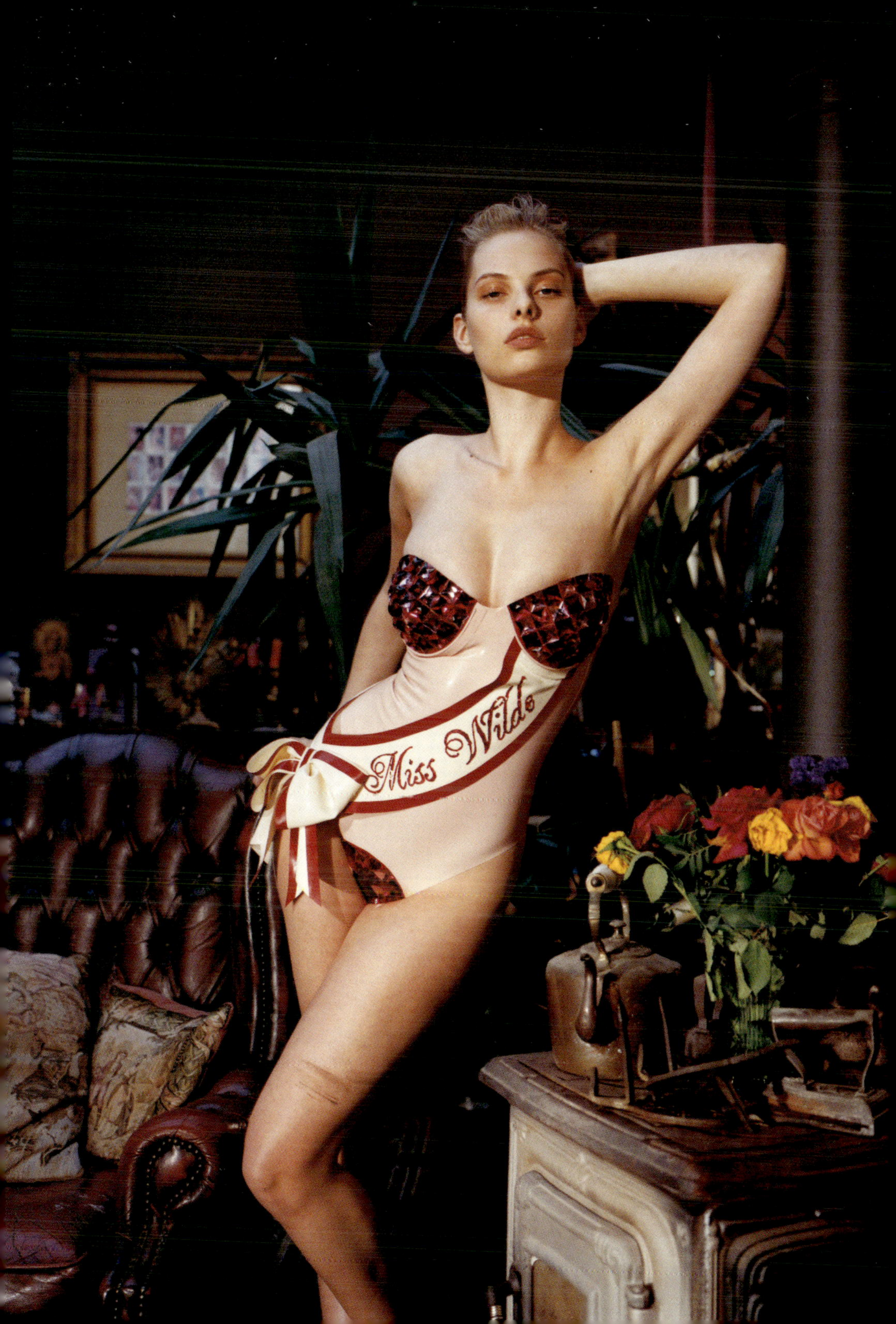
Miss Wilde

Tessa Kuragi Killing me softly with a Rope, June 2013, London

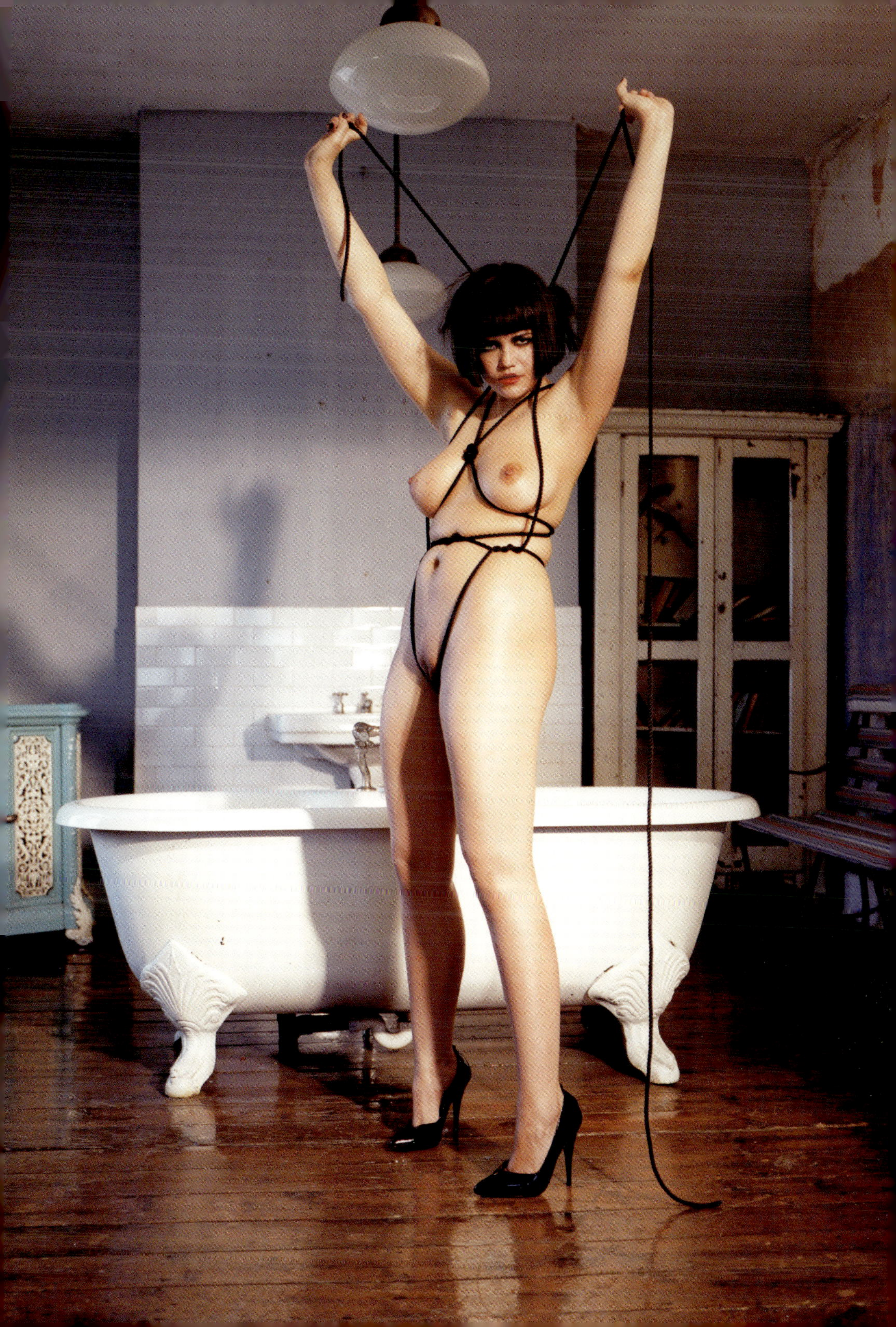

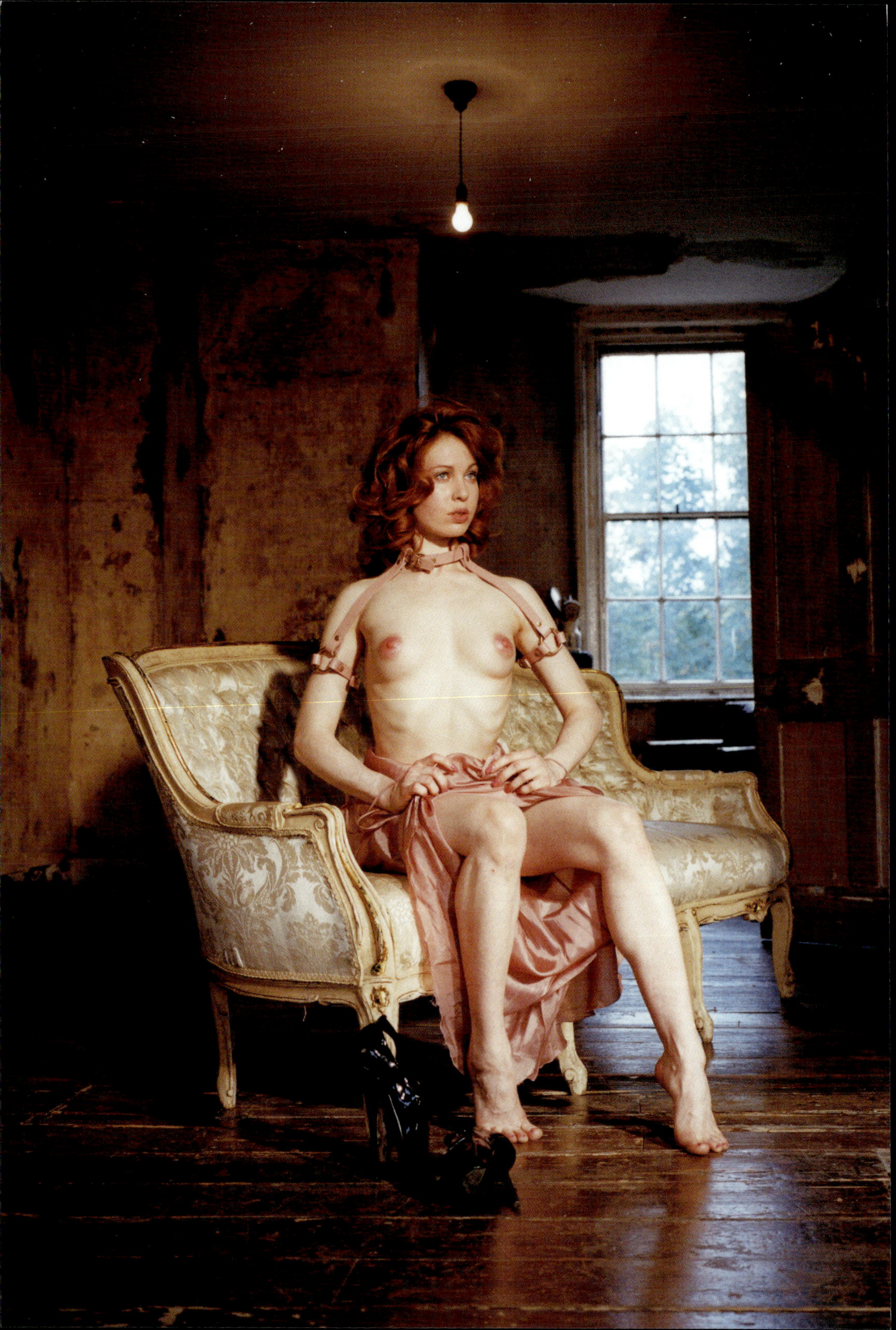

VOILÀ!

Voilà! Almost 40 years of photography – years, that have passed as if in a dream.
In this book, I have tried to pick out the finest moments of those years, creating a sort of autobiography in images.
Some of these images are well-known; others, drawn from my archives, have never been published before.
Images but also memories: my family, the people I love, the women that have inspired me, but also all those
that I only briefly photographed and who nevertheless touched my heart.
And then there are the teams that accompanied me: stylists, hairdressers, make-up artists.
All those who showed and defended my work: gallerists, museums, and the people who supported me by
writing texts that inspired new images.
The studio with its marvelous assistants, overflowing with talent, who patiently endured my changing moods.
And finally everyone who has accompanied me in the making of this book over the last year.
Without Serge Bramly, I should never have become a photographer and my life would have been less wonderful.
My husband Jean-Michel Darrois astounds me, moves me, and makes me laugh; I have loved him for 20 years.
With him, I have had the pleasure of watching Stanislas grow.
My son Virgile is everything to me and has presented me with the greatest daughter-in-law, Audrey.
And last but not least, to Alfred, just one year old: so that one day he will understand that his grandmother
was a very strange woman.

Voilà! Presque quarante années de photographie... Années qui ont passé comme dans un rêve.
J'ai essayé avec ce livre, d'en extraire les meilleurs moments, une sorte d'autobiographie en images. Des images
plutôt connues, d'autres complètement inédites, puisées dans mes archives. Mais aussi des souvenirs. Ma famille,
les gens que j'aime, les femmes qui m'ont inspirée, mais aussi celles et ceux que je n'ai que brièvement rencontrés
au cours d'une séance et qui m'ont touchée.
Et puis, il y a les équipes qui m'ont accompagnée. Les stylistes, les coiffeurs, les maquilleurs.
Ceux qui ont montré et défendu mon travail: les galeristes, les musées, ainsi que ceux qui l'ont soutenu en écrivant
des textes qui m'ont inspiré de nouvelles images.
Le Studio avec les assistants merveilleux et bourrés de talent qui ont eu la patience de supporter mes humeurs.
Enfin toutes les personnes qui pendant une année m'ont accompagnée dans la fabrication de ce livre.
Sans Serge Bramly, je ne serais pas devenue photographe, et ma vie aurait été moins belle.
Mon mari, Jean-Michel Darrois, me bouleverse, me fait rire et je l'aime depuis vingt ans.
Avec lui j'ai aussi eu le bonheur de voir grandir Stanislas.
Mon fils Virgile est tout pour moi, et il m'a offert la plus merveilleuse des belles-filles, Audrey.
Et enfin Alfred, tout juste un an, pour qu'il comprenne un jour que sa grand-mère était une bien étrange personne.

Voilà! Fast 40 Jahre Fotografie – Jahre, die wie im Traum vorübergegangen sind.
Für dieses Buch habe ich versucht, die besten Momente auszuwählen - eine Art Autobiografie in Bildern.
Einige der Bilder sind bekannt, andere hingegen wurden noch nie gezeigt und stammen aus den Tiefen meines Archivs.
Bilder, aber auch Erinnerungen: meine Familie; Menschen, die ich mag; Frauen, die mich inspirierten; aber auch all
diejenigen, die ich bei Shootings nur flüchtig kennenlernte und die mich trotzdem berührt haben.
Und dann sind da die Teams, die mich begleitet haben. Die Stylisten, Friseure und Visagisten.
Und jene, die meine Arbeit gezeigt und verteidigt haben: die Galeristen und Museen sowie diejenigen, die Texte geschrieben
und dadurch wieder neue Bilder inspiriert haben.
Das Studio mit seinen wunderbaren, hochtalentierten Assistenten, die mit Engelsgeduld meine Launen ertragen haben.
Und schließlich all diejenigen, die mir ein ganzes Jahr lang bei der Herstellung dieses Buches zur Seite standen.
Ohne Serge Bramly wäre ich nie Fotografin geworden, und mein Leben wäre weniger großartig gewesen.
Mein Mann Jean-Michel Darrois ist einfach umwerfend, er bringt mich zum Lachen, und ich liebe ihn seit 20 Jahren.
Mit ihm gemeinsam hatte ich das Glück, Stanislas aufwachsen zu sehen. Mein Sohn Virgile ist mein Ein und Alles,
und er hat mir mit Audrey die beste aller Schwiegertöchter geschenkt.
Und zu guter Letzt Alfred. Er ist gerade mal ein Jahr alt und soll eines Tages verstehen, was für eine merkwürdige
Person seine Großmutter war.

Bettina Rheims, April 2015, Paris

Fawnya Frolic looking like a fetish doll, June 2013, London

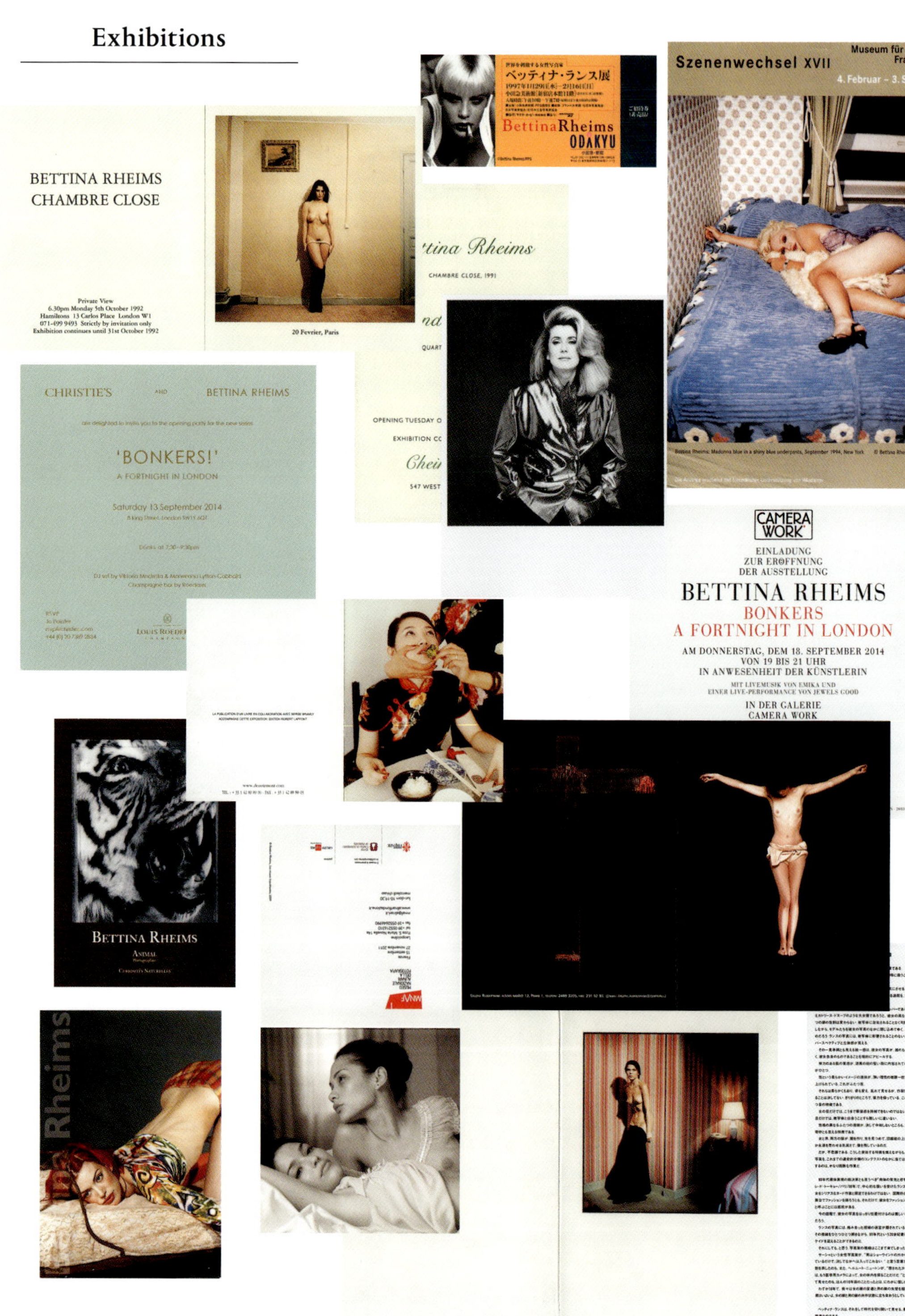

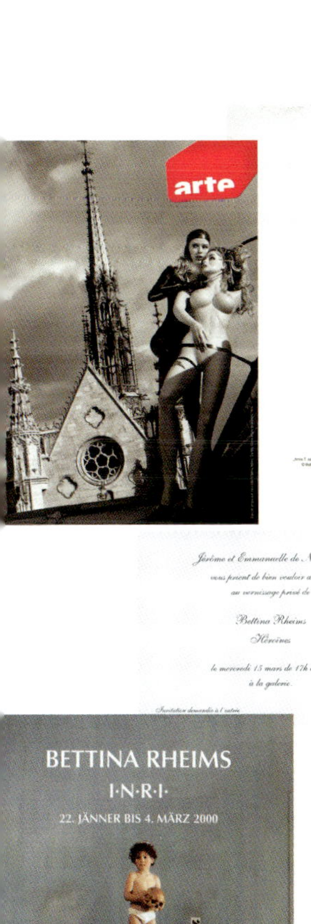

arte
BETTINA RHEIMS
I·N·R·I·
22. JÄNNER BIS 4. MÄRZ 2000
GALERIE THADDAEUS ROPAC
A-5020 SALZBURG · MIRABELLPLATZ 2 · TEL +43 (0)2 881 333 FAX 881 797

CO's
Wall
Cartier
B

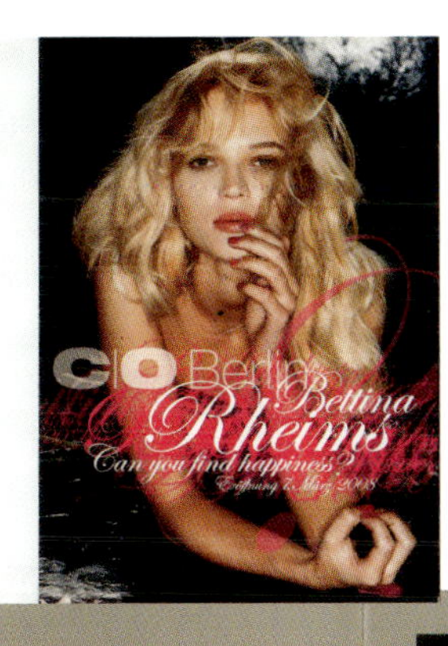

C/O Berlin
Bettina
Rheims
Can you find happiness?
Eröffnung 7. März 2008

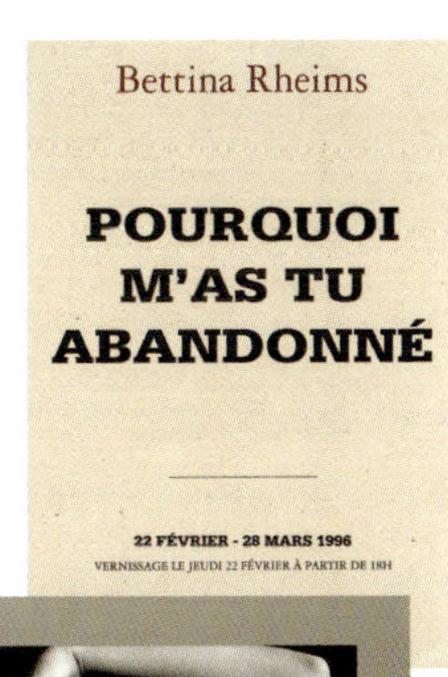

Bettina Rheims
POURQUOI
M'AS TU
ABANDONNÉ
22 FÉVRIER - 28 MARS 1996
VERNISSAGE LE JEUDI 22 FÉVRIER À PARTIR DE 18H

Jérôme et Emmanuelle de Noirmont
vous prient de bien vouloir assister
au vernissage privé de
Bettina Rheims
Héroïnes
le mercredi 15 mars de 17h à 20h
à la galerie.

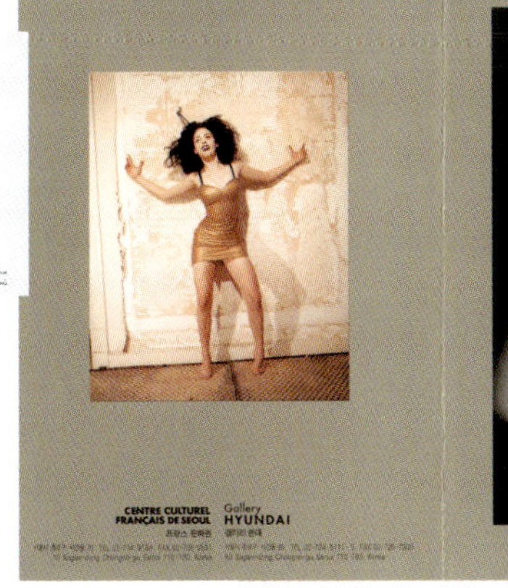

CENTRE CULTUREL   Gallery
FRANÇAIS DE SEOUL   HYUNDAI

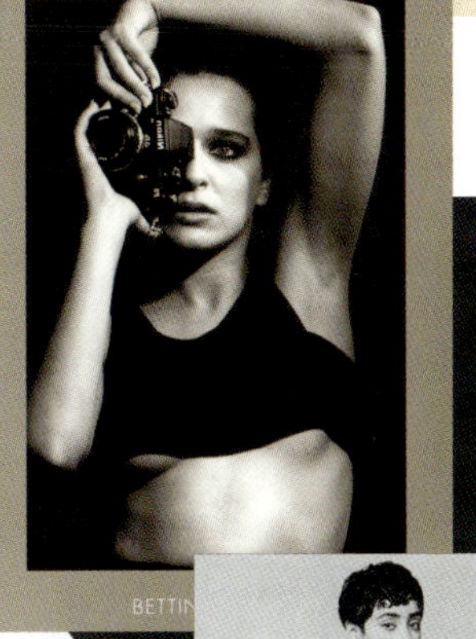

BETTINA
MAPPL
RH

DU
20 NOVEMBRE
AU
18 DÉCEMBRE 1981

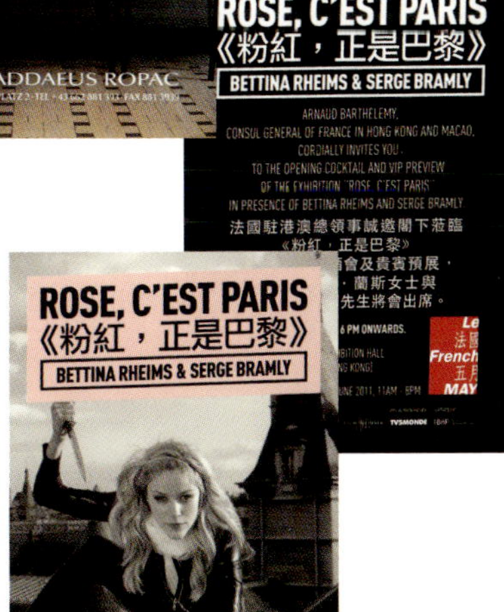

ROSE, C'EST PARIS
《粉紅，正是巴黎》
BETTINA RHEIMS & SERGE BRAMLY

ROSE, C'EST PARIS
《粉紅，正是巴黎》
BETTINA RHEIMS & SERGE BRAMLY

ARNAUD BARTHELEMY,
CONSUL GENERAL OF FRANCE IN HONG KONG AND MACAO,
CORDIALLY INVITES YOU
TO THE OPENING COCKTAIL AND VIP PREVIEW
OF THE EXHIBITION "ROSE, C'EST PARIS"
IN PRESENCE OF BETTINA RHEIMS AND SERGE BRAMLY

法國駐港澳總領事誠邀下蒞臨
《粉紅，正是巴黎》
展覽開幕酒會及貴賓預展，
蘭斯女士與
先生將會出席。

6 PM ONWARDS.

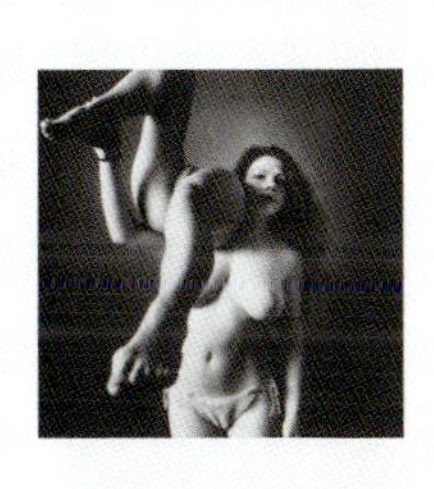

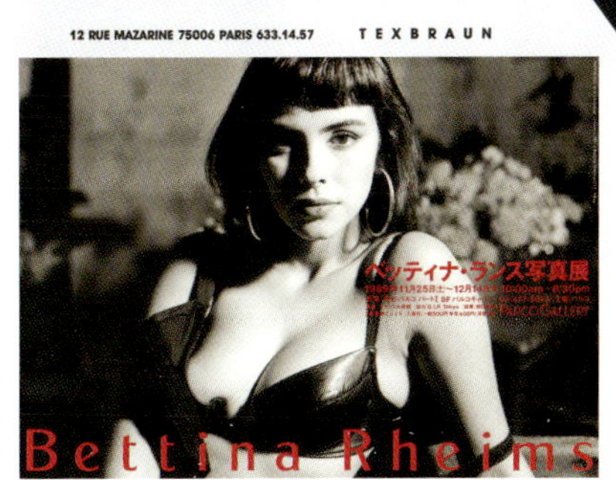

12 RUE MAZARINE 75006 PARIS 633.14.57   TEXBRAUN
ベッティナ・ランス写真展
Bettina Rheims

heims

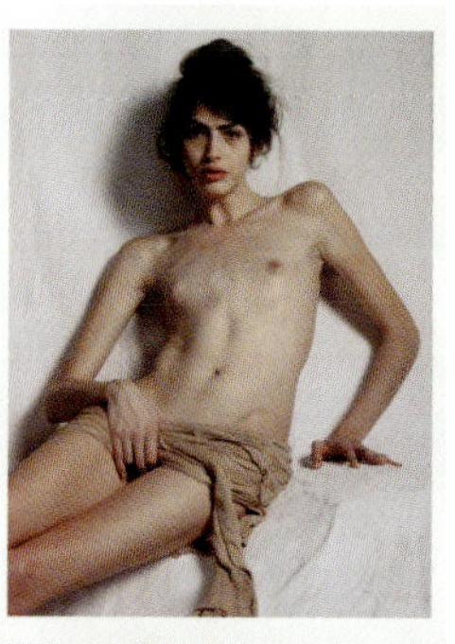

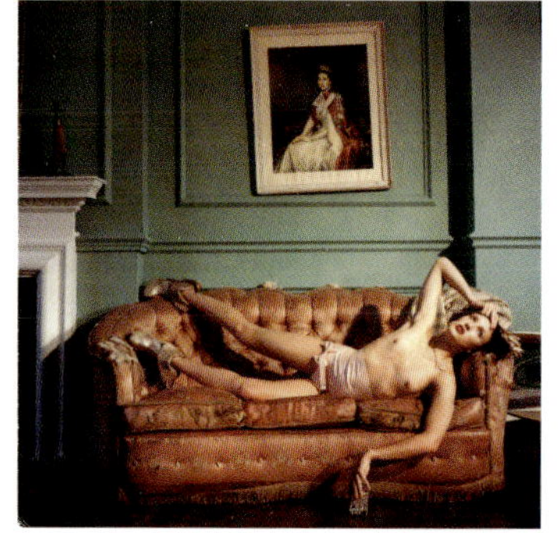

BETTINA RHEIMS: GENDER STUDIES. NRW-FORUM DUESSELDORF

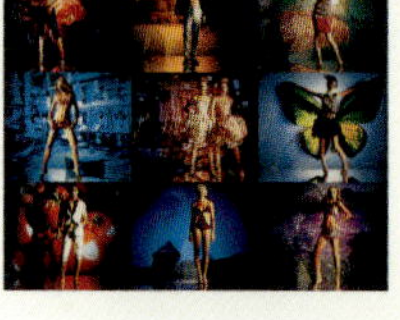

CHIC TACTIQUE AU PRINTEMPS VU PAR **BETTINA RHEIMS**

CATALOGUE FRANCAIS-ANGLAIS
TEXTE DE SERGE BRAMLY

The Gallery will be closed
from 24th December to 2nd January

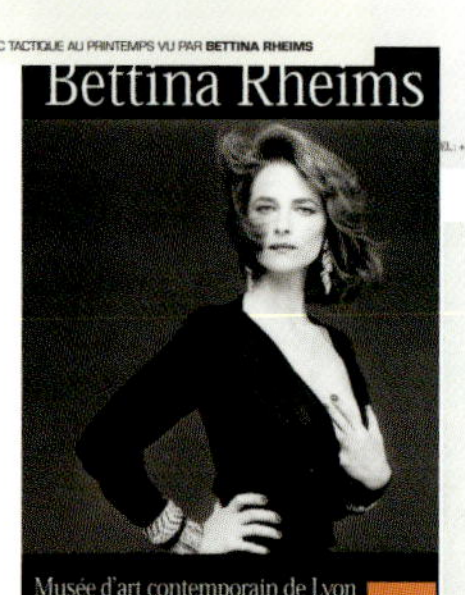

Bettina Rheims

Musée d'art contemporain de Lyon
retrospective
Du 16 juin au 13 août 2006

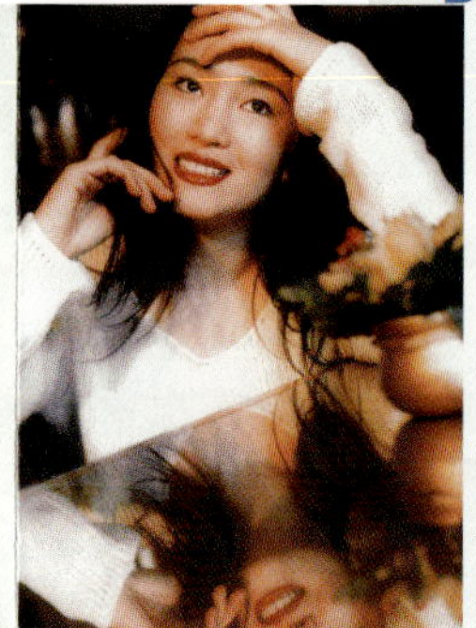

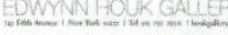

EDWYNN HOUK GALLERY
745 Fifth Avenue | New York 10151 | Tel 212 750 7070 | houkgallery.com

505 Nanjing Road East, Shanghai
Contact Person: Cedric
Telephone: 139 1802 8744
This invitation is valid for one person only

敬请回复 2002 年 11 月 20 日周三下午 4:00
海仑宾馆海天阁 (30 楼)
上海南京东路 505 号
联系人：Cedric
电话：139 1802 8744
此请柬仅限一人使用

They will exhibit and discuss their forthcoming works
on Shanghai Women soon to be published and exhibited
throughout the world.

邀请旅行法国已故的著名摄影师及作家 Bettina Rheims 和
Serge Bramly 威廉恩思出席并举行最新新闻发布会。同时，
他们将对上海女人这一主题的出版物及世界巡回的展览作详细
的介绍。

© Gong Li by Bettina Rheims

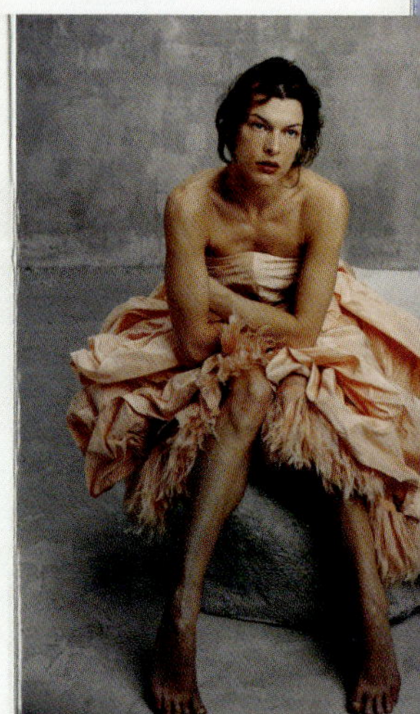

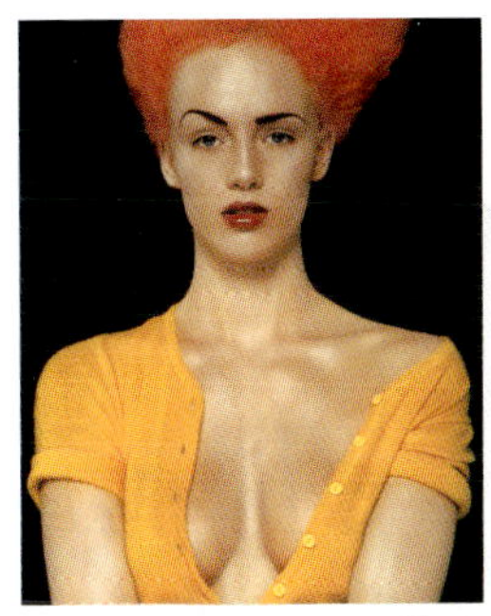

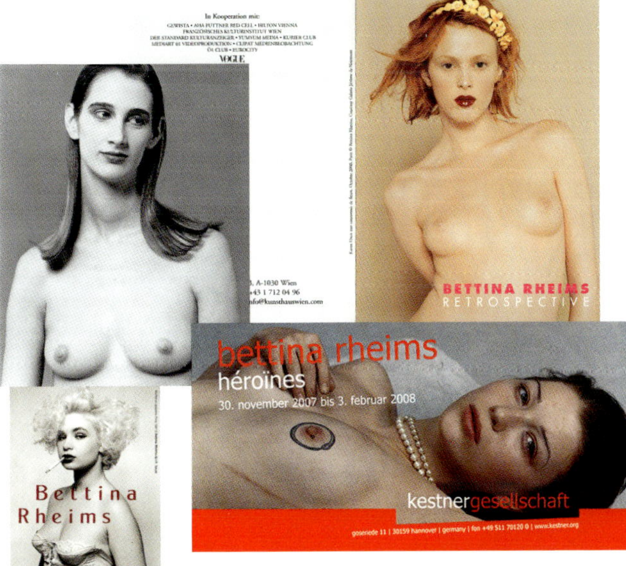
In Kooperation mit:
GEWISTA • AHA PUTTNER RED CELL • HILTON VIENNA
FRANZÖSISCHES KULTURINSTITUT WIEN
DER STANDARD KULTURANZEIGER • YUMYUM METRIA • KURIER CLUB
MEDIART 65 VIDEOPRODUKTIONEN • CLIPAT MEDIENBEOBACHTUNG
ÖL CLUB • EUROCITY
VOGUE

A-1030 Wien
+43 1 712 04 96
info@kunsthauwien.com

BETTINA RHEIMS
RETROSPECTIVE

bettina rheims
héroïnes
30. november 2007 bis 3. februar 2008

kestnergesellschaft

goseriede 11 | 30159 hannover | germany | fon +49 511 70120 0 | www.kestner.org

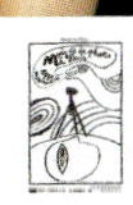

MUSTER FRAU

Fides Becker
Valie Export
Maki Na Kamura
Bettina Rheims
Annegret Soltau
Alba D'Urbano
Minnette Väri

14. 4. – 30. 6. 2002

KUNSTHALLE DARMSTADT

KUNSTHALLE DARMSTADT

Bettina
Rheims

ベッティナ・ランス写真展

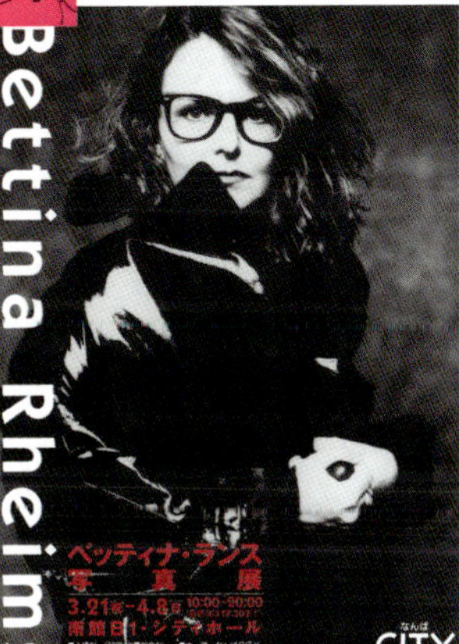
Bettina Rheims

ベッティナ・ランス
写　真　展
3.21㈯〜4.8㈰ 10:00〜20:00

CITY
なんば

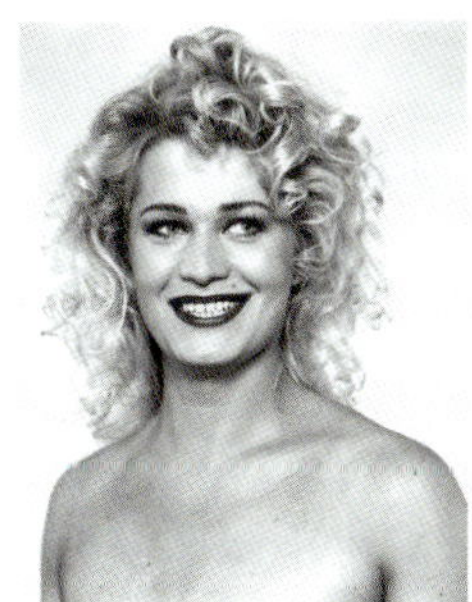

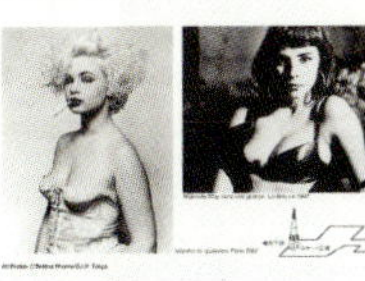

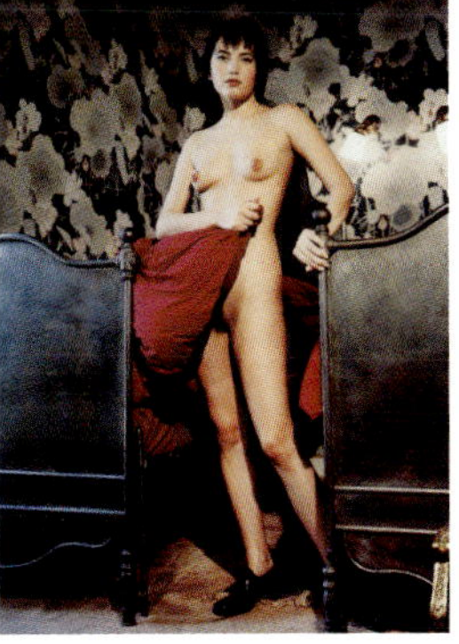
LA GALERIE SERA OUVERTE
LE MERCREDI 5 JUIN JUSQU'A 22 HEURES DANS LE CADRE DE LA
SOIRÉE DES ANTIQUAIRES, GALERISTES ET LIBRAIRES DU FAUBOURG SAINT-HONORÉ.

www.demoirxart.com
TEL. : +33 1 42 89 89 00 - FAX : +33 1 42 89 99 03

© 2024 TASCHEN GmbH
Hohenzollernring 53, 50672 Köln, Germany
www.taschen.com

Original edition: © 2016 TASCHEN GmbH
© 2024 Bettina Rheims, Paris

Art Direction Patrick Remy, Paris
Studio management Vanessa Mourot, Paris
Oriane Bault, Paris (assistance)
Design Mathieu Meyer, Paris
Cover Design Philippe Galowich, Paris; Andy Disl, Los Angeles
English translation Chris Miller, Oxford
French translation Jacques Bosser, Montesquiou
German translation Kristina Lowis, Jumilhac-le-Grand; Egbert Baqué, Berlin

ISBN 978-3-8365-9711-1
Printed in Bosnia-Herzegovina

BETTINA IS BACK

Since her first photographs in the late '70s, Bettina Rheims has defied the predictable. In this book she assembles more than 300 of her favorite pictures from the past 35 years. Shooting anonymous subjects and global icons like Kate Moss and Naomi Campbell, Rheims pushes at the breaking point between beauty and imperfection. This unique personal record of a defiant career spent shaking up codes of representation brings together renowned series like *Chambre close*, *Héroïnes*, and *Rose, c'est Paris*.

LE RETOUR DE BETTINA RHEIMS

Depuis ses premières photographies fin 1970, Bettina Rheims n'a cessé de bouleverser les codes. Pour cette publication, elle a choisi plus de 300 photographies parmi ses préférées tirées des 35 dernières années de sa carrière. Saisissant des inconnues comme des stars internationales telles que Kate Moss ou Naomi Campbell, l'artiste repousse les limites de la beauté et de l'imperfection. Cet ouvrage intime et unique retrace son parcours audacieux, libéré des codes de la représentation, en réunissant ses séries iconiques *Chambre close*, *Héroïnes* ou *Rose, c'est Paris*.

THEATER DES FRIVOLEN

Seit sie in den späten 70er-Jahren zur Fotografie fand, hat Bettina Rheims gängige Erwartungshaltungen torpediert. Für diesen Band hat sie über 300 ihrer Lieblingsaufnahmen aus den letzten 35 Jahren zusammengestellt – couragierte und provokante Fotografie aus berühmten Fotoreihen wie *Chambre close*, *Héroïnes* und *Rose, c'est Paris*. Makelloser Glamour trifft auf schlichte Schönheit, Kultiviertes auf Vulgares, strahlende Jugend auf Verfall Bettina Rheims liebt die Gegensätze.

> "The book is an object of desire."
> VOGUE

> "Bettina Rheims does not take photographs; she constructs compositions, like a painter."
> Le Monde

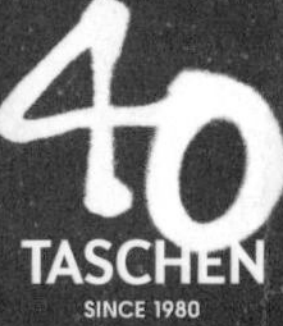

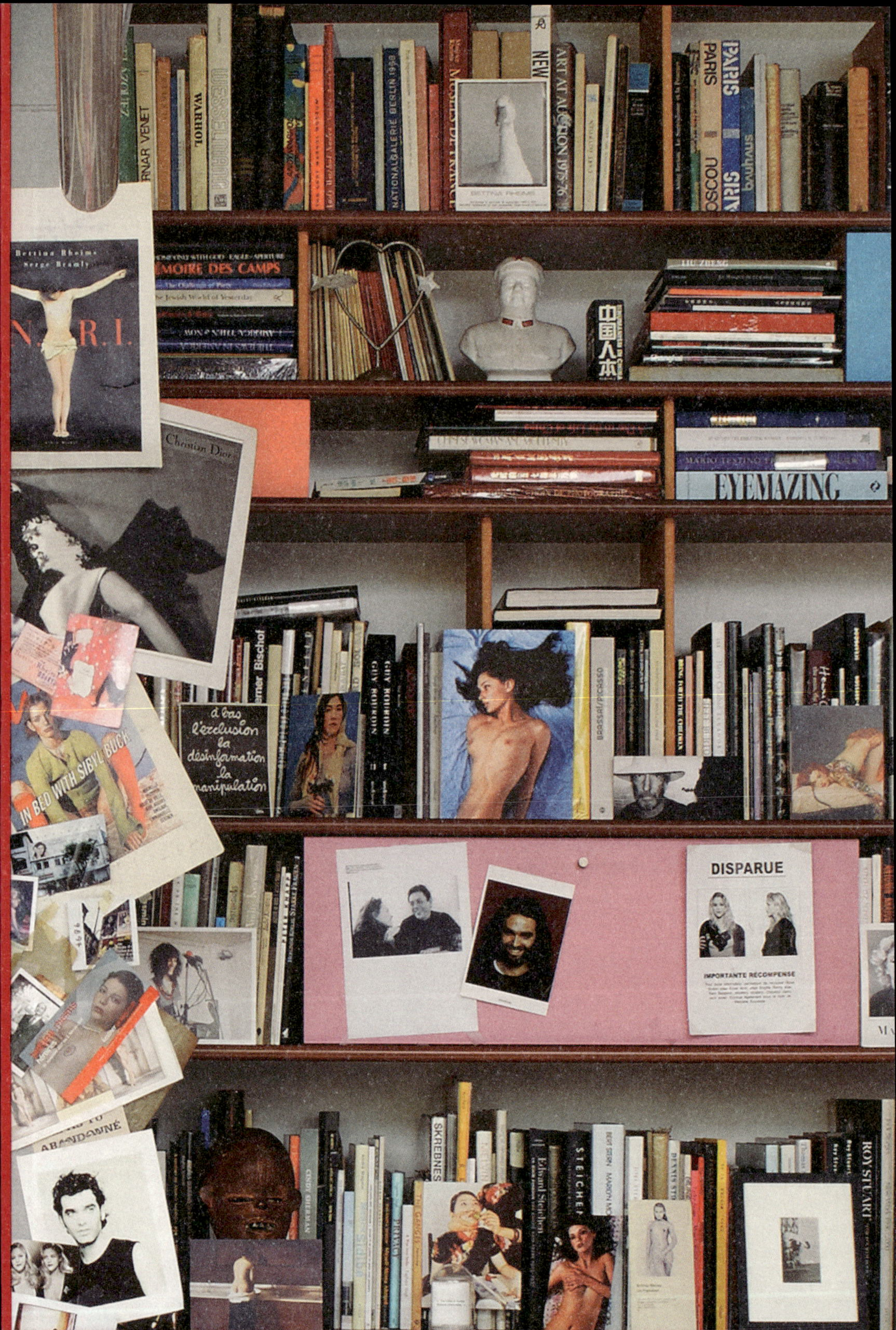